PAUL to CORINTH

Comments On

FIRST CORINTHIANS

And

SECOND CORINTHIANS

Comments are Based Upon
The Jonathan Mitchell New Testament, 2019 Edition

BY

JONATHAN MITCHELL, M.A.

CONTENTS

INTRODUCTION

BIBLIOGRAPHY and SOURCES

ABBREVIATIONS and APPARATUS

Copyright 2020 Harper Brown Publishing
ISBN 978-1-7321205-1-8
Cover Photo: iStock by Getty Images
New Testament text:
The New Testament, God's Message of Goodness, Ease and Well-Being, Which Brings God's Gifts of His Spirit, His Life, His Grace, His Power, His Fairness, His Peace and His Love, translated by Jonathan Mitchell; Copyright 2009, 2015 and 2019, all rights reserved; ISBN 978-1-4507-0505-9

Front Cover design and creation: Lynda Mitchell, Joshua Mitchell and Mishara Mitchell
Cover productions: Joshua Mitchell, Volcano Studios LLC

INTRODUCTION

The format and the methodology of these two commentaries follow those of our previous commentaries. They are based upon the author's original translations of the Greek New Testament, and are mostly verse-by-verse comments, while occasionally grouping a few verses together to treat them as a unit of thought. Occasional quotes from other commentaries, or scholars, are cited within the bodies of the texts. A short introduction is given before each of Paul's letters. A short excursus on a specific topic has from time to time been inserted.

Throughout the works, quotes of OT (Hebrew Scriptures) passages, as well as of Second Temple Jewish literature, are on offer to provide both historical and contemporary contexts of that may enlighten the thinking of Paul, along with the rhetoric of those days and Paul's use of language and figures of speech. Although most of Paul's writings are original to the revelations that he received, we are confident that just as he was aware of the works of Greek poets, he would have been aware of the thinking and manner of OT interpretation such as was used by his contemporary, Philo, of Alexandria.

In like manner, we view his theological environment as being a part of the larger Christian movement of his day, and so we have included quotes from other NT passages which, even if those writings were subsequent to the writings of these two letters, would have likely been representative of the ongoing developments in the oral traditions following the years of the ministry, and then the death, of Jesus Christ. Therefore, a bulk of our comments are in the form of quotes from 1st century Christian documents, along with occasional quotes from the period of Second Temple Judaism.

Added to the above are explanations of the imports of individual Greek words and their linguistic nuances, along with the author's exegesis and alternate renderings from the translations of the texts. We trust that this work will shed light on these two letters that were written to a specific community and were sent to address specific issues within the 1st century city of Corinth.

Jonathan Mitchell
Surprise AZ 2019

Other Bible translations used or referenced in this work:
A New English Translation of the Septuagint (N.E.T.S); *The Complete Bible, An American Translation* (J.M. Powis Smith); *Concordant Version of the Old Testament* (CVOT); *Concordant Literal New Testament* (CLNT); *English Standard Version*; *The Holy Bible, An American Translation* (W. Beck); *The Jerusalem Bible*; *New American Standard Bible*; *New International Version*; *New Revised Standard Version*; *Tanakh*; *The Emphasized Bible* (J.B. Rotherham); *The Emphatic Diaglott* (B. Wilson); *The Holy Bible in Modern English* (Ferrar Fenton); *The New English Bible* (NEG); *The New Testament, An Expanded Translation* (K. Wuest); *The Septuagint Bible* (Charles Thomson); *The Source New Testament* (Ann Nyland); *Young's Literal Translation*

BIBLIOGRAPHY and SOURCES

Ambrosiaster, *Ancient Christian Commentary on Scripture*, NT Vol. 6, 1-2 Corinthians, InterVarsity Press, 1999

Philipp Bachmann, in Conzelmann, ibid

Friedrich Buchsel, *TDNT* Vol. 2, Wm. B. Eerdmans, 1978

Robert Farrar Capon, *Kingdom, Grace, Judgment; Paradox, Outrage and Vindication in the Parables of Jesus*, Wm B Eerdmans Pub., 2002

J.H. Charlesworth, *The Old Testament Pseudepigrapha*, Vol. 2, Hendrickson Pub. 2013

Clement of Rome, *1 Clement*, Roberts-Donaldson trans., www.earlychristianwritings.com

Hans Conzelmann, *1 Corinthians, A Commentary on the First Epistle to the Corinthians*, in *Hermeneia – A Critical and Historical Commentary on the Bible*, Fortress Press, 1981

Delling, *TDNT*, Vol. 8, Wm. B. Eerdmans Pub., 1972

Tony Everett Denton (*Pertinent Parousia Passages, Second-Coming Scripture Studies*, 2016

J.D.G. Dunn, in Witherington, ibid

Arthur Eedle, personal email (cites: Ellicott, Barnes, Adam Clarke & John Gill)

Bart D. Ehrman, *A Brief Introduction to the New Testament*, Second Edition, Oxford University Press, 2009

Werner Foerster, *TDNT*, Vol. 3, Wm. B. Eerdmans Pub. 1978

Cameron Fultz, from his currently unpublished translation of Revelation, and personal emails

John Gavazzoni, "The Call to (Major) Repentance" www.greater-emmanuel.org/jg

Robert M. Grant, *The Gospel of Truth*, www.earlychristianwritings.com/text/gospeltruth.html

David Bentley Hart, *The New Testament, A Translation*, Yale Univ. Press 2017

Duncan Heaster, The Real Devil, A Biblical Exploration, www.realdevil.info/5-21.htm

Norman Hillyer, *The New Bible Commentary: Revised*, Wm. B. Eerdmans, 1973

C.A. Holladay, in Witherington, ibid

Wesley W. Isenberg, *The Gospel of Philip*, The Nag Hammadi Library, James M. Robinson, Gen. Ed., Harper & Row Pub. 1977

Robert Jamieson, A.R. Fausset, David Brown, *Commentary, Practical and Explanatory on the Whole Bible*, Zondervan Pub House, 1961

M.D. Johnson, *The Old Testament Pseudepigrapha*, Vol. 2, Hendrickson Pub. 2013

Dan Kaplan, personal communications

Ernst Kasemann, in Conzelmann, ibid

H.C. Kee, *The Old Testament Pseudepigrapha*, Vol 1, Hendrickson Pub. 2013

A.F.J. Klijn, *The Old Testament Pseudepigrapha*, Vol. 2, ibid

Werner G. Kummel, *Introduction to the New Testament*, Founded by P. Feine and J. Behm, Completely reedited by W.G. Kummel, 14th Revised Ed., trans. by A.J. Mattill, Jr., Abingdon Press, 1966

Thomas O. Lambdin, *The Gospel of Thomas*, in *The Nag Hammadi Library*, ibid

Jeremy Lopez, www.identitynetwork.net

Marcus Aurelius, in Conzelmann, ibid

D.B. Martin, in Witherington, ibid

G.R.S. Mead, www.sacred-texts.com

B.M. Metzger, *The Old Testament Pseudepigrapha*, Vol. 1, ibid

M.M. Mitchell, in Witherington, ibid

Mario Murillo, https://mariomurilloministries.wordpress.com/2019/04/16/if-this-was/

Ann Nyland, *The Source New Testament*, Smith and Stirling Publishing, 2004

Stephen J. Patterson, *The Lost Way, How Two forgotten Gospels Are Rewriting the Story of Christian Origins*. HarperOne, 2014

N.R. Petersen, in Witherington, ibid

Philo of Alexandria, *Internet Encyclopedia of Philosophy,* www.iep.utm.edu/philo/#H12, and in Conzelmann

Plutarch, in Conzelmann, ibid

Rutherford H. Platt, Jr, *The Testament of Levi,* www.sacred-texts.com/bib/fbe/fbe267.htm

Don K. Preston, *The Resurrection of Daniel 12:2, Fulfilled or Future,* JaDon Management, 2016

Richard Rohr, "Daily Meditation," March 26, 2018

Adolf Schlatter, in Conzelmann, ibid

Hans von Soden, in Conzelmann, ibid

Paul Tillich, *Systematic Theology III*; *Perspectives on 19th and 20th Century Protestant Theology*

Michael Wise, Martin Abegg, Jr., & Edward Cook, 1QS, *The Dead Sea Scrolls, A New Translation,* Harper Collins 1996

Ben Witherington III, *Conflict and Community in Corinth, A Socio-Rhetorical Commentary on 1 and 2 Corinthians,* Wm. B Eerdmans Pub., 1995

Robert Young *Analytical Concordance to the Bible,* Revised, 22nd American Ed., Wm. B. Eerdmans Pub.

ACKNOWLEDGEMENTS

We wish to acknowledge our gratitude to Dan Kaplan for his priceless input in numerous places throughout the reading of the original drafts, along with faithfully pointing out any typing errors noticed during this phase. We also want to thank my sister, Rebecca Mitchell, for her excellence in the final proofing of the text, and for her occasional editing suggestions. We wish to express our appreciation to our son, Joshua Mitchell, for his continued IT support and for the publishing of this work.

ABBREVIATIONS and TEXTUAL APPARATUS

ABBREVIATIONS:
CVOT: *Concordant Version of the Old Testament*
CLNT: *Concordant Literal New Testament*
DSS: Dead Sea Scrolls
JM: translations of the LXX by the author
LXX: The Septuagint – Greek version of the Old Testament
MS: manuscript; MSS: manuscripts
MT: Masoretic Text (Hebrew text of the Tanakh)
N.E.T.S.: *A New English Translation of the Septuagint*, A. Pietersma, B. Wright, Oxford Univ. Press, 2007
n: note
OT, NT: Old Testament, New Testament
Gen., Ex., Mat., Rom., etc.: commonly accepted indicators of the books of the Bible
Aleph, A, B, C, D, Ψ, etc.: indicate an individual codex or MS
p: signifies that the MS is a papyrus MS
TR: *Textus Receptus* (the "Received Text;" the "Majority Text")
cf. confer or compare
TDNT: *Theological Dictionary of the New Testament*, Ed. Gerhard Kittle, W.B. Eerdmans, 1977

APPARATUS:
Brackets, [ ]'s, have been used for the following situations:
>   to give a reading based upon other MSS
>   to insert notes or comments into the text
>   to insert words to aid in the reading of the English version
>   to indicate the reference of a quote from the Old Testament
>   to insert explanations

Parentheses, ( )'s, have been used for the following situations:
>   to give other possible meanings of a Greek word
>   to give alternate renderings of phrases or verses
>   to give a potential idiomatic translation

"=" has been placed before words for the following situations:
>   to signify that the following is a potential idiomatic translation, or paraphrase; to give another
>   spelling of a name or a suggested equivalent name; to give a Hebrew equivalent of a word or
>   name; to give an explanatory note

OTHER PUBLISHED WORKS BY THE AUTHOR

THE NEW TESTAMENT, Expanded, Amplified and with Multiple Renderings
PETER, PAUL & JACOB, Comments on First Peter, Philippians, Colossians, First Thessalonians, Second Thessalonians, First Timothy, Second Timothy, Titus, Jacob (James)
JOHN, JUDAH, PAUL & ?, Comments on First John, Second John, Third John, Judah (Jude), Hebrews, Galatians
JUST PAUL, Comments on Romans
PETER'S ENCORE & LATER PAUL, Comments on Second Peter & Ephesians
THE END of the OLD & THE BEGINNING of the NEW, Comments on Revelation

Available from Harper Brown Publishing, www.jonathanmitchellnewtestament.com

Comments on 1 Corinthians

Introduction

Scholars place the date of this letter at c. AD 55, just over a couple decades since the resurrection of Jesus Christ. He wrote it from Ephesus, near the end of a three-year stay there (*cf* 16:5-9, below, and Acts 20:31). Paul had heard from Cloe's household that the "summoned-forth, covenant community in Corinth" was experiencing a development of factions where different groups within the community were aligning themselves with different teachers, and they were also having disorders and behavioral inequities when the members gathered together. There was also a scandal about an incestuous relationship that was going on.

Ben Witherington III observes that, "Paul was the product of the confluence of three cultural orientations – Jewish, Hellenistic Greek, and Roman..." (*Conflict and Community in Corinth, A Socio-Rhetorical Commentary on 1 and 2 Corinthians*, Wm. B Eerdmans Pub., 1995 pp 1-2). We should be alert to this as we play close attention to how Paul put this letter together. Witherington dissects this work in accord with the principles of rhetoric that were commonly employed in Paul's time.

Hans Conzelmann concludes concerning Paul's theology in this letter, that it
> "is for him primarily the exposition of the event of salvation that is doctrinally formulated in the creed and actualized in the gospel..." (*1 Corinthians, A Commentary on the First Epistle to the Corinthians*, in *Hermeneia – A Critical and Historical Commentary on the Bible*, Fortress Press, 1981 p 9).

We will include more observations from Conzelmann in the body of this work. For now we will add from him:
> "Plainly in the mind of the Corinthians...their conduct is grounded on a freedom principle (6:12; 10:23); this in turn rests upon 'knowledge' (8:1), and the latter derives from experience of the Spirit (12:4ff). Their freedom is accordingly not moral indifference, but represents a speculative position" (ibid p 14).

The founding of this called-out community is described in Acts 18. This letter did not begin Paul's communication with the group, but from 5:9, below, we see that there was a previous letter from him to them, and from 7:1 we observe that he had received a letter from them. So we are here coming into the middle of, as it were, an ongoing conversation. Appropriate conduct for the community is one of the central themes of the letter, and thus his instructions have relevance for us today, as well. But beyond the particular issues that he addresses we find many gems of the revelation concerning Christ, and concerning the realities of the new age into which God had ushered the world. We will see disclosed here much insight into the character of God, the work of Christ, and Paul's understanding concerning the Resurrection (ch. 15). One thing that we will learn about this community (at the time of this writing) is that they had a wealth of the effects of grace (*charis-ma*) but in spiritual understanding they were still children.

Werner G. Kummel observes,
> "The Epistle clearly has no connected train of thought, and there are no connecting links between the separate sections.... Paul handles various questions about the life of the community.... It is striking that more than once (6:1ff; 9:1ff; 13:1ff) a connected theme is interrupted by an excursus" (*Introduction to the New Testament*, Founded by P. Feine and J. Behm, Completely reedited by W.G. Kummel, 14th Revised Ed., trans. by A.J. Mattill, Jr., Abingdon Press, 1966 p 199).

When describing the cultural setting of Corinth, at that time, Kummel remarks that, "Religious syncretism flourished in the heterogeneous population" (ibid). In discussing the issues in Corinth, he points out that,
> "there is no convincing proof that Paul in particular sections is turning against each of these

'parties' one at a time…. In [chapter] 1-4 he always polemizes against, or speaks to, the entire congregation (*cf* Munck). The division is not caused by the presence of different doctrines or tendencies in the congregation, but by the Corinthians' overestimation of human teachers and baptizers as the result of an understanding of baptism like that of the mystery religions (1:12ff; 4:15)" (ibid p 201; brackets added).

Chapter 1

1. **Paul, a called** (or: summoned) **one – one sent forth with a mission** (a representative; an emissary) **of, and from, Jesus Christ** [with other MSS: Christ Jesus' ambassador] **through God's will** (purpose; intent) – **and** (or: with) **Sosthenes, the brother** (one from out of the same womb),

This letter's salutation opens with Paul identifying himself, his function and his authority: **a called** (or: summoned) **one – one sent forth with a mission** (an emissary; a representative) **of, and from, Jesus Christ**. The term "called" echoes Jesus calling the twelve disciples. The term "summoned" (I have followed Moffatt, here) is an allusion to his Damascus road experience. It was a summoning by his Lord and Owner (as we see from the use of the term *kurios* that he uses in vss. 2 and 3). He did not volunteer for this duty. *Cf* vs. 26, below where the term "calling; summoning; vocation" is applied to the Corinthian community, as well.

2. **to God's called-out community** (or: summoned-forth, covenant group that has God as its source, and which belongs to God), **the one being within Corinth;**
> **to those having been set-apart within Christ Jesus** (or: made holy, sacred, different from the normal and sanctified, in union with an Anointing of, and from, Jesus);
> **to called** (or: summoned) **folks [and] to set-apart people** (holy ones; saints; sanctified folks; sacred ones) – **together with all those in every place constantly calling upon the Name of our Lord** [note: the phrase applied to Yahweh in Gen. 12:8; Zech. 13:9], **Jesus Christ** ([the] Anointed One) – **their [Lord and Messiah], as well as ours:**

Here, he gives recognition to the status of his listeners within the purpose, intent and will of God, and affirms that they are on the same level in God's reign as he is: "called ones."
> "**to those having been set-apart within Christ Jesus** (or: made holy, sacred, different from the normal and sanctified, in union with an Anointing of, and from, Jesus);"
This may be an allusion to Israel being set apart, as we read in Ex. 19:6. There, Israel was designated by Yahweh to be a set-apart ethnic group (or: nation) and a royal (pertaining to a King) priesthood (sacred-effect; LXX). Observe the "divine passive" – this setting-apart was done by God. They were set apart "**within Christ Jesus**" – He is now the sphere of their existence. They were now "in union with an Anointing of Jesus," which came "from Jesus." So they were really "different from the normal." Next, we see that, just like Paul, they were "**called** (or: summoned) **folks**," and were "**set-apart people**," just as Israel was. But they were not the only ones, for they were "**together with all those in every place constantly calling upon the Name of our Lord**…" This could be an allusion to Ps. 99:6, and more specifically, to Joel 2:32,
> "And it will be that everyone who shall call on the Name of Yahweh shall escape, for in Mount Zion and in Jerusalem, deliverance shall come – just as Yahweh says – among the survivors whom Yahweh is calling" (CVOT). *Cf* Acts 2:21

Furthermore, **Jesus Christ** was **their [Lord and Messiah]**, as well as the Lord and Messiah of Paul, and the Jews. In Rom. 11:17 he instructs us that the ethnic multitudes (the non-Jews; the Gentiles) were grafted into the "olive tree" (the produce of the anointing oil used by the Jews), which was a figure of the joining of Jew and Gentile (Eph. 2:15) so that in God's economy of dealing with humanity, there is now One New Humanity.

2

First, he reminds them that they have been "set-apart." The parenthetical expansion explains this: they have been "made holy," i.e., "different from the normal" way of life. They have been made "sacred," for God's purposes and – as we will later see in this letter – they have been "sanctified" to be God's home. Just think about this as being our purpose in life. Those of us who have been raised in Christianity often give no thought to this – if we are aware of it at all. It is not emphasized in normal Christian teaching. We are told that a building, or a particular location, is holy or sacred. Seldom are we reminded that we are holy and sacred. Paul uses the adjective form in the next line, identifying them as "set-apart people, holy ones, sanctified folks, sacred ones." What a way to think of yourself!

But what are we set-apart to? What is our location, in His purpose and in His reign? What is it that makes us "different from the normal" way of life, the profane existence? The prepositional phrase that follows the perfect, passive participle (perfect meaning that it is a completed action; passive meaning that God is the one that did the action) answers these rhetorical questions: our location is "within Christ Jesus." And again, we have been set-apart to be "in union with an Anointing (another meaning of the term "Christ") of, and from, Jesus." The preposition "within" can also be rendered "centered in." He is our center, and we are located "within the midst of Christ Jesus." This is what makes us "holy; sacred; sanctified." Recall that it was God's presence that made "the ground" holy at the burning bush that Moses encountered. Now it is Christ's presence (within Whom we now exist) that sets us apart for His intentions. Pondering Paul's words, here, calls to mind what God said to Peter,

> "**You are not to continue making, deeming or considering common** (or: profane) **[the] things which God cleansed** (or: cleanses) **and made** (or: makes) **clean!**" (Acts 10:15).

Paul identifies these Corinthians as "called folks." Called, or summoned, to what? To be and do God's will, intent and purpose – just as was Paul. Note that he emphasizes the "set-apart" nature of their new existence by saying this first with a participle, and then with an adjective. This is who they now are. Notice the mutual interplay of voices between God calling folks, and folks calling upon "the Name of the Lord." Also, observe the inserted note: this phrase was used in Gen. 12:8, where Abram "called upon the Name of the LORD (LXX; Yahweh in the Heb. text)." Then another example is Zech. 13:9 where Yahweh says, "they shall call upon My Name, and I will hear them: I will say, 'It [is] My People.'" In our text, here, the Lord is Jesus, the Messiah.

3. **With, among, for and to you folks [are] grace** (the influence of favor, kindness, goodwill in the joy-producing gratuitous act) **and peace-of-the-joining from God, our Father and Lord, Jesus Christ** (or: from our Father, God, and [the] Owner, [Messiah] Jesus).

This verse is often rendered as a blessing, e.g., "Grace to you…" There is no expressed verb in this verse, and so this is a legitimate rendering, taking it to be a greeting. However, a missing copula is very common in Greek syntax, and a form of the verb "to be" is normally inserted into the English rendering. I have taken this latter approach to reading the text, so we have:

> "**With, among, for and to you folks [are] grace** (the influence of favor, kindness, goodwill in the joy-producing gratuitous act) **and peace-of-the-joining from God, our Father and Lord, Jesus Christ** (or: from our Father, God, and [the] Owner, [Messiah] Jesus)."

I conflated the potential functions of the dative, plural personal pronoun "you," to offer the reader this variety of nuances that fit the text: "With, among, for and to you folks." I read Paul as telling his listeners that these two expressions of God "[are]" actually with, among, for and to them. This is an affirmation of the "Good News," not simply a greeting. We should refrain from putting Paul in the box of the common form of writing letters in his day. Most everything he says is "outside the box" of his day.

The term "**grace**" means "the influence of favor, kindness and goodwill" which came "**in the joy-producing gratuitous act**" from God. You see that I also expanded the word normally just rendered "**peace**." This Greek noun is from the verb that means "to join." The implications of this statement pervade the Good News. It is the joining of all the races and ethnic multitudes (circumcision and uncircumcision), as we read in Eph. 2:11-19, to be the "one new humanity." It is the joining of Christ to His bride, the Head to the body. It is the joining of "heaven and earth" (the New Jerusalem descending unto the earth – Rev. 21:10-26). It is the joining of conciliation (2 Cor. 5:17-20). It is the joining of the wild branches into Israel's olive tree (Rom. 11:17). When antagonists are joined, there is peace.

All of this has come from "God, our Father and Lord, Jesus Christ." Now we realize that this rendering sounds strange for this series of Greek nouns that are all in the genitive case. If you prefer, the prepositional phrases can also be rendered, "from our Father, God, and [the] Lord (or: Owner), Jesus Christ (or: [Messiah] Jesus)." There were no punctuation marks in the oldest Greek MSS. This latter rendering supports the later doctrine of the trinity. The former simply presents Jesus as being both the manifestation and the functioning agent of God, who is our Father and Lord. Observe that there is no definite article before the word Lord, which would separate it from the title "Father" and make it read "the Lord Jesus Christ." I added "[the]" for those who will feel more comfortable with the traditional rendering. But, leaving aside the traditional theories, we are given birth by the Word (1 Pet. 1:23), which is God (Jn. 1:1), Who became flesh (Jn. 1:14), Who is Jesus Christ. So with this line of reasoning, Jesus (as God, as the Word) is our Father. We lay this out for you so that you will not just think in old formulas, but will actually think, and notice the details.

4. **I always and progressively give thanks to** (or: for) **my God**
> (or: experience gratitude in my God; express the ease of grace by my God; experience the happy fortune of abundant favor with my God; = observe my God's competent and prosperous grace) **concerning you folks, upon the basis of God's grace** (favorable influence) **[which is] being given to you folks within and in union with Christ** (or: [the] Anointed One,) **Jesus,**

The verb, in the present tense, has been normally rendered "give thanks," as my bold rendering offers. Now the term "God" is in the dative case, with no expressed preposition, so with this first option we have "give thanks TO God." Given the context of the letter, this was likely Paul's intent. But rather than 'second-guessing' Paul, let us consider the other options. First of all, the verb: the Greek elements are *eu*- prefixed to the term *charis* (grace; favor) along with the verb ending. With this in mind, that our word "grace" is the stem of this verb, consider the expanded renderings together with the optional functions of
> a) experience gratitude IN my God
> b) express the ease of grace BY my God
> c) experience the happy fortune of abundant favor WITH my God
> d) = observe my God's competent and prosperous grace.

I have offered these options for the verb throughout my translation, since they make sense to the contexts. The phrase that follows, "concerning you folks," fits with all these options. The first clause means 1) that Paul is expressing thanks, or 2) experiencing gratitude, or 3) expressing grace in his thoughts or words, or 4) experiencing God's favor concerning the Corinthians, as God is experiencing it, or 5) is observing God's grace in action, with regard to them. In all of these expressions, Paul is intimately involved with what God has done and is doing with the folks at Corinth.

Paul continues with his theme of "grace' (beginning with this term in vs. 3, but the content of the grace was given in vs. 2) with the phrase, "upon the basis of God's grace." He then reminds them that all this was "being given" to them WITHIN and IN UNION WITH Christ Jesus. All this is an expression of the "Good News." Verses 2 through 4 are a synopsis of the Gospel. We could share this short message with folks to impregnate them with the Love of God. But Paul continues on…

5. **because in** (or: that within the midst of) **everything, and in union with all humanity, you folks are** (or: were) **made rich within, and in union with, Him* – within every thought** (in the midst of all [the] *Logos*; centered in all reason and information; in every word, idea, expression, eloquence and message) **and in all intimate, experiential knowledge and insight** (*gnosis*) –   [*, vs. 5, *cf* 2 Cor. 9:11]

4

Pause and ponder the first phrase. The conjunction can be read as "**because**," informing his listeners that what follows gives the reason for what he said in vs. 4, above. Or, it can be rendered as "that," in the sense of "for the fact that," which offers the explanation of what he was inferring in vs. 4 (*cf* Conzelmann, ibid p 25 n 3). The form of the word *pas* ("everything," or, "all") that is used here (which is, *panti*) functions for both neuter (things) and masculine (people). They are "made rich within, and in union with, Him" – "within the midst of everything," i.e., in all their situations, experiences, etc., and, "in union with all humanity." You see, what had been given to them was also given to all humanity – by way of "the joining," referred to in vs. 3.

He goes on to explain that the realm and sphere of all their "riches" are "within every thought and in all intimate, experiential knowledge and insight." But let us look at the details of these two phrases. Here, the prepositions are expressed, and in both places it is the particle "in; within; in the midst of; centered in." The object of the first phrase is "every *logos*." The semantic range of this word includes, "thought, idea, reason, information, word, expression and message." Read the parenthetical expansion that offers the various meanings of the preposition, as well as of the noun. Notice that in one options I capitalized and transliterated the Greek word "*Logos*." This is to alert the reader to consider the "Christ" aspect (from Jn. 1:1ff, as well as in its frequent uses in the book of Acts and elsewhere in the NT), for this "idea" was in everything that was shared in the messages to people. It was all about Christ, as the *Logos*, becoming incarnate in the rest of humanity. But to consider other nuances of Paul's expression, consider the parenthetical expansion and the semantic range of *logos*. They were rich in all of this: reason, information, word, idea, expression and message. From the translation by James W. Leitch and George W. MacRae, in Conzelmann (ibid pp 25, 27), I have also included the meaning "eloquence." This provides an added view of Paul's analysis and description of those in Corinth.

Paul speaks of their "riches" in 2 Cor. 9:11, but there it refers to another repository of wealth and of, "**being progressively enriched unto abundance within every person** (or: in union with everything)." We might also recall Paul's words to the Roman community, "**the riches** (or: wealth) **of His kind and gentle usefulness** (sweetly-disposed benevolence; kindness)" (2:4), and then in 11:33,
> "**O, the depth of [the] riches** (wealth; resources) **and wisdom and intimate, experiential knowledge and insight of God** (or: from God; which are God)! **How unsearchable** (inscrutable) **the effects of His decisions** (results of the distinctive separations, judicial awards, judgments and evaluations from Him), **and untrackable** (untraceable) **His ways** (paths; roads)."
Cf 3:21; 4:8, below; Mat. 11:27; Acts 17:24; 2 Cor. 7:11b; 8:7, 9, 16; 9:8, 11; and Phil. 4:19

This all was also "in (etc.) all intimate, experiential knowledge and insight" – which gives the central range of meaning for the word *gnosis* (which was a term that spawned an early form of Christianity, and had been a strain of Judaism, as well, in a variety of groups known as Gnostics). So, they were spiritually rich, because of union with Christ. They had the *Logos* together with intimate knowledge of Him. This was all because of grace (vs. 4). But there is more…

6. correspondingly, and in proportion, as Christ's witness (or: the testimony pertaining to and from the Anointed One; or: the evidence which is the Anointing) **was made certain, stable and established on good footing** (or: validated and confirmed) **within, and among, you folks,**
7. and as you people are not continuing trailing behind or constantly late, so as to be deficient or fall short – not even in one effect of grace (or: result of favor) **– being ones habitually receiving and taking away into your hands from out of our Lord's** [= Yahweh's, or Christ's] **unveiling: Jesus Christ**
> (or: from the midst of the uncovering and revelation of our Lord, Jesus [the] Anointed; or: forth from the disclosure from our Lord, which is Jesus Anointed).

Here, Paul gives further qualifications: all of the above (vss. 2-5) corresponded to how Christ's witness to them "**was made stable within [them].**" It was "**made certain and established**" on good footing among them, "in proportions as the testimony pertaining to and from the Anointed One" was given to them. The "evidence, which is the Anointing" that they had received was validated and confirmed IN them. In other words, they could trust what they had heard because of an inner, corresponding witness to the Truth of it. Also, the verb "**was made certain, stable and established on good footing** (or: validated and confirmed)" is in the passive voice, "the divine passive," indicating the God was the One who did this both within and among them. We find a corroborating witness of this in 2 Cor. 1:21,

> "**Now God [is] the One repeatedly placing us on good, firm footing** (constantly stabilizing and establishing us; or: confirming, guaranteeing and validating us as possessed by a purchase) **and completely** (or: instantly, in one point in time) **anointing us, together with you folks, into Christ**."

We also want to point out that here, in vs. 7, it is NOT speaking about "gifts," but rather about the "effect of grace," or "the result of favor." This refers to "the actual condition of the community" (Conzelmann, ibid p 27). The Greek word is the dative form of the noun *charis-ma*. We've already seen the word *charis*, above. The *–ma* ending of the noun signifies that it is speaking of "the effect," or "the result" of the noun to which it is attached. We will encounter teaching about this word again, in chapter 12, below. However here, Paul is affirming and expanding what he had said in vs. 5, above. As to the conflated phrase, "**continuing trailing behind or constantly late, so as to be deficient or fall short**," *cf* 2 Cor. 11:5, 9b and Phil. 4:12, for a contrast. These Corinthians, however, are rich in these things and have been given "everything," and 7b, here, explains how this supply of wealth continually comes to them…

In 7a Paul affirms their solid and reliable place "in the **effect of grace**," and "in the result of [God's] favor." Then 7b goes on to acknowledge what they were "**habitually receiving and taking away [as] in their own hands**." But what were they receiving? It was Jesus Christ, who they had been receiving "**from out of our Lord's unveiling**." Another way of rendering this is: "from the midst of the uncovering and revelation of our Lord, Jesus Christ." Or, it was "from the disclosure FROM our Lord, which is Jesus Anointed." But you might say, Wait, my version of the NT says that they were "waiting for the revelation of our Lord Jesus Christ!" Yes, this is what all the common versions say, but I strongly differ with this rendering of the present participle *apekdechomenous*. Note, first of all, that this word definitely does not mean "coming," as the old KJV rendered it. The verb is *apekdechomai*, which is *dechomai* (which means "to take and receive with the hands") which is prefixed with the preposition *apek-*, a contraction of *apo*, "from," and *ek*, "out of the midst of." This verb should not be translated "looking for," or "awaiting." We find this same verb in Heb. 9:28, where I have rendered it the same way as here:

> "**so also, the Christ – being once borne** (or: carried) **close into the many** (or: being offered once unto and for the many) **to carry failures** (errors; sins; mistakes; deviations; misses of the target) **back up again – will continue being made visible** (or: will be progressively seen) **forth from out of the midst of the second [place** (*cf* 9:3, 7 & 10:9; {comment: = the holy of holies})**] – apart from failure** (apart from sin; apart from a sin offering; apart from error in attempting to hit the target) **– in those** (or: by those; to those; for those) **habitually receiving** (or: progressively taking) **from out of the midst of Him, [progressing] into a deliverance** (or: [leading] into a rescue; with a view to health and wholeness; into the midst of salvation)."

Let us consider other places where Paul spoke of this revelation, in reference to the Gospel:

> "**for I myself neither received it to my side from a human** (or: from beside a person), **nor was I taught [it], but to the contrary, [it came] through an unveiling of Jesus Christ** (or: through an uncovering pertaining to Jesus [the Messiah]; through a revelation from Jesus Christ; by means of a disclosure which is [the] Anointed Jesus)." (Gal. 1:12).

Notice that Paul had already RECEIVED an unveiling from Jesus. Then we have a second witness of this in Eph. 3:2-3,

> "**Since indeed you folks heard the house-law** (or: detailed plan; the dispensing within the household; the administration; management of the household; or: the distribution) **of the grace of God – which is being given by me unto and into you folks – that, in accord with an**

unveiling (or: down from and in line with a revelation; in keeping with a disclosure), **the secret** (or: mystery) **was made known to me – even as I before wrote** (or: wrote aforetime), **in brief**." They had all been receiving from out of this unveiling of Jesus as the Messiah. *Cf* Rom. 16:25; 1 Cor. 14:6, 26; 2 Cor. 12:1, 7; Rev. 1:1. All these verses speak of His revelation/unveiling/disclosure. We are not waiting for this to happen. We feed from it now. We find Paul using the verb *apekdechomai* (used here, in vs. 7, and as quoted above, in Heb. 9:28) repeatedly, in Rom. 8:

> 19. **For the looking away and watching with the head stretched forward alertly** (or: the peak expectation, premonition or intuitive opinion; or: = the concentrated and undivided focus) **of the creation is constantly receiving and taking away from out of the unveiling of God's sons**
>> (or: = the uncovering and revealing of folks who have the character and qualities of God; or: the disclosure pertaining to the sons of God; or: the unveiling and revelation which belongs to God's sons; or, as an ablative: **the disclosure from God's sons**)....

It is receiving from this unveiling and disclosure that imparts ongoing expectation to us, as well as transformations (*cf* 2 Cor. 3:18). And again, in Rom. 8:

> 23. **Yet not only [this], but further, even we ourselves – constantly holding** (or: having; possessing) **the firstfruit of, and which is, the Spirit** (or: the Firstfruit whose source is the Breath-effect; or: the first offering, or first portion, which is spirit and breath, and is from the Attitude) **– we ourselves also continually sigh and groan within** (in the center of) **ourselves, continuously accepting and with our hands taking away from out of a placing in the condition of a son** (or: [the] deposit of the Son; a setting in place which is the Son; a constituting as a son; a placing in the Son): **the process of the release of our body from slavery** (or: [and] the loosing from destruction pertaining to the [corporate, old covenant] body, which is us; or: = the unbinding and release of the body [of Adam; of humanity], which belongs to us)....
> 25. **Yet since** (or: even if) **we continue expecting what we are not seeing** (or: observing), **we continue taking away and accepting from out of it through remaining under [our present situation and circumstances]** (or: through patient, humble, persistent, supportive endurance).

Again, the continued expecting derives from continued accepting from out of it, "through remaining under" our present circumstances in order to give support to others. He also used the same verb in Gal. 5:5,

> "**For you see, in union with [the] Spirit** (or: by [the] Breath-effect; with [the] Spirit; or: in spirit) **– forth from out of faithfulness** (or: [the] trust-faith-loyalty) **– we, ourselves, continuously** (or: progressively) **receive by taking away, as with our hands, from out of [the] expectation which belongs to, comes from and which is [the] rightwising, eschatological deliverance within the Way pointed out** (or: forth from the midst of [the] expected hope, which is the state of being liberated, pointed in the right direction, and included as a participant in the new covenant)."

And then, in Phil. 3:20,

> "**You see, our citizenship** (result of living in a free city; or: commonwealth-effects; political realm) **continues inherently existing** (or: continues humbly ruling; continuously subsists; repeatedly has its under-beginning) **resident within the midst of [the] atmospheres** (or: heavens), **from out of where** (or: which place) **we also continuously receive and take away in our hands from out of a Deliverer** (a Savior; One restoring us to the health and wholeness of our original state and condition): **[the] Lord** (or: a Master), **Jesus Christ**."

Take note that the word "citizenship" is the "result of living in a free CITY." Now what city would that be? We are informed of what city it is in Heb. 12:22, "**you folks have approached so that you are now at Mount Zion – even in a city of a continuously living God; in 'Jerusalem upon heaven'**."

Lastly, we find Peter using this verb in reference to the days of Noah,

> "**within [the] days of Noah, when** (or: while) **he was continuing to be receiving forth, and taking away from, out of God's state of emotional quietness** (taking a long time before rushing or being in a heat of passion; long-enduring patience; putting anger far away) **while [the] ark was progressively being prepared and equipped** (constructed to readiness)..." (1 Pet. 3:20).

This was not something new. We read of this supply from God in Ps. 46:1,

"God is our Refuge and Strength, a very present Help in trouble" (ESV; caps mine). 2 Thes. 1:7 speaks of our "**relaxation** (ease; a relaxing of a state of constriction; relief)… **within the midst of the uncovering** (the unveiling; the laying bare; the revelation; the disclosure) **of the Lord Jesus from [our] atmosphere**…" For more on that passage see my, *Peter, Paul & Jacob… comments on 2 Thes., et al*, Harper Brown, 2012 pp 135-6

Moving on, let us observe the durative (continuing) aspect of the future tense of the verb in the first clause of the next verse…

8. **Who will continue making you folks stable, certain and established on good footing until maturity** (attainment of the purposed goal; accomplishment of the intended and destined results; finished)**: people not [being] open to accusation** (or: those not in the midst of a [legal] charge, not being called into account, or considered in some category; unimpeachable ones), **within the midst of and in union with this Day of our Lord – Jesus Christ!**
> (or: in the, or this, Day which is our Lord, Jesus Christ; or: in the day of [Yahweh], which is our Master, Jesus [the] Anointed.).

Now he tells them that Jesus "will continue making you folks stable, certain and established on good footing until maturity…" We just read, in 6b, above, that the witness and testimony (which was a "disclosure" to them that made them a called-out community) "**was made certain, stable and established on good footing** (or: validated and confirmed) **within, and among**" them. *Cf* a similar statement in 2 Cor. 1:21. So now we read that He will continue to establish them, **until** they reach maturity. This calls to mind Eph. 4:13,
> "**until we – the whole of mankind** (all people) **– can** (or: would) **come down to the goal** (or: attain; arrive at; meet accordingly; meet down face-to-face)**: into the state of oneness from, and which is, The Faithfulness, and which is the full, experiential and intimate knowledge** (or: and from recognition; and of discovery; as well as pertaining to insight) **which is** (or: of; from; in reference to) **the Son of God, [growing] into [the] purposed and destined adult man** (complete, finished, full-grown, perfect, goal-attained, mature manhood) **– into (or: unto) [the] measure of [the] stature** (full age; prime of life) **of the entire content which comprises the Anointed One.**"

Take note, in vs.8, above, of the parenthetical expansion of "maturity." It means "attainment of the purposed goal; accomplishment of the intended and destined results; finished." But further, they would be "people [that are] not open to accusation (etc.)." How would this be accomplished? By being "within the midst of and in union with **this Day** of our Lord…" We find in 2 Cor. 6:2 that this Day is now! In 1 Thes. 5:5 we read that, "**for you see, you all are sons of** (from; associated with and having the qualities of; or: which are) **Light and sons of** (from; associated with and having qualities of; or: which are [the]) **Day!**" And in Rom. 13:13 Paul tells us, "**As within [the] Day, we should** (may; can) **walk about** (= live our lives) **respectably**." It is for these reasons that I chose the demonstrative use of the definite article, "**this**," in the bold rendering. The parenthetical expansion of the last compound phrase of vs. 8, above, offers the terms "our Lord Jesus Christ" as a genitive of apposition: "in the Day which is our Lord, Jesus Christ." Christ IS the Day of the Lord. This phrase was used by the OT prophets to signify God's influence and activity upon a people. Associating those prophecies with the Age of the Messiah (in which Paul was, and we are, living), on offer is, "in the day of [Yahweh], which is our Master, Jesus [the] Anointed." 2 Pet. 1:19 put it this way:
> "**And so, we continue having** (or: constantly hold) **the Idea which was spoken ahead of time in and as Light** (or: the prior-enlightened Thought and Reason; or: the Prophetic Word) **more confirmed** (validated; established; certain), **by which** (or: in which) **you folks continue doing beautifully** (performing ideally; producing finely), **while continuously holding** toward (= playing close attention to) **[it] as to a lamp continually shining within a parched place – until which**

[time or occasion] the Day may shine through and a light bearer [= a morning star] may rise within your hearts

(or: constantly heeding, as to a lamp progressively making things appear in a dark, dingy or dirty place, until that the Day can dawn, and a light-bringer can arise in union with your core and innermost being)."

The Day is within us (in the core of our being), and we are in the Day (Christ). But Paul concludes this affirmation describing the present state of being of his Corinthian listeners in the next verse:

9. **God [is] full of faith, trustworthy, loyal and faithful – through Whom you folks were called** (summoned) **into a common being of and existence from** (or: partnership, participation, fellowship, sharing and communion with) **His Son, Jesus Christ, our Lord** (Owner; Master).

Take note of the supplied copula "[is]" in this common Greek construction, as we found in vs. 3, above. This statement is a description of God: "full of faith, trustworthy, loyal and faithful." These adjectives describe God. When He forms us to be in His image (as seen in Jesus), then we too become full of faith, trustworthy, loyal and faithful. We find this statement repeated in 10:13, below:

"**Now God [is] faithful, loyal, trustworthy, and full of faith and trust – One who will not permit** (let, allow; or: let go; leave alone) **you folks to be tested, tried, tempted or made to undergo an ordeal above** (or: over; = beyond) **that which you people continue having ability and power [to handle or endure], but to the contrary, together with the trial** (or: ordeal), **He will also continually make the way out** (the egress; or: He also will habitually do the stepping forth from out of the midst; or: He will even progressively construct the out-come) **to continually enable and repeatedly empower you folks to undergo [it]** (to bear up under [it]; to carry on under [it], sustain [it], and lead on)."

We find another witness of this in 1 Thes. 5:21,

"**The One continuously calling you is faithful** (trustworthy; loyal; full of faith and trust), **Who will also perform** (do, make, form, construct, create, produce) **[it; this]!**"

This is echoed in Heb. 10:23b, "**the One promising [is] Faithful, Trustworthy and Loyal!**"

It is through Him that we were called (see vs. 2, above) and invited to participate in Him. This experience, and this new existence is described as coming "**into a common being of, and existence from, His Son.**" Put this way it seems hard to understand or accept, but the Greek word means exactly this. *Koinōnia* has as its root -*ōn*-, which is a present participle of the verb "to be; to exist." The prefix *koin*- means "common." We have been invited into a "common being" with His Son. A "common existence, from His Son." This is HOW we become His body, with Him as our Head. It happens through means of His call and invitation to us. This is the work of God (as seen in the passive voice); we do not choose to be involved in this **common being** (of God and us). It is a call to discipleship and to be His representatives to the world about us. Jesus put this plainly in Jn. 15:16,

"**You yourselves did not choose Me, but to the contrary I, Myself, selected and picked out** (or: chose) **you folks and placed** (or: set) **you, to the end that you would** (or: can; may) **progressively lead and bring [situations] under control** (or: humbly go your way) **and would** (or: can; should) **be constantly bearing** (bringing forth) **fruit…**"

The fruit is the fruit of the Spirit (Gal. 5:22-25), and its purpose is to feed the aggregate of humanity.

Now the extended meanings of the term, *koinōnia*, signify "partnership, participation, fellowship, sharing and communion with," but they are all watered-down meanings of the central meaning of the word. A partnership is a "common existence" in a business venture. Participation expresses personal involvement. Fellowship expresses association and interaction. Sharing is an incarnation of Love. And communion expresses intimacy. But none of these hit the core meaning of a "common existence" or a "common being" – both of which are ontological and existential expressions. What the primary message conveys is that WE have been called, and invited, into a COMMON EXISTENCE, or a common BEING, with Christ. If we render the genitive phrase as apposition we can get a picture of what theologians have

9

called "the mystical body of Christ," i.e.: "a common existence WHICH IS His Son," i.e., the corporate body of the last Adam, or, the Second Humanity. This is what Israel was made to become (Ex. 4:22). This is what UNION brings. Participation in His Son – being "in Christ." We recall here Gal. 4:4,

> "**Yet when the effect of the filling of the time came** (or: that which was filled up by time reached full term), **forth from out of a mission** (or: from out of the midst of [Himself]), **God sent-off His Son**…"

This speaks to us of Jn. 3:16,

> "**For thus God loves** (or: You see God, in this manner, fully gives Himself to and urges toward reunion with) **the aggregate of humanity so that He gives His**…"

And we should not forget Rom. 8:29,

> "**because those whom He foreknew He also marked out beforehand** (defined and designed in advance) **[as] copies of the image** (material likeness; mirrored image) **of His Son into the [situation for] Him to be the Firstborn among, within the center of, and in union with many brothers.**"

These verses help us complete the picture of our being called into a common existence with His Son.

10. **Now I am constantly performing as a paraclete, calling you alongside to aid, comfort and encourage you, brothers** (= fellow members), **through the Name of our Lord – Jesus Christ – to the end that you can** (should; may; would) **all keep on speaking the very same thing, and there may not continue being tearing splits-effects** (divisions; schisms; rifts) **among you folks, but you should** (or: would) **progressively be folks having been mended, knit together and restored so as to be adjusted down, attuned on the same level, fitly and completely united within the very same mind and in union with the very same result of knowing** (consensus of intent; opinion of purpose; effect of personal insightful-knowing [*gnōmē*]).

We first want to point out the Greek word that I translated "performing as a paraclete." This term has been brought into the English language, specifically in reference to the Holy Spirit, based upon Jn. 14:16-17a,

> "**I Myself will continue asking** (making a request of) **the Father, and He will proceed to be giving another Helper** (One called alongside to give assistance, relief, comfort and encouragement; Paraclete), **of like kind, to you folks – to the end that He** (or: It) **can continue being** [other MSS: would be constantly remaining and dwelling] **with you folks on into the midst of the Age – the Spirit of the Truth** (or: the spirit and breath of reality; the Breath-effect and Attitude which is this Reality)…"

The noun form is only used in Jn. 1416, 25; 15:26; 16:7, and in 1 Jn. 2:1,

> "**And if anyone should at some point fail** (or: suddenly commit sin, make a mistake or deviate), **we constantly have One called alongside to help, give relief and guide us toward the Father** (or: we continuously possess a Paraclete, face to face with the Father)**: Jesus Christ, [the] One in accord with the Way pointed out** (or: a Just One; [the] Righteous One; [the] Fair One who is in right relationship with all; a Rightwised One; [the] right one; a Person that is turned in the right direction)."

Now John also identifies the "Spirit of the Truth/Reality" (Jn. 14:17a), as "the Holy Spirit/Breath-effect," in Jn. 14:26,

> "**Now the Helper** (the One called alongside to aid, comfort, encourage and bring relief; the Paraclete), **the set-apart Spirit** (or: the Sacred Breath; the holy Breath-effect; the holy attitude), **which the Father will proceed sending within, and in union with, My Name, that One will be progressively teaching you all things** (everything) **and will continue reminding you of** (calling to your mind and causing you to think about) **everything** (all things) **which I, Myself, said to you.**"

Yet with all this, notice that Paul states (vs. 10, here) that he is constantly performing as a paraclete – by calling them alongside to aid, comfort and encourage them. This is the work of both Jesus, and the Holy

Spirit, i.e., "the Spirit and breath of reality." Dan Kaplan reminded us of the first Adam, and how God said that it is "not ideal for the human to continue existing, being alone. We should at some point form (make; produce; construct) help in him, on the level of him (or: help by or with him, corresponding to him; or: a helper for him that accords with him)" (Gen. 2:18, LXX; JM). She was taken from Adam's side to be a "paraclete" for him.

Next, let us observe that Paul is functioning this way "**through the Name of our Lord, Jesus Christ**." First of all, "the Name" represents the Person. Paul was now associated with, and commissioned by, Jesus Christ (vs. 1, above) and had been called into a common existence with God's Son (vs. 9), he operated in the Lord's name, and thus, in Christ's authority. In representing the Lord, he possessed the power that was invested in "the Name," and therefore was able to bring God's help to these Corinthians. This all had a specific purpose. It was, "**to the end that you can** (should; may; would) **all keep on speaking the very same thing, and there may not continue being tearing splits-effects** (divisions; schisms; rifts) **among you folks**." Observe that if they would "speak the very same thing" then there should be no "split-effects" or "divisions" among them. The unity of a "common existence" (vs. 9) should produce the peace from "the joining." This should be their situation, because they "**should** (or: would) **progressively be folks having been mended, knit together and restored so as to be adjusted down, attuned on the same level, fitly and completely united**."

The verb of this clause, "progressively be," is a present subjunctive of the verb "to be; to exist." What follows the verb is a description of WHAT they should and would be, in the form of a perfect participle (indicating action that was completed in the past). In other words, a past action (by God) would determine what they WOULD progressively BE. They would, and should, be "folks having been mended." This indicates a repairing of what had been torn, or worn out. On offer, following "mended," is a conflation of the semantic range of the participle: "knit together; restored so as to be adjusted down; attuned on the same level; fitly and completely united." Wow! What a description of what the body of Christ should be!

But wait, there is more: they would be completely united because of being, "**within the very same mind and in union with the very same result of knowing**." Notice the close association of the words "**mind**" and "**knowing**." Sounds logical, right? The SAME mind (Christ's – 2:16, below). The SAME "result" of knowing. Knowledge of, and from, God came via an unveiling of Christ. The word used here is a –*ma* form (signifying result or effect) of *gnosis*: intimate, experiential knowledge and insight. It came from the Light shining into our darkness. The mending, knitting, restoring, unifying, etc. was, in part, in the MIND. Now this calls to mind Rom. 12:2b,

> "**be progressively transformed** (transfigured; changed in form and semblance) **by the renewing** (or: in the renewal; for the making-back-up-new again) **of your mind** [with other MSS: from The Mind; of the intellect; pertaining to the faculties of perceiving and understanding; of the mindset, disposition, inner orientation and world view] **into the [situation and condition for] you folks to be habitually examining in order to be testing and, after scrutiny, distinguishing and approving what [is] God's will** (design; purpose; resolve; intent)**: the good and well-pleasing, even perfect** (finished, complete and destined)**!**"

This is one of Paul's many imperatives, but keep in mind that when Paul's was speaking the *Logos*, as Christ's representative, with the imperative also came the power to accomplish it. Paul was speaking a creative word into the Roman community. It would happen through the work of the Spirit, just as the mending, adjusting and unifying would come to be in the Corinthian community. He simply used different expressions to describe the same work of Christ with us. The last expression of 1:10b that we have been dissecting (same result of knowing) can also be rendered in the following, extended ways: "consensus of intent; opinion of purpose; effect of personal insightful-knowing." Opinions are often formed from personal insights or observations, using our minds to judge a matter. These can affect our counsel, resolve or disposition (*cf* Bultmann, *TDNT 1*, p 717). The readings, "**result** of knowing" and "**effect** of personal insight-knowing" give the literal, and in our opinion, best understanding of Paul in this verse. This work by the Spirit, of opening their understanding through the impartation of the mind of Christ, is the

ONLY means of unity. Their different lines of thought (as seen in vs. 11, below) very likely came from their listening to the different teachers (listed in vs. 12, below), but as Conzelmann observed (ibid p 32), they still remained as a single community, even if they were not yet "**completely united within the very same mind and in union with the very same result of knowing**."

11. **For it was made evident and is clear** (or: was declared by intelligible communication) **to me about** (or: concerning) **you folks, my brothers** (= family of believers), **by those of Chloe's [people; group; household], that there continue being quarrels** (situations of strife; discordant debates) **among you people** (or: contentious dispositions within you folks).

This is why they needed the services of Paul, in being a paraclete to them, and why he (in vs. 10) was focusing them on being in agreement (speaking the same thing and having the same mind) and in unity. Verses 12 through 16 set out examples of the division among them.

12. **Now I am saying this because each of you is in the habit of saying, "I, myself, am indeed [a follower] of Paul," yet [another], "I myself belong to Apollos," and [another], "As for me, I [am] of Cephas' [group]," but [another], "I, myself, [am] of** (or: from) **Christ."**

Some things never change. This was the beginning of the Christian denominations! There was as much bad form then as it is now. Religion and politics seem to always spawn "parties." The situation in Corinth apparently came from people making personal decisions about with whom they would identify, rather than being "led by the Spirit" (Rom. 8:14). Thus, they were NOT "united with the same mind," and differing opinions was the result. This may well have happened through each of the teachers, listed here, presented to them a different way of "knowing" or a different "personal insight." We still have this today.

For variety of expression, and since each person tends to express himself differently, the genitive/ablative cases in these phrases were rendered "of Paul;" "belong to Apollos;" and "from Christ." Teachers, or leaders became identity markers within the community. For more of Paul's thinking along these lines, see 3:21-23, below. We read of Apollos in Acts 18:24-28 where he had come to Ephesus. He was

> "**a native of Alexandria – an adult man of reason, thought, and a gifted speaker** (or: a learned and eloquent man; a man well-trained in rhetoric) **being able and powerful in the** Scriptures... one **having been orally instructed in the way** (or: path) **of the Lord and continuing boiling hot** (= fervent) **in** (or: by; for; with) **the Breath-effect** (the Spirit), **he kept on speaking and teaching accurately the things concerning** (or: about) **Jesus – versed in and acquainted with only the immersion** (or: baptism) **carried out by John**" (vss. 24-25).

Stephen J. Patterson (*The Lost Way, How Two forgotten Gospels Are Rewriting the Story of Christian Origins*. HarperOne, 2014) suggests that since he had been educated in the wisdom schools of Alexandria, and knew only the teaching, baptism and wisdom from John the baptist's teaching about Jesus, that Paul may have been referring to him in his comment about "**not in cleverness of word** (within [wisdom] of a message or an idea; not in skillfulness of rhetoric)," in vs. 17, below. This may have been prior to his meeting with "**Priscilla and Aquila [who] took him to themselves and more accurately exposed** (or: expounded; set out from the midst) **God's Way** (or: path)" (Acts 18:26). It was during this period that Gnosticism had been growing in some streams of Judaism, especially in Alexandria (the general area where the Gnostic writings of the Nag Hammadi Library was found). If Gnostic influence, which did not speak of the death and resurrection of Christ, was a part of what was causing division in Corinth, we may better understand Paul's re-emphasis on "Christ crucified" (2:2, below). John had preached a baptism, but not the crucifixion. Paul joins both concepts...

13. **Christ has been parted and remains divided into fragments!** (or, as a question: Has Christ been fragmented and portioned out into divided parts?)
Paul was not crucified (suspended from a pole; executed on a stake) **over** (on behalf of; [other MSS: concerning]) **you folks! Or were you baptized** (immersed) **into the name of Paul?**

My first rendering follows the lead of the *Concordant Literal NT* by making this a statement, rather than as a question, as the parenthetical rendering offers. The body of Christ IS, in fact, Christ, and in Corinth, at that time, Paul observed that Christ's body was divided. Keep in mind that the oldest MSS did not have punctuation marks. But most scholars cannot imagine "Christ" being divided, and so prefer this as a question, as if to imply that Paul means, "By no means! – so why are you folks divided?" Either reading makes sense; it depends upon our perspectives.

As can be deduced from vss. 14-16, below, apparently there was considered to be a connection between the person who immersed (baptized) folks and those who were immersed. But Paul makes a more serious association with the name to whom people claimed connection. Neither he nor these other teachers were crucified over, or on behalf of, humanity. These teachers were not the Savior! And for those who claimed association with Paul, he affirms that they were not baptized into his name. And this last statement instructs us as to the importance of "the Name." Some scholars have read the last statement of vs. 12 as Paul saying that he, himself, was of, or from, Christ – as were they all – and thus they should not be considering themselves to be a part of some human teacher, or group, nor a follower of his or that group's teaching. Other scholars have considered the "of Christ" identification as a reference to Gnostics within the community who identified themselves only with the realm of "spirit" – i.e., viewing themselves as being the superior, "spiritual" members of the community. If this was the case, then most likely their view of "baptism" was that it was spiritual, not physical (*cf* Mat. 3:11b; Tit. 3:5) – and thus there could be continuity from this verse to the next.

Note the phrase, "**into the name**." Conzelmann suggests that this indicated the ideas of ownership, subjection and protection (ibid p 35-36). But a deeper level is seen by what Paul says in Gal. 27,
> "**For you see** (or: It follows that) **as many of you folks as were immersed into Christ, at once clothed yourselves with Christ** (or: were plunged into so as to be enveloped by then saturated and permeated with Anointing – or, the Anointed One – instantly entered within and put on [the/an] Anointing)!" *Cf* Rom. 6:3ff.

14. I continue with goodness of grace (or: thankful; [other MSS: I constantly thank {others add: my} God] **that I baptized** (immersed) **NOT ONE of you folks – if not even Crispus and Gaius!**
15. – so that NO ONE could say that you folks were immersed (other MSS: that I baptized) **into MY OWN name!**

In these two verses, I put "**NOT ONE**" and "**NO ONE**" in all upper case for emphasis, and to call the reader's attention to the denials emphatically stated in both of these verses. Rotherham uses diacritical marks to show the emphasis in these verses. My purpose is to set the scene for my rendering the first sentence in vs. 16, below, as a question.

A common rendering of the last phrase of vs. 14 offers the conditional particle followed by the negative particle (*ei mē*) by the term "except." Although grammatically correct, this reading would say that Paul did indeed baptize two people among them – which would be a flat contradiction to his emphatic NOT ONE and NO ONE in these two verses! For this reason, I chose "**if not even**" (*ei* means "if" and *mē* means "not") as rhetorical emphasis: If he had immersed ANYONE in the community, it would have been these two men. Now Crispus was immersed (Acts 18:8), and this would have been natural for him to do so since he was the chief ruler of the synagogue in Corinth (and as we see from the work of John the Immerser, immersion was part of the Jewish customs) – but this does not mean that it was Paul who "baptized" him. Gaius is mentioned in Rom. 16:23 where it states that he had hosted Paul, and it was from the area of Corinth that Paul wrote to the community in Rome.

Notice also the emphasis: "the name of Paul" (vs. 13); and "**MY OWN** name," here. The personal pronoun "MY OWN" is in the emphatic position in the Greek text. He stood strongly against following, or identifying with, anyone other than Christ.

16. **Now, did I even baptize** (immerse) **the household of Stephanas? Furthermore, I have not seen or know whether** (or: if) **I immersed some other person!**

The household/family of Stephanas was the first group to become converted in the Province of Achaia, so if it was Paul's custom to teach physical immersion (baptism) as a part of the Good News, we would not expect his strong negations about his immersing NO ONE in vss. 14-15. The conventional rendering, "And I baptized also…" (KJV) would also fly in the face of vss. 14-15. Of course it is possible that Paul was conceding that what he had just said was not completely true, but reading it this way would seem to undercut his argument.

Paul does not want people following him or taking his name as an indication that they hold to his teachings more than to someone else's. Such practices only lead to more divisions, fragmenting Christ. In regard to the term "household," we find it repeatedly in Acts (11:14; 16:15, 32, 34; 18:8), and the nuance of corporate inclusion is evident.

17. **For you see, Christ did not send me off with a commission to be constantly baptizing** (immersing), **but rather to habitually announce the message of goodness** (to repeatedly bring the message of abundant well-being; to progressively declare the news of fortunate and ideal ease), **[though] not in cleverness of word** (within [wisdom] of a message or an idea; not in skillfulness of rhetoric) **– in order that the cross of the Christ** (the Anointed One's execution-stake) **cannot** (or: would not) **be made empty or void of content and purpose [by rhetoric].**

He makes a startling statement in vs. 17 that would seem to be contrary to the emphasis that has been observed both in evangelical Christianity, and in traditional segments that emphasize the "sacraments." He asserts to them that, "**Christ did not send me off with a commission to be constantly baptizing** (immersing)." This is a response to his rhetorical question to them in vs. 13, "**Or were you baptized** (immersed) **into the name of Paul?**" Here he is equating immersion into a name of someone with their divisive claims of belonging to the parties of himself, Apollos, Peter, etc. (vs. 12). Such thinking and such speaking was actually dividing Christ (vs. 13a), since His body was being divided. But their source of being Christ's body was not these folks, as he posits in vs. 13, in reference to himself: "**Paul was not crucified** (suspended from a pole; executed on a stake) **over** (on behalf of; [other MSS: concerning]) **you folks!**" In other words, it was Christ's crucifixion that had founded them all, making them "**those having been set-apart within Christ Jesus**" (vs. 2, above).

So rather than baptizing them, this was Paul's mission: "**rather to habitually announce the message of goodness** (to repeatedly bring the message of abundant well-being; to progressively declare the news of fortunate and ideal ease)" (vs. 17). This conveyance of information (spreading the *Logos*) brought them into knowledge and awareness that called for a change in their thinking about everything. The gift of the mind of Christ (via the proclamation) enabled them to have a new world view with new perspectives. The old had passed away, and the new had come (2 Cor. 5:17). It was this "**very same mind and in union with the very same result of knowing**" (vs. 10, above) – this revelation of, and from, the Christ – that was to be their unifying identity around which they should come together. The message was the important thing, not the human instrument that God had used to bring them into the new creation (2 Cor. 5:17).

We should not miss the import of the final clause of vs. 17, where Paul emphasizes the manner in which he had announced the message of goodness: "**not in cleverness of word** (within [wisdom] of a message or an idea; not in skillfulness of rhetoric) **– in order that the cross of the Christ** (the Anointed One's execution-stake) **cannot** (or: would not) **be made empty or void of content and purpose [by rhetoric]**." Paul develops his theology of "the cross of the Christ," beginning with the next verse. But let us consider his concern that it might be "made empty or void of content and purpose." In Rom. 4:14 he stated that,

> "**You see, if the ones out of law** (or: = those who have [the] Law as their origin) **[are] heirs** (inheritors and enjoyers of the allotment), **[then] the faith has been made empty** (void; vain) **and is now without content, and the Promise has been rendered useless** (has been permanently unemployed and idle; has been annulled and is inoperative)."

And in 1 Thes. 3:5b he expressed concern,

> "**lest** (or: in case) **somehow the One continuously putting [folks] to the proof** (or: the trier; [note: this could refer to God, or to one of His instruments, as with Job]) **put you to the proof** (tried or tested you), **and our exhausting labor** (or: = the trouble to which we went; toil; hardship; or: beating) **may be birthed into a void** (or: come to be [entered] into an empty place; or: exist in vain; = be to no purpose)."

Also, in Phil.2:16b, he informed them that,

> "**I do not** (or: did not) **run into emptiness** (that which is without content; a void), **nor do I** (or: did I) **become weary or struggle in labor into emptiness** (unto that which is without content; into the midst of a void)."

In referring to his visit to the Jewish believers in Jerusalem, he wrote to the Galatians that,

> "**I put up to them** (set back again for them; = submitted to them) **the message of goodness, ease and well-being, which I am habitually proclaiming as a public message within the multitudes** (or: among the nations and ethnic groups – non-Jews; Gentiles) **– yet [I did so] privately, to those continuing to be disposed to thinking and imagination** (or: for those being supposed to continue with a reputation; or: to ones yet forming opinions), **lest somehow I am progressively rushing forward and running, or had run, into emptiness** (or: for an empty thing; into something without content; = to no purpose; or: = in vain)" (Gal. 2:2).

Like Jesus, in Jn. 15:1ff, Paul focused upon fruit coming from his work in the Lord. Jesus was aware that unless folks would remain joined in intimate relationship with Him (abide, remain, and dwell, in Him) there would be no fruit of the Spirit in their lives. They would simply be an "empty" branch that would die off from a lack of the flow of His Life in them. So Paul did not just try to convince people by rhetoric or philosophical ideas. The cross of the Christ is about a life that is lived in a cruciform manner, as we remain "joined to the Lord" (6:17, below). Turning back to the Law would bring emptiness; testings and trials could make folks leave the Path; a public debate with the scribes or Pharisees would lead into an empty situation. However, we read in 15:10, below, "**Yet in** (or: by; for; with) **God's grace, and joyous favor which is God, I am what I am, and His [placed]-into-me grace** (or: [birthed]-into-me joyous favor) **was not birthed to be empty**." So despite his concern for his sheep in the called-out communities, he trusted in God's grace – and in him it would prove to be fruitful. He ends his long argument in 15:58, below, with a positive word for them:

> "**Consequently, my beloved brothers, progressively come to be seated and settled folks – immovable and unswerving people – continuing to always be surrounded by more than enough** (or: superabounding) **within the midst of the Lord's work** (= [Yahweh's or Christ's] deed or act), **having seen and now knowing that your fatiguing labor** (or: toil) **does not exist without contents** (is not empty) **within and in union with [the] Lord**."

His admonition for them to "progressively come to be seated and settled" metaphorically corresponds to Jesus' admonition "to abide" in Him. In 2 Cor. 6:1 he admonishes them,

> "**Now we, habitually** (or: continuously) **working together [with Him], are constantly calling you folks alongside to aid, comfort, direct and encourage you not to accept or receive God's grace into a void** (or: an empty or vain [situation; way of life])."

This danger seemed to be a constant concern. As Jesus said, the cares of this life can choke out the life of the Word that has been planted. Rocky soil can restrict the striking of a root. And we have all seen the reality of this in peoples' lives…

The history of the theological philosophy, within the development of church doctrines, displays a witness to the truth of Paul's words, here: the scope of the effect of the cross of the Anointed One was made void of content and purpose by philosophical theories that tried to box up Christ into formulas and creeds. Fortunately, as C.S. Lewis allegorized, "Aslan is not a tame lion." Christ cannot be held within orthodox boxes. And so he explains...

18. **You see, the message** (the word; the *Logos*) **of the cross** (or: the idea from, and the concept pertaining to, the execution-stake/suspension-pole) **is and continues being, on the one hand, stupidity** (nonsense; foolishness) **to** (or: for; in; with) **those folks constantly, progressively destroying themselves** (or, as a passive: being habitually lost or progressively undone); **yet, on the other hand, it is and continues being God's power** (or: the ability of and from God; the power which is God) **in us, to us and for us: in the folks being presently delivered**
> (or: for those being continually rescued, repeatedly saved and progressively restored to health and wholeness; or: with the ones being now salvaged and progressively restored).

Conzelmann posits that the section of 1:18-3:23 should be "taken as a unity" (ibid p 39).

How is "**the message of the cross... God's power**"? First of all take note that this "ability of, from, and which is God" is "**in us, to us and for us**." Jesus told His followers,
> "**you folks will progressively receive power and will continue taking to yourselves ability: a sudden** (point of time) **added, full coming of the Set-apart Breath-effect** (the Holy Spirit and Sacred Attitude) **upon you folks**" (Acts 1:8a).

The *Logos* enters within us as we listen to the announcement of the message. Then the *Logos* constructs a new creation within us, and makes all things new. This is what God meant when He told John,
> "**Consider this! I am presently making all things new** (or: habitually creating everything [to be] new and fresh; progressively forming [the] whole anew; or, reading *panta* as masculine: I am periodically making **all humanity** new, and progressively, one after another, producing and creating **every person** anew, while constantly constructing all people fresh and new, i.e., continuously renewing **everyone**)!" (Rev. 21:5) [*cf* Isa. 43:19-21; 65:17-25; 2 Cor. 5:17]

Now of course His **power** is "for us," and He gives His ability "to us." This is what "delivers" us. The parenthetical expansion of the present participle "**being presently delivered**," shows other aspects of the work of God within us. Observe the "divine passive" which indicates that God is the Actor: continually rescued; repeatedly saved and progressively restored to health and wholeness; now salvaged and progressively restored. These are the results of the Good News. It was happening in Paul's day, and it has continued happening to each person, in their own group or class (15:23, below). Paul put it this way, in Rom. 1:16,
> "**You see, God's power** (or: [the] ability of God; capacity from God; or: **a power which is God**) **is unto deliverance** (or: exists [leading] into rescue, salvation, health, wholeness and restoration to the original state and condition) **for everyone** (or: in all; to everyone) **– to, for, in and with the person continuously having faith and trusting** (or: believing and relying upon [it]; being faithful): **both for** (to; in) **[the] Jew first, also for** (to; in) **[the] Greek** (or: = non-Jew)
>> (or: – to not only the believing/trusting Jew, but also, firstly {or: primarily}, to the Hellenist as well)."

Peter spoke of this same power, and of a similar situation, when addressing the house of Cornelius,
> "**Jesus, the One from Nazareth – even as how God anointed Him with [a/the] set-apart Breath-effect** (or: Holy Spirit; Sacred Attitude) **even for** (or: and with) **power and ability – Who went throughout repeatedly doing works bringing goodness, ease and well-being, as well as constantly healing all the folks being continuously held down under power** (tyrannized and oppressed) **by the one that casts things through folks** (the accuser, slanderer, adversary)**... because God was with Him**" (Acts 10:38).

Now tying these to situations with Paul's letter to Corinth, here, is the opening of the Gospel of Mark:

"**A beginning of the good news, which is Jesus Christ, God's Son** (or: [The] beginning of the message of goodness, ease and well-being which pertains to Jesus Christ – Son of God; or: A starting point from the evangel of [the] Anointed Jesus [= Messiah Yahshua], a son from God)" (Mk. 1:1).

Here, in vs. 18, Paul instructs us that "the good news which is Jesus" is "**the message** (the word; the *Logos*) **of the cross**," which is a code word for the Christ Event. In Mk. 14:62 Jesus uses the word "Power" to refer to God, when referring to His soon exaltation to be "**by habit sitting at** (or: forth from the midst of) **[the] right [hand; section] of the Power**..." And in Eph. 3:20b we read of,

"**the power and ability [which is] continuously operating** (making itself effective; energizing itself; working and developing) **within US, and in union with US**."

Heb. 1:3b instructs us about how the Son is, "**continuously bearing** (or: progressively carrying; and then repeatedly bringing) **the whole** (all things; everything and all existence) **by the gush-effect which is His power**." The 1 Pet. 1:5 informs us about Peter's listeners who were,

"**being continuously garrisoned within** (or: kept, maintained and guarded in the center of) **God's power, in union with an ability which is God, through [His] faithfulness, into a deliverance** (a rescue which brings health, wholeness and a return to your original state and condition; salvation; a [period of] rescue)..."

And then 2 Pet. 1:16 speaks about their, "**experientially or intimately [making] known to you the power and presence** (or: ability and [the] being alongside; *parousia*) **of our Lord, Jesus Christ**." Peter and his associates did this through proclaiming to them "**the message** (the word; the *Logos*) **of the cross**," for it is "**God's power** (or: the ability of and from God; the power which is God) **in us, to us and for us: in the folks being presently delivered**." Paul explains part two of this message in Phil.3:10 when he speaks of, "**the ability – even the power – of His resurrection and also the common existence** (participation; partnership, sharing and fellowship) **of the results and from the effects of His experiences**." Before leaving this focus on "power and ability," let us visit 2 Cor. 13:3b-4, which speaks of Christ,

"**not being weak, but rather continues powerful** (or: capable) **within and in union with you folks. For even though He was crucified from out of weakness** (or: hung and put to death on a torture stake forth from the midst of weakness), **yet in contrast He is continuously living from out of the midst of God's power and ability. For you see, we ourselves also continue being weak, within** (or: in union with) **Him, but still we will continue on living unto you, together with** [other MSS: within] **Him, from out of the midst of God's power and ability**."

The perception of the message as being "stupidity, nonsense and foolishness" comes across this way "**to** (or: for; in) **those folks constantly, progressively destroying themselves** (or, as a passive: being habitually lost or progressively undone)." Recall Jesus' words in Jn. 3:16, God sent His Son so that the aggregate of humanity "**would not lose or destroy itself, or cause itself to fall into ruin, but rather can continuously have** (or: would habitually possess and hold) **eonian life**." Without having the Son, people can do nothing else than destroy themselves. When a person is imprisoned by an addiction, or is walking a path of self-absorbed over-desires, they are "progressively destroying themselves" and the message sounds crazy – until the Light breaks through into them. If someone is emotionally lost, or is progressively undone by ill health, their mental state of hopelessness can make "the idea from, or pertaining to, the cross" sound ridiculous. But we who have the Light, have been informed concerning the crucified Christ:

"**You see, the Son of the Man** (= the eschatological messianic figure) **came to seek after, and then to save, deliver and restore what is existing being lost and destroyed**" (Lu. 19:10).

Conzelmann (ibid p 41) points out that Paul does not contrast "stupidity/foolishness" with "wisdom," but rather with "God's power." The contrast is also between, "**those folks constantly, progressively destroying themselves** (or, as a passive: being habitually lost or progressively undone)," and "**the folks being presently delivered** (etc.)." He cites Adolf Schlatter as positing that "if the word of the cross were 'wisdom,' 'then it would instruct us as to how the community can help itself'" (ibid p 42). The dative case that is used in designating both of these groups, in Paul's argument, should be noted. Each potential function of the dative (represented by the prepositions "in; to; for; with") expresses the sphere (in), relationship (to), purpose and focus (for), and corporate association (with) between "the idea from, and the concept pertaining to, the execution-stake/suspension-pole," which points to the historic Event, and each existential group to which Paul points his arguments. It is the impartation, or the impregnation, of the *Logos* (the Living Word that is delivered in the message) that births faith and brings "deliverance" and "salvation." This is the core idea of Paul's reference to the "message" of the crucifixion. Here, once again, Paul's "second" letter to Corinth gives more detailed instruction, in 2 Cor. 4:

> 3. **because you are and continue being those continuously set in clear light and progressively manifested: Christ's letter** (a letter whose source is Christ, and which is Christ), **being one dispensed in attending service by us, being one having been written** (inscribed; imprinted; engraved), **not in black** (= not with ink), **but rather, by** (or: in; with) **God's Spirit: One continuously living** (or: in a Breath-effect which has its origin in God, Who is constantly living); **not in stone tablets** (or: on tablets composed of stone), **but rather within tablets which are hearts made of flesh** (or: on tablets in hearts composed of flesh). [*cf* Rom. 8:26-27]
> 4. **Now through the Christ we continuously possess** (or: So, by means of the Anointing we progressively have and hold) **this sort of persuaded trust and faith-based confidence [directed and leading] toward God** (or: face to face with God)
> 5. **– not that we are competent** (adequately enough; sufficiently qualified) **from ourselves to logically evaluate or count anything as it were forth from out of ourselves – but to the contrary, our competency** (adequacy; sufficiency; qualification) **[is] forth from out of the midst of** (having its source in) **God.**

The other group, "**constantly, progressively destroying themselves,**" are the "yet to be impregnated folks," those who are still living in the first Adam (15:45, below). Before moving on, let us consider an observation by Mario Murillo:

> "Preaching the entire Gospel releases power. 1 Cor. 1:18, 'For the message of the cross is foolishness to those who are perishing, but to us who are being saved it is the power of God.' Romans 1: 16, 'For I am not ashamed of the gospel of Christ, for it is the power of God unto salvation for everyone who believes...' Why is the phrase 'power of God' used in two verses that deal with the offense of the Gospel? Because it is the power of God that drives home truth, even when it offends. Paul understood the plan behind the offense. As a top-flight intellectual, he was keenly aware of the God-designed offense of the Cross. He refused to rely on his formidable skill in debate, saying instead: 'And my speech and my preaching were not with persuasive words of human wisdom, but in demonstration of the Spirit and of power, so that your faith should not be in the wisdom of men but in the power of God.' - 1 Cor. 2: 4-5"
> (https://mariomurilloministries.wordpress.com/2019/04/16/if-this-was/)

Paul continues developing his argument about what seems to be **stupidity**, in the following verses:

19. **For it has been written, and thus stands,**
> **"I will undo** (untie and loose-away; destroy) **the wisdom and cleverness of the wise ones, and I will set aside** (or: displace; invalidate) **the intelligence** (comprehension; understanding) **of the intellectual** (intelligent; comprehending) **people."** [Isa. 29:14]

Just what did this prophecy from Isa. 29 mean? "Undo the wisdom?" "Loose-away the cleverness?" "Set aside (displace; invalidate) the intelligence?" Who were these wise folks and intellectual people? Paul is taking something from Isaiah's day, applying it to the group in 1st century Corinth, and setting it forth as the proof of his thesis. Conzelmann makes this astounding observation: "The God of the OT speaks immediately through this book today" (ibid p 42). Every culture has had its "wise folks." So has every age and time. But what would "undo, destroy, displace and invalidate" human wisdom and intelligence? Paul gives the answer in vs 21, below: "**the wisdom of God**, or, Wisdom from, and which is, God." Verse 24, below, asserts that this Wisdom is manifested and embodied in Christ.

But still, who were the wise folks, and the intellectuals? For his listeners in Corinth, Plato and Socrates might first come to mind. The folks who questioned Paul in Athens (Acts 17) might also come to mind, as well as the schools of philosophy with which they might have been acquainted. Yet how about the Jewish listeners? Would Paul have been referring to such as Hillel or Gamaliel, or the authors of all the Jewish "wisdom literature"? Was he contrasting the Wisdom which was revealed in Christ with the traditions of the elders, or even the everyday wisdom of their cultures? If we look back to what Jesus taught, then I think we will have to answer, "Yes." What sort of wisdom advocates taking up one's execution stake and following a crucified Messiah? Christ's wisdom turned conventional wisdom on its head. This verse in Isa. is completely counter-cultural. Conzelmann posits that "wisdom" and "intelligence" also have reference to "attitude" (ibid), and so here we submit that these arise from spirit, and Spirit.

But just as Christ was rooted in the OT (Rom. 11:17; Lu. 24:27), God's wisdom was also found there. Richard Rohr ("Daily Meditation," March 26, 2018) offers these insights:

> "[In] the Wisdom Literature (many of the Psalms, Ecclesiastes, the Song of Songs, Wisdom, and the Book of Job)... you discover the language of mystery and paradox. This is what the second half of life is supposed to feel like. You are strong enough now to hold together contradictions in yourself, others, and the universe. And you can do so with compassion, forgiveness, and patience. You realize that your chosenness is for the sake of letting others know they are chosen too! I call this classic pattern of spiritual transformation 'order-disorder-reorder.' Paul calls it 'the foolishness of the cross' (see 1 Cor. 1:18-25). There is no nonstop flight from order to reorder. We have to go through a period of disruption and disordering. What we first call 'order' is almost always too small and too self-serving. The nexus point, the crossover moment, is one that neither conservatives nor liberals like or even understand. It will always feel like folly."

It is Christ, as the Wisdom of God, that both initiates and fulfills this transformation. We read of this wisdom in Jas. 3:17,

> "**But the wisdom from above is** (constantly exists being) **indeed first** (or: primarily) **pure, thereafter peaceable** (or: peaceful; pertaining to peace and harmonious joining), **suitable** (fair; reasonably lenient; yielding; unassertive; considerate), **compliant** (easily persuaded; receptive; reasonable; willing to yield), **full of mercy** (= practical help) **and good fruits, non-separating** (not discriminatory; undivided in evaluating; unwavering; unprejudiced), **unpretending** (or: not hyper-critical; not judging from a low point of view; not focusing on tiny distinctions; not overly judgmental; not under-estimating of reality)."

20. **Where [is] a wise one? Where [is] a scribe** (one learned in the Scriptures; [the] scholar or theologian)**? Where [is] a collaborating seeker** (a co-investigator; a learned sophist; a reasoner; a dialectician) **of, or from, this age? Does not God prove** (or: make) **stupid** (foolish; nonsensical) **the wisdom** (attitude; cleverness; learned skill) **of this ordered arrangement** (aggregate of humanity; domination System; world of culture, society, religion)**?** [cf Isa. 19:11f; 33:18; Bar. 3:15f, 23 (LXX)]

To have Paul's questions (and the situation at Corinth) addressed, we again turn to Jas. 3:

> 13. **Who [is] wise and understanding** (adept) **among you? Let him at once exhibit** (show; present to the sight and demonstrate) **his works and actions out of beautiful behavior** (fine, ideal, excellent and appropriate conduct) **in gentleness of** (or: considerateness from) **wisdom.**
> 14. **Yet if you folks continuously have bitter rivalry** (or: jealousy) **and selfish ambition** (or: faction) **in your heart, do not habitually boast** (exult) **and lie** (speak falsely or deceitfully) **concerning the truth or reality** (or: are you not now vaunting against and falsifying the truth?).
> 15. **This is not the wisdom continuously coming down from above, but rather [is] upon the earth** (or: earthly; terrestrial), **pertaining to or proceeding from the soul** (soulful; having the mind, will and emotions as its source; = natural), **pertaining to, or proceeding from, or having the characteristics of demons** [Hellenistic term and concept; = influences thought of in that period and culture as being animistic or personified].

19

[comment: note that the three adjectives "earthly," "natural/soulish," and "demonic" are tied together to this same context, as being of the same sphere of being – or, fruit of the same tree]

16. **For where [there is] jealousy** (rivalry) **and selfish ambition** (faction; intrigue), **in that place [is] instability** (disorder; an unsettled state) **and every ignoble** (base; vile; worthless) **practice.**

Notice that it is not "**this ordered arrangement**, aggregate of humanity, or world system" that God reveals to be "stupid; foolish." No, it is the thinking and attitude (the "wisdom") of humanity with its systems and philosophical schools that are foolish. Paul put it this way in Rom. 1:

22. **[So] continuously claiming** (asserting; alleging with pretense) **to be wise ones, they were made to be dull** (sluggish; moronic; stupid; foolish) [*vs. 23, below: cf Ps. 106:19-20; Ex. 32:4]
23. **and they at once changed** (or: exchange in barter; make other than it is) **the glory** (or: splendor and praise-inducing manifestation; or: esteem; opinion; imagination; supposition; thought; appearance; honorable consideration) **of the imperishable** (un-ruinable; unspoilable and incorruptible; non-decayable) **God within the result of a likeness** (resemblance; conformed similarity; copy-effect) **of an image** (form; appearance) **of a perishable** (corruptible; spoilable) **human, as well as of flying things and of four-footed [animals]* and of creeping things.**
24. **Wherefore** (or: On which account) **God gave** (or: hands) **them over** (or: delivered or transfers them into another's power), **within the full passions** (or: rushing passionate cravings; added earnest desires, wants and wishes; or: compiled angers and complete wrath) **of their hearts, into uncleanness** (or: ritual impurity), **to be continuously dishonored and shamed – with respect to** (or: pertaining to) **their bodies – among** (or: within) **themselves,**
25. **whichever folks altered or exchange God's truth** (or: the reality from and which is God, and which pertains to God) **to and for something else, within** (or: in union with) **The Lie, then they were adored and venerated with dread, and next rendered religious service to and for the creation** (or: creature; or: forming, framing, founding and settling which brought order from chaos) **alongside** (or: to the side of; parallel to; or: = rather than) **the Creator** (The One framing and founding) **Who is** (continuously exists being) **well spoken of** (praised; blessed; eulogized; or: is One filled with thoughts of goodness and well-being) **on into the ages. It is so** (Amen)**!**

Returning to Paul phrase, "**the wisdom** (attitude; cleverness; learned skill) **of this ordered arrangement** (aggregate of humanity; domination System; world of culture, society, religion)," it is possible that Paul had not only the Greek philosophers, but also the Jewish Platonism schools of Alexandria and the teachers such as Philo of Alexandria, or the wisdom literature generated by Second Temple Judaism, in general.

Cf 2:1, 4-7, 13; and 3:19, below, where Paul again addresses the topic of the two kinds of wisdom. But the keys lie here, in 1:24 and 30, below.

21. **For since, in view of the fact that – within the Wisdom of God** (or: centered in the wisdom from God; in the midst of the Wisdom which is God) **– the ordered arrangement and System of secular and religious culture** (or: the aggregate of humanity) **did not come to have an intimate, experiential knowledge of God through means of this Wisdom**

(or: You see, in as much as – in union with God's wisdom – the world of mankind did not recognize, or have insight into, God through means of [human] wisdom), **God delights and considers it profitable** (thinks it thoroughly competent and easy; imagines it well-done) **to deliver** (or: save; rescue; salvage and restore to health, wholeness and their original state and condition) **the folks habitually trusting, repeatedly faithing, progressively believing and constantly being loyal, through the stupidity of the proclamation**

(or: the aforementioned foolishness of that which is proclaimed; or: the dullness of the effect of heralding; or: the "nonsense" of the result of the message preached), Cf 2:6, below

The Wisdom of God is embedded within His creation (Rom. 1:18-20), and within the Hebrew Scriptures (Lu. 24:27). Nevertheless, "**the ordered arrangement and System of secular and religious culture** (i.e., the aggregate of humanity) **did not come to have an intimate, experiential knowledge of God through means of this Wisdom**." For this reason, God sent His *Logos*, incarnated in human weakness, to be a contrast to "**the wisdom** (cleverness; learned skill) **of this ordered arrangement** (domination System; world of culture, religion, economy and government)" (vs. 20b, above). So the news about the incarnation and work of God's *Logos* was not spread abroad through philosophical arguments (the wisdom of humans), but through "**the stupidity of the proclamation**." It was not meant to convince through human logic, but rather, through the power and ability of the Breath-effect – the Spirit of Life – that raised folks from out the death of their carnal reasoning into the Life of Christ. It was the impartation of the *Divine Logos* (Jn. 1:1) into "earthen vessels" (i.e., us: 2 Cor. 4:7) that united us with the Lord, making us to be "one Spirit" (1 Cor. 6:17) and a part of the Vine (Jn. 15:1ff).

We now see another aspect of God's character and attitude: He "**delights and considers it profitable** (thinks it thoroughly competent and easy; imagines it well-done) **to deliver** (or: save; rescue; salvage and restore to health, wholeness and their original state and condition)." As Jesus stated in Lu. 19:10,

> "**You see, the Son of the Man** (= the eschatological messianic figure; = Adam's son) **came to seek after, and then to save, deliver and restore what is existing being lost, ruined, demolished and destroyed**."

Christ's faithfulness (the work of the cross) imparts "**habitual trusting, repeated faithing, progressive believing and constant loyalty [into] folks, through the stupidity of the proclamation**." It was in this way that He would "**undo** (untie and loose-away; destroy) **the wisdom and cleverness of the wise ones**" (vs. 19, above). Likewise, it was "**within the Wisdom of God** [that] the world of mankind did not recognize, or have insight into, God through means of [human] wisdom." He had a different plan. He knew that human wisdom could not rescue humanity (were that the case, the Jews had abundant wisdom literature on offer). Even "centered in the wisdom from God, [or being] in the midst of the Wisdom which is God [as was Adam, in Eden], **the ordered arrangement and System of religious culture did NOT come to have an intimate, experiential knowledge of God through means of this Wisdom**." We saw this in Heb. 7:19a, that "**the Law perfects nothing** (brought nothing to its goal or destiny; finishes nothing)." And so, Heb. 7:19b informs us that through "**a fully leading-in of a superior** (stronger and better) **expectation we are continuously and progressively drawing near to and in, by and with, God**."

Sadly, in the centuries that followed, Paul's words went unheeded and the religious leaders that created the Christian religion turned to the philosophy of Plato and Aristotle and formed theological constructs to interpret God, Christ and the writings of the sent-forth folks. Now theories determined whether or not a person was "orthodox," rather than it being their Love or the Life of Christ within them. They created boxes that shut folks in and kept others out. The "wolves" brought in hateful distortions that were laden with pagan ideas. Christianity became a false witness about God (I owe this statement to a writing by John Gavazzoni, "The Call to {Major} Repentance" at www.greater-emmanuel.org/jg). The daughters of Mystery Babylon mounted the beast of empire, once again (Eccl. 3:15).

22. **in as much as, in fact, Jews constantly request** (habitually demand) **signs, while and Greeks** (those of the Hellenistic culture) **constantly seek** (habitually try to find) **wisdom!**

Conzelmann (ibid p 47) observed that these two human classifications (divided by race, religion and culture) really had two things in common: they both wanted some kind of proof that Jesus Christ was who His representatives said that He was, or that these teachings were based upon divine truth and reality. They simply wanted the proof in different ways. Mat. 12:39 and 16:4 give examples of the Jews' demand, and Acts 17:21-32 shows us an example of the Greeks (in Athens). The Gospel of John notes the "signs" that Jesus provided for the Jews to whom He ministered. The book of Revelation has signs that pertained to 1st century Jerusalem, from chapters 12-19 (KJV unfortunately calls them wonders and miracles). But neither of these two cultures were, in general, open to "the message of the cross."

Without knowing of, or about, Him, Christ was actually what those Greeks were trying to find. Paul knew that this is what all humanity was seeking, and we find him,

"**constantly making mention** (constructing a recollection; producing for myself a mental image) **upon the [occasions] of my speaking and thinking toward having wellness and goodness** (or: imparted desires; prayers), **to the end that the God of** (or: pertaining to; or, reading the genitive as in apposition: Who is) **our Lord Jesus Christ, the Father of the Glory** (or: the founder and archetype of, and which is, this manifestation which calls forth praise), **would give** (may suddenly impart; should at some point grant) **to you folks a spirit** (or: breath-effect; attitude) **of WISDOM and revelation** (unveiling; uncovering; disclosure) **within the midst of a full and accurate experiential and intimate knowledge of Himself**" (Eph. 1:16b-17).

In Col. 2:3, he instructs us about Christ,

"**within Whom** (or: in which) **are** (continually exist) **all the hidden-away** (or: concealed) **treasures** (or: treasure chests or vaults; storehouses) **of the wisdom and experiential, intimate knowledge and insight**."

The two human categories (Jews and Greeks), mentioned in vs. 22, serve as figures for the whole of humanity (as perceived in terms of the 1st century Roman Empire). The person that is focused upon either a sign (something from the supernatural being demonstrated in some material or literal way; e.g., *cf* Mat. 12:38-39), or upon human reason, finds the apparent failure of a crucified Messiah, or a message about the Grace of God, to be something foolish. But it is the foolish and the stupid that God uses, as Paul goes on to show…

23. **Yet as for us, we are constantly proclaiming** (habitually heralding) **Christ: One having been terminally crucified** (or: an executed, hung from a pole Anointed One) **– indeed, a trap-spring** (or: a snare; thus: an obstacle or cause for stumbling or being ensnared) **to** (or: with; for; among) **Jews** (those of the Jewish culture and religion); **yet stupidity** (foolishness; nonsense) **to and for [the] multitudes** (among [other] ethnic groups; in [the] nations; with the non-Jews),

Paul points to the practice of what he stated in vs. 18a, above. They were "habitually heralding an executed, hung from a pole Messiah." Why was this a "trap" or a "snare" to, for, with and among those of Second Temple Judaism? Because they either expected a militant Messiah that would deliver them from the Romans, or because the Jerusalem leadership (scribes, priests, Pharisees) were afraid of losing their status and prosperity, as well as possibly being displaced by Jesus (Jn. 11:45-12:19). But the death of the Judean Messiah also trapped the whole religion of Second Temple Judaism, signaling its end.

To the ethnic multitudes – the nations such as the Greeks and Romans, etc. (*ethnē*: the designation of foreigners in the LXX) – the whole idea of becoming a follower of a slain leader was simply nonsense and stupidity. The "King of the Judeans" had not conquered Caesar – except in the reality of the new creation (2 Cor. 5:17), and this was a sphere that was not a part of the domination System of "the world."

24. **and yet [it is] Christ: God's power and ability, as well as God's wisdom** (or: and so [we see the] Anointed One – a power from, and which is, God, as well as understanding insight and skillful cleverness from, and which is, God), **to, for, in, with and among those [who are] the called ones** (or: these summoned folks), **both Jews and Greeks!**

Observe that "God's **power** and **ability**" was "**the message** (the word; the *Logos*) **of the cross**," in vs. 18, above, but now this is further identified as "**Christ**," here in vs. 24. So the *Logos* of the cross is, in fact, Christ. He is also "**God's wisdom**." Here, Paul may be alluding to Prov. 2, 3, 8 and 9 – for the Jews in his audience – and especially Prov. 3:17-19. An alternate textual reading is found, in *p*46 and in

22

Clement of Alexandria, where the terms "Christ, power/ability and wisdom" are all in the nominative cases. This would make this verse as a stand-alone statement, instead of a continuation of vs. 23, and so would read, "Christ [is] God's power/ability and God's wisdom..." Both readings say the same thing in emphasizing the central, determining role of Christ in God's program of the deliverance of humanity. Conzelmann concludes that "Chris is God's 'nature'" (ibid p 48). *Cf* vs. 30, below.

The term "**the called ones** (those summoned)" is an echo from Jesus in Mat. 20:16 and His parable, in Mat. 22:9-14 (the king's son's wedding banquet). Take note of the dative case in the phrase, here. Christ is God's power and wisdom "**to, for, in, with and among... Jews and Greeks alike!**" This phrase that joins those who had been separated by the Law and the old covenant, are now made One New Humanity (Eph. 2:15). Paul also used the term "called" in Rom. 1:1, 6, 7; 8:28, and we find it in Rev. 17:14. The substantive "calling" is frequently found in Paul's writings (e.g., in 1:26, below; Rom. 11:29; Eph. 1:18; 4:1, 4; Phil. 3:14) and in Heb. 3:1. But Paul continues his theme of "stupid things"...

25. **Because God's stupid thing [or: plan; idea]** (or: the foolish act of God; nonsense from God) **continues being wiser than the human beings** (or: [than] from people), **and God's weak act** (or: the weak [thing; plan; idea] from God) **[is] stronger than the human beings** (or: [than] from people).

Paul presents to us a maxim in rhetorical parallelism where God's acts, which humans would judge to be either stupid (foolish; nonsense) or weak, are contrasted with what humans consider to be wise or strong. The cross, and the idea of a crucified Messiah, is stupid and expresses weakness, from having been overcome by the opposition – i.e., in the eyes of human reasoning. But this "weak act" proved to be stronger than the death which came by means of strong human beings. Christ's resurrection proved to be stronger than death, and so what appeared to be "nonsense from God," demonstrated God's Wisdom. From the death that came through the first Adam, God's attitude of grace and mercy brought Life through the Last (*eschatos*) Adam (15:22, 45, below). And not only this, the "foolishness of preaching the word of the cross" is found to be "the power of God" in the rescued and transformed lives as Christ raises them from the dead (the death of carnal wisdom, in the first Adam). The parallelism here echoes the contrast between the wisdom and cleverness of the "wise ones" (vs. 19, above) and the wisdom of God (vss. 21, 24, above).

26. **For, take a comprehensive look at** (or: as an indicative: To be sure, you folks are progressively seeing and observing) **your calling** (or: summoning; vocation; social station) **brothers, that [there are] not many wise folks – according to flesh [= folks with the wisdom of the world]**
    (or: corresponding to a flesh [system of philosophy or RELIGION]; on the level of the
    estranged human situation; with a consciousness oriented toward a domination System), **not many powerful ones** (those with [political; financial] ability), **not many well-born ones** (ones born to social ease and profit; those of noble birth; folks with distinguished genealogy),

Again, take note that he used the same term for them (**calling**; summoning) that he had used of himself (vs. 1, above). I find it curious that Moffatt did not use the term "summoning," here (it is a different form of the same Greek term), thus losing the sense of the solidarity of, and the nuance of equality between, Paul's and the community's being summoned to this new Life in Christ, as simply being different member of the same body with different functions (see ch. 12, below). Such inconsistency has tended to broaden the false division between the so-called clergy and the so-called laity. This division does not exist within the Christ.

27. **but to the contrary, God collects His thoughts and speaks forth** (or: selects and picks out; chose) **the stupid things** (or: the foolish ones) **of the organized System** (the world of religion, culture and its secular society; or: the cosmos; the universe), **to the end that He could** (or: would; may) **habitually disgrace and bring shame down on the wise ones; and God collects His thoughts and speaks forth** (or: selects, picks out and chooses) **the weak things** (or: the powerless or sickly ones) **of**

the System (world; arranged order), **so that He would bring disgrace and shame down on the strong things** (or: the robust and mighty ones),

Twice in verse 27, and again in the first clause of vs. 28, Paul instructs us that God does (or: did; – the verb is in the aorist tense) something. The verb is *eklegō*, and is normally rendered: "select; pick out; or, choose," and these options are on offer in the parenthetical expansion. But in the history of its use, it had also been used to mean "to levy taxes," or, "to declare." The Greek elements of the verb are the prefix *ek-* (forth; out of) plus the verb *legō* (from which comes the noun, *logos*) which means "to lay something out (as a thought or an idea); to say; to speak; to express (something); to tell; to make a declaration." Now since the subject of this sentence is God, and since we know from Scripture that when God is described as doing something, it is often termed using a verb of speaking a Word, my bold rendering presents the reading of the Greek as understanding that God, "**collects His thoughts and speaks forth**." Now consider that in the previous verse (26), Paul speaks of their "calling." That gives us the image of God using His Voice, as He did throughout Israel's history. The point to which I am leading is that God uses His Voice and speaks a *Logos* when He calls and summons us to a "vocation, a social role, a position, or a station" (vs. 26a).

Verse 26 informs us that He does not "**call** (summon)" many "**wise folks**" who have the wisdom of this world. Then vs. 27 instructs us that He "**speaks forth the stupid things**," or, He calls "the foolish ones." Furthermore, God does not call "**many powerful ones** (those with [political; financial] ability)." Look at the social status and financial abilities of His twelve disciples. Likewise, He did not call "**many well-born ones** (ones born to social ease and profit; those of noble birth; folks with distinguished genealogy)." No, He "picked out," or "called" folks of lower social standing. Verse 29, below, tells us why: so that no flesh, nor any wisdom of the world, can take glory to itself.

Now from the idea of taking "thought" before speaking, or having a plan, an idea, before initiating a program, I included the idea that is inherent in the verb *legō*, namely, that "**God collects His thoughts**." Consider what Paul said about God's plans and purpose, in Eph. 3:

> 8. **To me, the one far inferior to all of those set apart** (or: the saints), **was given this grace and joyous favor: to myself address the nations** (non-Jews; Gentiles; ethnic multitudes) **with the good news of the untrackable** (untraceable; or: not-searched-out and unexplored) **riches of the Christ**
> 9. **and to illuminate all people [as to] what [is] the execution of the detailed plan and household administration of the secret** (or: mystery) **pertaining to that having been hidden away, apart from the ages** (or: disassociated from the [past] periods of time), **within the midst of God – in the One forming and founding** (creating) **all things –**
> 10. **to the end that now** (at this present time), **in union with the heavenly people, God's greatly diversified wisdom could be made known – through the called-out community – to the governments** (or: rulers; sovereignties; chief ones) **as well as to the authorities and folks with privilege among those situated upon elevated positions**
> 11. **in accord with** (or: corresponding to) **a PURPOSE of the ages** (a fore-designed aim, PLAN and object [which He is bent on achieving] of the unspecified time-periods) **which He formed** (creates; produced) **within the Christ by our Lord and Owner, Jesus**."

And now His Plan was to speak forth foolish things (like a crucified Messiah), and stupid people (who could not understand Jesus' teachings) who were a part of "**the organized System** (the world of religion, culture and its secular society)." He selected ordinary people – representatives of the majority of Israel, and of humanity.

Is the term, "the **wise ones**," an allusion to the serpent of Gen. 3? Its wisdom pointed the humans toward the Law (which gives the knowledge of good and evil). Was Paul alluding to those of Corinth who were steeped in Greek philosophy, or to Jews that were steeped in Second Temple wisdom literature? Was he singling out Torah experts (scribes or Pharisees such as those who tried to trap Jesus in His words)?

Why would God purpose to "**habitually disgrace and bring shame down on the wise ones**"? Was it simply to discredit human wisdom in the face of God's revealed wisdom in Christ? Was His purpose to turn people away from the logic of religion so that they would focus their attention on the glory of Christ (2 Cor. 3:18)? Was His intent to "bring disgrace and shame down upon the strong folks" in order to counter their tendency toward pride? Jacob (James) instructs us:

> "**you folks must consequently be made low** (humbled; demoted; brought to a low station), **in the Lord's sight** (= in [Yahweh's, or Christ's] presence), **and then He will progressively lift you up** (or: continue elevating you)" (Jas. 4:10).

Jacob further informs us, in chapter 1,

> 9. **Now let the low-positioned** (not rising far from the ground; or: humble; or: down-hearted or depressed) **brother** (or: fellow member/believer) **continually boast** (or: be habitually loud-mouthed) **in his high position** (or: exaltation; or: height),
>
> 10. **but the rich, in his lowness** (or: humiliation; depression), **because he will be progressively passing by as a flower of grass** (or: = a wildflower).

Paul testified of his own need for weakness and a low position in 2 Cor. 12:

> 5. **... I will not continue boasting – except in my weaknesses,**
>
> 6. **for if I should ever want or intend to boast, I shall not be senseless** (unintelligent; unreasonable; imprudent), **for I will continue declaring reality** (truth). **Yet I continue being reticent** (continue refraining, with thrift,) **and so no one should account into me [anything] above** (or: over) **what he continues seeing [in] and observing [of] me, or hearing from me.**
>
> 7. **And now, in the excess of the unveilings** (or: with the transcendence of the revelations; by the extraordinary amount and surpassing nature of the disclosures), **through this [situation] and for this reason – so that I could not be progressively exalted** (or: would not continue being overly lifted up [in myself or by others]) **– something with [its] point in [my] flesh is given in me** (or: an impaling-stake for the human nature was given for me; or: a thorn to the natural realm, and a splinter by alienated humanity, was assigned to me): **an agent of** (or: a messenger from) **the adversary, to the end that he** (or: it) **could** (or: should; would) **repeatedly beat me in the face** (or: slap me on the ear) **with his** (or: its) **fist.**
>
> > [comment: this personification of the irritation may well be metaphorical and may refer to his social or cultural-religious situation]
>
> 8. **I called the Lord** [Christ or Yahweh] **alongside for relief, ease and comfort, and entreated [Him] three times over** (or: about) **this, so that he** (or: it) **would** (or: should) **at once stand away and withdraw from me,**
>
> 9. **and yet He has said to me – and His declaration stands, "My grace is continuously sufficient in you** (or: My joyous favor is constantly adequate to ward [it] off for you), **for you see, the ability** (or: the [other MSS read: My] power) **is habitually brought to its goal** (or: finished; perfected; matured) **within the midst of weakness** (or: in union with lack of strength and infirmity)." **Most gladly, therefore, I will rather continue boasting in** (or: centered within the midst of; and in union with) **the** [other MSS: my] **weaknesses, to the end that the ability of the Christ** (or: the Anointed One's power) **can pitch its tent** (or: should tabernacle) **upon me** (or: = set up residence upon me during this transient life and journey; perhaps: = fulfill the type of the Feast of Tabernacles with me; or: = be my house from heaven; [cf. 5:1, above])!
>
> 10. **Wherefore I habitually delight and take pleasure in weaknesses** (or: in union with lacks of strength and infirmities); **in the midst of outrageous insults and ignominious situations of mistreatment; in union with pressured necessities; in the midst of pursuits for persecution and cramped situations over and on behalf of Christ, for whenever I continue being** (or: may periodically be) **weak, then I am powerful** (or: I then exist being capable)!

His "excess of the unveilings" could have given rise to spiritual or intellectual pride, so our Father brought situations to counter-balance the great gift of understanding that Paul had.

Next we see that "**God collects His thoughts and speaks forth** (or: selects, picks out and chooses) **the weak things** (or: the powerless or sickly ones)," and this is so that "**He would bring disgrace and shame down on the strong things** (or: the robust and mighty ones)." Now all of this speaking forth and choosing has to do with His purpose, and for the role that these folks will play within that purpose. We read elsewhere that His plan was for humanity to bear His image and be in His likeness (Gen. 1:26). Later His plan was for Israel to be the Light of God to the ethnic multitudes of the world. Some would be Light-bearers; some would have that Light shown upon them by these Light-bearers. His present followers were given grace and mercy so that they could pass that grace and mercy on to the rest of the world, in multiplied progressions (like One Seed producing many seeds). The failure of the physically, politically or financially strong needed to have their human "grace and honor" removed, so that they would see their need and turn to Christ who would heal them and raise them from the dead. Paul was speaking in this way to folks who lived in an "honor-or-shame" society. This was a prime cultural-value system. It was a central structure in the domination System (the world of Empire), and this system (which fed on human pride) had to be demolished.

28. **and God collects His thoughts and speaks forth** (or: selects, picks out and chooses) **ignoble things**

(or: those of no family; those without known ancestry; the base ones; or: the things that are unborn or have not happened; the occurrences that have not come to be) **pertaining to the controlling System** (or: from the world or government, politics, religion or culture; of the realm of the non-religious; which are the social and religious outcasts), **and those that are looked down on, despised and regarded as having come from out of nothing – even those being nothing** (nonentities; or: the things not existing; or: the things that are "nothing") **– in order that He could make ineffective** (bring to "nothing"; bring down to idle uselessness) **the existing things** (or: the things that are "something"; or: = [domination systems] presently having being),

So God also "**speaks forth ignoble things**" such as the Way of the cross (Mat. 16:24; etc.). And He selects, picks out and chooses "those of no family; those without known ancestry; the base ones; or: the things that are unborn or have not happened; the occurrences that have not come to be." That parenthetical expansion shows the wide semantic range of the word that I first rendered "**ignoble things.**" Once again, God is not choosing or speaking forth "spiritual things" or "beings of the heavens," but rather things and people that are from the world, from the various controlling systems – many of whom were social and religious outcasts.

He goes on to characterize them as "**those that are looked down on, despised and regarded as having come from out of nothing – even those being nothing.**" Now the last clause, "those being nothing," can also be rendered, "the things not existing," or, "the things that are 'nothing.'" Let us consider these options:

a) those being nothing is rhetorical repetition for "those having come from out of nothing." The use of neuter particle refers to their station in life or to their character, rather than to their actual being;

b) the things not existing could refer to the new creation, the new arrangement (covenant), or the reign of God manifested on earth;

c) the things that are "nothing" could refer to either a) or b), but be a contrasting expression to "the things that are 'something,'" in the next clause.

The verb used in the last clause, *katargeō*, "**make ineffective** (bring to "nothing"; bring down to idle uselessness)," is also used in an eschatological sense in 2:4; 6:13; 13:8, 10; 15:24, 26, below. We also find it in 2 Cor. 3:7, 11, 12, and we will quote 2 Cor. 3:14,

"**But further, the results of their perceptions, concepts and understanding** (effects of directing the mind and thought processes) **were petrified** (were hardened into a stony concretion and made callous [note: a medical term for being covered with thick skin]), **for until this very day the same head-covering** (veil) **continues remaining** (dwelling; abiding) **upon the reading of**

the old covenant (arrangement; thorough placement) – **it** [i.e., the reading of the old, or the old covenant itself] **continues not being uncovered or unveiled – because it** [i.e., the old covenant and arrangement] **continues being progressively and fully unemployed and brought down to doing no work and being made useless, ineffective and nullified within Christ** (or: [the old arrangement and covenant] is abolished in union with an Anointing, and in the midst of Christ)."

And one of our favorite verses also uses this verb:

"**rendering useless** (nullifying; rendering down in accord with inactivity and unemployment) **the Law** (or: the custom; = the Torah) **of the implanted goals** (or: concerning impartations of the finished product within; from commandments; which was inward directives) **consisting in decrees** (or: prescribed ordinances), **to the end that He may frame** (create; found and settle from a state of wildness and disorder) **The Two into One qualitatively New and Different** [*p*46 & others: common] **Humanity centered within the midst of, and in union with, Himself, continuously making** (progressively creating) **Peace and Harmony** (a joining)."

Cf Heb. 2:14

These other references further explain Paul's meaning here in vs. 28. Now all this is...

29. so that no flesh [nature, government or religious system] – [including, or at] all – could boast in God's sight or presence (or: before God). *Cf* Rom. 3:27; Eph. 2:9

The "flesh" in this verse may refer to just people – as a general reference to the human race. Or, Paul may be using this term as a contrast to spirit, i.e., as referring to the human nature in its estranged, disconnected-from-the-Vine state of being, as discussed in Rom. 8:

4. **to the end that the effect of the just Deed of deliverance in which wrong was set right, resulting from being liberated and turned in the right direction within the Way pointed out, which is the principle,** (or: so that the effect of the fair relationships which come from [His] law and custom; or: in order that the result of the equity and rightness of the Law) **can** (would; could; may) **be fulfilled and become full within us – in those habitually walking about** (or: = for the folks ordering their behavior/living their lives) **not in accord with flesh** (or: = not corresponding to the human condition; or: = on the level of Torah-keeping boundary-markers), **but rather in accord with spirit** (or: down from [the] Spirit; corresponding to [His] Attitude; on the level of and in the sphere of Breath-effect). [*cf* 2 Cor. 3:3; 5:16]

5. **You see, those continuously existing in accord with flesh** (or: = in correspondence to Torah-keeping and cultural boundaries; or: = the human condition) **habitually think about, have an understanding and outlook based upon, are inclined to, set their mind on and are disposed to the things of the flesh** (= the human condition with its cultural traditions, religious cultus and national boundary markers), **yet those in accord with spirit** (or: down from [the] Spirit; on the level of Breath-effect; in line with [His] Attitude) **[think about; have an outlook from] the things and matters of the spirit** (or: the Spirit; Breath-effect; the Attitude).
6. **For the result of the thinking** (mind-set; effect of the way of thinking; disposition; result of understanding and inclination; the minding; the opinion; the thought; the outlook) **of the flesh** (= from the human condition or the System of culture and cultus; or: = Torah keeping) **[is; brings] death, yet the result of the thinking** (mind-set; disposition; thought and way of thinking; outlook) **of the spirit** (or: from the Spirit; which is the Breath-effect) **[is; brings] Life and Peace** (joining).
7. **Because of that, the result of the thinking** (disposition; thought processes; mind-set, outlook) **of the flesh** (= attention to Torah boundary-markers, custom and cultus; or: = from the human condition) **[is; brings] enmity, alienation and discord [streaming] into God** (or: hostility unto, or active hatred with a view to, God), **for it continues not being humbly aligned and supportive** (habitually placed under and submitted; or, as a middle: subjecting, humbly

arranging or marshaling itself) **to the principle and law which is God** (or: in God's principle; by the Law from God), **for neither is it able nor does it have power.**

8. **Now the folks continuously existing in the midst of** (or: So people being in union with, or centered in,) **flesh** (= the alienated human condition; or: = the religious system involving flesh sacrifices, Torah boundary-markers/customs) **have no power and are not able at any point to please God** (or: to fit or adapt to God; or: to be content with God; or: to be acceptable in God).
9. **Yet you folks are not constantly existing within the midst of flesh** (or: you are not in union with nor centered on [the alienated human condition, or Torah-keeping with flesh sacrifices]), **but rather within spirit, in union with Breath-effect and centered on [His] attitude, since indeed God's Spirit** (or: if so be that [the] Breath-effect which is God; or: if as is the fact that an attitude which corresponds to God) **is continuously housing Itself** (making His abode; residing; dwelling; by idiom: cohabiting; living together as husband and wife) **within and among you folks. Yet if anyone is not continuously having, or not habitually and progressively holding, Christ's Spirit and [the Messiah's] Attitude** (or: So if a certain person is not regularly possessing a Breath-effect which is Anointed), **this one is not habitually existing from Him as his Source** (or: is not now having His character or qualities; or: presently is not His).

30. **Now you folks are, and continuously exist being, forth from out of the midst of Him – within and in union with Christ Jesus, Who came to be** (or: is birthed) **wisdom in and among us** (or: to us; for us), **from God: both a rightwising, eschatological deliverance into righted, covenantal existence in fair relationships of equity in the Way pointed out** (or: likewise a just covenantal Act from God) **and a being set-apart to be different** (a being made sacred), **even a redemptive liberation** (an emancipation; a loosing-away from [a condition of bondage]) –

Paul begins a conclusion of his line of thought by returning their thinking to Christ Jesus, as their source, as in vs. 2, above, while affirming their place "**within, and in union with,**" Him. Then he restates what he had said in vs. 24, saying here that "Christ Jesus… came to be WISDOM in and among us – as well as to us and for us." And all of this is "**from God.**" This last phrase finds expanded expression in Rom. 11:36. And in Col. 2:3 we read of "**God's Secret: Christ,**"
> "**within Whom** (or: in which) **are** (continually exist) **all the hidden-away** (or: concealed) **treasures** (or: treasure chests or vaults; storehouses) **of the WISDOM and experiential, intimate knowledge and insight.**"

This WISDOM from God is then defined and explained in the rest of the verse, and this is, in fact, what Christ Jesus was birthed to BE:
> a) **a rightwising, eschatological deliverance into righted, covenantal existence in fair relationships of equity in the Way pointed out** (or: likewise a just covenantal Act from God);
> b) **a being set-apart to be different** (a being made sacred);
> c) **a redemptive liberation** (an emancipation; a loosing-away from [a condition of bondage]).

Now because we have, "**been set-apart within Christ Jesus** (or: made holy, sacred, different from the normal and sanctified, in union with an Anointing of, and from, Jesus)" (vs. 2, above), all that He IS also applies to us!

Item a), above, covers the semantic range of *dikaiosunē*, and the term "rightwising" refers to turning someone in the right direction. I owe the expression "eschatological deliverance" to Douglas A. Campbell's *The Deliverance of God, An Apocalyptic Rereading of Justification in Paul*, Wm. B. Eerdmans, 2009. The ideas of "covenantal existence" and "a just covenantal Act" are extrapolations from the writings of N.T. Wright (e.g., *The Day the Revolution Began, Reconsidering the Meaning of Jesus's Crucifixion*, HarperOne, 2016). "The Way pointed out" is the root idea of the Greek term which by extension also means "fair relationships." The phrase rendered, "likewise a just covenantal Act from God," refers to the Christ Event, as does Campbell's "eschatological deliverance." These two phrases are complementary descriptions of what Jesus' death accomplished, and are the content of "**the message** (the word; the *Logos*) **of the cross** (or: the idea from, and the concept pertaining to, the execution-stake/suspension-pole)" (vs. 18, above).

Christ IS also item b) for us: "a being set-apart to be different," which is an allusion to Israel, itself, when God chose it as a people to be a light for the nations. It is also an allusion to the Levites being set apart to serve God and maintain the tabernacle, as well as to perform the sacrificial cultus on behalf of the people of Israel.

And finally c), He IS "a redemptive liberation/emancipation from both death and slavery to sin. The literal meaning of the Greek term is "a loosing-away from," which signifies setting us free. We see this term, without the prefix *apo-*, in Lu. 1:68,

> "**[The] Lord, the God of Israel** (= Yahweh, Israel's God), **is characterized by good words and blessings,'** [Ps. 41:13] **because He visits and closely looks upon with attentiveness, and also creates** (or: produced) **a loosing and liberation, for** (or: in; to; among) **His people.**"

Following the words by Simeon, concerning Jesus, the prophetess Anna used this same term in Lu. 2:38,

> "**And so, taking a stand on [the scene] in that same hour, she began – in [Simeon's] place – saying similar things to God** (or: she began responding in like words while standing in the place for God; or: she continued in [His] presence making confessions in God) **and kept on speaking about Him [either: God; or: the Child] to all the folks habitually having a view toward welcoming, granting access to, and receiving a liberation of Jerusalem** (or: a release by payment of a ransom for Jerusalem; [with other MSS: a redemption in Jerusalem])."

In Lu. 21: 28, Jesus used the longer form of the term (with the prefix), just as did Paul here in vs. 30,

> "**Now as these things are beginning to be progressively happening, at once bend back up** (or: stand tall and erect), **and then lift up your heads** (= hold your heads high), **because your setting-free** (the loosing-away and release of you folks from prison; your redemption and liberation from slavery) **is progressively drawing near!**"

We find Paul using it again in Rom. 3:24, where he speaks of the Christ Event in similar terms:

> "**while being folks presently and progressively being made right, freed from guilt, placed in solidarity within the Way pointed out, and continuously set in right relationship** (or: being [all] one-after-another delivered and rightwised; being ones habitually turned in the right direction; being [all] presently justified [by covenant inclusion]) **freely** (as a gift; gratuitously) **by His grace** (or: in His favor; with His grace; by His gratuitous act which brought joy) **through means of the process of a release-from-an-enslaved-condition and a liberating-away-from-imprisonment, which is resident within Christ Jesus** (or: by the setting-free which is centered in [the] Anointed Jesus; or: through the redemption that is union with Jesus [the] Messiah)."

Cf Rom. 8:23; Eph. 1:7, 14; 4:30; Col. 1:14; Heb. 9:15; 11:35 – for other places where this word is used. Gal. 5:1 uses a different word, but expresses the same concept. The whole concept of both of liberation, and being set free, is Exodus terminology, alluding to Israel's historical liberation from Egypt. Christ brought a liberating Exodus to all humanity. It was "release-from-an-enslaved-condition," not "salvation" from a future judgment. The Christ Event saved us here, and now! It is all about the human predicament here in this life. In the next life we all return into God (Rom. 11:36, "**forth from out of the midst of Him, then through the midst of Him, and [finally] into the midst of Him, [is; will be] the whole** {everything}"). He will sort out what will be best for each person, then and there. "**Jesus Christ [is] the same yesterday and today and on into the ages**" (Heb. 13:8). But just as in that first phrase of Rom. 11:36, quoted above, note the ontological, existential statement that Paul makes about us, as he began this verse: "**Now you folks are, and continuously exist being, forth from out of the midst of Him...**" Let us call to mind 2 Cor. 5:18,

> "**Yet further, all things [are]** (or: the Whole [is]; = all the things that exist [are]) **forth from out of the midst of God – the One transforming us to be completely other [than we were]** (etc.)..."

Now with all the above in mind, look at what Paul said in 2 Cor. 5:21, "**for you see, He made** (or: formed) **the One not at any point knowing failure** (sin; error; mistake) **by intimate experience [to take the place of; to be] failure over us and our [situation]** (or: He constructed and produced a sin [offering], for our sake, the Person who was not having an experiential knowledge of missing the target or making a mistake), **to the end that we may be birthed God's just and rightwising act of eschatological deliverance** (or: would come to exist in righted and liberated relationships of equity, fairness and justice in the Way pointed out, and be participants in the new covenant from God; could become expressions of the well-ordered living of the way it should be, which is God), **within Him and in union with Him.**"

But here, reviewing this verse from the top, we must keep in mind the central message within it: "**Christ Jesus, Who came to be** (or: is birthed)…" all that follows in the verse. Conzelmann puts it well, in saying that this verse "is an interpretation of the being of the crucified Lord…. with the exposition of the cross" (ibid p 51-52). In 2 Cor. 5:21, we see that He has made us to be what He Himself is.

31. **to the end that, correspondingly as it has been and stands written,**
    "The one constantly boasting: let him habitually boast and constantly take pride in [the] Lord [= Yahweh].**"** [Jer. 9:23]

Paul reached back to the prophets, again, to make a preliminary conclusion that he introduces with the conjunction: "**to the end that**." What follows gives us the purpose for which Paul has been arguing in the previous verses. Our boasting is not to be in ourselves, nor in human brilliance, nor in human wisdom. Our boast and pride is to be "in [the] Lord." Notice that since Jer. 9:23 referred to Yahweh, I inserted His Name into this quote so that our readers would be aware of this, and of the continuity of Scripture.

Dan Kaplan just pointed out how the rest of Jer. 9:23 and vs. 24 fill out that to which Paul was pointing his listeners by making this quote (a partial quote of a passage usually was a signal to the listeners to recall the rest of what was said in the passage). So let us review those verses:
> "Now THIS is what [the] LORD (= Yahweh) proceeds in saying, 'Let not the wise person continue boasting in his wisdom, nor the strong person keep on boasting in his strength. And let not the rich person continue boasting in his riches! But to the contrary, let the person continually boasting keep on boasting in THIS: to progressively make things flow together so as to understand, and to continue intimately knowing by existential insight that I, Myself, am, and continue being, [the] LORD (= Yahweh) – the One continuously performing (producing; forming; constructing; creating) mercy and the effect of justice (the result of a right decision and act of what is right), that is (or: also), a rightwising, eschatological deliverance into righted, covenantal existence in fair relationships of equity in the Way pointed out (or: likewise a just covenantal Act) upon the Land (or: earth), because in THESE THINGS [are manifested] the result of My inclination and will (the effect of My resolve, purpose and design; the expression of the Desire which is Me),' [the] LORD (= Yahweh) is now saying" (Jer. 9:23-24, LXX; JM).

Chapter 2

Paul continues on from the previous discussion about human wisdom, and reminds them that he did not employ any such tactic when he came to them:

1. **And I myself, in coming toward you, brothers** (= fellow members), **did not come repeatedly announcing the message of God's secret** (or: constantly proclaiming the news of the mystery [other MSS: witness; testimony] from God) **down to you as down from an elevation of thought** (or: according to superiority of word [*logos*]), **or of wisdom and cleverness** (= with a message of transcendent rhetoric or philosophical subtlety and brilliance)

God's secret, or, the mystery from God, was not rhetoric or wisdom literature, but rather was an unveiling of God's program and purpose (or, plan) of the ages, which we will see in 15:44-57, below, involved a planting of the first humanity, Adam, as the Seed, and the sprouting and growth of that Seed, up out of the earth, to be the Last Adam, the Second Humanity. Paul calls this entire program a secret, once again, in 15:51. He had not presented them a philosophy of life, or an ontological scheme of creation such as the Gnostics had envisioned, or would later construct. What he brought to them was a disclosure, an unveiling of the goal – and this was Christ, the joining of heaven and earth, of God with humanity, that is a resurrection from the state of being dead in relation to God and His creation. No, his focus was on the main issue:

2. for I decided not to see, perceive or know anything within or among you folks, except Jesus Christ – and this One being one having been crucified (suspended from a pole; executed on a stake)!

Did this mean that he went around carrying a crucifix? No, he resolved to see, perceive and know, the crucified Jesus "**within and among them.**" He wanted to see them living what some have called "a cruciform life" – a life which is lived in conformity to the cross of Christ, as Jesus had instructed, in Mat. 16:24-25. He wanted to see them "laying down their soul-lives for their friends" (Jn. 15:13). He did not want to see the self-centered division which he had heard was existing among them. Cameron Fultz makes an insightful comment on this verse:

"This is Paul's key knowing! As long as Paul stays focused on the '**slain Lamb standing**,' knowing this One's heart and how He thinks and what kind of Person He is, then the Spirit will communicate what needs to communicated to others" (from a currently unpublished translation of Revelation).

Cameron then points us to Gal. 6:14,

"**Now may it not happen to me** (or: in me) **to take up the practice of boasting, except within the cross** (execution stake/pole) **of our Lord, Jesus Christ, through Whom** (or: through which [i.e., the cross]) **the organized System** (or: the world of culture, economy, government and religion) **has been, and continues being, crucified** (executed on the stake; hung from a pole, in rejection and dishonor) **in me** (or: to me; for me; by me; with me), **and I by** (to; in; with; for) **the organized System** (the world; = their culture, secular society, religion, and government)."

He further reminds us of what Paul said in Phil. 3:

7. **But to the contrary, whatever things were being gains** (advantages; assets) **to, for or in me, these things I have esteemed and now consider** (or: regard) **as a loss** (a penalty; a forfeit; disadvantage; a bad bargain; a detriment) **because of the Christ** (or: on account of the Anointing).

8. **But further – indeed, then, as a matter of fact – I even am habitually considering** (or: regarding) **all things to be a loss** (a disadvantage; a forfeit) **because of** (for the sake of) **the thing that is constantly holding things above and thus having all-surpassing value and superiority: that which pertains to and comes from the experience of the intimate knowledge of my Lord, Jesus Christ** (or: of, from and which is Christ Jesus, my Owner) **– because of, on account of and for the sake of Whom I undergo loss of all things and I continue considering** (or: regarding) **them to be [either] a lot of refuse and filth** (a pile of manure) **[or] things that are cast away from the table to the dogs** (garbage), **to the end that I may have the advantage of Christ** (or: could maintain the gain of [the] Anointing),

9. **and may be found within Him** (or: in union with Him; centered in Him) **– not continuing having my [previous] pointed-out way** (my fairness and equity; my relationships; my basis for what is right; my own righteousness) **from out of the Law or custom, but to the contrary, the [Way pointed-out which was a rightwising deliverance] through means of Christ's faithfulness** (or: the trust-conviction which is Christ; the faith of and from [the Messiah]): **the rightwising, eschatological deliverance into the new covenant fairness and equity of righted relationships within the Way pointed out [which is] forth from out of the midst of**

God as a source (or: the just Act from the midst of God) **[and based] upon that Faithfulness** (or: [Christ's/God's] loyal allegiance; or: the Trust and confident faith) –

10. **to intimately and with insight experientially know Him, and the ability – even the power – of His resurrection and also the common existence** (participation; partnership, sharing and fellowship) **of the results and from the effects of His experiences** [note: these include good times/feelings and passions, as well as sufferings] – **being a person that is being continuously conformed by** (being progressively brought together with the form of; being habitually configured to) **His death.**

Next, Cameron takes us to Phil. 2:

5. **You see, this way of thinking** (this attitude and disposition) **is continuously within and among you folks** (or, as an imperative: So let this minding be habitually within you folks) – **which [is] also within Christ Jesus,**

6. **Who, starting and continuing as inherently existing** (or: beginning under; subsisting) **within God's form** (or: in an outward mold which is God), **He does not consider the [situation] to be equals in and by God a plunder** (or: a pillaging; a robbery; a snatching; or: a thing or situation seized and held),

> (or: Who, [although] constantly humbly and supportively ruling in union with an external shape and an outward appearance from God, did not give consideration to a seizure: the [situation] to continuously exist being the same things with God, even on the same levels in God, or equal [things; aspects] to God,)

7. **but to the contrary, He empties Himself** (or: removed the contents of Himself; made Himself empty), **receiving** (or: taking; accepting) **a slave's form** (external shape; outward mold), **coming to be** (or: birthing Himself) **within an effect of humanity's** (mankind's; people's) **likeness.**

8. **And so, being found in an outward fashion, mode of circumstance, condition, form-appearance** (or: character, role, phase, configuration, manner) **as a human** (a person; a man), **He lowers Himself** (or: humbled Himself; made Himself low; degrades Himself; levels Himself off), **coming to be** (or: birthing Himself) **a submissive, obedient One** (one who gives the ear and listens) **as far as** (or: to the point of; until) **death – but death of a cross** (torture stake)!

All this is what Paul wanted to see and know among the Corinthians. It was his desire for them, as well as for the folks at Philippi.

> "He tells the church to have the same mind: this same heart attitude as Jesus. Jesus self-emptied Himself. He became a man of no reputation Who lowered Himself. Moreover, just when you thought He could not lower Himself anymore, He went further to become an enemy of the state, worthy of an official state execution. Rather than try to justify Himself or protect His legacy, He allowed Himself to be as a misunderstood as convicted criminal who looks to be in the wrong" (Fultz, ibid).

Living the kind of Life that Jesus lived, and DOING what He taught was the fruit of enlightenment and experiential insight and knowledge. Wisdom and attitude alone were not sufficient. The resurrection of Jesus became the delivery event that brought us His Spirit, which empowers us (vs. 4, below).

So next Paul reminds them of how he was when he had been with them, and why he made his proclamation in the manner in which he did…

3. **So I, myself, came to be with and toward you, and faced you folks, in lack of strength** (or: in union with weakness), **and in fear – even in much trembling and agitation of mind** (or: very nervous; shaking with reverence and respect; or: = with earnestness and much concern),

As we envision what Paul says here, the picture that comes to mind is Jesus, in Gethsemane. It was like a person facing a cross (which was the situation, when proclaiming the apparent stumbling block and the foolishness of "the word of the cross" to the multitudes). He often received, and so expected, violent rejection of his message. *Cf* 2 Cor. 7:15; Phil. 2:12b.

4. **so my message** (the *Logos*, or word, thought and Information, from me) **and my public proclamation [were; consisted] not in persuasive words of wisdom** (or: ideas from cleverness [MSS add: of, or from, a human]), **but to the contrary [were] in demonstration of spirit and attitude, as well as of power and from ability**

> (or: in the midst of a display of clear and logical proof from [the] Spirit, consisting of power and ability; in union with a documented manifestation which was Breath-effect and which was a means of influence and capability),

5. **to the end that your trust would not be in human wisdom** (your faith and reliance would not exist in cleverness of people), **but rather in God's power, means, influence and ability.**

We see a similar statement by Paul in 1 Thes. 1:5,

> "**[The] message of the goodness of our God** (or: our God's good news; the message of ease and well-being, which is God; [other MSS: the good news from us]) **was not birthed into you within word or thought only, but rather also within power and ability, even within a set-apart Breath-effect** (or: in union with [the] Holy Spirit; in the midst of [the] Sacred Breath), **as well as in much assurance having been brought to full measure**..." *Cf* 2 Cor. 1:18.

His life, among them, had been a "**demonstration of spirit and attitude, as well as of power and from ability**." He had simply been Christ to them. He lived the life of the Spirit among them, so that they had an opportunity to see what that looked like. It would have been a life of being joined to the Vine (Jn. 15:1ff) so that he was producing the fruit of the Breath-effect (Gal. 5:22; Eph. 5:9). As the parenthetical expansion reads, his life had been "in the midst of a display of clear and logical proof FROM [the] Spirit, consisting of power and ability." It was in union with a "documented manifestation which was Breath-effect and which was a means of influence and capability." It was the Life of Christ manifested within their midst. *Cf* Rom. 8:19.

Now the purpose of this was not to bring a great reputation to Paul, but was rather so that their "trust would NOT be in human wisdom." *Cf* 3:3, 4, below. He wanted THEIR trust to be "**in God's power, means, influence and ability**." He was not turning them to doctrines or creeds, but directing them to their relationship with Christ. For this reason, he had come to them "**in lack of strength** (or: in union with weakness), **and in fear – even in much trembling and agitation of mind** (or: very nervous; shaking with reverence and respect; or: = with earnestness and much concern)" – which does not sound very much like being a charismatic preacher drawing large crowds with his winning personality and clever presentations. The image of Christ which we are called to reflect would be more like we find in Isa. 53:2b-3,

> "... as a root in a thirsty region (Land), there is no form to him, or glory (reputation; assumed appearance; manifestation which calls forth praise). And so we saw him, and he had no form or beauty. But to the contrary, his form [was] ignoble and without honor or value – even continuously failing (repeatedly being completely inferior and falling short from the midst; or: habitually forsaking [all]) compared to (at the side of) the sons of the humans; a person continuously being in union with (centered in; within the midst of) calamity and affliction from a blow, and knowing (perceiving) [what it is] to bear sickness and to carry weakness and disease. Because his face (or: presence) had been turned away, he was dishonored (unvalued), and was not esteemed or taken into account" (LXX, JM).

Does this comparison sound strange? Perhaps it does when we think of today's nominal Christianity. But consider what Paul says of himself and his associates in 4:12b-13, below,

> "**Being constantly insulted** (reviled; cursed; verbally abused)... **being habitually pursued and persecuted... being incessantly defamed** (slandered; plied with ill-rumors; [other MSS: blasphemed]), **we regularly called them to our sides** (normally entreated and offered assistance). **We were made to be as that which comes from cleaning all around** (as the off-scouring results; as the filthy refuses) **of the world** (from the organized System of culture,

religion, economy and government) **– wiped-off filth and scum of all things and all people – until right now!"**

Consider, again, 2 Cor. 12:9-10, cited above. Also, recall in Acts 20:23 Paul's meeting with the older folks from Ephesus, while on his journey to Jerusalem, and his words to them at that time:

> "**the Set-apart Breath-effect** (or: Holy Spirit) **keeps repeatedly giving full witness and evidence to me, continually saying that bonds** (= imprisonments) **and pressures** (oppressions; afflictions; tribulations) **continue remaining and are still awaiting me**."

He was following Christ, in His way of the cross.

6. **Now we habitually speak wisdom among the mature folks** (or: in the midst of the finished, completed people; or: in union with perfected ones who have arrived at the goal and destiny), **yet not a wisdom of, from or belonging to, this age, neither of the rulers** (chief people; leaders) **of this age – of or from those progressively and successively being brought down to idleness and ineffective uselessness** (or: gradually nullified and rendered inoperative; = brought to nothing; = ones fired from their jobs).

Who are "**the mature folks** (or: in the midst of the finished, completed people; or: in union with perfected ones who have arrived at the goal and destiny)"? Verse 3:1, below, gives clarification:

> "**And yet I myself, brothers, was not able to speak to you folks as to spiritual people, but to the contrary as to fleshly folks – as to infants in Christ**."

Using the word "infants," he implies those who have been born (e.g., Jn. 3:3, 5-8), but has not yet "grown up." This is the language of "growth" that should lead to "maturity." We see it in Jesus' parable of the kingdom as being like a farmer planting seeds, and how "**the seed can be progressively sprouting** (germinating) **and continuing to lengthen** (= to grow).... **first a sprout** (or: [the] blade of grass; herbage), **then a stalk head** (ear) **and finally a full grain within the stalk head** (ear)" (Mk. 4:27, 28). Those in Corinth were at that time still young (perhaps babies) and immature (adolescents). Many were probably like the kids of Mat. 25:41-46 – clueless about the needs of other; lacking *agapē* (13:1-3, below). We read of the same immaturity in Heb. 5:11b-14,

> "**[You] have become sluggish** (dull) **for hearing. For also, being obligated to be teachers, because of the time [gone by], you again have a need of someone to be teaching you folks the elementary things** (or: fundamental principles) **of the beginning of the brief spoken words of and from God, and so you have become folks having need of MILK, and not solid food. For everyone partaking milk [is] untried** (inexperienced) **pertaining to [the] Word of the Way pointed out. But solid food belongs to perfected ones** (complete and mature ones; ones who are fully developed and have reached the goal of their destiny) **– those, because of habit, having organs of perception trained as in gymnastic exercise and thus being skilled, because of practice, and disciplined with a view to a discerning** (or: when facing the act of separating, making a distinction and then a decision about) **both good and evil** (both that which is excellent, ideal, of good quality, profitable and beautiful, as well as that which is of bad quality, worthless, ugly or of bad form; or: = between right and wrong)."

The word "**mature**" is *teleios* is the adjective cognate of *telos* (end; goal; finished product). Christ's corporate body is like a family (another metaphor for the same thing) that is comprised of from newborns to the elders. Paul spoke "wisdom," the "deep things of God" among the elders, but also within the hearing of the next generation. The plant/child needs to be fed and watered in every stage of development. Delling (*TDNT*, Vol. 8 p 70) informs us that "Stoicism develops an Aristotelian principle when it stresses the fact that only he who has all the moral talents... is *teleios*..." Conzelmann cites Philo who speaks of "the man who is just beginning his training, the man; the man who is making gradual progress; [and] the perfect man" (ibid n 37). What comes to mind from Paul is Eph. 4:13,

> "**[to go on] until we – the whole of mankind** (all people) **– can** (or: would) **come down to the goal** (or: attain; arrive at; meet accordingly; meet down face-to-face): **into the state of oneness from, and which is, The Faithfulness even which is the full, experiential and intimate**

knowledge which is (or: of; from; in reference to) **the Son of God, [growing] into [the] purposed and destined adult man** (complete, finished, full-grown, perfect, goal-attained, mature manhood) **– into** (or: unto) **[the] measure of [the] stature** (full age; prime of life) **of the entire content which comprises the Anointed One.**"

Again he stresses that what they habitually speak is "**not a wisdom of, from or belonging to, this age, neither of the rulers** (chief people; leaders) **of this age.**" This could of course refer to the wisdom of the Greek culture and the Roman Empire. But from knowing Paul's struggle against Judaizers, we should also see that his reference is to the age of the Mosaic Law and its embodiment in Second Temple Judaism. It was specifically the wisdom of THAT age which was being "brought down to idleness and ineffective uselessness (nullified and rendered inoperative)," as we read in Heb. 6:1-3; 8:5a-8, and 13. For the day-to-day operations of culture, government and economy within the Empire, natural wisdom continued useful – it was not being nullified or rendered inoperative. What had passed away (2 Cor. 5:17) was the wisdom of the old covenant, for there was now a new creation that operated on the principles of the Christ-Life. The teachings of Jesus set the wisdom of the old age on its head. The old wisdom no longer applied, for the followers of Christ. The reference to "rulers, leaders and chief people" could likely refer to chief priests, scribes and Pharisees. The "this age" in which Paul lived and wrote did not completely end until AD 70. However this could also be a reference to Caesar and his court, as well as to the schools of philosophy or religion (e.g., in Alexandria).

A passage in Baruch 3 may lend insight to the topic of the wisdom "**of the rulers** (chief people; leaders) **of this age.**" In vs. 9 we read,

> "Hear, O Israel, an imparted goal (inward directive and impartation of the finished product) of, and which is Life; you folks give ear to know a way of thinking that is with thoughtful prudence (gut-intelligence; mindful purpose and frame of mind; considered understanding) with personal insight."

Then vss. 12, 14 reminds them, "You have forsaken and left behind the fountain (spring) of wisdom…. Learn where a way of thinking that is with thoughtful prudence (gut-intelligence; a mindful purpose and frame of mind; considered understanding) continues existing…" and vs. 15 asks, "Who has found her place...?" Next we come to a question that uses the same term "**rulers** (chief people; leaders)" that Paul used in vs. 6, above. Baruch 3:16 asks, "Where are **the rulers** (chief people; leaders) of the nations (the ethnic multitudes)?" Verse 19 gives the answer:

> "They were made to vanish (disappear) and they descended into the grave (the Unseen) – and then other folks stood up in their stead (or: in their corresponding place)" (LXX, JM).

Such as these, we submit, are the rulers and chief people to which Paul referred here in vs. 6 (*Cf* vs. 8, below). Here he affirms that they all were, "**progressively and successively being brought down to idleness and ineffective uselessness** (or: gradually nullified and rendered inoperative; = brought to nothing; = ones fired from their jobs)." *Cf* 1:18, above. The leadership in 1st century Jerusalem was being "brought to nothing; rendered inoperative," because the Law and the old covenant we also being "brought down to idleness and ineffective uselessness" – *cf* 15:53-58, below; 2 Cor. 3:11, 13; Heb. 8:6-13.

The section, beginning with this verse and continuing through vs. 16, moves away from the eschatological terminology of "**folks being presently delivered**" contrasted with "**folks constantly, progressively destroying themselves,**" in 1:18, above, as well as from the subject of all that Christ came to be in and among us, in 1:30, above, and now picks up the topic of "**the wisdom of God**" that he had mentioned in 1:21, 24 and 30. So he turns to **secret** and **hidden** things, using the language of the mysteries of God that are related to "**the ages**"…

7. **To the contrary, we habitually speak God's wisdom within the midst of a secret** (or: we normally speak – in [the form or realm of] a mystery which only the initiated understand – the wisdom which is God)**: the [wisdom] having been hidden away and remaining concealed, which God marked out in**

advance and set its boundaries (or: previously designed) **– before the ages – [leading] into our glory and assumed appearance** (unto our praise-inducing manifestation and with a view to our reputation),

Notice the qualifier in this verse: "within the midst of **a secret**, a mystery." This wisdom was not common wisdom, nor even the wisdom of Solomon or of the Jewish wisdom literature. It, being "**God's wisdom, the wisdom which is God**," had been "**been hidden away and remaining concealed**." It needed to be uncovered – revealed. This happened,

> "**whenever the time should be reached when it** [= the heart] **can** (or: would; may; should; or: shall at some point) **twist and turn upon, so as to face toward, [the] Lord** [= Christ].... **having a face that has been uncovered and remains unveiled, being folks who by a mirror are continuously observing the Lord's** [= Yahweh's or Christ's] **glory, are presently being continuously and progressively transformed into the very same image, from glory into glory**" (2 Cor. 3:16, 18).

God's mystery, His hidden purpose, was Christ and His body. Consider these elements that are found together in Col. 3:3,

> "**for you folks [i.e., His Body] died, and your life has been HIDDEN so that it is now concealed together with the Christ, within the midst of God** (or: in union with God)."

The other side of this mystery (God's secret purpose) was given in Col. 1:27,

> "**the riches of the glory of this Secret** (mystery) **within the multitudes** (among the nations; in the Gentiles; IN UNION WITH the swarms of ethnic groups), **which is** (or: exists being) **Christ within you folks, the expectation of and from the glory**."

So His Secret, His mystery involved a plan for the whole world! Verse 7, here, and these complimentary verses from Col. 1 and 3, combine Jewish apocalyptic and wisdom language that resonated in the contemporary and later Gnostic traditions, as well. Paul's message of the cross would have touched many religious veins of the Roman Empire, in his day. This verse calls to mind Dan. 2:18-19, 28, "they began seeking mercy before the God of heaven concerning this mystery... Then the mystery was revealed to Daniel.... there is a God in heaven revealing mysteries..." Since Christ, the Wisdom of God, is a mystery, people can know Him and experience Him, only through a revelation, or an unveiling of their hearts (2 Cor. 3:13-14).

Thus it follows, that "**because those whom He foreknew** (whom He knows from previous intimate experience), **He also marked out beforehand** (determined, defined and designed in advance) **[as] copies** (joint-forms) **of the image** (material likeness; portrait; mirrored image) **of His Son**" (Rom. 8:29), this previously hidden-away wisdom was also "**marked out in advance and set its boundaries** (or: previously designed) **– before the ages**." This led "**into our glory and assumed appearance** (unto our praise-inducing manifestation and reputation)" – from having become bearers of God's image. Paul says it this way, in Rom. 9:23-24,

> "**[it is] to the end that He could and would** (or: may) **also at some point make known by intimate experience the wealth of His glory** (or: of His manifestation of that which calls forth praise; of the glory which is Him; which pertains to His reputation; from His imagination and opinion) **upon containers of mercy** (instruments of mercy), **which He beforehand prepares into [being]** (or: made ready and provides into the midst of) **a manifestation of [that] glory – even us, whom He calls** (or: at one point summoned; invites), **not only from out of the Jews, but further, even from out of the nations** (or: out of the ethnic multitudes, also; forth from the Gentiles, too)."

Cf Rom. 8:18, 21, 30; 2 Cor. 4:17.

This hidden wisdom was the Christ that had been hidden within the writings of the OT. It was the wisdom which is the Second Humanity, the "last" Adam (15:45-48, below), the new creation (2 Cor. 5:17), the One New Humanity (Eph. 2:15). This **glory**, which we now manifest when Christ is seen within us, giving us a new and assumed appearance (the appearance of Christ within us) is describe in 15:49, below, in these terms:

"**correspondingly as we bear and wear the image of the dusty person,** [*p*46 adds: doubtless] **we can and should** [B reads: will continue to] **also bear and wear the image of the supra-heavenly One** (or: belonging to the One having the quality and character of the finished and perfected atmosphere; or: from the fully-heaven [sphere]; of the added-sky person)."

These two "people" (the dusty and the atmospheric) are the embodiments to the two, contrasting wisdoms.

What we need to keep in mind is that this Wisdom, which is "within the midst of a secret," is God's wisdom of a crucified Messiah. This section about wisdom and (in vs. 13) spiritual things is explaining the foolishness of proclaiming the message of the cross. Paul is not changing his message. *Cf* Eph. 3:5, but let us quote Eph. 3:

9. **and to illuminate all people** (give light to everyone) **[as to] what [is] the execution of the detailed plan and household administration of the secret** (or: mystery) **pertaining to that having been hidden** (concealed) **away, apart from the ages** (or: disassociated from the [past] periods of time), **within the midst of God – in the One forming and founding** (framing, building and settling from a state of disorder and wildness; creating) **all things** (the Whole; everything) –
10. **to the end that now** (at this present time), **in union with the heavenly people, God's greatly diversified wisdom** (the exceedingly varied in colors [as in a tapestry or the Veil] wisdom which is God; or: the many-phased wisdom from God) **could be made known – through the called-out community – to the governments** (or: rulers; sovereignties; chief ones) **as well as to the authorities and folks with privilege among those situated upon elevated positions**
11. **in accord with** (or: down from; corresponding to) **a purpose of the ages** (a fore-designed aim, plan and object [which He is bent on achieving] of the unspecified time-periods) **which He formed** (forms; made; constructs; creates; produced) **within the Christ by our Lord and Owner, Jesus**. *Cf* Rom. 16:25; 2 Tim. 1:9-10; Tit. 1:2-3.

Similar is Col. 1:26-28,

26. **the Secret** (or: sacred mystery) **having been hidden away and remaining concealed away from the ages** (or: from [past] eons), **as well as away from the [past] generations, yet now** (at the present time) **is set in clear light in His set-apart folks** (or: was manifested to His holy ones; is caused to be seen by His saints; is shown for what it is, for His sacred people),
27. **to whom God wills** (or: at one point purposed; or: intends) **to make known by intimate experience, what [are] the riches of the glory of this Secret** (or: the wealth which has its source in this sacred mystery's manifestation which calls forth praise) **within the multitudes** (among the nations; in the Gentiles; IN UNION WITH the swarms of ethnic groups), **which is** (or: exists being) **Christ within you folks, the expectation of and from the glory**
> (or: which is [the] Anointed in union with you people: the [realized] hope of the manifestation which called forth praise; or: which is [the] Anointing [and the Messiah] within the midst of you folks – the expectation which is the glory),
28. **Whom** [other MSS: Which] **we ourselves habitually proclaim down the line** (or: announce in accord with the pattern), **constantly putting [Him] into the minds of every person** (or: human) **and repeatedly teaching every person** (or: human), **within the sphere of all wisdom, to the intent that we may place every person** (or: human) **finished** (mature; perfect with respect to purpose; complete; as having reached the goal of destiny) **by [our] side, within the midst of, centered in, and in union with, Christ.**

8. **which [wisdom] not one of the rulers** (leaders; chief people) **of this age know** (or: came to know) **by intimate experience or insight. For if they knew, THEY would not likely have crucified** (hung or suspended on a pole) **the Owner of, and Who is, the glory and the assumed appearance**
> (or: For if they know, they would not stake-execute the **Lord** of the Manifestation which calls forth praise, and Who is the source of imagination and a good reputation).

You see, they did not know or experience Christ, so they crucified Him. Observe how the concealed secret (vs. 7) had reference to the cross (vs. 8). The people that Paul terms as "THEY," here, are pictured in Rev. 17:3-6. They were the leaders of Judea who were in collusion with the Empire, as Peter affirmed in Acts 2:23. But what we do to others we are also doing to ourselves, for in Col. 2:15, Paul instructs us concerning the RESULTS of what they had done to their Messiah:

> "**after Himself causing the sinking out and away of** (or: stripping off and away [of power and abilities]; undressing [them of arms and glory]; putting off and laying away [of categories and classifications]; or: divesting Himself of) **the governments and the authorities** (or: the ruling folks or people of primacy, and the privileged folks). **And then He made a public exhibit, in a citizen's bold freedom of speaking the truth, leading them in a triumphal procession within it [i.e., the cross/suspension-pole].**
>
> > (or: Undressing Himself {or: Stripping [them] off from Himself}, He also made a public display of the rulers and the authorities, with boldness leading them as captives in His victory procession in it {or: in union with Him}.)"

This is how the cross – the death of Jesus, as the representative (i.e., the Messiah) of Israel, the King of the Judeans – brought the Victory of which we will read in 15:55-57, below. But until the "veil is removed from their hearts" (2 Cor. 3:14-16), folks are unable to see this Victory, or understand how Christ's resurrection did what is described in Col. 2:15, just quoted.

Christ is the Owner, or Lord, of the glory. He owns all manifestations which call forth praise to God. If we render the term "the glory" as a genitive of apposition, we have "**the Lord, Who IS the glory**." He is also the source of imagination. His glory is alive and dynamic. It is a manifestation of His Presence. And yet, Paul continues, grounding his argument in Israel's prophecies…

9. **But to the contrary, according as it has been and stands written,**
> **"Things which an eye has not seen and an ear does not hear, neither does it ascend** (climb up) **upon [the] heart of a human, so as to conceive – so many things God prepares and makes ready in, for and by the folks habitually loving** (accepting and urging toward reunion with; fully giving themselves to) **Him."** [cf Isa. 64:3; 52:15]

You see, Israel did not have eyes to see, nor ears to hear Jesus, and this kind of Messiah had not come up into their hearts to conceive that He was the Way, the Truth and the Life (Jn. 14:6).

In the *Gospel of Thomas* 17 we read:
> "Jesus said, 'I will give you what no eye has seen, what no ear has heard, what no hand has touched, what has not arisen in the human heart.'" (trans. by Stephen J. Patterson in, *The Complete Gospels*, Robert J. Miller, Ed., Polebridge Press, 1994 p 308)

This does not sound like having a literal King of the Jews sitting on a throne in the literal city of Jerusalem, as the Judeans had envisioned concerning the coming of their Messiah. Conzelmann comments that a saying such as vs. 9 would have resonated with the Gnostics (ibid p 64), as we readily see in the quote of *Thomas* 17.

The final phrase, "**for and by the folks habitually loving** (accepting and urging toward reunion with; fully giving themselves to) **Him**" is echoed in Rom. 8:28,
> "**to those habitually or progressively loving and giving themselves to God – to the folks being called and invited according to [the] purpose – He is constantly working all things together into good and is progressively working all humanity together into that which is advantageous, worthy of admiration, noble and of excellent qualities.**"

All of this is the work of God alone. This is speaking "**wisdom among the mature folks**" (vs. 6, above); "**God's wisdom within the midst of a secret** (mystery)" (vs. 7, above). We are reminded of 1 Jn. 4:19,

"**We ourselves are** [some MSS add: now] **habitually loving** (or, as a subjunctive: can and should be constantly loving) **BECAUSE He Himself first loved** (or: urges to reunion with) **us**" (*cf* Jn. 3:16).

This is how we can be "habitually loving Him." The loving – the ability of which is a gift – is simply the channel used by His Spirit to deliver these prepared things to us, and to humanity.

10. **Yet** [other MSS: For] **God unveils [them] in us** (reveals [them] to us; uncovers [them] for us; discloses [these] among us) **through the spirit** (or: the Spirit; the Breath-effect), **for you see, the spirit** (or: the Spirit; the Breath-effect; the Attitude) **constantly and progressively searches, examines and investigates all humanity, and everything** (or: all things) – **even the depths of, from, which pertain to, and which are, God!**

The conjunction "**Yet**" (MSS reading *de*) presents vs. 10 as a contrast to vs. 9. The MSS reading "For" (*gar*) presents vs. 10 as an explanation of vs. 9, i.e., a further development. Both readings have good MS witnesses.

Notice the verb of the first clause, *apokaluptō*: "unveils; reveals; uncovers; discloses." This describes a revelation, an apocalypse that is given to US! It comes through, "**a spirit** (or: breath-effect; attitude) **of wisdom and revelation** (unveiling; uncovering; disclosure) **within the midst of a full and accurate experiential and intimate knowledge of Himself**" (Eph. 1:17b). Behind this verse in Eph. is the LXX,
> "It follows that Wisdom [is] a human-loving Spirit (or: humanly friendly and affectionate Breath-effect, and a hospitable attitude)" (Wis. of Sol. 1:6a; JM).
> "I called upon [Yahweh], and then a Spirit of Wisdom (or: a Breath-effect from wisdom) came to me" (Wis. of Sol. 7:7b; JM).
> "But who intimately knows (or: became acquainted with or gained insight into) Your determined purpose (will; design; counsel), except You, Yourself, give Wisdom, and send Your Holy Breath-effect (set-apart Spirit; sacred Attitude), from Highest [realms; spheres]?" (Wis. of Sol. 9:17; JM).

In Rom. 11:33, Paul exclaimed,
> "**O, the depth of [the] riches and wisdom and intimate, experiential knowledge and insight of God** (or: from God; which are God)! **How unsearchable the effects of His decisions** (results of the distinctive separations, judicial awards, judgments and evaluations from Him), **and untrackable His ways** (paths; roads)."

But in Eph. 3 he prays:
> 16. **to the end that He would give to you folks, in accord with the riches of His glory, to be strengthened in power and with ability – through His Breath-effect – for the interior person**
> 17. **to inhabit the Christ through the faith and by means of the trust within your hearts, being folks having been rooted and now established and placed on a foundation within the midst of and in union with Love.**
> 18. **To this end, may you folks be fully powerful and thus act out of strength to grasp, together with all the set-apart folks, what [is] the width and length and height and depth,**
> 19. **and thus to know – and gain insight by intimate experience – the love of, from, and which is, the Christ [that is] continuously transcending personal experiential knowledge and insight, so that you folks would be filled unto all the effect of the fullness of God and the result of the filling from God.**

For a person not yet raised to Life in Christ, the natural eye does not see, and the "first Adam" ear does not hear. Christ came to give sight to the blind (Lu. 4:18). Those who became born from above (Jn. 3:3) were given "ears to hear" (*cf* Rev. 2:7, *et al*). These things embody the wisdom of God. These very things "**God prepares and makes ready in, for and by the folks habitually loving** (accepting and urging toward reunion with; fully giving themselves to) **Him**." Does this sound a little like "the kingdom of God is within us"? We suggest that these things are symbolically seen as a city descending out of the atmosphere, from God (Rev. 21:10b). You see, "**God unveils [them] in us**." He also reveals [them] to us, uncovers [them] for us, and discloses [these] among us. This all happens, "**through the spirit** (or: the Breath-effect; the Spirit [of God])." The Spirit is the power to reveal and disclose; our joined and unified Spirit/spirit (6:17, below) is the power to receive and understand. Now it follows that this spirit – the Spirit; the Breath-effect; the Attitude [of God] – "**constantly and progressively searches, examines and investigates all humanity, and everything**." What a cosmological, existential, theological statement! The word "all" in this clause is in a form that serves both as a masculine singular (all humanity) and as a neuter plural (all things). Really, there is nothing that the Spirit of God, or the spirit in the human, or the spirit in the universe of matter, does not continuously search, examine and investigate. What does this tell us about the character of God, and of we who are being formed in His/Her image? Contemplate the ramifications of this statement. Paul made a similar statement in Rom. 8:27,

> "**But the One continuously searching** (tracing; exploring; trying to find out [concerning]) **the hearts has seen, and thus knows and is aware of, what [is] the effect of the mind-set and way of thinking of the Breath-effect** (or: This Spirit's opinion and thinking; or: the frame of mind and thought of the [person's] spirit and attitude), **because** (or: that) **down from God** (or: in accord with God; on the level of and commensurate with God) **He** (or: It; it) **continually hits on target within** (encounters and falls in union; obtains within while interceding), **over [the situation of] and for the sake of [the] set-apart folks** (saints; holy ones; sacredly different people)."

But wait, there is more: "**even the depths of, from, which pertain to, and which are God!**" Now I did not want to seem pantheistic here, so I left the conjunction that joins this last phrase to the main clause as simply "even." But its use could be rendered, "that is to say…" Conflated in this rendering are four functions of the genitive/ablative form of the term "God." Paul is speaking of "the depths of God," or said another way, "the depths which are God." He is also referring to "the depths which come **from** God," and "which pertain to God." When we endeavor to plumb the depths of a person that we admire, we are trying to fully understand and appreciate that person. So it is, when our heart and spirit endeavor to search out and investigate God's depths. He is the One that put this desire within us. We are attracted to Him/Her, so we want to intimately, experientially and fully know Him/Her. And God has the same desire toward us. We love, because He loves us. This is all really beyond words. So just listen, and let His Spirit speak to you. Perhaps what Paul says in 6:17, below, will bring insight to what he has just given, here:

> "**Now the person continually joining himself** (or: being habitually glued in intimate union; in himself being continuously welded) **to** (or: in; with) **the Lord exists being one spirit** (or: one Breath-effect; one Attitude; one Spirit)."

All of this is a development of "the message of the cross," presenting what follows as a result of the historical Events. But Paul continues…

11. **For who, of humans** (from people), **has seen so as to know the things of the human** (or: the [matters] pertaining to the person), **except the spirit of the human** (or: the person's spirit) – **the one within the midst of him? So, too, no one** (or: not one) **experientially or intimately knows** (or: came to know or have insight and exercise "*gnosis*" regarding) **the things of God** (God's matters), **except the Spirit of God** (or: God's spirit; the Breath-effect which is God).

His rhetorical question speaks of the human condition, in general. Paul may be alluding to Zech. 12:1b which speaks of Yahweh "progressively forming (repeatedly fashioning; constantly molding) a spirit (Breath-effect) of a human, within the midst of him (or: centered in her; or: in union with Him)" (LXX; JM). He is speaking about an aspect of our inner being – what elsewhere may be referred to as our mind or our heart (vs. 9, above), or even "our gut knowing." But the important thing is that this question is building on what he had just said about our "spirit" in the previous verse. So here we should conclude that knowing God, as well as knowledge of the depths of God, must be in the realm of the spirit (as contrasted to what Paul call "the flesh"), as Paul asserts in Rom. 8:4b-6,

> "… **those habitually walking about** (or: = for the folks ordering their behavior/living their lives) **not in accord with flesh** (or: = not corresponding to the human condition; or: = on the level of

Torah-keeping boundary-markers), **but rather in accord with spirit** (or: down from [the] Spirit; corresponding to [His] Attitude; on the level of and in the sphere of Breath-effect). [*cf* 2 Cor. 3:3; 5:16] **You see, those continuously existing in accord with flesh** (or: = in correspondence to Torah-keeping and cultural boundaries; or: = the human condition) **habitually think about, have an understanding and outlook based upon, are inclined to, set their mind on and are disposed to the things of the flesh** (= the human condition with its cultural traditions, religious cultus and national boundary markers), **yet those in accord with spirit** (or: down from [the] Spirit; on the level of Breath-effect; in line with [His] Attitude) **[think about; have an outlook from] the things and matters of the spirit** (or: the Spirit; Breath-effect; the Attitude). **For the result of the thinking** (mind-set; effect of the way of thinking; disposition; result of understanding and inclination; the minding; the opinion; the thought; the outlook) **of the flesh** (= from the human condition or the System of culture and cultus; or: = Torah keeping) **[is; brings] death, yet the result of the thinking** (mind-set; disposition; thought and way of thinking; outlook) **of the spirit** (or: from the Spirit; which is the Breath-effect) **[is; brings] Life and Peace** (Joining)."

We must be joined to, and abide in, the Vine (Jn. 15:1ff), for only "**the Spirit of God** (or: God's spirit; the Breath-effect which is God)" – which He imparts to us, in Christ – "**experientially and intimately knows** (or: has insight and exercise "*gnosis*" regarding) **the things of God** (God's matters)." Not only that, Jesus told His disciples, "**apart from** (or: separated from) **Me you folks continue having ability and power to do** (make; construct; create; form; perform; produce) **nothing!**" (Jn. 15:5b). Apart from the Spirit of God, there is no True *Gnosis* (Knowledge of God), even though our spirits may "**be continuously seeking God, since really, in fact, they could feel about and grope, and then at some point might** (or: possibly) **find Him!**" (Acts 17:27a). Jesus observed this fact in His prayer that is recorded in Mat. 11:25-26,

> "**I continue outwardly acclaiming My concurrence with You, publicly saying the same thing as You, O Father – Owner, Lord and Master of the heaven and of the earth** (or: of the sky and atmosphere, as well as of the land) **– that You hide** (or: because You hid) **these things from 'wise folks'** (or: 'clever people') **and 'understanding, intelligent, intellectuals,' and You unveil** (or: revealed; disclosed) **them to infants** (babes who are not yet able to speak; = untutored, untaught, ordinary folks). **Yes Father, because in this way goodwill is birthed in front of You** (or: because thus does Your thought, imagination and presuming of ease and wellness come into existence in Your presence)!"

Observe that in Rom. 8:6b, above, "**thinking**" is described as a function "**of the spirit.**" Conzelmann instructs us that "through the whole of ancient philosophy" there was "the old principle 'like [explained] by like'" (ibid p 66; brackets mine). Spirit is often explained as Mind, and vice versa. They are alike, when we try to compare them. Having the Mind of Christ (vs. 16, below) is the same as having the Spirit of Christ.

12. **Now we did not receive** (or: do not accept or take to ourselves; do not take control of or grasp hold of) **the spirit of the System** (the world's spirit and atmosphere; the attitude of or from the domination system of government, economy or religion), **but to the contrary, that spirit** (or: the Spirit, Breath-effect or Attitude) **[which is] from out of the midst of God – to the end that we can see and know the things being freely and joyously given to and for us in grace** (or: being graciously bestowed, and favorably given in us) **by God,**

We suggest that "the spirit of the System (etc.)" is simply a collective, or corporate, mind-set of the various domination systems of human cultures. Every corporate entity has a dominant "spirit" and "attitude," or, "mind-set." If the members of these corporate entities are not joined to the Lord, then that entity will have "the result of the thinking of the flesh," and will produce "death" (Rom. 8:6, above). This is why Paul referred to humanity's pre-Christ existence as being "**dead ones by** (or: to; with; in) **the results and effects of your stumblings aside** (offenses; wrong steps) **and failures to hit the mark** (or:

mistakes; errors; times of falling short; sins; deviations)" (Eph. 2:1). The spirit (and attitude) of the System engenders death. This is why John said,

> "**You folks should not be habitually loving** (as indicative: are not normally accepting; as imperative: Stop constantly seeking reunion with) **the world** (secular realm and the controlling ordered System of culture, religion, economy and government), **neither the things within the world** (ordered system of domination). **If anyone is in the habit of** (or: keeps on) **loving the world** (the domination System and ordered arrangement of religion, or of secular society), **the Father's** [other MSS: God's] **Love** (or: the love which the Father has; the Love which is the Father) **does not exist within him, because everything within the world** (ordered but dominating System of the secular and the religious) **– the flesh's over-desire and the eyes' over-desire, and the arrogant ostentation** (haughty, presumptuous or pretentious egoism) **pertaining to living** (= the biological and sociological life we live), **is not out of the Father...**" (1 Jn. 2:15-16).

Then, in 1 Jn. 3:14 we are instructed:

> "**We ourselves have seen, and thus know** (or: are aware), **that we have walked together** (or: proceeded to change, passing from) **out of the Death into the Life, because we are habitually loving the brothers. The person not habitually loving continues remaining** (dwelling; abiding; staying) **within the Death.**"

This gives insight to Paul's statement in Eph. 2:1, above. Death and "missing the target" equates to "not habitually loving" others. But we can only love because of God's love of us, and so we again quote 1 Jn. 4:19, "**We ourselves are habitually loving** (or, as a subjunctive: can and should be constantly loving) **because He Himself first loved** (or: urges to reunion with) **us.**"

But Paul assures his listeners, in the second half of vs. 12: We received "**that spirit** (or: the Spirit, Breath-effect or Attitude) **[which is] from out of the midst of God.**" This gift has a wonderful result and effect: "**that we can see and know the things being freely and joyously given to and for us in grace** (or: being graciously bestowed, and favorably given in us) **by God.**" This means that we can know the things of the Spirit of God, and search out the "depths of God" (2:10, above). Observe that all of this is a GIFT; it comes by His GRACE, which ITSELF equates to being His Spirit! Paul put it this way, in Rom. 8:15,

> "**For you folks did** (or: do) **not receive again a spirit of slavery to fear** (or: get slavery's spirit or breath-effect again, unto fear; or: take an attitude which personifies being a slave [as in Egypt or under the Law, leading] into fear again), **but rather you received a spirit of being placed as a son** (or: a Breath-effect which set you in the position of a son; or: you receive an attitude of one having been adopted [in accord with Greek or Roman law]), **within which** (or: in union with Whom) **we are habitually crying out, 'Abba** (Dad), **O Father'!**"

He made the same contrast between "**the spirit of the System**" and "**that spirit [which is] from out of the midst of God**" in Gal. 3, where in vs. 2-3 he contrasted "works of Law" and "flesh" with "**receiving the Spirit... from out of a hearing of a report about faithfulness...**" along with "**making a beginning inwardly by spirit** (or: in breath-effect; by [the] Spirit; with [the] result of [the] Breath)."

13. **which things we are also habitually speaking – not in words** (*logoi*) **taught from human wisdom** (or: not centered in learned thoughts, ideas or messages instructed which pertain to human wisdom; or: not among those taught in, by or with words, patterns of information, or reasons which are human wisdom), **but rather in those [words] taught from spirit** (or: in union with and among those folks taught of [the] Spirit – from the effect of a Breath and an Attitude), **habitually evaluating, while combining or contrasting and comparing, and then deciding spiritual [matters] together by spiritual [means] and with qualities inherent in the Breath-effect**

> (or: constantly matching or comparing/contrasting things pertaining to attitude with things in spirit, or by [the] Spirit; or: progressively making collective assessments of pneumatic [concepts] to and for pneumatic people; or: normally interpreting spiritual things in spiritual [terms]).

Here Paul affirms what he and his associated "habitually speak," picking up his train of thought from vss. 1, 4 and 6. First he gives the negative:

> "**not in words** (*logoi*) **taught from human wisdom**."

Take note that he again weaves in his thought about human **wisdom**. This is an important point, for he keeps returning to it. Let us consider the options for rendering this compound phrase, on offer in the parenthetical expansion:

> a) "not centered in learned thoughts, ideas or messages instructed, which pertain to human wisdom" – this could refer to Jewish wisdom literature, of that time, or to the Greek schools of philosophy;
>
> b) "not AMONG those taught in, by or with words, patterns of information, or reasons which are human" – this could refer to a "**soulish person**," i.e., one who was termed *psychical; non-pneumatic*," as he discusses in the next verse. It could also apply to those who had sat under the "patterned of information" and "reasons" concerning the OT or intertestamental writings, in the Second Temple Judaism schools.

There are other forms of *logos* (*logoi* is the plural). They are false words, ideas and concepts. Human wisdom and religions are full of these. This is why Truth and Reality needed to be manifested and revealed – in the Christ.

Next Paul gives the positive:

> "**but rather in those [words] taught from spirit** (or: in union with and among those folks taught of [the] Spirit – from the effect of a Breath and an Attitude), **habitually evaluating, deciding, combining or contrasting spiritual [matters] together by spiritual [means] and with qualities inherent in the Breath-effect**."

Observe the source of these positive words: "**from spirit**" (not from flesh). Now since the term "word" is not in the text (notice that I inserted it), I offer an alternate rendering of the entire phrase: "in union with those folks taught of [the] Spirit (or: from the effect of a Breath and an Attitude)." This also makes sense, however, the structure of the verse, and especially the final clause, lends evidence toward contrasting parallelism as being Paul's intent. He seems to be contrasting "words" of human wisdom to "[words]" that have been "taught from [the] Spirit." There is no definite article before the word "spirit," so Paul may simply be speaking about the "realm" or "level" of spiritual reasoning that comes from the *Logos* that is within them.

Let us now consider the final clause. The present participle is from the verb "to evaluate and decide (or: judge)" prefixed by *sun-* (with; together). Paul is speaking of bringing "spiritual [things; matters; ideas; etc.]" together with other "spiritual [things; matters; ideas]." In the process, they are being "habitually evaluated, decided about, combined, compared and/or contrasted." This is just the opposite of reading or interpreting in a "literal" manner. The core meaning of this word is, 'to combine, bring together' joined to the idea of, 'to compare, explain or interpret.' The LXX uses it to refer to the interpretation of dreams (e.g., Dan. 2:4-5). The next two verses will provide statements that show a stark contrast between the process just outlined in this last clause, above, and those who use the "wisdom of this System" to teach about God and spiritual topics.

Because Paul did not specify an object of the plural adjective "**spiritual**," and gave no expressed preposition for the plural noun "**spiritual**" (which is in the dative case), I inserted "[matters]" for the adjective, and inserted "[means]" for the noun. I also conflated two possible functions of the dative, yielding "**by** spiritual [means]," and "**with** spiritual qualities." The final phrase is first given as, "**inherent in the Breath-effect**."

Because of the inherent ambiguities of the text, I also offer three other viable readings for the entire clause:

a) "constantly matching or comparing/contrasting things pertaining to attitude with things in spirit, or by [the] Spirit."
b) "progressively making collective assessments of pneumatic [concepts] to and for pneumatic people."
c) "normally interpreting spiritual things in spiritual [terms]."

Interestingly, the second offering, b), would be how Gnostic interpreters of Paul's day, and later, might have rendered this clause. Also notice how this comports with the parenthetical alternative rendering of the first part of this "positive" clause (i.e., "in union with and among those folks taught of [the] Spirit"). This interpretation finds currency in the subjects of the next two verses.

14. **But a soulish person** (one dominated by, or living focused on, his breath [= the present transient life], or by those things which characterize the soul [emotions; will; intellect; physical life; internal welfare; the self; the ego] or psyche; = an unspiritual, nonpneumatic person) **does not normally accept** (or: habitually get or welcomingly receive the offer of) **the things of God's Breath-effect** (or: which have the character and quality of the Spirit of God; pertaining to God's spirit and attitude), **for they are stupidity to him** (foolishness for him; nonsense in him), **and he continues unable and habitually has no power to intimately and experientially know [them] or get insight, because they continue being sifted and held up for close spiritual examination**

> (are normally evaluated spiritually above; are constantly brought back for spiritual separation and attitudinal discernment; are progressively re-evaluated through means of the Breath-effect and comparison to the Attitude; or: are pneumatically discerned and interpreted).

15. **Yet the spiritual person** (one dominated by and focused on spirit or the realm of the Spirit, and characterized by the qualities of spirit: the Wind which continuously moves across the land; or: the pneumatic person) **is, on the one hand, continuously sifting and re-evaluating** (habitually separating and deciding from above on; progressively holding things up for close examination of) **everything and all humanity, yet, on the other hand, he is being sifted and held up for close examination or decision by no one.**

Paul now develops his argument and contrasts of the two kinds of wisdom into a contrast of two ways of living, or two world views, or two manners of Scriptural interpretation. These are not existential or ontological contrasts of different species of people, but rather of different mind-sets, realms of thought, world views, understanding of spiritual matters, and of ways of reading Scripture. These two categories, that Paul describes here, have continued on into our present day. But there remains the question of who Paul would put into which group! Each group views the other group as being in error, or just wrong. So let us dissect what Paul wrote in these verses, to those in Corinth, and take into consideration their context. His previous contrasts of the two kinds of wisdom should enlighten our investigation.

We suggest that the best understanding of the literal phrase, "a soulish person," would be "a human which is dominated by, or living focused on, his breath [= the present transient life]."

Now the next expanded offering may also add light: "by those things which characterize the soul [emotions; will; intellect; physical life; internal welfare; the self; the ego] or psyche." Probably taking both of these together would be a well-rounded way to approach this verse. We suggest that Paul is using the term "soulish" in the same way that he used "**the result of the thinking** (disposition; thought processes; mind-set, outlook) **of the flesh**," in Rom. 8:7. If we see these two characterizations of a person's life as being parallel expressions, then I think we will properly understand Paul, here, as well as the later Gnostic Christians that took Paul as their "apostle" (cf The Gnostic Paul, Gnostic Exegesis of the Pauline Letters, by Elaine Pagels, Trinity Press Int'l., 1992). Continuing with Paul's argument in Rom. 8:8 we see that,

> "**Now the folks continuously existing in the midst of** (or: So people being in union with, or centered in,) **flesh** (= the alienated human condition; or: = the religious system involving flesh sacrifices, Torah boundary-markers/customs) **have no power and are not able at any point to please God** (or: to fit or adapt to God; or: to be content with God; or: to be acceptable in God)."

He expands this reasoning in Rom. 8:9b,

> "**Yet if anyone is not continuously having, or not habitually and progressively holding, Christ's Spirit and [the Messiah's] Attitude** (or: So if a certain person is not regularly possessing a Breath-effect which is Anointed), **this one is not habitually existing from Him as his Source** (or: is not now having His character or qualities; or: presently is not His)."

Let us note that in vs. 14, above, he says that the soulish person, "**does not normally accept the things of God's Breath-effect**." The verb can also be rendered, "habitually get or welcomingly receive the offer." This could be for a variety of reasons, but Jesus might have said of such a person that he or she was not blessed to have ears to hear things "which have the character and quality of the Spirit of God." But Paul gives us an explanation:

> "**for they are stupidity to him** (foolishness for him; nonsense in him), **and he continues unable and habitually has no power to intimately and experientially know [them] or get insight, because they continue being sifted and held up for close spiritual examination.**"

This would be like Jesus saying,

> "**Certainly that is so. I am now saying to you, unless anyone may be born forth from out of water and spirit** (or: – as well as Breath-effect and attitude –) **he continues being unable** (he remains having no power) **to enter into God's realm** (or: reign; kingdom). **The thing being birthed, having been born forth from out of the flesh, is flesh** (or: from the estranged human nature, continues being the estranged human nature; or: = from out of a flesh system is a flesh system), **and the thing being birthed, having been born forth from out of the Spirit, is spirit** (or: what is birthed out of the Breath-effect continues being Breath-effect; or: what is born from the Attitude is an attitude). **You should not be amazed** (or: begin to marvel; at some point be filled with wonder; suddenly be astonished; or: Don't be surprised) **that I said to you, 'It is necessary and binding for you folks to be born back up again to a higher place** (or: for you people to be given birth from above)" (Jn. 3:5-7).

We are back to the Vine and the branch metaphor, as well.

The soulish person needs the Spirit, the Breath-effect, so that he or she can become a "spiritual person" (vs. 15), "**because they** [i.e., spiritual matters] **continue being sifted and held up for close SPIRITUAL examination**

> (or: are normally evaluated spiritually above; are constantly brought back for spiritual separation and attitudinal discernment; are progressively re-evaluated through means of the Breath-effect and comparison to the Attitude; or: are pneumatically discerned)."

Now in contrast, "**Yet the spiritual person** (one dominated by and focused on spirit or the realm of the Spirit, and characterized by the qualities of spirit: the Wind which continuously moves across the land; or: the pneumatic person) **is, on the one hand, continuously sifting and re-evaluating** (habitually separating and deciding from above on; progressively holding things up for close examination of) **everything and all humanity**." In Eph. 4, Paul describes such folks this way:

> 20. **But you folks did not learn the Christ in this way,**
> 21. **since, in fact, at one point you heard and so listen to Him, and within Him as well as in union with Him and centered in Him you were and are taught – just as Truth and Reality continuously exist within Jesus** (or: in union with the One, Jesus) –
> 22. **to put off from yourselves** [as clothing or habits] **what accords to the former entangled manner of living** (or: twisted up behavior): **the old humanity** (or: the past, worn-out person) – **the one continuously in process of being corrupted** (spoiled; ruined) **down from and in accord with the passionate desires** (the full-covering, swelling emotions) **of the deceptions** (or: seductive desires) –
> 23. **and then to be continuously renewed** (or: from time to time, or, progressively made young again) **by** (or: in; with) **the spirit** (or: attitude; breath-effect) **of your mind** (or: from the mind which is you folks; or: by the Spirit which is your [collective] mind),

45

24. **and to enter within** (or: clothe yourselves with) **the new humanity** (or: the Person that is different and innovative in kind and quality) **– the one in accord with and corresponding to God** (or: the person at the Divine level) **– being formed** (framed, built, founded and settled from a state of disorder and wildness; created) **within the Way pointed out** (or: in union with fair and equitable dealings with rightwised relationships, justice, righteousness and covenant participation; centered in [His] eschatological deliverance) **and reverent dedication** (or: benign relationship with nature) **pertaining to the Truth** (or: in intrinsic alignment with reality, which is the Truth).

Eph. 4:22 uses the term "the old humanity (or: the past, worn-out person)" and this corresponds to "the soulish person." But the "continuously renewed by, in and with the spirit of [one's] MIND" person (Eph. 4:23) corresponds to the "spiritual person" of vs. 15, here in 1 Cor. 2. We see that Eph. 4:24 calls this "the new humanity – the one in accord with and corresponding to God," which equates to "the second humanity" of 15:47, below. So there you have it. The same thing, just said in different ways. Verse 15 goes on to explain that these folks are, "**continuously sifting and re-evaluating** (habitually separating and deciding from above on; progressively holding things up for close examination of) **everything and all humanity**."

Now what does he mean by the final, contrasting clause, "**yet, on the other hand, he is being sifted and held up for close examination or decision by no one**"? Does Paul simply mean that people who still live in the realm of the old humanity (or, the old covenant) simply do not have "eyes to see"? Is it that the spiritual folks are now living in the spiritual realm (Eph. 2:6) where the soulish person has no vision to see (as, e.g., with those of 2 Cor. 3:15, who have a veil lying upon their hearts)? The Greek verb means that others cannot make a decision about (or, judge) the spiritual person. This may be because of what Paul wrote in Rom. 8:

> 1. **Nothing, consequently, [is] now a result of condemnation in** (or: a commensurate effect of a decision for; a corresponding result of a negative evaluation which falls in line with a decision or follows the pattern which divides [folks] down, with) **those within Christ Jesus**
> 2. **For the principle and law of, from and which is the spirit and attitude of 'The Life within Christ Jesus'**
> > (or: For you see, the Law of Life's spirit, joined with [the] Anointing of Jesus; or: For the Spirit's law of life within Christ Jesus; or: the Law [= Torah] from the Breath-effect, which is Life in union   with [the] Anointed Jesus)
> **frees you away from the Law of the Sin and of the Death**
> > (or: immediately set you [other MSS: me] at liberty from the principle of the failure, or of the missing of the target, and from the death; exempts you from this code involved with error and deviation from the goal, as well as from the death; emancipated you from this law from the mistake, and which is the Death).

16. **For,**
> **"Who intimately knows** (or: experientially knew) **[the] Lord's** [= Yahweh's] **mind? Who will proceed to co-habit with** (or: so that he will mount, as male with female, or come together so as to unite with and be knit with) **Him?"** [Isa. 40:13, LXX; note: for **mind** the Heb. text has Spirit]
Yet we, ourselves, are continuously holding (or: progressively having) **Christ's mind** (a mind which is Anointed, and which is Christ [other MSS: {the} Lord])**!**

Paul also quoted Isa. 40:13, in Rom. 11:34, but there he uses a different verb (perhaps from reading a different MS, at the time) in the second question. There it asks, "**Or, who becomes** (or: came to be) **His planning adviser** (His design counselor; the one who makes determinations with Him)**?**"

This verse reaches back to vss. 10b-13, above, using the quote of Isa. 40:13 as the grounds and basis for his argument, answering Isaiah's question with a statement of the new Reality/Creation, in Christ: We "**are continuously holding** (or: progressively having) **Christ's mind**." Paul is affirming that he, and the covenant community in Corinth DO actually have the Spirit (vs. 12, above) – they are pneumatics, not "people of the flesh (3:1, below)," or the psychical folks. This echoes 1:10b, above, where the same word, "mind," is used. An application of having **Christ's mind** can be seen in Phil. 2:2, 5-6 (although a different word is used in that passage) which echoes what Paul will address in 3:3ff, below. No wonder we can search the depths of God (vs. 10b, above). This gift, through being joined to Him, is beyond calculation.

Note the progressive reading of the present tense of the verb "have; **hold**." The parenthetical expansion is both practical, "a mind which is Anointed [by the Spirit of God]," and paradoxically mystical, "which is Christ" (which is an appositional rendering of the genitive case; other MS witnesses read "Lord"). But it all makes sense – to the spiritual person. God indwells us; we are one Spirit – from being joined to Him. These are aspects of the Good News, in Jesus Christ, which only the Spirit of God can unveil to us. The wisdom of the world is of no value here. Recall Jn. 3:8,

> **"The Spirit** (or: Breath-effect, or, exhaled Breath; Attitude) **habitually breathes and blows where It** (or: He) **is presently intending** (willing; purposing), **and you continually hear Its** (or: His) **voice, but yet you have not seen, and thus do not know, from what source It continuously comes, and where It progressively goes and habitually brings [things and folks] under [Its] control.**
>
>> (or: The wind constantly blows where it presently sets its will, and you constantly hear it's sound, but yet you have not seen and do not know from where it is coming, nor where it is going; or: = The wind continuously blows and the Spirit normally breathes – in the place that each has purpose. And so you are often hearing the sound that either makes, although you have not perceived from what place it is presently coming, as well as to what place it is presently leading, under [its influence or control].)
>
> **Thus is everyone** (or: does everyone constantly exist being) **– the person** (or: the [corporate] Person [= the Second Humanity]) **being birthed, having been born forth from out of the midst of the Spirit**
>
>> (or: In this manner exists all mankind, which is in the state of being born from the Breath-effect)."

Chapter 3

1. **And yet I myself, brothers, was not able to speak to you folks as to spiritual people** (*pneumatics;* e.g., having the effect of the Breath; led by the Spirit/Attitude; = people of spirit), **but to the contrary as to fleshly folks** (= those focused on what affects the flesh; = as "natural" people, unaffected by the Breath/Spirit; = people of flesh) **– as to infants in Christ** (or: babies/adolescents in Anointing).
2. **I gave you folks milk to drink, not solid food, for you were continuing not as yet being able or having power. But then, neither are you yet now** (at present) **able** (or: having power), **for you are still fleshly ones** (continue being people of flesh, focused on ordinary life, with natural thinking).

Observe that in vs. 1 he substitutes the word "**fleshly**" for the word "**soulish**," which he used in 2:14, above. This should alert us that the two words are synonyms, for Paul. Fleshly folks are soulish people. So we can conclude that even though they had received Christ and were a called-out covenant community, Paul did not regard them as "spiritual people." They were not experiencing the "effect of the Breath," and therefore were not being "led by the Attitude" – and thus the division among them; the absence of the Peace that came from the Joining (to Christ and to one another). They were spiritual infants in Christ and required milk to drink – as though not yet having teeth to chew solid food. They were still weak (for they as yet had no power or ability) – e.g., as in Rom. 14:1-2. Insight here will be gained by rushing ahead to 14:20, below:

> "**Brothers** (= Fellow members of the community)! **Stop becoming little boys and girls in or by [your] way of thinking and use of intellect, but still be infants – non-speaking babies! – in the worthless, the ugly and the poor of quality or the evil. Yet progressively come to be**

mature as folks which manifest the purpose (full-grown; perfect; ones having reached the goal and express the destiny; or: = adults) **in [your] way of thinking and use of intellect**."

Conzelmann (ibid p 71) sees Paul's "language of the mysteries" being replaced by "the terminology of education," i.e., "child-training," the term used in 14:20, rendered "boys and girls." Not only does Paul use varieties of terminologies, he freely mixes metaphors, as in vs. 9, below, calling the Corinthians first a farm, and then a building. He seems to use whatever it takes to get his points across.

These descriptions of the condition of the believers in Corinth informs us that there is a growth process, from being born from above on unto mature adulthood in Christ (Eph. 4:12-16). We are not told how long it had been since he was last with them, but the problems which he addresses in this letter to them is evidence to him that they still "have no power or ability" – i.e., they were "still **fleshly** ones," even though they were, "**not continuing trailing behind or constantly late, so as to be deficient or fall short – not even in one effect of grace** (or: result of favor)" (1:7, above). Paul gave one definition of "fleshly" in Rom. 7:14b,

"**I** [= Israel? or, Adam] **myself am** (or: exist being) **fleshly** (composed of flesh; carnal; flesh-oriented; or: = affected by the alienated self), **being one having been and now remaining sold under [the power and control of] the Sin** (under failure and the miss of the Target [of Torah?])."

But why does he determine this about those in Corinth? Because…

3. **For you see, in which place** (or: insofar as) **[there is] jealousy and strife and folks standing apart** (divisions and disunities) **among you folks – are you not existing being fleshly folks** (people adapted to flesh and self), **even constantly walking around** (= living your life) **according to, on the level of, in the sphere of, and corresponding to, humanity?**
4. **For whenever anyone repeatedly says, "I myself am indeed of Paul** (belong to Paul; have my association with Paul)**," yet a different one [says], "I, myself, of Apollos" – are you not continuing being fleshly humans** (= people acting like the estranged flesh; = non-spiritual)**?**

The jealousy and strife are from living in the first Adam, as "**fleshly humans**,"

"**The first human** (or: man), **Adam, came for existence** (or: was birthed) **into [being] a living SOUL**" [Gen. 2:7] (15:45a, below).

There, he contrasts existence as a "soul" with, "**the Last Adam into [being] a continuously life-making** (life-producing; life-creating; life-forming) **Spirit** (or: Breath-effect; Attitude)" (15:45b).

Paul explains "**being fleshly folks**" as, "**constantly walking around** (= living your life) **according to, on the level of, in the sphere of, and corresponding to humanity**." This equals "the first human, Adam," and is the exact opposite of being "set-apart" unto God, living in His reign, and being "led by the Spirit" (Rom. 8:14). It is "**having the character and quality of moist soil or mud**" (15:48, below); it means to "**bear and wear the image of the dusty person**" (15:49, below). This is why Paul later informed them that "**flesh and blood** (= humans in their estranged condition; = people of dust who have not been resurrected) **have no power and continue unable to inherit or receive and participate in an allotted portion of God's reign** (kingdom or sovereign action)" (15:50, below). These Corinthians were "**continuing being fleshly humans**," and it is only the "spiritual" – those who are "**habitually walking about** (or: = for the folks ordering their behavior/living their lives)… **in accord with spirit** (or: down from [the] Spirit; corresponding to [His] Attitude; on the level of and in the sphere of Breath-effect)" that can participate in God's sovereign activities; it is not those who walk "**in accord with flesh** (or: = not corresponding to the human condition; or: = on the level of Torah-keeping boundary-markers)" (Rom. 8:4). And further, Rom. 8 informs us:

5. **You see, those continuously existing in accord with flesh** (or: = in correspondence to Torah-keeping and cultural boundaries; or: = the human condition) **habitually think about, have an understanding and outlook based upon, are inclined to, set their mind on and are disposed to the things of the flesh** (= the human condition with its cultural traditions, religious cultus and national boundary markers), **yet those in accord with spirit** (or: down from [the]

Spirit; on the level of Breath-effect; in line with [His] Attitude) **[think about; have an outlook from] the things and matters of the spirit** (or: the Spirit; Breath-effect; the Attitude).
6. **For the result of the thinking** (mind-set; effect of the way of thinking; disposition; result of understanding and inclination; the minding; the opinion; the thought; the outlook) **of the flesh** (= from the human condition or the System of culture and cultus; or: = Torah keeping) **[is; brings] death**... (*cf* vss. 7-8, as well)

The "spiritual person" is simply one who "abides in the Vine" (Jn. 15:1ff), i.e., "is joined to the Lord" (6:17, below), and Rom. 8:6b instructs us:
> "**yet the result of the thinking** (mind-set; disposition; thought and way of thinking; outlook) **of the spirit** (or: from the Spirit; which is the Breath-effect) **[is; brings] Life and Peace** (joining)."

5. **What, then** [other MSS: So then, what], **is Apollos? And what is Paul? [They are] attending servants and dispensers of [spiritual] provisions, through whom you folks came to believe and trust – even as the Lord** [= Christ or Yahweh] **gave** (or: gives) **to and in each one.**

The "apostles (literally: sent-forth folks)" were simply "**attending servants and dispensers of [spiritual] provisions.**" They were incarnations of the Paraclete and were conduits of the Life of Christ, bringing Him to humanity. What they do (being "**attending servants and dispensers...**" is what they are, to the body of Christ. This is similar to what Jesus said in Lu. 17:10,
> "**Thus also, whenever you yourselves may do all the things being fully arranged** (specifically assigned) **to you folks, be habitually saying, 'We are unnecessary, useless** (= good-for-nothing and unprofitable; or: = ordinary) **slaves. We have done that which we were constantly obliged and indebted to do.'**"

In other words, Paul is telling his listeners that he and Apollos are nothing special, of themselves. Consider how Paul introduced himself to the community in Rome, in saying, "**Paul, Jesus Christ's slave...**" (Rom. 1:1).

In a letter that emphasized aspects of "the group," i.e., "the corporate community" – the corporate body, it is interesting how often Paul uses the term "each one." He uses it five times in this chapter alone, in vss. 5-13. Paul uses this word 23 times in this letter, as compared to only twice in 2 Cor., and only a few times in each of his other letters. The corporate is his man focus, but each member of the body has importance to Christ – none are without significance (*cf* 12:7-30, below).

6. **I myself plant** (or: planted), **Apollos irrigated** (or: waters; caused [you] to drink), **but then God was causing [it/you] to progressively grow up and increase** (be augmented).

Below, in chapter 12, let us observe how he explains it, using the human body as a metaphor:
> 14. **You see then, the body is not one member** (or: part), **but to the contrary, [it is] many.**
> 15. **In case the foot should ever say, "Because I am not a hand, I am not from out of the midst of** (= a part of) **the body," not for this reason is it not from out of the midst of the body** (or: = it is not from this statement that it does not exist with the body being its source and that it is not a part of the body)**!**
> 16. **And if the ear should ever say, "Because I am not an eye, I am not forth from** (= a part of) **the body," not alongside of this** (= not for this reason) **is it not forth from** (= a part of) **the body!**
> 17. **If the whole body [were] an eye, where [would be] the hearing** (or: the ability to hear)**? If [the] whole [were] hearing** (the ability to hear), **where [would be] the sense of smell?**
> 18. **Yet, at this present time** (or: = But as things are), **God, for Himself, places** (or: at once set in Himself) **the members** (or: parts) – **each one of them – within the midst of and in union with the body, just as He intends** (purposed; wills).
> 19. **Now if the whole** (or: all) **were one member, where [would be] the body?**

The Corinthians were "God's field" (vs. 9, below), or perhaps, "God's vineyard," in which Paul and Apollos functioned as farmers, to bring forth Christ in the lives that comprise the community. Here, he is speaking of the corporate, not the individual. But both Apollos and Paul are God's "hired hands" (vs. 8, below). It is God that owns the farm/vineyard. Furthermore, it was obvious the God causes plants to grow. But inherent in this observation is the fact that God is the source of Life, which in turn causes the growth. Notice, also, the "point in time" aorist tense of the verbs "plant/planted" and "irrigated/waters," but then the ongoing action indicated in the imperfect tense of God's action: He "**was causing [it/you] to progressively grow up and increase**." Paul expands this argument and this picture below:

7. **So that neither is the one habitually planting anything [special]** (anyone [of importance]), **nor the one habitually irrigating** (watering; giving drink), **but rather God: the One habitually and progressively causing growth and increase.**

In other words, don't get your eyes on the minister, or the ministry. Keep your eyes on Christ (2 Cor. 3:18), and as we read in Heb. 12:2,

> "**turning [our] eyes away from other things and fixing them** (or: looking away) **into Jesus, the Inaugurator** (First Leader; Prime Author) **and Perfecter** (Finisher; the Bringer-to-maturity and fruition; He who purposes and accomplishes the destiny) **of the faith, trust, confidence and loyal allegiance.**"

Observe the rhetorical emphasis in the restatement: that it is God who is "**habitually and progressively causing growth and increase**," (here, the present tense of the verb). This is God's job, His function in the field. WE do not need to worry about growth, or increase. What a relief! And just where does growth occur? WITHIN the plant. This is an inside job – not something "applied" to the plant. Cf Phil. 2:13, quoted below. Not only is Christ continually walking among the called out communities (Rev. 1:20-2:1b), He is within each individual plant. He is the Water of Life of the whole transpiration process. Cf Acts 5:36; Gal. 2:6; furthermore, consider Gal. 6:15. It is all about God and His farm, His new creation.

8. **Now the one continually planting and the one continually irrigating are one** (exist being a unit), **yet each one will receive his own wage** (pay; compensation) **corresponding to his own labor** (toil). 9. **For we are God's fellow-workers** (or: we are co-workers of, and from, God, and are people who work together with God; we exist being workings-together who belong to God, synergies of God; attending deeds which are God). **You folks are God's farm** (or: field under cultivation), **God's building** (or: construction project from God; structure which is God; or: an act of building pertaining to God).

So we should conclude that, since Paul, Apollos and Cephas "**are one**," there should be no division within the community. They "exist being a unit," but we see that they had different functions. Thus, they were not necessarily saying the same things (planting is different from watering), nor was it needful for them to theologically or ontologically agree or have the same spiritual perceptions. The sent-forth folks are laborers in God's vineyard, and God says and does different things to different people, and at different times. Both the Seed and the Water have Life, but they are not existentially identical. Even their "labor" is different. Still, they are all "fellow-workers," not one being above or more important than another. The called-out, covenant communities comprised "God's farm."

Notice that those who "**labor**" in God's field/farm/vineyard will receive compensation, a "salary." God is fair. He does not treat us as slaves, even though He owns us (6:20; 7:23, below; Mat. 13:46). The word "labor" in vs. 8 is synonymous with the term "work," in vs. 13, below. Paul speaks of "hard work" in 15:10 and 16:16, below, as well as in 1 Thes. 3:5; Gal. 4:11; Rom. 16:12. This is an important concept for Paul.

These folks are "**God's fellow-workers**." What a statement! What a privilege. What a vocation! Consider the other options that are on offer:

a) we are co-workers of, and from, God, and are people who work together with God;
b) we exist being workings-together who belong to God;
c) we are synergies of God;
d) we are attending deeds which are God.

Notice the semantic range between being a "worker," and being a "working/synergy/deed" that is "of" and "belongs to" God. The options b, c and d picture them as embodiments, or incarnations, of the workings of God. We (both individually and corporately) are the vessel that He has formed; we are God's opus – cf Jer.1:9; 12:14-14; 18:2-6; 24:6 – God's new creation (or, "God's construction project" – vs. 9). But being a "fellow-worker," or "a co-worker of, and from, God" puts them, and us, right alongside God: people working in the same field where God is working, laboring on the same farm, right alongside Him, where He is LABORING. Yes, God is still here, working among us. Recall what Jesus said, in Jn. 5:17,

> "**My Father is continuously working and keeps on being in action until the present moment** (or: up to right now); **I, Myself, also am continually working** (or: and so I, Myself, continue active, regularly performing in [His] trade)."

Then there is Phil. 2:13,

> "**for you see, God is the One habitually operating with inward activity, repeatedly working within, constantly causing function and progressively producing effects within, among and in union with you folks – both the [condition] to be habitually willing** (intending; purposing; resolving) **and the [situation] to be continuously effecting the action, repeatedly operating to cause function and habitually setting at work so as to produce – for the sake of and over the pleasing good form and the thinking of goodness in delightful imagination.**"

Now the last phrase, "**God's building** (etc.)," changes the metaphor, but the subject remains the same: Paul, Apollos, Cephas – or whoever God would send forth to continue building His temple. Have you ever thought of yourself as "God's construction project"? It's the same as being the pot that is being molded, on His potter's wheel (Jer. 18:2-6). Note here that the Greek *oikodomē* can also be rendered "act of building," and so answers to "attending deeds, etc.," of 9a, above. The two pictures fit well together. *Cf* 2 Cor. 6:1; Phil. 4:3; 1 Thes. 3:2; Philemon 24.

The genitive/ablative form of the term "God" offer's these rendering which could modify either of the terms "farm" or "building." For simplicity I only applied them to the second word: "construction project from God (the ablative); structure which is God (apposition); or: an act of building pertaining to God (genitive of relationship)." Each rendering is worthy of our consideration and meditation. Regarding of his work among them, in 2 Cor. 10:8 Paul spoke,

> "**concerning our privilege from out of Being** (or: right and authority) – **which the Lord** [= Christ or Yahweh] **gives us with a view unto edification and up-building** (construction into being a house)…"

Then in 2 Cor. 12:19b we read:

> "**Down [here] in God's stead and place, we are constantly speaking within Christ and in union with [the] Anointing. And the whole** (all [these] things), **beloved ones, [is** (are)**] over** (on behalf of) **your edification** (your upbuilding; the construction of your house)."

10. **Corresponding to, in accord with, and to the level of, God's grace and favor [which are] being given to** (or: by) **me, as [being] a skillful master-carpenter** (wise chief-builder; clever head-artisan; learned, insightful leading-stonemason; like a wise architect, engineer, foreman or director of works) **I lay** [other MSS: have laid] **a foundation** (or: laid a foundation [Stone]), **yet another is progressively building a house upon [it]. Now let each one continue watching to observe** (= take care) **how he keeps on building the house upon [it]** (or: upon the house),

11. **for you see** (or: For it follows that) **no one can** (or: continues able to; is having power to) **lay another foundation** (or: to place or set another foundation [Stone] of the same kind) **beside** (or: in

addition to and distinct from) **the One lying** (or: continuing being laid)**: which is** (continues being) **Jesus Christ** (Jesus [the] Anointed One; = Jesus, [the] Messiah).

In the first clause of vs. 10, I conflated three ways of rendering the preposition *kata*, which lead us to ponder the fact that Paul worked among them:

a) **Corresponding to God's grace and favor**; -- all that he did in presenting Christ crucified to them corresponded to God' grace and favor; laying the Foundation among them was not in relation to the Law, but to grace;

b) **In accord with God's grace**; -- there was an accord between the grace of God and the work of Jesus Christ;

c) **To the level of, God's grace and favor**; -- this calls to mind Rom. 8:38-39,

"**For you see, I have been persuaded and now stand convinced that neither death, nor life** (or: living existence), **nor agents** (or: messengers), **nor sovereignties** (rulers; those in prime position; or: beginnings), **nor things being now here** (being placed within, at present), **nor things about to be** (impending, or about to consecutively come), **nor powers** (or: capabilities), **nor height** (effect of being high), **nor depth** (or: deep places), **nor any other or different created thing** (or: founded thing; institution; = the Law; = old covenant; = adversaries) **will be having power or be able to separate, divide or part us from God's Love** (or: from the acceptance from God; from the urge toward reunion, which is God; God's full giving of Himself to us) **which is within Christ Jesus, our Owner** (Lord; Master; Possessor)."

The level of His Grace is the level of His Love – both aspect of Him are what we call "infinite."

The indirect object "**me**," which follows the verb "**being given**" (i.e., by God – the divine passive) is in the dative case which can be rendered "**to me**," signifying that Paul is the recipient of this gift of grace, or, it can function as instrumental, "**by me**," indicating that Paul is the "dispenser" of the Grace-and-Favor from God, or which is God. The next word that introduces Paul's building metaphor can be rendered as a simile, "**as [being]**," or as a metaphor, "**like**," as given in the parenthetical expansion. I owe this observation to Conzelmann (ibid p 75). Either makes sense, and the difference is a fine point: had he acted "like a wise architect, etc.," and all the detail-oriented considerations which that would imply, or had he more existentially worked with them "**as [being]**" God's "**skillful master-carpenter, etc.**"? Probably both. But just consider all that these terms (in their expressions of the semantic range of the word *architektōn*) imply. This is so much more than simply preaching a little sermon. And here, Paul is speaking only about "laying a foundation" of the Christ community in Corinth. Following his work among them, "**another is progressively building a house upon [it]**." Specifically, Apollos.

The first clause of vs. 11 is likely an allusion to Isa. 28:16-17,

"Behold, I am laying a foundation stone in Zion, a choice stone, a precious corner, a well-formed foundation…. And I will make right judgment the measuring tape, and righteousness the plummet…" (CVOT). *Cf* Ps. 118:22; Eph. 2:20; 1 Pet. 2:6-8

Now keep in mind the subject of Paul's discussion is still speaking of Apollos, Cephas and himself (or; others like them, i.e., sent-forth emissaries, teachers, community leaders, etc.; in other words, God's fellow-workers), in vs. 10, not about the Corinthians, themselves. The Corinthian community was the building UPON which these folks were working. Paul recognizes that the work that he does among the called-out groups is "skilled" work, because of the "level of God's" grace that was being given through him. He had laid the foundation for their community – which vs. 11 identifies as being **Jesus Christ** – and now he is speaking to, and about, other "builders" and "artisans" that had, and still would, come among them. But as with the agriculture metaphor, above, where the increase comes from God, so too here, the progressive building of His house was a work of God's Spirit within, and among, the people. Jesus identified Himself as doing this, in Mat. 16:18,

"**I will progressively be constructing and building up My house – the called-out, covenant community**."

Paul said it this way, in Eph. 2:

> 19. **Consequently then, you folks no longer continuously exist being strangers** (foreigners) **and sojourners, but in contrast, you continually exist being fellow-citizens of those set apart to be sacred people** (or: folks residing together in a City belonging to, and composed of, the holy ones)**: even God's family** (members of God's household),
> 20. **being fully built as a house upon the foundation from the sent-forth representatives and prophets, Jesus Christ continuously being a corner-foundation [stone] of it,**
> 21. **within, and in union with, Whom all the home-building, being continuously fitted [and] progressively framed together** (closely and harmoniously joined together; made a common joint by a word), **is continuously and progressively growing into a set-apart temple within [the] Lord.**

So Paul continues by giving a warning admonition: "**let each one continue watching to observe** (= take care) **how he keeps on building.**" They are not to try to lay some other foundation (vs. 11). The continued building of the communities should not be based upon either philosophies or on past traditions, such as those of the old covenant. This was not a continuation of the Law and the Prophets. Recall what God said to Peter, Jacob and John when Moses (a figure of the Law) and Elijah (a figure of the Prophets) had appeared with Jesus on the mount:

> "**This Man continues existing being My Son!... Make it a habit to listen, to continue paying attention, and then to [really] hear Him** (implies: obey Him)!" (Mat. 17:5)

Now look at Mat. 17:8, "**Now, upon lifting up their eyes, they saw no one** (or: not even one person) **except Him – only Jesus.**" They were no longer to be listening to either the Law, or the Prophets. We have a second witness to this in Heb. 1:1-2,

> "**Long ago, in many parts and in** (or: with; by) **much-traveled ways consisting of many turns and directions, God, having spoken to the fathers – in the prophets – yet upon [the] last of these days He spoke to** (or: speaks for and concerning; discourses in; makes conversation with) **us in a Son whom He placed [as; to be] Heir of all** (or: One who receives all humanity as an allotment)."

Considering the letters which Paul wrote to Galatia, and then would later write to Rome, we suspect that Paul was referring to the Judaizers, who desired to bring the Corinthians under the Law of Moses. But there were also Jewish strains of Gnosticism developing in areas such as Alexandria, and Paul may have had concerns about these. Much of his secret/mystery language may have been aimed at reaching folks in those religions, as well. The admonition, here, would apply to any sort of building that folks might do, but this one aspect of other teachers seems to have been Paul's immediate concern. They were not to construct another religion, or even form a new sect of Judaism.

Furthermore, if they were attempting to build upon the Christ, "**no one can** (or: continues able to; is having power to) **lay another foundation** (or: to place or set another foundation [Stone] of the same kind)." If they were to do so, it would not be a body of Christ. It may have truth in it, but it would be someone else's building – even perhaps Moses', again (Heb. 3:2)? To what might Heb. 6:1b-2 refer?

> "**not again repeatedly conceiving** (or: laying; casting down; putting down) **a foundation which involves a change of mind with a turning away from dead works** (or: observances), **and of faith and trust upon God; of teachings of immersions** (baptisms), **besides a placing-on of hands; and then of resurrection of dead ones – as well as of the results of an eonian decision** (or: the effects of an unspecified separation, or a judgment which pertains to and has the quality of an age)!"

Would this describe the baptism of John the immerser? His movement carried on, after him (Acts 18:25). Since that is what Apollos had known, could Paul be referring to that movement as a different foundation? Whichever, even on the true Foundation, they were to take care how they built. So…

12. **Now if anyone proceeds building a house** (a superstructure) **upon the** [other MSS: this] **Foundation – gold and silver [with] precious** (valuable) **stones; wood [and] thatching: herbage** (or: grass; hay) **[or] stalk** (or: straw; stubble) –

13. **each one's work will make itself to be visible in clear light** (or: will become apparent), **for the Day will continue making [it] evident** (showing [it] plainly). **Because it is being progressively unveiled** (continually revealed) **within the midst of Fire, and the Fire, Itself, will progressively test, examine and put to the proof what sort of work each one's exists being**.

The "clear light" come from "the midst of the Fire." The Fire comes to "**progressively test, examine and put to the proof what sort of work each one's exists being**." This may be an allusion to Mal. 3:

> "[The] Lord, whom you folks seek, will suddenly come to His temple…. for He [is] like a refiner's Fire… and He will sit [as] a refiner and purifier of silver the sons of Levi [= those of the priesthood] and will purify them as gold and silver" (vss. 1-3).

Correct translation of the verb "**unveiled** (revealed)," in the third clause, is vital for understanding the proper context and time frame of vss. 12-13. The NIV, ESV, NRSV all render the verb as being in the future tense. The NASV renders it properly, as the present tense that it is, but then they add "to be" (in italics), "is *to be* revealed." These versions reflect biased translating that fits into an interpretation that assumes Paul to be speaking of a future event, rather than an ongoing process, as the Greek text clearly shows. Because it is an ongoing process, Paul uses future tense in the other verbs, "will make itself to be visible,.. will continue making [it] evident… will progressively test…" But the Fire of God is always at work, and our ongoing, or completed, work "**is being progressively unveiled** (continually revealed) **within the midst of Fire**." This is not speaking about some future, so-called "End Time" event. It is "continually revealed" as to what sort of work it is. Building inspectors check the progress being made by the workmen, as a building is being constructed. When they find that errors have been made, they issue a "stop work" order, until corrections are made. They do not wait until the project is finished to order corrections, if they see that inferior or improper material is being used. The work is repeatedly checked against the plans and the appropriate building codes. God does not wait until "the end of time" or some theoretical return of Christ to institute corrective measure.

Fire was a time-honored figure for "testing" the quality of work, the purity of the materials or the honesty of the workmen/builders. Notice that Paul says exactly is: "**the Fire, Itself, will progressively test, examine and put to the proof what sort of work each one's exists being**." In Scripture, Fire is a symbol for God in His creative or corrective work within His creation, and among the people that He has made. In Paul's metaphor, the "building" is His people (vs. 9, above). Specifically here, it is the corporate community in Corinth, for in vs. 17, below, he affirms to them (regarding the building of which he is speaking in vss. 12-17) that it is: "**God's Temple – which you folks, yourselves, are** (exist being)."

A literal fulfillment of this symbolic Fire came upon the Judean leadership in AD 70, and the temple was burned, along with the city. That was a "Day" of the Lord. But the term "Day" also symbolized the time of the Messiah – which came with Jesus, and continued on into our present time. It was a Day of deliverance (6:2, below), and they were "**sons of** (from; associated with and having the qualities of; or: which are) **Light and sons of** (from; associated with and having qualities of; or: which are [the]) **Day!**" (1 Thes. 5:5). The work of the Spirit, among them, was shining the Light on the works of the people at that very time – and this is why Paul was able to see the wood, hay and stubble that had been placed among them causing division and other maladies. Paul was "the Light of the world" for them (Mat. 5:14a), and the City of Corinth (which was symbolically on Mt. Zion – Heb. 12:22) could not be hidden from him (Mat. 5:14b). Before his eyes, they were standing at the "judgment seat of Christ" (5:3, below; *cf* Rom. 14:10; 2 Cor. 5:10).

Now do not miss or confuse the purpose of the Fire: it is not to burn the person, but rather, quoting this again, it is to "**test, examine and put to the proof what sort of work each one's exists being**." Paul was observing that the divisive adherence to one teacher against another was the result of building with inappropriate materials (selfish, dividing attitudes that lacked love for one another). His words to them here were like what we read of God's witnesses, in Rev. 11:5, "Fire [the Spirit of God] was proceeding out of [his] mouth." We read about another example of this in Acts 16:18. These are just examples of Christ's ongoing evaluations and decisions among humans. Consider this context with his words in 6:3, below:

> "**Have you not seen so as to know that we shall continue sifting, separating, evaluating and making decisions about agents** (or: will continue judging messengers) **– why not, indeed, the affairs and business matters of everyday life?**"

Also, observe what he says to the entire community, below, in ch. 14:

> 29. **Now let two or three prophets be speaking, one after another, and let the other folks continue thoroughly sifting and sorting so as to fully evaluate and reach a decision.**
> 30. **Yet if it may** (or: should) **be unveiled** (revealed; disclosed) **to another being seated, let the first hush, and keep silent,**
> 31. **for you all continue able** (constantly have power) **to be repeatedly prophesying, one by one, to the end that everyone** (all) **can be learning, and everyone** (all) **can be called alongside to receive relief, aid, comfort and encouragement** (may receive the benefits of the Paraclete).

Their "decision" should be burning out wood, hay and stubble – immediately! Someone may be adding junk to the Corinthian community – and that would need to cease at once. We are seeing Paul as bringing a Fire to that situation (via this letter, etc.). Just as Jesus confronted Saul on the road to Damascus, so now Paul here confronts the community leaders to renounce these divisions and center on "Christ crucified." More and more we are seeing the "judgment seat of God/Christ" as being here and now, through the Anointing of His witnesses and "workers."

Why would the Lord wait until some future time to make the correction of getting rid of the "wood, hay and stubble"? His Fire is here with us now (as it was on the Day of Pentecost, which made the covenant communities to be Lampstands (Rev. 1:20b) -- the Light/Fire of the world). God's judgment is not "punishment," but correction and adjustment. We need to rid ourselves of thinking in terms of some far off "end of time" mentality. Paul was not giving the Corinthians eschatology that would have no benefit to them. He was speaking to his and their present time. They needed to immediately let God's Fire burn out all that wood, hay and stubble. Notice that the One constantly walking among the communities (Rev. 2:1) had "**feet like white brass** (or: bronze; fine copper) **as having been set on fire in a furnace**" (Rev. 1:15). And His words to them, in those two chapters (Rev. 2 & 3), were words of judgment and adjustment -- for right then and there, in Asia Minor.

Here, the gold, silver and jewels (or: valuable stones – as in Rev. 21:11-12, 18-21) – were people within the community who had been tested by God's Fire, and could now be trusted to speak God's wisdom and revelation/teaching. The New, heavenly Jerusalem of Rev. 21 is a composite City that is made up of all the "buildings" such as the one being described here, in 1 Cor. 3. These metaphors describe those who are "joined to the Lord," as described in 6:17, below.

14. **If anyone's work which he or she built upon [it] will remain, he or she will proceed in receiving wages** (pay; compensation).
15. **If anyone's work will be burned down, he or she will proceed in incurring a loss** (sustaining the damage; forfeiting), **yet he himself or she herself will be saved** (rescued and delivered; healed; restored; made whole; kept safe), **and as in this way – through Fire!**

Observe that in vss. 14 and 15 he is speaking about a person's WORK, not about the person himself/herself, yet the Fire has a direct relationship with the workman. There may be here an allusion to the passage from the Prophets, where Amos speaks to Israel on behalf of Yahweh,

"I overturn among you like Elohim's overturning of Sodom and Gomorrah, and you are becoming like a wooden poker rescued from the burning, yet you do not return unto Me, averring is Yahweh" (Amos 4:11; CVOT).

Then there is Zech. 3:2,

"And Yahweh says... [even] Yahweh Who is choosing Jerusalem... Is not this wooden poker being rescued from the fire?" (CVOT)

In Judah (Jude) we read:

"**be continuously delivering** (or: repeatedly rescuing and saving, restoring to health and wholeness) **others, snatching them from out of the midst of the Fire; be repeatedly extending compassionate mercy in reverent fear, while hating and radically detaching from even the garment having been stained** (or: spotted) **from the flesh**" (vs. 23).

Take note that in vs. 14 Paul is speaking of "wages, pay and compensation." We saw a parallel to this in Jesus' kingdom parable in Mat. 20:1-15, about the laborers in the vineyard. Cf Mat. 9:37-38. So this is not speaking about "works-righteousness" or "works-salvation," but about functioning in God's field, or working on His building. God is a fair Employer; He does not expect work for free. One can never lose by working on His projects – even if one is not aware of it. Remember the parable of the "sheep and the kids," in Mat. 25?

34. **"At that time** (or: point), **the King** (or: Reigning One) **will proceed saying to the folks at [the places to] His right, 'Come here, you folks having received words of ease and wellness from** (or: spoken well of by; or: having received the blessing of; or: bearing thoughts, ideas, expressions and the Word of goodness from) **My Father! At once come into possession of the inheritance of, and enjoy the allotment of,** [the period of, place of, or realm of] **the reign** (or: kingdom; influence and activity of sovereignty) **having been prepared and made ready from a founding** (a casting down [as of a foundation; or: of seed]) **of a system** (or: of [the] adorned arrangement; of an arranged order; of [the] world).

35. **"You see, I was hungry** (or: I hunger) **and you folks gave** (or: give) **to Me [something] to eat; I was thirsty** (or: I thirst), **and you folks gave [something for]** (or: cause) **Me to drink; I was existing being a foreigner** (or: stranger), **and you people gathered Me together [with you]** (= showed Me hospitality and oneness with your group);

36. **"[I was/am] naked, and you people clothed** (or: clothe) **Me; I fell sick** (or: become weak), **and you folks carefully looked upon** (or: = visit and look out for; took oversight of) **Me; [I was/am] in prison** (or: jail), **and you came to Me** (or: come and set your face on Me).

Read vss. 37-40 for His explanation of how they had lovingly served Him. But let this compensation, stated in vs. 34, sink in.

Jesus' parable of "the talents" (Mat. 25:14-30) gives us another picture of what Paul lays out here in vss. 14-15. In that parable there were both rewards (compensation by advancement in the business, etc.) and loss. The loss was the losing of a job for the "unprofitable servant." The "outer darkness" was being without employment, which, as in the parable of the vineyard workers (Mat. 20) meant that an unemployed person might not have the basics of food and shelter (they were day-laborers, next to being destitute) – definitely a situation for "weeping and regret" (Mat. 25:30). Those parables spoke to the same situation (the kingdom/reign; the work of building Christ's called-out communities – His vineyard; His temple) that Paul addresses here in vss. 12-17.

But notice the grace involved in this arrangement: "**yet he himself or she herself will be saved** (rescued and delivered; healed; restored; made whole; kept safe), **and as in this way – through Fire!**" Let us see a parallel case of "judgment" that we find in 5:5, below:

"**hand over such a man, with the adversarial [spirit]** (or: in the adversary; by the opponent; or: to *satan*), **into a loss of the flesh** (or: an undoing and destruction of this [distorted human nature]; a loss of [his "dominated existence" – Walter Wink]) **– to the end that the spirit may be saved** (rescued; delivered; restored to health, wholeness)**: within the midst of and in union**

with the Day of (or: in this day from, or, which is) **the Lord** [= Christ or Yahweh; other MSS add: Jesus; others read: our Lord, Jesus Christ]." [*cf* 1 Tim. 1:20; Job 2:6, LXX]

Notice that the "Fire" only destroyed the sub-standard work. Recall the purpose of God's Fire in the quote of Mal. 3, above. It was the loss that "saved" him. The "wood, hay and stubble" of 3:12, 15a, above, correspond to the "flesh" of 5:5, quoted here. And now, let us meditate on the expanded semantic range of the word rendered **saved**: rescued and delivered; healed; restored; made whole; kept safe. This is very much like Rom. 11:32,

> "**You see, God encloses, shuts up and locks all mankind** (everyone; the entire lot of folks) **into incompliance** (disobedience; stubbornness; lack of being convinced), **to the end that He could** (or: would; should) **mercy all mankind** (may make everyone, the all, recipients of mercy)!"

He treats everyone the same. And everyone eventually enters into His Mercy (Christ). All the worthless building that was added to the foundation of Christ, over the centuries, will be (and much has already been) burned up – in His time, and in the appropriate season. Another agricultural picture is given in Heb. 6:7-8, where the good field was burned off, to remove the "thorns and briers" that had overgrown it. That prepares the field to receive good Seed again.

In regard to the quality of the work done, 11:31 shines a Light (from His Fire) on how the Fire continues disclosing its value: "**The God and Father of the Lord Jesus... has seen and thus knows**." And now Paul brings this metaphor of farm workers and builders to an explanation and a conclusion:

16. **Have you folks not seen, to now know, that you people continuously exist being God's Temple** (Divine habitation; holy place and holy of holies; inner sanctuary), **and God's Spirit is constantly dwelling** (God's Breath is making Its home; the Wind which is God is housing Himself; the Attitude from God is progressively co-habiting) **within the midst of** (in union with) **you folks?**
17. **If anyone habitually spoils, ruins, wrecks or corrupts God's Temple, God will spoil, ruin, wreck and corrupt this person; for you see, God's Temple – which you folks, yourselves, are** (exist being) **– is set-apart** (holy; sacred; different from the common).

Already, before the destruction of the physical temple in Jerusalem, Paul asserts that a called-out community now exists being "**God's Temple** (Divine habitation; holy place and holy of holies; inner sanctuary)." This is revolutionary. We suppose that it was an unheard-of idea. It eliminates physical sacrifices, as well as the need for a priesthood to perform rituals in a physical building. We suggest that it eliminates rituals in any formal system. Jesus prophesied of this situation in Jn. 4:21, 24.

> "**an hour is progressively coming when neither within this mountain nor within Jerusalem will you folks continue giving worship to the Father**.... **God [is] spirit** (or: [is the] Spirit; [gives] Breath; [becomes] Wind; [is] a Breath-effect and Attitude), **and it is binding** (or: necessary) **for the ones continuously worshiping Him to be constantly worshiping in union with spirit and Truth** (in Breath-effect and Reality; within the midst of [the] Spirit and [the] Fact; centered in [life]-attitude, as well as non-concealed genuineness and open actuality)."

The fact of the Corinthians being **God's Temple** answers to Rev. 3:12, "**The one habitually conquering** (repeatedly overcoming so as to be the victor) **– I will continue making** (forming; constructing; creating; producing) **him [to be] a pillar** (or: column) **in the Temple that is My God**." And what is a temple? The HOME of a Deity. Paul is saying that they should realize that because of the Spirit indwelling them, that they are where God lives: "**God's Spirit is constantly dwelling** (God's Breath is making Its home; the Wind which is God is housing Himself; the Attitude from God is progressively co-habiting) **within the midst of**" THEM! The preposition of this last phrase can also be rendered "in union with." Union speaks of marriage, as Paul suggests in 6:17, below. We co-habit with the Spirit, and thus produce the "fruit of the Spirit" (Gal. 5:22-23), and in Gal. 5:25 Paul puts it this way: "**Since** (or: If) **we continue living in and by spirit** (or: for [the] Spirit; to Breath-effect; or: with attitude)..." Living IN, and BY the Breath-effect! Paul would call this being "spiritual," as opposed to being "soulish" or "fleshly." With the Spirit of God living within us, we are enabled to be led by this same Spirit (Rom. 8:14). We are God's sons and daughters.

Verse 16 is a corporate statement, but each "cell" (individual) of the corporate body must live in, and be saturated with, the Spirit, or it will be like a branch that is not dwelling within the Vine (Jn. 15:1ff). In order not to build with "combustible materials" when building on the Christ Foundation, they needed "**to buy from [Him] gold having been refined** (set ablaze) **forth from out of fire**" (Rev. 3:18a). Again, the temple metaphor here is seen in the metaphor of a City, in Rev. 21:10-27. Notice the gold and precious stones in the New Jerusalem's description in that passage. Gold was a symbol of deity, or the divine nature. The physical elements of gold, silver and precious stones were the most precious and valuable materials known in Paul's day. Peter describes our present passage in 1 Cor. 3 in this way:

> "**you yourselves are, as living stones, continuously being erected** (or: progressively constructed and built up), **[being] a spiritual house** (a building with its source being the Spirit, with the characteristics of a Breath-effect), **into a set-apart** (or: holy; sacred; different-from-the-ordinary) **priesthood to bear up spiritual sacrifices** (or: offerings) **well** (or: most) **acceptable in God** (or: by God; to God; with God), **through Jesus Christ**" (1 Pet. 2:5).

Now vs. 17 moves to his previous thread of thought, concerning INDIVIDUALS (**anyone**) who might "**habitually spoils, ruins, wrecks or corrupts God's Temple**." This has been repeatedly done, all down through history, to our present day. We should keep in mind the immediate context of this verse: Paul is still focused on those who build with their faulty teaching. He brings up himself, Apollos and Cephas again, in vs. 22, below. Also note that the temple (the members of the community of Corinth) was not spoiling or corrupting itself, it was those who brought "wood, hay and stubble." This has been done through political leaders introducing systems of control, teachers introducing pagan philosophies and cosmologies, and even well-meaning individuals who read the Scriptures with carnal understanding instead of illumination from the Spirit. Daughters of Jerusalem mounted another beast of human reasoning, human political structures, us-and-them exclusionary theories, soulish and "fleshly" returns to old-covenant-type cultus, rules and domination systems. And the "church" became darkness, rather than light – for the lampstand had been removed (Rev. 2:5). As in first century Corinth, the historical church became divided – and mostly as the result of decisions about what doctrines were "orthodox," and which ones were "heretical." But progress is still being made, for He periodically brings in Fire to burn the wood, hay and stubble. God does not wait "until the end of time" to do this. He works throughout the ages.

A stern warning was given concerning those who might spoil or corrupt His Temple. Paul said, "**God will spoil, ruin, wreck and corrupt this person**." He had explained this in metaphorical terms, in vs. 15, above. The Fire of God will bring this person into ruin. Yet, we see that this spoiling and ruining of the person refers to the works that he or she had done, and the result is deliverance and salvation of that person. God sends the Physician to heal the sick and bind-up the wounded. He sends the Good Shepherd to find the "spoiled sheep" that goes its own way. He puts Incorruption upon corruption (15:53, below). He plants them, they die, and then they are resurrected as a new plant, for 15:42, below, instructs us:

> "**It is habitually** (repeatedly; presently; one after another) **being sown within corruption** (or: in union with decay and ruin; in perishability); **it is being habitually** (or: presently; repeatedly; one after another) **awakened and raised up within incorruption** (non-decayability; imperishableness)."

Robert Farrar Capon makes an interesting observation about the parable of the "Good Samaritan" (Lu. 10:30-36):

> "The defining character – the one to who the other three respond by being non-neighbor or neighbor – is the man who fell among thieves" (*Kingdom, Grace, Judgment; Paradox, Outrage and Vindication in the Parables of Jesus*, Wm B Eerdmans Pub., 2002, p 212).

This man had been ruined and wrecked. But despite the hindrances of the current religious system (the reasons for why the priest and the Levite would not help), the story has the ruined person cared for and healed. The prodigal son (Lu. 15) had a self-centered attitude, and the father made it possible for him to go off into ruin and death. But that was his path to deliverance and salvation. If we read Paul correctly, concerning his struggles with those who were actually building upon (adding things to) the covenant communities – but with inappropriate materials – it is those who were adding the old covenant Law and religious cultus onto the backs of these folks. Using the term "circumcision" as a code word for the Law, Paul informs the Galatians in ch. 5:

> 3. **Now I continue solemnly asserting** (attesting; affirming; witnessing), **again, to every person** (or: human) **proceeding to be circumcised, that he is, and continues being, a debtor** (one under obligation) **to do** (to perform; to produce) **the whole Law** [= the entire Torah]!
> 4. **You people who in union with** (or: centered in; [remaining] within) **Law continue being "liberated, rightwised and placed in covenant," were at once discharged** (made inactive, idle, useless, unproductive and without effect; or: voided, nullified, exempted) **away from Christ** (or: [the] Anointing) – **you folks fell out from the grace** (or: fall from the midst of the favor)!

What does "falling out from the grace" mean? He gives us the answer by the common agricultural metaphor in Gal. 6:

> 7. **Do not be continually led astray** (or: Stop being caused to wander and being deceived); **God is not one to be sneered at** (to have a nose turned up at; to be scorned, mocked or treated like a fool), **for "whatever a person is in the habit of sowing, this also he will reap,"**
> 8. **because the person continually sowing into the flesh of himself** (= his estranged inner being), **will progressively reap corruption** (spoil; ruin; decay) **forth from out of the flesh** (= the estranged inner being);
> > (or: the one habitually sowing into the flesh [system], of himself will continue to reap decay from out of the flesh [system]).

Adding rules and purity codes from the Law into the lives of the called-out folks (those who were called out and away from religious identity markers) was sowing into their flesh, with a system of flesh rituals.

Paul ends this section by a positive re-statement of the Truth of who they were: "**God's Temple – which you folks, yourselves, are** (exist being) **– is set-apart** (holy; sacred; different from the common)." They were not like the domination systems of religion, or the beast-systems of empire; they were "set-apart" from both. They were "different from the common." In 1 Time. 3:15, we read of,

> "**God's household** (or: to be treated, conducted or caused to behave in God's **HOUSE**), **which is** (or: exists being) **a called-out community of [the] Living God** (or: whose source is a living God; which has the qualities and character of [the] living God; or: which is a living god), **a pillar and foundational seat of The Truth** (or: a base from and an effect of a settling of reality)."

God's House was another term for God's Temple. The opening line, in vs. 17, "**If anyone habitually spoils, ruins, wrecks or corrupts God's Temple,**" is parallel to, and explains, "**Now if anyone proceeds building a house**... [with] **wood [and] thatching: herbage** (or: grass; hay) **[or] stalk** (or: straw; stubble)," of vs. 12, above. But Paul now returns to the topic of wisdom...

18. **Let no one continue to be completely cheating, tricking, deceiving or deluding himself: if anyone among you folks habitually imagines** (thinks; supposes; presumes) **[himself] to be wise** (to exist being a clever one) **within this age** (this era; this period of time), **let him come to be** (or: birth himself) **stupid** (dull; foolish; a fool) **– to the end that he can come to be** (or: may birth himself) **wise.**

Paul was living within the conjunction of the old and new ages. The temple in Jerusalem had not yet been destroyed. We suggest that "the wisdom of [the old] age" was that with which he was constantly contending. Keep in mind that his arguments are still against the false builders. For centuries the Jews had lived by the wisdom of Moses and the Prophets. It only seemed reasonable, to the natural mind, that people should still live by all those rules. We find the same thing in much of Christianity, even today. For everyday morality, folks usually turn back to the OT for guidance of how they should live their lives. Many still want to keep the feast days, etc. They forget that Paul instructs us that:

> "**Law and custom at one point entered in alongside** (or: intruded into the situation by the side) **to the end that the effect of the fall to the side** (or: so that the result of the offense and the stumbling aside) **would increase to be more than enough** (should greatly abound and become more intense)" (Rom. 5:20).

Even the Jewish wisdom literature, such as Proverbs – which gave good, human reasoning against being a fool – was to be set aside if folks were to follow the radical teachings of Jesus and the "upside-down world" of God's kingdom. Now Paul advises those who were "**wise** (to exist being a clever one) **within this age**" to "**come to be** (or: birth himself) **stupid** (dull; foolish; a fool)" for the sake of the Good News. Leaving all to follow Christ and be "led by the Spirit" (instead of by the Law) would seem to be the most stupid thing one could do – in fact, it would get a person killed. The natural, soulish person would want nothing of this. They thought Paul was mad (insane; out of his mind – Acts 26:24-25). But the truth was just the opposite…

19. **For you see, the wisdom** (cleverness; skill) **of this world System** (or: pertaining to this ordered and controlling arrangement of cultures, religions and politics; or: from this society of domination; of the aggregate of humanity) **is stupidity** (exists as nonsense and foolishness) **[when put] beside or next to God** (or: in God's presence). **For it has been written,**

> "**He is the One habitually laying hold of and catching in His fist the wise** (clever) **ones, within the midst of their every act** (or: capability and readiness to do or work; cunning; craftiness)." [Job. 5:13]

20. **And again,**

> "**[The] Lord** [= Yahweh] **continues, by intimate experience, knowing the reasonings** (thought processes; designs) **of the wise ones, that they are and continue being fruitless, useless and to no purpose.**" [Ps. 94:11]

The wisdom of the domination system was the wisdom that humanity gained by partaking of the fruit of the tree of the knowledge of good and evil. Yes, it made sense, but it was not the wisdom of the tree of Life (the wisdom of the cross). The wisdom pertaining to human systems does not produce the fruit of the Spirit, it only keeps folks in bondage and leads to death (the curse of the Law). In quoting this Psalm (Ps. 93 in the LXX), Paul changes the OT reading, which has the phrase "reasonings of the humans" (LXX), to the "designs (etc.) of the wise ones," thus fitting it to the topic of his discussion, here. In this we can see another witness to the fact that Paul seems to equate "the wisdom of this world System (etc.)" to "the thought processes (etc.) of the wise ones." Paul sees the work of Christ, and the Event of the Cross, as an example of God "**habitually laying hold of and catching in His fist the wise** (clever) **ones.**"

Dan Kaplan brought to mind Gen. 3:1-6 where he pointed out that the "woman," as it were "mounted the beast" (received the wisdom of the serpent) and then partook of the fruit of the tree that would "make one wise."

21. **Hence** (or: And so)**, let no one continue boasting in people** (among, or in union with, humans)**. You see, here it is: all things [are] yours** (or: all things pertain to you),

Boasting in people – or in philosophical systems of reason – is not the wisdom from God. It obviously had led to dividing the body of Christ. It still does, today. They did not have to cling to the wisdom of the ages, or to any particular person or group, because in the Life of God's reign "all things belonged to, and pertained to," them – and us. And now Paul gives examples of this…

22. **whether Paul, or Apollos, or Cephas; whether [the] world** (System of culture, religion, economy or government; human aggregate), **or life, or death; whether things standing or having been placed**

within [your situation], or things being about to be (impending things), all things [are] yours (or: everything pertains to you, belongs to you, and [is] from you folks),

With all these things belonging to the Corinthians (and by extension, to us), let us read what Paul said about some of these same things in Rom. 8:

> 38. **For you see, I have been persuaded and now stand convinced that neither death, nor life** (or: living existence), **nor agents** (or: messengers), **nor sovereignties** (rulers; those in prime position; or: beginnings), **nor things being now here** (being placed within, at present), **nor things about to be** (impending, or about to consecutively come), **nor powers** (or: capabilities),
> 39. **nor height** (effect of being high), **nor depth** (or: deep places), **nor any other or different created thing** (or: founded thing; institution; = the Law; = old covenant; = adversaries) **will be having power or be able to separate, divide or part us from God's Love** (or: from the acceptance from God; from the urge toward reunion, which is God; God's full giving of Himself to us) **which is within Christ Jesus, our Owner** (Lord; Master; Possessor).

Since none of these things can separate us from God's Love (which is to say, from God Himself), no wonder all these things "belong to us." Consider the alternate renderings of the last clause of vs. 22,

a) "everything pertains to you" – no wonder He works them into good; EVERYTHING affects us and is in relation to us;

b) "everything belongs to you" – and thus, belongs in our life; everything is accessible for our benefit, even if only in our thoughts;

c) "everything [is] from you" – this is the ablative reading, and may seem overstated – considering our finite condition – but consider how this may apply to our lives: a great part of our relationship with others, and with our personal environment, does come "from us."

The System, life and death, their present circumstances, impending situations – all of this was theirs and pertained to them. They need not choose one person or ideology against another. They did not even have to "choose life" (like those under Moses; Deut. 30:19). Both life AND death belonged to them: death (following Christ, bearing one's own cross) was the path (the Way) to Life. Arguments, debates about doctrines, divisions for any reason, etc., were all fruitless. For those with eyes to see, God

> **"is constantly working all things together into good and is progressively working all humanity together into that which is advantageous, worthy of admiration, noble and of excellent qualities,**
>> [with other MSS: Yet we know that God is continuously joining everything together (or: working together with everything) into goodness by those continuously loving God...]
> (Rom. 8:28).

There might also be some irony in Paul's words, here, for in 4:6, 8, below, he give admonition, and then, almost sarcasm:

> **"learn not to set your thoughts** (be disposed; put your intellect and opinion; entertain sentiments) **on things over and above things which have been written**.... **You folks already continuously exist being ones having become completely satiated, with the result that you are now fully satisfied. You are already suddenly rich. You people suddenly reign as kings – apart from us!** [note: these three statements could also be questions: Are you... Are you... Do you...?] **And would that you surely did reign, so that we could also reign as kings together with you!"**

It may also be "wisdom" to keep in mind the words given to Timothy,

> **"since we are continuously remaining under for support** (or: if we continue patiently enduring), **we will also continue reigning** (performing royal activities and influence) **together with [Him]**..." (2 Tim. 2:12). Cf Rev. 20:4-6 for an apocalyptic picture of a then-present reality.

23. yet you folks [are] Christ's – yet Christ [is] God's!

(or: Now you have your source and origin in [the] Anointed, and [the] Anointed has His source and origin in God; or: But you belong to [Messiah]; [Messiah] belongs to God.)

This is the bottom line, and all else is mere rubbish by comparison. It is because of this that vs. 22 has any validity. We belong to Christ. He bought us and we are His possession. And all that Christ is belongs to God. As can be observed in the parenthetical expansion, the terms Christ and God can be read as ablatives, which was a function to show "source." Our source and origin is the Anointed, and the Anointed has His source and origin in God. God is the destiny of everything – Rom. 11:36, "**into Him are all things.**" The reality that is in Christ is Paul's answer for all human conflicts and divisions. He said it this way, in Col. 3:3,

> "**for you folks died, and your life has been hidden so that it is now concealed together with the Christ, within the midst of God** (or: in union with God)."

And this is further explained in 2 Cor. 5:14-15a,

> "**[We are] deciding** (discerning and concluding; judging) **this: that** [some MSS add: since] **One Person** (or: Man) **died over [the situation of] all people** (or: for the sake of all humans); **consequently all people died** (or: accordingly, then, all humans died). [*cf* Rom. 5:12; the death of the first Adam is reversed] **And further, He died over all people** (over [the situation] of, and for the sake of all humans)…"

Conzelmann concludes, regarding vss. 22-23, that, "the event of salvation is given concrete shape and definition of existence in its relation to the world." Amen! The next chapter begins with explanations of how the Corinthians should regard Paul, Apollos, Cephas, and other teachers…

Chapter 4

1. **Thus, let a person** (a human) **continue logically considering** (or: measuring and classifying) **us as God's subordinates** (God's deputies; those under God's orders; God's under-rowers) **and house-managers** (or: administrators) **of God's secrets** (or: mysteries from God which require initiation for receiving; secrets which are God).

Now observe that he does NOT refer to himself, Apollos, or other teachers as "house-managers" of PEOPLE. No, they are dispensers of the Christ, Who is the Secret that was hidden from past ages, and which is best explained in Col. 1, where we also learn of Paul's goal in being "**God's subordinate,**"

> 26. **the Secret** (or: sacred mystery) **having been hidden away and remaining concealed away from the ages** (or: from [past] eons), **as well as away from the [past] generations, yet now** (at the present time) **is set in clear light in His set-apart folks** (or: was manifested to His holy ones; is caused to be seen by His saints; is shown for what it is, for His sacred people),
> 27. **to whom God wills** (or: at one point purposed; or: intends) **to make known by intimate experience, what [are] the riches of the glory of this Secret** (or: the wealth which has its source in this sacred mystery's manifestation which calls forth praise) **within the multitudes** (among the nations; in the Gentiles; IN UNION WITH the swarms of ethnic groups), **which is** (or: exists being) **Christ within you folks, the expectation of and from the glory**
> > (or: which is [the] Anointed in union with you people: the [realized] hope of the manifestation which called forth praise; or: which is [the] Anointing [and the Messiah] within the midst of you folks – the expectation which is the glory),
> 28. **Whom** [other MSS: Which] **we ourselves habitually proclaim down the line** (or: announce in accord with the pattern), **constantly putting [Him] into the minds of every person** (or: human) **and repeatedly teaching every person** (or: human), **within the sphere of all wisdom, to the intent that we may place every person** (or: human) **finished** (mature; perfect with respect to purpose; complete; as having reached the goal of destiny) **by [our] side, within the midst of, centered in, and in union with, Christ** [other MSS add: Jesus],
> 29. **unto which [goal] I habitually work hard** (or: progressively toil on) **and become weary, constantly struggling as in a contest, corresponding to** (or: down from, yet on the level of)

His inward working (or: energy and operation)**: the One continuously operating (energizing and inwardly working) within me – within power and in union with ability.**

As he said above, he and other sent-forth folk are simply workers on God's farm, God's building. Those in Corinth should not think of them as more than this. The opening adverb, "**Thus,**" is being used as an intensifier pointing back to what has just preceded it, summing up what he has just presented in 3:21. This is our position in God's reign. Paul has returned to his topic of 3:5ff, above.

2. **In this situation, furthermore, it is constantly being looked for and sought after, in house-managers** (administrators)**, that this person may be found [to be] full of faith** (loyal; reliable; trustworthy; faithful). *Cf* Tit. 1:7; 1 Pet. 4:10

3. **Now to** (or: for) **me, it is of little importance** (a very trivial matter) **that I am being constantly critiqued** (sifted, critically reviewed and evaluated; put up for judgment) **by you folks, or by a human day** (= day of reckoning; man's tribunal or day in court). **In contrast, by habit, neither do I set myself up for critique** (or: review, evaluate or judge myself).

4. **For, in and regarding** (or: [as] to; for) **myself, I have been conscious of nothing; but yet [it is] not in this [that] I have been set forth as** (or: made to be) **fair and equitable** (just and rightwised with right relationship in the Way pointed out). **Now the One continually setting me up for evaluation** (sifting, reviewing and deciding about me) **is [the] Lord** [= Christ or Yahweh].

In the service to the King, those operating as His representatives must be "**full of faith** (loyal; reliable; trustworthy; faithful)." This is seen in the parable of the unjust or worthless servants (figures of the Judean leadership of the 1st century) in Jesus' parables.

In vs. 4 he assures his listeners that he is not aware of any personal fault, but then goes to posit that having a clear conscience is not the basis for a person having been "rightwised with right relationship in the Way pointed out." In 8:7, below, he points out that a person can have a "**conscience** (integrated inner knowing; perceptive awareness) [that is] **being weak**." Our being "**set forth as** (or: made to be) **fair and equitable** (just)" was the work of Christ, in His death and resurrection. We do not base our place in the new creation on what we may or may not be conscious about, any more than we are to be critiquing ourselves (vs. 3). We are confident is the Lord's "**continually setting [us] up for evaluation,**" and sifting us to remove the chaff from His grain, that He has produced in us. This is the ongoing "judgment seat of Christ/God." For this reason "**it is of little importance** (a very trivial matter) **that [he was] being constantly critiqued** (sifted, critically reviewed and evaluated; put up for judgment) **by [them].**" Recall Rom. 14:4,

> "**You, who are the person constantly judging** (separating away; making a distinction or a decision about) **another man's house-servant** (domestic)**! By** (In; To; For; With) **his own Lord** (Master; Owner) **he continues standing, or, he is falling. Yet he will repeatedly be made to stand, for you see, the Lord** [= Yahweh or Christ] **is constantly able** (perpetually powerful) **to make him stand.**"

We need to remember this admonition as it applies to us, as well. But let us drink in Paul's conclusion…

5. **Hence** (or: And so)**, do not be constantly evaluating** (or: stop judging, making decisions about or critiquing) **anything before [its] season** (before a fitting, due or appointed situation; prior to a fertile moment)**: until the Lord** [= Yahweh or Christ] **would come – Who will continue giving light to** (or: shine upon and illuminate) **the hidden things of the Darkness** (or: the hiding things which are things in the shadows and dimness of obscurity)**, and will progressively set in clear light** (or: keep on manifesting) **the intentions and purposes** (designs, dispositions, motives and counsels) **of the hearts – and then the praise and applause from God will repeatedly be birthed** (happen; come into being) **in each human** (or: for every person)**!**

This verse has traditionally had a futuristic spin put to it as though it related to a "coming of Christ" that supposedly has not yet happened. But that is yanking the verse out of its context. Read again the last statement of vs. 4. In this admonition of vs. 5, Paul is of necessity speaking of a future situation, for this is always the case when speaking in imperatives, such as, "**do not be constantly evaluating** (or: stop judging, making decisions about or critiquing) **anything before [its] season** (before a fitting, due or appointed situation; prior to a fertile moment)." But he is speaking into their current lives and to a potential, immediate future – within first century Corinth! And so next he goes on to define what he means by the term "season" (fitting or appointed situation; fertile moment [in their lives]): and that would be whenever "**the Lord** [= Yahweh or Christ] **would come.**" Now this is not an eschatological, end-of-the-age scenario. It is apocalyptic language, but this is normal to Paul as he "unveils" what was being disclosed to him, and what he says of the Lord's coming, here, is likely analogous to what he said in 2 Tim. 4:17a, "**Yet the Lord** [= Christ or Yahweh] **took a stand beside me** (or: stood alongside in me) – **and He empowered me** (enabled me; gave me inward ability)..." It would be comparable to what the risen Christ had John write to Ephesus,

> "**Yet if not, I am continuously** (repeatedly; habitually) **coming to you** [as a group], **and I will proceed removing** (or: moving) **your lampstand out of its place, if ever you** [as a group] **may not change your way of thinking** (your mind-set and paradigm) (Rev. 2:5; cf Rev. 2:16; 2:22-23; 3:3; 3:11, for other examples).

No, this was not speaking of the false teaching of a "second coming of Christ." It was speaking of the Lord coming, by His Spirit (we no longer know Him in the sphere of the flesh – 2 Cor. 5:16) to illuminate the situations that needed their evaluations and decisions, and they were to wait for the Lord's "**giving light to** (or: shine upon and illuminate) **the hidden things of the Darkness** (or: the hiding things which are things in the shadows and dimness of obscurity)." In Jn. 1:4 we read, "**the life was continuing being, and began progressively existing as, the Light of mankind,**" and the next verse tells us, "**the Light is constantly shining in the dim and shadowed places, and keeps on progressively giving light within the gloomy darkness where there is no light**" (Jn. 1:5). This might very likely happen through someone such as Paul (cf 5:3, below), or through someone within their community where there is given "**an effect of grace,**" such as "**a word** (thought; message; expression; [the] reason) **of intimate, experiential knowledge, insight or realization** (gnosis) **– in accord with** (or: down from; in the sphere of; in line with) **the same Breath** (or: Spirit)." (12:4, 8b, below).

When Jesus sent out his disciples to the towns and villages, he gave them His power and authority – and they were effective representatives of Him (cf Lu. 10:17, 19). Therefore, when they had come to villages they were to announce that God's kingdom (the presence and actions of the Lord) had come to them (Lu. 10:9). Here Paul instructs those at Corinth that the Lord's coming would "**progressively set in clear light** (or: keep on manifesting) **the intentions and purposes** (designs, dispositions, motives and counsels) **of the hearts.**" We saw an example of this with Peter, in the incident of Ananias and Sapphira (Acts 5:1-10). We see this ongoing situation, spoken of here in vs. 5, presented as a metaphor of "a step, platform, stage or place ascended by steps to speak in public assembly in the center of a city" in 2 Cor. 5:10. There, Paul sets the scene in vs. 9, "**Therefore we are constantly loving the value** (or: ambitious for the honor)... **to constantly be folks [that are] well-pleasing to Him.**" Why? Verse 10 gives the answer:

> "**for it continues** (or: is repeatedly) **necessary for us – the all** (= the whole of humanity) **– to be manifested in front of Christ's elevated place** (a step, platform, stage, or place ascended by steps to speak in public assembly in the center of a city; or: = an official bench of a judge or public official), **to the end that each one may himself take into kindly keeping, for care and provision** (= be responsible for), **the things [done] through** (or: by means of; or: [during our passing] through the midst of) **the Body – [oriented] toward, and facing, what things he practices** (or: she accomplishes), **whether good or bad, whether serviceable or inefficient, whether fair or foul, whether capable or careless.**

(or: for you see that it continues binding for us all to be set in light so as to be clearly seen in the presence of the judgment seat which is Christ, so that each should keep and provide for the things performed throughout [His] body, with a view to, and face to face with, what things [were practiced], whether virtuous or vile)." [cf 3:9-17, above]

Notice the second half of vs. 10: the reason for living *coram Deo* (in God's presence) is for evaluation of what we have been doing, in regard to the body of Christ. The purpose is "to take [these things] into kindly keeping, for care and provision (= be responsible for)" our actions and "practices." This implies facing up to what we have been doing, so that we can make corrections, if necessary.

Paul brings up the topic of "judging [one's] brother" in Rom. 14:10, and then reminds them, "**For you see, we will all continue standing in attendance alongside on God's elevated place**," and then in 14:12 informs them,

> "**Consequently, then, each one of us will continue giving a word** (presenting a message; rendering an account) **about himself to God** (or: for God; by God; in God)."

This is like the accounting of a manager to the owner, in the parables of Jesus. This is not a one-time thing, but a periodic necessity.

6. **Now I refashioned these things** (or: transposed and transfer these things into a figure; change the distinctive form to apply and exemplify; or: = changed the form of the metaphor), **brothers – with a view to Apollos and myself – because of you folks, to the end that in us you could learn not to set your thoughts** (be disposed; put your intellect and opinion; entertain sentiments) **on things over and above things which have been written, so that you do not continue being puffed up – one over and above another, [and] down on the different one.**

Paul has said all this about himself and Apollos as an example for them, so that they would not "set [their] thoughts on things beyond what has been written." So often, pride is the motivation behind factions and divisions. Paul did not want them to be "puffed up" with an inflated self-disposition of being intellectually or spiritually superior to others – especially toward folks that were "different," so as to look down on them. This sort of opinion or sentiment engenders an "us-and-them" cliquishness that brings division, instead of "joined unity."

Of what was he speaking, when he referred to, "**things over and above things which have been written**"? The first thing that came to our minds was, "the Scriptures." This would mean the plan of the ages (Eph. 3:11), the Alpha to the Omega. No need to go into theories and philosophies of human speculations. But further, the lyrics of Gerry Rafferty come to mind: "Whatever's written in your heart, that's all that matters," or as Heb. 10:16 put it,

> "**Continuously giving My laws upon their hearts, I will even progressively write them upon their mental perception** (or: comprehension; that which passes through the mind)."

Reading Paul's admonition of vs. 6 in the light of this quote from Heb. 10 seems to us to best align with Paul's teachings. He had received unveilings that were "over and above" what had been written in the OT writings. Those unveilings were rooted in the old covenant (Rom. 11:17), but everything in the new covenant was growth "above" the roots. With the insight of things being written our hearts, they would be the real from which we can give honest witness to the Way, the Truth and the Life that came through Jesus. But speculations on things that are beyond our grasp, things that are not being lived-out, leads to intellectual, heady ideas that simply gender pride and prejudice, usually ending in divisions and factions.

Also, as Dan Kaplan reminds us, Paul told these folks,

> "**You yourselves are and continue being our letter**.... **you are and continue being those continuously set in clear light and progressively manifested: Christ's letter** (a letter whose source is Christ, and which is Christ), **being one dispensed in attending service by us, being one having been written** (inscribed; imprinted; engraved), **not in black** (= not with ink), **but rather, by** (or: in; with) **God's Spirit: One continuously living** (or: in a Breath-effect which has

65

its origin in God, Who is constantly living); **not in stone tablets** (or: on tablets composed of stone), **but rather within tablets which are hearts made of flesh** (or: on tablets in hearts composed of flesh)" (2 Cor. 3:2-3; [cf Rom. 8:24-25]).

This seems to be a second witness as to what Paul was meaning, concerning what has been written. And now, observe how he continues his thoughts…

7. **For who continues making you to discriminate** (or: who is now thoroughly separating or dividing you through the midst, for evaluation; or: who is repeatedly discerning or distinguishing you; or: what makes you completely different, separated or exceptional)**? And what are you habitually holding** (constantly having) **which you did not receive? Now since** (or: if) **also you received [it], why do you continue boasting, as though not receiving [it]?**

Since they had all received the same effects of grace, why would they discriminate against those that they deemed inferior for some reason? Why would they boast about what had been freely given to them? Those who feel that they are "the elect" can be tempted to think of themselves as "special" or superior to those who, in their eyes, are apparently not a part of "the chosen." Paul is challenging them in regard to their practice of "discriminating," and challenging their assumption that they are "completely different, separated (from others in the community) or exceptional." Next he characterized their self-assumptions using irony…

8. **You folks already continuously exist being ones having become completely satiated, with the result that you are now fully and excessively satisfied. You are already suddenly rich. You people suddenly reign as kings** (or: attained to sovereignty) **– apart from us!** [note: these three statements could also be questions: Are you… Are you… Do you…?] **And would that you surely did reign** (function as kings) **so that we could also reign as kings together with you!**

Taken as a statement about them, Paul might be using sarcasm to combat their apparent airs of superiority. But the Greek could be read as a series of rhetorical questions that would call them to reconsider their attitudes towards others. He is striking at the root of the divisions that have been tearing at the unity of the community. The final statement, "**would that you surely did reign**…" tells us that Paul does not think that they are really reigning at this point. But consider what he said in 2 Tim. 2:12,

> "**since we are continuously remaining under for support** (or: if we continue patiently
> enduring), **we will also continue reigning** (performing royal activities and influence) **together**…"

There are conditions for reigning. Jesus asked His disciples, in regard to this,

> "**Are you folks now able and do you continue having power to drink at once the cup which
> I, Myself, am continuing about to be progressively drinking?**" (Mat. 20:22)

Obviously, Paul considers them as still being children (3:2, above; 9:7, below; Heb. 5:12, 13). His terminology about "reigning" is an allusion to the concept of God's reign and kingdom, and points to the goal of being leaders in God's sovereign activities (Mat. 20:21), in contrast to seeking success in the domination systems of the Empire, or in society.

Another point to observe here is Paul's assessment of their being satisfied with their present level of spiritual growth. He characterizes them as being "satiated" and "fully and excessively satisfied." Paul, on the other hand, does not consider himself to have yet "attained." To Philippi he would write concerning himself,

> "**not because I already take it by the hand** (grasp, lay hold of it; or: obtained) **or even have
> been already brought to the purposed goal and destiny**" (Phil. 3:12),

but rather, he was,

> "**continuously pressing forward, pursuing down toward** [the; or: an] **object in view** (a mark
> on which the eye is fixed)**: into the awarded contest prize of God's** (or: the award which is

God's) **invitation to an above place** (or: the prize from, and which is, the upward calling from, and which is, the God) **within the midst of and in union with Christ Jesus**" (Phil. 3:14). These folks had attached themselves to one or another of the "anointed preachers or teachers" of their day, and apparently felt that this was their ticket to being a part of the "in crowd," the "winners circle." He wants them to face their present reality, and then adjust their attitudes. They apparently had a lack of humility and thought that they had finished their course, in following Christ. Their immaturity demonstrated the fact that they were not "reigning as kings" in God's kingdom. They also apparently saw themselves as independent of the rest of Christ's body – as we see in Paul's words: "**apart from us!**" The risen Christ described a similar situation in Rev. 3:15-20.

9. **Indeed, it continues seeming to me that** (or: I regularly suppose that; I am presently thinking that) **God shows us off** (exhibits us) – **the last ones sent off with a mission** (or: displayed the emissaries and representatives last) – **as men condemned to die in the public arena** [e.g., as gladiators, or as thrown to the lions], **because we were made to be a theater** (= an observed public spectacle) **for the world** (or: to the organized, domination System of culture, religion, economy and politics; or: in the cosmos!), **even to messengers** (or: for [government] agents; among folks with the Message), **and for humans** (or: to and among peoples [in general]). *Cf* 15:31, below; Rom. 8:36; 2 Cor. 4:10.
10. **We [are] stupid folks** (fools; ones led by nonsense) **because of Christ, yet you folks [are] sensible and intelligent ones** (ones with understanding) **within, and in union with, Christ; we [are] weak ones, yet you people [are] strong ones; you [are] folks in glory and illustrious reputation, yet we [are] dishonored and unvalued ones.** *Cf* 1:26-27, above.
11. **Until the present hour** (or: Up to now – this very minute), **we also continue being hungry, constantly thirsty, habitually naked** (= scantily clothed), **repeatedly being struck on the ear with a fist** (= treated roughly) **and are continuously unsettled** (= homeless and wanderers).

Here he is contrasting the low position of himself and his associates (the "us" and "we" in these verses) to the Corinthians' boastful, false, self-image. He is being both literal (vss. 9 and 11) and sarcastic in vs. 10, where we see three sets of antitheses linked together. Observe the last statement, "**we [are] dishonored and unvalued**" – in general, yes, but he is pointedly saying that this is how those in the Corinthian community both treat and regard him and his associates. That should have pricked their consciences. He is reflecting back to them a cruciform life of following the Path of the Master, as contrasted to their supposed intelligence, strength and glorious repute. The Corinthians had been Paul's disciples, but they had forgotten or not taken to heart what Jesus had said:

> "**A student** (or: disciple) **is not over or above the teacher, nor [is] a slave over or above his owner. [It is] sufficient and enough for the student** (or: disciple) **that he can come to be as his teacher, and the slave as his owner**" (Mat. 10:24, 25a).

The last clause of vs. 9 gives us a glimpse of Paul's world view, when he speaks of having been "made to be in a theater for the organized, domination System." He adds two categories of those who had been observing them "as a public spectacle." The agents/messengers could have been folks of higher rank or function within religions or governments, or other people that were proclaiming the Message of Christ, or they could have been folks like those described in Heb. 12:23,

> "**ten-thousands** (or: myriads) **of agents and messengers** (people with a/the message)" and "**an assembly of an entire people** (or: an assembly of all; a universal convocation) **and in** (or: to) **a summoning forth** (or: a called-out and gathered community) **of firstborn folks having been copied** (from-written, as from a pattern; or: enrolled; registered) **within [the; or: various] atmospheres** (or: heavens)."

Whichever he meant by the "agents/messengers," the other category is "**and for humans** (or: to and among peoples [in general])," which gives us pause, as to his meaning here. He might have simply meant "everyday people of other cultures," by this second category. We, today, will interpret his meaning according to our own world view and cosmology, but his point was probably not to make a cosmological statement, but to dramatically say that they had been "exposed" to the critical view of the whole world.

Verse 11 sure gives a different picture than of those in "the ministry" in American Christianity today. And for this, we are thankful. But it may accurately picture those who presently serve in developing countries. In 2 Cor. 6:3-13 he gives a similar description of his and his companions' experiences and mode of life, where in vs. 11 he assured them, "**our heart has been broadened and is now enlarged [toward you]**," and then ending the passage by saying to them, "**You folks also be broadened and enlarged**"

Conzelmann observes Paul presenting to Corinth the witness of preservation within adverse situations as speaking to the "divine power" that was associated with their ministry (ibid p 89 n 43).

12. **Further, we continue toiling** (laboring) **to weariness – habitually active in work with our own hands** [note: the Greek culture despised manual labor]. **Being constantly insulted** (reviled; cursed; verbally abused), **we are repeatedly speaking words of goodness** (or: blessing); **being habitually pursued and persecuted, we are continuously holding up and bearing [it]** (or: holding back [i.e., from retaliation]);
13. **being incessantly defamed** (slandered; plied with ill-rumors; [other MSS: blasphemed]), **we regularly called them to our sides** (normally entreated and offered assistance). **We were made to be as that which comes from cleaning all around** (as the off-scouring results; as the filthy refuses) **of the world** (from the organized System of culture, religion, economy and government) **– wiped-off filth and scum of all things and all people – until right now!**

Yes, they lived a cruciform life and reflected the image of their Lord. What a contrast for a people that were apparently proud and boastful – and as Paul put it, who "reigned as kings." Paul's life sounds more like those recorded in Heb. 11:

> 36. **But different ones took a trial** (or: received a test) **of mockings** (scoffings), **and of scourgings, and further, of bonds and imprisonment** (= put in chains and thrown in jail).
> 37. **They were stoned, they were cut in two with a saw, they were put to the proof** (tried; tested), **they passed away in a slaughter** (or: by murder) **with sword, they went around** (wandered) **in sheepskins, in goat skins, continuously being behind** (being in want; being in the rear), **being constantly pressed** (squeezed; afflicted), **habitually being held in the bad** (being maltreated; having it bad) – [cf 2 Ki. 2:13 (LXX): Elijah's mantle a sheepskin – Denton]
> 38. **of whom the System** (the ordered arrangement; the world or culture, secular society, religions and government) **was not worthy** (was not of equal value) **– being continually deceived** (led astray; caused to wander) **in deserts and mountains and caves and the holes of the earth** (or: ground).

In vs. 12 we observe that he and his companions "blessed, and did not curse" (Rom. 12:14). We find here simply statements of facts, not complaints about how bad the world is. Notice in vs. 13 that he says, "We were made to be the off-scouring results, the filthy refuses, of the world." Today we do not hear many messages about the Christian life described in such terms. In vs. 16b, below, Paul tells these folks, "**Progressively come to be** (or: Keep on becoming) **my imitators** (ones who copy or mimic me)." Now the immediate context of that imperative (vs. 16a) refers to him being their paraclete, but his function as that for them is certainly not far from his descriptions (vss. 12-13) of all that they had gone through.

14. **I am not continuing to write these things [to be] constantly shaming you folks** (or: turning you back within yourselves), **but to the contrary, as my beloved children** (accepted born-ones to whom I urge for reunion), **I am progressively placing things in your minds.**

His admonitions to them were "placing into their minds" the proper world view for a Christ follower: to take up their crosses and follow the Life that Jesus lives; to walk (live their lives) the Way (Path) that Jesus walks. They, too, are called to be co-laborers with Christ (3:9, above). Jesus is still walking out His reality (Truth), both within and among them. Paul had just described what this might look like for them (vss. 10-13, above). He is treating them in the manner that a good parent brings correction to his or her children. Paul was "looking unto Jesus" (Heb. 12:2a) as the Pattern and Leader on the Path – and he was following Him in that way (as noted in Heb. 12:2b). And the reason for "**turning [our] eyes away from other things and fixing them** (or: looking away) **into Jesus**" (2a) is the same reason that Paul had rehearsed his own life to them: "**to the end that you may not tire with exertion** (or: labor to weariness), **being continuously dissolved** (be enfeebled and exhausted; caused to fall apart) **in your inner selves** (or: by your souls; = in your lives)" (Heb. 12:3b). The next verses in Heb. 12 go into more details about the topic of Paul's present admonitions to those in Corinth, so let us review them:

4. **You folks do not yet resist** (or: did not as yet take a stand down against, or fully put in place opposition) **as far as blood** (= to the point of bloodshed; or, as a figure: = to the depth of your soul-life), **toward constantly struggling against** (or: repeatedly contending and fighting in opposition to) **the failure** (the sin; the error; the miss of the target; missing the point).

5. **And further, you have entirely forgotten** (or: been oblivious of) **the calling-near** (the relief, aid, comfort and encouragement) **which keeps on speaking-through** (discoursing; reasoning through and conversing; laying out the issue in every direction) **to you folks, as to sons:**

"**My son, do not be neglecting** (giving little care to) **the Lord's discipline** (education; child-training), **neither be exhausted** (dissolved; = fall apart) **while being continually scrutinized or convicted** (exposed and put to the test; or: reproved) **by** (or: under) **Him,**

6. **for whom the Lord** [= Yahweh] **is loving** (urging toward reunion and acceptance), **He is continuously and progressively educating** (or: disciplining; child-training), **and He is periodically scourging every son whom He is taking alongside with His hands** (accepting; receiving).**"** [Prov. 3:11-12; *cf* Job 5:17; Ps. 94:12; Phil. 1:29]

7. **[So] be constantly enduring** (or: You folks are continuing to remain supportively under) **with a view to education, discipline and child-training: as to sons is God Himself continuously bringing [it] to you. For who is a son** (or: what son is there) **whom a father is not disciplining, educating and training?** [*cf* Jas. 1:12; Rev. 3:19]

8. **But if you are without education, discipline and training, of which all have become partakers** (common participants; partners), **accordingly you are really illegitimates** (= rabbinic term *mamzer*: child of a prohibited marriage [Lev. 18], or of uncertain fatherhood) **and not sons.**

The phrase, "**as my beloved children,**" should not be taken as a simile, but as a spiritual reality which he explains in the next verse. This phrase should be interpreted in the sense of "since you ARE my beloved children." Just as a father teaches his children (as noted in the passage from Heb. 12, just cited), Paul was "**progressively placing things in [their] minds**" – the literal meaning of the Greek word, *noutheteō* (from *nous* + *tithēmi*) which is often rendered as "warn" (KJV; Nyland) or "admonish." Yes, those extended meanings apply, but Paul was actually planting seeds (placing [Gr.: *tithēmi*] the *Logos*) in their minds (*nous*). This calls to mind his words to the Roman community,

"**be progressively transformed** (transfigured; changed in form and semblance) **by the renewing** (or: in the renewal; for the making-back-up-new again) **of your mind**" (Rom. 12:2).

15. **For should you folks proceed to have a vast multitude** (a myriad; ten thousand) **of child-escorts and guardians within Christ** (or: tutors or educators in an Anointing), **in contrast [you do] not [have] many fathers** (or: parents), **because in one moment I myself fathered** (gave birth to; generated) **you people within and in union with Christ Jesus – through means of the message of abundant wellness** (the news of fortunate, ideal ease and goodness).

God was the Father of Jesus; Jesus became a father to Paul; now Paul functions as a father to the communities he founded, in Christ. Here we may have a preview of a similar generational/family metaphor that he presents in 11:3, below:

"**the Christ is** (or: exists being) **the Source** (or: Head) **of every adult male** (or: the Anointing is the head of every husband); **in turn the adult male [was] a source of woman** (or: the husband

[is] a head of a wife); **and yet God [is the] Source of the Christ** (or: [is] Head of the Anointed One)!"

But, returning to the "**father**" metaphor, here, let us consider more from Heb. 12:

9. **Then again, we indeed used to have instructors** (educators; teachers of boys; discipliners) **– the fathers of our flesh** (= human parents) **– and we continued being repeatedly turned among [them]** (or: turned within and caused to reflect; = we listened to them and obeyed). **To a much greater extent, shall we not be continually placed under and humbly arranged and aligned by the Father of the spirits** (or: the Progenitor of breath-effects and Mentor of attitudes)**? And then we shall proceed living** (or: progressively live)**!** [*cf* Nu. 27:16; Eph. 6:2-3]
10. … **upon this [instruction, arrangement and alignment] He is continuously bringing [things; situations] together** (progressively collecting unto profitability) **– unto this: to mutually partake of His set-apartness** (or: to take by the hands together, share and mutually receive from the holiness and sacredness which is Him).
11. **Now on the one hand, all discipline** (instruction; child-training; education) **with a view to** (or: face to face with) **what is presently at hand, does not at the time seem to be joyous or fun, but to the contrary [is] painful and full of sorrow and grief; however afterwards** (or: subsequently), **to, for, in and by those having been gymnastically trained** (exercised without clothing; = working-out while stripped of self-works) **through it, it is constantly and** [*cf* Jas. 3:18] **progressively yielding fruit which has the character and qualities of peace and harmony – which equates to fair and equitable dealings in rightwised relationships which are in line with the Way pointed out, and justice** (also: = from covenant inclusion and participation).

Paul "fathered" them, "**through means of the message of abundant wellness** (the news of fortunate, ideal ease and goodness)." This, of course, took place "**within and in union with Christ Jesus.**" This phrase is a compact description of the Gospel, the new covenant and the new creation. Apart from Him, we can do nothing (Jn. 15:5b)! Union, and dwelling "within" says it all. But as then, so now: **not many fathers** (or: parents); not many who will follow through on the job of "parenting." And as the next verse admonishes us, let us progressively mimic Paul in this function, as well.

16. **Therefore, I am repeatedly performing as a paraclete for you** (calling you to my side to aid, comfort, encourage and advise you). **Progressively come to be** (or: Keep on becoming) **my imitators** (ones who copy or mimic me).

If we take the verb "repeatedly performing as a paraclete" as meaning "advising," then he is "advising and encouraging" them to imitate the cruciform life that he had just described to them, in vss. 10-13, above. Again, this also means that they (and we) should "father" other people! The functioning as a paraclete is the "parenting" of those we "father." Children need training, educating and encouraging – and they need solid food when they are ready for it. This means that WE need to have "meat" to share with them.

Paul did not tell these folks to "follow" him – the KJV is a mistranslation here. Rather, he presents himself as an example of a follower of Jesus Christ.

"[Paul] does not present himself as a Christian personality. This summons is always bound up with the paradox that he is an example inasmuch as he is nothing and he suffers." (Conzelmann, ibid p 92).

17. **Because of this, I sent Timothy to you folks – he who is my beloved child** (accepted born-one) **and one full of faith** (or: a loyal, reliable, faithful and trustworthy person) **within and in union with [the] Lord** [= Christ or Yahweh], **who will continue calling you back to remembrance** (will be repeatedly reminding you) **of my ways** (roads; paths) **– the ones in union with an Anointing** [other MSS: in the midst of Christ Jesus (or: in {the} Anointing of Jesus); others: within {the} Lord Jesus; others: in Jesus] **– correspondingly as** (according as; along the lines as and to the level as) **I am habitually teaching**

everywhere, within the midst of every called-out community (ecclesia; summoned forth covenant assembly).

Observe that Paul said that Timothy will repeatedly remind them of "[his] **ways** (roads; paths) – **the ones in union with an Anointing** [other MSS: in the midst of Christ Jesus (or: in {the} Anointing of Jesus); others: within {the} Lord Jesus; others: in Jesus]." Paul's way of life, and the Path that he followed was a living parable and example for them. And he was consistent in teaching along these lines – and to this level of understanding – among every called-out community. So to have what he taught clearly in mind, we suggest repeatedly reading over again 4:1-16, above. Again, being a father to those who he birthed into the kingdom was one of his "ways" of following the Way. Being led by the Spirit (Rom. 8:14) is, of course, central to his road. Notice his emphasis on *en christō* (centered with the midst of and in union with Christ/the Anointing) which he had just used in vs. 15, above, and now again here. THIS is the Good News – where we are, and with Whom we are joined in intimate union. This is what he was "**habitually teaching everywhere, within the midst of every called-out community** (ecclesia; summoned forth covenant assembly)." Notice also his child-rearing style: repetition of information. Timothy was to "**continue calling you back to remembrance** (will be repeatedly reminding you)." And he was to remind them "**CORRESPONDINGLY as** (ACCORDING as; ALONG THE LINES as and TO THE LEVEL as) [Paul was] habitually teaching.**" Paul therefore had great confidence in Timothy. We all need this sort of reminding. Also observe how Paul qualifies Timothy: **one full of faith** (or: a loyal, reliable, faithful and trustworthy person)." This is the primary attribute that the called-out need to have in their representatives.

Paul's use of the term "**ways**" here may also be alluding to the "way" of other teachers that had been among them. Apollos, e.g., had been "**one having been orally instructed in the way** (or: path) **of the Lord** [= Yahweh]," but he was "**versed in and acquainted with only the immersion** (or: baptism) **carried out by John**" (Acts 18:24). Aquila and Priscilla "**took him to themselves and more accurately exposed** (or: expounded; set out from the midst) **God's Way** (or: path)" (Acts 18:26b). Concerning John, Jesus had said, "**You see, John came toward you men within the path** (or: on the road) **of fairness and equity, in accord with the way pointed out, and in the right relationship which pertains to justice,**" (Mat. 21:32a), but he was still in the old covenant (the Law), and had not received the full revelation of Christ, who WAS the Path (the Road; the Way).

18. **Now certain ones were puffed up** (= became arrogant; were bloated [from pride or self-esteem]), **as though I [were] not proceeding to be coming to you.**
19. **Yet I will proceed quickly** (speedily) **coming to you folks, if the Lord** [= Christ or Yahweh] **should intend** (purpose; will) **[it], and I will progress in knowing by intimate experience not the word** (thought; idea; message; verbal expression; information) **of, or from, those having been puffed up, but to the contrary, [their] ability and power.**

Paul is a representative of Christ. The summoned folks in Corinth were his children. If Paul came to them again, it would be the Lord coming to them. It would be a time of accounting for those who became arrogant and bloated. He would test what sort of "power" they actually had. Dan Kaplan pointed to a similar potential situation that Jesus described for the disciples that He was sending out unto the lost sheep of Israel,

> "**And if, indeed, the house should be suitable and worthy, you men let your peace** (the joining from and which is you folks; [= shalom]) **come upon it – yet if it may not be suitable or worthy, let your peace** (this joining from you) **be returned back upon yourselves**" (Mat. 10:13).

20. **For God's reign** (or: the kingdom which is God; the sovereign influence or activity from God) **[is; lies] not within an idea** (a *logos*; information; a thought; a word; a message; a verbal expression), **but rather within ability, in union with capability, or in the midst of power.**

21. **What do you folks want** (presently desire; normally intend; by habit purpose)**? Should I come to you people within [the realm of] a rod** (staff; = with corrective measures), **or within love** (solidarity), **and in a spirit of gentle friendliness and tender kindness** (or: meekness)**?**

God's reign lies within lives that are lived out – not in theories, philosophies or doctrines. God's sovereign influence embodies "**ability, capability and power**" within those who live "**in union with an Anointing**" (vs. 17, above). Paul is affirming that he is operating in union with God's reign, which is present to him, not some future "coming." He will not come with just ideas or thoughts, but within it power and ability. But as he said in Rom. 14:17,

> "**for you see, God's kingdom** (or: the reign-and-dominion which is God; the expression, influence and activity of God's sovereignty) **is not** (or: does not exist being) **solid food and drink, but rather, eschatological deliverance into fair and equitable dealing which brings justice and right relationship in the Way pointed out** (being turned in the right direction; rightwisedness; also = covenant inclusion and participation), **peace and harmony from the joining** (= shalom) **and joy** (or: happiness; rejoicing) **within set-apart Breath-effect** (or: in union with and amidst a dedicated spirit and a sacred attitude; or: in [the] Holy Spirit)."

So that "power and ability" is a good thing! When rightly understood, who would not want this?

Notice that vs. 21 offers the Corinthians two different aspects of "the judgment seat of Christ" – "corrective measures," or "**love** (solidarity), **and in a spirit of gentle friendliness and tender kindness.**" As a member of Christ's body, Paul functioned AS Christ for those who were his "children." The "rod" is a shepherd's staff, used to herd the sheep and protect the entire flock from those who would bring in the wood, hay and stubble. When folks are still spiritual "children" (3:1-2, above), they still need the direct involvement of fathers. Paul may be alluding, here, to Prov. 10:13b,

> "A rod [is] for the back of a person that is void of (or: who lacks) understanding."

Or, perhaps, to Prov. 13:24,

> "He who spares his rod hates his son; but he who loves him disciplines him diligently."

Or, Prov. 29:15a, "The rod and reproof give wisdom..."

We read in Rev. 2:27 where the resurrected Jesus spoke of this function as seen in Paul,

> "**he will continue shepherding** (i.e., feeding, tending and guarding) **them with a staff made of iron, as he is being continuously broken [like] pottery vessels,** [Ps. 2:8-9] **as I also have received from My Father**."

What also comes to mind is "the rod of God" (Ex. 4:20) which was a rod of deliverance and freedom, seen again as the rod of the priesthood (Heb. 9:4). We should also recall what Paul said to those in Galatia:

> "**Now the works** (actions; deeds) **of the flesh [are] seen and made apparent in clear light, which are.... those habitually practicing** (or: performing) **such [religious, or personal,] things will not be inheriting** (receiving and enjoying a distributed allotment of) **God's reign** (kingdom; sovereign influence and activities)" (Gal. 5:19, 21b).

Also, his admonition in 1 Thes. 2:12 is worth remembering:

> "**be continuously walking about worthily of the God** (= living your lives in a manner equal in value with regard to the God) **[Who is] continuously calling** (or: repeatedly inviting) **you people into His own royal activity** (or: reign; sovereign influence; kingdom) **and glory** (or: reputation; manifestation which calls forth praise; or: opinion and imagination; or: = manifest presence)."

Chapter 5

1. **It is actually** (or: generally; everywhere) **being repeatedly heard [that there is] prostitution among you folks – and such a sort of prostitution which is not even being mentioned** (or: named) **among the ethnic multitudes** (nations; non-Jewish groups)**: so as someone continues to hold** (or: a certain person is repeatedly having) **[his] father's woman** (or: wife; or, thus: [his] stepmother)! [cf Lev. 18:8ff]

Paul now moves to specifics of misconducts, and addresses them as a father would to his son. The present tense of the infinitive, "to hold; to have," informs us that this was an ongoing or repetitive situation. From Paul's description of the social aspects, this was apparently considered to be an outrageous affair, even among other cultures in that day. The issue has often been considered to be incest (and thus Nyland renders the term), but "**prostitution**" is the basic meaning of the word, as seen in the LXX usage, and elsewhere. We address this in greater detail under vs. 9, below. In beginning our investigation of this chapter, we should keep Israel's history in mind, for as we will see, in vss. 6-8, below, Paul references the Jewish practice of cleansing their houses in preparation for Passover, then returns to the topic of prostitution and a catalogue of vices, in vs. 9. Prostitution (especially spiritual: being unfaithful to Yahweh) was a recurring issue with Israel. *Cf* Isa. 1:21 and the book of Hosea. But considering the individual matter at hand, *cf* 7:2, below, and Jn. 4:18. Also, *cf* Gen. 35:22.

We suggest that this entire chapter be read as speaking to the situation given here, in vss. 1-2. It should be noted here that the complaint that Paul lodges is directed to the entire community. As we will see, below, the main concern was that God's Temple (the Corinthian community of believers) should be clean. It was a corporate matter.

2. **And now you folks, yourselves, have been puffed up and remain inflated with pride! And still you do not rather mourn and grieve** (or: lament and express sorrow), **so that the man performing this act would** (or: that the man practicing this deed should) **at once be caused to depart** (or: be picked up, removed or taken away) **from out of your midst.**

Notice that Paul is seeming to say that if they had "**mourned and grieved** (etc.)" that "**the man performing this act would** (or: that the man practicing this deed should) **at once be caused to depart** (or: be picked up, removed or taken away) **from out of your midst**." Does this mean that God would have intervened – is this the "divine passive" potentially at work in Paul's words? But why would Paul think that he should depart from being a part of the community? Let us recall Peter's words to Simon, in Acts 8:

> "**There is neither a part nor a lot for you within this Word** (or: this *Logos*; this Idea and Reason; this expressed verbal communication; or: this message; or: this matter). **You see, your heart is not straight and level with a position answering to God** (or: in front of God, in His presence). **So change your mind and your way of thinking – away from this worthlessness** (or: ugliness; baseness; badness of quality; malice) **of yours – and then at once urgently ask of the Lord** [= Christ or Yahweh] **if consequently** (or: since in that case) **the thought and purpose of your heart will be caused to flow away** (or: will be divorced from [you]; will be forgiven and sent away)" (vss. 21-22).

The main concern for both Peter and Paul was the witness of Christ (the Word of the cross) to the world that environed the called-out groups. Both Peter (in this Acts situation) and Paul (there in Corinth) held out a good end for these individuals.

The misconducts involved at least two individuals (only one seems to be the focus of this instance – the man, who seems to be seen as the one responsible for the issue; it is possible that the woman was not a member of the covenant community, and thus her part was not being considered). But Paul's thrust is to the lack of response by the called-out folks, together with the fact that amidst this situation the community remains "**inflated with pride**." He expects an opposite reaction to this situation than what has been reported to him, and says with apparent amazement: "**And still you do not rather mourn and grieve** (or: lament and express sorrow)." Instead, they have been, and continue "puffed up." The situation was apparently not something that concerned them. Paul was expecting immediate action by the group, and note how he put it: "**that the man performing this act would at once be caused to depart** (or: be picked up, removed or taken away) **from out of your midst**." Conzelmann rightly observes (ibid p 94) that this verse can also be rendered as a question – thus, more emphatically expressing his amazement about the situation.

For some folks, today, this suggestion and what Paul instructed them to do, in vs. 5 below, may sound harsh and exclusionary. In our current pluralistic society of acceptance of different lifestyles, Paul would be considered as being "politically incorrect." But even today, many people of the Christian religion apply Paul's words, here, in a literal manner for their particular group. Yet others look at these verses as examples of cultural norms of Paul's time and place, and decide that they no longer of necessity apply to our day and changing world.

This latter view is a classic example of what might be called "liberal interpretation" versus "conservative interpretation." Behind this lies our view of "the authority of Scripture" from one time and culture upon the lives of later times and cultures. Groups are divided about whether or not the behavior codes from Moses apply to the followers of Christ. We certainly do not follow Moses' instructions in Lev. 20:9, "anyone who curses his father or his mother shall surely be put to death." Also, in many cases an issue involves variant views about "the authority of the church/denomination." Today, more and more laws, and then potential lawsuits, must be considered before making decisions about other peoples' lives. Furthermore, many people, though still being followers of Christ, have left the formal, corporate life of institutional "churches."

Before we judge Paul on this matter, let us consider the culture of his day, his relationship to this specific group of people, and how his theology classified them in relation to Jesus Christ. This entire chapter is devoted to this same general subject, and he ends it (vs. 13, below) by quoting from Deut. 13 as being the guide for their corporate action concerning this individual.

Paul portrays himself as their father, and thus as having a right to discipline their group conduct. His main concern is the called-out community. The issue that he is addressing was considered wrong in his own culture, and apparently (from vs. 1, above) was considered wrong by society at large (the "ethnic multitudes; nations; non-Jews") – at least in the Roman Empire. Next, considering that the called-out, covenant communities were to be "the Light of the world" – "a city set on a hill" (Mat. 5:14), these folks had been called to live a pure life (by the standards given to them by Paul when they first converted). They were a people that had been "set-apart" to be different from their surrounding societies. They were to represent, and to be, Christ in their world. Call to mind what Paul said in Rom. 14:1-16, about eating meat that had been slaughtered at a pagan temple. He ended that section by admonishing the group in Rome,

> 15. **For instance, if because of solid food** (or: the effect of something eaten) **your brother is continually made sad** (made sorry, distressed or grieved), **you are no longer continuing to walk about** (= living your life) **in accord with** (or: down from and on the level of) **Love** (or: you are not yet habitually walking [your path] in participation with transcendent unity of unambiguous, uniting acceptance toward others). **Do not, by your food** (or: for your solid food), **progressively destroy away** (lose by ruining; bring to loss) **that person over whom Christ died.**
> 16. **Do not cause your good thing** (or: the excellence and virtue which pertain to you) **to be slandered** (defamed; insulted; blasphemed; vilified; have its light hindered).

From those early days of Jesus and Paul, things have changed – over the centuries. The Light has not gone out, but many perceptions of what it means to be a follower of Jesus have changed. And these differences of perceptions/interpretations have resulted in Christ's body becoming completely fragmented.

3. **For I myself, indeed, continuing being absent – in the body – yet continuously being present alongside – in** (or: by; with) **the spirit** (or: Breath-effect; or: attitude) **– have, as being present, already sifted, evaluated and decided about the man thus working down to this effect:**

Notice Paul's actual union with the community in Corinth. It was a spiritual union, and the physical distance between them had no effect on his "**continuously being present alongside**" with them. In his spirit, he has discerned the situation, and by the Spirit had "**sifted, evaluated and decided**." Verse three gives us another example of "the judgment seat of Christ." Paul obviously made this evaluation of the situation through the grace-effect of spiritually discerning (12:8-10, below), from what had been reported to him (vs. 1, above).

4. **[Upon] your being gathered together within** (or: centered in) **the Name of our Lord, Jesus Christ, then together with my spirit** (or: attitude) **– in, by and with the power and ability of our Lord Jesus –** 5. **[you are] to commit** (surrender; hand-over) **such a man, with the adversarial [spirit]** (or: in the adversary; by the opponent; or: to *satan*), **into a loss of the flesh** (or: an undoing and destruction of this [distorted human nature]; a loss of [his "dominated existence" – Walter Wink]) **– to the end that the spirit may be saved** (rescued; delivered; restored to health, wholeness): **within the midst of and in union with the Day of** (or: in this day from, or, which is) **the Lord** [= Christ or Yahweh; other MSS add: Jesus; others read: our Lord, Jesus Christ]. [*cf* 3:15, above; 1 Tim. 1:20; Job 2:6]

Now he directs them – as a group – to "**gather together within** (or: centered in) **the Name of our Lord, Jesus Christ, and together with [his] spirit**." Notice Paul's spiritual solidarity with them. He wanted them to have the same "attitude" toward this brother as he had: the man's ultimate restoration.

But there is more: they were to do this "**in, by and with the power and ability of our Lord Jesus**." This is an astounding statement. Many today, and in the past (as reported to us), have claimed to have "the power and ability of Jesus Christ," but seemingly more often than not, the results proved that they did not embody this power – they only claimed it by organizational positions that they held. Usually it was not the authority of a cruciform life, but the brute power of the domination system (beast) upon which they had been stationed by man, not God. But Paul sets two criteria: they must existentially be "**together within** (or: centered in) **the Name of our Lord, Jesus Christ**," and also, "**together with my spirit** (or: attitude)." They could not follow his instructions if they were not in union with the Lord, and if they did not have the same spirit and attitude that Paul embodied: ultimate restoration of the offending party – a spirit of grace and mercy.

Nonetheless, he instructs them to convene a "judgment seat" in Christ. Now the common rendering of the first clause of vs. 5 instructs the Corinthian assembly to "hand this man over to *satan*." The term *satan* is merely a transliteration of the Greek word, which is the LXX rendering of the Hebrew word that means "adversary; opponent." So the Greek term also means "adversary; opponent." But here, the term is in the dative case, without an expressed preposition. My first offering is reading the dative function as "with," interpreting the phrase as meaning "**the man WITH the adversarial** [spirit]." This phrase is immediately followed by a second prepositional phrase, "**into a loss of the flesh**," which tells us the preliminary purpose of "the handing-over, or, the committing." The word "**loss**" can be rendered as "an undoing" (the core meaning of the term), and thus, "a destruction." Observe the parenthetical expansion of the significance of the word "flesh." In Paul this does not refer to the physical body, but to "the distorted human nature" or, as Walter Wink defines it, his "dominated existence." *Cf* Wink's trilogy, *Naming the Powers; Unmasking the Powers; Engaging the Powers*.

The ultimate purpose for this "committing; surrendering; handing-over" is expressed in the subordinate clause: "**to the end that the spirit may be saved** (rescued; delivered; restored to health, wholeness)." This is the purpose of all "judgment."

Also on offer is the rendering, "surrender such a man, in the adversary, into a loss..." This interpretation of the dative case says that this man was "in the adversary," rather than abiding in the Vine. He was not producing the fruit of the Vine, so this would be like "casting him into the Fire" (Jn. 15:6b; Heb. 6:7, 8). It is an example of 3:13, 15, above. Next is the option, "hand [him] over by the opponent." This calls to mind "the Sabeans; lightning (Fire of God); the Chaldeans; the storm wind; bodily sores" in Job 1 and 2. All of those things were to loose Job from aspects of his disconnected flesh nature with which he wrestled until God showed up in ch. 38:1. There Yahweh answered Job from out of the very "storm wind" that had been Job's "adversary" in Job. 1:19.

The final rendering on offer in our present verse is the traditional rendering of the dative, "to," with the common transliteration of the Greek term *satan*. This would also be an allusion to God doing the same act, in Job 1 and 2. However, although all these functions fit the context, reading the first clause as "the man with the adversarial [spirit; attitude; behavior]" seems best to us. The loss of his flesh will be the work of God, and will work toward his deliverance, so reading that phrase as "describing" the man makes the most sense to us.

The final, modifying phrases, "**within the midst of and in union with the Day of** (or: in this day from, or, which is) **the Lord**" refers to the Day (Christ) in which they were presently living. Paul's desire was for this man to immediately be made whole – right there as he lived the rest of his life. He had simply failed, morally, as we all have in one way or another. He was a lost sheep, and needed a time of "lost-ness," as did the prodigal son. A similar situation is presented in 1 Tim. 1:20. The adversary (*satan*) is always used to enhance the condition of the person to whom it is directed against.

Paul, in the Spirit, is coming to them with the first option of 4:21, above: with a rod of correction. Conzelmann informs us: "According to Jewish law, the man who lies with his father's wife is to be stoned" (ibid p 96 n 28). Paul's spirit and action are grace! Dan Kaplan reminded us of the beautiful passage in 1 Pet. 4:

> 8. **Before all people** (or: = More than anything), **continue being folks constantly holding the outstretching and extending Love** (unambiguous, uniting acceptance) **unto yourselves** (i.e., into each other) – **"because Love** (the urge toward union; self-giving) **is constantly covering*** (habitually throwing a veil over; progressively concealing) **a multitude of failures** (mistakes; errors; misses of the target; sins)." [Prov. 10:12]
> 9. **[Continue being] those [who are] stranger-loving unto one another** (= friendly, kind and hospitable to strangers, foreigners and aliens [inviting them] into the midst of each other's [homes and/or societies]), **without expressing dissatisfaction** (complaining; grumbling; murmuring),
> 10. **each one, according as he receives an effect of grace** (or: received a result of favor), **continuously giving supporting service and dispensing it unto yourselves** (i.e., into each other), **as beautiful** (fine; ideal) **house managers** (administrators) **of God's varied grace** (or: of [the] diverse favor which is God; [as] of a many-colored [tapestry] of grace whose source and character are from God).

This attitude and this thinking echo what we have seen in the heart of Paul, and of course is the heart of Christ.

6. **The effect of your boast is not beautiful, fine, ideal or good form. Have you not seen so as to know that a little leaven** (or: yeast) **progressively leavens** (permeates) **[the] whole lump of dough** (the result of that which has been uniformly mixed and kneaded together)?
7. **At once completely clean out the old leaven, so that you folks would progressively be a fresh, new lump of dough with uniform mix-effect, just as you are free from ferment**
> (or: in that you have continued being an aggregation which has been freshly mixed and kneaded together – correspondingly as you are continuing being unleavened ones). **For also Christ, our Passover** [= Passover lamb], **was slaughtered** (or: sacrificed; slain for food).
8. **Consequently, we can** (or: should) **be continuously keeping and celebrating the Feast** (7-day Festival of Unleavened Bread) – **not in union with old leaven** (or: yeast in old dough, from the previous batch), **neither in union with or in the midst of a leaven of bad quality** (worthlessness; ugliness; what ought not to be; malice) **and painful misery** (hard labor; evil disposition; mischief; wickedness) – **but in contrast, in union with and in the midst of unleavened cakes** (matzah) **of genuineness** (or: which are integrity and sincerity; from that which has been tested by sunlight and found to be pure and unadulterated) **as well as truth and unhidden reality.** [cf Deut. 16:3; Lu. 12:1; Rev. 5]

The "boast" to which he refers, in vs. 6, is their "**remaining inflated with pride**," in vs. 2 above, as well as to his statements in 4:6, 7 and 18. The effect of this was "**not beautiful, fine, ideal or good form**." Now he did not say here that the failure of the man, above, was bad form (although it obviously was), but he is now addressing the second misconduct: that of the community in boasting in something other than Christ. It was their pride, and their boast, that was "progressively leavening the whole lump" – i.e., the whole community. The "**effect of their boast**" was permeating the whole group (the **lump of dough** – recall that they are "one loaf of bread" – 10:17, below). So Paul was instructing them to "**clean out the old leaven**" of boasting in things that are not "beautiful, fine or ideal" – i.e., that are not Christ. In Mat. 16:6, Jesus used the figure of leaven in instructing His disciples:

> "**be constantly seeing, and be then attentive in holding [yourselves] away from the leaven** (yeast) **which comes from, characterizes, [and puffs up or permeates] the Pharisees and Sadducees**."

In vs. 12 Matthew explains the He was referring to "**the teaching which belongs to, comes from and characterizes the Pharisees and Sadducees**." As Paul reminds the Corinthians, even "**a little leaven progressively leavens** (permeates) **[the] whole lump of dough**." So even though the issue that he is addressing in this chapter might seem like something of no great consequence (a "little" leaven), its effects would spread throughout the entire community. So when he says, "**At once completely clean out the old leaven**," he is speaking of the man's behavior and the community's inflation with pride that are both examples of the old Adamic life that would end up "fermenting them." They needed to be refreshed so that they would be a new lump (a body of believers that were free from that which would inflate their egos).

Next he reminds them that "**Christ, our Passover** [= Passover lamb], **was slaughtered**." This was a past event, and so now,

> "**the blood of, from, and which is Jesus, His Son, keeps continually and repeatedly cleansing us** (or: is progressively rendering us pure) **from every sin** (or: from all error, failure, deviation, mistake, and from every shot that is off target [when it occurs])" (1 Jn. 1:7b).

Both Paul and John are keeping the Christ Event of the cross, and of Jesus' death, centered in Israel's story. The Passover reference speaks of the deliverance of Israel from their slavery in Egypt. Paul's use of the term "slaughtered" alluded to the evening meal that they were to eat (thus Jesus' reference to eating His flesh, in Jn. 6:53, and in Mat. 26:26, *et al*) in order to have strength for the next day's journey (Ex. 12:9-11, 29-41). But in that event, the blood was an identification marker for the Israelites; there was no mention of sin. Yet Christ served as the fulfillment of another Feast, the Day of Atonement, to which John's letter, above, would be referring. Christ's blood served multiple functions. Jesus also spoke of our need for LIFE:

> "**unless you folks should at some point eat the flesh of the Son of the Human** (the Son of man; = the eschatological messianic figure), **and then would drink His blood** (or: since you would not eat the flesh which is the Human Being, and further, drink His blood), **you are continuing not holding** (or: habitually having or presently possessing) **LIFE within yourselves**" (Jn. 6:53).

This is the only place that Paul brings up Christ as being "our Passover." The only other NT letter that uses this term is Heb. 11:28, a reference to Moses. That Paul almost casually mentions the phrase tells us that they had been instructed about it. But we should observe that it is not stated here that he was using it in reference to the deliverance or salvation of the Corinthians. The point of the allusion is given in vs. 7, "**At once completely clean out the old leaven**," where in vs. 13, below, he explains this by saying, "**Carry forth** (Expel; Remove) **the degenerate person!**" He was using the historical, Jewish preparation for the Passover Feast as a foundation for his argument that they needed to "clean up their act," to use a modern phrase. Also, as Heb. 9:23-26 instruct us, even the Day of Atonement had been fulfilled in the work of Christ, and thus Heb. 9:28 informs us of the ongoing situation for His followers:

> "**so also, the Christ – being once borne** (or: carried) **close into the many** (or: being offered once unto and for the many) **to carry failures** (errors; sins; mistakes; deviations; misses of the target) **back up again – will continue being made visible** (or: will be progressively seen) **forth from out of the midst of the second [place** (*cf* 9:3, 7 & 10:9; {comment: = the holy of holies})**] – apart from failure** (apart from sin; apart from a sin offering; apart from error in attempting to hit the target) **– in those** (or: by those; to those; for those) **habitually receiving** (or: progressively taking) **from out of the midst of Him, [progressing] into a deliverance** (or: [leading] into a rescue; with a view to health and wholeness; into the midst of salvation)."

The works of both deliverance (Passover) and cleansing (Atonement) had been completed in the Christ, as a combined historical Event. And thus, "**Consequently, we can** (or: should) **be continuously keeping and celebrating the Feast**... **in union with and in the midst of unleavened cakes of genuineness**." Note: he did not say "once a year keep the Feast." He was using this part of Israel's history to make his point. They were the "heavenly temple" into which Jesus had entered, with His blood (Life) and the new mercy seat (in their hearts) had been "sprinkled" (Heb. 10:19-22), within the spiritual "holy of holies," which they now were (6:19, below). The old covenant was a thing of the past for the Corinthian community (2 Cor. 5:17). Although the Jews were still celebrating the Feasts of the old covenant (in those pre-AD 70 days), those outward rituals no longer applied to the Body of Christ. They were no longer slaves in the domination System (or either Egypt, in Israel's past, or Rome, in Israel's present) but had entered into "the promised Land" of the Spirit, the kingdom of the Atmospheres (heavens). In Gal. 5:1 Paul affirmed that the called-out had been brought into freedom. They could be "**habitually receiving** (or: progressively taking) **from out of the midst of Him**" (Heb. 9:28), the Christ that was continuously dwelling both within and among them.

So it is in the context of the Day of Preparation, and then the seven days of unleavened bread that followed the Feast of Passover, to which he is alluding. And the context is about **cleansing** their community (vs. 7a) so that they would not have the "old leaven" (vs. 8) in their midst. They were to get rid of "**leaven of bad quality** (worthlessness; ugliness; what ought not to be; malice) **and painful misery** (hard labor; evil disposition; mischief; wickedness)" (vs. 8). Everything that he had just brought up, as a critique of them, was something that had bad quality, was worthless, was ugly, and it was that which ought not to be in a new covenant community. And somehow their situation had puffed them up. Their eyes must have become blind, as did the eyes of the Pharisees (Mat. 23:26), and the community in Laodicea (Rev. 3:18b).

Paul instructed them that they could metaphorically "**be continuously keeping and celebrating the Feast**," not with "old leaven" that inflated them with pride (or, for the Jews of the community, not with the old covenant ceremonies or ritual cultus), but rather – and IN CONTRAST – "**in union with and in the midst of unleavened cakes** (matzah) **of genuineness** (or: which are integrity and sincerity; from that which has been tested by sunlight and found to be pure and unadulterated)." So he is figuratively talking about living genuine lives which are comprised of integrity and sincerity. Lives that have been tested by Sunlight, and found to be pure and unadulterated with pride or the wisdom of the domination System.

Added to the genuineness is "**truth and unhidden reality**." All of this is about the life that they were living as a called-out community of Christ. I conflated the meaning of one Greek word that equally means "truth, reality and that which is open to view – i.e., unhidden." The Secret (Christ) has been unveiled and is no longer hidden in a sacrificial system or a physical temple.

Paul now presents a catalogue of vices that are examples of "**leaven of bad quality**"... and thus continues his topic concerning the need for the community to be pure – free from adulterations which do not reflect the image of God. Jesus listed some of these in Mk. 7:21-23,

> "**for you see, from inside of the person – from out of the midst of the heart – the worthless reasonings** (base conversations; dialogues of poor quality; evil thoughts and schemes; bad ideas and designs) **constantly issue forth: [for example], prostitutions; thefts; murders;**

adulteries; situations of wanting more than one's share (thoughts of greed; feelings of coveting), **bad conditions which bring pain, gushes of misery, anguish or hard labor** (or: acts of wickedness; malicious deeds; evil doings); **bait to catch someone with deceit, treachery, guile or fraud; loose conduct** (indecency); **an evil eye** (= a focus toward malice or mischief); **villainous and light-hindering slander, harmful and abusive speech, or blasphemy** (a hindering of light); **pride, arrogance and haughtiness; acting without thinking** (or: imprudence; unreasonableness; inconsiderateness; lack of purpose; folly). **All these bad situations and misery-causing things are habitually issuing forth from within, and repeatedly contaminate the person** (continuously make the human common, polluted and ritually unclean)." *Cf* Mt. 15:29; Rom. 1:29-31; 13:13; 2 Cor. 12:20f; Gal. 5:19-21; Eph. 5:3-5; *et al*

9. **I wrote to you folks, in the letter: not to keep on mixing yourselves together again with men who make a practice of whoring, or who are male prostitutes** (or: not to be repeatedly intermingled again with male paramours or boys who sell themselves) –

10. **and [I am] not wholly or altogether [referring] to this world's** (or: secular society's) **prostitutes** (or: the male prostitutes of this cultural, religious and political system [note: the concept of sexual misconduct also has a figurative aspect in Scripture, denoting unfaithfulness to God]); **or to those who are greedy and want to have more than, and to take advantage of, others and/or [are] folks who snatch things away, as extortionists; or [who are] idolaters** (or: hirelings of the idols). **Otherwise, in that case, you folks continue under obligation to consequently exit the System** (go forth from out of the midst of the world of religion, culture and society) –

In vss. 9 and 10, on offer are a number of renderings from the lexicons for the word *pornos*: **whoring, male prostitute; fornicator or male paramour**; along with the parenthetical expansions. There are differing opinions among scholars as to the meaning of this term (here in the plural). Because of this, the common, modern translations have opted for rendering it "immoral" or "sexually immoral." The problem that I see with these modern choices is that they are too general, and today's readers will interpret these general terms in a variety of ways. What constitutes immoral (NASB rendering) for one person may well be different for another. The more specific, "sexual immorality," can also have different interpretations, depending on our cultural conditioning. Nyland, *The Source NT*, does not translate the word, but rather brings it transliterated into her text, stating that there is no equivalent English term. Her research directs us to acts condemned in the Law of Moses. Paul instructions may be an allusion to Deut. 23:17,

> "There will not continue being a prostitute from among the daughters of Israel; there will not continue being one that is habitually practicing prostitution from among the sons of Israel" (LXX, JM).

He has moved to general situations regarding the group's ongoing way of life, but it flows from his metaphor of "**leaven of bad quality**," in vs. 8, and is really a continuation of the topic begun in vs. 1. He cites immoral behavior in vss. 9-10a, then gives other examples of "bad form": **those who are greedy and want to have more than, and to take advantage of, others**; and/or, **folks who snatch things away, as extortionists**, or, **idolaters** (or: hirelings of the idols). These were all examples of typical vices, as a teaching device – he was not insinuating that the community in Corinth had these conditions.

In 10a he gives a qualifier: **[I am] not wholly or altogether [referring] to this world's** (or: secular society's) **fornicators**. Then the last statement explains what he means by this: "**Otherwise, in that case, you folks continue under obligation to consequently exit the System** (go forth from out of the midst of the world of religion, culture and society)." And he is not suggesting that they should do such a thing. After all, they are to be the Light in Corinth. His statement in Rom. 7:6 sheds further light on what he means, here:

> "**But now** (at the present time), **we** [= Israel] **are** (or: were instantly) **rendered inactive** (brought down to living without labor, released from employment, made unproductive; discharged) **away from the Law** (= the Torah; [some MSS add: of Death]), **dying within that in which we were**

constantly being held down (held in possession and detained), **so that it is [for] us to be habitually performing as slaves within newness of spirit** (a newness pertaining to spirit and has its source in the Breath-effect; freshness and new quality of attitude) **and not in oldness** (obsoleteness; outdatedness) **of Letter** (or: not in outwornness of written Scripture)."

11. **yet at this time** (or: so now) **I write for you folks not to continue mixing yourselves back together with anyone being regularly recognized as** (usually designated; habitually named or called) **a "brother," if he should continue being a prostitute, or a covetous and greedy person, or an idolater, or a verbally abusive one, or a drunkard, or a snatching one** (or: an extortioner) **– to not even be habitually eating with such a person.**

Notice the continuous or habitual action that Paul is speaking about, since he chose the present tense for the words "continue mixing," and "continue being," and "habitually eating." If the community regularly did these things they would not present themselves to Corinth as being different from the norm (or: set-apart). The image that they would bear would be the same as the image of their surrounding society. But Paul is not telling them to be as the Pharisees or even the Jews (who were not to have intimate dealings with non-Jews; *cf* Peter's concern about this in Acts 10).

Now is this different from the pattern that Jesus demonstrated by eating with the outcasts of the Jewish society (sinners, tax collectors, prostitutes, etc.)? It would appear to be. Is Paul stressing purity laws for those at Corinth? To the first question, we would say, "Yes." To the second question, we would say, "No." We suspect that the reason is that Paul is writing to those who are immature in Christ, and thus, could be led astray, or would be too weak to maintain the kind of witness of the Truth, the Way and the Life that Jesus was able to maintain. Recall "the weak" in Rom. 14, cited above. Furthermore, Roman society already considered the Christians as atheists (they denied the pagan gods). Secondly, history records that Christians were accused of immorality, and other false charges, by their Roman opponents. Walking circumspectly would be the wisdom of God for these situations.

The sequence of the terms, "**a covetous and greedy person, or an idolater**," may be an echo of the 2nd century BC *Testaments of the Twelve Patriarchs, Judah* 19:1,
> "My children, love of money leads to idolatry, because once they are led astray by money, they designate as gods those who are not gods" (trans. by H.C. Kee in *The Old Testament Pseudepigrapha*, Vol 1, Hendrickson Pub. 2013 p 800).

Similar prohibitions in Judean ethics carried on into the 1st century AD:
> "**every prostitute** (or: male prostitute; paramour), **or unclean** (impure [in character]; morally indecent) **person, or greedy one** (person who is covetous: insatiably desiring advantage or more than one's due), **[i.e.,] the person who exists as** (or: that is) **an idolater, is not now holding enjoyment of an inheritance** (does not currently continue having use of an allotment) **within the Christ's and God's reign or sphere of sovereign activity**" (Eph. 5:5). *Cf* 6:9, below; Gal. 5:20

Then Paul puts it this way in Col. 3:5-6,
> "**Make dead, therefore, these members** (body parts; = aspects of your life) **upon the earth: prostitution, uncleanness, [unbridled] passion, worthless over-desire** (rushing upon bad things; obsessive, evil cravings), **and the desire to have more and gain advantage over another** (or: selfish, greedy, grasping thoughts and behavior) **– which is idolatry** (the worship of forms, shapes, images or figures; or: service to pagan concepts) **– because of which things God's inherent fervor** (natural impulse and propensity; internal swelling and teeming passion of desire; or: anger; wrath) **is repeatedly** (or: continuously; progressively) **coming.**"

12. **For what [right is it] for me to be making decisions about or judging those [who are] "outside"? Are you yourselves not repeatedly sifting and critiquing** (or: separating and judging) **those "inside"? Now those "outside" God habitually sifts and makes decisions about** (is constantly judging).

13. **"Lift up out and carry forth** (Expel; Remove) **the degenerate person** (the misery-gushed, worthless, base or evil one who brings pain) **out of the midst of yourselves."** [Deut. 13:5; 17:7; etc.]

Verse 12a is missing a finite verb, so the text is ambiguous. The *Concordant Literal NT* reads, "For what [is it] to me to be judging..." Since the last clause of this verse says that it is God who is judging those "outside" the community, in the first clause I have added the word [right] with the ellipsis [is it]. He is saying that it is NOT right for him to be judging all the folks he has just, above, told the community not to continuously hang around. That is God's business. He "**habitually sifts and makes decisions about** (is constantly judging) **those 'outside'**" the community. This calls to mind Jn. 3:36b,

"**the person now continuing being unpersuaded by the Son** (or: presently being constantly incompliant, disobedient or disbelieving to the Son; being repeatedly stubborn toward the Son) **will not be catching sight of** (seeing; observing; perceiving) **[this] life. To the contrary** (or: Yet, nevertheless), **God's personal emotion and inherent fervor**

(or: the teeming passion and **swelling desire, which is God**; the mental bent, natural impulse, propensity and disposition **from God**; or: the ire, anger, wrath or indignation **having the quality and character of God**)

presently continues remaining (keeps on resting, dwelling and abiding) **upon him**."

But then he challenges them: are they not repeatedly evaluating and making decisions concerning those in their own covenant community? This rhetorical question would expect a "Yes," from his listeners.

We want to point out the present tense (continuous or habitual action) that Paul uses of God's judging. Yes, God is CONTINUOUSLY judging those outside the called-out communities. He is NOT waiting for some imaginary "end of time" to do this. God is constantly involved in world affairs and among the peoples of the world. But He has not informed us, so as to answer our little questions, such as: "Why don't You do this? Why do You allow that? Etc." We are called to live a life of trust in God, and put our faith in His good Character. God never gave Job an answer to Job's "Why?"

For the practical situation with which this chapter has been dealing, Paul quotes the Torah. You see, His grace is sufficient to deal with this person who would now become one that was "outside." Jesus spoke of doing this to the Jewish leadership, who would within His generation be fired from their jobs of representing God's reign, and would be cast into outer darkness – outside the ongoing sovereign activities of Christ's movement of bringing Light into the world. This community in Corinth represented God's kingdom, His sovereign activities and influences in the world. So just as the Jewish leadership of the first century had the kingdom taken from them for not properly representing God to the world, this individual was to lose his place within the called-out of Corinth: he was "old leaven" to them. But like the unbelieving Jews, he too could later be "grafted back in again" (Rom. 11:23).

By quoting Deut. 13, Paul is understanding that the man referenced in vs. 1, above, is a "degenerate person." As the parenthetical expansion offers, the semantic range of the word could indicate that this situation was bringing someone pain, and thus the entire community was being affected (*cf* 12:26, below). The next chapter opens in dealing with another situation, but Paul is still addressing the community's need to take action concerning disruptive things that arise. In 6:12a, he states that,

"**To me, all things are presently out-of-Being** (Everything continues from existence for me; or: All is authorized, allowed, permitted by and in me). **But yet not everything proceeds to bear together for advantage, profit or help**."

The "advantage, profit and help" is the same as "**building the house**" in 3:10, above. The ongoing behavior of the man in vs. 1, above, was adding wood, hay and stubble to the Corinthian temple of God. Paul's assessment, and the directives given in vs. 5, above, and here in vs. 13, was "**fire issuing** (or: proceeding) **out of [his] mouth**" (Rev. 11:5) to burn up this worthless behavior. His words are the "rod" of which he spoke, in 4:21, above.

If we consider the "garden" descriptions of the New Jerusalem (Rev. 22:1-5) and perceive that this is an allusion to the Garden of Eden (Gen. 2:8-16) we may be able to see the correlation between the New Jerusalem (the City was now God's temple/dwelling place) and the community in Corinth, which Paul describes as "the temple of God." This being the case, and bringing in the concept of God's reign and "kingdom" (*cf* 6:9-10, below), just as Adam and Eve were ejected from the original Garden, we can better understand why Paul followed suit in his instructions about the man who partook of the "tree" of intimate knowledge of "evil" in this chapter.

Chapter 6

1. **Does anyone of you folks [who] are continuing holding a result of some deed done** (or: the effect of a practice; or: = a court case) **toward someone else**

> (or: are now having a business transaction focused toward another; continue in having a dispute or law-suit proceeding toward the different person) **now dare or boldly presume to continue to be judged upon the basis** (or: = in the place or court) **of unjust folks** (people who are unfair and are not in the way pointed out; = those outside the called-out community), **and not upon the [basis; place; court] of the set-apart folks** (the saints; the holy ones)**?**

This calls to mind Jacob's question, in Jas. 2:6b,

> "**Are not the rich people continuously exploiting you people, repeatedly exercising [their] power and abilities against you? Are they not continually dragging you into courts of law for judicial hearings?**"

Now keep in mind that vs. 1, above, is an immediate continuation of what Paul has been saying in ch. 5, so we should conclude that the judgment that he has just made was "**upon the [basis; place; court] of the set-apart folks**" – i.e., the "judgment seat of Christ." He expects the community to do the same thing. They should NOT turn to the courts of "unjust folks," i.e., folks that do not belong to the called-out community. In 5:13, above, he termed these folks "**those 'outside.'**" In vs. 6b, below, he refers to them as "**unbelievers.**" Whether it was the 12 or the 70, with Jesus, or the 120 in the Upper Room (Acts 2), or the Jerusalem called-out community, the body of Christ was expected to be a kind of sub-culture in its corporate manifestations within every geographical location. They were to remain "**set-apart**" from the dominant System that surrounded them. Jesus taught His disciples,

> "**If you had been and yet had your being from out of the System** (or: controlling world of culture, religion and politics) **as a source, the System** (world with its control by religion and politics) **would have been being friendly toward and fond of its own production and possession. Yet now, because you do not exist from out of the System** (world) **as a source – but to the contrary I have selected** (or: chosen) **and picked you out from the midst of the System** (from the world's culture, religion and politics)" (Jn. 15:19).

He repeated this idea in His prayer in Jn. 17:16-17a,

> "**They do not exist** (are not being) **from out of the System** (world of society, religion or politics) **as a source or origin, just as I, Myself, am not from the System** (world) **as a source or origin. Set them apart** (or: Make them different from the norm) **within the midst of the Truth** (or: in union with, and centered in, reality)."

Paul described the distinction between the System and the called-out in 1 Thes. 5:5,

> "**for you see, you all are** (or: exist being) **sons of** (from; associated with and having the qualities of; or: which are) **Light and sons of** (from; associated with and having qualities of; or: which are [the]) **Day! We are** (exist) **not of night, nor of darkness** (or: we do not belong to or have the characteristics of night, nor to or of dim obscurity from shadows and gloom)."

2. **Or have you not seen so as to know that the set-apart folks** (the saints; the holy, sacred people; the different-from-the-profane folks) **will habitually sift, separate, evaluate and decide about the**

organized System (the world of culture, religion and government; or: secular society; or: = the Empire)**?
So since** (or: if) **centered in, among and in relation to, you folks the domination System is being
habitually** (progressively; repeatedly) **evaluated and decided about** (or judged)**, are you people
unworthy or unfit in regard to deciding about very trivial controversies**
> (or: not of equal value to the smallest standards by which to sift and evaluate; or: of [holding the]
> least tribunals or places for court)**?**

This situation to which he refers may be reflected in what we read in Eph. 2:6, where the called-out are
seated with Christ in the atmospheres (realm of God's reign). It may also be an allusion to what Jesus
said in Mat. 19:28 (*cf* Lu. 22:30),
> "**I am now laying it out and saying to you men – in** (in union with) **the Rebirth** (Birth-back-
> again) **when the Son of the Man** (or: = the eschatological messianic figure; or: the Human
> Being) **would** (or: should; may) **sit upon the throne of His glory** (or: of his reputation and
> manifestation which calls forth praise; which is His assumed Appearance), **you yourselves – the
> folks following Me – you also will be habitually sitting down upon twelve thrones** (or: seats)
> **repeatedly separating-out [issues], evaluating and making decisions for, or administering
> justice to, the twelve tribes of Israel**."

The called-out in Corinth were at that time living in "the Rebirth." Upon His resurrection Jesus (the Son of
the Man; the eschatological Human Being) was enthroned and was immediately sitting upon the throne of
His glory, as we read in Rev. 3:21,
> "**To** (or: In; For) **the person who is habitually conquering** (repeatedly overcoming; normally
> victorious) **I will continue giving** [the right? the ability? the honor?] **to sit** (or: be seated) **with Me
> within My throne, as I also conquer** (or: conquered; overcome; overcame and was victorious)
> **and sit** (or: sat down) **with My Father within His throne**."

But what does this look like? How was God's temple in Corinth judging the domination System? The
covenant community itself was "within the System" (Jn. 17:15, 18b), but the System was not their source
(Jn. 17:14b, 16). Jesus Christ was now Lord, not Caesar. They had been "**Set apart** (or: Made different
from the norm) **within the midst of the Truth** (or: in union with, and centered in, reality)" (Jn. 17:17). But
they were expected to, "**habitually sift, separate, evaluate and decide about the organized System**
(the world of culture, religion and government; or: secular society; or: = the Empire)." They were called to
follow Christ, not the culture or the religions that surrounded them. This did not mean that they were to
condemn others, but they were to sift things out, and throw out the things that they did not see their
Father doing (Jn. 5:19-20). Being led by the Spirit (Rom. 8:14) meant that they were to "obey God, rather
than humans" (Acts 5:29). As Jesus had taught, this often meant turning cultural norms on their heads.

In Acts 2:23b and Acts 3:13-15, Peter evaluated the actions of the Judean leaders when they crucified
Jesus. He "judged the System" as having been in the wrong. Paul judged the Judaizers in Gal. 5:2-12,
where in vs. 9 he informed them that, "**A little yeast** (or: leaven) **is progressively permeating so as to
ferment** (to be leavening) **the whole batch of kneaded dough**." He was there referring to the "art of
persuasion" (vs. 8) of the Judaizers. Also, Paul's listing of the "works of the flesh" (Gal. 5:19-21a) was a
judgment about the System. The cruciform life was a living parable that judged the cultures, and their
domination systems.

3. **Have you not seen so as to know that we shall continue sifting, separating, evaluating and
making decisions about agents** (or: will continue judging messengers, i.e., folks with the message) **–
why not, indeed, the affairs and business matters of everyday life?**

Paul, himself, was one of the set-apart folks that was sifting "agents" (e.g., Apollos, Cephas, and those in
Corinth). Furthermore, consider his instructions to the whole community in 14:29, below,
> "**Now let two or three prophets be speaking, one after another, and let the other folks
> continue thoroughly sifting and sorting so as to fully evaluate and reach a decision**."

The entire community was to function as the "judgment seat" of Christ, which, incidentally, was also known as the "mercy seat" within the heart of the temple (and the called-out of Corinth were now that Temple). But observe that the ending rhetorical question is set in contrast to the first rhetorical question. Things pertaining to "agents," or, "folks with the MESSAGE," were about aspects of God's reign among them. They were "spiritual" things, not "the affairs and business matters of everyday life." Nonetheless, if the Spirit of God that indwelt them and qualified them to sift out "spiritual matters," then surely the wisdom of God would be present among the members for sorting out things within community life.

Take note of the durative function of the future tense of the verb in the first clause: "**we shall continue sifting, separating, evaluating and making decisions**." This implies that it was at that time an ongoing function of called-out communities, and that it would thus continue on throughout the Age of the Messiah.

This is one of the reasons that Paul mentioned the ongoing spiritual status of the called-out folks:
> "**He jointly roused and raised** (or: suddenly awakens and raises) **[us] up, and caused [us] to sit** (or: seats [us]; = enthroned [us]) **together within the things situated upon** [thus, above] **the heavens within and in union with Christ Jesus**" (Eph. 2:6).

Also, we see this pictured in Heb. 12:22-24,
> "**you folks have approached so that you are now at Mount Zion – even in a city of a continuously living God; in 'Jerusalem upon heaven'**.... **in** (or: to; with) **God, a Judge** (an Evaluator and Decider) **of all mankind, even among** (or: to; with) **spirits of just folks** (or: breath-effects from those who are fair and equitable and in right relationship within the Way pointed out) **having been brought to the destined goal**... **and in** (or: to) **Jesus, a Medium** (or: an agency; an intervening substance; a middle state; one in a middle position; a go-between; an Umpire; a Mediator) **of a new and fresh** (young; recently-born) **arrangement**... **to and in blood of sprinkling** [i.e., at the mercy/judgment seat in the Temple]..."

It was the same for those in Corinth as it was for those in Colossae, "**Christ within and among you folks, the expectation of and from the glory** (the manifestation which calls forth praise)" (Col. 2:27b), for they,
> "**were awakened and are raised up together in the Christ** (or: If, then, you are aroused and raised with the Anointed One), **be constantly seeking and trying to find the upward things** (or: the things being above), **where the Christ is** (exists being), **continuously sitting within the right [side]** (or: at the right [hand]; = at the place of receiving, and in the place of honor and the power) **of God**" (Col. 3:1).

Paul alluded to this same situation, based upon our union with Christ, in Rom. 6:4,
> "**just as** (or: in the same manner as) **Christ was roused and raised forth from out of the midst of dead folks THROUGH** (through means of) **THE GLORY of The Father** (or: which is the Father), **thus also we can walk around** (or: we also should likewise conduct ourselves and order our behavior) **within newness of life**."

All of this informs us about how and why we are to evaluate and make decisions about His agents (His folks with the message).

4. **Indeed, therefore, if you may continue having tribunals** (places or situations for trying things; or: standards for evaluating controversies) **pertaining to life's affairs and business matters, make it a practice to seat [as judges] those in the local called-out community [who] have been regarded as amounting to nothing and are treated with contempt and scorn** (those least esteemed and of humble station in life).
> (or, as a question: are you making it a practice to seat [as judges] those looked down upon, disregarded or without repute and "standing" within the congregation?)

Observe Paul's terminology: "**tribunals** (places or situations for trying things; or: standards for evaluating controversies)." Once again, this is a reference to a judgment seat of Christ (Rom. 14:10; 2 Cor. 5:10). But what is Paul saying about "seating" members into this function? Is Paul making a statement about what sort of person to seat, or is he questioning their practice when they seat folks for trying "life's affairs and business matters"?

The form of the verb "to seat [as judges]," in the second clause, can be read either as an imperative (the bold rendering) or as an indicative (the parenthetical rendering). If we read it as an imperative, Paul is saying to seat the humbled folks on the tribunals, not the proud that he has been verbally chastising. But if we read it as an indicative, Paul is likely questioning their practice of using folks for this function that most likely lack wisdom and have no reputation, among their fellows, as being spiritually mature. Verse 5, below, fits with either reading, here.

Cf Rev. 2:26-27; 3:21, which were promises to those 1st century communities that could be experienced then and there.

5. **I am saying [this] to direct you folks toward turning back within [your community or yourself, and so, to reconsider]. Is there thus not one wise person** (one skilled with insight) **among you folks who will continue able to thoroughly sift and hold up [things] for evaluation and decision** (to adjudicate back) **in his brother's midst?**

The first sentence is commonly rendered as though Paul is endeavoring to "move them to shame or embarrassment." But this need not be the case. The deciding phrase literally means "**toward a turning back within**." I have inserted the purpose for this in the brackets. He wants them to look at themselves as a community, and as individuals, so that they will reconsider the way they have been acting. This is why he has taken pains to lay out their situation before their eyes. Bringing shame would be to hold their improper behavior against them – and God does not do this (2 Cor. 5:19). Also, remember Rom. 8:1.

So now he reasons with them through the question that he presents to them. He wants them to consider whether there is not someone qualified to adjudicate the situation that is a brother within the community.

6. **But to the contrary, a brother is constantly being brought to court** (sued; judged; evaluated and decided about) **with a brother** (= by a fellow believer; or: member of the same family) **– and this upon [the basis and situation] of unbelievers!**

Jacob (or: James) addressed a similar situation:
> "**Are not the rich people continuously exploiting you people, repeatedly exercising [their] power and abilities against you? Are they not continually dragging you into courts of law for judicial hearings?**" (Jas. 2:6).

They have been turning to those outside the covenant community to bring a legal suit against another member of the called-out. They have been seeking "unbelievers" (i.e., folks who are not followers of the Way – those that are "outside") to adjudicate "civil" matters. Conzelmann, and the translators in his commentary, feel that this verse should be rendered as a question (ibid p 105), and in our view either reading works with the context.

7. **Indeed, it is already** (or: to begin with [= even before going to court]) **therefore wholly an effect of a lessened condition in** (a defeat: a result of a diminishing from an overthrow for) **you folks – that you continue having lawsuits with one another. Why not rather continue suffering wrong** (or: be repeatedly treated unfairly and unjustly)**? Why not rather continue being defrauded** (or: being deprived from; or, as a middle: allowing yourselves to be cheated)**?**

Paul is saying that the community has lost ground, into "an effect of a lessened condition; a defeat: a result of a diminishing" in their bearing God's image and Christ's glory. They are acting like the domination System, and not like folks who bring God's reign to the ethnic multitudes.

The two rhetorical questions are unthinkable to those who are trying to keep themselves safe (Mat. 16:25a). But Paul expects each one to,

> "**completely say, 'No,' to, deny and disown himself, and then in one move lift up his execution stake** (pole for suspending a corpse; cross), **and after that proceed to be by habit continuously following after [Christ]**" (Mat. 16:24).

He expects them to remember Jesus' teaching in Mat. 5:40,

> "**And further, to the person continuing in desiring** (wanting; purposing) **for you to be judged** (or: sued; or: presently intending to litigate with you) **and even to take your inner garment** (tunic; = shirt), **at once send off to him your outer garment** (cloak; coat) **as well!**"

Or perhaps he is alluding to Mat. 5:42,

> "**Give at once to the person presently, or repeatedly, asking of you, and you should not be turned away from the one continuously wanting** (or: purposing) **to borrow money from you.**"

This was so that they would have the character of, and properly represent, their Father – the One that is within the atmospheres (Mat. 5:45). As a counter-balance to "**suffering wrong**" or "**being defrauded,**" we have Paul's perspective in Rom. 8:18,

> "**You see, I have come to a reasoned conclusion that the effects of the sensible experiences – sufferings, impressions, passions or feelings – of the current season** (or: of the situation fitted to the present time) **[are] not equivalent [being] face to face with the glory which is progressively about to be disclosed unto us, and for us** (or: unveiled into our midst; revealed to and [enter] into us)." *Cf* Mat. 5:29

Likewise, we have the example of Jesus,

> "**turning [our] eyes away from other things and fixing them** (or: looking away) **into Jesus, the Inaugurator and Perfecter of the faith, trust, confidence and loyal allegiance, Who, instead of and in place of the joy** (or: in the position on the opposite side from the happiness) **continuously lying before Him** (or: lying in the forefront within Him; lying ahead for Him), **remained under a cross – despising shame**" (Heb. 12:2).

And then there is another witness of Christ, in 1 Pet. 2:23,

> "**Who, being repeatedly reviled** (harshly and bitingly rebuked and insulted), **was not reviling back** (answering insult with insult; taking the position of harsh, biting rebuke); **continuously** (or: repeatedly) **suffering** (experiencing ill treatment), **he was not threatening, but kept on giving [the situation] over to** (committing [it] with; entrusting [it] in) **the One at His side: the One constantly sifting, separating and deciding** (or: judging) **fairly** (equitably; following the Path of the Way pointed out, bringing situations to a rightwised condition)."

8. **Yet instead, you yourselves are constantly committing wrong** (being unfair and unjust; living contrary to the Way pointed out) **and are repeatedly defrauding** (cheating; depriving from [someone]) **– and this [to] brothers** (folks from the same womb; = fellow believers; = members of the Family)!

They had been living in the realm of the first Adam (the soul/self-oriented person), instead of the "eschatos" (last) Adam (15:45, below). They had not continued to dwell in the Vine (Jn. 15:1ff), and so they were unable to produce the fruit of the Vine (*cf* Gal. 5:22-23). They were not following Paul's advice, as he wrote to the province of Galatia, in Gal. 5:

> 24. **Now those whose source and origin is Christ Jesus** (or: those who belong to the Anointed Jesus) **crucified the flesh** (or: put the flesh [system] on an execution stake; or: = associate their old estranged human nature as being put to death along with Christ Jesus), **together with the results and effects of the experiences** (emotions; feelings; sufferings; passions) **and the over-desires** (rushing passionately upon things; full-rushing emotions).
> 25. **Since** (or: If) **we continue living in and by spirit** (or: for [the] Spirit; to Breath-effect; or: with attitude), **we also can habitually advance orderly in line in regard to, or amidst, elementary principles** (or: [observing] rudimentary elements), **in and by spirit** (or: for [the] Spirit; by Breath-effect; with attitude; or: = walk in rank following [the footsteps] behind the Spirit). [*cf* Rom. 4:12]

26. **We can** (or: should) **not repeatedly** (or: habitually) **come to be** (or: Let us stop becoming) **folks with empty glory** (or: a vacuous reputation; = to be egotistical or conceited), **continually being those challenging one another [as to combat], constantly envying one another.**

The Corinthians had not been living the cruciform life, but instead had lived like the domination System of the Empire. Being a disciple of Christ is more than just "accepting the Lord as one's personal Savior."

9. **Or have you not seen so as to know that unfair** (unjust; inequitable; wrongly-turned) **folks will not proceed to inherit a kingdom from God** (or: receive an allotment in God's sovereign reign or activities)**? Do not be repeatedly misled or constantly caused to wander** (or: be deceived). **Neither sexually licentious folks** (paramours; fornicators; [note: may also refer to men associating at idol temple-feasts]), **nor idolaters, nor adulterers** [may = participation in pagan religions; *cf* Isa. 1:21; Ezk. 16:15], **nor unmanly** (men who wear soft clothes [Mat. 11:8]; soft, delicate, weak folks; = untrained and undeveloped, so unable to bear a load?), **nor men who lie in beds** (= lazy folks? or: sex-traffickers? [note: meaning uncertain; *cf* LXX: Lev. 18:22; 20:13 have been associated with these passages; = those following an off-target direction?]),

10. **nor thieves, nor greedy** (covetous) **ones; not drunkards, not verbal abusers, not people who ravenously snatch, swindle or extort, will proceed to inherit a kingdom from God** (or: will continue in receiving an allotment in God's sovereign reign and activities).

Both vss. 9 and 10 use the term "**inherit** (receive an allotment)." This concept is an allusion Israel's history, in many situations, but the most notable is what the Land of Israel was allotted among the twelve tribes. The creation of Israel as a nation, with God as their King, was the first manifestation of God's kingdom, among the nations of the earth. Israel's exiles had removed the kingdom from them, and so Jesus has his followers pray,

> "**Make Your reign and kingdom come. Make Your will** (the effect of Your intent and purpose) **come into existence** (happen; come to be; be birthed) **– as within heaven** (or: [the] atmosphere), **so also upon earth**" (Mat. 6:10).

Earth is to be the central focus of the manifestation of God's kingdom, even though it is not a part of the organized systems of empires or religions (Jn. 18:36). Instead,

> "**The reign** (or: kingdom) **of the dominating, ordered System** (of the world of religion, culture, government and economy; or: of the realm of the religious and secular; or: of the aggregate of humanity) **suddenly came to belong to our Lord** [= Yahweh or Christ] **and to the anointed of Him, and so He will continue reigning** (ruling as King) **on into the ages**" (Rev. 11:15b).

In Lu. 12:32, Jesus told His disciples,

> "**Stop fearing** (or: Do not continue being wary), **little flock, because it delights the Father** (or: because the Father thought it good, and thus, approved) **to give the reign** (rule; kingship; kingdom; sovereign influence and activities) **to you folks.**"

These traditions and teachings lie behind Paul's reference to inheriting a kingdom from God. In 15:50, below, Paul further explains what he is saying here in vss. 9-10:

> "**Now I am saying this, brothers** (= fellow members and believers), **that flesh and blood** (= humans in their estranged condition; = people of dust who have not been resurrected) **have no power and continue unable to inherit or receive and participate in an allotted portion of God's reign** (kingdom or sovereign action) **– neither is corruption and decay** (the perishable) **continuing on to inherit** (participate in the allotment of) **the Incorruption** (Imperishability)."

In that passage Paul had been contrasting the two Adams, the two Humanities (vss. 45-49). These two also represented the two covenants (one of slavery, the second of freedom) and so in Gal. 5:30 he concludes his allegory in saying, "**by no means will the son of the servant girl** (the slave-girl; the maid) **be an heir** (take possession of and enjoy the distributed allotment) **with the son of the freewoman.**" In Mat. 5:5, Jesus gave this characterization:

> "'**The kind, considerate, gentle, mild-tempered, humane and nonviolent folks** (people who do not use force)' **[are] happy and blessed because they, themselves, 'will proceed to be inheriting the Land** (or: be receiving and enjoying the earth as an allotment)!'" [Ps. 37:11]

Then in Mat. 25, He said that the sheep – those who lived love and mercy to others:

"**At once come into possession of the inheritance of, and enjoy the allotment of,** [the place of, or realm of] **the reign** (or: kingdom; influence and activity of sovereignty) **having been prepared and made ready from a founding** (a casting down [as of a foundation; or: of seed]) **of a system** (or: of [the] aggregate of humanity; of an arranged order; of [the] world)."

Another view of this whole new arrangement is seen in Rev. 21:7, "**The one habitually being victorious** (or: progressively overcoming) **will proceed inheriting** (acquiring by lot) **these things, and I will continue being a God for him** (in him; to him) **and he will continue being a son for** (to; in; with) **Me.**" Much more could be said concerning "inheriting the kingdom of God," but that is a study in itself.

Take note that Paul brings up the "kingdom from God; God's sovereign reign and activities." They had been acting like prodigals that had left the Father's house (Lu. 15:13ff). We are reminded of Jesus' words in Lu. 14:27,

"**Whoever is not habitually picking up and carrying his own execution stake** (or: the cross of himself; the suspending-pole which pertains to, or is, himself) **and then continuing in coming behind Me – he has no power and is unable to be My disciple** (apprentice)!"

Those who are "constantly committing wrong" (vs. 8, above), "being licentious," and the rest of the list in vss. 9-10, disqualify themselves from discipleship – i.e., being active in God's reign and representing Him – because they are living lives that are centered in themselves, rather than in Christ. They had been eating from the tree of the knowledge of good and evil. Now this has nothing to do with any "heaven or hell" false dichotomy, it is about being a living branch within the Vine; it is about being a living stone of His Temple (1 Pet. 2:5) – here and now. It is about being a "sheep" (one who is following the Shepherd and knows His voice – Jn. 10:3-5), rather than a "kid" (Mat. 25:34, 41-46). *Cf* Gal. 5:21

11. **And some of you were these things. But now you folks bathed yourselves off** (took a bath to cleanse things away). **Even more than that, you were set apart** (made holy; sanctified). **But yet more, you were eschatologically delivered, rightwised and placed in the Way pointed out** (turned in the right direction, made just, and then joined in right, covenantal relationship with God and mankind) **in union with and within the midst of the Name of our Lord, Jesus Christ – even in union with and within the midst of the Spirit of our God** (or: that is, centered in the Breath-effect from our God and the Attitude which is our God)**!**

The turn-around, begun in the second clause, is an echo of Isa. 1:16a,

"You folks at once bathe and wash yourselves: become (birth yourselves to be) clean! Take away (separate and remove) the painful labor (or: bad condition; unsound situation; unprofitable or malicious deed) from your souls..." (LXX, JM)·

Paul has in the previous verses set the dark, contrasting background; now he reminds the "disciples" in Corinth of who they really are now. Some had been a part of the dark background, but were now transformed. They had:

a) "bathed" themselves – as figured in Rev. 7:14, "washed their robes;" they had experienced "**a bath of and from a birth-back-again** (or: [the] bathing of a regeneration) – Tit. 3:5; they had gone through, "**cleansing** (purging) **by the bath of the Water [that is] within a result of a flow** (or: in union with a gush-effect; or: in the midst of a spoken word, a declaration, or an utterance)" (Eph. 5:26);

Observe that both Isa. 1:16 and this present clause are in the middle voice. Because of the passive voice in the following clauses, most translations (and most scholars) render this clause as being passive – but it is not. Isaiah was writing to Israel: God's people. So is Paul. Isaiah used the imperative mood and the middle voice; Paul the indicative, middle – since he was referring to a past action. Paul said the same thing as Isaiah, but just used different metaphors, in Rom. 13:12,

"**We should put, then, the acts of the Darkness** (works from the realm of the shadows; actions that belong to dimness and obscurity) **away from ourselves** (or: take off and put away the deeds pertaining to darkness; = ignorance; that which was before the light arrived), **and clothe ourselves with the instruments** (tools; weapons; implements; [some MSS: works; deeds]) **of Light** (or: The Light)."

Here in his letter to Corinth, Paul is simply referring to a past act of those who were already in Christ: they had cleansed away prior behaviors from their lives, through the work of the Spirit. This is not referring to a ritual of "baptism." These folks had done what Paul directed in Eph. 6:11, but there using a different metaphor:

"**you folks must at some point, for yourselves, enter within** (or: clothe yourselves with) **the full suit of armor and implements of war** (panoply; the complete equipment for men-at-arms) **which is God** (or: which comes from and belongs to God), **in order for you to be continuously able and powerful to stand**..."

But the following clauses speak of what God, in Christ, had done to and for these folks. All three clauses begin with a strong, adversative conjunction indicating contrast and difference. Because of the different statements of these clauses, I rendered them: "**But now**... **Even more than that**... **But yet more**," in order to emphasize the nuances of the rhetorical construction. The first clause notes the contrasting change since they had cleansed themselves by acting upon the implanted *Logos* (the message of the cross). The second and third clauses remind them of what the Christ Event had done to, and for, them:

b) they had BEEN "**eschatologically delivered, rightwised and placed in the Way pointed out** (turned in the right direction, made just, and then joined in right, covenantal relationship with God and mankind);" – **But yet more**...

c) they had BEEN "put in covenant **in union with and within the midst of the Name of our Lord, Jesus Christ**;" – and THUS...

d) they were, "**in union with and within the midst of the Spirit of our God** (or: that is, centered in the Breath-effect from our God and the Attitude which is our God)!" *Cf* 1 Thes. 4:1-2.

Now, it doesn't get much better than that. They were back in the Garden; they were the New Jerusalem. With this affirmed, Paul moves on in his arguments...

12. **To me, all things are presently out-of-Being** (or: All things continue from existence for me; or: All is authorized, right and permitted by and in me). **But yet not everything proceeds to bear together for advantage, profit, help, or are for the best. To me, all things are authorized, permitted and out of [His] Being, but still I myself will not proceed in being brought under authority by anyone.**
(or: With, to and for me, all is from the source of Being, and continues with right and privilege. However, all is not habitually carrying together. With, to and for me, all is from the source of Being, and continues with right and privilege; nonetheless, I will not continue being put in subjection to rights and privileges under any person or under any certain thing, pertaining to me. or: All have rights with me, but on the other hand, not all things are advantageous. All, from [his, her or its] existence, has privilege with me, although, as for me, I will not proceed in being subdued under anyone's privilege.)

Statements that are almost identical to the first two sentences in this verse are made by Paul in 10:23, below. Something said twice has significance and importance. Even within these two verses, the idea is repeated; there is parallelism.

Now some read the first statement as "all is allowed for or by me" – an "anything goes" statement that Paul counters in the following statement, in both pairs of the parallelism. Ann Nyland's *The Source NT* renders both this verse and 10:23 in a manner that suggests that Paul is citing a saying by some

Corinthian libertarians. These interpretations have merit, but we shall investigate this verse as though it comes from Paul, since viewing it as quoting someone else is interpretive conjecture.

The personal pronoun "me" is in the dative case, so on offer are "to me, for me; by me and with me," all of which make sense to the context. The verb is considered to be an impersonal verb. It is the third person, singular, present tense of the verb "to be; to exist" that is prefixed by the preposition which means "from; out of; forth from the midst of." The common versions render this verb "allowed; authorized; permitted; lawful." These are extended meanings, and make sense to the context, but they obscure the root idea in the Greek thought that bases its the meaning on a verb of "being," or "existence." The noun associated with this verb is *exousia* and is found in Jn. 1:12b, "**It [The Logos] gives** (or: He gave) **to them** (or: for them; in them; among them) **authority** ([the] right; or: privilege from out of the midst of Being) **to be birthed God's children**." Since these cognates are based upon the same verb and the same prefixed preposition, I have stressed the idea of "being" and "existence" in my renderings. Therefore, we have "**all things are presently out-of-Being**," or the alternatives, "All things continue from existence," and "All is authorized, right and permitted," in the first clause. *Cf* 12:4, below.

Paul says that these statements have a relation to him. It is "to his perception or his world view" that "all things come out of Being." This would be similar to his statement in Rom. 11:36a, "**forth from out of the midst of Him**..." are all things. As Paul Tillich has put it, God is the Ground [i.e., Source – my word, here] of Being.

Now the next option, "All things continue from existence for me," would suggest that Paul views the entire universe exists for him – meaning, of course, for humanity. Or, God made this world for us. But offering the verbal meanings of authorization, right and permission would be saying that these could be used by him or were in him. All of this makes sense, when we consider Paul's place and function in God's reign.

But we see Paul's wisdom: he recognizes that "**not everything proceeds to bear together for advantage, profit, help, or are for the best**" with regard to building God's Temple (as stated in ch. 3, above). But what about the corresponding parallel in the last part of the verse: **I myself will not proceed in being brought under authority by anyone**? Was Paul rebellious? Or was this a reference to his relationship to the Jerusalem congregation, or perhaps, to Corinth itself? The object of the preposition "by," or, "under," functions to signify either "anyone," or "anything." So he could be referring to religious or political systems, or even the emperor.

In the parenthetical expansion, I followed the lead of the *Concordant Literal New Testament* and rendered the subject of the first and third sentences as simply "all." When this term is used as the subject of a sentence, it is plural and neuter, or neutral. However, the majority of the time where we find "all" in the NT it is speaking about people. NT Greek does not always follow the exact rules of Greek grammar. We suggest that it is possible to read these "all's" as referring to people, and so offer it this way.

Following the first, **bold**, rendering are two optional renderings of the entire verse. The second option offers other meanings of the Greek words, and the third option offers a reading where "all" refers to people, instead of "things." We suggest meditating on all three renderings, and let the Spirit disclose the possibilities of interpretive nuances.

In this verse, Paul is not taking away their freedom in Christ (Gal. 5:1), but is pointing them to the Wisdom of God for the benefit of the community. Our liberty should not harm the community (Rom. 14:13-16). After repeating the first half of vs. 1, above, in 10:23a, below, the explanation of 10:23b-24 enlightens us here:

> "**but yet not all things progressively edify or build up the house. Let no one be habitually seeking the [interest, advantage, profit, welfare or edification] of, or pertaining to, himself,**

but to the contrary, the [interest, advantage, profit, welfare and edification] of the other (or: pertaining to the different) **person.**"
This all points us back to 3:21-23, above: "**all things [are] yours**.... **yet you folks [are] Christ's.**" Paul is still on the same theme as begun in 5:1, above, and this same theme continues on, below.

13. **The foods** (The things eaten) **[are meant] for the stomach, and the stomach [is meant] for the things eaten, yet God will make both it and them useless and unprofitable** (or: will also bring this and these down to being idle).
Now the body [is] not for prostitution (or: sexual immorality; or: = idolatry), **but rather for the Lord – and further, the Lord [is] in** (or: for; with) **the body.**
14. **Yet God both aroused** (awakened) **and raised up the Lord, and He is presently and progressively** (or: one-after-another repeatedly; or: keeps on) **arousing and raising us up out of the midst** [reading with p11.46*, A, D*, P and others; or: p46c2, B and others read: He fully aroused and raised us up (or: at one point arouses and raises us up out); or: p46c1, Aleph, C, D2 and others read: He will continue raising us up out] **through His power and ability.**

In vs. 13a, Paul seems to begin speaking to the idea of things that "**bear together for advantage, profit, help, or are for the best**" (vs. 12) in the community, with regard to "**foods**" and "**the stomach.**" But then he breaks off from this topic and does not address it until 8:4, below. In 13b he takes up the topic of "**prostitution**" and brings in the word "**body.**" Now the word that I have rendered "**stomach**" (*koilia*) literally means "cavity," and thus could refer to either the organ of digestion or of sex, and sex is the underlying topic for the rest of the chapter, and on through chapter 7. Is Paul perhaps simply quoting a proverb or "saying" but with the intent on emphasizing the transient nature of all of this, in 13b? With the term "**body,**" as Paul uses the term, there are two levels of meaning and different layers of interpretation. Perhaps Paul had Sirach 23:6 (LXX) in mind when he said this:

"Let not the belly's appetite and sexual intercourse seize me, and do not give me over to a shameless soul" (*A New English Translation of the Septuagint*, Oxford Univ. Press, 2007 p 737).

Or, perhaps this was an allusion to Mk. 7:19 where Jesus spoke of what went into the "belly" and then into the sewer. Paul does not explain what he means by "**God will make both it and them useless and unprofitable** (or: will also bring this and these down to being idle)," especially considering that he goes on to say "**the body [is]... for the Lord – and further, the Lord [is] in** (or: for; with) **the body.**" Of course, a spiritual/metaphorical meaning of "body" makes sense, here, and even our physical bodies belong to the Lord – He is our Owner/Master.

We can see Paul's practical concerns for both the physical and the corporate bodies: both are "**for the Lord.**" This calls to mind vss. 19b-20, below: we are not our own. Verse 13b is a logical conclusion of being "set-apart" to God, and this is in contrast to the temple prostitutes of pagan religions of the time. But there is a spiritual level to this topic of prostitution. It is an allusion to Israel having turned away from Yahweh and to pagan gods. We find the same situation presented in the visionary picture of "Babylon" in Rev. 17. We will cite just one instance from Israel's' history, during the time of Isaiah: "Alas, the Faithful City has become a prostitute!" (Isa. 1:21).

Verse 14 is echoed in Eph. 2:6, as noted above. The term which I have conflated as "**aroused and raised up**" speaks of resurrection – a topic to which Paul will devote much of chapter 15, below. Note the present tense of this verb. It was an ongoing event (or, a "one-after-another" event) in Paul's day. We suggest that it has been going on ever since. In 15:29 Paul rhetorically asks a question containing the subordinate clause, "**If dead folks are not altogether** (actually; absolutely; generally speaking) **being habitually awakened and presently raised up...?**" Notice the other MSS that have the verb in the past tense, and others that have it in the future progressive. This was, is and will be (conflating all the MS witnesses) done "**through His power and ability.**" And it is worthwhile to quote Col. 3:1a, again,

"**Since, therefore, you folks were awakened and are raised up together in the Christ** (or: If, then, you are aroused and raised with the Anointed One)..."

Paul experienced this spiritual resurrection as a present reality, as did the writer of Heb. 12:22, "**you folks have approached so that you are NOW at Mount Zion – even IN a city of a continuously living God; in 'Jerusalem upon heaven.'**"

15. **Have you folks not seen so as to know that your** [other MSS: our] **bodies are** (exist being) **members** (body parts) **of Christ? Upon lifting up and carrying off** (or: bearing away) **the members** (body parts) **of the Christ, will I proceed then in making** (or: could or should I at any point yield) **[them] members** (body parts) **of a prostitute? May it not come to be or happen** (= Heaven forbid; = No way)! 16. **Or, have you folks not seen so as to know that the man continually joining himself** (or: being habitually glued in intimate union) **to** (or: in) **a prostitute exists being one body [with her]? For, He says,**

> **"The two will continue existing, being [joined] into one flesh."** [Gen. 2:24] *Cf* Mat. 19:5

Being a "**member**, or body part, **of Christ**" was and is a spiritual reality that is expressed in a "**body**" metaphor. Paul will further develop this symbolic picture in chapters 11 and 12, below. However, many of Paul's audience were "soulish" (2:14, above; *cf* Jas. 3:15; Jude 19) and "carnally minded" (Rom. 8:6), and they were still spiritual children (3:2, above), so he speaks to both the physical and the spiritual levels here. Both levels are also addressed in vs. 16, where he cites Gen. 2:24. Our life in the kingdom, here, is a living metaphor in the living letters that we are (2 Cor. 3:1-2). He will develop his reference to "prostitution" below. *Cf* the connection between the terms "body" and "flesh" in Eph. 5:28-29.

17. **Now the person continually joining himself** (or: being habitually glued in intimate union; in himself being continuously welded) **to** (or: in; with) **the Lord exists being one spirit** (or: one Breath-effect; one Attitude; one Spirit).

This is one of the deepest and most beautiful statements in all of Scripture. This statement is parallel to vs. 16, above, and he is, of course, speaking of a spiritual reality, but we suggest that it is also an existential reality – just as our being His home (temple) and His child are existential realities. Since God is Spirit, and we are spirit, this is not just a metaphor. But Paul is contrasting this present reality of "the body of Christ" to the potential reality of prostituting it – on both natural and spiritual levels. What he is describing here is the union of marriage. The language of vss. 15-16 is speaking about sexual union. In this verse, it is the spiritual marriage between the body of Christ and Christ Himself, just as there was this same relationship between Israel and Yahweh, under the old covenant. Read Ezk. 16, as well as the imagery in Hosea. Paul is in this verse using the physical sexual union of a man and a woman as a metaphor for our relationship to God. On the physical plane, it is the greatest union that people can experience. Thus our being joined to the Lord would by comparison be the greatest spiritual union that we can experience. With the explanation given by this verse, we have a key to Paul's teaching about the body of Christ, which will follow. It is a spiritual Body, composed of physical/spiritual people.

Take note of the semantic range of the word **joining**: "glued in intimate union; welded." The Spirit Himself must reveal to us what it means to be "**one spirit/Spirit/Breath-effect.**" The idea of a "spirit" being an "attitude" is more easily seen: one Attitude – like having the mind of Christ. But the potentially ontological reading of Paul, here, can blow our minds – even if we understand the metaphor of the joining of Husband-wife, which is how Paul is speaking. In Ps. 73:28 (72:28 in LXX) we read:

> "Now it continues being good for me (in me; with me) to be continuously joined face-to-face with God (or as a middle: to repeatedly glue myself focused in God), and to place my expectation in union with the LORD (set my expectant hope centered in [Yahweh])" (LXX, JM).

18. **Constantly flee** (Repeatedly take flight [from]) **the prostitution.** [note: this would also apply to idolatry in pagan temples which used prostitutes as part of the idol worship] **The effect** (or: result) **of every sin** (failure to hit the target; error; mistake; deviation) **– whatsoever a person may do – exists**

being outside of the body. Yet the one habitually committing prostitution (practicing sexual immorality) **is habitually sinning** (sowing errors and mistakes) **into his own body.** [note: both his physical body, and the body of the called-out community]

Notice the imperative: **Constantly flee** (Repeatedly take flight [from]) **the prostitution.** This calls to mind Rev. 18:4, "Come out of her, My people." But it also implies, "stay away from situations that could lead to involvement with a prostitute" – whether it be an individual, or a corporate, situation. Most of the prostitution that Israel fell into was primarily that of corporate idolatry. But temple prostitutes also profaned the individual, if he got involved in it. *Cf* Prov. 6:25-35. In 10:14, below, we find the same verb as used here: "**be habitually fleeing away from the idolatry.**" In 1 Tim. 6:11, Timothy is advised to FLEE the love of money (vs. 10), and "**continuously PURSUE fair and equitable dealings in right relationships in the Way pointed out** (rightwisedness; justice; = loyal covenantal living), **faith** (trust; trustworthiness; loyalty), **love**... (etc.)."

On the corporate, and thus spiritual, level, this meant to not be involved with an institution that God considered to be a prostitute. Israel's leaders had both done that, and become that, as in Ezk. 16:15ff.

This admonition applies on both levels. Paul put it this way in 2 Cor. 6:14,
> "**Do not of yourself continue** (or: Stop) **becoming yoked differently** (or: unevenly yoked; yoked with ones of a different sort) **with folks without faith** (or: by those without trust; to unbelievers; with disloyal people), **for, what mutual holding** (having-with: sharing; partnership; communion; membership) **[have] rightwised living and lawlessness** (or: fairness/equity, and a lack of following rules; deliverance to right relationship which accords with the Way pointed out, and [the] inequity or wrong which come from violation of law), **or what common existing** (participation; partnership; sharing of Being) **[is] in Light [directed] toward, or face to face with, darkness** (or: [is there] for light with dimness from murky obscurity in the realm of shadows)**?**"

Failure to hit the target of bearing the image of God, or of reflecting the glory of the Lord (2 Cor. 3:18) might be something that was an error or a mistake that was "outside of the [corporate or individual] body." But prostitution implied intimacy with one that was not a spouse, and therefore it violates the sacred union of the marriage (whether this be an individual matter, or a corporate situation).

19. **Or, have you folks not seen so as to know that your body** (or: the body of you folks) **is a temple of the set-apart spirit** (or: a sanctuary belonging to the Holy Spirit; a holy place and a holy of holies which pertains to the Sacred Breath; or: that the body, which is you folks, exists being a divine habitation which has the qualities and characteristics of the Holy Attitude) – **within the midst of you** (or: in union with you folks; or: among you people) – **which you people constantly hold and progressively possess from God? And further, you are not folks belonging to yourselves** (or: Also then, you people do not exist from yourselves),
20. **for you people were bought, as at a marketplace: [there was] value and honor involved in the price** (or: [you are] of value)
> (or: = you see, you folks were bought and paid for; or: it follows that from a valuable price you folks were bought at market).

By all means then, glorify God (bring a good reputation to God; manifest that which calls forth praise to God) **within your body** (or: within the midst of the body which you folks are)!

Verse 19a repeats what he said in 3:16, above. Here, depending on how one reads the genitive case of the plural, personal pronoun "**your**/of you folks," the "**temple**" is either the individual, or the corporate body. The "**the set-apart spirit**" can refer to the "Attitude" that was imparted into the group from hearing the Good News from Paul. But this is also the Holy Spirit, or, God's Sacred Breath, which had taken up residence within, and among them. Existential experience attests to the Breath-effect/Spirit inhabiting the individual – this is how we come alive in Christ. We can get more insights into what he is saying here, by reading his later letter to Rome. In Rom. 8:

> 10. **But since Christ** (or: Yet if [the] Anointing) **[is] within you folks, on the one hand the body is dead** (lifeless) **BECAUSE OF sin** (through failure, deviation and missing the target), **yet on the other hand, the Spirit, Attitude and Breath-effect [is] Life BECAUSE OF an eschatological act of justice that brought a rightwising deliverance into equitable, covenantal relationships within the Way pointed-out** (or: on account of the covenantal Faithfulness of a liberating Turn into the Right Direction of the Living Way/Path).
>
> 11. **Now since the Breath-effect** (or: Spirit; Attitude) **of the One arousing and raising Jesus forth from out of the midst of dead folks is continuously housing Itself** (making His abode; residing; making His home; by idiom: living together as husband and wife) **within, and in union with, you folks, the One raising Christ Jesus forth from out of dead ones will also continue progressively giving Life to** (or: will even habitually make alive) **the mortal bodies of you folks** (or: your mortal bodies) **through the constant indwelling of His Spirit** (or: the continual in-housing of His Breath-effect; the continuous internal residing of the Attitude, which is Him,) [other MSS: because of His habitually-indwelling Spirit] **within and among you folks.**

Notice the near identity of the terms "Christ/Anointing" and "Breath-effect/Spirit/His Spirit" in these two verses. You have One, you have the Other.

Notice that what he says in 19b is something that they "**constantly hold and progressively possess from God.**" So what had they received, so that they now possess it? May we suggest that it was "**a new creation** (or: [it is] a framing and founding of a different kind; [he or she is] an act of creation having a fresh character and a new quality)" (2 Cor. 5:17). It was the framing of the "divine habitation" which God had founded within and among them. They possessed "a holy place and a holy of holies which pertains to the Sacred Breath, the Holy Spirit." Paul spoke of this in 2 Cor. 5:1, where he uses the term "tabernacle" (which later was replaced by the temple),

> "**You see, we have seen, perceived and know that if our House – from the Tabernacle which was pitched on the Land – would at some point be dismantled** (or: that whenever our house, which is this tent upon the earth, should be loosed down), **we constantly have** (continuously hold; presently possess) **a dwelling structure or place** (a building for an abode; or: **a household**; = a family or a possession) **forth from out of the midst of God: an eonian act of building a roofed house** (or: a covered building for dwelling having qualities and character which pertain to the Age [of the Messiah]; a structure of edification for, and pertaining to, the ages) **– not made by hands** [cf Heb. 9:1-8, 11; Dan. 2:34, 45; Eph. 2:11; Col. 2:11] **– resident within the atmospheres** (or: in union with the heavens)." [cf 6:16, below; 1 Tim. 3:15; Heb. 9:24]

Notice, in this quote, that Paul uses the same verb: we "**constantly have** (continuously hold; presently possess)" it. And notice that in this letter he also refers to it as "**a dwelling structure or place** (a building for an abode)." And just as in vs. 19, above, here in 2 Cor. 5:1 this structure is "**forth from out of the midst of God.**" In both passages, this "temple" or "dwelling structure" can be seen on both the individual and the corporate levels.

Their corporate body is "a sanctuary belonging to the Holy Spirit," and it has "the qualities and characteristics of the Holy Attitude." That Holy Attitude was one of taking the place and form of a servant and living a cruciform life. This is why they, as a covenant community, have been "set-apart" for God. In vs. 20 Paul uses a marketplace metaphor and term to remind them that they "**were bought,**" and that there was "**value and honor involved in the price** (or: [you are] of value)." So it follows that "they do not belong to themselves." If we ponder the metaphor that Paul uses here, we can see that they (and, thus, likewise we) had no choice or say in the matter. They had been like slaves that were bought at the marketplace. Now they belonged to God and Christ; they had a new Master. Now, as God's possession, "**By all means then, glorify God** (bring a good reputation to God; manifest that which calls forth praise to God) **within your body** (or: within the midst of the body which you folks are)!" Once again we have the potential readings of this referring either to the individual, or to the group. They were to be living their lives like members of the Household of God; they represented God and were, in fact, God's home. This, by the very nature of the situation, brought a responsibility to them – but God's grace and power were what would enable them to meet this responsibility.

Now most Christians are not normally taught this. The words, "**your body** (or: the body of you folks) **is a temple of the set-apart spirit** (or: a sanctuary belonging to the Holy Spirit)," often seem to be only "mouthed," or are that to which assent is given, and then passed over without further meditation upon the proclamation. But Paul is going to great lengths to enlighten them as to their new existential situation. They need to be living like they are God's house; His new creation; His special possession. If this attitude permeated them, there would be no thought of prostitution or idolatry. Conzelmann makes a cogent observation: "The body is the place and the means of glorifying God" (ibid p 113). They had been "**jointly roused and raised** (or: suddenly awakens and raises) **[us] up, and caused [us] to sit** (= enthroned) **together within the things situated upon** [thus, above] **the heavens**" (Eph. 2:6).

Chapter 7

1. **Yet concerning the things which you folks wrote: "Is it fine for a man to by habit not touch a woman so as to hold or kindle her as a wife?"**
    (or: = Now about what you wrote: "Is it ideal for a man to live in celibacy as a way of life?")

Most translations offer as a statement – which would mean it expresses Paul's pronouncement about the issue – what I have chosen to render as a question. Because of Paul's reply in the following verses, this seems to be the best way of reading the text (keep in mind that the earliest MSS had no punctuation marks). Paul is restating the question which the Corinthians had written to him, and then he proceeds to answer that question.

2. **Well, because of prostitutions** (= the dangers of sexual immorality, or the lure of pagan temple prostitutes), **let each man continually hold and be permanently having a wife** (or: woman) **for himself, and each woman be constantly holding and permanently having her own husband.**

He is saying, and history seems to have proved him right, that for most people who live in a close community such as those of the called-out folks of the 1st century, it is best for the members to be married. Prostitution was quite common in the surrounding culture, and the normal sexual drives might well prove to be stronger than one's commitment to celibacy and the result would be guilt and shame.

3. **Let the husband habitually render** (give away in answer to claim and expectation) **to the wife [her] due** (what is owed to her; the obligation; the debt), **yet likewise the wife, also, to the husband.**

Furthermore, he advises normal sexual relations between the married couple. In that culture this was considered to be a marital obligation, what a person "owed" to the spouse.

4. **The wife continues having no right or authority pertaining to her own body, but to the contrary, the husband [does]. Now likewise the husband, also, continues having no right or authority pertaining to his own body, but to the contrary, the wife [does].**

This is a "leveling of the field" for marriage roles, and it is astounding, considering the norms for what we know of the surrounding society in the 1st century Roman Empire. Paul is saying that the husband and the wife are equals in their physical relationship.

5. **Do not habitually deprive** (defraud; rob) **one another, except anytime** (or: unless perhaps) **it should [be] from out of mutual consent** (spoken agreement) **with a view toward a specific period** (or: appointed season; fertile situation or condition) **so that you [both] may be at leisure in activities**

that lead toward having goodness and well-being (or: could be otherwise unoccupied for prayer; can give each other time for thoughts of ease or to be unemployed with a view to wellness), **and then you [both] may proceed being** [other MSS: should come together] **again [putting your attention] upon this very thing [i.e., resume your physical relationship], so that the adversary** (the opponent; the adversarial [situation or attitude]) **may not keep on testing you** (endeavoring to put you to the proof; trying you; tempting you) **because of your lack of strength** (through your lack of control; because of your incontinence).

> [note: continued sexual relations in marriage was a duty, under Jewish law and custom; failure to do so was grounds for divorce – Ex. 21:10-11; vs. 4 is a step toward equality]

With vs. 3, above, in mind, Paul is advising that there should be mutual consent to abstain from the normal physical relationship, and that it should be "for a specific period of time." Notice the emphasis on "goodness and well-being" during these situations of "leisure in activities," i.e., temporary release from the "obligation."

The mention of a testing from the adversary – because of peoples' "lack of strength" in the area of sexual relationships – would be the trial from one's normal inner-drives. The "flesh" is our normal battleground, and this is why Paul often advises "living in the spirit, and by the Spirit." Paul made this clear in Gal. 5:16,

> "**So I continue saying, be habitually walking about** (= living your life) **in spirit** (or: by [the] Spirit; with a Breath-effect), **and you should under no circumstance** (or: would by no means) **bring to fruition** (carry to its goal; end up with; bring to maturity) **the full rushing passion** (the over-desire; craving) **originating in flesh.**"

6. **Now I am saying this in accord with the common knowledge of experience, not down from an arrangement put upon [you]** (or: not in response to an imposed disposition or injunction).

Notice that Paul is not imposing any law or rule upon them. He respected their freedom, but offers words of wisdom that were based upon "common knowledge of experience."

7. **You see** [other MSS: Now], **I normally want** (keep on wishing; repeatedly set my will for) **all people** (all mankind; all humans) **to habitually exist being even as myself! But of course each one continues having and holding his own effect and result of grace and favor** (or: gracious gift) **from out of God: on the one hand, one person in this way, and on the other hand, another in that way.**

The first statement in this verse seems to be only something that Paul would like to have, for those who are "imitating" him. It corresponds to "**not down from an arrangement put upon [you]** (or: not in response to an imposed disposition or injunction)," in vs. 6, above. Verse 9 explains that this is not his expectation for everyone.

Observe that Paul was not teaching "uniformity of behavior," but as we have seen, above, a unity of spirit. The noun rendered "**effect and result of grace and favor**" is the *–ma* form of the word "**grace**" or "**favor**." We briefly spoke of this word in 1:7, above, but sense that Paul's use of it in this verse bears more explanation. This noun ending indicates "the effect or result" of grace, or of a favor. This might be in the form of what we would term a "gift," but not necessarily so. Grace inhabits us through the presence of God's Spirit in us. Grace is an aspect of God, and this aspect (grace) affects us. God's Spirit affects us, and the effect is what we term "favor." His presence "favors us," or "graces us." His Presence is manifested or experienced in many expressions of Himself – in us, and through us. In Eph. 3:10 Paul described such expressions as being:

> "**God's greatly diversified wisdom** (the exceedingly varied in colors [as in a tapestry or the Veil] wisdom which is God; or: the many-phased wisdom from God) [which] **could be made known – through the called-out community.**"

The very fact that God inhabits us is a gift from Him/Her to us. We call this "grace." What Paul is speaking of here in vs. 7 is an "effect" or "a result" of His favoring us with Himself in a specific way that enables and empowers us in relationships with a person of the opposite sex. This is a "gracious gift," but it is the "effect and result" of God being joined to us, and it comes "**from out of God.**" A beautiful aspect of this is that it is not a "mechanical" thing, but is personal in, and for, us: "**on the one hand, one person in this way, and on the other hand, another in that way.**" Further insight on this is gained from 16b, below: "**as the Lord has divided, apportioned and distributed a part to** (or: in; for) **each one.**"

We will come across this term *charisma* five times in chapter 12, below, but he uses this word only once in 2 Cor.,

> "**Your habitually cooperating and working together in undergirding support over us** (= on behalf of us, or, concerning our situation), **even in the need** (or: and by the [or: your] petition regarding [our] need), **[gives the result] that forth from out of many faces** (= people; or: = outward appearances) **[and] through many folks, the effect and result of grace and favor can be sent** (or: given) **unto us in the goodness, ease and well-being of grace** (or: from favor) **over our [situation]** (or: may be given in gratitude on our behalf)" (1:11).

8. **Now I am saying to the unmarried** (= single; without a spouse, i.e., not married; can refer to: widowed, or, separated – Alain Decaux) **people, and to the widows, that [it is] fine for them** (or: beautiful in them; ideal to them) **if they can** (may; should; would) **remain even as I [am].**
> [note: from Acts 26:10, where Paul says "I cast my vote," being a member of the Sanhedrin, he likely would have been a married man at that time]

9. **Yet if they are not habitually having inner strength and control, [then] they must at once marry, for it is better to proceed to marry** (or: to continue married) **than to be repeatedly set on fire** (or, as a middle: to progressively burn oneself [= with passion and desire]).

Lack of inner strength and control are situations that are common to the human condition. Paul was not placing extreme requirements upon them, but to the contrary, he shows that he was sensitive to these folks simply being human beings.

10. **Now beside this, I – not I myself, but rather, the Lord** (or: Master) **– am giving an added message to those being married: a wife is not at any point to be separated** (disunited so as to be apart from) **[her] husband**
11. **– yet, even if she should get separated or be caused to depart, let her remain unmarried or else she must at once be reconciled to [her] husband – and a husband is not to proceed in divorcing** (or: leaving, or sending away) **[his] wife!**

We see here both cultural influence in Paul's directives, and that this admonition is from the Lord. This was wisdom for the health of this unique community. Healthy relationships within the community were vital to it continuing to be a temple of God. These folks were members of the spreading of the Christ movement as it reached out into the world at large. Take note of the sense of equity in the roles (the wife/husband relationships) that is seen in these verses. This is a step beyond such relationships under the old covenant (Deut. 24:1). Verse 10b sounds like a wife could initiate a separation, but in the covenant community this was not to be the case. Likewise, in vs. 11b, the husband was not to either initiate or follow through with this. Note 13b, below, "**let her not divorce** (or: leave or send away) **[her] husband.**"

12. **Now to the rest, I, myself – not the Lord** (or: Master) **– am speaking: if any brother is having an unbelieving wife** (or: a woman not full of faith; or: unfaithful?), **and she continues mutually content** (habitually thinks it jointly profitable and easy; with [him] is agreeable and approving) **to continue dwelling and making a home with him, let him not proceed to divorce her** (or: leave her, or send her away). [note: observe the equality in vss. 12-16]

13. And a wife who is having an unbelieving husband (or: a man not full of faith; or: unfaithful?), **and this man continues mutually content to continue dwelling and making a home with her, let her not divorce** (or: leave or send away) **[her] husband.**
14. You see, the unbelieving husband (man void of faith) **has been made set-apart and remains holy and sacred within** (or: in union with) **the wife, and the unbelieving wife** (woman void of faith) **has been made set-apart and remains holy and sacred within** (or: in union with) **the brother** (= the believing husband) **– otherwise, the consequence is your children being unclean. Yet now they are set-apart** (holy and sacred ones; folks different from the common).

The equality of women and men, within the community, can be seen in how Paul lays out the same relationship situation: first from the standpoint of **the wife**, and then from the standpoint of the husband, in vs. 14 referred to as "**the brother**."

The state, or condition, of being "**made set-apart, holy and sacred**" should be understood in context of their being a part of the set-apart, called-out community within Corinth. Temples were set-apart (sacred; holy) locations. They were the residence of a deity. So being married to a person who was a member of "God's Temple" would automatically make the couple set-apart, just as being "joined to the Lord" makes a person "one spirit" with the Lord (6:17, above). We see from 14b that Paul understands the concepts of "being clean" as synonymous with "being set-apart." Here is another underlying concept: being joined to what is clean (be it a person, or the Lord) now makes a person clean. This is the new arrangement (covenant) – which is just the opposite of the old arrangement, where contact with what was unclean made a person unclean. This is why the new covenant/arrangement is such Good News. People who are joined to a member of a covenant community become members of that community and are actually now a part of God's Temple in which God displays Himself through the unveiling of His glory (Jesus Christ) within and among them.

Scholars have lost sleep over the situation concerning children, in vs. 14. Paul does not fully explain what he means by the potential of them "**being unclean**," but we can see that he is speaking metaphorically in terms of the community being God's Temple, and he is setting the minds of his listeners at ease: "**now they are set-apart** (holy and sacred ones; folks different from the common)." They, too were a part of the called-out community. The principle seems to be that just as being joined to the Lord makes us sacred/holy/set-apart; the children who are a part of this community, through being a part of a "sacred family" are also "sacred/holy and set-apart." It is God's presence that makes EVERYTHING holy, as we have come to learn. Instructive is Clement of Rome, 1st Epistle to the Corinthians (circa AD 95):
> "Join (Glue; Weld; Adhere) yourselves closely to (among; with) the set-apart (holy; sacred) folks, because the people continuously joining closely (gluing; welding; adhering; cleaving) to (among; with) them will be progressively be made holy (sacred; set-apart)."

15. So if the unbelieving (or: faith-lacking; trust-void) **one proceeds to be separating** (disuniting so as to be apart), **let this one continue separating and departing: the brother or the sister has not been nor is now enslaved** (has not been bound in servitude nor is under compulsion) **within such situations – for God has given you** [other MSS: us] **a permanent call within the midst of, and in union with, peace that is centered in harmony of the joining** [= shalom].

There is no bondage or slavery involved with being a part of a called-out community. There is freedom (Gal. 5:1). This community is an example of true freedom. The call is to a joining which is peace and harmony. The call continues within the midst of the peaceful joining which the folks of the called-out continue to embody.

16. For what have you seen or how do you know, O wife (or: dear lady; woman) **– whether you will bring health and wholeness to** (or: will rescue, save and deliver) **[your] husband** (or: man)**? Or what have you seen and how do you know, O husband** (or: dear sir; O man) **– whether you will bring**

health and wholeness to (or: will rescue, save and deliver) **[your] wife** (or: woman), **except as the Lord** [= Christ or Yahweh] **has divided, apportioned and distributed** [other MSS: parts and distributes] **a part to** (or: in; for) **each one?**

From vs. 12, above, we see that the ideal situation is for unbelieving partners to remain with their spouse and continue as a part of the community. This environment (where Christ is being manifested through the members) is the most likely place that this person that is void of trust and faith can be made whole, rescued and delivered. The timing for this to happen is up to the Lord (15:23, below), when He will "**divide, apportion and distribute a part** (Question: A "**part**" of what? A part of His life; of Himself; of the reign; of the promised inheritance; of a saved existence; of freedom, of the Fruit of the Spirit; etc.) **to, in and for each person**." What a wonderful arrangement! Paul may be alluding to Sirach 45:20, here:

> "And He placed toward (thus: added to) Aaron glory (an assumed appearance; a manifestation which called forth praise; an esteemed reputation), and gave to him an allotted inheritance; He **divided, apportioned and distributed** to them [the] first fruits of [the] increase of the first products; He prepared abundant bread in the midst of [the] first things" (LXX, JM).

We find a similar thought in the last clause of Rom. 12:3,

> "**as God divides, apportions and distributes** (or: parted) **to, in and for each one a measure of faith** (a meted amount of firm persuasion; a measured portion of trust; a [specific or allotted] ration of confidence and loyalty)."

Also instructive is Paul's statement in 2 Cor. 10:13, where he uses the same verb:

> "**Now we ourselves will not boast into what is not measured** (or: about the things that cannot be measured), **but rather, corresponding to the measure of the measuring rod** (rule; standard; canon; = sphere of allocated influence) **which God divided, apportions and gives as a part to** (in; for) **us – of a measure** (or: = sphere of influence) **to reach even as far as upon you folks**."

It is this new existence, in the new covenant, in the new creation (2 Cor. 5:17), in the realm of the Spirit… that has the very practical effect upon the relationships of wives and husbands. This is a "grace-effect," the result of the Good News of Christ within us (Col. 1:27), our expectation of manifestations that call forth praise.

Now most translations place what I have given as the last clause of vs. 16 (I follow the lead, here, of the *CLNT*) as the beginning of vs. 17 (along with what follows, here, "Let each one…"). The last part of this clause, that begins with, "**except as the Lord**," seems best fitted to Paul's rhetorical questions (here in vs. 16), and as being in line with Paul's reasoning here. Also, linguistically, what I (and the *CLNT*) have rendered "**except**" (*ei mē*) is the most often chosen rendering of these particles, which in themselves are literally "if not." Another suggested rendering is, "aside from that…" Next, let us ponder the implications of what I have set off as the final statement of this verse…

Let each one thus be habitually walking about (= continue living your life in this way), **as God has permanently called** (summoned) **[him].**

We suggest that Paul has two layers of meaning in this admonition. We will first discuss the spiritual layer, and then with vs. 17, below, functioning as a transition to second layer concerning life in the community, we will, beginning with vs. 18, be following Paul into the practical applications.

Keep in mind the last statement of vs. 15, which is, "**a permanent call within the midst of, and in union with, peace that is centered in harmony of the joining**" (*cf* Eph. 2:15). The core idea of God "calling or summoning" people is to be His followers, His called-out community, His Temple. We see this in Gal. 1:6,

> "**I am constantly amazed** (or: I continue filled with wonder) **that you folks are so quickly being progressively transplanted** (or, as a middle voice: are thus now quickly transferring yourselves or changing your stand) **from the One** (or: that [message]) **calling** (summoning) **you people, within Christ's grace** (or: in [the] favor of the Anointed One), **on into a different sort of**

"message of goodness" (unto a different evangel, "good news," or gospel; = into an imitation and alternative message of goodness, ease or well-being) – **which is NOT "another" one of the same kind** (= not just another version)!"

Another view of this is seen in 1 Thes. 4:7,

"**For God did not call us on the basis of uncleanness** (or: does not invite us [to be] on [a path lived in] a soiled condition or a dirty environment), **but rather within the sphere of set-apartness** (or: sacred difference; = in a manner commensurate to covenant living)."

And we also have Eph. 4:4,

"**[being] one body and one spirit** (attitude and effect of the Breath), **according as you folks were** (or: are) **also called** (summoned) **within the midst of one expectation** (or: in union with one expectant hope) **of your calling** (or: summons; invitation)."

Now Paul did NOT say, "as this person has personally decided and chosen." No, the distribution of the parts of God's reign (or, body, temple, Life, etc.) are "**as GOD has given a permanent call**" to each person. The verb "**call/summon**" is in the perfect tense, which means that the action has lasting, or permanent, results. The "**divided, apportioned and distributed**" in this verse is parallel to "**permanently called** (summoned)." Both verbs in the perfect tense are introduced by "**as.**" "**As the Lord... as God...**" Both of these speak of the works of God within the individual. The Father/Mother is the One that gives birth to the child; the child is the result of THEIR union, and remains as such. Even Jesus passed through this process, as being one of us, as we read in Acts 13:33,

"**God has filled this out of [our] midst** (or: has fully fulfilled this) **for** (or: to; in) **our children** [other MSS: us, their children,] **in raising** (resurrecting; standing back up again) **Jesus – even as it has been written in the second Psalm,**

'**You are My Son; I Myself have given birth to You today** (or: today I Myself have become Your Father).'" [Ps. 2:7]

That this had reference to Christ's position (the Chief Corner-stone of the Temple) and function (the Chief Priest of the new priesthood, of the order of Melchizedek) is seen in Heb. 5:5-6,

"**Thus also, Christ did not glorify Himself** (give Himself a reputation; have an opinion of Himself) **to be born** (or: to come to be) **a Chief Priest, but to the contrary, [it was] the One at one point speaking to Him,**

'**You are My Son; today I have given birth to** (or: conceived) **You** (= become Your Father).' [Ps. 2:7]

Just as also in a different place He is saying,

'**You [are] a Priest on into the Age, down from** (or: in accord and in line with) **Melchizedek's station** (order; lineup; alignment; placement; appointment; succession).'"
[Ps. 110:4]

In the same way, vs. 16b, here, speaks of membership, or being a constituent part, of the Temple (in Corinth, and elsewhere). It was also a call to priesthood (Rev. 1:6). We should also observe that the last statement of vs. 16 leads directly into vs. 17ff, and that Paul's expanded explanation of being "called" reflects back on the practical level of what he has just said.

17. **And thus am I habitually arranging throughout** (or: thoroughly setting in order; fully prescribing or distributing; or: arranging the troops) – **within the midst of** (or: in union with) **all the called-out communities** (or: among all the summoned-forth folks).

18. **Was anyone called** (invited; summoned) **being a person having been circumcised? Let him not be de-circumcised** (have the marks of circumcision covered over)! **Has anyone been called [being] in [the condition of, or, among the group termed] uncircumcision? He is not to proceed in being circumcised!**

19. **The circumcision is nothing, and the uncircumcision is nothing – but to the contrary [what matters is the] observing and keeping of the goals implanted from God** (or: the impartations of the finished product within, which is God; or: God's inward directives to [His] end).

Verse 19 is an expression of the central theme of the Good News that came through Paul. The old covenant markers (figured by the term "circumcision") have passed away (2 Cor. 5:17). Likewise, Gentile inclusion (those that were not circumcised) is not the entirety of the new game (*cf* Rom. 11:17ff). There was now "ONE NEW HUMANITY" (Eph. 2:15, and its context). Now the new covenant/arrangement was "**progressively giving My Laws into their thought** (into that which goes through their mind; into their perception and comprehension), **and I shall progressively imprint them** (write or inscribe marks) **upon their hearts**" (Heb. 8:10). It is the work of the Holy Spirit to "**implant** (write)" His **goals** and impart "the finished product [Christ] within" as we are being led by the Spirit (Rom. 8:14) from God's "inward directives."

Our outward vocation (calling; summoning) or position in society has no bearing upon God's reign within and among us. So Paul continues...

20. **Let each person – within the midst of the calling** (vocation; = station, position, situation or circumstances) **in which** (or: to which) **he was** (or: is) **called** (summoned) **– keep on remaining** (dwelling; abiding) **within this.**

This has a dual meaning: practical and spiritual. It is almost a restatement of 16b, above:
> "**Let each one thus be habitually walking about** (= continue living your life in this way), **as God has permanently called** (summoned) **[him]**."
But in the next verse, he speaks to the natural realm...

21. **Were you called** (summoned) **[while being] a slave? Quit letting it be a concern or worry for you** (Do not continue to let it be a care to you). **But nonetheless, if you also continue to have the power and ability to become free** (or: a freeman), **make very much use of** (or: all the more employ) **[it]!**
> (or: Instead, even if you presently have means to come to be at liberty, [choose] rather to use [your present situation].)

22. **In fact, the person within the Lord** [= Christ or Yahweh] **– being one that was called** (summoned) **[when being] a slave – is [the] Lord's freed-person** (or: exists being [Christ's or Yahweh's] emancipated slave). **Likewise, the person being one that was called** (summoned) **[when being] free, or a freedman, is Christ's slave.**

Verse 22 instructs us about how Paul felt about social position and slavery. In the light of God's reign, such issues were insignificant. Yet vs. 21 informs us of his views concerning everyday life on the natural plane, and thus explains vs. 20. Notice how many times he uses the word "**called** (summoned)" in vs. 18, above, and now in these three verses (20-22). This is instructs us as to what is paramount for our lives: our **summons** to be a part of His Temple, a member of the Christ Body within the earth, our place for functioning as representatives of His reign among the nations. Conzelmann observes in all of this that "Paul does not distinguish between outward and inward and does not make freedom the result of taking ourselves in hand" (ibid p 126 n 14). This being true, we see in Gal. 3:27-28 that he spoke to a different level, or sphere, of existence for the called-out communities:
> "**For you see** (or: It follows that) **as many of you folks as were immersed into Christ, at once clothed yourselves with Christ** (or: were plunged into so as to be enveloped by then saturated and permeated with Anointing – or, the Anointed One – instantly entered within and put on [the/an] Anointing)! **Within** [Him; us], **there is not** (there does not exist) **Jew nor Greek** (or: Hellenist); **within, there is not** (does not exist) **slave nor freeman; within, there is not** (does not exist) **'male and female'; for it follows that, you folks all exist being one within Christ Jesus** (or: for you see, all you people are one person, centered in, and in union with, an Anointing from Jesus)."
And in 12:13, below, we observe:

> "**For we, ourselves – within the midst of one Spirit** (or: in union with one Breath-effect and attitude) **– are all submerged into one body** (or: were all immersed into, so as to be enveloped by, one body) **– whether Jews or Greeks** (or: Hellenists), **whether slaves or free folks – and we all are** (or: were) **made** (or: caused) **to drink one Spirit** (or: spirit; Breath-effect; Attitude)."

A third witness is Col. 3:9b-11,

> "**[Be] folks at once stripping off from yourselves** (undressing yourselves from; or: go out and away from) **the old humanity** (the old human; = the old Adam), **together with its practices, and then [be] suddenly clothing yourselves with** (or: entering within) **the new one** (the fresh one which existed only recently), **the one being continuously** (or: repeatedly; habitually; progressively) **renewed** (made back up new again, in kind and character) **into full, accurate, added, intimate and experiential knowledge and insight which is down from and corresponds to the image** (an exactly formed visible likeness) **of its Creator** (of the One framing and founding it from a state of wildness and disorder), **wherein** (or: in which place) **there is no Greek** [figure of the multitudes who are non-Jews, and of those who are cultured and civilized] **and Jew** [figure of a covenant people of God], **circumcision and uncircumcision** [figure for religious in-groups and out-groups; there is no longer a covenant people versus non-covenant people], **barbarian** [foreigner who speaks a different language], **Scythian** [figure or example of wild, uncivilized groups], **slave, freeman, but to the contrary, Christ [is] all, and within all**
> > (or: Christ [is] all humanity, and within all mankind; or: Christ [is] everything or all things, and within everything and all things; [note: the Greek is plural, and is either masculine, signifying "mankind," or neuter, signifying all creation, in these phrases])."

The two statements in this verse, connected by "**Likewise**," are parallel, both presenting the eschatological reality of the new creation, even though they are contrasting metaphors. Paul was both. The Lord (Christ Jesus) had freed Him from the Law (*cf* Rom. 6-7; Gal. 5:1), but he called Christ "Master (Lord; Owner)," and thus termed himself "a slave of Jesus Christ" (Rom. 1:1). Paul states the same admonition twice (indicating its importance) in Rom. 6:18, 22a,

> "**Now, being set free** (or: liberated) **from the Sin** (failure; error), **you folks are** (or: were suddenly) **enslaved** (made slaves) **to justice** (= to covenant participation in solidarity)
> > (or: in the Way pointed out; for fair and equitable dealings; by the Well-ordered, Righteous Existence [in Christ]; to rightwised relationship and [covenantal] behavior)....
> **But now being folks set free from the Sin** (from failure; from error; from missing the target; from deviation) **yet being enslaved by** (to; in; for) **God, you folks continue having** (habitually hold and possess) **your fruit unto the quality and sphere of being set-apart** (into a sacred difference)."

So viewing vss. 21-22 on the metaphorical level, a Jew could remain a Jew that was emancipated from the Law and into Christ, and the pagan who had lived free from the Law of Moses now could experience the spiritual freedom which was considered to be a slave of Christ – through being "joined" to the Lord.

23. **You folks were bought, as at a marketplace: [you are] of value** (or: [there was] value, worth and honor involved in the price). **Do not continue becoming slaves of humanity** (or: Do not repeatedly come to be slaves of people).

They had been purchased when they were slaves (to sin, to addictions, to self-interests, etc. – and to the Law, if they were a part of Second Temple Judaism), but now they were "the Lord's freed-person" (vs. 22). Paul said it this way, in Rom. 8:2,

> "**For you see, the Law of Life's spirit, joined with [the] Anointing of Jesus emancipated you from this law from the Mistake, and which is the Death.**"

Now the common rendering of the first statement of vs. 23 is represented by the ESV: "You were bought with a price." The word "price" is *timē*, and one of the lexical meanings is "price." But the "price" indicates "an estimate of worth, or value." As recognition of another's "worth," this word means that we "honor" the person, and have "respect" for him or her. The verb *timaō* means to "honor, revere, respect," when dealing with people. When dealing with things it means "set a price, assess the value, etc." Now there are only two words in this sentence, in the Greek text: the verb ("you were purchased"), and the noun *timē* (in the genitive or ablative case). Since "purchasing" involves "paying a price" for something, it seemed redundant to add the word in the sense of "price." All that Paul needed to say was, "You folks were bought, as at a marketplace" (this last phrase is inherent in the verb). That means "a price was paid." This reading of Paul puts the emphasis on the "money" of the transaction. Now this interpretation has its place, and its "value," but we think that it leaves important nuances on the table.

By inserting the copulative "**[you are]**," the simple genitive, "**of value**," makes perfect sense and strongly leads into the second statement of the verse: "**Do not continue becoming slaves**..." The second option for a copula, "**[there was]**," reads Paul as saying that there was something of "**value, worth and honor involved in the price**," which could allude to the death of Christ, and the value/honor in the price that He paid for submitting to the death of the cross (which, of course, is true), or it could also mean that He saw "**value**, worth and honor" in that which He **bought** (like "the pearl of great price" in Mat. 13:46). Art White points us to Mat. 13:44, as well:

> "**The reign** (or: kingdom; sovereignty; dominion) **of the heavens and atmospheres exists being** (or: is) **like a treasure – having been hidden** (or: being concealed) **within the midst of a field – which, upon finding, a person hid** (concealed) **[again] and then, from the joy he has, he proceeds leaving [it] and one after another sells as many things as he is then possessing and is proceeding in PURCHASING THAT FIELD**."

Art pointed out that in Mat. 13:38 Jesus had defined His metaphor of "the field" as being "the world" – i.e., the aggregate of humanity. Dan Kaplan sees the same indication in regard to the "pearl of great price/value" in vs. 46, noting that pearls are "grown" in the sea, which is another symbol for humanity. He further saw the "clam" as a picture of the Law that had the pearl hidden within it, until it was opened up.

The rendering of 23a, above, "**[you are] of value**," calls to mind an interesting thought that is presented in *The Gospel of Philip* (p 64, plate 110 – via Jean-Yves Leloup edition),

> "When the pearl is cast down into mud, it does not become greatly despised (= lose its value; Leloup)... Compare the sons of God, wherever they may be. They still have value in the eyes of their Father" (trans. by Wesley W. Isenberg, *The Nag Hammadi Library*, James M. Robinson, Gen. Ed., Harper & Row Pub. 1977 p 137).

So in the realm of the kingdom/reign/sovereign-influence of God, they should no longer live as enslaved people, becoming enslaved to human systems (religious, political or social) or "the will of people" (in the sphere of God's reign), but rather, they should be "led by the Spirit" and do what they "see [their] Father doing" (*cf* Jn. 5:19).

24. **Let each person, brothers** (folks from the same womb; = fellow believers; family members) **– within that in which he was** (or: she is) **called** (summoned) **– keep on remaining** (dwelling; abiding) **at God's side and presence within the midst of this.**

He is speaking their "calling/summoning" here on the level of their outward social position, in the stratified society of the Roman Empire – in the condition within which he or she existed when the summons came. This admonition is parallel to 16b, above, but with a change of verb – and so a change of emphasis. In vs. 16 the emphasis was on the daily way of living a life; here it is on where and in what realm one is dwelling, remaining, abiding. The clause "**remaining** (dwelling; abiding) **at God's side and presence**" speaks of the realm of God's reign (or: "abiding in the Vine" – Jn. 15:1ff), and His Presence – "**within the midst of**" which, their life is hidden with Christ, in the midst of God (Col. 3:3). The object of the preposition is the term "**this**," which refers back to "**within that in which he was** (or: she is) **called** (summoned)," i.e., whether being "a slave or a freed-person" (vs. 22). That existential situation, in this life, had no bearing on dwelling at God's side and presence. God has come to dwell with US! *Cf* Rev. 21:3.

This verse presents two "**within**" phrases. Paul's point, and emphasis, is the second one – the one within which they are to "**keep on remaining** (dwelling; abiding)" – "**at God's side and presence.**" He referred to this in Eph. 2:6. We are to continue living/dwelling in this realm – He is our abiding place!
> "O Yahweh, You Yourself have become our Habitation (dwelling place) in generation after generation" (Ps. 90:1; CVOT; additions mine).
> "He who is dwelling in the concealment of the Supreme shall lodge in the shadow of Him Who-Suffices" (Ps. 91:1; CVOT).

Before moving on to the next section of Paul's letter, let us hear the admonitions from Peter, in 1 Pet. 2:
> 11. **Folks that are loved** (Beloved ones)**: I am presently calling you alongside to encourage, aid, comfort and admonish you, as resident aliens** (exiles; sojourners; ones dwelling beside citizens in a foreign country) **and temporary residents** (expatriates; strangers) **to continually hold yourselves away from the fleshly over-desires** (passions; full-rushing upon things), **which things are constantly warring** (doing military service; battling) **down against the soul** (the inner self and being),
> 12. **continuously holding your beautiful behavior** (your fine and ideal turning yourselves back around) **among the multitudes** (the companies; the associations; the ethnic groups; the nations; the castes; the non-Jews, or, Gentiles), **to the end that, within what thing they are continually speaking down pertaining to you folks** (repeatedly speaking against you) **as of ones constantly doing the worthless and things of bad quality** (or: as of evildoers or criminals; as of those repeatedly creating bad situations or forming what not ought to be), **repeatedly looking upon and observing as eyewitnesses the outcome from the beautiful actions** (the fine deeds; the ideal and honorable works), **they may glorify** (or: give a good opinion of) **God, within a day of inspection and overseeing care.**
> 13. **Because of, and by, the Lord** [= Yahweh or Christ], **you folks are to be humbly aligned in and to every human creation and with every societal invention**
>> (or: be subordinated to every human framing; let yourselves be arranged under for support of every founding or institution pertaining to mankind which brings order to a state of wildness)**: whether to** (or: by; for) **a king, as to** (or: by; for) **one being superior** (or: constantly holding over [others]; = as a prominent cultural institution),
> 14. **or to** (or; by; for) **governors** (government officials; rulers; leaders; guides), **as to** (or: by; for; with) **those being regularly sent** (or: dispatched) **by Him unto a maintaining of right, in regard to doers of worthlessness**
>> (or: into a correction from out of the way pointed out pertaining to those creating bad situations; unto an administering of justice, fairness and equity of situations affected by evildoers) – **yet on the other hand, [sent] unto a commendation** (a praise; applause) **of those habitually doing good things** (performing with virtue; constructing excellence).
> 15. **Because thus is God's will** (or: For God's intent and purpose exists in this manner)**: folks habitually doing good things** (constructing excellence; performing with virtues; creating goodness) **to repeatedly muzzle** (continuously gag; thus: progressively silence) **the ignorance of senseless and thoughtless people** (humans without intellect and prudence; unreasonable folks);
> 16. **as free folks** (those not bound) – **and not continually holding** (or: having) **the freedom as a covering** (or: a veil) **of worthlessness** (bad quality; evil; poorness of situation) – **but still, as God's slaves.**
> 17. **Value everyone** (Honor all)! **Habitually love** (Keep up the urge toward union of; Repeatedly accept) **the brotherhood** (= the organism of fellow-believers)! **Practice reverence to God** (or: Habitually fear God; Be constantly respecting and revering God)! **Be continuously valuing and showing honor to the king** (or: the One Who reigns).

18. **The domestics** (house servants or slaves; members of a household), **those habitually being subordinated** (being humbly aligned and subjected for support) **by** (or: to; for) **the owners** (masters)**: [conduct yourselves] in all fear and respect – not only to the good and lenient** (reasonable, suitable; equitable; gentle; considerate) **ones, but also to the crooked folks –**

19. **for this [is] grace: if through [the] conscience, which is God,** (or: through awareness pertaining to God; or: by means of a joint-knowing with God; or: because of consciousness of God), **someone is continuing to bear and hold up under distress or pains** (griefs; sorrows; anxieties; sufferings), **continuously experiencing it wrongfully** (unjustly; contrarily, in regard to fairness and right relationship; undeservedly)**!**

20. **For what sort of credible report** (honorable rumor; credit; fame; praiseworthy reputation) **[is it] if, being ones habitually doing what is wrong** (failing to hit the target; sinning) **and being repeatedly beaten and struck with a fist** [*p*72 & other MSS: repeatedly lopped-off and pruned], **you folks will continue** [*p*72 & other MSS read: you are constantly] **remaining under and enduring [it]? But to the contrary, if while habitually practicing virtue** (doing good; constructing excellence) **and [at the same time] repeatedly experiencing such bad treatment** (or: continually suffering) **you will continue** [*p*72 reads: you are constantly] **humbly remaining under, enduring and supporting [it], this [is] grace at the side of** (or: from beside; = in the presence of) **God,**

21. **for into this you are called** (or: were invited), **because Christ also experienced [this]** (or: suffered) **over you folks** (or: for your sakes), **leaving continuously below** (or: behind) **in you** (or: with and for you) **an underwriting** (a writing under which you are to write or copy; hence: a pattern; a model) **to the end that you could** (or: would) **follow-on in the footprints of Him**

22.   **"Who does not make a mistake** (Who did not perform failure; Who does no sin; Who does not construct failure to hit the target), **nor is** (or: was) **deceitful bait** (fraud; guile) **found in His mouth;"** [Isa. 53:9]

23. **Who, being repeatedly reviled** (harshly and bitingly rebuked and insulted), **was not reviling back** (answering insult with insult; taking the position of harsh, biting rebuke); **continuously** (or: repeatedly) **suffering** (experiencing ill treatment), **he was not threatening, but kept on giving [the situation] over to** (committing [it] with; entrusting [it] in) **the One at His side: the One constantly sifting, separating and deciding** (or: judging) **fairly** (equitably; following the Path of the Way pointed out, bringing situations to a rightwised condition),

24. **Who, Himself, bore back up again our failures** (our mistakes; our times of falling short or to the side of the target; our sins and errors) [Isa. 53:4, 12] **within His body upon the tree** (the wood; the stake), **to the end that, being folks suddenly coming to be parted away from the failures** (mistakes; errors; sins; misses of the target), **we can** (or: would; may) **live in** (or: by; for; with) **the eschatological deliverance to fairness and equity, in rightwised relationships, in the Path of the Way pointed out** (or: = in covenant participation), **where "you folks are** (or: were) **healed** (or: cured) **in the wound** (or: by the welt; in the bruise of the blow)." [Isa. 53:5]

25. **For you folks were continuing to be "like sheep, being habitually caused to wander** (being led astray; or, as a middle: people constantly wandering away)," [Isa. 53:6] **but now in contrast, "you are** (or: were) **turned around and made to return, upon" [the will of; the herding of] the Shepherd and Overseer of** (Supervisor of; the One who watches over) **your souls** (your inner beings).

But now Paul returns to practical matters for this special community. Verses 25-40 appear to be answers to questions that the group in Corinth has sent to him.

25. **Now about the virgins** (or: unmarried girls of marriageable age) **and celibate women, I do not hold** (or: have) **an arrangement put upon [you]** (or: an imposed disposition or injunction) **which originates from [the] Lord** [= Yahweh, or Christ]**, but I continue giving [you] the result of experience-gained knowledge, as being one having been mercied** (shown mercy) **by** (or: under) **[the] Lord, to exist being one full of faith** (or: to be trustworthy, loyal and faithful).

26. I therefore reason from custom [that] this continues to be inherently beautiful (fine; ideal; good form) – **because of the present necessity which has been placed within through compulsion** (= a time or circumstance of stress) – **that it is ideal** (fine; beautiful) **for a person to continue being thus** (= as he is; or: for humanity to continue existing in this way)**:**
27. Have you been bound together so that you are now tied to a wife? Stop (or: Do not continue) **seeking loosing or release. Have you been released so that you are now loosed from a wife? Stop** (or: Do not continue) **seeking a wife.**
28. Yet even if you should marry, you are not making a mistake (or: missing the goal). **And if the virgin or celibate woman should marry, she does not fail** (is not making a mistake or missing the goal). **Still, such folks** (= those who do) **will continue or proceed having pressure and constricting stress, in the flesh** (= their natural lives) – **and as for myself, I [would] spare you folks [that]** (or: I advise thrift and restraint [in this] for you people).

In considering these verses, we should keep in mind that Paul was speaking to relational situations that pertained to them being a group that was functioning as God's Temple, His holy place within the city of Corinth. Notice, in vs. 26, that Paul says that he is "reasoning from custom." We, almost 2000 years later, should not extract from this specific situation anything more than an understanding of that time, that situation, and how God was leading Paul to be a paraclete for 1st century Corinth. We should be led by God's Spirit for our own special times and situations.

Notice, again from vs. 26, that he was speaking "**because of the present necessity which has been placed within through compulsion** (= a time or circumstance of stress)." Paul was viewing all this from the eschatological window of the 1st century, and what he apparently perceived was the closing season of the old age, and the birth-pangs (Rom. 8:22) that the new creation was experiencing at that time – throughout the Empire. The Jewish rebellion brought a time of great stress. Paul may have been recalling Jesus' words, later recorded in Mat. 24:

> 16. "**at that time, let the people within the midst of Judea progressively escape** (flee; take flight) **into the hills and mountains.**
> 17. "**Let the person upon the housetop** (roof) **not descend** (= go downstairs) **to pick up or carry away the things** (= his possessions) **from out of his house,**
> 18. "**and let not the one in the midst of the field turn back behind to pick up his cloak** (= to get a coat or outer garment).
> 19. "**Now it will progressively be a difficult or tragic time for the pregnant women and nursing mothers in those days**....
> 37. "**For you see, even as [it was in] the days of Noah, thus** (in this same way) **will progressively be the presence of the Son of the Man** (= Adam's son; = the son who is human; = the eschatological Messianic figure).
> 38. "**For as people kept on being** (or: habitually were) **within those days – the ones before the down-wash** (the deluge; the flood; the cataclysm) – **habitually eating and drinking; by custom marrying and by habit giving** (or: taking) **in marriage, up to the day in which Noah entered into the ark;**
> 39. "**and they did not know** (were not aware; took no note of the situation) **until the down-wash** (deluge; flood; cataclysm) **came and washed [the] whole population away** (or: picked up all [the] people to sweep [them] away)...

29. Now I forcefully declare this, brothers (folks from the same womb; = family)**, the season** (fitting and appointed situation; fertile moment) **now exists being one that has been contracted** (drawn together so as to be shortened, curtailed and limited)**! So that for the remaining [time]** (for the rest of [the season]; henceforth)**, those presently having wives** (or: the men now holding a woman) **should proceed in being as not presently having [them],**
> [note: in the culture and time which Paul is here addressing, the term "married," or, "having a woman" referred to both formal marriage, and to a man and a woman living together]

30. **and those presently weeping** (lamenting; shedding tears), **[should be] as [if] not weeping, and those presently rejoicing, [should be] as [if] not rejoicing, and those habitually buying at the market place, [should be] as [if] not constantly holding on to it** (owning it; keeping it held down; retaining it; = not being possessive),

31. **and those habitually employing** (making use of) **the System** (the ordered arrangement and world of culture, economy, religion and government; or: secular society) **as not folks who are constantly using it down** (exploiting it; making excessive employment or over-use of it), **for the outward fashion, mode of circumstance, condition, form-appearance** (or: character, role, phase, configuration, manner) **of this System** (ordered world of culture, religion and society) **is progressively passing by** (= the present scheme of things is changing and passing away).

The "**season**" or "appointed situation" to which Paul was referring was the time in which he was living: the transition period between the old age of the Law and the new age of the Messiah. This "season," or "fertile moment" in history had been called "the Day of the Lord," by the prophets, as in Zeph. 1:14-15,

"Because the great Day of [the] LORD [is] near: near and exceedingly soon (or: quick; swift). [The] Voice (or: sound) of (or: from) [the] Day of [the] LORD has been set and in now arranged as bitter and harsh (sharp; hard to accept) – an able, powerful Day of swelling emotion (the inherent fervor; the internal swelling that gives rise to an impulse and mental bent which may be expressed in strong emotion, such as anger or wrath; a vigorous upsurge of [God's] nature) [will be] That Day; a Day of anguish (affliction) and distress; a Day of disappearance and losing sight-of; a Day of a thick cloud and darkness; a Day of cloud and vapor (mist; fog)" (LXX, JM).

This was apocalyptic language that pointed to the end of the Mosaic age: a period from the execution of Jesus until the destruction of Jerusalem, and of the temple (that would "disappear" – Zeph. 1:15). *Cf* Dan. 12:1. In Mat. 24:8-9, Jesus told His followers:

"**Yet all these things [are but] a beginning of birth pangs** [note: = travail to birth something {new}; also: = a time of distress]. **At that time people will be repeatedly handing you men over into pressure** (squeezing; tribulation; affliction), **and then, they will, one after another, kill you. Further, you will continue being men that were detached [by society], repeatedly treated with ill-will, and constantly hated by all the ethnic multitudes** (or: the nations) – **because of My Name.**"

So, how was the "season" being "**contracted**, shortened and curtailed" (vs. 29, above)? This, most likely, was an allusion to Jesus' words concerning the end of the Mosaic age (the old covenant arrangement) in Mat. 24. There Jesus said,

21. **"You see, 'at that time there will be great pressure** (squeezing; compression; affliction; tribulation) **of the sort that has not happened** (occurred; been birthed; come to be) **from [the] beginning of [this] ordered arrangement** (system; adorned order; systematic disposition; world) **until now – neither under any circumstances could it have occurred** (happened; come to be).' [Joel 2:2; Dan. 12:1]

22. **"Furthermore, if those days were not curtailed** (or: except those days be cut short), **no flesh** (= people) **[at] all would likely be rescued** (delivered; kept safe). **Yet, because of the picked out and chosen folks, those days will proceed being curtailed** (cut short).

When Paul wrote this letter, it was within the generation of which Jesus said that these things would happen (Mat. 24:34). Similarly, what He said as recorded in Lu. 21:6-36 was spoken to His disciples, for their lives and in their time. Consider Mat. 16:28,

"**there are some of the folks presently standing here who under no circumstances can taste** (= partake of, or, experience) **death, until they would** (or: should) **perceive and see the Son of the Man** (= the eschatological Messianic figure) **progressively coming.**"

Cf also Mat. 23:36.

That season (that ended with the Jewish war with Rome, AD 66-70) would reach a climax in just over a decade, and the Jewish world would be changed forever. Paul knew that they were living in a conjunction of two ages: one ending and another one beginning. It was a season in which the old arrangement was passing away and the new one was in the process of being brought to birth. As Jesus put it, in Mat. 24:8, "**all these things [are but] a beginning of birth pangs**." Rev. 12:1-17 gives an apocalyptic picture of the season that began with the advent of Jesus as Israel's Messiah being born and then continued in the resulting situations being played out throughout Paul's days – which involved the birthing of the Body of the Messiah (often called the period of the "early church"). So for Paul, in Corinth and the other cities of the Empire (especially where the covenant communities included Jews), life was soon to drastically change. The center of Second Temple Judaism was about to be destroyed.

With all of this in mind, we can better understand Paul's advice from 29b-31 to live in a non-normal way: it is an apocalyptic perspective; it's not "business as usual" and the "times" are calling for drastic measures. Think back to some of Jesus' sayings which were counter-cultural because of what was soon to come. In Lu. 12 He told a parable of a "senseless farmer" who said to himself, "**Soul** (Self), **you are now possessing many goods [that] continue lying [in storage] on unto many years. Continue resting and taking it easy: eat, drink, continue easy-minded and keep on being merry**" (vs. 19). And that night, he died. So Jesus said to His disciples, "**On account of this I am now saying to you folks, Quit being anxious and overly concerned for the soul – what you should eat! Nor for your body – what you should put on**" (vs. 22). There are many other examples.

In vs. 31, here, Paul tells them that "**the outward fashion, mode of circumstance, condition, form-appearance** (or: character, role, phase, configuration, manner) **of this System** (ordered world of culture, religion and society) **is progressively passing by** (= the present scheme of things is changing and passing away)." After AD 70 the physical temple in Jerusalem would be gone – as would the "called-out community" in Jerusalem. They were living in a "fertile moment" that would soon be "curtailed and limited (vs. 29)," so they should be thinking ahead to realize that soon it would not be as it always had been. The destruction of Jerusalem had far-reaching effects.

However, there was another level of meaning to his admonitions in these verses. Their very existence as now being "the temple of God" had changed everything for them. Paul had said, elsewhere, that the ethnic multitudes (Gentiles) had been grafted into Israel's olive tree (Rom. 11:17) and were now, "**come to be** (were birthed; are generated; are suddenly become) **near**" the Promise, because Christ had,

> "**destroyed the middle wall of the fenced enclosure** (or: the partition or barrier wall)**: the enmity** (cause of hate, alienation, discord and hostility; characteristics of an enemy), **rendering useless** (nullifying; rendering down in accord with inactivity and unemployment) **the Law** (or: the custom; = the Torah)..." (Eph. 2:12-15a).

Furthermore, in God's reign,

> "**Within** [Him; us]**, there is not** (there does not exist) **Jew nor Greek** (or: Hellenist)**; within, there is not** (does not exist) **slave nor freeman; within, there is not** (does not exist) **'male and female'; for it follows that, you folks all exist being one within Christ Jesus**" (Gal. 3:28).

Talk about the fashion and mode of existence changing for the called-out folks! With these things in mind, we can better perceive Paul's point of view that he was sharing, here, with the Corinthians. As we look back, over the centuries, we can see how many times the form and fashion of the outward System changed, throughout all the world. But, life in the kingdom was life in the resurrection, and in the resurrection,

> "**men neither continue marrying** (taking wives)**, nor [are women] continuing being given in marriage, but to the contrary, they continue being** (or: constantly exist being)**, as it were, agents – within the atmospheres** (or: like messengers in the midst of the heavens; or: as folks with the message, centered in the skies)**!**" (Mk. 12:25).

The coming of Christ, and then the giving of God's Spirit, changed everything for those who had been apprehended to be Christ in the earth. Christ was on the move, continually "coming and going" (Rev. 1:8, *JMNT*). And as we read in Acts 6:7, "**the *Logos* of God** (or: God's idea, message; the Word from God, which was God) **kept on progressively growing and increasing** (also: = God's Reason was spreading out like a growing Vine)." Witherington observes: "This is not a model of asceticism, but of putting all earthly goods into a heavenly perspective..." He quotes N.R. Petersen, *Rediscovering Paul: Philemon and the Sociology of Paul's Narrative World*, Fortress, 1985 p 135,

> "Paul integrates his social instructions within a symbolic universe rather than a social one, for the consequences of compliance or non-compliance are not determined socially, that is by social actors, but eschatologically by the Lord..." (ibid p 180 n 42).

So now, Paul continues by giving examples of what he means...

32. **Now I intend** (purpose and want) **you folks to constantly exist being free from anxiety** (care; concern; worry). **The unmarried one** (= the person who is not co-habiting; the single person) **is habitually concerned about and caring for the Lord's things** (= the issues pertaining to Yahweh; the matters that come from and belong to Christ)**: how he or she can please** (be accommodating to) **the Lord.**

The first statement, here, reveals Paul's intent for all these admonitions. It was not to bind them with rules, but rather to help them be "**free from anxiety** (care; concern; worry)." His reasoning is easy to follow. To the called-out folks in Thessalonica, he wrote in 1 Thes. 5:

> 1. **But concerning the times and the fitting situations** (or: specific seasons or occasions; fertile periods; mature moments), **brothers, you have no need [for it] to be continually written to you,**
> 2. **for you yourselves are accurately aware** (know exactly from having seen) **that a day of, from and which is the Lord thus continually comes** (is habitually and repeatedly coming and going; is presently coming) **as a thief in a night** (or: within [the] night).
>> [comment: the day of Yahweh was a term that figured a time of judging and hard times, in the Old Testament; e.g., *cf* Joel 1:15 and 2:1-2; Jer. 30:7; Amos 5:18]
> 3. **So whenever they may be repeatedly saying, "Peace and security from falling** (or: safety; stability)**," then** (at that time) **sudden and unexpected ruin** (or: a surprise of destruction) **is presently standing upon them, just as the birth-pang for the pregnant woman** (or: to the one having [a child] in the womb), **and they may by no means flee out or make an escape.**
> 4. **Yet you yourselves, brothers, are not continuously in darkness to the end that the day may** (or: would) **suddenly take you down** (grasp or seize you in a corresponding manner) **as a thief,**
> 5. **for you see, you all are sons of** (or: which are) **Light and sons of** (or: which are [the]) **Day! We are not of night, nor of darkness.**

In 1 Jn. 2:18a we read,

> "**O undeveloped ones or folks of the age to be educated** (or: servants, little boys and little girls who might be hit in training and for discipline), **it continues being** (or: is progressively) **a last hour** (= an *eschaton* of the Day, or the closing moment [of the age]..."

It was this kind of awareness that fits with Paul's advice to the folks in Corinth.

33. **Yet the one being married is constantly concerned about and repeatedly caring for the involvements of the System** (the issues pertaining to his world of culture, religion, economy and government)**: how he can please and be accommodating to the woman** ([his] wife), **and thus, he has been divided so as to be distributed in parts!**

The last clause of this verse crystalizes Paul's point for this whole passage. The follower of Christ, who is to live AS BEING God's Temple, cannot have a divided mind.

> "**A two-souled** (or: = divided-willed; or: = emotionally split) **adult male** (or: person) **[is] unstable** (unfixed; inconstant; turbulent; fickle; or: = indecisive) **in all his ways and paths**" (Jas. 1:8).

Jesus had put it in these terms:

> "**No one continues being able to continue being, or performing as, a slave for two owners. You see, he will either proceed in hating** (or: inwardly detaching from or: regarding with ill will)

the one and will continue loving the different one, or he will continue holding firmly to and having instead the one, and will proceed despising (having a negative attitude and disposition toward) **the different one. You folks are not able to continue being, or performing as, slaves for God and at the same time for money and riches!**" (Mat. 6:24)

This same point is said another way, in 2 Tim. 2:4,

"**No one serving a tour of duty as a soldier** (currently performing military service or being at war) **habitually intertwines or entangles himself in** (or: by; with) **everyday affairs of the course of life, in order that he may please the one enlisting him in military service.**"

34. **Further, the unmarried** (or: = single) **woman – as well as the virgin** (or: unmarried mature young woman of marriageable age) **– is habitually concerned about and caring for the Lord's things** (= issues; matters)**: [i.e.,] that she may continually exist being set-apart** (holy; sacred; different from the profane) **– both in [her] body and in [her] spirit** (with other MSS: so that she would be sacred with the body as well as with the spirit; that she should be holy both for the Body, and for the Spirit). **However, the woman being married is constantly concerned about and repeatedly caring for the involvements of the System** ([her] world)**: how she can please and be accommodating to the man** ([her] husband).

Yes, it takes adjustments to live within two worlds at the same time, until maturity is attained and the two become one. This is the New Jerusalem (our Life in Christ) settling down on earth to open her gates (those 12 pearls – Rev. 21:10, 21) to the world. Here, the woman's being spoken of as being "**set-apart** (holy; different from the profane)" would be speaking in the sense of dedicated to God, consecrated, sacred, i.e., focused on God and His reign. It means being focused on her existential membership as a "living stone" of the Temple (1 Pet. 2:5). She would therefore NOT be "**divided so as to be distributed in parts**" (vs. 33, above).

The reference to "**[her] body and in [her] spirit**" simply means her whole being. This calls to mind what Jesus said in Mk. 12:30,

"'**And so, you folks will be loving** (fully giving yourselves to; urging toward reunion with) **[the] Lord** [= Yahweh] **your God from out of the midst of your whole heart** (core feelings; seat of emotions), **and from out of the midst of your whole soul** (or: inner self-life; person; consciousness), **and from out of the midst of your whole intellect** (throughout the midst of your entire comprehension and full mental ability), **and from out of the midst of your whole strength.**'" [Deut. 6:4-5]

The parenthetical readings, "with the other MSS" also give the dative cases of the nouns in different functions: "so that she would be sacred with the body as well as with the spirit; that she should be holy both for the Body, and for the Spirit." The second of those options, which reads "for the Body and for the Spirit," offers the idea that "body" here refers to the corporate body of the called-out community, and that her "holiness" is for God's Spirit.

35. **Now I am saying this with a view toward your personal advantage** (that which brings benefits together to your very selves) **– not so that I can throw a noose** (a lasso; or: a halter; = a leash) **upon you folks! To the contrary, [it is] with a view toward good form** (the well-fashioned [life]; the scene of ease and competent-appearing action) **and a good seating, [being] undistracted beside the Lord** (or: a close seat of ease, undistractedly sitting in the Lord).

"With a view toward good form, and a good seating, being undistracted, beside the Lord." The **good form** is the image of Christ that should presented to the world around them. The parenthetical expansion further defines what Paul means. The **good seating** is the place where their spirits are dwelling (Eph. 2:6), in the heavens, or the atmospheres of the Spirit (i.e., in the Temple, with the Lamb of God, on the mercy seat). Being "**undistracted beside the Lord** (or: a close seat of ease, undistractedly sitting in the Lord)" is like "**being free from anxiety** (care; concern; worry)" (vs. 32). Being undistracted is the exact opposite of being "**divided so as to be distributed in parts**" (vs. 33). Paul does not want us to "multi-task" in different "worlds" at the same time. Hitting the target requires focus and attention. Maintaining "**a good seating**" (in Him) allows for this.

The term *brochon* had a number of meanings. The first rendering, **noose**, has the idea of either choking them, or even "hanging them." In other words, he is not metaphorically trying to choke the "life" out of them, or even to kill them! The idea of "lasso," would have the sense of trying to capture them or reign them in. The idea of using a "halter" or a "leash" would signify trying to control them. His words are not meant to do any of these things.

36. **Now if anyone continues reasoning about custom [so as] to go on bringing the appearance of bad form** (or: is behaving dishonorably or indecently – that which is contrary to the accepted fashion) **upon [the situation of] his virgin [daughter; or: fiancée] – if she may be over her prime** (= beyond marriageable age; past the bloom of youth) **– and thus** (or: in this way) **he has obligation [for it] to proceed in occurring, let him continue to do what he is wanting and intending – he is not making a mistake or missing the goal: let them be marrying.**

Paul is addressing some specifics that pertained to their time and culture. He knew that his audience would understand his words – even if they may be confusing to us, at this great distance from their time and place.

This general situation was discussed in *Sirach* 42:
> "A daughter is a hidden sleeplessness to a father, and anxiety about her takes away sleep – in her youth, lest she become past her prime and having married, lest she be hated, in virginity, lest she be defiled and she become pregnant in her father's house…" (vss. 9-10a; *cf* vss. 10b-14; N.E.T.S)

We suggest that the final imperative, "**let them be marrying**" is a general reference to the unmarried, older virgin women within the community. This statement makes a concession, and an exception, to the preference as expressed in vss. 32-34. Paul is affirming the freedom of folks to do what they think is best for their own: "**what [each one] is wanting and intending**." There is no error, "**mistake or missing the goal**" in such a decision – despite the eschatological times in which they were living. Grace is sufficient.

Worthy of consideration, in this context, is what Paul wrote to Timothy,
> "**yet she will be delivered** (rescued; saved; made whole and restored to her original state and condition) **through the Birth** (or: birthing) **of the Child – should they dwell** (abide) **within trust** (or: faith; faithfulness and loyalty) **and love** (acceptance) **and the results of being set-apart** (holiness; the quality of sacred difference), **with soundness of mind** (sanity; sensibility). **The Word** (*Logos*) **[is] full of faith!** (or: Trustworthy [is] this idea and message.)" (1 Tim. 2:15).

37. **Now [he] who has been standing firm and is now settled in the seat of his heart – presently having no necessity** (continuing to hold no compulsion) **but holds authority concerning** (or: has a right pertaining to) **his own will and has decided this in his own heart – to continue keeping watch over and guarding his virgin** [daughter; fiancée; or, perhaps: his own virginity], **will be doing beautifully** (finely; ideally).

Simply notice the freedom that Paul is expressing: "standing firm and is now settled in the seat of his heart… holds authority concerning his own will… decided… in his own heart… will be doing beautifully, ideally." The decision rests with the individual. But note the remaining responsibility: "**to continue keeping watch over and guarding his virgin**." The inserted brackets indicate some of the thoughts that interpreters have suggested as being the meaning of "his virgin." The next verse offers these same optional readings in brackets and in the parenthetical expansion of the first clause.

38. **Consequently, also, the one giving his virgin [daughter] in marriage** (or: the one marrying his virgin [fiancée]; or: the one giving the virginity of himself in marriage) **is doing** [other MSS: will be doing] **beautifully, and yet the one not giving in marriage or getting married will be doing better.**

39. **A wife, by law and custom, has been bound upon and remains tied to her husband for as much time as he continues living. Yet if the husband may fall asleep in death, she exists being free to be married to whom she continues intending** (willing; purposing) **– only within** (or: centered in; in union with) **[the] Lord.**

The first level of exegesis pertains to the practical matters of life in the Corinthian community, but we see in Paul's letter to the Roman community that he took the same sort of practical example to teach a second level of interpretation. So we will let Paul expound on the spiritual dimension of his words here, by quoting him from Rom. 7:

1. **Or are you continuing to be ignorant** (are you remaining without experiential knowledge and insight), **brothers** (= fellow covenant members) **– for I am speaking to those having intimate experiential knowledge of Law** (= those who understand Torah) **– that the Law** (or: culture; Torah) **continuously performs as lord** (owner; master) **of the man for as long as he is living?**

2. **For instance, the married woman** (the woman under subjection to a husband or to an adult male) **has been bound and remains tied up by Law and custom to the living husband** (or: has been wrapped up and stands tied to law [= Torah; or: custom] by the living man). **Yet if the husband may die, she has been released from employment and stands idle** (or: has been brought down to living without labor and rendered inactive; she is discharged and brought down to unproductivity, being idled down) **away from the husband's law** (or: from pertaining to the Law [= Torah] and custom of the adult man).

3. **Consequently** (or: Accordingly), **then, [with the] continued living of the husband, she will be dealing as an adulteress** (or: bear the title "adulteress") **if she should become [attached] to, or [a lover] for, or [involved] with a different man** (or: husband); **but if the husband may die, she is free** (she exists in a state of freedom) **from the Law** [= Torah], **not to be an adulteress, pertaining to her becoming [a wife] for** (or: to) **a different man** (or: husband).

4. **So that, my brothers** (folks from the same womb), **you folks also were made dead to the Law** (or: were put to death by the Law [=Torah] and with the Law), **through the body of the Christ, [proceeding] into the situation to become [the wife] for** (or: to; in; with) **a different One – in** (to; for) **the One being roused and raised forth from out of the midst of dead folks – to the end that we may bear fruit by God** (or: produce a harvest in, for, to and with God).

40. **Yet, she continues** (or: exists) **being happier** (more blessed) **if she remains as she is, according to the knowledge gained from my experience. Now I also continue seeming to hold** (or: have; possess) **God's spirit** (a Breath-effect from God [on this matter])
(or: For I, myself, am also continuing to presume to constantly possess God's Spirit and Attitude).

Again we see Paul sharing his wisdom, which he is convinced is God's attitude on these matters. But these admonitions applied to those days and that culture. Let us simply extract the Lord's wisdom in these words, and apply that Wisdom (Christ) to our own situations.

Chapter 8

1. **Now concerning [foods] that were offered in sacrifice to idols, we have seen and know that we all continue having insight and knowledge** (*gnosis*) **gained by personal experience.** [note: this may have been a quotation from their letter to Paul]

Paul has moved on to another situation: foods, most likely meat purchased from butchers who were an outlet for surplus meats from the pagan temple offerings. Conzelmann informs us that the Greek word rendered, "**[foods] offered in sacrifice to idols**," was a Jewish term aimed at the term "**offered in a temple or a sacred sacrifice**," which Paul addresses in 10:28, below. The problem, in general, was that there was no way for members of the covenant community to know whether or not the meat that they purchase came from such a source. He will return to this topic in vs. 4, below, but now he pauses to address the subject of "insight and knowledge (*gnosis*)." We should recall 6:12-13, above, where he states that, "**To me, all things are presently out-of-Being** (or: All things continue from existence for me; or: All is authorized, right and permitted by and in me). **But yet not everything proceeds to bear together for advantage, profit, help, or are for the best**," and then makes a reference to "**foods**." Some interpreters view this as part of the letter from the Corinthians, claiming to have superior insight into the freedom in Christ, to the end that "meat sacrificed to idols" is not an issue to them. There is validity to this view, but a straightforward reading – that these are Paul's thoughts – would understand this as Paul introducing the subject of "knowledge," and he is acknowledging that all followers of Christ have insight from the fact of God's Spirit being within them. But Paul, even from his days of being a Pharisee and his observation of those Jews who felt superior to non-Jews, from their knowledge of God (via the Law, the Prophets and the Writings – the OT and the Mosaic covenant) – would know from this personal experience what "knowledge (insight; *gnosis*)" could produce in a person. Remember Eve, and what she "learned/experienced" through heeding the serpent. So in 1b he reminds them…

The (or: This) **knowledge** (*gnosis*) **keeps on puffing [you; us] up** (progressively inflates), **but** (or: yet) **The Love** (*agapē*: urge toward unambiguous, participating, accepting reunion; fully giving of oneself to others in solidarity) **progressively edifies and builds up the house!**

"Knowledge," apart from the humility that comes from Christ's Love, will always puff people up and inflate the ego: "Because of MY knowledge, I am superior to YOU." This is a potential pitfall for anyone. So now Paul introduces a topic upon which he will later expand. But this one element, *agapē* -- first referenced in 4:21 above, is the one protection from the pitfall, and the one cure, for pride. Not only that, it "**progressively edifies and builds up the house!**" He comes back to chapter 3, here. There was to be a building of God's Temple, but "knowledge" without "Love" would not survive the Fires of the tests that would certainly confront the community, as Peter instructed his communities,

> "**within the midst of and in union with [this] last season** (or: resident within a final fitting situation; in a final fertile moment; on [this] last occasion), **within which [season and deliverance] you folks are presently feeling constant joy and happiness and are continuing to rejoice exceedingly – though for a little while, at present, since** (or: if) **it continues being binding and necessary, being pained** (distressed; grieved; sorrowed) **within various tests** (or: different trials and ordeals) **to put you to the proof. [This is] to the end that the examined and tested approval of your faith** (of the trust and faithfulness of you folks) **– [being] of much greater value and worth, and more precious, than of gold that constantly loses itself away** (perishes of itself) **despite being progressively tested and examined through fire**…" (1 Pet. 1:5b-7a; *cf* 2 Thes. 1:4-8).

Notice that Peter also brings up the comment about "gold," as did Paul in ch. 3, above. Peter speaks of trials and tests again, in the same letter, 1 Pet. 4:

> 1. **Christ, then, having undergone experiences and suffering in flesh** (or: being physically and emotionally affected to the point of suffering) **over us** (or: over our [situation] and for our sakes), **you folks also arm and equip yourselves with the same mental inclination** (idea; thought; way of thinking; frame of mind; attitude), **because the person [thus] suffering or going through physical or emotional experiences which affect him in [the] flesh** (or: = by [his] estranged humanity or alienated self) **has in and for himself put a stop to failures, errors and mistakes** (or: sins) [or, with other MSS: has been caused to cease from sin],
>
> 2. **[and comes] into the [condition or situation] to no longer live out the additional remaining course [of his] time within [the] flesh** (= in the natural realm) **in the midst of** (or: in union with) **[the] full passions** (or: for [the] over-desires; to [the] rushings of emotions upon

things) **of humans** (or: pertaining to or originating in mankind), **but to the contrary, in God's will** (or: for God's intent; to God's purpose). *Cf* 1 Pet. 4:12-13

All of this is part and parcel of "building" and "testing" the House of the Lord – His people. Knowledge must be joined to Love (*cf* 13:1-3, below).

2. **If anyone continues imagining** (supposing; presuming) **to have come to know anything through his experience, he not as yet knows according as it continues binding and necessary [for him] to personally know** (or: he does not yet have insight in the sphere as, or correspondingly as, he ought to have insight).

Now Paul is not saying here that such a person needs MORE knowledge! No, it is that if anyone is in the habit of "imagining, supposing or presuming" to have come to know something, "**he not as yet knows ACCORDING AS** (or: in the sphere as; correspondingly as) **it continues binding and necessary [for him] to personally know.**" Why did Paul use the verb "imagining (etc.)"? He is saying that this person's experiential knowledge is not in the realm of Reality, or Truth. It is "imagined, supposed or presumed" knowledge. It is not knowledge that has come from intimate union with God.

And what is that sphere in which it continues binding for him, or in what way ought he, to have insight? Verse 3 gives us the answer: in the sphere of "loving God." Or, correspondingly as he is habitually urging toward union with, and fully giving oneself to, God!"

We are also instructed as to the sphere, and to what true knowledge must correspond, in 1 Jn. 2:27,
> "**the effect of the anointing which you folks received** (or: receive) **from Him constantly remains** (abides; dwells; makes its home) **within you folks, and you continually have no use** (or: you are not constantly having a need) **that anyone should keep on teaching you** (or: be repeatedly giving you a course of lessons; coach you; instruct you), **but rather, just as the effect of His anointing is continuously and progressively teaching you about everything** (or: concerning all people), **and is continuously true, and real, and is not a lie, even according as it taught** (or: as He instructs) **you: you are continuously abiding** (remaining; dwelling; being at home) **within and in union with Him** (or, reading as an imperative: be constantly remaining, abiding, staying and dwelling within the midst of Him)."

3. **Yet if anyone is continuously or habitually loving** (urging toward union with; fully giving oneself to) **God, this person has been personally and intimately known by Him and continues under the experience of His knowledge** (or: this One has been intimately known by him [i.e., by the one progressively loving God]).

How is anyone "continuously or habitually loving God"? "**We ourselves are** [some MSS add: now] **habitually loving** (or, as a subjunctive: can and should be constantly loving) **because He Himself first loved** (or: urges to reunion with) **us**" (1 Jn. 4:19).

Next, Paul instructs us that such a person that is abiding in this love relationship with God, "**has been personally and intimately known by Him and continues under the experience of His knowledge.**" This expanded expression is a rendering of the perfect tense of the verb: a completed past action that continues on in its completed state. This calls to mind the contrast, in the parable concerning the "foolish virgins," where the person who answered the door said, "'**I now say in truth to you folks, I have not seen you nor am I presently acquainted with you people**" (Mat. 25:12). A parallel to this verse is seen in 13:12b, below,
> "**Right now I am progressively coming to intimately and experientially know from out of a part** (gain insight from a piece; be acquainted with a portion of the whole), **but thereupon I shall continue accurately knowing and recognizing, from full intimate experience and added insight, correspondingly as I am also fully and accurately known, by intimate experience.**"

Notice, also, Gal. 4:9a,

> "**Yet now, coming to know God by intimate experience and personal insight – or, rather, being known intimately by God**..."

To intimately know someone, in the sense of the Greek verb used here in vs. 3 and in these last two quoted verses, there is a mutual knowing and experiencing – a spiritual, inter-penetrating, mutual correspondence. Knowing involves "being known." This has been the historical path of the mystic. We should all be mystics. We find this OT quote in 2 Tim. 2:19,

> ""**[The] Lord** [= Yahweh] **knows** (or: knew) **by intimate experience those being of Him** (or: the ones that belong to Him; those having Him as their source)." [Num. 16:5; Nah. 1:7]

Now this final clause can also be rendered: "this One has been intimately known by him [i.e., by the one progressively loving God]" i.e., God has been intimately known by the person habitually loving Him. Either reading of the Greek gives us beautiful truth and reality. The oldest MSS were in what we would call "all caps," – all the letters were the same size, so the subject could be either "this person," or, "this One (i.e., God)," depending upon whether "this" has "anyone" as its antecedent, or "God" as its antecedent. Grammatically, it can read either way. If the first way, "this person," then we are informed that what God knows of us, through His testing us, is learned in a relationship of mutual Love. If the second way, "the One," it instructs us that knowledge (*gnosis*) of God comes ACCORDING AS we love Him. Both readings express the intimate experience which comes from the union of two lovers.

Verses 3 has a different reading in *p*46, an important early MS, which omits the word "God" and the phrase "by Him"" in vs. 3. Clement of Alexandria quotes verse 3 as it is given in *p* 46, and MSS Aleph* and 33 also omit "by Him." So the abbreviated reading would be:

> "**Now if anyone is continuously loving, this person has been intimately experienced, and continues with the results of this intimacy**."

It could be that the "divine passive" of the Greek verb prompted later MS editors to insert the words "God" and "by Him."

Conzelmann points us to *Corpus Hermeticum* 10:15,

> "For it follows that God does not ignore the human (or: has no insight into, or awareness of, or acquaintance with, humanity), but to the contrary (or: but rather) also knows [him] fully (has very intimate knowledge and is quite acquainted with [her]) and furthermore, He continuously wants, wills and intends to be intimately and experientially known" (trans., JM).

We also find an interesting statement in *The Gospel of Thomas*, 3:4,

> "When you come to know yourselves, then you will become known, and you will realize that that it is you who are the sons of the living Father" (trans., Thomas O. Lambdin, *Nag Hammadi Library*, ibid p 118).

In *Gnosticism*, Robert M. Grant (Harper & Brothers, 1961 pp 146—61), translates *The Gospel of Truth* (from the *Nag Hammadi Library*), circa AD 140-180, and attested in the *Adversus Haereses* (3.11.9) of Irenaeus,

> "The gospel of truth is joy to those who have received from the Father of truth the gift of knowing him by the power of the Logos.... Those who were wise in their own estimation came to put him to the test. But he discredited them as empty-headed people. They hated him because they really were not wise men. After all these came also the little children, those who possess the knowledge of the Father. When they became strong they were taught the aspects of the Father's face. They came to know and they were known. They were glorified and they gave glory. In their heart, the living book of the Living was manifest, the book which was written in the thought and in the mind of the Father and, from before the foundation of the All, is in that incomprehensible part of him" (www.earlychristianwritings.com/text/gospeltruth.html).

4. **Therefore, concerning the eating of the [foods] that were offered in sacrifice to idols, we** (or: I, indeed,) **have seen and know that an idol [is] nothing** (or: = meaningless) **within [the] System** (or: not

even one idol [exists] in the world of [our] culture or religion, or within the midst of the created universe, or among the aggregate of humanity), **and that [there is] no other God, except One.** [*cf* Deut. 6:4]

While pointing to the topic of "food," which he does not address until 7b, below, he first affirms two things that the corporate "**we**" **have seen and know**, and which establish the basis and rationale for his arguments. They had seen these things from the OT Scriptures. Paul is founding his reasoning on what God had revealed to Moses, at Mt. Sinai, and was affirmed in the Prophets. These complementary facts are:

> a) **an idol [is] nothing** (or: = meaningless) **within [the] System** (or: not even one idol [exists] in the world of [our] culture or religion, or within the midst of the created universe, or among the aggregate of humanity) [Isa. 41:24];
> b) **[there is] no other God, except One.** [Deut. 4:39; Isa. 44:8b]

In the semantic range of "[the] System (*kosmos*)," we find "within the midst of the created universe." There is no place or realm where **idols** are a reality. **Idols** are NOTHING. They represent the imaginations of human thought. People personify ideas and give to them names as though they are some sort of spiritual entities or metaphysical beings with supernatural powers – but Paul instructs us that they are NOTHING. They only exist as mental concepts or negative attitudes within people's minds and emotions. It is of such imaginations that Paul wrote, in 2 Cor. 10:4b-6a,

> "**pulling down** (demolition) **of effects of fortifications** (or: strongholds; strongly entrenched positions [of the "Domination System" – Walter Wink, *Engaging the Powers*]), **progressively tearing down and demolishing conceptions** (concepts; the effects of thoughts, calculations, imaginations, reasonings and reflections) **and every height** (or: high position; high-effect) **and lofty [attitude, purpose or obstacle] that is habitually lifting itself up against** (or: elevating itself up on so as to put down) **the intimate and experiential knowledge of God, and then taking captive every effect of perception, concept and understanding** (result from directing one's mind) **– one after another – and leading them prisoner into the hearing obedience of the Christ** (or: the humble attentive listening, which comes from the Anointed One; or: the submissive paying attention, which is the Anointing), **even continuously holding [them] in a ready state and prepared condition to support justice and equity**…"

This is also why Paul admonished, and DESCRIBED, people:

> "**Women** (or: Wives) **[of the community], similarly, [should be] serious** (dignified with majestic gravity, inspiring awe), **not devils** (or: adversaries; women who thrust things through folks)" (1 Tim. 3:11b).
> "**the people** (the humans; mankind) **will continue being**…. **devils** (adversarial slanderers; folks who throw or thrust something through people to hurt or cause divisions)…" (2 Tim. 3:2-3).

Conzelmann quotes Marcus Aurelius Antoninus, *Meditationes* 7:9,

> "It follows that [there is] both one cosmos (universe; ordered system) from out of which [are] all things (or: made up of all things), and One God, through the midst of (or: immanent in) all things, and One Being (or: existing; Substance) and one Law" (ibid p 142 n 26; trans., JM).

Isa. 44:6 proclaims,

> "Thus continues saying God, the King of Israel, even God Sabaoth, delivering him. I [am] First and I [am] after these things. Besides (In addition to) Me there is no god!" (LXX, JM)

Cf 10:19ff; 12:2, below; Isa. 44:6-20; 46:1-7; Wis. of Sol. 13-14.

5. **For even though certainly there are ones being habitually termed, called or laid down in ideas as "gods" – whether within heaven or upon earth** (or: in sky and atmosphere, or on land) **– just as there are many "gods" and many "lords"** (or: masters; owners),

Here he is speaking about the common ideas and world views of his day. But what vs. 4 makes clear is that the "gods" of the ethnic multitudes are non-existent. In Isa. 65:3 we read,

> "[The people of Israel] are repeatedly sacrificing (keep on making offerings) in the gardens, and constantly burn incense upon the bricks, to and for the demons (Hellenistic term and concept for assumed animistic influences) – which things DO NOT exist!" (LXX, JM)

The phrase "**within heaven or upon earth**," which can also be rendered, "in sky and atmosphere, or on land," was a common way that the ancient peoples described the perceived universe. It was a way of saying "anywhere." It included all the realms of their world views. *Cf* Gen. 1:1; Acts 17:24.

Paul was aware that all cultures had their "gods," and that even some men were called "gods," e.g., Caesar and other rulers. In regard to the final clause, "**there are many "gods" and many "lords"** (or: masters; owners)," Werner Foerster comments,

> "There are many so-called gods in heaven and on earth – Paul remembers that rulers, too are equated with gods.... There are also many lords, many things on which men are dependent, and these are real powers. Paul, then, does not make any distinction between *theos* and *kurios* as though *kurios* were an intermediary god; there are no instances of any such usage in the world contemporary with primitive Christianity. *Kurios* is here a concept of relationship. It denotes that on which men make themselves, or are, in fact, dependent" (*TDNT*, Vol. 3, Wm. B. Eerdmans Pub. 1978 p 1091).

Paul makes this clear, in Gal. 4:8,

> "**But on the other hand, at that time, in fact, having not perceived and thus not knowing God, you folks were, and performed as, slaves to** (or: for) **those [who], by nature, are not gods.**"

6. **to the contrary, to us** (or: yet for us; however with us) **[there is] one God, the Father, from out of the midst of Whom [is] the whole** (the All; or: [are] all things) **– and we [proceeding] into Him – even one Lord** (or: as well as one Owner and Master), **Jesus Christ: through Whom [is] the whole** (or: [are; exist] all things) **– and we through means of and through the midst of Him!**

For those with the knowledge of God, there is "**one God, the Father.**" This was the OT view, upon which Paul has been drawing.

Now observe the cosmological ontology that defines this One God: "**from out of the midst of Whom [is] the whole** (the All; or: [are] all things) **– and we [proceeding] into Him.**" Conzelmann states, "[T]a panta is the All. The prepositions *ek* 'from,' and *eis* 'toward,' define God as its origin and goal, that is, its sum total" (ibid). We find Paul later saying the same thing, in Rom. 11:36a,

> "**Because, forth from out of the midst of Him, then through the midst of Him** (or: through means of Him), **and [finally] into the midst of Him, [is; will be] the whole** (everything; [are] all things; or: = Because He is the source, means and goal/destiny of all things – everything leads into Him)."

This has in view:

> "**that God can be all things within the midst of and in union with all humans** (or: may be everything in all things; or: should exist being All in all; or: would exist being everything, within the midst of everyone)" (15:28b, below).

He is our focus and our Goal. The last compound phrase, "**and we through means of and through the midst of Him,**" echoes Acts 17:28. The second reference to "one" is "**one Lord** (or: as well as one Owner and Master), **Jesus Christ: through Whom [is] the whole** (or: [are; exist] all things)." This echoes Jn. 1:3,

> "**All things suddenly happened and came to be** (or: occur and come to be; were birthed) **by means of It, or Him** (or: He at some point gives birth to all humanity through It), **and apart from**

> **It** (or: Him) **not even one thing comes into being** (occurs; was birthed; came into being;
> happens) **which has come into being** (which has occurred; which has happened)."

It refers to the *Logos*, which became flesh (so we now term the *Logos*, He; Him) – Jn. 1:14. It is "through
means of" Jesus Christ that we existentially "return" **into Him (the Father – the one God** of the first
clause of vs. 6, here)." The rendering "through the midst of Him" corresponds to the image of a Ladder, in
Jn. 1:51, and is a direct reference to Rom. 6:3-5, "baptized into His death…. And resurrection." Paul has
in this one verse encapsulated the entire Gospel and the "plan of the ages" (Eph. 3:11)!

Now he gives an expanded edition of all this in Col. 1, from which is this sample:

> **12. [We are folks who are] constantly giving thanks to the Father: the One calling you**
> [other MSS: us] **– as well as making [you; us] competent** (sufficient; qualified; fit; suitable) **–
> into the divided share of the lot of the inheritance of the set-apart folks** (or: belonging to the
> saints; from the sacred people; which is the different-from-the-ordinary folks) **within the Light;**
> **13. He who drags us out of danger** (or: rescued us) **forth from out of the midst of the
> authority of the Darkness** (from Darkness's jurisdiction and right; from existing out of gloomy
> shadows and obscure dimness; = the privilege of ignorance), **and changes [our] position** (or:
> transported [us], thus, giving [us] a change of standing, and transferred [us]) **into the midst of
> the reign of the Son of His love, and which is His love and drive toward union,**
> **14. in Whom** (or: in union with [which Son]) **we continuously have and hold the release into
> freedom from slavery or imprisonment** (the liberation from our predicament) **[which results
> in] the sending away of the failures** (or: the dismissal of the errors pertaining to falling short
> and straying to the side of the target; the flowing away of the sins; the divorce from mistakes).
> **15. It is [this Son] Who is the Image** (portrait; the Exact Formed Likeness; the Figure and
> Representation; visible likeness and manifestation) **of the not-seen God** (or: the unable to be
> seen God; the invisible God), **the Firstborn of all creation**
> **16. because within Him was created the whole** (or: in union with Him everything is founded
> and settled, is built and planted, is brought into being, is produced and established; or: within the
> midst of Him all things were brought from chaos into order) **– the things within the skies and
> atmospheres, and the things upon the earth** (or: those [situations, conditions and/or people] in
> the heavens and on the land); **the visible things, and the unseen** (or: unable to be seen;
> invisible) **things: whether thrones** (seats of power) **or lordships** (ownership systems) **or
> governments** (rulers; leadership systems; sovereignties) **or authorities – the whole has been
> created and all things continue founded, put in order and stand framed through means of
> Him, and [proceeds, or were placed] into Him** (or: = He is the agent and goal of all creation).
> **17. And He is before** (prior to; or: maintains precedence of) **all things and all people, and the
> whole has** (or: all things have) **been placed together and now continues to jointly-stand**
> (stands cohesively; is made to have a co-standing) **within the midst of and in union with Him,**
> **18. and so He is the Head** (or: Source) **of the body – which is the called-out community** (the
> summoned congregation) **– Who is the Beginning** (or: the Source, Origin and Ruling Principle;
> the Beginning Power and Ability of the process), **a Firstborn forth from out of the midst of
> dead folks, to the end that He would be birthed** (may come into existence; or: could come to
> be) **within all things and in all people: He continuously holding first place**
> > (or: constantly being preeminent; or: habitually being the First One; or: continuing being
> > the First Man [note: this phrase has in Greek literature been used as a title for a person]),
> **19. because WITHIN Him all – the entire contents** (the result of that which fills everything; all
> the effect of the full measure [of things]) **– delights to settle down and dwell as in a house** (or:
> because He approved all the fullness [of all existence] to permanently reside within Him)
> **20. and THROUGH Him at once to transfer the all** (the whole; = all of existential creation),
> **away from a certain state to the level of another which is quite different**
> > (or: to change all things, bringing movement away from being down; to reconcile all
> > things; to change everything from estrangement and alienation to friendship and harmony

and move all), **INTO Him – making** (constructing; forming; creating) **peace** (harmonious joining) **through the blood of His cross: through Him, whether the things upon the earth** (or: land) **or the things within the atmospheres and heavens!**

But next Paul returns to the topic opened up in vs. 1, above…

7. **Nevertheless, this intimate, experiential knowledge, insight and awareness** (*gnosis*) **[of this is presently] not within** (or: centered in; resident in) **everyone** (or: all folks). **Now some – by joint custom and mutual habit pertaining to the idol, until right now – are continually eating [food] as something sacrificed to an idol, and their conscience** (or: integrated inner knowing; perceptive awareness) **being weak is repeatedly being stained** (polluted; defiled).

Not everyone is yet aware of what Paul had just said – "**this intimate, experiential knowledge, insight and awareness** (*gnosis*) **[of this is presently] not within** (or: centered in; resident in) **everyone** (or: all folks)." This comes through being joined into the Vine (Jn. 15:1ff). It comes from being raised from the dead (Eph. 2:1-6). It comes from being born back up from above (Jn. 3:3).

Some folks were still living with an old covenant (more literally: Second Temple Judaism) world view of regarding sacrificial meat (that came from an idol temple) in the same way as they previously regarded it, i.e., as something defiled. And so when they endeavored to live in the freedom of Christ (e.g., Gal. 5:1) and would go ahead and eat meat that they regarded as ceremonially unclean, they were "**repeatedly being stained** (polluted; defiled)" – since "**their conscience [was] weak.**" *Cf* Rom. 14.

The other potential renderings for the term first offered as "**conscience**," may grant us a better understanding of what Paul meant by using this term. Some of these folks, due to "joint custom and mutual habit pertaining to the idol," had not yet had their "integrated inner knowing" or their "perceptive awareness" aligned and attuned to the new covenant in these areas of their thinking. They were mixing the old (which in God's economy had been caused to pass away – 2 Cor. 5:17) with the new which Paul had proclaimed. They were acting one way while "believing" another. It was concerning this same topic that Paul instructed the community in Rome that,

"**everything which [is] not forth from out of faith** (or: [does] not arise from trust and conviction) **is a failure to hit the target** (exists being an error; is a deviation from the goal; continues being sin and a mistake)" (Rom. 14:23b).

This is because our living and very life is to have the goal of living from out of trust and faith (Hab. 2:4; Rom. 1:17; 4:3ff). And brother Jacob wrote,

"**A two-souled** (or: = divided-willed; or: = emotionally split) **adult male** (or: person) **[is] unstable** (unfixed; inconstant; turbulent; fickle; or: = indecisive) **in all his ways and paths**" (Jas. 1:8).

Conzelmann notices that "Paul gives no advice either to the strong or to the weak on the question of how the weak consciences could be strengthened" (ibid p 147). This comes with spiritual growth and insight that is given by the Breath-effect, not by rules or regulations. It comes from abiding in the Vine, which automatically nourishes the branches. *Cf* Rom. 14:3-4. Here, to Corinth, he speaks of the "**conscience** (or: integrated inner knowing; perceptive awareness) **being weak.**" In Rom. 14:1-2 he speaks of "**the one continuing without strength in the faith**" as being "**the person being constantly weak** (without strength) [and] **continues** (or: is normally) **eating vegetables**," and then in vs. 2a contrasts that one to the person "**habitually trusting** (continually believing; continuing to have faith) **to eat everything.**" Can we deduce from this that Paul associate the ideas of conscience (which can be weak or strong, depending upon one's spiritual growth and "perceptive awareness") with trust and faith? We think that the two go hand in hand.

8. **Yet food** (something eaten) **will not proceed placing us beside, nor continue causing us to stand in the presence of, God. Neither if we should not eat are we continually behind time or being in**

the rear (also = falling short or failing to attain, thus being inferior), **nor if we should eat are we constantly attaining superabundance** (surrounding ourselves with more than enough; exceeding; = spiritually or morally advancing ourselves).

The dietary codes of the old Jewish covenant had nothing to do with "**placing us beside, nor causing us to stand in the presence of, God.**" These things were accomplished through the death and resurrection of Jesus. Eating or not eating are both irrelevant. Furthermore, "not eating" (whether keeping dietary codes or fasting) does not make a person "inferior" or a "second class" follower of Christ. At the same time, if we live in Christ's freedom and eat as the Spirit leads us, this in itself does not equate to "**attaining superabundance.**" But what does this phrase mean?

The parenthetical expansion sheds light here: "surrounding ourselves with more than enough; exceeding." In other words, it does not make us part of some elite group, or suggest that we are "super Christians." On offer is the interpretive paraphrase, "spiritually or morally advancing ourselves," by ignoring dietary codes or by the idea of abstinence. No, it is about loving our neighbors, and doing what Jesus taught.

Rom. 14:6 put it this way,
> "**the one habitually eating, in the Lord is he eating, for he habitually gives thanks to God** (constantly expresses gratitude by God, for God and in God). **And the one not eating is not eating in God** (to God; for God), **and still is habitually expresses gratitude for God** (in God; gives thanks to God)."

Food, itself, is neutral:
> "**for it follows from, 'the earth** (or: land; soil) **and the results of its filling** (entire contents; that which fills it up) **belong to and have their origin in the Lord** [= Yahweh].'" (10:26, below; [Ps: 24:1; etc.])

9. **So continue to be on watch and take notice lest somehow this "right"** (privilege and authority from out of existence; license; = liberty) **of yours should come to be a tripping-effect to, or an obstacle that results in, stumbling for, or in, the weak folks.**

Letting Paul explain himself, we again cite Rom. 14:
> 15. **For instance, if because of solid food** (or: the effect of something eaten) **your brother is continually made sad** (made sorry, distressed or grieved), **you are no longer continuing to walk about** (= living your life) **in accord with** (or: down from and on the level of) **Love** (or: you are not yet habitually walking [your path] in participation with transcendent unity of unambiguous, uniting acceptance toward others). **Do not, by your food** (or: for your solid food), **progressively destroy away** (lose by ruining; bring to loss) **that person over whom Christ died.**
> 16. **Do not cause your good thing** (or: the excellence and virtue which pertain to you) **to be slandered** (defamed; insulted; blasphemed; vilified; have its light hindered),
> 17. **for you see, God's kingdom** (or: the reign-and-dominion which is God; the expression, influence and activity of God's sovereignty) **is not** (or: does not exist being) **solid food and drink, but rather, eschatological deliverance into fair and equitable dealing which brings justice and right relationship in the Way pointed out** (being turned in the right direction; rightwisedness; also = covenant inclusion and participation), **peace and harmony from the joining** (= shalom) **and joy** (or: happiness; rejoicing) **within set-apart Breath-effect** (or: in union with and amidst a dedicated spirit and a sacred attitude; or: in [the] Holy Spirit).

10. **For if anyone should see you – the one presently having** (continuing in holding and in possession of) **experiential, intimate knowledge or insight** (*gnosis*) **– repeatedly lying down** (habitually reclining at a meal during a sacrificial banquet) **within an idol's temple dining room, will not his conscience** (or: integrated inner knowing; perceptive awareness) **– he being a weak person – be progressively**

"built up" unto the [rationalizations for him] to be habitually eating [foods] having been offered in sacrifice to idols?

Here Paul addresses behavior within the community, not what is being eaten, and points out that the folks within such a community who continue with "**experiential, intimate knowledge or insight**" have a responsibility as being role models for those who are not yet strong in the Lord. The "weak" might think, "If those leaders of the community can do this, then it must be OK for us, too, even though it does not seem right." The situation that he describes here might be compared to a person who is known to be a follower of Christ repeatedly patronizing a "strip club" or participating in a "worship service" of a religion that the local community considers to be a "false" religion. We should note the continuous action (repeatedly; habitually) that is indicated by the present tense of the verb "lying down; reclining at a meal." This suggests a lifestyle, not an incidental event. So Paul is not laying out legalistic rules, but speaking of patterns of behavior that could send the wrong message to "**a weak person**."

Observe that Paul uses the verb "**built up**" – another reference to 3:10-17, above. Our behavior can "build" the thinking of another person: with either precious things, or with worthless materials. The building described in this verse would not survive God's purifying and testing Fire. This also instructs us as to what Paul meant by his metaphor of building a temple, in ch. 3.

11. **You see, [thus] the one being habitually weak is being progressively lost-away, brought to loss and ruined** (or: is destroying himself) **by** (with; in; for) **your "knowledge"** (*gnosis*) **– the brother** (= fellow believer; member from the same womb and Family) **because of whom Christ died!**

Take note of Paul's use of the verb, "**lost-away, brought to loss and ruined**." We may surmise that Jesus used this term in a similar way. But also note that Paul informs us, in vs. 12, that such "**ruined**" folks are still a part of Christ! Just because of a failure a person does not cease to be a "brother."

Our "**knowledge**" affects our behavior. Both knowledge and behavior can "destroy" another person's life, making them a "lost sheep." Sheep follow those who are shepherding them, and so can be led astray by the shepherd's tainted (or, incomplete) "knowledge." This is not living in Love, if we mislead others. He gives similar advice, here about food, in Rom. 14:15,

> "**For instance, if because of solid food** (or: the effect of something eaten) **your brother is continually made sad** (made sorry, distressed or grieved), **you are no longer continuing to walk about** (= living your life) **in accord with** (or: down from and on the level of) **Love** (or: you are not yet habitually walking [your path] in participation with transcendent unity of unambiguous, uniting acceptance toward others). **Do not, by your food** (or: for your solid food), **progressively destroy away** (lose by ruining; bring to loss) **that person over whom Christ died.**"

Nonetheless, we know that, "**Jesus Christ [is] the same yesterday and today and on into the ages**" (Heb. 13:8), and Jesus said,

> "**You see, the Son of the Man came to seek after, and then to save, deliver and restore what is existing being lost, ruined, demolished and destroyed**" (Lu. 19:19).

12. **Now by continually doing error** (repeatedly failing and missing the goal; habitually sinning or acting amiss; proceeding in deviation) **unto the brothers** (or: So while from time to time [casting this] mistake into the [hearts] of [your] fellow believers from the same womb and Family) **in this way, and repeatedly beating or striking and thus wounding their weak conscience** (or: integrated inner knowing; perceptive awareness), **you folks are constantly doing error** (failing; sinning; acting amiss) **unto Christ!**

Note, again, the present tense (continual or repeated action) of the verb in the first clause: **continually doing error** (repeatedly failing and missing the goal; habitually sinning or acting amiss; proceeding in deviation). Paul considers our "stumble-causing freedom" as **"repeatedly beating or striking and thus wounding"** someone who was birthed from the same womb (God; the Jerusalem above – Gal. 4:26) – if that person has a **weak conscience** (or: integrated inner knowing; perceptive awareness). Jesus addressed this same sort of situation, in Lu. 17:

> 1. **So** (or: Now) **He said to His disciples, "It continues being inadmissible** (or: unallowable; or: unavoidable; or: = incredible) **that the entrapments and causes for stumbling are not to come. Nevertheless, tragic is the fate of the person through whom it continues coming**
>> (or: It is inwardly unacceptable [that] snares [will] not be [set in place], but all the more, [it will be] a grievous experience for the person who keeps on [setting them])!
>
> 2. **"It continues being an advantage to, and a profit for, him** (or: It progressively looses him to the goal) **if a stone from a [hand] mill continues lying around** (= tied to and hanged from) **his neck and then he had been tossed** (or: pitched; hurled) **into the sea, than that he should cause one of these little ones to stumble or be ensnared.**
>
> 3. **"Be habitually holding your attention and your selves toward each other, and thus be considerate of and devoted to one another. If your brother** (or: fellow believer; group or family member) **should make a mistake or fail** (may miss the goal or fall short; or: happens to sin or go into error), **respectfully give him honorable advice and let him know of his value. Then, if he should change his mind and his thinking [while turning to Yahweh and neighborliness], make the [issue] flow away from him** (or: forgive and release him).
>
> 4. **"Even if he should** (or: may) **be a failure unto you** (or: sin into you) **seven times a day, and then seven times should turn around to you, time after time saying, 'I continue in the process of changing my thinking [and am turning to neighborliness],' you will proceed making it flow away from him** (or: be repeatedly forgiving and habitually releasing him)."

So what is done to a brother is done to Christ. Where have we heard this before? Mat. 25:40,

> **"And then, giving a decided reply, the King will proceed saying to them, 'I am truly now saying to** (or: It is true, I now tell) **you folks, Upon such an amount** (or: = To the extent) **that you did** (or: do) **and perform(ed) [it] to** (or: for) **one of these belonging to the least of My brothers** (used collectively: = the members of My family; or: = those of My group or brotherhood), **you did and perform [it] to and for Me!"**

Once again we see that Jesus and Paul had the same message…

13. **Because of this very reason, if food is habitually being a snare-stick to entrap my brother** (= fellow believer; Family member) **or cause him to stumble, I should under no circumstances eat meat** (flesh [i.e., referring to what was offered to idols]) **– on into the midst of the Age! – so that I should not be a snare-stick to entrap my brother** (or: group member) **or cause him to stumble.**

This is what Jesus meant, when He said,

> **"If anyone continues intending** (purposing; willing; wanting) **to come on behind Me, let him at once completely say, 'No,' to, deny and disown himself, and then in one move lift up his execution stake** (pole for suspending a corpse; cross), **and after that proceed to be by habit continuously following after Me!"** (Mat. 16:24).

Paul was ready to say, "No," to eating meat, if that behavior would **"be a snare-stick to entrap my brother."** Why? Because in those cities, such as Corinth, meat was usually available only through a butcher, who got his meat supply from a local idol-temple. It was a matter of association with idolatry, which in turn would stumble a weak member of the community, which made this a vital issue for Paul. He made similar remarks in Rom. 14:21,

> **"[It is] beautiful** (fine; as it ought to be; profitable; ideal) **not to eat meat** (animal flesh), **neither to drink wine, nor even that in which your brother habitually stumbles** (strikes himself against [it]), **or is being constantly snared, or is continually weak."**

Conzelmann makes a cogent observation, here: "The strong man's renunciation, too, is an act of freedom…" (ibid p 150). *Cf* Rom. 14:13. And yet, all this must be taken with the time, the culture and the audience relevance in mind. It was about a behavior that a person comes to realize to be a stumbling block for the young or the weak. Much more than eating meat is on the table, here. How about business practices, or "church government," or social exclusion?

Chapter 9

1. **Am I not free** (Do I not exist being a free man)**? Am I not one sent forth with a mission** (a representative; an emissary; a commissioned agent)**? Have I not seen Jesus, our Lord** (Owner; Master)**? Are you folks not my work within the Lord** (or: = in union with Christ or centered in Yahweh)**?**
2. **If I am not one sent off with a mission to or for other folks, nevertheless I surely am to and for you people – for you, yourselves, are my seal of the expedition** (or: the legally valid attestation document of my sent-off mission)**, within, and in union with, the Lord** (or: = centered in the Master).
3. **– this is my defense** (my verbal reply) **to or for those continuously examining me and sifting the evidence about me –**

Even though this seems to be a change of subject, it flows from 8:13 where some might think that his stance there would indicate a kind of bondage to what other people think. His first question, "Do I not exist being a free man?" explains that what he has just said in vs. 13 does not eliminate his freedom. Recall his bold proclamation in Gal. 5:1,

> "**For this freedom, Christ immediately set us free** (or: [The] Anointed One at once frees us in, to, for and with freedom)**! Keep on standing firm, therefore, and do not again be habitually held within a yoke of slavery**
>> (or: Continuously stand firm, then, in the freedom [to which the] Anointing sets us free, and let not yourselves be progressively confined again by a yoke pertaining to servitude)!"

His second question is answered by his third question, and in vs. 2 – their very existence as a called-out community testifies to the fact that he was sent-out on a mission as Christ's representative. His third question affirms that it was Jesus Himself who commissioned him as an agent. He repeats this fact of having seen Jesus, in 15:8, below, and in Gal. 1 he explains how he had received the message that he proclaims:

> 11. **You see, I am habitually making it intimately known to you folks by experience, brothers: that the message of goodness and well-being – the one being announced and proclaimed as "good" news by** (or: under) **me – is not down from or according to a person** (or: is not corresponding to something human; is not on the level of or in the sphere of humanity),
> 12. **for I myself neither received it to my side from a human** (or: from beside a person)**, nor was I taught [it], but to the contrary, [it came] through an unveiling of Jesus Christ** (or: through an uncovering pertaining to Jesus [the Messiah]; through a revelation from Jesus Christ; by means of a disclosure which is [the] Anointed Jesus).

Verse 1, here both answers that potential assumption and weaves his arguments back to the topic of the sectarianism that had developed in the Corinthian community – its division into followers of himself, Apollos, Cephas, etc. He is free in Christ, and Christ has sent him forth as His representative to the nations. He is qualified – perhaps, in this context, even beyond Apollos of whom it is not said that he had "seen Jesus" – and his listeners are the evidence: they are his "**work within the Lord**." *Cf* 15:10, below, and in 2 Cor. 3 we read:

> 2. **You yourselves are and continue being our letter – being one having been written** (inscribed; imprinted; engraved) **within your hearts** [other MSS: our hearts]**; one progressively being experientially known and continuously read** (or: periodically recognized and experienced again) **by all people** (human beings) –
> 3. **because you are and continue being those continuously set in clear light and progressively manifested: Christ's letter** (a letter whose source is Christ, and which is Christ),

being one dispensed in attending service by us, being one having been written (inscribed; imprinted; engraved), **not in black** (= not with ink), **but rather, by** (or: in; with) **God's Spirit: One continuously living** (or: in a Breath-effect which has its origin in God, Who is constantly living); **not in stone tablets** (or: on tablets composed of stone), **but rather within tablets which are hearts made of flesh** (or: on tablets in hearts composed of flesh). [*cf* Rom. 8:26-27]

They, themselves, were his "**seal of the expedition**," or, "the validated document of [his] sent-off mission." Notice that, in vs. 2, he repeats the phrase, "**within, and in union with, the Lord**." So the Lord is his authority, and the community itself was his "**defense to or for those continuously examining**" him (vs. 3). We suspect that those who were "**sifting the evidence**" about him were Judaizers who may have inferred that he had parted from the true path of the Christ (which, in their eyes, would have been to remain in the old covenant while accepting Jesus as the Messiah). Or, they may have been those of the various factions (the followers of the other teachers and emissaries). He does not single any of them out, he simply presents his case to the whole community. But now he continues with more rhetoric:

4. **Are we not in any way continuing to have [the] right** (privilege from out of being; authority) **to eat and to drink?**
5. **Are we not in any way continuing to have [the] right** (authority; privilege from existence) **to be habitually leading around a sister [as] a wife – as also the rest of those sent out on a mission and the Lord's brothers, and Cephas?**

The clause, "**the rest of those sent out on a mission**," tells us that there were numerous sent-forth representatives that were going out into the Empire. Much more was happening than is recorded in the NT reports that remain for us. The questions in these two verses address the matter of personal conduct with regard to the sent-forth folks. Apparently some folks have criticized his conduct, misconstruing it, and were using it as a personal attack against him. Conzelmann (ibid p 153) brings up the point, here, that what would be involved with "**leading around a sister [as] a wife**," was that this would bring an extra expense to the communities that were supporting these missionary efforts. Wives apparently traveled with these emissaries, just as women traveled with Jesus. Some interpreters, however, consider this phrase as simply meaning, "to be married." There was probably no set pattern of behavior among the various emissaries, as Paul himself exhibits.

6. **Or, are only Barnabas and I continuing to have no right** (privilege; authority; license) **not to be habitually active in a trade** (not to be constantly working)**?**
7. **Who is at any time habitually performing military service** (serving as a soldier) **at his own expense** (by his private rations)**? Who makes a habit of planting a vineyard and then is not eating its fruit? Or who habitually tends** (or: shepherds) **a flock and then is not eating** (nourishing himself) **from out of the flock's milk?** [*cf* 2 Tim. 2:6]

Observe that his "**defense**" continues in the form of rhetorical questions. He throws out a series of questions that would expect an affirmative answer. This will set the minds of his listeners on his side. They could not help but say, "Yes, yes, yes..."

Notice his reference to "eating," once again, in vs. 4. He is maintaining the "right" – the "privilege from out of being" in union with Christ – "to eat and to drink." But 8:13, above, shows that he will not abuse this privilege, for he is a disciple of Jesus.

In vss. 5 and 6 we are informed that following Jesus did not demand a renunciation of living a normal life. Paul makes his own decisions, as he is led by the Spirit (Rom. 8:14), but he does not preach asceticism. Neither does he promote a monastic way of life, nor a withdrawal from society (as, e.g., with the Qumran community of the Essenes).

However, in vs. 7 he uses the military, agricultural and animal husbandry metaphors to indicate that those who are called to live in full-time service to the called-out communities, and in evangelism, have the right to receive sustenance from those communities. Verse 6 affirms that those in full-time ministry have the right to devote all of their time to the ministry, and not have to do other work to maintain themselves. Jesus termed this activity as "labor; work" in Mat. 9:37 and in Jn. 4:35-38. When Jesus sent out the twelve and then the seventy, they were expected to receive hospitality – indeed, this was a central element of the Jewish culture in those days. We find this emphasized in 1 Tim. 5:17b-18,

> **"especially those being continually wearied and spent with labor in [the] Word** (or: in the midst of the message) **and by teaching** (or: instruction and training), **for the Scripture is saying, 'You shall not muzzle a bull** (or: ox) **when it is threshing out grain,'** [Deut. 25:4] **and, 'The worker [is] worthy** (of equal value) **of his wages.'"** [Luke 10:7] *Cf* 2 Tim. 2:15

So what Paul is saying here is speaking of receiving daily rations of bed and board – but not about becoming rich at the expense of those communities. This latter came when the Christ movement became institutionalized.

8. **Am I not speaking these things to accord with [what is] human** (or: in line with and in the sphere of humanity)? **Or is not the Law also saying these things?**
9. **For you see, within the Law of Moses it has been written:**

> **"You will not continue muzzling an ox** (bull; cow) **[that] is progressively treading in threshing."** [Deut. 25:4]

Is the attention and concern to (or: by; for) **God [here perhaps] not about the oxen?** (or: It is not a care with God that has reference to bulls!)

He substantiates what he has just said by first a call to the example of ordinary life within their culture, and then uses the Law as his foundation, citing an animal husbandry reference in Deut. 25:4, and extrapolating that principle to be applied to their present daily lives. Notice that the last sentence of vs. 9 can be either a rhetorical question, or an interpretive affirmation. We should take note of Paul's exegesis and hermeneutic! Paul makes his case for the "rightness" of the communities supporting those who work in the kingdom full-time, but as for himself, see 2 Cor. 11:7-9 for a record of his "freedom" to choose not to avail himself of this privilege. He explains himself in more detail in vss. 16-18, below.

Although the Law, as stated in Deut. 25:4, had in focus the care of animals, Conzelmann notes:

> "Paul, however, expounds the statement according to the Hellenistic Jewish principle that God's concern is with higher things; that accordingly the detailed prescriptions of the law are to be allegorically expounded" (Ibid p 155).

He then cites Philo, a contemporary of Paul,

> "For the law does not prescribe for unreasoning creatures, but for those who have mind and reason" (*Spec. leg. 1260;* ibid n 37)

10. **Or, is He** (or: it) **undoubtedly saying [this] entirely** (everywhere and in all circumstances) **because of us? Because of us! For it was written that the one progressively plowing ought normally** (or: is constantly obliged) **to be habitually plowing upon [the basis of] an expectation** (or: expectant hope), **and the person habitually threshing [to do so] on an expectation of the [result]: to continue participating in his share [of the produce].**

Next he poses a leading rhetorical question, followed immediately by an affirmative answer. His explanation takes the form of an agricultural metaphor (he follows the teaching method demonstrated by Jesus) to present the idea of working while holding an "**expectation**" concerning the results of that work. Now he ties this in to the worker "**participating in his share [of the produce].**"

Paul's statement following, "for it was written," has been assumed by some scholars to have reference to an apocryphon: a "secret writing," plural apocrypha – a Greek term for a genre of Jewish and Early

Christian writings that were meant to impart "secret teachings" or "gnosis" (knowledge and insight) that should not be publicly taught. Others understand this to be an exposition of OT passages. Paul freely quoted a Greek poet in Acts 17:28. Truth is truth, whoever speaks it. But he continues his line of thought…

11. **Since, upon [the ground of] an expectation, we ourselves sowed the spiritual things in** (to; for; with; among) **you folks, [is it] a great thing if we ourselves shall reap a harvest of your fleshly things** (= natural or material goods pertaining to the material life)**?**

Now he presents to them a present time/situation application of his rhetoric, as a conclusion to all his rhetorical questions, above.. He and Barnabas had "**sowed the spiritual things in** (to; for; with; among) **[those] folks**." Here, he has taken the agricultural metaphor of the citation in vs. 10 and has applied it to their missionary endeavors. They had (switching to another of Paul's metaphors) "built" this community with gold, silver and precious stones (ch. 3, above). Is it "a great thing" for them to harvest some stubble (**fleshly things**) and be materially fed from their fields, vineyards and flocks? This last phrase refers to physical sustenance. Once again he brings up the contrast between "spiritual things" (i.e., God's reign) and "fleshly things" (the normal life). This calls to mind Rom. 15:27,

> "**For they take delight and were well-pleased, and are their debtors, for since the ethnic multitudes** (the nations; the Gentiles; the non-Jews) **have common participation and shared existence in their spiritual things, they also continue indebted to perform communal service to and for them in things pertaining to the material life** (or: fleshly things)."

12. **Since, or if, others are continually sharing and participating in your right from existing** (privilege; authority), **[why] not rather** (or: all the more) **we? But to the contrary, we do not** (or: did not) **make use of this right** (privilege from being; authority), **but rather we are habitually putting a roof over, and thus covering** (perhaps: = putting up with) **all people, and all things [or: situations], so that we should not give any hindrance to the progress of Christ's good news**

> (or: would not offer any incision which blocks the way for the message of abundant goodness, wellness and fortunate ease which pertains to and has its origin in the Anointing, and which is the Anointed One).

Notice that he called their material "harvest" (vs. 11) a "**right from existing** (privilege; authority)" – something that they now had "access to, and control over." I gave the literal rendering of *ex-ousia* first: a right or privilege that comes from out of existing (or: Being, i.e., God – the Creator of grains and animals that sustain us). He notes that these other teachers had shared in this privilege, so it was only logical that he and Barnabas should likewise be participants.

Nonetheless, they were not making use of this right. Instead, they were "**habitually putting a roof over, and thus covering** (perhaps: = putting up with) **all people, and all things [or: situations]**." It is interesting to note that the verb in this clause is the same verb that is used in the first clause of 13:7, below:

> "**[Love] continuously covers all mankind** (It [i.e., unambiguous acceptance] progressively puts a protecting roof over all things)…"

And his reason was an expression of loving concern: "**so that we should not give any hindrance to the progress of Christ's good news**." Take time to meditate on the parenthetical expansion on offer, which is an alternate rendering of the clause. Note the picture described in the phrase, "incision [i.e., presented by Paul and Barnabas entering their community] which blocks the way." Paul's central concern is "the message of abundant goodness, wellness and fortunate ease." This goodness (etc.) has its origin in the Anointing, and (rendering the phrase as apposition) the Goodness IS the Anointed One. It is the message that itself is Christ. The word *christos* means both "anointing" and "anointed one." The Anointing comes via the Spirit, and in that Anointing is The Anointed One.

He spoke similarly in 1 Thes. 2:9,

> **"For you are remembering, brothers, our exhausting labor** (or: = the trouble to which we went; toil; hardship; or: beating) **and hard work, continuously working night and day towards not being burdensome** (or: a weight) **upon any of you, [and] after the manner of a herald we proclaimed God's message of goodness** (the good news from God; or: the message of ease and well-being which is God) **into the midst of** (or: unto) **you folks."** *Cf* 2 Cor. 12:13.

13. Have you folks not seen so as to know that those habitually working at (performing the duties of; engaged in the business pertaining to) **the sacred things of the temple are habitually eating from out of the things of the temple** (the holy place of the sanctuary)**? Those constantly sitting beside and attending to the altar are habitually sharing jointly in a portion of the altar** (= the offerings sacrificed there).

He continues by giving them a more direct analogy, since the called-out community in Corinth is a Temple of God, as a result of being joined to the Lord (6:17, above). The Levites (the tribe from whom the priests would come) were not given an inheritance of land; they were separated from the other tribes in order to bear the ark of the covenant and to minister to Yahweh, in the temple, so Yahweh was their inheritance (Deut. 10:8-9). In this arrangement they would therefore neither work the land (raise crops) nor herd livestock. Thus, their food came from the temple sacrifices and offerings that the people brought to Yahweh. For example, we read in Lev. 6:16-17 that after the priests offered a portion of a mixture of flour, oil and frankincense before Yahweh,

> "The rest of it Aaron and his sons shall eat; as unleavened [bread] shall it be eaten in a holy place. In the court of the tent of appointment shall they eat it... as their portion I give it from My fire offerings" (CVOT).

In the case of the sin offering, Lev. 6:25b-26a instructed them,

> "In the place where the burnt offering is killed... The priest that offered it for sin shall eat it..."

From this background, Paul continues...

14. Thus also, the Lord [= Yahweh or Christ] **thoroughly arranged for those habitually bringing down the announcement of the message of goodness** (of the abundant wellness, good fortune and ease) **to be continuously living from out of the message of goodness** (= the announcement of ease, well-being and goodness is to be the source of their living).

Now he relates his example to their present situation concerning **"those habitually bringing down the announcement of the message of goodness."** The Lord arranged for these people **"to be continuously living from out of the message of goodness,"** in the same manner as did the priests of the old covenant. It is a perfect correlation: the same principle, but in new situations.

15. Yet I myself have not made use of nor do I now employ even one of these things – and I do not write these things so that it should come to be thus in me (or: = in my case)**: for to me [it would be] fine** (beautiful; ideal; good form)**, rather, to die than that anyone should** [other MSS: shall proceed to] **make the result of my boast empty and void,**

Nonetheless, Paul did not make use of this arrangement, and he is not saying this to the Corinthians so that they will feel obliged to support him. No, he would rather "die" than do this. Keeping in mind that Paul was a part of an "honor/shame" society, he is focused on the "honor" side of that dichotomy, and it was normal for folks in that culture to "boast" in what was honor to them. So he viewed his occasional working of his trade, and the dependence on people's hospitality as being "his boast." And so, he would rather **"die than that anyone should make the result of my boast empty and void."** But he explains...

16. for it is not the result of a boast for [other MSS: for is it not grace to...?] **me if I should habitually announce good news, for you see, a compressed necessity** (a compulsion) **continues laid upon me.**

For it is a woe (a condition or situation at which I would say, "Alas!") **to and for me, if ever I should not constantly bring and announce the message of Goodness.**

His mission is not something of which he boasts, for "**a compressed necessity** (a compulsion) **continues laid upon**" him. Notice the "divine passive" voice of the verb: this is not a matter of Paul's "free will" or choice; his use of the passive voice demonstrates his understanding that God laid this charge upon him, and he regarded it as a "**compressed necessity.**" This was like having "the hand of the Lord" placing this mission on him. Recall Rom. 1:1 where Paul identifies himself as "a slave of Jesus Christ."

The words that he uses reveal how important it is for him to "**constantly bring and announce the message of Goodness.**" If ever he should not do this it would be "**a woe to him.**" For him, such a situation would be something of which he would say, "Alas!" In other words, it could bring him into depression or despair if he should not fulfill this mission that he was given. This reveals Paul's commitment to the Lord. No wonder he described his life as a sent-forth representative as that of having been "**taken down by hand** (fully seized; forcefully grasped and taken possession of) **by, and under [the control of], Christ Jesus**" (Phil. 3:12b).

17. **For if I willingly continue performing this** (voluntarily from my being keep on executing this action), **I continue having compensation** (pay; a wage; a reward). **However, since** (or: if) **unwillingly, involuntarily, and not from my being I have been persuaded, caused to believe [in] and given faith [for] the management of a Household** (or: entrusted [with] a stewardship),

This all had happened to him "**unwillingly and involuntarily.**" Recall his Damascus Road experience, in Acts 9. We have two contrasting adverbs in this verse, *ekōn* and *akōn* (a contraction of *aekōn*, a negation of *ekōn*). The *ek-* means "out of," or, "from." *Ōn* is the present participle of "to be; to exist." For this reason, I conflated the first adverb as "willingly… voluntarily… from my being," and the second adverb as negations of the first adverb: "**unwillingly, involuntarily, and not from my being.**" Each of these three English terms and phrase give a true picture, but with different nuances, especially in the negative forms. Paul could have accepted his summons as an involuntary response to Christ's call: he just found himself responding – his will was not even involved; it was like breathing, or like suddenly falling to the ground from the Voice and the Light (Acts 9). Or, he may have not wanted to follow this Path, but was persuaded against his will ("Not my will, but Yours"). The third option suggests that the act of taking on the management of Christ's Household (the called-out communities) did not come from within him – he did not decide to do this; it was not his idea; it did not come "from his being." Observe the "divine passive" of the verb *pisteuō*: "**I have been persuaded, caused to believe [in] and given faith [for]** (or: been entrusted [with])."

One who works for compensation or wages is termed a hireling. Paul was not a hireling. Jesus said, in Jn. 10:12-13,
> "**The hireling** (hired hand working for wages) **– not even being a shepherd [and] the sheep are not his own – continues attentively watching the wolf progressively coming, and proceeds to abandon the sheep and to take flight – and the wolf continues ravenously snatching them away and progressively scattering and dispersing them – because he is a hireling and it is not a concern to him** (or: a care for him) **about the sheep.**"

Paul's life and letters witness to the fact that he was a shepherd, not someone working for pay. And since he had been apprehended (Phil. 3:12b; KJV) for this call, he had "**been given faith [for], and entrusted with, the management of a Household.**" And this was not "compensation," but added "**compressed necessity**" (vs. 16, above) of responsibility. That household was God's Family, as represented by the called-out communities. So we suggest that Paul's next part of this rhetorical question (vs. 18a, below) is irony, as he takes the supposed position that is not really the case…

18. **what then is my compensation** (pay; wage; reward)? **That while repeatedly announcing the message of Goodness, I will continually** (or: can) **deposit** (put; set; place) **the good news** (the message of abundant wellness and fortunate ease) **without cost** (or: expense; or: = free of charge), **[leading] into the [situation so as] not to make downright use of my right or privilege within the good news** (or: not to fully employ or abuse my authority from being in union with the message of Goodness).

The answer that he gives is not really "compensation," but rather continued responsibility that will end in costing him the rest of his life, as a slave, yet free (vs. 19, below). Conzelmann observes, "Paul has shown that his behavior is not a matter of free decision. Yet it is precisely in acting in accordance with this constraint that he exercises his freedom..." (ibid p 158), and he noted Wettstein as observing that Paul's "reward [was] to receive no reward" (ibid n 28). But still, Paul looks at this life as,

> "**continuously pressing forward, pursuing down toward** [the; or: an] **object in view** (a mark on which the eye is fixed)**: into the awarded contest prize of God's** (or: the award which is God's) **invitation to an above place** (or: the prize from, and which is, the upward calling from, and which is, the God) **within the midst of and in union with Christ Jesus**" (Phil. 3:14).

He had explained of what the "contest prize" and "the award" consists, in 1 Thes. 2:

> 19. **For WHO** (or: what) **is our expectation** (or: expectant hope) **or joy, or shall continue being a crown** (VICTOR'S WREATH; encirclement) **of boasting and glorying in front of our Lord Jesus, in His presence** (or: in the place facing toward our Master, Jesus, within the midst of His being present alongside [us])**, if not even YOU folks?**
> 20. **For you see** (or: For it follows that), **YOU yourselves are our glory** (or: our reputation; our manifestation which calls forth praise) **and joy!**

What Paul explains in the rest of vs. 18, here, may give us insights as to what he regarded as the "**contest prize**" in that letter to the Philippians, and in the above verse from 1 Thes. 2. It was to be able to "**continually deposit** (put; set; place) **the good news** (the message of abundant wellness and fortunate ease) **without cost** (or: expense; or: = free of charge)" was the "joy that was set before him" (Heb. 12:2). "**Not to make use of**" his privilege was something of value to him, as he explained it in vs. 15, above. His position on this issue is just the opposite of what he advised against in 7:31, above: "**constantly using it down** (= making excessive employment or over-use of it)." We saw this same attitude in 8:13, above. He explained this perspective in 2 Cor. 6:10b, "**as [one] possessing** (having or holding) **nothing, and yet continuously possessing all things to the full.**"

19. **You see, continually being free from out of the midst of all things and from all people** (or: independent of everyone and from everything), **I enslave myself to all people** (or: to everything and for everyone), **to the end that I can** (may; would) **gain [all] the more folks.**

In terming himself "**free from out of the midst of all things and from all people,**" we suggest that he was not talking about his freedom as a Roman citizen, but rather, was speaking of freedom from the Law, and from the cultural limitations both of the Jews and of Second Temple Judaism. This is the freedom of which he spoke in Gal. 5:1. This very freedom, however, allows him to "**enslave [himself] to all people,**" and this takes the lived-out form of service to others. It calls to mind Jesus' words in Lu. 22:27b,

> "**I Myself am in your midst as the person constantly giving attending service.**"

Peter had a similar thought:

> "**[Be] habitually with humility aligning yourselves** (arranging yourselves for support) **that if any are habitually unpersuaded by the Word** (or: uncompliant or disobedient to the message; unconvinced with the thought, reason or idea), **they will continue being profited** (will progressively receive advantage; or: will proceed in being **acquired as gain**) **without a word** (or: message; reason), **through the behavior** (or: conduct; way of life)..." (1 Pet. 3:1).

Our behavior, and attitude, proclaims the Good News.

The apparent paradox of this statement can be explained by recognizing the existential reality of "**continually being free**," in Christ, while concretely being a slave "to everything and for everyone" with both his attitude and by his life of cruciform service to humanity. The ending purpose clause, "**to the end that I can** (may; would) **gain [all] the more folks**," leads directly into his explanations of his methods of "enslaving [himself]," in vss. 20-23...

20. **So I come to be** (or: became) **as a Jew for** (or: to; with; among) **the Jews, to the end that I can** (would; may) **gain Jews; as under Law for** (or: to; with; among) **those under Law, to the end that I can** (or: would; should; may) **gain those under Law;**

We saw this in the way that he presented "the message of goodness, ease and well-being" in the synagogues, arguing from the OT that Jesus is the Messiah, as recorded of his activities in the book of Acts. We see another example in Acts 21:23-27, where, at the request of the Jewish believers in Jerusalem, he joined four men who had taken a vow. He was operating from the perspective of Eph. 2:15, where God had broken down the dividing wall (which was the Law) and had made both Jew and Gentile (circumcision and uncircumcision) into One New Humanity (the Second Human, the last Adam, of 15:45-47, below.

21. **as without law** (or: as lawless) – **[though] not continually being without a law pertaining to God, but to the contrary, within a principle which is Christ** (or: Christ's law; the custom which has the character and quality of Christ; or: [the] law which is [the] Anointing) – **to those without law** (for and with the lawless ones), **to the end that I will progressively** [other MSS: can; may; would] **gain the folks without law** (the lawless ones).

He related to everyone according to where they were, in God's economy. For Paul, "**The circumcision is nothing, and the uncircumcision is nothing**" (7:19, above). Paul makes his point by rhetorical parallelism in reference to how he behaves both toward Jews and toward Gentiles. He was, of course, a Jew, so that part would come naturally. But in his behavior toward the Gentiles, we see from vs. 20 that it requires him to "**come to be**" as a Gentile, i.e., "**as without law**," or "without The Law."

Those to whom he refers as being "without law" may be of two categories:
      a) the ethnic multitudes (the nations) to whom the Law of Moses never applied;
      b) the Zealots who were planning a revolt against Rome, or those who simply lived lawlessly.

He clarifies what he meant about himself being "**as without law** (or: as lawless)" by the disclaimer, "**not continually being without a law pertaining to God**." He always lived "**within a principle which is Christ** (or: Christ's law; the custom which has the character and quality of Christ; or: [the] law which is [the] Anointing)." Each of the four renderings, that relate "principle/law/custom" to Christ, offers an optional understanding of what Paul meant: a principle; a law; or a custom. The genitive case of the term "Christ" is offered in the functions of a) apposition, b) possession, c) description. This apparent ambiguity offers us multiple views into Paul's thoughts here. The appositional "[the] law which is [the] Anointing" points us to Rom. 8:14 – being led by the Spirit.

Conzelmann posits that Paul is not suggesting that there is some kind of "new" law, but that Christ is "the norm." Understanding the term "law" as a principle of "being" seems to clarify Paul's meaning. There is a New Being (Paul Tillich's term) in the New Humanity (Eph. 2:15). The New Creation (2 Cor. 5:17) operates with new principles of that "kingdom existence."

22. **To** (For; Among; With) **those without strength** (the weak ones), **I become** (or: came to be) **as without strength** (weak), **to the end that I would** (can; may) **gain those without strength** (the weak ones). **I have become and continue to be all things for** (to; among; with) **all folks** (or: peoples), **to the**

end that I can (would; may) **by every means** (in every way; under all circumstances; entirely; everywhere) **save** (rescue; deliver; restore to health, wholeness and their original condition) **anybody!**

The first clause may refer to such as he made reference in Rom. 14 (concerning dietary issues), or to those referred to above who were weak in "conscience," or perhaps to those who were economically stressed, socially on a low level (like outcasts), or suffering with chronic illness. Like our Master, Jesus, Paul lived in solidarity with everyone. He would work "**by every means** (in every way; under all circumstances; entirely; everywhere)." This is what he meant by the clause in vs. 19, above, "**I enslave myself to all people.**" The clause, "**I have become and continue to be all things for** (to; among; with) **all folks** (or: peoples)" is a summation of vss. 20-22a.

The second half of the verse is ambiguously "all-inclusive." His target audience was "**anybody.**" As far as deliverance, rescue, salvation, restoration and wholeness were concerned, Paul did not have a theology of some being "elect" or "the chosen," while others were not. Such a concept is an invention of later theology, as Christ's followers became institutionalized and led astray from the Love of God. Paul saw rescue and deliverance (salvation) as happening to everyone – to each one in his or her own group, class or order (15:23, below).

23. **Now I habitually do all things** (or: everything) **because of the message of abundant wellness** (the good news; the message of prosperous and ideal ease, and Goodness), **to the end that I would** (could; can) **for myself come to be its** (or: His) **joint participant** (co-partner; sharer-in-common, along with others; equal fellow in communion and common Being).

Paul's whole life was dedicated to "the message" with the aim of being a "**joint-participant**" of this good news, as well as of Him. The genitive pronoun serves both the masculine and the neuter, so it can be rendered either "Him," or "it." Paul never assumes himself to "have arrived," so his focus is to "**come to be**" an "equal fellow in communion and common Being," or a "co-partner with the message," or, a "sharer-in-common with Christ," or a "**joint-participant in the message of abundant wellness** (etc.)." The word "**joint-participant** (etc.)" is the Green *sun-* (co-; joint-; share- fellow-) prefixed to *koinōnos* (common being; common existence). What a statement of unification and solidarity! The term "common Being" is the corporate Christ, the Second Humanity (15:47b, below). He will next explain HOW he "habitually does all things," by using a metaphor from the athletic contests held in the stadiums...

24. **Have you folks not seen, so as to know, that those progressively running, on the race-course within a stadium, are indeed all progressively running** (or: constantly and repeatedly racing), **yet one normally** (= each time) **grasps** (takes; receives) **the contest prize** (victor's award)? **Be habitually running** (progressively racing) **so that you folks can** (may; would) **seize and take [it] down in your hands!**

This metaphor builds upon vs. 23. He is not talking about a person's "ultimate salvation," or about bringing glory or fame to one's self. He is talking about how they should be living their lives, here and now: with total commitment to full participation within the "**common Being.**" He is talking about living as though one were running a race – with all their heart, soul, mind and strength – and continuing this way until they reach the "finish line," which is the end of their physical life here. Verses 24-27 all have the same message, and we saw this encapsulated in the quote of Phil. 3:14, under vs. 18, above. We find a similar admonition in Heb. 12:1b,

> "**after at once putting off from ourselves all bulk and encumbrance** (every weight; all that is prominent; or: getting rid of every arrow point within us) **and the easily-environing** (skillfully-surrounding; well-placed encircling) **failure** (sin; error; mistake; shooting off-target; missing of the point), **we can and should through persistent remaining-under** (or: relentless patient endurance and giving of support) **keep on running the racecourse continuously lying before us** (or: lying in the forefront within us; or: lying ahead, among us)."

This is practically interpreted in living out the reply by Jesus in regard to the Law – which is a synopsis of the Spirit of the Law and the Prophets, but only enabled to fully accomplish under the new covenant by the power of the indwelling Spirit:

> "**You will continue loving** (fully giving yourself to; urging toward reunion with) **[the] Lord** [= Yahweh], **your God, in union with your whole heart – and within the midst of the core of your being, and in union with your whole soul – and within the midst of your entire soul-life, and in union with your whole intellectual capacity – and within the midst of your whole thinking process and comprehension**" (Mat. 22:37; Deut. 6:5).

Paul expounds this theme in chapter 13, below. But here, his analogy continues...

25. **Now every person habitually engaging in a contest** (participating in the violent struggle of the public athletic games) **constantly exercises inner strength and self-control in all things, and among all folks: those, of course, therefore [do it] so that they may** (can; would) **grasp** (take; receive) **a corruptible wreath that will soon wither, yet we an incorruptible** (un-withering) **one.**

The verb, "**constantly exercises inner strength and self-control**" speaks of the contestant's habit of personal training. But in Gal. 5:23, we find the cognate of this verb in the noun, "**inner strength** (self-control)," which describes one aspect of "the fruit of the Spirit." So our training involves "abiding in the Vine" (Jn. 15:1ff), in order to produce the Spirit's fruit. But abiding, like training, involves focus and connected union with the source of Life.

So to what is he referring, in using the metaphor of "an incorruptible wreath"? What is the spiritual "prize" in the analogy of vs. 24? This metaphor served different purposes to different writers. For Paul, it was the people that he served, as he stated in Phil. 4:1,

> "**my brothers** (= fellow believers; Family) **– loved ones and longed-for folks** (people missed with a craving), **my joy and winner's** (or: festal) **wreath**..."

Jacob used this "goal" metaphor in this way:

> "**Happy and blessed is the adult male** (or: person; [A and other MSS: human]) **who is continuously remaining under a proving** (a putting to the proof; or: a trial; an ordeal), **because upon being birthed approved** (or: growing and becoming proved and accepted) **he or she will continue laying hold of the circle of the life** (or: life's crown; life's encirclement; the encirclement from this living existence; or: the wreath which is the Life) **which He** [some MSS: the Lord (= Yahweh or Christ)] **Himself promised to those continuously loving, and urging toward union with, Him**" (Jas. 1:12).

Note the parenthetical expansion of "the circle of the life... the wreath which is the Life," and that "he or she will CONTINUE laying hold" of it. And what is the basis for remaining in this Christ Life? It is "**continuously loving, and urging toward union with, Him**." Jesus informed us that we love Him when we are loving "the least of His brothers" (Mat. 25:40). And then Peter combined the metaphor with his admonition in 1 Pet. 5:3b-4,

> "**progressively becoming beaten models** (types made by the strike of a hammer; examples) **for the little flock, and so, with the Chief Shepherd** (or: the Original and Ruling Shepherd) **[thus] being made visible** (being shown in clear light), **you folks will continue bringing to yourselves – with care and kindly keeping – the un-withering and unfading wreath of the glory** (or: the assumed appearance)."

What Paul referred to as being "**incorruptible**," Peter described as "**un-withering and unfading**." These descriptions are figures for that which continues on without death: God Himself. Paul uses the term "incorruption" in 15:42, below: "**the resurrection of the dead people... is being habitually** (or: presently; repeatedly; one after another) **awakened and raised up within incorruption**." We suggest that what Paul refers to, here in vs. 25, and that of which Peter spoke of, above, is the same thing that was spoken to John in Rev. 2:10b,

"**Progressively come to be a faithful and reliable person** (or: You must be being birthed a trusting and loyal one) **until death, and I will continue giving Life's wreath to you** (or: for you the wreath of The Life; or: the victor's symbol, which is life in you)."

We find this same term employed in 2 Tim. 4:8,

"**For the rest** (or: Henceforth) **the winner's wreath of the Course having been pointed out** (the athlete's laurel wreath consisting of the rightwised relationship in fair and equitable dealings, and pertaining to the justice of right behavior on the course; or: = the wreath from covenant inclusion and participation) **continues laid away for me** (or: **is presently reserved in me**), **which the Lord, the Fair** (Equitable; Just; Rightwising; [Covenant]) **Judge** [of the games], **will proceed to pay to** (or: **award in**) **me within the sphere of that Day – yet not only to me! ... but further, also, to and in all those being ones having loved** (urged toward union with; totally gave themselves to; unambiguously accepted) **His full appearance in Light** (or: the complete manifestation of Him; His fully bringing things to light; the shining upon things pertaining to Him; His full and accurate manifestation)."

These metaphors may be echoes from the *Wisdom of Solomon*:

"Now just people (folks living in the pointed-out Way) will continue living on into the Age [of the Messiah], and thus their reward [is] within the midst of, centered in, and in union with, [the] LORD, and their care [is] at the side of, and in the presence of, [the] Most High. Because of this they will one-after-another receive the attractive crown of state (or: royal dwelling of this dignity), even the beautiful diadem, from out of [the] Hand of [the] LORD, because with the Right Hand He will constantly shelter, cover, hide and protect them, and with the Arm He will continually shield them (defend and cover them with a shield)" (LXX; JM).

Putting on such a wreath is the same thing as admonished in Rom. 13:14,

"**You folks must clothe yourselves with** (or: enter within and put on) **the Lord, Jesus Christ, and stop** (or: do not continue) **making forethought** (constructing provision; planning ahead; performing provident care) **into excessive desires of the flesh** (= into rushing upon emotions which pertain to the inner self or the estranged humanity; = into the setting of feelings and longings upon something of the human nature that is oriented to the System)."

Conzelmann quotes Hans von Soden, "Sakrament und Ethik," 7, stating that,

"It is the case of 'the asceticism of the competitor who is out to win, the behavior of the man who does not roam the vast field of what is permitted, but presses forward on the narrow path of what is beneficial'" (ibid p 162 n 30).

Paul wrote in Gal. 2:2b of the possibility of his "**progressively rushing forward and running, or had run, into emptiness** (or: for an empty thing; into something without content; = to no purpose; or: = in vain)." Then in 5:7a he said to the Galatians, "**You folks have been running beautifully** (finely; ideally; with good form)! **Who** (or: What) **cut in on you folks, to hinder or thwart you...?**" But keeping all this in balance is Rom. 9:16,

"**Consequently, then, [it is] not of or from the one constantly exercising [his] will** (or: [it does] not pertain or belong to habitually intending or designing), **nor of the one constantly rushing forward** (or: nor does it pertain or belong to the one continuously running or habitually racing), **but rather of, from, pertaining to and belonging to God, the One constantly being merciful.**"

26. **So now, I myself am constantly running** (racing) **in this manner – not as without clear visibility of the goal** (not in an uncertain or aimless manner which lacks clear purpose); **thus I am habitually boxing – not as repeatedly flaying** (thrashing; = punching) **air.**

We have two metaphors from the games: running and boxing. Paul offers his own life as an example for the Corinthian group. It was a life of constant focus on the goal; a life of habitual energy spent "to overcome even as He overcame" (Rev. 3:21) – and He overcame through a cruciform Life that was joined to the Vine. He did not thrash about as a boxer that has no skill or training. He embodied what he has said in vs. 25, above.

27. **To the contrary, I am repeatedly "striking my face below my eyes and beating my body black and blue"** (= treating my body severely by discipline and hardship) **and continually leading [it] as a slave** (or: causing it to lead the life of a slave), **lest somehow, while proclaiming** (heralding; preaching; [note: at the games it means to announce the rules of the game and call out the competitors]) **to** (or: for; among) **others, I myself should** (can; may; would) **come to be one that does not stand the test** (or: unproved; or: without the approval which comes from testing; or: disapproved and disqualified).

Paul presents his own body as his opponent in the game of boxing. He causes his body to "**lead the life of a slave.**" He is fully aware of how this personal opponent can overcome him and thus disqualify him from his function of being Christ's representative. The risen Christ warned the entire called-out community in Ephesus that they would be disqualified as functioning as His temple there – symbolized by His threat to remove their lampstand (Rev. 2:5) – unless they "**change their thinking**" and do "**the first works**," which was in their "**first love**" (vs. 4).

But now he takes his audience back to the Roots (Rom. 11:18): he once again grounds them in the types from the OT. Don't miss his mode of exegesis as he draws from Israel's experiences…

Chapter 10

1. **So I am not intending** (or: willing; wanting) **you folks to continue being ignorant, brothers, that our fathers** (= ancestors) **were all continually existing under the cloud, and everyone passed completely through the midst of the sea,**
2. **and so they all immersed themselves into Moses** (or: got themselves baptized [other MSS: were baptized] unto Moses), **within the cloud and within the sea,** [cf Ex. 13:24; 14:21f]

Ps. 104:39 remembers the cloud experience:
> "He spread out a Cloud for a covering shelter for (or: on) them, and a Fire to give Light for (on; among) them, at night" (LXX; JM).

The writer of The Wisdom of Solomon (LXX) interpreted this incident as the work of "Wisdom," personified:
> "She did not abandon (leave down in the midst) a just man when he was being sold as a slave, but rather (to the contrary) She, by Herself, rescued him from out of the midst of a sin (from [that] mistake). She descended together in him, into a pit (or: She stepped down with him into a dungeon), and then did not abandon, leave or neglect him [when] in the midst of chains, until She brought him a scepter of a kingdom, and privilege from this existence (right; authority) over his constant tyrannizers (= those who had been constantly ruling as tyrants over him). She both showed to be false those finding fault with him (demonstrated to be liars those blaming and accusing him) and She gave age-lasting glory for him (life-long fame to him). She rescued a pious (devoted to God) people and a blameless seed from out of a continuously oppressing nation (or: a nation of folks that were constantly pressing and afflicting). She entered into [the] soul of an attending care-provider from [the] LORD (or: [Yahweh's] attendant), and She stood against dreadful kings, within the midst of wonders and signs. She paid to a pious and devoted people a wage (or: reward) for their labors; She guided and led them on an astonishing Path (within the midst of a wonderful Way; centered in a marvelous Road), and came to be a Covering Shelter on (or: for) them by day, and then a Flame of (or: from) stars, by night. She mounted and

caused them to go (or: transported them) through the midst of the Red Sea, and brought them through – through the midst of much (abundant) water" (Wis. 10:13-18, LXX; JM).
The incident is recounted again in Wis. 19, where in vs. 7 we read that, "The Cloud [was] continuously overshadowing the camp (the encampment [of Israel])."

This description of ancient Israel's experiences (passing through the Red Sea and then "**continually existing under the cloud**") is a picture for explaining our immersion into Christ, and our being "led by the Spirit" (Rom. 8:14). Take note of the repetition, and thus emphasis, of the word "**all**" in vss. 1-4. God delivered the whole of Israel, and took the entire nation through all the experiences listed here: and vs. 11, below, instructs us that all these things were types of what would happen at the conjunction of the ages – in which Paul was then living. Israel's experiences were types, examples for the whole world – all of humanity.

The clause, "**immersed themselves into Moses**," sets the picture for the called-out folks being "immersed into Christ" (Rom. 6:3b-5). This entire people became "the body of Moses" (Jude 9). Hereafter, they would identify themselves with him, and hold the Law that he brought to them. Just as Rom. 6:5 associates immersion (the dipping into and then arising out of) as death and then resurrection, so Israel died to their old way of life as slaves in Egypt and then emerged from the Red Sea into a life of freedom. Paul obviously see Christ and the "new Moses" of a "new Exodus." He used this typology from Israel's story as a pattern for the deliverance that we have in Christ. Paul follows the genre of a Jewish Midrash.

3. **and they all ate the same spiritual food,** [*cf* Ex. 16:4, 14-18]

In Ps. 77:22-24, the psalmist spoke of Israel's wilderness history:
> "... they did not trust in God (have faith centered in God), nor did they place expectation upon His deliverance, and yet He, Himself, put His goal and purpose in (implanted His inner directive for; imparted of the finished product by) clouds from above, and then opened up [the] doors of [the] atmosphere ([the] sky; heaven) and rained on (or: among) them manna to eat, that is, He gave to, for and among, them bread from [the] atmosphere (made of sky; having the quality of heaven; heaven's bread). Humanity ate bread from agents (messengers' bread; bread that had the character and quality of folks with a message). He sent off to, and for, them a store of provisions, unto abundance (to fullness)" (LXX; JM).

Notice how Paul interprets what they physically ate as being "spiritual food." He is following Jesus' interpretation in this...
In Jn. 6, Jesus tells the people who were asking him for a sign,
> 32. **Therefore Jesus says to them, "Count on this** (Amen, amen): **I am now [emphatically] saying to you folks, Moses did NOT give the bread from out of the atmosphere** (or: the sky; heaven) **to YOU folks! But rather, My Father is presently** (or: continually; progressively) **giving the true, real, genuine bread from out of the heaven** (or: the atmosphere) **to, for and among you people.**
> 33. **"For God's bread is** (or: You see the bread which is God, and comes from God, exists being) **the One repeatedly descending** (continually or habitually stepping down) **from out of the midst of the atmosphere** (or: heaven) **and constantly** (or: habitually and progressively) **giving Life to the world** (or: in the organized system and secular society; or: for the aggregate of humanity and in the universe)."

The "manna" from the sky was a type for what Jesus said in Jn. 6:56-58,
> "**The person habitually eating My flesh and repeatedly drinking My blood is continuously remaining** (abiding; dwelling) **within, and in union with, Me – and I Myself within, and in union with, him. Just as** (or: In corresponding accordance as) **the continuously-living Father**

135

sent Me off (or: forth) **as an Emissary** (or: commissions Me as a Representative and sends Me on a mission), **and I Myself am continuously living through** (or: because of) **the Father, likewise the person who is habitually eating Me, that person will also continue living, through** (or: because of; by means of) **Me. This is the Bread: the One stepping down** (or: descending) **from out of the midst of heaven** (or: [the] sky and atmosphere) **– not according as the fathers ate and died. The person habitually eating this Bread will continue living on into the Age.**"

4. and they all drank the same spiritual drink, for they kept on drinking from out of a spiritual bedrock (or: cliff rock; rock mass) **– one continually following along behind** (or: progressively accompanying [them]). **Now the bedrock** (or: cliff rock) **was the Christ** (or: the rock mass was existing being the Anointing). [*cf* Ex. 17:6; Num. 20:7-13]

With Paul not giving the background of these statements, we can assume that these stories must have been familiar to his listeners. Since Philo was a contemporary of Paul, let us quote a bit more of his allegorical exegesis on this topic:

> "According to Philo, Moses called manna 'the most ancient Logos of God (*Det.* 118).' Next Philo explains that men are 'nourished by the whole word (Logos) of God, and by every portion of it ... Accordingly, the soul of the more perfect man is nourished by the whole word (Logos); but we must be contented if we are nourished by a portion of it' (LA 3.175-176). And 'the Wisdom of God, which is the nurse and foster-mother and educator of those who desire incorruptible food ... immediately supplies food to those which are brought forth by her ... but the fountain of divine wisdom is borne along, at one time in a more gentle and moderate stream, and at another with greater rapidity and a more exceeding violence and impetuosity....' (*Det.* 115-117). This Wisdom as the Daughter of God 'has obtained a nature intact and undefiled both because of her own propriety and the dignity of him who begot her.'" (*Internet Encyclopedia of Philosophy*, Philo of Alexandria, cir. 20 BC to AD 40; www.iep.utm.edu/philo/#H12)

This kind of Jewish interpretation of their Scriptures should instruct us in regard to Paul's understanding of what that OT story meant, as it pertained to Christ and to the called-out communities. Thus, rather than try to make logical sense of this verse in any literal interpretation, we are well advised to simply follow Paul's thinking and hear his argument: the work of God in the OT was Christ, or a manifestation of the Anointing (itself being a figure for the Spirit of God). The Anointing (which made Jesus "the Christ") was the "**bedrock**" of God's actions in the OT accounts. And thus, following the Spirit's leading, in our own lives, defines us as "sons of God" (Rom. 8:14). Witherington notes that J.D.G. Dunn (*Christology in the Making*, Westminster, 1980 pp 183f) "maintains that Paul is saying that Christ is now the equivalent of what the rock was then" (ibid p 221 n 14).

If we are not familiar with Israel's wilderness history, it behooves us to go back and learn their stories.

The **bedrock** here corresponds to Mat. 7:24-25, where Jesus spoke of "building a house upon bedrock" so that it would survive the floods of adversity that would come against His followers. This is alluded to by the "Foundation Stone" (Christ) of 3:10-11, above. The new city of the new covenant, New Jerusalem (the Jerusalem which is above – Gal. 4:26), is the "temple" that Paul has reference to in 3:10-17, above, and in Rev. 21:19-20 we find twelve foundations of twelve precious stones. These were the beginnings of the corporate Christ of the 1st century AD (note Rev. 21:14 where these twelve foundations have the names of the little Lamb's twelve original sent-forth folks) and was typologically figured by the twelve precious stones of the high priest's breastplate (Ex. 28:17-21) – each one inscribed with the name of one of the tribes of Israel. You see, this foundation, which forms the "roots" of the City, is apocalyptically rooted in OT Israel and corresponds to the "roots" of the olive tree metaphor in Rom. 11:17-18. What was "existential" on the physical realm for Israel in the wilderness is now "existential" for us in the spiritual realm (the atmosphere of the "heavens"). He will take up the topic of everyone drinking "**the same spiritual drink**" once more, in vs. 16, below.

5. **But still, God did not take delight** (was not well-pleased; did not approve) **in the majority of them, for it followed that, they were strewn down flat on the ground** (scattered and laid low) **within the midst of the wilderness** (desolate place; desert; uninhabited place). [*cf* Num. 14:16]

This short paragraph (vss. 1-5) reaches back to Israel's history as support for what he had just said, concerning himself, in 9:27b above, and for what he is now about to apply to everyone (the "**us**" in vs. 6a, below). Deliverance (from Egypt, any empire, or our own personal bondage) is not the end of the journey. Immersion is his term for this deliverance of Israel from Egypt, as well as for the present deliverance (through the work of Christ) from the 1st Adam, from the humanity of dust (15:44-50, below) and from death via our immersion into Him, in the present time.

By analogy, Paul is telling the Corinthian community that they, too, can yet be "**strewn down flat on the ground** (scattered and laid low)" during what remains of their journey through this life, as a part of the "called-out" folks (just as Israel was "called-out" of Egypt, yet the "old generation" among them did not enter into the promised land, which is that to which Paul is referring in vs. 5). These folks in Corinth were not now making a physical journey unto a literal land, but just as those in Moses' day "**drank a spiritual drink**" that came from "the Anointing" that was on Moses, so now these folks were drinking a spiritual drink that was the Living Water, which is Christ:

> "**Just as the Scripture says, 'Rivers** (or: Floods; Torrents) **of living water will continuously flow** (or: gush; flood) **from out of the midst of His cavity** (His innermost being or part; or: the hollow of his belly; [used of the womb])'**" (Jn. 7:38). [*cf* Isa. 58:11; Ezk. 47:1; Joel 3:18; Zech. 13:1; 14:8]

Even though the parent generation of Israel, who came out of Egypt, lived the rest of their lives in the wilderness, and did not enter into His rest (Heb. 4:6), still they were led by the Spirit (the Cloud), they were fed (the manna) and, in Deut. 8:4, Moses reminded them: "Your clothing has not worn out on you, nor did your foot swell these forty years." In Deut. 29:5 he said, "When I conducted you forty years in the wilderness, your clothes did not decay on you, and your sandal, it did not decay on your foot." Even in their unbelief, God cared for them for the rest of their lives. They simply missed out on a higher calling – to come into His rest (Hebrews way of speaking of "the promised land," the place of resting from wandering). But don't forget... even Moses was not allowed to enter into that rest; it was his time to die, along with the rest of that generation. Now we can see this as a type (as per vs. 6, below): Moses represented the Law, and the old covenant. Those were NOT to come into the "rest," which is a type of the new covenant. Those today who bring the Law into the new covenant are also doomed to die in the wilderness in this life, unable to enter into His rest. The Law, which represents "works of the Law" for eschatological deliverance and being rightwised (Gal. 2:16), has no place in the "rest" of the new creation.

This is one of the clearest examples of how to read Israel's history (the OT) and then to draw a spiritual analogy, or distil practical application, for the followers of Christ. Obviously Christ, for Paul, was the new Moses, the new Deliverer. As Paul goes on to say...

6. **Now these things were made to be types of us** (or: were birthed to be examples for, and typological figures pertaining to, us), **[directed] into this [goal]: [for] us not to habitually be those who set their strong passions** (rushing emotions; ardor; cravings) **upon worthless things** (ugly things of bad quality), **just** (correspondingly; along the same lines) **as those also set their passionate emotions and cravings on [such things].**

Let us observe his use of the term "**worthless things** (ugly things of bad quality)." This may be an allusion to the wood, hay and stubble of ch. 3, above. But it could also be setting a contrast to the spiritual bread and the spiritual drink that he discussed, above. Also, as we read in vs. 5, these things would be anything in which "**God [does] not take delight** ([is] not well-pleased; [does] not approve)." A red flag for us would be whatever arouses "**strong passions** (rushing emotions; ardor; cravings)."

7. **Neither continue on to become** (or: Stop becoming) **idolaters, just** (or: correspondingly; along the same lines) **as some of them, even as it has been written,**
> **"The people sit down to continually eat and drink, and they stand up** (arise again) **to repeatedly engage in childish play** (sport; amusement)." [Ex. 32:6]

The context of Ex. 32:1-5 is Aaron listening to the people and then making a molten calf of gold. Having completed it, the LXX has him saying, "These are your gods, Israel, who brought you up from the land of Egypt." The Masoretic Text (Heb.) has the people saying this. Following that, Aaron built an altar in front of it, and the next day people "rose up early and offered burnt-offerings, and presented thank-offerings" (vs. 6a). Then they sat down to eat from the offerings that were presented to the idol. Here we can see why Paul brought up this incident, since eating at idol temples – or eating meat that had been sacrificed to an idol – were issues in the Corinthian community, and thus his instructions here in this verse. Notice that the verb is in the imperative!

8. **Neither may we continue practicing prostitution just** (correspondingly; in the same sphere) **as some of them practiced prostitution – and twenty-three thousand fell in** (or: on) **one day.**

The main issue to which Paul alludes was the "prostitution" of Baal worship, as recorded in Num. 25:1-9. That was also the issue in Ex. 32, cited above in vs. 7. Paul was not addressing personal morality here, but corporate "prostitution" in the form of idolatry. He had dealt with personal morality in 5:1-13, above, and ended with instructing the community to "**Lift up out and carry forth** (Expel; Remove) **the degenerate person** (the misery-gushed, worthless, base or evil one who brings pain) **out of the midst of yourselves**" (vs. 13). He touched again on the personal dangers in 7:2-6, once again. So personal morality was a given – something that was assumed as a requirement for functioning as a "temple of God." We saw the same line of thinking in 6:15-20 where admonitions against prostitution were correlated with their corporate body being a temple of the Holy Spirit, and with being "joined to the Lord." This carries on into the associated issues that we see here in vss. 9-10, below. In Isa. 1:21, Yahweh asks concerning Jerusalem, "How is the faithful city become a prostitute?" We find this same city in Rev. 17:1-6, where we read in vss. 5-6,
> "**A MYSTERY** (A SECRET; a matter that to gain the knowledge of which initiation is necessary) – **BABYLON the GREAT: The <u>Mother</u> of the Prostitutes and of The Abominations** (Detestable Things) **of The Land** (or: from the earth). **Then I saw the woman, being continuously drunk from out of the blood of the set-apart folks and from out of the blood of the witnesses of Jesus**..." Cf Mat. 24:15

Does this seem fantastic that this would refer to 1st century Jerusalem? Consider Mat. 23:
> 35. **"so that upon you, yourselves, can** (or: should) **come all [the] just** (equitable; rightwised) **blood being continuously poured out** (or: spilled) **upon the Land – from the blood of rightwised** (just; fair; in-right-relationship) **Abel, until the blood of Zechariah, the son of Barachiah** (or: Baruch), **whom you people murdered between the Temple and the altar.**
> 36. **"Assuredly, I am now saying to you people, it will progressively move toward this point, and then arrive – all these things! – upon this generation!**
> 37. **"O Jerusalem, Jerusalem! The one repeatedly killing the prophets, and habitually stoning the people sent off with a mission to her**...

And in Lu. 13:33b we read, "**it continues being inadmissible** (not acceptable; = unthinkable) **for a prophet to be destroyed outside of Jerusalem!**" The individual member of the body is important, but Paul's (and the resurrected Jesus, in Rev. 2 & 3) primary concerns involved the community as a whole. Paul commended the whole community of Thessalonica:

"**you turned about toward God from the idols** (forms; images seen; external appearances; pagan concepts and world views) **to continuously be a slave to, for and with the living and true** (or: real) **God**" (1 Thes. 1:9)

And then in 1 Thes. 4:3 he instructed them:

"**You see, this is the will** (intent, purpose) **of God: your state of being set apart from the common use or condition** (or: sacred difference; = covenant living) **– you are to continuously hold yourself from** (be distant from; abstain from) **all of the prostitution.**" [note: figuratively, the worship of idols or false religions, and a break from covenant]

In Israel's history we read how idolatry led them away from God. The Son of God reached back to 1 Ki. 16:31 for the story of Jezebel (who brought Baal-worship to Israel in her time) to critique Thyatira concerning someone in their community that answered to her description. In Rev. 2:20 we read of:

"**Jezebel: she is habitually calling herself a prophetess and she is continually teaching and deceiving** (seducing) **My slaves to practice prostitution and** (or: that is,) **to eat things sacrificed to idols** (things offered to forms and outward appearances)."

In Rev. 14:8; 17:2, 4; 18:3 and 19:2 we read of Babylon's (aka: Jerusalem) prostitution – which was the central reason for her judgment in AD 70.

There is additional insight in Wisdom of Solomon 14:

"You see, an added thought, a devising and an invention of idols [was] a beginning of prostitution, and a discovery of them [the; a] corruption of life. For it follows that this were neither from [the] beginning, nor will it continue existing on into the Age [of Messiah]" (Wis. 14:12-13, LXX; JM).

The issue is turning away from God to become involved in any sort of idolatry – anything that takes the place of God in our lives. Corinth could become a "**daughter**" of Jerusalem. Paul addresses the corporate "us" here in vs. 8, and compares it to "them" (**twenty-three thousand**) in Israel's history (Num. 25:9).

9. **Neither should** (or: may) **we keep on putting the Anointed One** (or: Christ) **to outrageous tests** [with other MSS: put the LORD [= Yahweh] to the proof, out of {personal motives}; with others: try-out God] **just as some of them tested and tried [Him] – and they kept on being destroyed** (lost and ruined-away) **by the serpents, day by day.** [Num. 21:5-9]

10. **Neither continue habitually murmuring** (grumbling with a buzz of under-toned mutterings of critical and discontented comments; [Num. 16:41]) **exactly as some of them murmured – and lost and ruined themselves away** (or: affected their own destruction) **by the Destroyer** [note: same word used in Ex. 12:23, LXX].

These past five verses list that the Corinthians (and thus we, as well) were NOT "to habitually be… continue on to become… continue practicing… or keep on putting, Christ **to outrageous tests.**" Notice God's judgments on Israel in the OT situations that he cited. Keep in mind that all of this stems from what Paul said of himself, in 9:27, above, so these verses here were warnings to the called-out communities! They, and WE, can fall prey to the same pitfalls as did the Israelites of old. Verses 8, 9 and 10 all speak of God's judgment upon His people. But we also read in Heb. 11:23-29 of the trust and faith of Moses during God's visitation upon Egypt through this same "Destroyer," Who is mentioned in Heb. 11:28.

We may well ask, "How has the Destroyer been causing us to become lost, ruining us away from Christ, or causing us to destroy ourselves, because of our habitual '**murmuring** (grumbling with a buzz of under-toned mutterings of critical and discontented comments)'?" Keep in mind that Paul is writing this to the called-out, covenant community – not to the world at large! Take note of the condition of the community in Sardis:

"**I have seen, and thus know** (am aware of) **your works** (actions; deeds) **[and] that you have a name** (= reputation) **that you are living, and yet you are dead!**" (Rev. 3:1)

Or then, there was Laodicea, where He said, "**because you continue being lukewarm** (tepid), **and are neither boiling hot nor cold, I am about to vomit you out of My mouth**" (Rev. 3:16). The Destroyer may or may not bring physical death, but if a branch does not abide in the Vine, the Life of the Vine ceases to flow through the Vine, and the branch is destroyed (the Destroyer is simply the Death that brings lostness and ruin). It is usually the mind's focus on the flesh that breaks the union with the Spirit:

> "**For the result of the thinking** (mind-set; effect of the way of thinking; disposition; result of understanding and inclination; the minding; the opinion; the thought; the outlook) **of the flesh** (= from the human condition or the System of culture and cultus; or: = Torah keeping) **[is; brings] death, yet the result of the thinking** (mind-set; disposition; thought and way of thinking; outlook) **of the spirit** (or: from the Spirit; which is the Breath-effect) **[is; brings] Life and Peace** (joining)" (Rom. 8:6).

In regard to the "**habitually murmuring**," Witherington points us to the complaint from the "mixed multitude" that they had not "meat" to eat (Num. 11:4, 13) in the wilderness. He comments that,

> "These examples are especially apt, then, in Paul's effort to promote the idea of concord in a group of factious Corinthians willing to sacrifice the concord of the body of Christ for the sake of eating meat" (ibid p 218).

11. **Now all these things went on progressively** (or: from time to time) **stepping together among** (or: to; with) **those folks by way of types** (as examples; figuratively), **and it was written with a view toward a placing [of them] into the minds of us: ones unto whom** (directed into the midst of whom) **the ends** (= conjunctions; or: consummations; goals) **of the** (or: these) **ages have come down to** (or: arrived at and meet) **and are now face to face [with us]**.

> [note: "the ends," plural, may describe a picture of a succession, where "one end" meets and touches "another end," this latter being really the beginning of another indefinite time-period, stretched out like a rope; each rope in the time-line having "two ends."]

Verse 11 should be scribed deeply into our hearts. It should guide us as we read the OT, and it should make plain to us the value that the OT should have for us – primarily, as here, in the area of our behavior – to walk in the Spirit, not in the flesh. But we should keep in mind that what they did physically, we can be led astray to do spiritually. Paul obviously saw the value of the old stories as examples for admonition.

A similar statement to the last clause of this verse in found in Heb. 9:

> 25. **Nor yet [is it] that many times He would be repeatedly offering Himself, even as the chief priest is repeatedly entering into the set-apart** (or: holy) **places yearly in blood belonging to another,**
> 26. **otherwise** (or: in that case) **it was continually binding Him to experience [it]** (or: to suffer; to have sense-experiences and to feel) **many times from the founding of the organized System of [their] religion and culture** (or: the casting down of the world or universe). **Yet now** (at this time), **once, upon a conjunction** (a joined destiny; a bringing of [two] ends together ["denoting the joining of two age-times" – E.W. Bullinger, *The Companion Bible*]) **of the ages, He has been and remains manifested** (has been brought to light and continues visible) **into a displacement of the failure** (from the error, sin and deviation from the target) **through the sacrifice of Himself** (or: through His sacrifice; or: by means of the sacrificial altar-offering which was Himself). [*cf* Rom. 6:9-10]
> 27. **And now, according to as much as it continues lying-away** (or: laid away; reserved-off; stored) **in** (or: with; for; to) **mankind** (or: people) **to die-away once, but after this a process of evaluating** (a separating and making a distinction to be a judging and determining; a deciding),

12. **Consequently, let the person habitually supposing** (thinking; imagining) **to have taken a stand – and presuming to still be standing – be continually taking notice and observing so as to heed [that] he should** (or: [and] he would) **not fall.**

Verse 12 echoes the same sentiment that he had said of himself, in 9:27, above. This is a call for attentive living, so that WE would "**be continually taking notice and observing so as to heed [that] WE should** (or: [and] WE would) **not fall**." The author of Hebrews put it this way, in ch. 4:

> 1. **With [the] announced promise to enter into His rest** (or; the ceasing which is Him) **continuing in being remaining left behind down on this level [for us] and fully left [open], we should, then, be at once caused to fear** (= take respectful care and be attentive), **lest at some point anyone from among you folks may be appearing** (or: seeming; or: being of the opinion) **to have been behind** (to have come to be in the rear; or: to be deficient; or: = to have missed it)!
>
> 2. **For you see, we are people having been addressed with goodness** (or: being brought a message of ease and well-being), **even as those folks, also. But the Word** (or: message; thought; idea; Logos) **which they heard did not profit** (or: benefit) **those folks – [it] not having been mixed and blended together with faith, trust or loyalty in** (or: by; for; with) **those at that time hearing [it].**
>
>> [with other MSS: – {they} not being folks that had been co-mingled by conviction and loyalty with those paying attention and listening.]
>
> 3. **For we, those at this point believing and trusting, are progressively entering into the rest** (or: the stopping)…

Paul gave a similar warning in Rom. 11:20b-21,

> "**Stop being haughty** (Don't constantly have high opinions; Do not continually think lofty things), **but to the contrary, [be constantly having] an attitude and mindset of respectful awe** (or: [Godly] fear; healthy respect)! **For you see, since** (or: if) **God spares not** (or: was not thrifty with) **the natural branches** (the branches down from, or, in accord with, nature), **neither will He continue sparing you!**"

And lest we start feeling insecure, brother Judah said THIS of our Lord, in Jude:

> 24. **Now in and by** (or: with; to; for) **Him being powerful and able to keep and guard you folks from stumbling** (or: tripping) **and from harm, and then to stand you flawless and blameless** (or: unblemished; without defect or stain) **in the presence of His glory** (or: down in sight of the manifestation of Him which calls forth praise and yields a good opinion and reputation; or: down in the center of a view of the assumed appearance which is Him) **in extreme joy** (in the center of a much-jumping exultation; in union with body-moving celebration).
>
> 25. **By [the] only God** (or: To and for God alone; In and with God alone), **our Deliverer** (Rescuer; Safe-keeper; Savior; Restorer) – **through Jesus Christ our Lord** (Master; Owner) – **[is] glory** (or: a manifestation of that which calls forth praise; a good reputation; opinion; imagination), **greatness, strength, honor and authority** (right and privilege from out of Being) **before all of the Age** (or: in front of the Age's entirety and all that is the Age), **both now and on into all the ages** (eons; indefinite periods of time)! **Amen** (It is so; Count on it).

The writer of *The Testament of Levi* (one of twelve books that are biographies written between 107 and 137 BC) spoke of "the ends of the ages,"

> "11 Therefore, my children, I have learnt that at the end [Gr. text: ends] of the ages ye will transgress against the Lord, stretching out hands to wickedness against Him; and to all the Gentiles shall ye become a scorn" (trans. by Rutherford H. Platt, Jr., *The Forgotten Books of Eden*, 1926, www.sacred-texts.com/bib/fbe/fbe267.htm; brackets mine)

Another witness comes from the Qumran community in scroll 1QS, Col. 4, lines 20-23,

> "By His truth God shall then purify all human deeds, and refine some of humanity so as to extinguish every perverse spirit from the inward parts of the flesh, cleansing from every wicked deed by a holy spirit. Like purifying waters, He shall sprinkle each with a spirit of truth, effectual

against all abominations of lying and sullying by an unclean spirit. Thereby He shall give the upright insight into the knowledge of the Most High… making wise those following the perfect Way. Indeed God has chosen them for an eternal [pertaining to the Age of Messiah] covenant; all the glory of Adam shall be theirs… Perversity shall be extinct…" (*The Dead Sea Scrolls, A New Translation*, Michael Wise, Martin Abegg, Jr., & Edward Cook, Harper Collins 1996 p 131; brackets mine).

Paul now adds assurances for them…

13. **No trial** (or: ordeal; temptation; putting to the proof; effect of probing and testing) **has laid hold of or seized you folks except a human one** (something pertaining to the human nature and situation). **Now God [is] faithful, loyal, trustworthy, and full of faith and trust – One who will not permit** (let, allow; or: let go; leave alone) **you folks to be tested, tried, tempted or made to undergo an ordeal above** (or: over; = beyond) **that which you people continue having ability and power [to handle or endure], but to the contrary, together with the trial** (or: ordeal), **He will also continually make the way out** (the egress; or: He also will habitually do the stepping forth from out of the midst; or: He will even progressively construct the out-come) **to continually enable and repeatedly empower you folks to undergo [it]** (to bear up under [it]; to carry on under [it], sustain [it], and lead on).

This first statement completely shatters the Zoroastrian dualistic-conceptions that the Jews brought from Persia, and which was later woven into the fabric of the Christian religion. Their trials are NOT due to "*satan*" or demons (i.e., metaphysical entities or animistic influences of the spirit world) coming against them. Their ordeals were "**human ones**." They were testings by "something pertaining to the human nature and situation."

Furthermore, the next statement declares God's control of our tests, trials, temptations and ordeals. This is reminiscent of Job 1 and 2 where God put limitations upon the spirit of adversity (which, by the way were all manifested in humans or through His creation). This apocalyptic scene had God telling His servant that it could go this far, but no farther. We suggest reading those two chapters without wearing dualistic glasses. God was in total control, and even instigated the situations for Job's trials. Concerning vs. 13, here, we can observe that God is intimately involved in these trials.

And so he assures them that "**God [is] faithful, loyal, trustworthy, and full of faith and trust**." Furthermore, He is "**One who will not permit** (let, allow; or: let go; leave alone) **you folks to be tested, tried, tempted or made to undergo an ordeal above** (or: over; = beyond) **that which you people continue having ability and power [to handle or endure]**." What can possibly show us the "rubber-meets-the-road" involvement of God in our daily lives, more than this statement? As the saying goes, "We can take this to the bank" – it is currency backed by Gold (well, actually, by God). Now wait a minute, do we really believe this? Well, William Paul Young projected the trials of his life into *The Shack*. If you've read that novel, he painted a really horrific story that echoed the pain of his own shattered life. And God brought him through it. It is only by the trust that He gives us – and that is really Him putting Himself into us – that can make this true for us. This is the situation as described by Paul in Gal. 2:20,

> "**I was crucified together with Christ, and thus it remains… yet I continue living! [It is] no longer I, but it is Christ continuously living and alive within me! Now that which I, at the present moment, continue living within flesh** (= a physical body), **I am constantly living within [His] faithfulness – in and by that [faithfulness] which is the Son of God** (or: in union with the trust and confidence that is from God's Son; [with other MSS: in the faith and fidelity belonging to God and Christ]), **the One loving me and giving Himself over to another for the sake of me**."

Paul is speaking to a called-out community that has been "joined to the Lord" (6:17, above). Only in such an existential situation can Paul's statement in vs. 13, here, be true. So he goes on to lay it out for them:

> "**To the contrary, together with the trial** (or: ordeal), **He will also continually make the way out** (the egress; or: He also will habitually do the stepping forth from out of the midst; or: He will

even progressively construct the out-come) **to continually enable and repeatedly empower you folks to undergo [it]** (to bear up under [it]; to carry on under [it], sustain [it], and lead on)."
Let us consider the alternate renderings on off parenthetically:

a) "He also will habitually do the stepping forth from out of the midst" – Wow! He not only will "**continually make the way out** (the egress)," He will "walk it out" for us. Remember:

"God is the One habitually operating with inward activity, repeatedly working within, constantly causing function and progressively producing effects within, among and in union with you folks" (Phil. 2:13).

b) "He will even progressively construct the out-come" – that statement needs no comment.
This, too, we can take to the bank. This is true, because: "**God [is] faithful, loyal and trustworthy.**"

14. **Wherefore by all means, my beloved ones, be habitually fleeing away from the idolatry** (the religious service of form, figures or image, and of what is seen; phantoms of the mind; impressions or fancies; ideas and concepts).

Here Paul picks up the same tone of instruction that we saw in vss. 6b-10, in regard to their behavior. Also observe that he returns to the topic of "**idolatry**," similar to what he just said in vs. 7, which he then joined to "**prostitution**" in vs. 8. "In vs. 14 Paul gives the directive that all of chs. 8-10 has been arguing for: Flee from idolatry" (Witherington, ibid p 224).

The parenthetical expansion of the term "idolatry" is worth noting. The Greek *eidōlon* properly means: a form, shape figure; external appearance; image or statue; an idol, an image of a god. It comes from the verb *eidō* which meant: to see. With this in mind, consider what is on offer:

a) the religious service of "form" – this can refer to a cultus or way of performing a religious act;
b) figures or image – these can apply to non-religious, cultural ideals or presentations; icons;
c) what is seen – either mental imaging or what the physical eye beholds;
d) phantoms of the mind – visions, imaginations, inventions (Wis. 14:12, above);
e) impressions or fancies – responses to what we've seen; attachment to ideals;
f) ideas and concepts – theories; philosophies; doctrines; world views; etc.

Now none of these things are of themselves "idolatry," but we can turn them into idols and even subconsciously "worship" them – hold them in contrast to Christ and the knowledge of God. A sinister aspect of idolatry was that it could become what folks thought of as a way of controlling God (or: a god, as they perceived it). Today Christian enthusiasts can come close to this by thinking that they can use God's Word to control Him. "He said it, so He has to do it!" – or so they say. Manipulation was usually a companion to religious practices – even if its purpose was simply to have it rain on their crops, or protect them from harm. Most often, an idol was something (or someone) that people "used."

With this verse in mind, which warns of idolatry, consider its relation to his topic that begins in vs. 16…

15. **I am now saying [this] as to and for sensible and thoughtful people** (ones with a prudent and intelligent frame of mind; discreet and discerning folks)**: you, yourselves, sift and decide about** (or: separate and judge) **what I continually affirm and mean.**

Now in these verses he returns to a central theme – something that must have been plaguing this community: idolatry. He tells them to actually "run" from it, in vs. 14. Well, this has been, and still is, a core issue that is common to all humanity, from Eve, in the Garden, to the Greeks of Paul's day (both were seeking wisdom, to the point of placing that before God).

In vs. 15 he appeals to their mental capacities and their "intelligent frame of mind," as well as their "discretion and discernment." He knows them. He knows that if they take his words to heart, they are "smart enough" to perceive and apply what he has been saying. So he puts it to their own judgment of these issues, and asks them to sift out any straw or unrefined particles before they eat it. This call for their discernment especially applies to the next two verses...

16. **The cup of The Blessing** (or: The cup which is the Word of Goodness, ease and well-being; the cup of the Idea from Goodness) **which we are habitually blessing** (speaking well of; speaking of with reference to goodness, ease and wellness), **is it not** (does it not exist being) **the common existing and sharing with, participation in, fellowship of, communion of being with and partnership of, and from, Christ's blood** (or: the blood which is the Anointing)**?**
The bread (or: loaf of bread) **which we are habitually breaking, is it not** (does it not exist being) **the common existing and sharing with, participation in, fellowship of, communion of being with, and partnership of, and from, Christ's body** (or: the body which is anointed)**?**

Since this verse twice uses the term that has its semantic range conflated as "**common existing and sharing with, participation in, fellowship of, communion of being with and partnership,**" we feel that the opening phrase, "**The cup of The Blessing,**" might have multiple allusions. What first comes to mind is the corporate metaphor found in Isa. 65:8,

> "Thus says Yahweh: 'As new wine [LXX reads: grape] is found in the cluster, and someone says, "Do not destroy it, for a blessing [LXX adds: of the LORD] is in it," so will I do for the sake of my servants so as not to ruin and destroy the whole [nation] [LXX reads: for the sake of the one who is subject to Me, for this one, I will not proceed to ruin or destroy them all].'"

The point is that the "new wine [or, grape]" is a part of "the cluster" – the body of Israel, at that time. Because of His Servant, He would not ruin and destroy the whole of Israel. And even with them, "the BLESSING" was in them: they carried IT. Another picture adds to this scene:

> "**to the end that the Good Word** (the Blessing; the Word of wellness and goodness) **pertaining to Abraham** (belonging to and possessed by Abraham; whose intermediary source is Abraham) **could within Jesus Christ suddenly birth Itself** (or: may from Itself, within Anointed Jesus, at once come into being [and be dispersed]) **into the multitudes** (the nations; the ethnic groups; the Gentiles), **so that we** [note: "we" = the new "one" mankind; *cf* Eph. 2:11-16] **could receive the Spirit's promise through the Faithfulness [of Christ]**" (Gal. 3:14).

The Cup also represented "the Blessing of Abraham," which was for the ethnic multitudes of the world, and was further defined as "the Spirit's promise (or: the Promise from the Breath-effect; or: the Promise, which is the Spirit)." Or, as is written in 1 Pet. 3:9b,

> "**constantly speaking things that embody wellness or give a Blessing, because into this you are called** (or: were invited), **to the end that you folks may inherit a word embodying wellness** (a Blessing; a message of goodness; a thought bringing ease)."

In Rom. 15:29, Paul uses the word "blessing" (*eulogias*) in a way that is instructive:

> "**Now I have seen and thus know** (or: am aware) **that when coming** (or: going) **to you I will continue coming** (or: going) **in an effect of the fullness of Christ's message of Goodness**
> (or: within that which fills up pertaining to [the] good word {*Logos*} about Christ; in a result of the entire contents of well-speech from [the] Anointing; in union with an effect of the filling of [the] Blessing, which is [the] Anointed One)."

So, "The Cup of THE Blessing" is all of this. And since we will read in vs. 17, below, that "**the bread**" symbolizes "**The Many,**" the common "**cup,**" may also signify the called-out community, from which the world may drink of His Life. We therefore suggest viewing its significance as more than a cultic ritual. But let us continue...

We now extract the two realities that he draws from "**the cup**" – clearly a reference to the "**spiritual drink**" of vs. 4, above, which was a part of their natural sustenance in the wilderness – and "**the bread,**" that is an echo of the "**spiritual food,**" in vs. 3, above:

> a) **the common existing and sharing with, participation in, fellowship of, communion of being with and partnership of, and from, Christ's blood** (or: the blood which is the Anointing);

b) **the common existing and sharing with, participation in, fellowship of, communion of being with, and partnership of, and from, Christ's body** (or: the body which is anointed).

Israel, in the wilderness, had a "common existence." They depended on God for something to drink and something to eat. Likewise with the Corinthian community that existed within the "wilderness" of the Roman Empire and a Hellenistic society. They needed "spiritual food and drink" – both of which were aspects of Christ's Life (His blood, which was also the Anointing – *cf* Heb. 10:22, "**hearts having been sprinkled**... **the body having been bathed**" – and His body, which is "**true, real, genuine food** -- Jn. 6:55).

So observe this: both **the cup** and **the bread** were their "**common existing and sharing**." The cup and the bread are the Life and the Body which is, in fact, the called-out covenant community in Corinth. On offer is a conflation of the semantic range of the Greek term *koinōnia*: "common existing (the root of this term is *ōn*, a present participle of the verb "to exist," and it is prefixed by *koin*, from the adjective *koinos*, 'common; belonging equally to several; shared; etc.')... partnership" which can be seen in both a) and b), above. This community in Corinth is "the body of Christ" (*cf*, e.g., 12:27, below) – both of these metaphors (cup and bread) refer to this group of people, or to any called-out community. Paul seems to be defining the community with these words. He gives further explanation by saying...

17. **Because we, The Many, are** (exist being) **One Bread** (one loaf of bread), **One Body, it follows that we, The All** (the all of humanity), **are continuously holding a share with others and are co-partaking from out of the One Bread** (or: this one loaf of bread).

This calls to mind the theme of ONE, in Eph. 4:2b-6,
> "**continuously holding one another up** (or: bearing with each other with tolerance) **within the sphere of, and in union with, love** (unqualified acceptance and the urge toward union), **repeatedly hurrying to make every effort to constantly keep** (watch over to guard and protect; maintain) **the Spirit's oneness** (or: the unity from the Breath-effect, and of spirit; the oneness which is the Spirit) **within the bond** (the link, tie and connection that joins two things; the binding conjunction which results in union) **of the Peace** (or: which is from THE JOINING), **[making] ONE BODY and ONE SPIRIT** (attitude and effect of the Breath), **according as you folks were** (or: are) **also called** (summoned) **within the midst of ONE expectation of your calling** (or: summons; invitation), **[with] ONE Lord** (Master), **ONE faith** (or: loyalty, confidence and trust), **ONE effect of submersion and envelopment which brings absorption and permeation to the point of saturation, ONE God and Father of all humans – the One upon all people and [moving] through all people, and within the midst of all humanity and in union with all people and all things**."

One Bread also means "**One Body**." On the first level of interpretation, he is speaking of the spiritual unity of relationship among the membership of the community. He is not talking about a cracker and a sip of grape juice! He is not speaking of a symbolic ritual, but of an existential relationship that is a "common existence." He will develop this theme in ch. 12, below. Now on another level, just as Paul used one human, Adam, to represent all humanity, in Rom. 5:12-21 as well as in 15:44-49, below, and then in 15:50 he instructs us that he is not speaking of "flesh and blood," i.e., of the physical existence, here the Body of Christ is representative of, a picture of, and a living parable of, "**The All (the all of humanity)**." The body of Christ is the firstfruit of the later harvest of all of humanity. Jacob made this same analogy in Jas. 1:18,
> "**Being purposed** (intended; willed), **from being pregnant He gave birth to us** (brought us forth; prolifically produced us) **by a Word** (in a collected thought; for an expressed idea; with a message) **of Truth and from Reality – into the [situation for] us to be** (or: to continuously exist being) **a specific** (or: a certain; some) **firstfruit of His created beings** (or: of the effects of His

act of creating; or: from the results of the founding and creation which is Himself; [other MSS: of the Himself-creatures])."

In the types found in Israel's annual feasts, we find the waving of the sheaf of the firstfruits (Lev. 2:10-14). This was done prior to the general harvest (*cf* all of Lev. 23).

It is interesting that Paul used the definite article with both "Many" and "All," in this verse. The common versions usually do not translate the article (e.g., NRSV, NASB, ESV, KJV, NIV), however Kenneth Wuest's *Expanded Translation* renders it with the first noun, "the many," but not with the second noun, "all." Why is this important? When Paul used the phrase, "the many," in Rom. 5:15 and 5:19, he was using it to refer to "all humanity" in 5:12 and 5:18. Here Paul is associating these two phrases as referring to the same, corporate group: mankind as a whole.

Thus the "**we**," found twice in vs. 17, here, should also be seen as speaking of "the all of humanity," i.e., the corporate Adam of ch. 15, below, and of "the many" of Rom. 5:12ff. On the firstfruits level, Paul was referring to "the called-out," but on the humanity-wide level it applies to Adam ("**who is, and continues being, a replication** {an impress; a pattern; a type; a pre-figure} **of and from the One being repeatedly about to [be]** {or: the One habitually impending}," – Rom. 5:14b), whom he uses to refer to all humanity in 15:45 and 47, below. You see, the "world" is supposed to partake of us as we partake of Jesus. The Corinthian community was "one loaf of bread" that was "**continuously holding a share with others and are co-partaking from out of the one Bread**," i.e., Jesus Christ. Now the called-out that is "joined to the Lord" is "one loaf of bread" from out of whom a greater loaf of bread (the rest of humanity, in its time and class – 15:23, below) will continuously hold a share and co-partake of the Christ. This time-tiered presentation (firstfruits, then the rest of the harvest) is similar to the association of the various "heads/sources" in 11:3, below.

The idea of humanity being in God's likeness was incarnated in humanity's oneness: the One New Humanity of Eph. 2:15. The "common existing" of the called-out is a figure for the "common existing" of all of humanity. When everyone sees Him, they will all be like Him (1 Jn. 3:2), for they will see Him as He is – not as the institutional church has painted Him to be.

The concept of God's Temple (a called-out community) being integral to the whole of humanity can be seen in Jesus' parable of the kingdom (reign) in Mat. 13:33,

> "**The reign** (kingdom; sovereignty; dominion) **of the heavens and atmospheres exists being (is) like leaven** (or: yeast) **which a woman, upon getting** (taking; receiving) **[it], hides within** (= mixes in) **three large measures** (1.5 pecks, or 12 quarts, per measure) **of wheat flour, or meal, until [the] whole [batch] is leavened to thus be fermented, risen [and teeming with life]!**"

The kingdom/reign, which is represented in Paul in the "community-temple" metaphor, permeates all humanity, raising it higher, as it becomes One Loaf that is ready for His Fire of purification.

Another picture from Jesus is found in Mat. 13:44,

> "**The reign** (or: kingdom; sovereignty; dominion) **of the heavens and atmospheres exists being (or: is) like a treasure – having been hidden** (or: being concealed) **within the midst of a field...**"

Now recall that Jesus instructed them in Mat. 13:38, "**Now the field is the organized System** (the ordered arrangement; the world of religion, economy, culture and government; = the realm of society; or: the aggregate of humanity)." Covenant communities are the treasure hidden within "**The Many**."

18. **Take an extended look at Israel, according to [the] flesh, and be observing [their cultural situation]: are not those habitually eating the things sacrificed common-beings of the altar** (partners, partakers and ones who share common participation pertaining to the altar)**?**

When he speaks of Israel "**according to [the] flesh**," he is referring to historic Israel, as the human nation whose story is recorded in the OT. In Rom. 9:3b, Paul refers to Israel as, "**my brothers, my relatives** (kinsmen; joint or commonly born ones; fellow countrymen) **according to flesh** (= in the sphere of natural human birth)." Then, in 9:5, he even speaks of Christ in this way, tying Him to:

> "**the fathers** (= ancestors) **and forth from out of the midst of whom [is] the Christ** (= the Messiah), **the [descendant] down the line of flesh** (or: according to and on the level of the human realm) – **the One continuously being upon all mankind: God, worthy of praise and blessing on into the ages!**"

Thus he is grounding his arguments, and his listeners, in the OT and their spiritual "roots." We, too, need to "**take an extended look at Israel**" – to find Christ in its shadows and types (Lu. 24:27). The history of Israel is a source of spiritual understanding, especially for when endeavoring to perceive Paul's metaphors concerning the new creation (keeping in mind that Israel, by comparison, was the "old" creation that has passed away – 2 Cor. 5:17).

Here in vs. 18, Paul is alluding to Lev. 7:1-6, 15, and Deut. 18:1-4. These Scriptures instituted the communal meals for the priests in Israel, when sacrifices or offerings were made for Yahweh. In Deut. 12:11ff, Moses instructs the people concerning some of the tithes and offerings that they bring to the priests. The people, as well, were to "eat them before Yahweh [their] God, in the place which Yahweh [would] choose" (Deut. 12:18). This was one of the ways that the priests were fed, too. Witherington reports:

> "According to Philo (*De Spec. Leg.* 1.221), 'he to whom sacrifice has been offered makes the group (*koinōnon*) of worshippers partners in the altar and of one table'" (ibid p 225).

So Paul was not the only one who held such views. Both the Jews and the "strong" – those with "knowledge" – would probably been familiar with Philo.

Now there is a new priesthood (e.g., Rev. 1:6; *cf* Heb. 7:11-28), and we are able to eat and be nourished from His altar – for as being His new priesthood, we participate with "**common-being**" in His altar and sacrifice.

This may have been the original saying of, "You are what you eat." The implication of Paul's rhetorical question is that, "Yes, they are." Eating part of the sacrifice made one a participant, so that he had "common-being" in the whole event. Let us stress the fact, again: in ancient Israel, the sacrifices physically sustained the priests who actually performed the ritual. It became part of an actual meal for the priests. The altar of the sacrificial cult corresponded to the table fellowship of the "new priests" of the "new arrangement/covenant." So there was a symbolic, spiritual aspect of the communal meals of the called-out communities. The cup, and the bread that they were breaking together (vs. 16, above), was an actual "common existence" that the members of the community shared together.

19. What, then, am I now meaning and affirming? That what is sacrificed to an idol is anything? Or, that an idol is anything (= something more than just an idol)**?**

No, obviously he was not saying those things about either the sacrifice or an idol, as he affirms in the next verse. He is rhetorically taking his listeners back to what he had said in 8:5-6, above, to re-introduce his theme on "idolatry." To those in Galatia, he made it clear:

> "**[At] that time, in fact, having not perceived and thus not knowing God, you folks were, and performed as, slaves to** (or: for) **those [who], by nature, are not gods**" (4:8).

In Isa. 65:3, Yahweh complains about the behavior of Israel:

> "This people [is] the one constantly provoking Me through everything – in My very presence! (or: in the thing or place that is opposite to Me; in union with that which is in place of Me; or: in My sight!) They are repeatedly sacrificing (keep on making offerings) in the gardens, and constantly burn incense upon the bricks, to and for **the demons** (Hellenistic term and concept for assumed animistic influences) – which things **DO NOT exist**!" (LXX: JM)

147

J.M. Powis Smith, *et al, The Complete Bible, An American Translation*, renders Ps. 96:5a,
> "For all the gods of the peoples are non-entities…"

The *Tanakh* renders the predicate: "are mere idols." In Rotherham: "are things of naught." CVOT: "are useless [idols]." William F. Beck: "are worthless idols." *The Jerusalem Bible* gives us: "Nothingness, all the gods of the nations."

So, in the next verse, he goes on to answer his rhetorical questions, and to address the situation that was being practiced by some members of the group…

20. **To the contrary** (or: Not at all!)**: that which the multitudes of ethnic groups** (the nations; the pagans; the Gentiles) **habitually sacrifice, they continue sacrificing to, for or by demons** (Hellenistic concept and term: = animistic influences; personified concepts), **and not to, for or by God** (or: even to or by a non-god, or a no-god), **and I am not intending for** (willing; wanting) **you folks to proceed to becoming partakers of and thus common-beings with the demons**
> (= partners and ones who share common participation pertaining to the animistic influences [possibly: = evil or deranged spirits, mental conditions or attitudes]).

Was he affirming the reality or the existence of "demons" by what he has just said? We do not think so. What we suggest that he means is that it was the INTENT, and the purpose, of these pagans to make their offerings and sacrifices to "animistic influences" or "personified concepts" – which Paul goes on to say were "non-gods," or, "no gods" – but which THEY believed to be real. He was also affirming that these Gentiles were NOT doing this "**to, for or by God.**" All of the OT spoke against such things. What Paul is addressing, here, is the practice of eating meals at the dining halls of the idol temples. By what he had just laid out as an existential principle, in vs.18, was that to eat something that was a part of a sacrifice was to come into "common-being" with that sacrifice. So to eat what was offered to a false god was to become a "partaker" of their altar, and thus participate in idolatry.

We read Paul as using the term "demons" as derogatory rhetoric to devalue sacrifices to idols and show them in a very negative light. Jesus had come casting out "demons" which were also termed "deranged or evil spirits," or what we might call "bad attitudes" or "mental illness." Paul did not want members of God's temple to have any common-existence with the concepts of animism or any such superstitions.

21. **You folks are unable to continue to drink** (or: You cannot habitually drink) **[the] cup of the Lord** (or: the Owner's cup; or: = the cup pertaining to Christ; or: [Yahweh's] cup; *cf* John 18:11) **and a cup of demons** (or: a cup pertaining to animistic influences [possibly: = evil attitudes; deranged mental conditions; evil spirits]); **you are unable to continue to** (or: to habitually) **hold a share with and co-partake of [the] Lord's** [= Christ's or Yahweh's] **table and also a table of demons** (pertaining to or having its source in animistic influences [possibly: = evil attitudes or qualities]).

We notice that Mal. 1:7 refers to the altar of burnt-offering as "the table of the Lord;" Isa. 65:11, Jer. 7:18 and Ezk. 16:18; 23:41 use the term "table" with reference to pagan idol-feasts. Thus, Paul may be using the terms "cup" and "table" figuratively, and not referring to specific ceremonies. We see from vs. 20 that his concern is that they NOT "**becoming partakers of and thus common-beings with**" idols (which he terms "demons," for the Hellenistic audience to which he is writing).

Paul did not budge an inch on this issue. Again, the term "**cup**" signifies participation, and noted in Jn. 18:11. In Mk. 10:38, Jesus asked Jacob (James) and John,
> "**Do you now have power and do you continue able to drink the cup which I Myself am now progressively drinking, or to be immersed in** (or: baptized with) **the immersion** (baptism) **which I Myself am now progressively being immersed** (baptized)**?**"

Drinking the cup signified participation and experiencing the same sort of ordeal that Jesus was about to endure. Here, Paul once again is signifying "common existence" and "common experience" by use of this metaphor.

The note which I have inserted into my translation of this verse, above, gives OT references and explanations for the meaning of the term "**table**." Participating in idol-feasts was not compatible with membership in the called-out community. Such activities were entering into a partnership with the idol.

22. **Or are we proceeding to cause the Lord's emotions to boil over the side** (constantly inciting the Lord [= Christ, or Yahweh; *cf* Deut. 32:21, LXX] to jealous indignation)**? We are not stronger than He!**

Here Paul expresses what he knows would be the Lord's feelings and response about this issue. Recall the risen Christ's messages to the Asia Minor communities in Rev. 2 and 3. He had harsh words for the community in Thyatira about "**that woman, Jezebel**" that was "**continually teaching and deceiving** (seducing) **My slaves to practice prostitution** (adultery; fornication) **and** (or: that is,) **to eat things sacrificed to idols** (things offered to forms and outward appearances)" (Rev. 2:20).

Paul's second question suggests that the Lord would indeed use His strength to correct the Corinthian community (*cf* Rev. 2:22-23, which instructs us of His intent toward that Jezebel and her "children"). It behooves us to ask our Father to point out any areas of idolatry in our lives and cultures.

Paul continues his teaching on this topic...

23. **All things are presently out-of-Being** (or: All things continue from existence; or: All is authorized, right and permitted), **but yet not all things proceed to bear together for advantage, profit or expedience. All things are authorized, permitted and out of [His] Being, but yet not all things progressively edify or build up the house**
> (or: All exists from out of [His] Being, but not all keeps on bringing [things] together; all is from Existence, but not all continues to edify).

The first half of this couplet repeats 6:12a, above, but the second half now points to the community as being the focus of concern regarding our behavior. Yes, all things come from out of God (Rom. 11:36), but our concern is now about **building up His House**. If something does not "**bear together for advantage, profit or expedience**," then it should not be a part of the life of the community. And so he continues...

24. **Let no one be habitually seeking the [interest, advantage, profit, welfare or edification] of, or pertaining to, himself, but to the contrary, the [interest, advantage, profit, welfare and edification] of the other** (or: pertaining to the different) **person.**

Once again, the answer is a cruciform life, with a view to how one's life affects the lives of others. This was the pattern and example of Jesus, and now again in Paul, and he wants this pattern to spread. This is Love that is lived out.

25. **Go on habitually eating everything that is normally being sold in** (or: at) **a meat market, while examining nothing because of** (or: sifting not one thing back through) **the conscience,**
26. **for it follows from,**
> "**the earth** (or: land; soil) **and the results of its filling** (entire contents; that which fills it up) **belong to and have their origin in the Lord** [= Yahweh]." [Ps: 24:1; etc.]

So here is practical advice from which we can extract a principle for living that reaches beyond the specific situation in Corinth and other 1st century communities. We live seeing God both behind and within everything.

27. **If anyone of the unbelievers** (or: of those not full of faith and void of trust) **is periodically inviting you folks [to be his guest], and you are wanting** (or: intending) **to go, keep on habitually eating everything that is normally being placed beside** (or: = set before) **you, while examining nothing because of** (or: sifting not one thing back through) **the conscience** (integrated inner knowing).
28. **Yet if anyone should say to you folks, "This is [meat; something] offered in a temple or a sacred sacrifice to an idol," do not proceed to eat [it], because of that person pointing it out** (disclosing it) **and [on account of] the conscience** (integrated inner knowing; perceptive awareness).
29. **Now I am not speaking [about] your own conscience, but rather the other person's. For to what purpose is my freedom now being decided by another person's conscience?**

Paul moves to a more specific example, and the central issue is the conscience (the inner level of awareness in regard to the new creation and the new covenant) of BOTH parties involved. We do not lose our freedom in Christ when we sacrifice that freedom for the benefit of someone who lacks the perceptive awareness of the new Being, the anointed Temple that has been called to reflect Christ's glory (2 Cor. 3:18).

30. **If I myself am continuously participating** (holding a share with [others] and co-partaking) **in grace and favor** (or: with gratitude), **why am I being repeatedly blasphemed** (spoken abusively about; vilified; injuriously misrepresented; or: hindered in regard to the Light) **over what I myself am habitually receiving in good grace and for which I am expressing gratitude?**

He said it this way, in Rom. 8:1,

> "**Nothing, consequently, [is] now a result of condemnation in** (or: a commensurate effect of a decision for; a corresponding result of a negative evaluation which falls in line with a decision or follows the pattern which divides [folks] down, with) **those within Christ Jesus**
> > (or: In that case, therefore, [there is] now not one thing [that is] really an effect of a downward-judging to, in or with the folks in union with or centered in [the] Anointing of Jesus)!"

In using the word "**blasphemed**" in application to himself, we are given a window into the semantic range and usage of this term in that day. Notice that it can also mean "spoken abusively about; vilified," or, "injuriously misrepresented." These give us understanding of the practical ways that a person could "blaspheme" another person. But on offer is a meaning that is based upon the Greek elements that compose the word: "hindered in regard to the Light." We see another example of these meanings in Acts 13:45,

> "**Yet upon seeing the crowds, the Jews were filled with jealousy and began contradicting the things being spoken by Paul, while repeatedly speaking abusively** (or: arguing with slander and invectives; speaking light-hindering misrepresentations; defaming with accusations of villainy)." Cf 4:13, above; Acts 18:6

31. **Therefore whether you folks are habitually eating or continually drinking, or anything you are constantly doing, be continuously doing all things unto God's glory**
> (or: performing everything [directed toward and leading] into a good reputation pertaining to God; making all things into a manifestation which calls forth praise to God; forming all people into an assumed appearance from God).

This is a conclusion of what he was saying in vss. 27 and 28, and is first of all speaking into the context of this passage. However, taking his last clause not as simply a cliché, this points us to what can be the restraining side of Rom. 8:14 (being led by the Spirit) and is, in fact, a central, guiding Light for how we live our lives: **doing all things unto God's glory**. This should give insight into any questions concerning our behavior or decisions about our businesses and corporate relationships. Let us pause to consider the alternate renderings of this last clause:

> a) performing everything [directed toward and leading] into a good reputation pertaining to God'
> b) making all things into a manifestation which calls forth praise to God;
> c) forming all people into an assumed appearance from God.

It is this last rendering, "c," that speaks the most to us. This would speak of our affect upon other people, as being their fathers (4:15, above), as the child-training of a parent "forms" the children that they are raising. We want the "appearance" (one of the meanings of "glory") that they "assume" (another meaning of "glory") to be that which comes from God, so that their appearance will reflect His image and likeness.

We find a similar thought in Eph. 5:10,

> "**repeatedly testing so as to prove and approve** (or: continuously showing proof of) **what is** (or: continually exists being) **fully pleasing and compatible** (happily acceptable; well pleasing; good pleasure) **to** (or: for; in; with) **the Lord**." *Cf* 2 Cor. 5:9; Phil. 1:20

32. **Progressively come to be people who are not obstacles or causes for stumbling** (= become inoffensive) **– both to, or among, Jews and to Greeks** (or: among those of the Hellenistic culture), **as well as to God's called-out community** (or: God's called-out person),

Paul gave this admonition in Rom. 14:13,

> "**No longer, then, should we continue judging** (making decisions about; discriminating against; separating away) **one another, but rather, to a greater extent you folks must decide this: not to continue placing** (or: setting) **the stumbling-block** (that which results in tripping) **for or in the brother; neither a snare** (a trap-spring; a cause for tripping or becoming trapped)."

We find similar instruction in Phil. 1:10-11,

> "**habitually test, examine, distinguish and determine the things that carry through and are thus of consequence or make a difference, so that you may constantly be folks judged by the light of the sun** (thus: clearly sincere and with integrity) **and ones [that are] not stumbling or jarring against [anything] nor striking toward [someone] and causing trouble, on into the midst of a Day of, and which is, Christ** [*p*46: the Day from Christ (or: an anointing)], **being people having been filled full with [the] Fruit of fair and equitable dealings which bring right relationship within the Way pointed out: the one [that is] through Jesus Christ [that is] leading into God's glory**."

Everyone needs to be reminded of these things. They are admonitions for universal application.

33. **correspondingly as I myself am also habitually accommodating and pleasing all folks in all things, not continually seeking the thing that bears together for advantage, profit, welfare and expedience of myself, but to the contrary, that which pertains to The Many – to the end that they can and would be saved** (rescued, delivered, healed, kept safe, made whole and restored to their original state and condition)**!**

Witherington observes:

> ""The rule is 'consider others first.' Verse 33 explains further that Paul strives to fit in with everyone in all such matters… in order to save many for Christ" (ibid p 228).

This is a synopsis, a recap, of all that he has just been saying. Notice in vs. 33 that he once again uses the phrase, "The Many," and that this is speaking with a view to their being "**saved** and **delivered** (etc.)." This is an example of what Jesus said, "**the works** (actions; deeds) **which I Myself am constantly doing** (habitually performing; progressively making, constructing, creating, forming) **that person also will proceed doing** (performing; making; creating; producing), **and he will progressively be doing and producing greater than these**" (Jn. 14:12).

Christ completed His work, but now we are called to carry on that same work. Paul is saying that our behavior and our way of life is meant to be the vehicle of salvation, healing, deliverance and restoration for those of "The Many" with whom He brings us into contact. There is no greater calling than this. And it is because we are joined to the Lord, are one Spirit with the Lord, and we "house" the Lord. We no longer live, but Christ lives within us – provided we "abide in the Vine."

1. Progressively come to be imitators of me, correspondingly as I, myself, also [am] of Christ and from [the/an] Anointing.

I have moved this verse from the beginning of ch. 11 to be joined closely with Paul's thoughts in 10:33 where he is speaking of his own behavior and way of life. Because he lives as described in vs. 33, he can say what he does in 11:1, given here. As often done, I have conflated the final prepositional phrase of this verse rendering the Greek form as first a genitive (of Christ) and then an ablative (from [the/an] Anointing). Notice that Paul did NOT tell them to follow him. No, they are to be led by the Spirit, and imitate Paul by following Christ – just as he is following Christ. The Anointing is just one description of how we experience Christ within us.

Paul takes the role of the teacher and sets the Corinthians in the role of students. Witherington posits that since these folks were immature (3:1ff, above), "Paul must tell them to use the elementary pedagogical device of imitation" (ibid p 230). Perhaps Paul had in mind the same thought that he wrote to the Philippians,

> "**You see, this way of thinking** (this attitude and disposition) **is continuously within and among you folks** (or, as an imperative: So let this minding be habitually within you folks) – **which [is] also within Christ Jesus**.... **He empties Himself** (or: made Himself empty), **receiving** (or: taking; accepting) **a slave's form** (outward mold), **coming to be within an effect of humanity's likeness. And so, being found in an outward fashion, mode of circumstance, condition, form-appearance** (or: character, role, manner) **as a human, He lowers Himself** (or: humbled Himself; made Himself low), **coming to be a submissive, obedient One** (one who gives the ear and listens) **as far as** (or: to the point of) **death – but death of a cross!**" (Phil. 2:5, 7, 8).

He had written this to the Thessalonians,

> "**within much pressure** (or: squeezing; oppression) **you yourselves were birthed** (produced, made to be) **imitators of us and of the Lord, receiving** (taking in hand) **the Word** (or: idea; thought; message;) **with [the] joy of [the] set-apart Breath-effect**" (1 Thes. 1:6).

And in Phil. 3:17 he said,

> "**Brothers** (Folks from the same womb; Family; Fellows), **be progressively birthed to be joint-imitators of me** (or: unite in becoming my imitators), **and continually keep a watchful eye on and take note of those habitually walking about thus** (i.e., those who thus live their lives), **according as you folks continue having us as a pattern** (model; example; type)."

Paul's life was a living parable, and a letter to be read by all. May we imitate his example.

Chapter 11

2. Now I am continually commending and appreciating (or: applauding; adding praise upon) **you folks because you have called to mind and still remember everything that originated with me** (or: that came from and had its source with me; that is mine and of me), **and habitually keep possession of** (or: hold down and retain) **the traditions** (things handed on; *cf* vs. 23, below) **just as I handed [them] on** (or: transmitted [them]) **to** (or: for; among) **you people.**

Paul has just been delivering some intense admonition to his listeners (keep in mind that this letter was being read, and performed to include non-verbal communications, by whoever was acting as the rhetor for the audience in Corinth), and as preparation of his audience, by a good rhetor, he breaks the intense flow with a commendation to his audience to keep them drawn-in to what is being presented. This compliment also affirms to them his feelings about, and opinion of, them and reinforces his solidarity with them. It would praise them to hear Paul saying, "**you have called to mind and still remember everything that originated with me** (etc.)." Then by continuing with, "**[you] habitually keep possession of** (or: hold down and retain) **the traditions** (things handed on; *cf* vs. 23, below) **just as I handed [them] on** (or: transmitted [them]) **to** (or: for; among) **you people**," he prepares them for what he is next about to say…

3. **Now I continue intending** (willing; wanting; purposing) **you folks to be aware, from having seen and thus knowing, that the Christ is** (or: exists being) **the Source** (or: Head) **of every adult male** (or: the Anointing is the head of every husband); **in turn the adult Male [was] a source of Woman** (or: the husband [is] a head of a wife); **and yet God [is the] Source of the Christ, and the Anointing** (or: [is] Head of the Anointed One)!

He grounds his next topic in Christ, and then builds from there. Conzelmann (ibid p 182) notes that Paul is not making this argument based upon a Christian tradition, but rather on Hellenistic-Jewish speculative tradition. Because of the carnal abuse of the term "head," first on offer in my translation is the broader meaning of the term: "Source." The "head" of a river is its "source." In Gen. 2:10 we have this example: "A river… began to be divided and was, as it were, four heads" (J. Wash Watts). We have another use of the term in Mat. 21:42 where, "**A stone… comes to be for a head of a corner.**" Linguistically, the word *kephalē* has a broad semantic range. Among its usages are for: the head of a person or an animal; a source or origin; a starting-point; a headdress; one's life (e.g., putting one's head on a chopping block – *cf* Nyland, *The Source NT*, pp 323-4); and (metaphorically) a crown, an extremity, end point, completion, top, brim, or even, Aries – the *kephalē* of the cosmos; (*cf* Liddell and Scott). In vss. 8, 9 and 12, below, the idea of "source" can be clearly seen. Furthermore, Paul is not describing a monstrous multi-headed being, nor, we suggest, is he setting up a social or spiritual hierarchy. Nyland (ibid p 324) argues against Paul speaking of a hierarchy, due to the word order of Christ and God being listed last. She points out that this rather suggests a chronological order in God's development of His purposes: first the man, then the woman… and then Christ, from God. In regard to the OT use of *kephalē*, Conzelmann posits that "'Head' does not there denote the sovereignty of one person over another, but over a community" (ibid p 183 n 21). An example of this is Judg. 11:11, "the people made him head and ruler over them" (LXX). In David's song of deliverance and salvation (2 Cam. 22), in vs. 44, the last clause reads, "You will continue preserving (guarding; watching over; keeping) me to [be] a head (*kephalē*) of ethnic multitudes (nations)" (LXX; JM). In Isa. 7:8 we read, "But the head of Aram is Damascus, and the head of Damascus, Rasim… (etc.)" (LXX).

Witherington (ibid p 237) raises the question of *kephalē* meaning "source" in our present passage (vss. 2-16), and then asks, "Is Paul really also arguing that Christ's source is God?" He admits the possibility of this being the case. As you see, I have rendered vs. 3 to say just that! The story of Jesus' conception by the Holy Spirit, and His becoming "the Anointed One" when the Spirit descended upon Him at His immersion in the Jordan, both bear witness to this interpretation.

It is noteworthy that Paul does not continue on to develop any sort of cosmology from what he has just said, but rather move on to specifics of a cultural/religious issue, in vs. 4ff.

Perhaps Paul is drawing from the apocalyptic imagery of the living beings of Ezk. 1:5-6 where each one had "four faces," and each faces was a symbol. Here, Paul presents four "faces," or presentations: God, Christ, the adult Male, and a Woman. The four comprise one Unity, God, in Christ, in His Temple (the joined Man-Woman of the Last Adam, the Second Humanity – 15:45, 47; i.e., the "spiritual," 15:46, below). In 12b, below, he affirms that God is the Source of everything, i.e., all is "out of God." The topic that he is going to discuss has to do with communal behavior, specifically "head coverings" as an item for showing respect.

Notice the dual meanings of "adult male/husband" and "woman/wife." The first of each of these is more general, and is likely here Paul's intent, rather than the more specific terms, "husband/wife," that would apply to individual relationships in that culture and time. Christ bookends this picture, and the "adult Male" is mentioned twice: once in relation to Christ, and the second time in relation to the Woman. In the Garden of Eden story, Adam was literally "the source of the woman." However, in the new creation, the Second Man (Christ) is the source of the "last Adam," since He is "**a continuously life-making** (life-producing; life-creating; life-forming) **Spirit** (or: Breath-effect)," and "**the Second Human** (Person; Humanity; [other MSS add: {is} the Lord]) **[is made] out of heaven** (or: [is] from atmosphere and sky; [*p*46 reads: {is} spiritual])" (*cf* 15:45-49, below). Considering the later development, in ch. 15, it may be wise to keep this layer of meaning in view. The understanding that "the Source/Head of every adult male is Christ" speaks to this spiritual interpretation of Paul's words.

On the more individual and specific level, in the called-out community it would seem fitting that "the Anointing [should be] the head of every husband." This being true, then even though "the husband is the head of a wife," the headship pertaining to the wife leads back to the Anointing as being the ultimate headship, or leadership. In Col. 3 we read the admonishment to put on "**the Love, which continues being a joining link and uniting band of perfection**" (vs. 14), and then, "**let the peace** (or: joining) **of the Christ** [God] **continuously umpire** (act as a judge in the games) **within your hearts**" (vs. 15), and also, "**let Christ's Word be continuously making its home within you**" (vs. 16), summing all this up with the general admonition of vs. 17:

> "**And everything – whatsoever you may be habitually doing, in word or in action – [do] everything within and in union with [the] Name of [the] Lord, Jesus, constantly giving thanks**…"

Now following these admonitions to continue abiding in the Vine and living in the Spirit for the ability to do what he next instruct them, he gives practical instruction to wives, husbands, children, fathers and servants (vss. 18-22). Then he bookends that passage with vs. 23, "**Everything – whatever you folks may be habitually doing – be constantly working from out of soul, as to** (for; in; with) **the Lord**…" – which mirrors vs. 17, and is echoed here, above, in 10:31. The pattern is the same: the affirmations toward kingdom living, because of our life and relationship in Christ, the Vine, followed by instructions for living in the covenant community in a way that accords with this new creation in Christ.

Paul is delivering spiritual realities in terms of cultural perceptions of the day. And so he proceeds to cultural norms for expanding his arguments, and settling some first-level issues that involve ethnic customs…

4. **Every adult male** (or: husband) **habitually speaking to having well-being** (or: praying) **or prophesying while holding down [the; his] Source** (or: having [a head-covering {kalumma}] on, down from [his] head), **is continually bringing shame** (disgrace; dishonor) **to his Source** (or: Head).
> [note: according to A.T. Robertson (*Word Pictures in the NT*, vol. 4, p.159) there is no certainty that the *tallith* was used at this time]

Norman Hillyer explains: "The Christian man is not to pray in public (or to prophesy: see on 12:10), as the Jew did, *with his head covered*, a sign of submission to another person (*cf* Gen. 24:65). To do so *dishonors his 'head'*, i.e., Christ, the only one to whom he owes submission" (ibid p 1065). Paul made clear, in vs. 3, that of which he was speaking as being the "**Source**/Head" of the adult male: Christ, or, the Anointing. From this cultural statement (by acting in this manner), we can distil the idea that any behavior within our own culture that would bring shame or disgrace to Christ should be avoided.

5. Now every woman (or: wife) **normally speaking to having well-being** (or: praying) **or prophesying [publicly] with the head uncovered** (or: [her] source not veiled down) **is continually bringing shame** (disgrace; dishonor) **to her head** (or: source), **for it is one and the very same thing with the woman having been shaved.**

> [note on shaved: a dishonor as punishment for adultery, or for a prostitute; a custom for women slaves]

Witherington notes that,

> "Roman males also covered their heads when offering sacrifice" (ibid p 233 n 9), and points out that the situation is about "praying and prophesying in Christian worship" (ibid p 235). He concludes that "Paul created in the church a social force of a unique kind…. an alternative society to the civil order as a whole" (ibid p 236 n 18).
>
> "He is setting up new customs… deeply grounded in his theological understanding of creation, redemption, their interrelation, and how they should be manifested…" (ibid p 238).

Hillyer offers this interpretation: "In Paul's day [praying unveiled in public] meant she repudiated [her husband's] authority" (ibid; brackets mine). Harvey comments, "if shaving off the hair is a disgrace for a woman, so presumably is taking off the veil" (A.E. Harvey, *The New English Bible Companion to the New Testament*, Oxford Univ. Press 1970 p 558). The main issue seems to be that of showing honor and respect for others, as is appropriate for the cultural context. The primary focus of this honor, and respect, is for God and Christ, but when these are given to others, they are also given to Them. So for both men and women, the instruction from Paul is to show appropriate respect.

6. You see, if a wife (or: woman) **is not habitually covering herself down with a veil, let her also shear herself. Now since** (or: if) **[it is] ugliness** (deformity [of custom]; thus: a social disgrace, shame, dishonor and bad form) **for** (or: to) **a wife or a woman at any point to shear or shave herself, let her habitually veil herself down** (or: completely cover herself).

Paul has just equated "**a wife or a woman at any point to shearing or shaving herself**" with the situation of her publicly praying or prophesying "**with the head uncovered.**" He now characterizes such an act as "**ugliness** (deformity [of custom]; thus: a social disgrace, shame, dishonor and bad form)." Since he, and apparently others, viewed this to be the case, then we can understand why he instructs them, "**let her habitually veil herself down** (or: completely cover herself)." In a called-out, covenant community, **ugliness** (etc.) reflects on the image of Christ that the community is summoned to bear.

7. So a husband (or: a mature Male), **on the one hand, is continually obligated not to be covering [his] Source** (or: veiling down the head) **– [he] being inherently** (or: constantly being under the rule and headship of) **God's image** (resemblance; likeness; portrait) **and glory** (reflection; reputation; splendor; manifestation which calls forth praise; assumed appearance). **On the other hand, the wife** (or: Woman) **is, and continuously exists being, a husband's** (or: a mature Male's) **glory** (reflection; reputation; splendor; manifestation which calls forth praise; mirrored appearance).

> [note: a reference to Gen. 1:28; 2:26; *cf* 2 Cor. 3:18]

Being God's "image-bearer" is what is at stake in these arguments. This transcends any and all cultural issues. The equivalent counterpart of this should be seen in the Woman, who by reflecting the glory of the Man (who IS the Glory of God) would thus also reflect God's splendor and assumed appearance, or glory.

8. You see, [the] mature Male is not (or: a husband does not exist being) **forth from out of the midst of Woman** (or: a wife), **for to the contrary, [the] Woman** ([the] Wife) **[is] forth from out of the midst of [the] mature Male** ([the] Husband)!

> (or: It follows that one is not a husband from a wife, but [one is] a wife from a husband.)

Paul is alluding to the forming of Adam and Eve, and this bold reading can be seen as an echo of Gen. 2:21, 22. For this reason, I capitalized "Man" and "Woman," since he is not speaking of normal human birth, but of the archetypal story of humanity's creation and beginning. We find Paul using Adam this way in both Rom. 5, and in chapter 15, below.

The parenthetical readings, with the generalized "a husband" and "a wife" (both nouns have these dual meanings), present a functional, or a role, aspect to Paul's statement. If we read the masculine and feminine nouns from this perspective, we have a cultural picture from a patriarchal, male-dominated society – which was indeed the society to which Paul was writing. With this picture his argument is drawing from the societal roles of the time and place of 1st century Corinth (and throughout the Empire). Paul drew from this functional model in Eph. 5:25, using Christ and the called-out as his example:

> "**O husbands, be constantly loving, and urging to unity with, [your] wives** (or: Men, continue giving yourselves for and accepting the women), **accordingly and correspondingly as the Christ also loved** (or: to the degree that, and commensurately as, the Anointed One loves and unambiguously accepts) **the called-out community, and gave Himself up** (or: commits and transfers Himself over) **in behalf of** (for the sake of; over [the situation of]) **her**."

But we suggest that the higher (bold, symbolic) reading of vs. 8, here, is echoed from what he said of that passage in Eph. 5, explaining that where he had been speaking about husbands and wives, he was really talking about the Lord in relation to the corporate community, as laid out there in vs. 32:

> "**This secret** (or: mystery) **is great** (= important), **but I am speaking unto** (or: into; with a view to) **Christ, even** (or: and; as well as) **unto** (or: into; with a view to) **the called-out community** (or: the called-out person; or: the summoned-forth covenant assembly)."

9. **For also, [the] mature Male** (or: Husband) **was not created through** (or: because of) **the Woman** (or: Wife), **but to the contrary, [the] Woman** (or: Wife) **through** (or: because of) **the mature Male** (or: the Husband).

Notice that both vss. 8 and 9 seem to be an allusion to Adam and Eve – and the very beginnings of the Jewish culture and of the plan of God. Once again, the allusion is to Gen. 2, but we suggest that Paul's subtle implication is that the called-out community was created/birthed through Christ. Verse 9 is a rhetorical re-statement of vs. 8, for emphasis – so that they won't miss his point. He is not speaking of natural birth in these verses. He is speaking typologically.

10. **Because of this, the Woman** (or: wife) **is continually obligated to be habitually having privilege and right from being** (or: permission) **upon [her] head – because of the agents**
> (or: normally ought to constantly hold authority from out of being herself, [based] upon the Source, [as shown] through the messengers [= ancestors and prophets]). [comment: she ought to veil her glory, just as Moses veiled the glory that was on him – 2 Cor. 3:13]

This pronouncement has always presented modern readers with an enigma. If he had ended it with, "because of our tradition," it would have made more sense to us. But perhaps this is what he is saying, using the term "agents/messengers" to refer to Moses and the Prophets, etc., as did the author of Hebrews (which may well have been Paul). In the first chapter of that book, vss. 4-7 speaks to the topic of "agents/messengers" (*cf* my Comments on Hebrews, in *John, Judah, Paul & ?*, Harper Brown Publishing, 2013 pp 94-97).

Witherington concedes, "That the *angeloi* mentioned in vs. 10 are human emissaries of the *ekklēsia* [called-out communities] is possible…" (ibid p 236 n 22; brackets mine). However, he does not seem to embrace this view.

The expanded meanings of the noun, "privilege and right from being; permission; authority" seems to point to the origins of their culture, specifically via the OT Scriptures. The parenthetical alternative rendering on offer here gives a reading that also points in this same direction of interpretation. The preposition for the last phrase (*dia*) that is usually rendered "because" is given as "through" in this second rendering, and this also supports the idea that Paul may have been referring to the writers of the OT. This final phrase with *dia*, "through the messengers (or: = the folks with the message about Christ)," may answer as parallel to "through the mature Male," in vs. 9. Consider the parenthetical reading of vs. 10, "normally ought to constantly hold authority from out of being herself, [based] upon the Source…" Paul's writings were always saying something beyond the first-level reading. This came naturally, from his training in Hellenistic-Judaism. So we need to read him with the eyes of the Spirit.

11. **Nevertheless** (Of course), **in union with – and in the midst of – the Lord neither [is] Woman severed, separate or apart from mature Male** (or: a wife disunited from a husband), **nor [is] mature Male severed, separate or apart from Woman** (or: a husband disunited from a wife).
12. **For you see, just as the Woman [was] forth from out of the midst of the mature Male, in the same manner, the mature Male [is] through the Woman – yet all things [are]** (or: the whole [comes]) **forth from out of the midst of God.** [*cf* Rom. 11:36]

Here Paul seems to be saying that the new arrangement in Christ turns their traditions on their heads. Verse 11 proclaims the oneness of the sexes in the sphere of Christ and God's reign. It also proclaims the union and oneness of Christ and His Wife, His Body. Jesus spoke of this in Jn. 17:21,

> "**to the end that all humans would** (or: all people can and should) **continuously exist being one, correspondingly as You, O Father** [other MSS: Father], **[are] within the midst of Me, and I [am] within the midst of You – so that they, themselves, may and would also continuously exist being within the midst of Us, to the end that the aggregate of humanity** (the System: world of culture, religion and government; or: secular society) **can** (may; would) **continuously trust and progressively believe that You sent Me forth as an Emissary with a mission.**"

Recall Gal. 3:

> 27. **For you see, as many of you folks as were immersed into Christ, at once clothed yourselves with Christ** (or: were plunged into so as to be enveloped by then saturated and permeated with Anointing – or, the Anointed One – instantly entered within and put on [the/an] Anointing)!
> 28. **Within** [Him; us], **there is not** (there does not exist) **Jew nor Greek** (or: Hellenist); **within, there is not** (does not exist) **slave nor freeman; within, there is not** (does not exist) **'male and female'; for it follows that, you folks all exist being one within Christ Jesus** (or: for you see, all you people are one person, centered in, and in union with, an Anointing from Jesus).

Verse 12 alludes to Gen. 2:21-22, then flips the picture to natural birth. But this can also be seen on a different level, for Adam was a type of Christ (Rom. 5:14b). Adam was not deceived by the serpent (1 Tim. 2:14), but rather, with eyes opened he entered into the death that Eve was experiencing in order to accompany Eve (be the Seed that falls into the ground, and dies – Jn. 12:24) and ultimately redeem the flesh of his flesh and bone of his bones. Many have seen the figure of the blood and water flowing from the side of Jesus, when having died on the cross, as a figure for the birth of the Wife of the Lamb, Christ's body (bone of His bone; flesh of His flesh). By being placed into the immersion of His death (Rom. 6:3-4) humanity was raised with Him (to experience this existentially one-at-a-time – 15:23, below), and this is the spiritual understanding of "**the woman [comes] forth from out of the midst of the mature Male.**" But just as Jesus (the Head of the Body of Christ) was born of Mary, the rest of His body is born from "the **Jerusalem which is above**" (Gal. 4:26) and proceeds to grow "**into [the] purposed and destined adult man** (complete, finished, full-grown, perfect, goal-attained, mature manhood) **– into** (or: unto) **[the] measure of [the] stature** (full age; prime of life) **of the entire content which comprises the Anointed One**" (Eph. 4:13).

What Paul has been saying in vss. 11-12, along with the other quotes on offer, is speaking of the restored state of the archetypal, New Humanity (Eph. 2:15). He is speaking of the new creation (2 Cor. 5:17), and we have been focusing on the corporate aspects of all of this. But there is an individual level of understanding in which the spirit and soul can be perceived. We suggest that there is an allusion to Gen. 2:21-24, i.e., God's work of forming the new soul within us (Mat. 16:25b-26) as the Last Adam, that can be seen in Heb. 4:12,

> "**You see, the Word of God** (or: God's thought, idea and message; or: the expressed *Logos* from God; or: the Word which is God) **[is] living** (or: alive), **and active** (working; operative; energetic; at work; productive) **and more cutting above every two-mouthed sword, even passing through** (penetrating) **as far as a dividing** (or: parting; partitioning) **of soul and spirit** (or: of inner self-life/consciousness and breath-effect), **both of joints and marrows, even able to discern** (separate; judge; decide) **concerning thoughts** (ponderings; reflections; in-rushings; passions) **and intentions** (notions; purposes) **of a heart** (= core of the being)."

As with Adam and Eve, that dividing and forming has in view a renewed union and oneness. It is of this finished product that Paul spoke in 1 Thes. 5:23, where,

> "**the God of the Peace** (the Joining) **Himself** (or: Yet the very God who is peace and joined-harmony can) **set you folks apart [being] completely whole** (or: wholly perfect; entirely mature; wholly finished and at the goal), **and may your whole allotment** (= every part) – **the spirit, the soul and the body – be kept** (guarded; maintained) **blameless** (without fault) **within, and in union with, the presence of our Lord** (Master; Owner), **Jesus Christ**."

The work of the Word and the Spirit also enters into the very structure (house; temple) of our being: the "joints and marrows" of the skeletal system. From this picture, we can also reflect back upon the corporate dimension, as well, with its "connecting parts" (Eph. 4:16) and "pillars" (Rev. 3:12), as we mix the metaphors, in good Pauline style!

The final clause, "**all things [are]** (or: the whole [is]) **forth from out of the midst of God**," is echoed in Rom. 11:36a, "**Because, forth from out of the midst of Him, then through the midst of Him** (or: through means of Him), **and [finally] into the midst of Him, [is; will be] the whole** (everything; [are] all things)." But having established these points, he continues his arguments by asking his audience to consider more aspects of the issue...

13. **Sift, sort-out and decide among yourselves: is it appropriate** (fitting and proper) **[for; in] a woman** (or: wife) **to [in public] be habitually praying uncovered** (not veiled down) **to God?**
14. **Does not even the essence and nature of what our culture has produced, itself, consistently teach you folks that if an adult male should ever plume himself or give himself airs with long hair** (tresses or long ringlets; = hair ornamentally arranged like a woman's style) **it is a dishonor to him** (is degrading for him)**?**

Now Paul's rhetoric turns toward an appeal to their cultural norms (vs. 13) and then "nature" itself (vs. 14). This moves from the theological realm to everyday situations to which his listeners could easily relate. He is doing the same kind of teaching from the essence of their culture (vs. 14a) and the nature of creation (a woman's hair, vs. 15) that Jesus did from nature:

> "**Focus your mind down on and consider the ravens** (or: rooks; jackdaws).... **Focus your mind down on and consider the lilies – how it progressively** (or: repeatedly) **grows and increases**..." (Lu. 12:24, 27).

All of our environment can be used by the Spirit to guide our behavior and impart wisdom.

15. **Yet if a woman should have plumes or long, luxuriant hair** (tresses and long ringlets that are ornamentally arranged) **it is a glory to her** (is a good appearance, reflection and reputation for her; is splendor and a manifestation which calls forth praise for her), **because the long, ornamentally arranged**

hair has been given to her as a permanent endowment, instead of an article of clothing or mantle cast around [her head, or as a coat or cloak].

Having dealt with "males" in vs. 14, he rounds out his example by addressing the "female" side of his illustration. And keep in mind that he has opened these two sides by saying (in vs. 13a), "**Sift, sort-out and decide among yourselves**." So this was not an issue that was essential to the Good News, but rather a point within their own social context and which applied only to them – and, of course, others who may have had the same cultural norms.

Another insight from vs. 15 comes from the fact that Paul attributes the woman's "**luxuriant hair**" as being HER glory. It is a "reflection and reputation for HER." Making a public appearance, and speaking, would draw attention to HER, and would be "a manifestation which would call forth praise to HER."

Now move this insight to the corporate level: it is not any glory of her that should be seen, but rather that of her Husband. The exact opposite of this is seen in Rev. 17:4, where the woman is sitting upon the beast System, and is "**clothed [with] purple and crimson** (scarlet). **And having been adorned** (overlaid; gilded) **with gold and precious stones and pearls, she is continuously holding in her hand a golden cup** (goblet)…" This is counterfeit religion, which is the exact opposite of what John saw in Rev. 21:10b-11a,

> "**the set-apart** (or: holy; sacred) **city, Jerusalem, progressively** (or: habitually; or: presently) **descending out of the atmosphere** (or: heaven), **from God – continuously having** (holding; or: = bringing with it) **the glory of God** (God's glory; God's reputation; or: God's appearance; or: the opinion from God; the manifest presence, which is God), **her illuminator** (that which gives her light; the cause of her light)…"

16. **Still, if anyone continues presuming to be habitually fond of quarreling** (likes to argue, dispute or be contentious and cause strife), **we ourselves do not habitually hold to** (or: have) **such a custom or mutual habit – neither [do] God's called-out folks** (or: communities).

This statement seals the issue as being a local, cultural topic – it is nothing that Paul would carry over to other called-out communities.

17. **Now while bringing along this announcement** (giving this notification to [your] side), **I do not now bring praise, or offer applause and commendation upon [you], because you folks are not continually coming together into more strength and for the better, but to the contrary, into the inferior: a diminished situation** (= the less profitable; = your gatherings do more harm than good).

Now Paul moves to a more serious, relational issue, within the community, in which the collective has come into an inferior, diminished situation that is less profitable than that which had been present with them before. Now, their gatherings were doing "more harm than good." So he explains what he is talking about…

18. **You see, in the first place, in your repeated coming together within an assembly of the called-out, I am constantly hearing there to be the results of tearing, and split-effects** (= separations into cliques; divisions), **continually inherent among you folks – and a certain part of it I am now believing!**

He is broaching a subject first brought up in 1:11ff. Furthermore, this was not just an occasional situation, but it was "**continually inherent among [them]**." What he had discussed in ch. 1 had developed into ongoing "**split-effects**" within the community. The "**results of tearing**" was being manifested in fleshly, social situations that were showing lack of love and lack of common courtesy, much less, "common existing," for "a temple of God." The situation was the exact opposite of "building up" the community, for these tearing, split-effects would be the destruction of the community, if they were allowed to continue. And so he explains…

19. **Then you see, it also continues to be necessary and binding for there constantly to be choices and options among you folks** (or: For there must even be sects, factions, a mixture of doctrinal stances, or even heresies in your midst), **to the end that those who have been examined, tested and approved among you may also come to be** (or: be birthed) **manifested ones** (folks shown in clear light).

Because of the results and effects of the splits within the community, there had to be "choices" and "options" among them. This created "sects, factions, a mixture of doctrinal stances, or even heresies in [their] midst." The Greek term, *hairesis* means, primarily: a choice; an option. By extension it referred to a sect, a faction. In practical terms it came to refer to a different doctrinal stance or view. In later times, when folks organized into structured entities, the dominant parties declared the view(s) of the minority parties as heresy(s). But here, Paul is saying that because the community has splits and tears, the folks now have choices of what teacher they would embrace… whether Paul, or Apollos, or Peter, etc.

The "**end**" of all this was "**examinations**" and "**tests for approval**." Paul is ambiguous here: Who is doing the examining and the testing? Is it the sects examining folks to see if they qualify to be a member of their sect? Or is it God examining them in accord with their choices within the community? Is He testing them to see what options they take? In either case, this was happening among them so that the community (Paul uses the plural throughout this verse) may be "folks shown in clear light." Despite their actions, God would manifest them as they really were, and would at some point work this into their good (Rom. 8:28). This would also allow them to see themselves as they were behaving.

Another interpretation of "**choices and options**" being "**necessary**" is because of the freedom that they now have in Christ (Gal. 5:1). Because of this, as a part of their "child-training" in the Lord, there must be times of testing so that folks can manifest the growth of maturity for fruit-bearing (i.e., the fruit of the Spirit). We who have been freed from the bondage of religion (and the control of religious structures and hierarchies) are free to choose what thread of theology or Christology or ecclesiology that we will follow. We are free to be led by the Spirit. But this freedom is only as we abide "in Christ," where we are bound by His Love, and "**the principle and law of, from and which is the spirit and attitude of 'The Life within Christ Jesus'**" (Rom. 8:2). And so he continues…

20. **So then, on the [occasion] of your periodically coming together at the same [time and place], it is not to be eating an evening meal having the character or qualities of the Lord** (or: a supper for, or pertaining to, the Owner; or: a Lord's [= Yahweh's or Christ's] dinner; a supper belonging to the Master; an evening meal validating, and directed by, the Master).
21. **for each person, in the midst of the progressive eating, is habitually taking his own meal before [another person], who, in this second case, is also constantly hungry, [or] who, in another situation, is repeatedly drunk** (or: constantly intoxicated).

Since Paul would naturally be addressing the leadership in the community (who could correct this bad behavior), about this situation, we wonder if he had in mind Ezk. 34:2-31, especially vs. 18, where Yahweh says to the "shepherds,"
> "[You] have eaten up the good pasture, but must you tread down with your feet the residue of your pastures? And you have drunk of the deep waters, but must you foul the residue with your feet [= behavior]?"

Verse 21 explains why vs. 20 says that their group meal was "**NOT to be eating an evening meal having the character or qualities of the Lord**." It was because they were being selfish or behaving in a way that Paul would call "the flesh," as opposed to "the spirit." There was an obvious lack of Christ's

Love, and a demonstration of being thoughtless in regard to other people. An example of the second case (vs. 21) could be of slaves who were not released from their duties in time to arrive before most of the food had been eaten. In our day, arriving late at a pot-luck or a community meal can mean that bare pickings are left, especially if some were unable to bring food, for various reasons. The topic of Paul's discussion, here, is not a symbolic meal, later described by organized Christianity as "the Lord's Supper (or: communion)," but rather a real community meal.

This Corinthian community was not having "table-fellowship," but, like some of the followers of Jesus, they came for the food and drink:

> "**Jesus decidedly answered them, and says, 'It is certainly true, I am saying to you folks, you people continue seeking Me not because you saw signs, but rather because you ate from out of the loaves, and you were fed until satisfied. Stop continuously working or doing business for the food which is continuously disintegrating of itself** (destroying itself), **but rather [for] the Food continuously remaining** (abiding; dwelling) **into eonian Life**" (Jn. 6:26-27a).

In our day many come primarily for the good music, the "blessing" or the good feelings. There is often little contact or care for those who are not part of the "inner circle," or for the marginalized who might attend, as strangers to the group. And yes, some are "**repeatedly drunk**" (metaphorically), in their forms of "worship." The "individualized" religion of Christianity tends to be geared for "personal, progressive eating" and "**habitually taking [one's] own meal**." As the organizations grow, sometimes those vying for top positions are "**made drunk from out of the wine of her prostitution** (idolatry)" (Rev. 17:2), as were the leaders in 1st century AD Jerusalem.

22. **So do you folks by no means continue having houses for the habitual eating and drinking? Or are you constantly despising** (holding a negative attitude toward) **God's called-out community, and are you repeatedly pouring shame and disgrace down on those presently having nothing? What should I say to you? Am I supposed to now praise and commend you folks? In this I am not now sending praise, applause or commendation upon [you]!**

He asks two rhetorical questions: first, concerning their personal living situations (and the taking of sustenance); second, concerning their attitudes toward other members of the called-out community, or towards the entire group, as BEING God's covenant community. The behavior described in vs. 21 would be poor form even on the natural level, but it certainly should not happen during the communal meals of God's Temple, which they are!

As regards his second question, Paul sees their behavior as either "despising" or "holding a negative attitude" toward the group as a whole. The third question was in regard to the poor, who were "**presently having nothing**." Keep in mind that theirs was an "honor/shame" based culture. Their behavior was "manifesting them in clear light" (19b, above). Obviously he was not praising or commending such behavior. He was chiding them, and calling them to account. They were now appearing before Christ's judgment seat, through Paul.

23. **For you see, I myself received to myself and accepted from the Lord** [= Christ or Yahweh] **that which I also passed along** (or: transmitted; commended; committed; hand on as a tradition; *cf* vs. 2, above) **to you folks, that the Lord Jesus, within the night in which He was in process of being handed over** (or: transferred), **received and took a loaf of bread,**
24. **and then, with gratitude and expressing the ease of grace, broke it in pieces and said, "**[some MSS add: You folks take {it}; eat {it}.] **This is My body, being now broken over [the situation and condition of] you folks** (or: for you people; on your behalf). **Keep doing this, into the calling up of the memory pertaining to Me** (or: with a view to remembering Me; or: unto a remembering of what is Mine)."

Paul is referencing, in vs. 23a, the tradition that was passed along to him and which he had then passed along to those in Corinth. This tradition he identifies and recites, in 23b-25: it is the one that describes the final meal that Jesus had with His disciples before His crucifixion, as recorded in the Gospels in Lu. 22:19-20; Mk. 14:22-24; and Mat. 26:26-28. One reason for which they are called to remember Christ, is to keep in mind His words (messages; Jn. 14:23) and to Love one another (Jn. 13:35). Wis. 16:5-6 recalls Israel's judgments from God (snake bites) which was "a warning, [while] possessing a symbol of salvation [the bronze snake on the pole] to REMIND them of the command of Your Law" (N.E.T.S.: brackets mine). They would also be reminded that they were now in a New Covenant. The old covenant had passed away (2 Cor. 5:17).

But let us look at another level of interpretation. Recall 10:17, above: "**Because we, The Many, are (exist being) One Bread** (one loaf of bread), **One Body…**" As followers and imitators of Christ, THEY should be "**broken**" for those in need among and around them. Notice the rest of the tradition: "**Keep doing this, into the calling up of the memory pertaining to Me**!" They are called to remember the One whom they are to imitate, and how He lived His life. He gave Himself for others; they (and we) are to do the same! His followers are called to do the works that He did:

> "**It is certainly true, I am saying to you folks, the person habitually trusting and progressively believing into Me, the works** (actions; deeds) **which I Myself am constantly doing** (habitually performing; progressively making, constructing, creating, forming) **that person also will proceed doing…**" (Jn. 14:12).

Dan Kaplan points us to Jesus' definition of "bread" (literally: food) in Jn. 4:34,

> "**My food is** (or: exists being) **that I should do** (can perform; would produce; [other MSS: can continuously be doing; or: habitually do]) **the will, intent and purpose of the One sending Me, and that I should and would bring His work to its purposed goal and destiny** (or: can complete His act; may finish and perfect His deed)."

He also took us back to the tabernacle/temple setting, where in the holy place (a figure of the called-out community {Rev. 1:20b} and the realm of the ministry of the priests) there was the Table of the "Bread of the Presence" (Ex. 25:30 that was food for the priests. There were twelve loaves put on that Table, daily (their "daily bread" – Mat. 6:11), each loaf representing one of the twelve tribes, a figure of the universal Body of Christ. As Christ's priests, we are to partake of Him (the Bread of Life) daily. While our thoughts are on this setting, let us share more of Dan's insights:

> In the holy place, there was also the Lampstand (Ex. 25:31-37), which had 7 branches (alluded to in the 7 communities in Rev. 2-3). Dan sees the center one, as Christ (the Vine; the Head/Source of the Lampstand), and the remaining 6 branches as a figure of the humanity of this Lampstand. He also noted that this Lampstand was the only article of furniture in the holy place that had no measurements given to it (which calls to mind the Spirit being given "without measure" – Jn. 3:34), and as Dan says, "The Holy Spirit cannot be measured."

> The Lampstand burned olive oil (a figure of God's Spirit, the Source of the Anointing, and of Light, within the holy place) – a figure of God consuming Himself (Fire burning the Oil of the Spirit) to give us the Light. Dan posits that the oil was the "blood" of the Lampstand, and was a picture of the blood of Christ giving Life and Light to the communities. Without His Fire, there was no Light in the holy place. Dan pointed out that the Lamp "illuminates our hearts," while the Bread "feeds us."

> In Lev. 9:23-24 we read that, "the glory of Yahweh appeared unto all the people, and there came Fire out from before Yahweh, and consumed upon the altar the burnt offering…" That fire was to be kept burning, with embers carried during their wilderness journey. It was from the coals of this fire that the lampstand was lit. In Lev. 10:1-2 we read of the incident of using "strange fire" (i.e., embers from a source other than the altar of burnt offering) to offer incense in the holy place – and of the judgment on them for doing this. This was a lived out parable that taught against using

"fire" from a source other than Yahweh (in other words, an injunction against bring idolatry into the worship of Yahweh; the "strange fire" represented a "strange god"). From this typology, Dan posits that all "light" had to come into the called-out community by way of the sacrifice of Christ – the work of God, through the Spirit of God. The Fire from that altar entered into the tabernacle/temple (Us) and gave Light and fueled incense (prayers). The blood from the Sacrifice sanctified and cleansed the holy place and entered into the heart of the tabernacle/temple (the holy of holies; the hearts of the people), which was the goal (Christ; the Mercy Seat; the Throne of God) of the Life of Christ, given for all.

Dan also pointed out that the sacrificial Lamb represented Adam, and all the blood had to be drained from it (the life of the old Adam had to be drained out). The soul was in the blood, and in this sacrifice (figure of the cross), the old man of the heart (the soul of the old Adam) was destroyed (Mat. 16:25), in order to "find" the new soul (Mat. 16:25) of the Second Humanity (15:45-49, below).

25. Similarly, [He took] the cup also, after the eating of the supper, saying, "This cup is the new arrangement within My blood (or: exists being the thorough placing and setting – which is new in kind and character – in the sphere of My blood; or: is the different covenant [being made] in union with My blood). **Keep on doing this, whenever you may be normally drinking, into the calling up of the memory pertaining to Me** (or: with a view to remembering Me)."

Because Paul has referenced this historical and symbolic meal, traditional interpretations of this passage have normally assumed that either this whole passage on communal meals in the covenant community was instruction concerning the group having "Communion," the "Eucharist," or the "Lord's Supper" (as it is variously termed), or that it is addressing "table fellowship" of the community on two different levels, and actually two different meals – one being the symbolic "Eucharist (etc.)," the other a regular community dinner.

He began talking about an "evening meal" in vs. 20, and, because of their behavior at it, he disqualifies it as "**having the character or qualities of the Lord**." Let us now examine the optional renderings of this phrase, as given in vs. 20:
     a) a supper for, or pertaining to, the Owner
     b) a Lord's [= Yahweh's or Christ's] dinner
     c) a supper belonging to the Master
     d) an evening meal validating, and directed by, the Master.
As we ponder these five renderings of the phrase, we can observe a variety of meanings. The question is, Were the communal meals that they were having (as described in vss. 21-22) SUPPOSED to be what Paul presents as the "tradition" in 23b-25? Verse 21 would seem to say, "No!" Verse 22 would seem to answer an even stronger "No!!" as we see Paul's reference to "despising" and "negative attitudes," along with their "**repeatedly pouring shame and disgrace down on those presently having nothing**." So up to vs. 23, it would NOT seem that Paul was talking about what would later be called "the Eucharist (etc.)," i.e., the grape juice and the cracker. Also, the five descriptions in vs. 20, listed above, do not necessarily point to a symbolic meal, but rather a meal that would be appropriate for a community that had been set-apart for the Lord. All that they were to do in their lives was to be for His glory (10:31, above).

Furthermore, in 12:13, below we read Paul's thinking on "drinking":
     "**For we, ourselves – within the midst of one Spirit** (or: in union with one Breath-effect and Attitude) **– are all submerged into one body** (or: were all immersed into, so as to be enveloped by, one body) **– whether Jews or Greeks** (or: Hellenists), **whether slaves or free folks – and we all are** (or: were) **made** (or: caused) **to drink one Spirit** (or: spirit; Breath-effect; Attitude)."
This is not speaking about the "drinking" half of the Eucharist; it's about the life of the body, which is the called-out folks.

So why did Paul rehearse "the Last Supper" of Jesus in this context, especially following a discussion of their taking meals in a disreputable way? Was he, perhaps, reminding them that they are a COVENANT community, and that they should act that way toward one another? Was he merely alluding to the final meal that Jesus had with his group (which symbolically established the new covenant, and the partaking of the life of Christ), as contrasted to the very different "table fellowship" that these Corinthians were displaying? In other words, was he holding up before them that standard and example of to what table fellowship (having a communal meal together) should compare? Was he simply saying, remember the kind of meals that Jesus had with the poor and the outcasts, and how His final meal was as a parable, revealing what common meals in His kingdom represented?

In vs. 22, above, he challenged their table behavior that was shaming those who had "nothing" – i.e., they were obviously poor. It was the custom in that time and culture for the upper class of society to eat first, and those of the lower class to eat last – when often the best parts of the meal had already been consumed. The situation in Corinth reminds us of Jacob's instructions for the called-out folks (Jas. 2:1-7). There, in vs. 1, he instructs them not to hold Christ's faithfulness (i.e., the Life of Christ) "**in respect of persons or appearances**." Then he gives an example of how rich guests are treated, as contrasted to how the poor are treated, and points out that in this disparity they "**dishonor and devalue the poor**" (vs. 6). Now returning to Paul…

26. **It follows that,** (or: For) **whenever** (or: as often as) **you folks may be repeatedly eating this loaf of bread and may be habitually drinking the** [other MSS: this] **cup, you are continuing to proclaim and bring down the announcement of the death of the Lord – until which point He may come** (or: up to the point at which He should come; or: until the time where He would suddenly come).

When he says "**this loaf**" (recall that he has called them, the whole community, "one loaf" in 10:17, above) and "**this cup**," is he referring to their common existence and reminding them that all their meals should reflect the COVENANT of which they are all partakers? Does their table fellowship "**continue to proclaim and bring down the announcement of the death of the Lord**"? Recall what he said to them, in 2:2, above? "**I decided not to see, perceive or know anything within or among you folks, except Jesus Christ – and this One being one having been crucified.**" Paul wants to see a cruciform life among these Corinthians; that their lives together would proclaim His death for humanity, by their self-giving love for one another. He wanted to perceive the crucified Lord within them. Specifically, he wanted their "table fellowship" to reflect the covenant, death and life that was proclaimed by the symbolic meal that Jesus had with His first disciples.

We see Christ talking about coming to the seven called-out communities is Rev. 2 and 3. He is repeatedly "**coming and going**" (Rev. 1:8), while "**continuously walking about within the midst of the seven golden lampstands** (i.e., called-out communities – Rev. 1:20-2:1)." He would come to Corinth, as well, but perhaps Paul was referring to His coming WITHIN their lives and behaviors. Or, He might visit the community, as He did in Laodicea,

> "**Consider! I have stood, and continue standing, upon** (= at) **the door** (entrance), **and I am constantly knocking; if ever anyone may** (or: can) **hear My voice** (or: sound) **and would open the door, I will proceed entering** (coming or going in) **toward him, and then I will continue eating the evening meal with him, and he with Me**" (Rev. 3:20).

Dan Kaplan pointed us to Lu. 24:13-53, where the risen Jesus, after joining the disciples on the Road to Emmaus, in "**beginning from Moses, and then from all the prophets, He continued to fully interpret and explain to** (or: for) **them the things pertaining to** (or: the references about) **Himself within all the Scriptures**" (vs. 27), so the disciples pressed Him to stay in the village with them. Then,

> "**during the** [situation for] **Him to be reclining** [at the meal] **with them! After taking** (or: receiving) **the loaf of bread, He spoke words of well-being and blessing. Then, after breaking** [it], **He began giving** [it] **to them**" (vs. 30).

But notice what happened next: "**At that their eyes were at once fully opened wide, and they experienced full recognition of Him**" (vs. 31). In vs. 35 we read that, "**He came to be known to them** (or: personally recognized by them) **in the breaking of the loaf of bread.**" Keep in mind that in this setting, and in the Rev. 3:20 situation, it was simply eating a normal meal – but it was in His presence. A.T. Robertson has pointed out that the recognition did not come in His exegesis of Scripture, but at the meal and His serving them.

27. So that whoever may habitually eat the loaf of bread, or should be drinking the cup, pertaining to (or: with reference to) **the Lord in a manner or situation without equal value** (or: unworthily; unsuitably), **he or she will proceed in coming to be one held within** (or: embraced by and possessed within the sphere of; or: will continue being a possession that is engulfed within) **the body and the blood of the Lord.**

Now notice that Paul returns to the subject of bad form, which started this passage in vs. 20, above. He is speaking of their BEHAVIOR: **eating or drinking… in a manner or situation without equal value** (or: unworthily; unsuitably). Behavior towards others, both here and in the next two verses, is the point of his instructions. Now think back to his discussion of their meals, in 10:16-21, above, where in vs. 18 he said, "**are not those habitually eating the things sacrificed common-beings of the altar.**" He was referencing the temple priests of the old covenant. But now, the members of the Corinthian "temple" are the priests of the new covenant, and so ALL of their meals are temple meals; they all are "**pertaining to** (or: with reference to) **the Lord.**" And again, in 10:31, above, he admonished them, "**whether you folks are habitually eating or continually drinking, or anything you are constantly doing, be continuously doing all things unto God's glory.**" We suggest that this is the same thing to which he is referring, here in 11:27. *Cf* Col. 3:23

The second half of vs. 27 is normally read as a kind of judgment against the person eating or drinking "unsuitably or unworthily," and in one sense it is, as vs. 29, below, explains. But we rather suggest that this offense is also covered by His blood, and that the literal rendering, "**one held within** (or: embraced by and possessed within the sphere of… engulfed within)," is a positive promise. John said it this way:

> "**the blood of, from, and which is Jesus, His Son, keeps continually and repeatedly cleansing us** (or: is progressively rendering us pure) **from every sin** (or: from all error, failure, deviation, mistake, and from every shot that is off target [when it occurs])" (1 Jn. 1:7b).

That is continually happening within the community, since the "blood" is a figure of the Life of Christ which flows among the members of His body. Therefore, we can see another practical application of 27b, here: "**the body and the blood of the Lord**" is the Life and manifestation (the Loaf) of Christ incarnated in the group at Corinth. The "body" of Christ-followers would "embrace and engulf" such a person.

28. **So let a person habitually examine, test and evaluate himself** (or: regularly approve and accept himself [i.e., his attitude and behavior in the occasion]), **and in this manner let him be habitually eating from out of the loaf of bread and drinking from out of the cup,**

What a person is to examine and evaluate is his or her behavior and attitude towards others within the group, at these communal meals. All too often, "churches" have come to be places of gossip and back-biting. The common meals should be "love feasts" but those of vs. 21, above, could be as those described in Jude 12,

> "**These folks are sharply-cleft portions of rocks** (or: reefs; = menaces) **in your love [relationship]s** (or: love-feasts and table fellowships; movements toward acceptance with the drive for reunion), **repeatedly feasting well together, by habit fearlessly shepherding themselves.**"

29. **for the one continually eating and drinking in a manner or situation without equal value** (or: in an unworthy or unsuitable way) **is repeatedly eating and drinking the effect of an evaluation and the**

result of a decision (or: a sifting and a judgment) **in** (or: to; for) **himself – by not habitually discerning the body**

> (or: in not regularly distinguishing the body; not completely evaluating the body; not discriminating for, discerning about, or making a distinction of, the body [of believers]; not now passing judging throughout the body; [other MSS add: of the Lord]).

Again, what Paul is speaking about is the "**manner or situation without equal value** (or: in an unworthy or unsuitable way)." It is a rhetorical restatement of the point in vs. 27, for emphasis. He is not saying that the person is without equal value or unworthy. He has come back to the opening of this topic (vss. 20-21, above), and now gives further instruction about the situation:

> a) "**an evaluation and the result of a decision** (or: a sifting and a judgment) **in** (or: to; for) **himself**," but…
> b) "**by not habitually discerning the body**."

This calls to mind how Paul dealt with the individual member, in 5:5-7, above, and b) would indicate that this person was not discerning that the Corinthian community was in fact "**the body**" of Christ, and so would need an adjustment in perception and attitude. But let us consider the options on offer for the last clause, in the parenthetical expansion:

> a) in not regularly distinguishing the body;
> b) not completely evaluating the body;
> c) not discriminating for, discerning about, or making a distinction of, the body [of believers].
> d) not now passing judging through the body.

With a) it is saying that the sifting was due to not treating the body as being sacred and distinct from the pagan society around him; he made no distinction. Then b) would show that the individual evaluation would not come to a complete evaluation of the entire body. Now c), may expand upon this person's "evaluation, in himself," concerning the other members: being self-centered and "not discriminating for (i.e., on behalf of)" the others, or not "discerning about" them, or "not making a distinction of" the group – in relation to the surrounding community. The final offer, d), would say that the judgment was just for the individual; he would not be passing it throughout the body. There is ambiguity in Paul's construction of the final clause of this verse.

30. **Because of this, many among you folks [are] without strength** (or: weak and infirm) **and without health** (ailing; chronically ill), **and a considerable number** (or: quite a few) **are habitually asleep** (or: continuously sleeping; or: = dead).

The "this" to which he refers is the lack of Christ's love that is demonstrated in the bad form and unworthy behavior. Any time there is a split in a group, the entire group is weakened. Those who create the factions separate themselves from others by doing so. If one is separated, that person becomes weak, then without health, and finally dies (either metaphorically, or literally). They become a branch that is no longer abiding in the Vine (Jn. 15:1ff), and the result is that the entire community becomes "sick."

31. **But if we were** (or: had been) **in the habit of thoroughly evaluating, sifting throughout and passing discerning judgment on ourselves, we would not have been being sifted, separated, evaluated and judged.**

God continues at work within and upon the community. As we abide in Him, we see with His eyes and are able to evaluate our walk with Him, sift out the issues with which we are dealing, and then pass discerning judgment in regard to any adjustments that we need to make, as Christ empowers us to do so. This is what is meant in Heb. 5:14,

> "**But solid food belongs to perfected ones** (complete and mature ones; ones who are fully developed and have reached the goal of their destiny) **– those, because of habit, having organs of perception trained as in gymnastic exercise and thus being skilled, because of practice, and disciplined with a view to a discerning** (or: when facing the act of separating,

making a distinction and then a decision about) **both good and evil** (both that which is excellent, ideal, of good quality, profitable and beautiful, as well as that which is of bad quality, worthless, ugly or of bad form; or: = between right and wrong)."

Notice the metaphor of food in this verse; it fits nicely with Paul's present topic.

The potential "**being sifted, separated, evaluated and judged**" has reference to the potential ill health (both in the natural, as well as in the realm of our spirits) referenced in vs. 30, above, and vs. 34b, below. This potential can become a reality, as shown in the next verse...

32. **Yet, being folks habitually being sifted, separated, evaluated and judged by, and under, the Lord** [= Christ or Yahweh], **we are being continuously child-trained, educated, disciplined or corrected [by the Lord or His agent], to the end that we should not at any point be correspondingly evaluated or commensurately decided about** (separated-down or condemned; or: = have sentence passed on us) **together, and in company with, the organized and controlling System** (the world of culture, religion, economy, government and mankind).

The corrective and guiding work of the Lord is always for our benefit and growth – it is "child-training" and calls to mind Heb. 12:3-11 which is an admonition that follows the reference to the cruciform life of our Lord, in vs. 2 there, and how He endured the cross. That passage in Heb. 12, about child-training, closes with instruction that would apply well here in vs. 30, above:

> 12. **Because of which [education],**
> > "**straighten up** (or: build anew and restore) **those hands hanging down helplessly, and those knees having been paralyzed or loosened at the sides,**" [Isa. 35:3]
> 13. **and then,**
> > "**make straight and upraised wheel-tracks for your feet,**" [Prov. 4:26]

This is a call to solidarity and mutual love among the community members. Take care of the weak (vs. 30, above); help others adjust and rightwise the paths of their lives.

A benefit of this is that the Corinthian community (and we, likewise) would not need to be adjusted in the same manner as "**the organized and controlling System** (the world of culture, religion, economy, government and mankind)," where God continuously makes "**corresponding evaluations or commensurate decisions**." We saw the same thing stated in 5:12b, above: "**Now those "outside" God habitually sifts and makes decisions about** (is constantly judging)."

33. **So that, my brothers** (= fellow believers; folks from the same womb), **while repeatedly coming together into the [situation or occasion] to be normally eating, be constantly receiving from out of one another, taking them in your arms and welcoming them from out of the midst [of the group].** 34. **Now if anyone is habitually hungry, let him be regularly eating at home, so that you may not be constantly coming together** (gathering) **into a result of judgment** (the effect of a separation, an evaluation and then a decision).

Paul summarizes the instruction, begun in vs. 20, closing with the same topic of "**normally eating**" at times of "**repeatedly coming together**." They should take each other in their arms and welcome the weak and the outcasts, or those of lower social status. Verse 34 gives them practical advice in order that they might not come together and have the Lord address them as He did the seven called-out communities in Rev. 2 and 3. Can you picture the regular Sunday morning, or Wednesday evening, service and find that you have gathered "**into a result of judgment** (the effect of a separation, an evaluation and then a decision)"? Well, we suggest that many do this without realizing it: they may have been spewed out of His mouth; the lampstand might just be missing; they might have a reputation that they are a really "alive" congregation, but in fact they are metaphorically "dead" and asleep to the fact.

If we are correct in our interpretation of vss. 20-34, does this call into question the long traditions of the Eucharist which substituted a symbolic ritual for something that was to be communally lived-out in the lives of the called-out folks?

But I will myself thoroughly set the remaining matters [which you asked about] in order whenever I can come.

Since there were "**remaining matters**," we can assume that what Paul has been discussing were matters of great importance to him, and to the Lord.

Chapter 12

1. **Yet once again** (or: Now then), **brothers** (= fellow believers, or, members of the Family), **I do not intend** (purpose; want; desire) **you folks to continue being ignorant concerning the things** (or: matters) **of the spirit and attitude**
    (or: the [qualities; characteristics] which are the Spirit; the [aspects] of, or [workings] from the Breath-effect; or: spiritual folks).

The opening phrase, "**Yet once again** (or: Now then)," is my rendering of *de* as a transitional particle joining what he had just said in the previous verse, about a future visit to them, to the large topics that will follow. He was putting off discussing "**the remaining matters**" (11:34), but now he emphasizes that there are things of which he does not want them to continue being ignorant – and these things won't wait for a future visit. Everything he has been saying in this letter, up to this point, had been said so that they would not "continue being ignorant." And so, "once again" he returns to his instruction. A milder version of opening this new topic is, "Now then, brothers…" A conventional, and legitimate, reading of the text is, "Now concerning…" This has led some scholar to conclude that Paul is beginning an answer to questions that had been sent to him from Corinth (which would involve chapters 12-14). My rendering would make that suppositional conclusion unnecessary, and seems more rhetorically emphatic for his transition to the foundational topics of these next chapters. The insertion of the designation, "**brothers** (etc.),**" also lends currency to this reading. He wants the rhetor who reads this letter to those in Corinth to have his or her audience "sit up and pay attention!"

From this statement we see that Paul is moving to a new topic: "**the things** (or: matters) **of the spirit and attitude** (etc.)." We might conclude from this that what he has just been speaking to them about were not "things or matters of the spirit, or attitude," and as we saw, they were primarily behavioral issues: fleshly matters. And since he did not want the Corinthians to be "**ignorant**" concerning "the [characteristics or qualities] which are the Spirit," we can conclude that he assumes that they have no knowledge of these issues. And these are not "peripheral" issues.

Before moving on, we should first of all take notice of the fact that the word "gifts" is not in the Greek text of this verse, but is often supplied in the common versions. You will see, below, why I did not choose to insert the word "gifts" as an option for the potential bracketed insertions. The Greek word is a plural form of the adverb *pneumatikōs*, preceded by the definite article, "the," in a form that serves for masculine, feminine or neuter (neutral) nouns. The other options on offer are:
     a) "the [qualities; characteristics] which are the Spirit;" this is rendering of the genitive as apposition, which defines that of which Paul is speaking (whether things, matters, qualities or characteristics) – they are in fact speaking about, or manifestations of, the Spirit (Breath-effect). Notice that in vs. 3, below, the subject matter is "**speaking within God's Spirit.**" Then the Spirit is involved in vss. 4-11.
     b) "the [aspects] of, or [workings] from the Breath-effect" [note: second reading is an ablative];
     c) "spiritual folks."

Even though the word "spirit" is neuter, or neutral (neither masculine nor feminine), an adverb does not carry gender and the form of the plural definite article that is used here can be read as masculine. For this reason I included "c)" – Paul may be speaking of "spiritual folks." Take note that he carries on in the next verse speaking about people. So Paul's word, *pneumatikōs*, may be referring to all the renderings that are on offer for this word…

2. **You have seen, and know, that when you were being** (or: continued existing being) **ethnic multitudes** ([the] nations; Gentiles; non-Jews) **how you were folks being constantly led astray** (or: led off [the path] and away) **toward the voiceless idols** (silent images; mute forms; silent rituals) **– as often as you were being periodically and progressively led** (or: conducted up).

What an unusual statement opens this verse! It echoes Eph. 2:15 and shows that he really meant what he said in Gal. 3:28, "**there is neither Jew nor Greek** [i.e., Gentile]." Here he says, "**WHEN you were Gentiles** (non-Jews)." In other words, since He has made of the TWO (Jew and Gentile) ONE new HUMANITY (Eph. 2:15), those to whom he was writing in Corinth were no longer Gentiles, in God's new economy/new creation.

Paul may have had Hab. 2:18 in mind when he spoke of "voiceless idols,"
> "What use is a carved image, because one carved it? He shaped it a molten image, a deceptive representation (or: a false appearance; a lying vision), because its shaper trusts in (or: places faith upon) his (or: its) shape, to make idols dumb (or: dumb idols)!" (N.E.T.S.; parenthetical expansions mine, LXX).

In their old existence they had been "**constantly led astray toward the voiceless idols**." The Greek conception of the term "idol," used here, was also used of "reflections in water" and to speak of shadows, and even for "the inhabitants of the underworld," or "apparitions." It was parallel to the term "false" and was "opposite of truth and reality." (Friedrich Buchsel, *TDNT* Vol. 2, Wm. B. Eerdmans, 1978 pp 375-377) This lends a broader meaning to what Paul may have been inferring (e.g., a false god, in the Jewish use of the word, as used in the LXX). It speaks of such as superstition, ideologies, philosophies and general animism – things that were not real, but supposed.

Notice that they were "**periodically and progressively led**." This suggests that they were not free, but were slaves. They were being controlled. Paul explains this condition in Rom. 7:14-24. It was the law of the Sin.

The Greek text of the final clause can be read, *ōs an ēgesthe* (giving the bold rendering, above), or: *ōs anēgesthe* (giving the parenthetical rendering, "conducted up"). The parenthetical rendering would mean "being conducted up to offer a sacrifice" – i.e., in an idol temple. Either rendering makes sense, since Paul was speaking about being led astray "toward voiceless idols." Notice the imperfect tense of the verb: this had been an ongoing, or periodic, activity – or, it was progressive: leading them deeper into the mysteries of the cult. But the old things had now passed away (2 Cor. 5:17) since they were in the new covenant, which is a new creation. Because of this, things have changed, and so…

3. **Wherefore, I am now proceeding to make known to you folks that no one – speaking within God's Spirit** (or: speaking in union with the Breath-effect of God; speaking in the sphere of a Breath which is God) **– is in the habit of saying, "Jesus [is] a result of something set up as an offering to a deity** (or thus: Jesus [was] devoted as a sacrifice to God; or [negatively] accursed)**!" And no one is able** (normally has power) **to say, "Jesus [is] Lord** (or: O Lord Jesus; or: O [Yahweh]… Yahshua [= Yah is Savior])**!" except within and in union with [the] Holy Spirit** (or: in the midst of a set-apart Breathe-effect; in consecrated spirit and attitude; centered in [the] Sacred Breath).

First of all, notice that it is possible for someone to be "**speaking within God's Spirit** (or: speaking in union with the Breath-effect of God; speaking in the sphere of a Breath which is God)." This, in itself, is amazing. Let all three of these optional renderings sink in. Meditate on this!

> "**Let Christ's Word** (or: the *Logos*, which is the Christ; the Idea which is the Anointing; or: the message of and from the Christ [other MSS: of God; of {the} Lord]) **be continuously making its home within you folks** (or: progressively indwelling and residing – centered in and in union with you) **richly, within the midst of and in union with all wisdom**..." (Col. 3:16; *cf* Jas. 3:13-18).

But Paul sets limitations here: a person who is speaking in union with God's spirit "**is [not] in the habit of saying, 'Jesus [is] a result of something set up as an offering to a deity!'**" This bold rendering is the original and central meaning of *anathema*; the second of the parenthetical renderings is a later, profaned use. But let us consider the first parenthetical option: "Jesus [was] devoted as a sacrifice to God." Now that is what is implied, if not outright stated, in the unfortunate doctrine of Penal Substitutionary Atonement. Think about that! But no, the Spirit would not prompt someone to say that. Only pagan teachings would. What we see Paul saying here is that Jesus was NOT offered to God to appease His wrath (as pagans offered sacrifices to appease what they thought were deities). We will read in 2 Cor. 5:19 that God was WITHIN Christ, reconciling the aggregate of humanity to Himself. God was offering Himself to US! The typology of the cross was based upon the old covenant Day of Atonement, but the Hebrew word for "atonement" meant "covering," not appeasing. It was used of Noah putting a sealing (like pitch) upon the outside of the ark, to keep the ship afloat. On the Day of Atonement, the blood of the sacrifice was to "cleanse" the furnishings of the Tabernacle from Israel's failures (sins). The scapegoat was a figure for God taking those failures away from Israel's camp, or later, Land. Christ's blood was for us, not for God. It was God giving His Life to, and for, US. You see,

> "**Love** (the urge toward union; self-giving) **is constantly covering*** (habitually throwing a veil over; progressively concealing; [and with other MSS: will continue covering]) **a multitude of failures** (mistakes; errors; misses of the target; sins)" (1 Pet. 4:8b; *cf* Prov. 10:12; *cf* 13:7, below).

Of course, a follower of Christ would never call Him "accursed." But by their behavior, if they are "**falling by the side** (or: falling aside along the way)... **[they are] continuously suspending back up** (or: hanging on a pole; crucifying) **again in, with, to, for and by themselves the Son of God, and [are] constantly exposing [Him] to public shame/disgrace**" (Heb. 6:6).

But more than this, "**no one is able** (normally has power) **to say, "Jesus [is] Lord except within and in union with [the] Holy Spirit**." If a person is not abiding in the Vine, or walking in the Spirit, he or she cannot claim Him as being their Lord, for they are either not yet alive to Him, and in Him, or else have separated themselves from the Vine. So it follows that when,

> "**within The Name: Jesus! every knee** (= person) **– of the folks upon the heaven** (of those belonging to the super-heaven, or [situated] upon the atmosphere) **and of the people existing upon the earth and of the folks dwelling down under the ground** (or: on the level of or pertaining to subterranean ones; [comment: note the ancient science of the day – a three-tiered universe]) **– may bend** (or: would bow) **in prayer, submission and allegiance, and then every tongue** (= person) **may speak out the same thing** (should and would openly agree, confess, avow and acclaim) **that Jesus Christ [is] Lord** (Master; Owner) **– [leading] into [the] glory of Father God** (or: unto Father God's good reputation; [progressing] into a manifestation which calls forth praise unto God [our] Father)!" (Phil. 2:10)

Thus they will say this "**within and in union with [the] Holy Spirit**."

4. **Now there continue being different distributions** (divided-out, assigned apportionments) **of the effects of favor and the results of grace, yet the same Spirit** (Breath-effect; Attitude),

What I have rendered "**the effects of favor and the results of grace**" is a literal translation of the term *charisma*. *Charis* is the word for "favor" or "grace." The *–ma* ending informs us that this form of the noun indicates that it is "the effect" or the "result" of what that noun means. David Bentley Hart renders the whole phrase "graces bestowed" in his recent translation. The *Concordant Literal NT* gives us "apportionments of graces" for this phrase. The Greek word *dōrea* and its cognates signify "gift; present; benefit; grant." But what are discussed in the chapter are "**different distributions** (divided-out apportionments)" of what has come with God's grace to us: the effects and results of His favor. Verse 7, below, describes each effect as a "**manifestation** (clear display in light) **of the Breath-effect**." We should keep these things in mind as Paul continues his instructions on them.

Now with these "different distributions" he informs us that it is "**the same Spirit** (Breath-effect; Attitude)" that makes, and is the Source of, these "divided-out apportionments." Now observe that he references the Spirit/Breath-effect immediately following a reference to this "**same**" Spirit/Breath-effect in 3:b, above, the One by Whom a person has power and ability to say, "**Jesus [is] Lord**." That One also divides-out, apportions and assigns "**the effects of favor and the results of grace**."

5. and there are different distributions of attending services (divided-out apportionments and assignments of dispensings), **and yet the same Lord** (or: Owner; Master; [= Christ or Yahweh]);

He now singles out another aspect of God's Household, His Temple, His Reign: the sovereign activities of God in His relationship to humans and cultures. From Him, "**the same Lord**," we receive "**attending services**," or "assigned dispensings." This would seem to indicate supply and support to maintain the communities. We receive these through Christ's "servants." In today's English, we could consider what is meant by this profane Greek concept of *diakonia* as the provision of "goods and services." We first come across this noun in Lu. 10:40 (the only place this noun is used in the Gospels), along with its verb form:

> "**But Martha kept on being pulled from all around and was thus distracted concerning much serving** (or: = attending to many duties).... [telling Jesus that her] **sister is leaving [her] completely alone to be continuously giving attending service**..."

Luke uses this same noun in Acts 1:17, in speaking about Judah (Judas),

> "**he obtained by lot the allotted portion** (or: share) **of this attending service**." (Also in 1:25)

You see, Jesus used the noun form that means "one who gives attending service or runs errands" in Mat. 20:26,

> "**whoever may be now wanting or should continue intending to become great** (or: = to make himself to be important) **among you, he will continue** (or: proceed in) **being your attending servant**." *Cf* Acts 6:1, 4, where contrasting functions use this same term; also Acts 11:29; 12:25; 20:24; 12:19

This noun and its cognates were frequently used in the NT, but unfortunately the KJV renders it mostly as "ministry; ministers," and in 1 Tim. 3:8, 12 and 4:6, pronounces these "servants and errand runners" as being "deacons" – making them people who hold a church office, when the KJV was translated, rather than those who give attending service to the community. In modern, organized Christianity, the "minister" is commonly a person who has a staff to serve him or her. It is a place of church leadership, while in Mat. 20:25-27 Jesus told His disciples,

> "**The rulers and chiefs of the ethnic multitudes** (the nations or people groups) **habitually lord it over [people]**.... **It is not this way among you folks**.... **whoever may now be wanting or should continue intending to be first** (or: foremost; = prominent) **among you folks, he will continue** (or: proceed in) **being your slave**."

Notice that how Paul correlates the idea of "attending service" to the title, "**Lord** (or: Owner; Master)," reaching to the current cultural relationship of those two contrasted social position of his day: master/slave or lord/attending servant. We suggest that this contrast was intentional. In 16:15, below, he sets forth examples:

> "**the household of Stephanas and Fortunatus, that it is [the] firstfruit of Achaia, and they orderly arranged themselves into attending service for and among the set-apart folks**."

A picture of this is found in Mat. 25:34-36, where it speaks of the sheep's observed activities.

In 2 Cor. 3:7, Paul spoke of, "**the attending service of the Death,**" as a reference to the Law, Israel and Moses, and then in vs. 9a describe that old service as, "**the attending service and dispensing of the corresponding evaluations and commensurate decisions which follow the pattern** (or: separations for condemnation; judgments which are down-decisions against folks)." But in verses 8 and 9, he gave the contrasting "services": those of, "**the attending service and dispensing of the provision of the Spirit** (or: which has its source in the Breath-effect)" and "**the attending service and the dispensing of the eschatological deliverance into fairness and equity in rightwised relationships.**"
In 2 Cor. 5:18, he described what we now have (*cf* 2 Cor. 4:1) as that of Christ,

> "**giving to us the attending service of, and the dispensing from, the complete transformation [for folks] to be other [than before]** (or: the change into another [position]; the changing to correspond with other [situations; perceptions]; the alteration to be another [person]; the change from enmity to friendship; the reconciliation)."

These aspects of the new covenant, and the new creation in Christ, are that to which everyone is called: unto service to the world, and all members of the Body of Christ have a part in this.

6. **also there continue being different assigned distributions of the results of inner workings** (effects of inward operations), **and still, the same God – the One continuously working inwardly** (progressively activating) **all things within and in union with all humans** (or: constantly energizing, activating and operating the whole, centered within the midst of all things).

In light of Paul's citing Spirit, Lord and God, here in vss. 4-6, Conzelmann points us to 2 Cor. 13:14,

> "**The grace and joyous favor of, from and which is the LORD, Jesus Christ – even the Love which is GOD** (or: and the unambiguous, uniting acceptance and participation of, from and which characterizes God), **and the common-existence, partnership, sharing, communion and participation which is the set-apart Breath-effect** (or: of and from the Holy SPIRIT and that sacred spirit-attitude) **– [continue being; are] with all of you folks…**"

And then he points us to Eph. 4:

> "**the Bond** (the link, tie and connection) **of the Peace** (or: which is from THE JOINING), **[making] ONE BODY and ONE SPIRIT** (attitude and effect of the Breath), **according as you folks were** (or: are) **also called** (summoned) **within the midst of ONE expectation of your calling** (or: from your summons), **[with] ONE LORD** (or: Master; Owner), **ONE FAITH** (or: faithfulness, fidelity, loyalty, reliability, confidence, conviction, assurance, and trust), **ONE effect of SUBMERSION and envelopment which brings absorption and permeation to the point of saturation, ONE GOD and Father of all humans – the One upon all people and [moving] through all people, and within the midst of all humanity and in union with all people and all things**" (vss. 3b-6). Also, *cf* 1 Pet. 1:2 for a similar triad of terms.

In our present text (12:4-6, above) Conzelmann interprets this as a progression that "builds up to a climax…. [in] a series toward God as it goal" (ibid p 207 and n 5), similar to what he saw in 3:23, above, "**you folks [are] Christ's – yet Christ [is] God's.**" We are reminded of the Path of circularity seen in Rom. 11:36, "out of Him… through Him… and into [God]." It is the Journey from the Garden, in Gen. 3, to the "Garden City" in Gen. 22. The Path of Humanity.

Now another aspect of His functioning within His called-out are "**the results of inner workings and the effects of inward operations**" – presumably both individual and corporate. This time he informs us that these "**different distributions**" come from "**the same God.**" Taking these last three verses together, it would seem that we are to equate Spirit/Breath-effect, Lord and God as being One and the Same. Are these terms interchangeable? Is this close proximity of ambiguity done on purpose? Can we take the second half of this verse as an answer to these questions? Are these three terms just different ways of speaking of "**the One continuously working inwardly and progressively activating all things within**

and in union with all humans"? Does our theology need to be a bit flexible? However we understand God, He provides us with grace, attending service, an inner workings/operations. That is Good News.

We should not miss the inclusivity in this statement: the universal reference to "**all humans**." The form of the word "all" here serves both masculine and neuter subjects, so the last part of the verse can include "constantly energizing, activating and operating the whole, centered within the midst of all things." There is NOTHING in which God is not both present and involved. This is the Biblical worldview. Modern folks have abandoned this worldview, but we suggest that it has been to their loss and disadvantage – they wind up thinking of God as distant and uninvolved, if they think of Him at all.

7. Yet in (to; for; with) **each person the manifestation** (clear display in light) **of the Breath-effect** (from, and which is, the Spirit) **is continuously being given with a view to and [leading] toward progressively bringing [folks; things] together, face-to-face with the constant mutual bearing-together for benefit, advantage, expedience and the common good.**

This verse provides a summation of the previous three verses, calling them "**the manifestation** (clear display in light) **of the Breath-effect** (from, and which is, the Spirit)." This can mean either, a manifestation that is created by the Spirit, or it is the Spirit, which is given through the manifestation. Both interpretations are correct!

God's "continuous inward working" is "**for benefit, advantage, expedience and the common good** [of all]," yet it is also "**in, to, for and with each person**." Each individual "**manifestation** (clear display in light) **of the Breath-effect** (or: from the Spirit)" – as described in vss. 4-6, above – is "**continuously being given [with a view] to and [leading] toward progressively bringing [folks or things] together, face-to-face with the constant mutual bearing-together**." That is a mouthful, but it describes the up-close and personal way that these benefits are coming from God. They are intended to be "**progressively bringing [folks or things] together;**" they are "**constant mutual bearings-together**" that are brought "**face-to-face with**" us – and all of this is for "**the common good**." Even if we don't understand the particular "**manifestation**," we can trust the Spirit; God has a Good Attitude towards us. What assurance this should give us! This reminds us of Rom. 8:28.

But now Paul becomes more specific about what he has been describing...

8. **For you see, on the one hand, in** (or: to; for; with; by) **one person a word** (a thought, message or expression; a *logos*) **of wisdom** (or: patterned information from Wisdom; reason which is wisdom; a wise idea) **is repeatedly or from time-to-time or progressively being given. In** (or: To; For; With; By) **another person, on the other hand, [is given] a word** (thought; message; expression; [the] reason) **of, or from, intimate, experiential knowledge, insight or realization** (*gnosis*) **– in accord with** (or: down from; in the sphere of; in line with) **the same Breath-effect** (or: Spirit).

Two manifestations of the Breath-effect (vs. 7) are given here, and both of them are "**a word** – a *Logos*":
      a) **of wisdom** (or: a wise idea);
      b) **of intimate, experiential knowledge, insight or realization** (*gnosis*).
One word is "**repeatedly or from time-to-time or progressively being given by one person** – or it is given to this person; or it is given in this person (an inward word); or it is given for this person (the word applies to, or is of benefit for, him or her); or this word comes with (the presence of) this person. This word imparts God's **wisdom**, or a wise idea. Considering the vast amount of Jewish "wisdom literature" available to Paul, was he thinking in terms of personification, "patterned information from Wisdom [God]," both personalizing Wisdom, and rendering it as an ablative? Another rendering, as apposition, gives us "reason which is wisdom." This all may simply be "a wise idea."

Consider what our brother Jacob said in Jas 3:

13. **Who [is] wise and understanding** (adept) **among you? Let him at once exhibit** (show; present to the sight and demonstrate) **his works and actions out of beautiful behavior** (fine, ideal, excellent and appropriate conduct) **in gentleness of** (or: considerateness from) **wisdom.**

14. **Yet if you folks continuously have bitter rivalry** (or: jealousy) **and selfish ambition** (or: faction) **in your heart, do not habitually boast** (exult) **and lie** (speak falsely or deceitfully) **concerning the truth or reality** (or: are you not now vaunting against and falsifying the truth?).

15. **This is not the wisdom continuously coming down from above, but rather [is] upon the earth** (or: earthly; terrestrial), **pertaining to or proceeding from the soul** (soulful; having the mind, will and emotions as its source; = natural), **pertaining to, or proceeding from, or having the characteristics of demons** [Hellenistic term and concept; = influences thought of in that period and culture as being animistic or personified].

> [comment: note that the three adjectives "earthly," "natural/soulish," and "demonic" are tied together to this same context, as being of the same sphere of being – or, fruit of the same tree]

16. **For where [there is] jealousy** (rivalry) **and selfish ambition** (faction; intrigue), **in that place [is] instability** (disorder; an unsettled state) **and every ignoble** (base; vile; worthless) **practice.**

17. **But the wisdom from above is** (constantly exists being) **indeed first** (or: primarily) **pure, thereafter peaceable** (or: peaceful; pertaining to peace and harmonious joining), **suitable** (fair; reasonably lenient; yielding; unassertive; considerate), **compliant** (easily persuaded; receptive; reasonable; willing to yield), **full of mercy** (= practical help) **and good fruits, non-separating** (not discriminatory; undivided in evaluating; unwavering; unprejudiced), **unpretending** (or: not hyper-critical; not judging from a low point of view; not focusing on tiny distinctions; not overly judgmental; not under-estimating of reality).

18. **Now the fruit of fair and equitable dealing** (eschatological deliverance which brings justice and right relationship in accord with the Way pointed out; the condition of being rightwised, or turned in the right direction; also: = covenant participation) **is continuously being sown in peace and harmonious joining by and for those habitually performing** (making; doing; producing) **peace and harmonious joining.**

> [comment: this is the fruit of the Spirit, or, from the Tree of Life]

The other word imparts *gnosis*: "**intimate, experiential knowledge, insight or realization**." Once again, this word is given "**In** (or: To; For; With; By)" this person.

Even though there are different manifestations or aspects of God that are given, Paul wants his listeners to know that these are not coming from different gods (as with the polytheism of paganism), but are in fact "**in accord with** (or: down from; in the sphere of; in line with) **the same Breath** (or: Spirit)." The semantic range of the preposition "in accord with, etc.," lends us insight to how these words are associated with God. They come down from Him (in a spacial metaphor: God is up, we are down); these words are "in the sphere of the Breath-effect," and are "in line with" the Spirit's intent and character. They "**accord with**" the Spirit of God. If they do not meet these criteria, we should question that they have come from God. We also see the familiar "Devine passive" voice, "**being given**," which was the common rhetorical device that was used to acknowledge God as the Source.

9. **In** (To; For; With; By) **a different person [is given] faithfulness** (trust; loyalty; belief; conviction; faith; trustworthiness), **within and in union with the same effect of the Breath** (or: Spirit; Attitude); **yet in** (to; for; by; with) **another the effects of grace, and the results of joyous favor, which result in healings – within and in union with the one Breath-effect** (or: Spirit; Attitude).

The "**same effect of the Breath**" of Life; the "**one Breath-effect**," brought both **faithfulness** and **healings** to the called out community. Ponder the semantic range of the word first rendered "faithfulness." Its potential power and ability, rendered as "**faith and trust**," can be seen in 13:2, below. As an aspect of the "fruit of the Spirit," we see it listed in Gal. 5:22. As an essence, empowerment or characteristic that "**continues remaining and habitually dwells**, see 13:13, below. Interpreters, thinking of this particular reference to "faith" as being "a gift," have wanted to separate it from the "faith" that a person needs "to be saved." But Paul says nothing of the sort. Faith is one of **the effects of grace**." Deliverance and salvation do indeed involve faith, but hear how it is put in Eph. 2:8,

> "**For you see, by** (or: to; in; for; with) **the grace and joyous favor you are** (you continuously exist being) **folks having been delivered** (rescued; kept safe; saved; made whole; restored to your original state and condition) **so as to now be enjoying salvation through** [some MSS add: the] **faithfulness** (or: loyalty; trust; faith; confidence), **and even this not forth from out of you folks, [it is] the gift of and from God** (or: the gift which is God; or: the gift pertains to God)."

In that verse, the word "gift" is *dōron*: a gift; a present. It is not something a person is expected to have, unless it is given to him or her. Notice the appositional rendering: the gift which IS God. Also the ablative rendering: the gift FROM God. God, the Spirit, gives faith, faithfulness (etc.) to us. THIS is the Good News. He provides Himself to us through growing His Fruit (faith, love, etc.) from within us, when the Seed of the Vine, planted within our hearts/spirits sprouts from the darkness of our Adamic soil, and grows up in His Resurrection Life, as,

> "**the One who shines forth within the midst of our hearts, with a view to illumination of the intimate and experiential knowledge of God's glory – in a face of Christ**" (2 Cor. 4:6b).

As you can observe, both of the terms "a different person" and "another" are in the dative case, with no expressed preposition. So on offer are the various functions of the dative case: in, to, for, by, with. This verse builds off of vs. 8, so, as in 8b, the verb "**given**" in 8a is inserted in 9a, here. Notice what is given "**within and in union with**" this One Spirit: faith (etc.) and healings. These are given "in" these folks, or "to" these folks, or "for" these folks, or "with" these folks, or/and "by' these folks. So "faith, trust, loyalty, belief, conviction and trustworthiness" can come to someone, within that very person. Or, it/they can come by someone else, who as a carrier of the Spirit imparts it/them. Faith (etc.) can come "to" a person directly from being in union with the Spirit (the Spirit, as it were, impregnates a person with trust and loyalty). The idea of "within" implies that these people are dwelling within the Breath-effect (Acts 17:28). We think it important to emphasize, again, that "**faith/trust**" issues directly from the Spirit, as an "**effect of the Breath**," or from union with the Spirit.

Now it is the same with healings, except Paul specifically identifies these as "**the effects of grace, and the results of joyous favor**." Those effects and results emanate from the presence of the Spirit being with and in these folks. Paul makes a fine distinction here. Grace is a gift that has effects and results. Healings is just one of them. He does not say what kind of healings, so this could be "wholeness," physical healing, mental and emotional healings, etc. They might refer to the healings of Adam that comes to individuals as they are made alive in Christ (15:22-23, below) – which is the central meaning of Isa. 53:5,

> "Now He was wounded through and because of our failures (sins; deviations), and He was weakened and made sick through our acts of lawlessness: child-training and discipline, which had a view to our peace-from-the-joining, [came] upon Him; by His bruise we were suddenly and miraculously healed" (LXX, JM).

10. **Yet in** (to; for) **another person [is given] the effects and results of inner workings and operations of abilities, powers and influences; still in** (to; for; by) **another [is given] a prophecy** (or: light ahead of time), **and in** (to; for; by) **another [is given] thorough discernings, distinguishings, discriminations or evaluations pertaining to spirits**

> (or: separations from spirits throughout [oneself]; [the] siftings and complete separations which lead to a thorough decision or judgment of spirits or attitudes). **Yet, in** (to; for; by) **a different person [are given] races and species** (families; classes; kinds) **of languages** (or: tongues), **then in** (to; for; by) **another one [are given] translations and interpretations of languages** (tongues).

What applied about the "persons" in vss. 7-9 applies here, as well. So let us examine what Paul lays out concerning what the Spirit is doing in, to and for these folks"

a) **the effects and results of inner workings and operations of abilities, powers and influences**: the inward presence of the Holy Spirit is the One doing the "inner workings," and is the Source of "abilities, powers and influences" (these terms are a conflation of the Greek *dunamis*); this is a restatement of vs. 6, above both within and through individual members of the body;

b) **a prophecy** (or: light ahead of time): notice that I added the dative function "by," for this prophecy (that brings "light ahead of time" – a rendering based upon the Greek elements of the word) can come by, or through, a person; it can also come in, to or for a person; Paul discusses this further in 14:6 and 22ff, below'

c) **thorough discernings, distinguishings discriminations or evaluations pertaining to spirits**: the adjective "thorough" comes from the prefix *dia-* that is added as an intensifier for the word *krisis*, which means "a discerning; a distinguishing; a discrimination; an evaluation." Now what is meant by the term "spirit" in this context? In the parenthetical expansion is included the term "attitudes." When people harbor attitudes, they can be either positive and good, or negative and harmful to the body (both the physical body, and the corporate group). One can have a spirit of Love, or a spirit of hate; one can have a spirit of compassion, or a spirit of greed and avarice; one can be filled with the Spirit of God, or with the spirit of the dominant society; one can have a spirit of joy, or a spirit of sadness, grief or anger. We do not think that Paul is speaking of metaphysical entities, but rather of the rainbow colors of Light, or the many shades of darkness that are all aspects of His creation, and of the capabilities of our own beings; for an in-depth investigation into the topic of "spirits" and other metaphysical terms that were used in the 1st century Roman Empire, and in the times before, I recommend Walter Wink's, *Naming the Powers, The Language of Power in the New Testament*, 1984. This effect of grace is more fully explained in 14:24f, below;

d) **races and species** (families and classes) **of languages** (or: tongues): this may refer to "supernatural," ecstatic abilities and manifestations, or to gifts and abilities in our natural minds for use with folks that speak a different language than we do; he speaks of this in vss. 28 and 30, below, and he devotes 14:2-39, below, addressing issues of the public use of these;

e) **translations and interpretations of languages** (tongues): these, again, can be in either category as those of languages: spiritual/supernatural, or natural abilities. Paul will speak more about the functioning of the "spiritual; ecstatic" aspects of these, and of languages in ch. 14, below. But notice, in our next verse, both the Source and the operation of all that has been given...

11. **Now the One and the same Spirit** (or: Breath-effect; Attitude) **is habitually working within** (energizing, activating and operating) **all these things, constantly dividing, apportioning and distributing in** (to; for) **each person his own [effect of grace], correspondingly as He** (She; It) **progressively intends** (is habitually willing; continuously purposes; keeps on pleasing [to do]).

It is **the same Spirit** (or: Breath-effect; Attitude), just as we saw above, that "**is habitually working within** (energizing, activating and operating) **all these things**." He began emphasizing "the same Spirit in vs. 4ff, above, and then in vs. 9b (as here in vs. 11) uses the term "**in union with the ONE Breath-effect** (or: Spirit)." Why this emphasis on "**the One and the same Spirit**"? We know that Jesus instructed us that "**God [is] spirit** (or: [is] Spirit; [gives] Breath; [becomes] Wind; [is] a Breath-effect and Attitude)," in Jn. 4:24, so what should we take away from Paul's repeated emphasis? Unfortunately, he did not explain himself about this, here, but it 2 Cor. 3:17 he informs us,

> "**Now the Lord** [= Christ or Yahweh] **continuously exists being the Spirit** (or: Yet the Breath-effect is the LORD), **so where [the] Lord's Breath-effect** (Spirit; Attitude) **[blows, there is] freedom** (or: and so in the place in which the Breath-effect – the Spirit – which is [the] Lord [= Christ or Yahweh] [blows; exists], liberty [comes; arises])."

It seems to us that he simply wants us to recognize God, in His Spirit, as the Source and manifested activity in all of these results, of and from God's grace, that are given to us. These letters were written before the later theologians came up with the idea and doctrine of God being a "Trinity."

Now the distributions of all that he has been describing is not just a one-time thing. God is "**constantly dividing, apportioning and distributing in** (to; for) **each person his own [effect of grace]**." Furthermore, Paul assures us that this constant activity by God is done "**correspondingly as He progressively intends** (is habitually willing; continuously purposes)." Do you get the idea that God is intimately and functionally involved with the people that comprise His Temple? We would say that this is a definite, "YES!" And you know... He is the same: yesterday, today and on through the ages (Heb. 13:8). Dan Kaplan has seen in the "apportioning and distributing" an allusion to Moses (a figure of the working of the Spirit) setting up the Tabernacle, in Ex. 40. In vss. 18-19 we find:

> "Moses set up the tabernacle; he laid its bases and set up its frames, and put in its poles, and raised up its pillars; and he spread the tent over the tabernacle, and put the covering of the tent over it; as the LORD had commanded Moses" (NRSV).

We suggest that in this same way, the Spirit sets up the Body of Christ, placing each "part" in its proper place for its intended function. Reading all of Ex. 40 (along with Lev. 8 and Num. 9) will be instructive for understanding Paul's metaphor of a "body" to describe the makeup of God's Temple, which in turn is a picture of us, His called-out community.

From vss. 7-11 Paul has been focusing on "**each person**," and the grace-effects that have been individually given to various individuals, but all along emphasizing that it is One Spirit in which they have these results of the Christ event, which sets his audience up for what he will say next...

12. **You see, correspondingly as the [human] body is one [body] and continuously has** (possesses; holds) **many members** (body parts), **and all the members of the one body – being many – are one body, in this way, also, [is] the Christ** (or: even thus [is] the Anointed One and the Anointing).

The Christ, and the Anointing which is the Spirit, has been the aim of Paul's reasoning in this passage. The Spirit joins and bonds all the "**many members**" into being One Body, which is the corporate Christ. The Christ was not just Jesus. As Paul will explain in 15:44-49, below, "**the Last Adam** (Christ, the Second Humanity) **[was born] into [being] a continuously life-making** (life-producing; life-creating; life-forming) **Spirit**." And thus, the essence and substance of **the Christ** is Spirit (Breath-effect): "**the Second Human** (Person; Humanity) **[is made] out of heaven** (atmosphere)" – 15:47, below. We suggest that he was speaking of the Christ when, in 15:46, he said, "**the spiritual [is] not first, but rather the one having the qualities and characteristics of a soul; then afterwards, the spiritual** (that pertaining to and having the qualities of Breath-effect)." This would, of course, apply to both the first Adam and to the last Adam. Both were ultimately corporate bodies, with many members (*cf* Rom. 5:15-19).

So now Paul has moved to an analogy of the human body, in order to make clear all that he has been saying since vs. 4, above. Is it not interesting that God created the human body to be an image and likeness of Himself, and now Paul is reflecting back to these Corinthians that the Christ, the Anointed Human (for the term Christ means "Anointed," which signifies God flowing as Oil upon the Second Humanity – 15:47, below), is like the body of a human, which has "**many members**," and is still "**one body**"?

Witherington provides some interesting observations (similarly noted by a number of scholars) that, "The image or metaphor of the body has a considerable history. One important instance is from M. Agrippa, who draws an analogy between the state and the human body..." (ibid p 253). He also cites M.M. Mitchell, *Paul and the Rhetoric of Reconciliation* (Tubingen: Mohr, 1991 pp 157-64) where she says that, "the crucial point is that this metaphor or example had a history of use against factions..." (ibid. p 254 n 3). He further says, "But it is not merely an analogy, since he believes that it describes a real supernatural entity..." (ibid. p 255). Clement of Rome (*circa* AD 80-140) wrote:

"Let us take our body for an example. The head is nothing without the feet, and the feet are nothing without the head; yea, the very smallest members of our body are necessary and useful to the whole body. But all work harmoniously together, and are under one common rule for the preservation of the whole body" (*1 Clement* 37:5, Roberts-Donaldson trans., www.earlychristianwritings.com).

That Paul thought of the body of Christ as an actual organism is seen from vs. 26, below, "whether one member is continuing to experience the effect of something, or constantly undergoes suffering, all the members continually experience the effect or the suffering together..." Witherington points out that in our present verse, the term "**the Christ**" is "a synonym for the *ekklēsia*, the body of Christ" (ibid p 258). Now we should meditate long on this. You see, WE are the Christ (God's Anointed) in the earth, today.

13. **For indeed** (or: also) **we, ourselves – within the midst of one Spirit** (or: in union with one Breath-effect and Attitude) **– are all submerged into one Body** (or: were all immersed into, so as to be enveloped by, one body) **– whether Jews or Greeks** (or: Hellenists), **whether slaves or free folks – and we all are** (or: were) **made** (or: caused) **to drink one Spirit** (or: spirit; Breath-effect; Attitude).

OK, now just what are "**we, ourselves within the midst of**"? "**One Spirit.**" Yes,
> "**For you see, within the midst of and in union with Him we continuously live** (or, as a subjunctive: could be constantly living), **and are constantly moved about and put into motion, and continue existing** (experiencing Being)" (Acts 17:28).

Now, being within the midst of the Spirit, "**are all submerged into one Body,**" and so, it would seem, the Body "is already there" (Conzelmann, ibid p 212 n 13) "when believers are taken up into it..." Remember when we cited 15:45, below, "**the Last Adam INTO a continuously life-making** (life-producing; life-creating; life-forming) **Spirit.**" That is the corporate "New Humanity" (Eph. 2:15; the Second Humanity, 15:47, below), and this includes us. Then in 15:48 we read,
> "**and likewise, as [is] the Added, Imposed, Heavenly Person** (or: the one made of and having the quality and character of the added-heaven – i.e., Christ), **of such sort also [are] the added, imposed, heavenly people – those made of and having the quality and character of the added, imposed, heaven** (or: the finished and perfected atmosphere)."

This equates to our now being "IN Christ," were we now "**made** (or: caused) **to drink one Spirit,**" which equates to "**drinking [His] blood**" (Jn. 6:54) – which is to say, "drinking His Life" – and this leads us to Jn. 7:37, where,
> "**Jesus, after having taken a stand, stood and then suddenly cries out, saying, 'If ever anyone may continue being thirsty, let him be habitually coming toward** (or: face-to-face with) **Me, and then let the person continuously trusting and progressively believing into Me be constantly** (habitually; repeatedly) **drinking!**'" [*cf* Isa. 12:3; 55:1]

And so now Paul explains Jesus' meaning to us, here in vs. 13. It means "**to drink one Spirit** (or: spirit; Breath-effect; Attitude)," and this is that to which Paul was referring in 11:25-26, above.

Now not only are we "IN Christ," and "IN the One Spirit," we find a slightly different picture, put in a different metaphor, in Col. 3:10-11,
> "**[be] suddenly clothing yourselves with** (or: ENTERING WITHIN) **the new one, the one being continuously** (or: repeatedly; habitually; progressively) **renewed into full, accurate, added, intimate and experiential knowledge and insight which is down from and corresponds to the image of its Creator, wherein there is no Greek and Jew, circumcision and uncircumcision, barbarian, Scythian, slave, freeman, but to the contrary, Christ [is] all, and within all.**"

And in Gal. 3:27, Paul instructs us,
> "**For you see** (or: It follows that) **as many of you folks as were immersed into Christ, at once clothed yourselves with Christ** (or: were plunged into so as to be enveloped by then saturated and permeated with Anointing – or, the Anointed One – instantly ENTERED within and put on [the/an] Anointing)!**"

So, comparing Gal. 3:27 with vs. 13, here, it seems that Paul equated the One Spirit, with Christ, into Whom we have been immersed. Joining this to 13a, above, can we conclude, again, that the "Body of Christ" is in fact the Spirit? It seems that it is the Spirit that creates the Body out of Himself. Furthermore, Gal. 3:28 speaks similarly re: Jew and Greek, slave and free, but adds: "**there is not** (does not exist) **'male and female'; for it follows that, you folks all exist being one within Christ Jesus**." This is the "new creation" of which he spoke in 2 Cor. 5:17. Paul was teaching these same things to those in Corinth, and here in vs. 13, he is using the metaphor of a body, into which we were "all immersed into, so as to be enveloped." And while you are in Gal. 3, you might as well read vs. 29 where he informs us that because of all this, we are "**Abraham's Seed: heirs** (possessors and enjoyers of the distributed allotment), **down from, corresponding to and in the sphere of Promise!**" Can you see all the threads tying together, creating the beautiful tapestry that tells the story from the Alpha to the Omega? But there is more…

Since we just called attention to Adam, in the comments on vs. 12, let us recall 10:17, above, where Paul said, "**we, The Many, are** (exist being) **one bread** (one loaf of bread), **one body**… **we, The All** (the all of humanity), **are continuously holding a share with others and are co-partaking**." And, once again, he affirms the oneness and joined union of this body, in saying "**whether Jews or Greeks** (or: Hellenists)." This is definitely a NEW arrangement (covenant) and in Eph. 2:11-18, where in vs. 15 he speaks of God now having made these Two Group into "One New Humanity," and then in vs. 18-22 he affirms (and note the similar language and metaphors as we find here in Corinthians) that…

> 18. … **The Both, continuously have the procurement of access** (conduct toward the presence; admission, being led), **within one Spirit** (or: in union with one Breath-effect and Attitude), **to** (or: toward; face to face with) **the Father.**
> 19. **Consequently then, you folks no longer continuously exist being strangers** (foreigners) **and sojourners** (folks being or living beside a house; temporary residents in a foreign land), **but in contrast, you continually exist being fellow-citizens of those set apart to be sacred people** (or: folks residing together in a City belonging to, and composed of, the holy ones): **even God's family** (members of God's household),
> 20. **being fully built as a house upon the foundation of the sent-forth representatives** (or: emissaries) **and prophets** (folks who had light ahead of time), **Jesus Christ continuously being a corner-foundation [stone] of it** (or: there being an extreme point and head of the corner, or, capstone/keystone: Jesus Christ Himself),
> 21. **within and in union with Whom all the home-building** (all the construction of the house; or: the entire building), **being continuously fitted [and] progressively framed together** (closely and harmoniously joined together; made a common joint by a word), **is continuously and progressively growing into a set-apart temple within [the] Lord** [= Christ, or, Yahweh]:
> 22. **within the midst of** (or: in union with) **Whom you folks, also, are continuously and progressively being formed a constituent part of the structure** (or: being built together into a house) – **into God's down-home place** (place of settling down to dwell; abode; permanent dwelling) **within [the] Spirit** (or: in spirit; or: in the midst of a Breath-effect and an attitude).

Wow! What a *Logos* to us. And in this house/temple, there is no social differentiation or distinction between "slaves and free folks." Now notice that these two, contrasting genetic and social groups are ALL "**made** (or: caused) **to drink one Spirit**." The universal unification inherent in Paul's words is hard to miss. It's a new arrangement (new creation): the former outsiders are now insiders.

14. **It follows then, the Body is not one member** (or: part), **but to the contrary, [it is] many.**

This now informs 11:27b and 29, above. The Body IS the many members.

15. **In case the foot should ever say, "Because I am not a hand, I am not from out of the midst of** (= a part of) **the Body," not for this reason is it not from out of the midst of the body** (or: = it is not

from this statement that it does not exist with the body being its source and that it is not a part of the body)**!**

16. **And if the ear should ever say, "Because I am not an eye, I am not forth from** (= a part of) **the Body," not alongside of this** (= not for this reason) **is it not forth from** (= a part of) **the Body!**

17. **If the whole Body [were] an eye, where [would be] the hearing** (or: the ability to hear; the ear)**? If [the] whole [were] hearing** (the ability to hear), **where [would be] the sense of smell?**

He has affirmed that every "member" is a part of the Body. Then he instructs them that each member has a function FOR, and IN, the body. His analogies are crystal clear – no enigmas, here!

Cf the importance of "**hearing**" in Heb. 5:11; 2 Tim. 4:3-4; and Lu. 7:1, where it speaks of "**the hearing of the people** (or: into the people's ability to hear)."

18. **Yet, at this present time** (or: = But as things are), **God, for Himself, places** (or: at once set in Himself) **the members** (or: parts) – **each one of them – within the midst of and in union with the Body, just as He intends** (purposed; wills).

We are again tied to chapter 15 in Paul's present metaphor, for in teaching on the resurrection, vs. 38 instructs us that, "**Yet God habitually gives a body to** (or: for) **it, according as He wills, and to** (or: for; with) **each of the seeds its own body**." God doing what He will, purposes and intends, is a central theme throughout all of Paul's teaching.

Don't complain that you don't see visions or hear prophesies, or that you are not laid (being a hand) upon someone to heal them: what you do and how you function in the Body are "**just as He intends** (purposed; wills)." And underline this: **God, for Himself, places the members – each one of them!** There is Personal, intimate involvement of God in the life of each individual.

The verb "places/set" is aorist (either a simple English present tense, or a simple English past tense), in the middle voice. This voice indicates that the subject (God) acts for Himself, or upon Himself. I rendered the former in bold, and the latter in lightface: "at once set in Himself." We are set in the Body FOR God's use and purposes in the kingdom, but the wonderful reality is that He places us IN Himself (i.e., in His Spirit).

> "**Since, therefore, you folks were awakened and are raised up together in the Christ**.... **You folks died, and your life has been hidden so that it is now concealed together with the Christ, within the midst of God** (or: in union with God)" (Col. 3:1a, 3).

19. **Now if the whole** (or: all) **were one member, where [would be] the Body?**

As he will begin showing in vs. 21, by the word "**member**," used here, his analogy refers to a body part. Here, Eph. 4 comes to mind:

> 15. **But continuously being real and true** (living in accord with reality and the facts; holding to, speaking, pursuing and walking in Truth; truthing it) **within, and in union with, Love** (or: centered in unambiguous acceptance; a full giving of ourselves with an urge toward union), **we can grow up** (enlarge; increase) **into Him – the ALL which is the Head: Christ** (or: [and] we would in love make all things grow up into Him Who is the head and source: [the] Anointed One)!
> 16. **– from out of Whom** (or: out from the midst of Which) **all the Body** (or: the entire body) **being continuously fitted and framed together** (made a common joint by a word; laid out and closely joined together) **and constantly being knit together and caused to mount up united through every fastening** (or: joint) **of the supply of rich furnishings** (or: through every assimilation of the full supply of funds; through every touch {kindling; setting on fire} of the completely supplied requirements) **in accord with** (or: down from; commensurate to; in the sphere and to the degree of) **the operation** (operative, effectual energy) **within [the] measure of**

each one part [other MSS: member], **is itself continually making** (or: is for itself progressively producing and forming) **the growth and increase of the Body, [focused on and leading] into house-construction** (or: unto building [up] and edification) **of itself within the midst of, and in union with, love** (full self-giving in an unambiguous urge toward union or reunion; acceptance).

20. **But, at this present time** (now) **[there are], indeed, many members** (or: parts), **yet one Body.**

As noted, in parentheses, he is speaking of "many body parts." So the Body of Christ is made up of many "parts" and each part needs the other parts, as he goes on to say...

21. **Now the eye continues unable** (habitually has no power) **to say to the hand, "I continue having no need of you," or, again, the head [cannot say] to the feet, "I continue having no need of you [two]."**

Each of the community members that regularly met together, even as presented in 11:20-34, above, all needed each other. There needed to be profitable dialogue between the members, not a suggestion of exclusion or a desire for separation between the members. Vision needs the ability of working – the hand to be used in building the Temple (chapter 3). The head needs the ability to stand, and it needs mobility. Richard Rohr wrote an insightful book, *Everything Belongs*, and his title says it all. Look at what environmental biologists have learned about ecosystems. Everything is here for His purpose, and for ours, as well. Again we are reminded of Eph. 4:

> 2. **with all lowliness of attitude** (or: humility in frame of mind) **and gentle kindness and friendliness, with longsuffering** (even-tempered, forbearing patience; a long wait before rushing in passion; putting anger far away; passionate perseverance unto the goal), **continuously holding one another up** (or: bearing with each other with tolerance) **within the sphere of, and in union with, love** (unqualified acceptance and the urge toward union),
>
> 3. **repeatedly hurrying to make every effort to constantly keep** (watch over to guard and protect; maintain) **the Spirit's oneness** (or: the unity from the Breath-effect, and of spirit; the oneness which is the Spirit; = agreement of [your] attitude) **within the Bond** (the link, tie and connection that joins two things; the binding conjunction which results in union) **of the Peace** (or: which is from THE JOINING).

22. **On the contrary, much rather, the members of the body habitually seeming or appearing to be inherently weaker are** (or: exist being) **pressingly necessary and indispensable,**

Is he saying, by this analogy, that "**God's weak act** (or: the weak [thing; plan; idea] from God) **[is] stronger than the humans** ([than] from people)"? (1:25, above). Or, that,

> "**God collects His thoughts and speaks forth** (or: selects, picks out and chooses) **the weak things** (or: the powerless or sickly ones) **of the System** (world; arranged order), **so that He would bring disgrace and shame down on the strong things** (or: the robust and mighty ones)"? (1:27, above).

Is this why Jesus said that tax-collectors and prostitutes would enter God's reign before the religiously respectable folks? In the physical body, it is easy to see Paul's point. But regarding the calling to follow Christ, this may be like what he said in 1:26, above: "**[there are] not many wise folks – according to flesh, not many powerful ones** (those with ability), **not many well-born ones**." This is the reason that the "**inherently weaker [members] are** (or: exist being) **pressingly necessary and indispensable**."

Dan Kaplan points us back to Israel's history to observe that with their patriarchs God normally chose contrary to cultural practices by choosing not the firstborn son, but a younger one, or a weaker one, to receive the main or larger inheritance and leadership for the next generation. Recall the stories of Isaac, Jacob, Judah, Joseph (Israel's first savior that first became rejected by his brothers, sold into slavery and then wrongly sent into prison for years, before coming into his calling). A socially inconsequential man,

Gideon, became another deliverer of Israel, and later the overlooked younger son David, who tended the family's flocks, became Israel's greatest king. Heb. 11 gives a generalized listing of other apparent "losers" who were considered "heroes" of faith and trust:

> 36. **But different ones took a trial** (or: received a test) **of mockings** (scoffings), **and of scourgings, and further, of bonds and imprisonment** (= put in chains and thrown in jail).
> 37. **They were stoned, they were cut in two with a saw, they were put to the proof** (tried; tested), **they passed away in a slaughter** (or: by murder) **with sword, they went around** (wandered) **in sheepskins, in goat skins, continuously being behind** (being in want; being in the rear), **being constantly pressed** (squeezed; afflicted), **habitually being held in the bad** (being maltreated; having it bad) – [cf 2 Ki. 2:13 (LXX): Elijah's mantle a sheepskin – Denton]
> 38. **of whom the System** (the ordered arrangement; the world of culture, secular society, religions and government) **was not worthy** (was not of equal value) – **being continually deceived** (led astray; caused to wander) **in deserts and mountains and caves and the holes of the earth** (or: ground).

Jesus took the form of a servant to fulfill God's plan of the ages. He was born to an obscure family and was considered to have had an illegitimate birth. By human standards these all would have been considered to be "**inherently weaker [members]**" of their groups. Even Paul said of himself, "**Who is continuing weak and I am not proceeding to be weak** (= sharing their weakness)?.... **I will boast concerning the things pertaining to, from, and which are, my weakness**" (2 Cor. 11:29-30).

23. **and ones which we habitually presume** (or: suppose; deem; think) **to be less valuable and less honorable [parts] of the body, we are constantly surrounding these with more abundant honor** (or: habitually place [things] of exceeding value around these), **and so our unattractive** (deformed; indecent; unfashionable) **[members] are constantly having** (habitually holding) **more exceeding and abundant good form** (or: presentability; respectability; modesty; good appearance).

24. **Now our well-formed** (or: respectable; presentable; profitably fashioned) **[members] continue having no need, but God mixed and blended the Body together, giving more abundant value and honor to those habitually or repeatedly being left behind in the rear** (or: being made defective, deficient, or below standard),

Does this sound like Jesus saying, "The first shall be last"? God raises up the humble and resists the exalted (Mat. 23:12; Jas. 4:6). He sends the rich to the fires, and the wretched to Abraham's bosom (Lu. 16:23ff). Here in this life, "**God mixed and blended the Body together, giving more abundant value and honor to those habitually or repeatedly being left behind in the rear** (or: being made defective, deficient, or below standard)." Regardless of how we understand or interpret Paul's analogy in vss. 23-24a, his application in 24b, and God's reason for it, seems clear. All are needed for the proper functioning of the Body. God's reign brings this balance. We read in Lu. 1:

> 52. "**He takes down folks of power and ability from thrones, and then lifts up high folks of low status** (or: He also exalts humble folks). [Ps. 113:7]
> 53. "**He in-fills with good things folks who are habitually hungry, and yet He sends out and away empty folks who are habitually rich.** [cf Mat. 5:6]

The Corinthian community had not been following this example. So why does God do this?

25. **to the end that there should be no tearing split-effect, causing division, within the body, but rather that the members should constantly show the same care over, and have the same concern about, the welfare of one another.**

So that they all "**constantly show the same care over, and have the same concern about, the welfare of one another.**" What a simple explanation of how God does things, and why. He does not want "**tearing split-effect, causing division, within [His] body.**" Ah, but look at "church history!" Even in Paul's day, in the province of Galatia he observed, in Gal. 4:

15. **Now since, or if, you folks are habitually biting and repeatedly eating one another down, watch out, lest you may be used up and consumed by** (or: under) **one another.**
16. **So I continue saying, be habitually walking about** (= living your life) **in spirit** (or: by [the] Spirit; with a Breath-effect), **and you should under no circumstance** (or: would by no means) **bring to fruition** (carry to its goal; end up with; bring to maturity) **the full rushing passion** (the over-desire; craving) **originating in flesh**
> (= pertaining to the estranged human nature, or the self which has been dominated by a system of culture or religion; or: corresponding to flesh-[righteousness]; belonging to [a religious system] of flesh-works).
17. **For the flesh [system or nature] is constantly rushing passionately down upon** (or: against) **the spirit** (or: Breath-effect), **and the spirit** (or: Breath-effect) **down on** (or: against) **the flesh [nature, or, system of religion], for these things are constantly lying in opposition to each other** (lying set to displace each other), **so that – whatever you may habitually be intending** (wanting; willing; purposing) **– these things you repeatedly cannot be doing.**

Jeremy Lopez offers insights for today's situations in the called-out communities:
> "This dismissiveness of others over 'differences' stifles the miraculous and the working of the supernatural within the Body of Christ more than all else. This dismissiveness of others – this judgment – is actually a form of blasphemy against the Holy Ghost because it says, 'I don't trust the Holy Spirit to lead others into truth.' This judgmental dismissal of others seemingly different from us shouts, 'If you're different, then you're wrong.' How absurd and how audacious this spirit is. How very arrogant and prideful. Is it any wonder we often fail to see the miraculous now working within our churches? Rather than loving, we would rather protest against the rights and beliefs of others. Rather that honoring those seemingly unlike us, we would rather seek to discredit and to malign them, slandering them for not agreeing with us…. This judgment and pride is rebellion in the Kingdom and a spirit of witchcraft - manipulation and a desire to control others, disguising itself as 'faith.' It's the work of an Antichrist spirit. Will He not do the work of drawing all men and women unto Himself as He promised? Is He not the head of all things? Aren't all things in Him and even by Him? Even those which seem different? The 'unity of the faith' says, 'I trust the Holy Spirit to lead all men and all women into truth.' The 'bond of peace,' though, says, 'In spite of our many differences, I can respect the unique journeys of others.' This message is a clarion call not only for unity within the Body but also a call for common decency, respect, and civility again. If you truly want to experience a revival of miracles, signs, and wonders, begin by seeking a revival of love again." (from: a Facebook post, 12/7/2018; www.identitynetwork.net)

26. **And further, whether one member is continuing to experience the effect of something, or constantly undergoes suffering, all the members continually experience the effect or the suffering together with [it; her; him]; or if a member is being constantly glorified, normally given an assumed appearance, or is progressively receiving a good reputation, all the members are continuously rejoicing together with [him; her; it].**

Now Paul lays out the realities of a body of Christ: when "**one member is continuing to experience the effect of something, or constantly undergoes suffering, all the members continually experience the effect or the suffering together with [it; her; him].**" This statement means more than members being sympathetic toward the suffering of other members. It is existential co-experiencing. In this we see how connected all the members are to one another. This is existential solidarity. The second half of the verse gives us the positive side of this spiritual union in Christ: mutual **glory** and constant "**rejoicing together.**" This is what it means to be "a body." Now, what if we take this "spirit-connectedness" to a greater level, beyond a localized "temple of God"? Yes, being within the midst of Him, we live, are moved about, and exist connected to everything, and everyone (Acts 17:28).

Paul could have gone on to give lots of specific examples for what he has laid out here, but keeping these statements as generalizations allows them to be applied to a multitude of particular situations – and keeps them from being turned into "laws" for behavior. Paul's words are spirit, and they are life. Christ's body would grow and reproduce into to many different contexts, cultures and times. Each of these can draw from the Way that he has pointed-out.

27. **Now you folks yourselves are, and continuously exist being, Christ's Body** (or: a body which is Anointed; or: a body whose source and character is Christ, and which is Christ) **– and [you folks are] members of** (or: from out of) **a part [of it] –**

Consider the magnitude of this statement – the overwhelming ramifications! We are not just a group that belongs to Christ – although that of course is true, as well. But what Paul says here is a summation of the implications of all that he has been saying about "a body" up to this point. We are a physical manifestation that is inhabited by Christ; we are a present-day incarnation of Christ; we are "a body which is Anointed;" we are "a body whose source and character is Christ, **and which is Christ**." Could Paul have said it more plainly?

28. **whom also God Himself, indeed, placed in union with the covenant community** (or: set, centered within the called-out). **[Now] first [it was] those sent off on a mission** (emissaries; representatives); **second [it was] folks who have light ahead of time and speak it before others publicly [on behalf of God]** (spokesmen [for God]; prophets); **third [it was] people who teach. Then after that [He gave] abilities and powers, adding then effects of grace which result in cures and healings. [He also gave] folks who take [things] in hand, in place of another, and grasp with their mind and apprehend the replaced [situation] and exchange**
　　　　(or: those who lay hold of the other side of something in order to aid and assist; or:
　　　　occasions of receiving in turn or in exchange; or: = helpful services; supports given in turn) **[and provided] situations and skills for steering the course** (or: abilities to guide and direct action; acts of pilotage; helmsman abilities and services; wise counsel and guidance; = administrative and managerial skills). **[He then gave] species** (or: families; races; kinds) **of languages** (or: tongues).

This verse is a continuation of vs. 27, and it can be read both individually (each listener that was hearing this letter read was a person "**whom also God Himself, indeed, placed in union with the covenant community**" in Corinth). Or, corporately, the community in Corinth had been placed in union with the worldwide, ages-inclusive called-out community that comprised the entirety of the Christ.

Next he explains how God **placed** the beginning members **in union with the covenant community**, at large. First were "**those sent off on a mission** (emissaries; representatives)." Next He placed "**folks who have light ahead of time and speak it before others publicly [on behalf of God]** (spokesmen [for God]; prophets)." Following that He set "**people who teach**." Notice the "logic" of the *Logos*, as God was building His Temple. "**Then after that [He gave] abilities and powers**" within the communities. He also added "**effects of grace which result in cures and healings**." Each member of His body had a different function that was to attend, feed and care for His flock, His body, His temple. And, by the way, the purposes of these "different members" were for FUNCTION, and were not about establishing "offices" within a human "organization." It is a spiritual reality that incarnated the Way, the Truth and the Life. Paul describes Christ's Body as an organism that lives in and by the Holy Spirit.

As the groups came together He saw the need for "**folks who take [things] in hand, in place of another, and grasp with their mind and apprehend the replaced [situation] and exchange**." The called-out communities were a new culture; a new society – their lives had changed, and needed "those who lay hold of the other side of something in order to aid and assist in occasions of receiving in turn or in exchange, i.e., helpful services and supports given in turn." Their communities were to operate as a "well-anointed manifestation of the Reign of the heavens."

The Spirt then provided "**situations and skills for steering the course** (or: abilities to guide and direct action; acts of pilotage; helmsman abilities and services; wise counsel and guidance; = administrative and managerial skills)." These were all for management of His Household. Since the communities were now composed of multiple races and ethnic origins, He gave "**species** (or: families; races; kinds) **of languages**" – for the multi-lingual communities, as well as for those sent out into areas that spoke different languages. He is still doing this, in our own day.

29. **[So you see that] not all [are] folks sent off on a mission** (representatives; envoys; emissaries). **Not all [are] those who have light ahead of time and speak it before others in public** (prophets). **Not all [are] people who teach** (teachers; instructors). **Not all [have] abilities or powers**. 30. **Not all constantly hold** (habitually have or possess) **effects of grace which result in cures and healings. Not all habitually speak in multiple languages** (or: are constantly speaking by tongues; or: normally talk to tongues [figure of people groups of other cultures]). **Not all are continually interpreting** (or: habitually translating).

As a good rhetor, Paul employs repetition and restatement to affirm that everyone does not have the same function in the body – they are all different "body parts." These verses are often rendered as questions, but they need not be. The repetition of "**Not all**" – seven times – alerts us to his rhetorical emphasis, and drives home his point of God's plan of diversity in the functions of the members of the body. Our culture (both religious and secular) has led us to strive for places of importance, in the eyes of people. But having laid out this seven-fold negation, consider well the contrast that he now presents to them...

31. **Yet, you folks be constantly boiling with fervor** (or: are habitually fervent in zeal) **[for; seeking; supporting; in devotion to] the greater effects of grace and favor! And still, I am now progressively pointing out and showing you folks a path** ([the] Way) **corresponding to transcendence**
> (or: a road which accords with a casting-something-over [someone] on their behalf; a pathway in the sphere of excess and extravagance; = an incomparable way)**:**

The imperative of the first clause, modified by his teaching in ch. 13, below, will be picked up again, in 14:1, below: "**Now with boiling fervor and affection, be habitually** (or: you are constantly) **welling-up and zealous in regard to the things of the spirit**..." The "things of the spirit/Spirit" are the "effects of grace and favor!" Take note that the verb in both of these verses can be read either as an imperative, or as an indicative (statement of fact). This ambiguity would serve two different situations appropriately.

He is NOT telling them to seek "the more important *gifts*!" He is instructing them to be fervent in zeal of "**the greater effects of grace and favor**" which he immediately explains as being "**a path** ([the] Way) **corresponding to transcendence**." On offer are two other renderings of this, and a paraphrase:
> a) a road which accords with a casting-something-over [someone] on their behalf;
> b) a pathway in the sphere of excess and extravagance;
> c) = an incomparable way.

This Way (the Christ-Life) is founded and grounded in the effects of grace, but it is a road that is to be walked, the Path to be followed, that leads on into "transcendence." The next chapter charts this Path:

Chapter 13

This chapter is a rhetorical diversion that is different in both form and style from what has just preceded it, and from what immediately follows, in 14:1. In 8:1b, above, Paul brought up the topic of Love, saying, "**The Love** (*agape*: urge toward unambiguous, participating, accepting reunion; fully giving of oneself to others in solidarity) **progressively edifies and builds up the house**," in contrasting it to "knowledge." In

10:23b, above, he made the point that, "**All things are authorized, permitted and out of [His] Being, but yet not all things progressively edify or build up the house**." In the verses below he will go into specifics. The word Love (*agapē*) is used most frequently in the Gospel of John, and in 1, 2 & 3 John, but is common in Paul's other letters. Becoming familiar with its uses in these other texts will inform a reading of Paul, here. Harvey says of *agapē*, "Indeed, so far as we can tell, the word did not belong to ordinary speech at all, the commonest expressions being *erōs*... and *philia* (friendship).... The word, in fact, is not psychological at all, but is a technical term of the Christian vocabulary. It derives its meaning from the act of God in Christ..." (ibid p 561-2). This chapter can be divided into three sections: vss. 1-3, 4-7 and 8-13. Here Paul presents the antidote to the factionalism in Corinth, which this letter has confronted. It should be noted that the Love that is discussed in this chapter is not "a gift," unless we see that this Love is God Himself, given to us in and through His Spirit. This Love (which we can think of as describing Christ) is in fact "the FRUIT of the Spirit" (Gal. 5:22). The Fruit of the Spirit is the Anointing, the Son of God (as in the case of Jesus, born of Mary), and Paul is speaking of the "same Spirit, same Lord and same God" of which he spoke in 12:4-6, above. This *Agapē* is God, Himself/Herself:

"**God continuously exists being Love** (or: God is Love and Acceptance)" (1 Jn. 4:8).

So as we read through this chapter, when we see the word Love, let us think of God, Christ, the Spirit. This chapter is about The Way, the Truth and the Life. The rhetoric is similar to Rom. 7: Paul sets himself (the speaker, "I") in vss. 1-3, then gives instruction in vss. 4-10, and returns to himself in vss. 11-12. Verses 12-13 inform us of both their present situation and the aspects of it that continue dwelling with us.

1. **If ever I could habitually speak** (or as an indicative: If I continuously speak) **in or with the languages of the human groups** (or: by the tongues of mankind) **– or even of the agents** (or: messengers) **– yet am not constantly having and continuously holding Love** (a drive toward reunion with, unrestricted acceptance of, and full giving of myself to, others) **I have come to be a continuously sounding** (or: blaring; booming out; resounding) **[piece of] brass** (or: copper; bronze) **or a repeatedly clashing basin or a continuously clanging cymbal!**

Paul now selects one of the **effects of grace** that he listed in 12:10, above: "languages." Now recall the opening chapter of this letter where he said that he "**always and progressively gives thanks to** (or: for) **my God concerning [them], upon the basis of God's grace**" (1:4).... because "**you people are not continuing trailing behind or constantly late, so as to be deficient or fall short – not even in one effect of grace**." So this chapter addresses the central element that must infuse and be displayed in ALL of the effects of grace: **Love**. Without this, their habitual speaking, no matter what language it may be, is mere noise. Continuous sounding will soon be ignored. Repeated clashing becomes an affront. Continuous clanging is nothing but irritation. But perhaps Paul had the old covenant, or Jewish practices in mind, as exhorted in Ps. 150:5b, "praise Him on the high sounding cymbals."

If there is no **Love** in it, more harm is done than good. Paul uses this as a code word for God, for this is really the only source for "a drive toward reunion with, unrestricted acceptance of, and full giving of myself to, others."

Call to mind the situation in Acts 12:21-23, where the people responded to Herod's oration by shouting, "**[This is] a voice of a god, and not of a human!**" Paul may be using irony and hyperbole, here. However, consider what he said in 2 Cor. 12:3-4,

"**I have seen and know such a person... snatched away into the Paradise and heard inexpressible gush-effects and utterances** (unutterable sayings and results of a flow; inexpressible matters and declarations) **which are not being from out of existence in a person** (for a human) **to at any point speak**."

Cf 14:7-12, below.

2. **Even if I am continuously holding light ahead of time** (or: repeatedly have prophecy), **and I may have seen, and thus know, all the secrets** (or: every mystery) **and all the intimate knowledge** (or:

insight; *gnosis*), **and if I now continuously possess all the faith and trust – so as to repeatedly transport mountains** (or: to change the place and position of mountain after mountain) **– yet do not habitually possess** (or: progressively have) **Love and unambiguous, unrestricted acceptance, I am** (I exist being) **nothing!** [*cf* Mk. 11:23]

Here he cites two more results of grace, of which he spoke in 12:8, 9 and 28, above. These three, prophecy, knowledge and faith/trust, are core ingredients of the Good News. We should notice the definite article before the terms "mysteries/secrets" and "knowledge/insight." In Eph. 5:32 we read of one secret,

> "**This secret** (or: mystery) **is great** (= important), **but I am speaking unto** (or: into; with a view to) **Christ, even** (or: and; as well as) **unto** (or: into; with a view to) **the called-out community** (or: the called-out person; or: the summoned-forth covenant assembly)."

In Eph. 3:9 Paul instructs those in Asia Minor that he was given the privilege,

> "**to illuminate all people** (give light to everyone) **[as to] what [is] the execution of the detailed plan and household administration of the secret** (or: mystery) **pertaining to that having been hidden** (concealed) **away, apart from the ages** (or: disassociated from the [past] periods of time), **within the midst of God...**"

Paul was, of course, speaking as being a follower of Christ, in order to "**have seen, and thus know, all the secrets** (or: every mystery)," for we read in Col. 2:2b-3 about,

> "**God's Secret: Christ, within Whom** (or: in which) **are all the hidden-away** (or: concealed) **treasures of the wisdom and experiential, intimate knowledge and insight.**"

A person would have to be "in Christ" in order to "**continuously possess all the faith and trust.**" His rhetorical target is, of course, those of the Corinthian community who might think that they possess special knowledge and spiritual abilities.

We find a summation in Rom. 16:25-27, where Paul uses the term "**secret** (mystery)" in a more general context:

> "**Now by the One** (in the One; to the One) **being continuously able and powerful to set you steadfast** (to make you stand firm and settled) **in accord with** (or: corresponding to; in the sphere of; in line with) **my message of goodness and well-being – even the preaching and public heralding of the message of and from Jesus Christ – down from** (in accord with; in line with) **an unveiling of a secret** (or: a revelation and a disclosure of a mystery) **that had been being kept silent** (or: quiet) **in eonian times** (or: for time periods of the [preceding] ages; to [the] times [that would] pertain to the Age [of Messiah]), **but now is being brought to light and manifested, and through prophetic Scriptures, down from** (in accord with, on the level of and in line with) **a command of the eonian God**
>> (from the God Who exists through and comprises the ages; of God in relation to the ages; or: = from the God who created, inhabits, owns and rules the ages), **[which leads] into hearing obedience from faith as well as a humble listening and paying attention belonging to trust, pertaining to confidence and which comprises loyalty – suddenly being made known unto all the ethnic multitudes** (nations; Gentiles; pagans; non-Israelites) **by God** (or: with God; in God), **alone wise, through Jesus Christ, in Whom [is] the glory** (by Whom [is] the reputation) **on into the ages of the ages. It is so** (Count on it; Amen)!"

Paul is also probably alluding to Jesus' words in Mat. 13:11,

> "**To** (or: For; With) **you folks it has been given to intimately experience and insightfully know the secrets** (mysteries) **of the reign and dominion of the heavens** (or: the kingdom which is the heavens; the royal rule which pertains to and has its origin in the heavens, and which emanates from the atmospheres), **yet it has not been given to those people.**"

It was the unveiling (revealing) of these secrets that gave Christ's followers knowledge of the Truth, the Way (or: Path) and the Life (eonian life of the Age of the Messiah). Understanding of all the secrets (mysteries) and now knowing all the knowledge are set in Paul's argument as giving the possessors of these things a specific power or ability: "**so as to repeatedly transport mountains** (or: to change the place and position of mountain after mountain)." Was Paul speaking of geography or geology? No, he was speaking of kingdoms, governments or empires. These political organizations were commonly spoken of by the symbol of a mountain. Mount Zion was often used to refer to the kingdom of Israel, and then Judea, and in the prophecies of the OT it was a reference to God's coming kingdom. In Dan. 2:35b the king's dream of the successive kingdoms ended with a stone that was "cut out of the mountain without hands (= supernaturally).... That struck the image [and then] became a great mountain, and filled the whole land (or: earth)" – Dan. 2:3-35). In vss. 44-45 of that same chapter, Daniel explains that the stone, that became a mountain, was a figure for God's kingdom.

All of this may lend insight to the enigmatic saying of Jesus in Mat.17:20,

> "**I am now saying to you people, if you can progressively hold trust, habitually have faith and continue possessing fidelity** (faithfulness) **– as a mustard seed** (grain of mustard), **you folks will be saying to this mountain, 'Transfer** (Move in step with, and after) **from this place [to] there!' and it will be progressively transferring** (moving)."

Jesus added to this last statement, in Mat. 21:21, "**you can also say to this mountain range** (or: hill country; mountain), **'Be uplifted, and then be flung** (cast) **into the midst of the lake** (or: sea)!'**" To what mountain might He have been referring? Was it perhaps the kingdom of which Jerusalem was the capital? Was this a figure of God's kingdom being taken away from the Jews and cast into the sea of humanity? Was the lake perhaps the Lake of Tiberias (or: Sea of Galilee), which was considered a Gentile region? Paul's use of this clause here in vs. 2 may also refer to the setting of what he said in Eph. 6:12, the princes and governments of the domination systems,

> "**because for us** [other MSS: for you] **the wrestling is not against** (toward; with a view to) **blood and flesh** (= physical bodies), **but rather against** (toward; i.e., "face to face" with) **the beginning controls and rules**
>> (or: original rulings; or: rulers and controllers; governments; those things or people in first position; the beginning things or people; the original ones; the princes) **and face to face with the rights and privileges** (or: liberties to do as one pleases; or: authorities; or: aspects from out of existence), **with a view to the strengths of the System** (or: strengths of the ordered arrangement; or: universal powers of domination; the world's strong-ones; or: the strengths from the aggregate of humanity)..."

The "beginning controls and rules" of this verse may be a symbolic reference to Mt. Sinai, and the old covenant that would be moved out of its place in God's economy.

Yet if the Corinthians (and we), as individuals or as a community, "**do not habitually possess** (or: progressively have) **love and unambiguous, unrestricted acceptance**," they (and we) are **NOTHING**. This means that they would cease being God's temple. John made it quite clear:

> "**The one not habitually loving has not come to know God by intimate experience**..." (1 Jn. 4:8a).

John went on to instruct us,

> "**Within this exists** (or: is) **the Love, NOT that we ourselves have loved** [other MSS: not that we ourselves love or accept] **God, BUT, in contrast, that He Himself loves us and sends** (or: urged toward reunion with us and sent) **His Son as a Representative** (Emissary)**: a cleansing, sheltering covering around our sins** (failures to hit the target, errors, mistakes, deviations). **Beloved ones, since thus** (or: in that manner) **God loves** (or: loved) **us, we also are constantly indebted** (or: under obligation) **to habitually love and accept one another**" (1 Jn. 4:10-11).

So Paul is also reaching back to 11:21, 28 and 29. It is not just in their behavior (when eating the common meal together) that they should examine, it is also their attitude, spirit and behavior when they function in one or another of the grace-effects. John called habitual love and acceptance an obligation, a debt, to folks. Non-acceptance causes a severing of relationship; absence of love leads to divisions – which leads to "nothingness." The Light is extinguished, the branch is removed from the Vine. Loss of love leads to a removal of the lampstand (Rev. 2:4-5). History has seen the disappearance of many "churches."

3. If further I should dole out all my habitual subsistences in morsels of food – even if I should hand over (commit) **my body! – so that I could boast** [C, D and other, later MSS read: so that I will be burned], **and yet do not habitually possess and progressively have Love, I continue being benefited** (furthered; augmented; helped; profited) **in not even one thing.**

> [note: love (*agapē*) – "unambiguous love;" "an ecstatic manifestation of the Spiritual Presence;" "the drive toward reunion;" "participation in the other one;" "the acceptance of the other one as a person... the power of reunion with the other person as one standing on the same ultimate ground..." – Paul Tillich, *Systematic Theology III*, pp 134-137; *Perspectives on 19th and 20th Century Protestant Theology*, p 200]

It may seem hard to imagine acts of mercy and humanitarian deeds as not being inherently loving activities, but Paul is digging into the depths of our motivations, e.g., "**so that I could boast**." Keep in mind that this was written to a society that held human honoring as an uppermost aspect of community life. The alternate MSS readings, "so that I will be burned," may stem from a MS tradition that had Paul speaking in hyperbole, giving the most extreme act of apparent "self-sacrifice" that would somehow bring a glorious reputation to that person's life. That would be the extreme opposite to being a criminal and having the Romans throw one's body in the city garbage dump (that would have been Gehenna, in Jerusalem) – no honor in that! This reading seems to us to be less plausible. His audience could more readily relate to doing something so that a person could boast. However, Conzelmann points to the ancient custom in India of voluntarily burning oneself that was spoken of by ancient writers (ibid p 223 n 48).

On offer are two possible implications of the present tense that Paul chose for the verb "possess; have." Rather than choosing the aorist tense, as found for the verb "love" in Jn. 3:16, he chose the tense that can mean either habitual action or progressive action. We can habitually possess God's love, but more than that, we can "progressively have" it: it can grow in us so that what we have multiplies to 30, 60 or a hundred fold (Mat. 13:8, 23; Lu. 8:8). Love is one description of the Fruit of the Spirit (Gal. 5:22-23; *cf* Jn. 15:1ff).

So boasting over something that does not have the character of God intrinsic in the action brings no benefit, augmentation or profit to the person that does "good works." The kingdom of God grows only by the Life of God, just as a "branch" only grows by the flow of the sap (figure of the Spirit) from the Vine. Jesus informed His followers: "**apart from** (or: separated from) **Me you folks continue having ability and power to do** (make; construct; create; form; perform; produce) **nothing!**" (Jn. 15:5b) The author of *The Gospel of Philip*, saying #45, reads, "Faith receives; love gives... No one will be able to give without love... we believe, but it is so that we may love and give..." (Isenberg ibid p 137).

Throughout my translation I have drawn from the exegesis of Paul Tillich on the Greek word *agapē*. See the note following verse 3, above. This word meant vastly more than the feeling or sentiment that is normally understood by our English word, "love." But Paul writes more, below (by way of a personifying style that is characteristic of Jewish wisdom literature), to better define "The *Agapē*," i.e., God, and to inform us of it qualities, and how it behaves.

4. The Love (or: This unrestricted acceptance, etc.) **is habitually even-tempered, taking a long time to be in a heat of passion** (is constantly long-enduring/suffering and patient; keeps on putting anger far away; continues slow to progress toward rushing emotions which cause violent breathing; continues passionately persevering unto the goal) **– it continues being usefully kind.**

The Love (or: This urge toward unambiguous, accepting reunion and giving of oneself) **is not constantly boiling with jealousy and envy. The Love is not continuously bragging or "showing off" – it is not habitually being puffed up; it is not conceited or arrogant.**
5. **It is not repeatedly indecent in manner or behavior** (it does not continually display lack of [good] form, rudeness or improper demeanor); **it is not habitually self-seeking** (or: not constantly pursuing its own interests or rights); **it is not continually caused to be sharp [in response] nor aroused to irritation or upset emotions; it is not habitually keeping account of the worthless thing, nor logically considering something of bad quality, nor counting the injury.**
6. **It does not continue to rejoice upon [seeing or hearing of] the injustice, nor is it happy about dishonesty, inequity, or lack of the qualities of the Way pointed out, yet it repeatedly rejoices with the Truth** (or: takes delight together in Reality).

These affirmations about **The Love** (i.e., God) need little comment, except to say be sure to read them as qualities of God, and see what comes to you. Verse 4a gives a positive statement, then 4b-6 are all statements about what The Love (God) is NOT! God is habitually **even-tempered**, and continues being "**usefully kind**." Wow. And in vs. 5, "[God] is not habitually keeping account of the worthless thing..." Does this remind you of 2 Cor. 5:19, "**not accounting to them** (not putting to their account; not logically considering for them; not reasoning in them) **the results and effects of their falls to the side** (their trespasses and offenses)"?

Paul's own life was a lived-out parable of this Love, so what he is saying here is not an impossibility for the Corinthians to live-out, for all of this is the work/Being of God. In 2 Cor. 6, Paul recounted how he and his associates lived their service to the called-out communities, and in vs. 6 states,

> "**[We have served and dispensed] with pureness** (or: centered in [a life of] purity); **in personally experienced knowledge; with forbearing patience** (in taking a long time before becoming emotional or rushing with passion); **with useful kindness; in a set-apart** (holy) **spirit** (or: within the midst of [the] Holy Spirit; within a hallowed breath-effect; in a set-apart attitude); **centered in, and with, uncritical love** (or: acceptance that is free from prejudice and from a separating for evaluation; love that is not based on making distinctions, fault-finding or judging)."

He was not boasting, but was presenting an example to his listeners. Also, from their LXX, they had the admonition of Sirach 2:4,

> "Accept whatever befalls you, and in times of humiliation be patient" (NRSV).

They would have also had *The Testament of Joseph*,

> "In ten testings he showed that I was approved, and in all of them I persevered, because perseverance is a powerful medicine and endurance provides many good things" (Kee, ibid p 819).

Prov. 19:11 adds another witness:

> "Those with good sense are slow to anger, and it is their glory to overlook an offense" (NRSV).

In Rom. 9:22, Paul reveals this, concerning God,

> "**Now since God – habitually willing to display and demonstrate inherent fervor, natural impulse, propensity and disposition** (or: teeming passion; swelling desire; or: anger, wrath and indignation), **and also to make known by personal experience His power and ability – in much long-suffering** (long-breathing state of inner quietness; forbearance; pushing anger far away) **bears and carries** (or: brought forth and produced; or: enduringly supports while moving) **containers** (vessels) **of natural impulse** (belonging to a passionate disposition; displaying inherent fervor; from teeming passion and swelling desire; or: of anger; having the character of wrath; owned by indignation)..."

But now consider Paul's glorious, affirming conclusion of this section:

7. [Love] continuously covers all mankind; it is habitually loyal to all humanity; it constantly has an expectation for all mankind; it is continuously remaining under and giving support to all people.

> (or, since "all" can also be neuter: It [i.e., unambiguous acceptance] progressively puts a protecting roof over all things; it is habitually trusting in, and believing for, all things; it is continually hoping in or for all things; it keeps on patiently enduring all things.)

The bold rendering gives "all" as masculine readings: "**all mankind; all humanity; all people**." Now look carefully as what God's Love does: It (**HE**) **continuously covers all mankind** (this is "atonement"), **is habitually loyal to all humanity, constantly has an expectation for all mankind** and **is continuously remaining under and giving support to all people**.

The concept of "**covers**" is an allusion to the Heb. word *kaphar*, which literally means "to cover," and in Ex., Lev. and Nu. Is conventionally rendered "to make atonement." In the NT, we are reminded of 1 Pet. 4:8b,

> "**Love** (the urge toward union; self-giving) **is constantly covering*** (habitually throwing a veil over; progressively concealing; [and with other MSS: will continue covering]) **a multitude of failures** (mistakes; errors; misses of the target; sins)." [*cf* Prov. 10:12]

The neuter reading of "all" is also beautiful. The subject, It, is still the Love that is the subject of this chapter, and specifically of vss. 4-8a. Look at what God's unambiguous acceptance does! His Love keeps on "patiently enduring all things." Also take note of the present tense of all the verbs. There is no end to any of this! And when God's love is active within us... just think of the possibilities.

8. The Love (or: This unrestricted, self-giving drive toward reunion) **never – not even once – fails** (collapses or falls into decay; = becomes fruitless or ineffectual; [other MSS: falls out or lapses]).

Apply this rock-solid (Christ-solid) statement to all of God's intents, purposes, desires, plans and goals. None of them fail – even once! This calls to mind Eph. 1:11b,

> "**in keeping with** (or: down from; corresponding to; in accord with) **a before-placed** (or: predetermined-by-setting-forth; destined) **aim, design and purpose of the One continuously operating** (effecting; energizing) **all things** (or: the whole) **in accord with** (or: down from; in line with; in correspondence to; following the pattern of) **the deliberated purpose** (intent; design; plan; determined counsel) **of His will** (or: resultant decision of His resolve; effect of His desire)."

It also echoes Isa. 46:10,

> "declaring the end from the beginning and from ancient times things not yet done, saying, 'My purpose shall stand established, and I will accomplish all my purpose and intention.'"

Of course we must include at least one of His specific "wills,"

> "**God, our Deliverer, is constantly willing** (continuously intending and purposing) **all humans** (all humanity; all mankind) **to be saved** (delivered; rescued; made healthy and whole), **and** (or: even) **to come into a full, accurate, experiential and intimate knowledge and insight of Truth** (or: that is, to go or come into a complete realization of reality)" (1 Tim. 2:3b-4).

But now, in 8b, Paul's style of instruction changes again. As a good rhetor, he is keeping his audience awake. He now explains how the communal manifestations of the results of grace are not the Spirit's ultimate goal, but are effects of His favor for the journey, as he begins, in 8b:

Now, whether prophecies (or: situations of light ahead of time) **will be rendered useless and unproductive** (or: idled-down to be inactive and unemployed, discarded or, nullified) **or languages will stop themselves** (or: tongues will restrain themselves so as to cease [speaking]; "utterances of ecstasy" will cease of themselves), **or whether intimate or experiential knowledge** (or: insight; *gnosis*) **will be rendered useless and unproductive** (be idled-down to be inactive and unemployed, discarded or, nullified)

When will a prophecy be rendered useless and unproductive, or, idled-down to be inactive and unemployed, discarded or nullified? When they have been fulfilled and when the time and situation has passed. When that to which it pointed no longer exists. The OT is full of these. Consider what Jesus said in Lu. 21:22,

> "**because these are days of executing justice** (or: from deciding the case, with a view to the maintenance of right: whether vindication or retribution) **– of bringing about what is fair and right and of establishing what accords with the Way pointed out – with a view to have fulfilled all the things having been written** (or: for all that is written to be fulfilled)!"

Jesus was referring to what would happen, in AD 70.

When would the same thing happen to knowledge? Mainly when new knowledge comes to displace what was "known" before. People knew what the old covenant had taught. Of their teachings, Jesus said,

> "**You folks hear** (or: heard) **that it was declared**…. **Yet I, Myself, am now saying to you people**…" (Mat. 5:27a, 28a).

The knowledge of all the laws concerning the Levitical priesthood became obsolete with the coming of the Melchizedek priesthood. *Cf* Heb. 6:20-7:28

2 Cor. 3:11 points first to 8b, here, and then to 13:13, below:

> "**You see, since that which was being progressively unemployed and brought down to doing no work – even being made ineffective and nullified – [came] through glory, to a much greater extent is the continuously remaining one** (the dwelling, abiding and enduring one) **[existing] within the midst of glory, and in union with [greater] imagination** (repute)."

9. **– for we are progressively gaining intimate and experiential knowledge from out of a part** (insight from a piece or a fragment; *gnosis* from the midst of a portion of the whole), **and we are habitually prophesying** (speaking publicly before others and sharing light ahead of time) **from out of a part** (a portion; a fragment; a piece of the whole) **–**

10. **still, whenever the destined goal** (the mature person; the finished product; maturity; the complete attainment of the purpose; perfection) **comes** (arrives), **that which is out of a part** (a piece; a portion; a fragment; partial) **will progressively be rendered useless and unproductive** (idled-down to be inactive, unemployed or discarded).

What was the "part" of which he spoke in these verses? What is the destined goal? What was in Paul's day becoming "useless and unproductive"? We suggest that "the part" referred to what Heb. 1:1 spoke of: "**Long ago** (or: In the old days), **in many parts** (or: with fragments; by divided portions; = bit by bit)… **God, having spoken to** (or: in talking with; when discoursing by; making vocal utterances for) **the fathers – in** (in union with; centered in; = through; in [the words of]) **the prophets**…"

The **destined goal** (vs. 10) was the coming of the Messiah and the new creation of the new Humanity that would exist in the new arrangement/covenant. Humanity was "**under those to whom the trust is committed** (guardians; ones entrusted with control and right to turn upon their charges) **and house managers** (estate stewards; administrators) **until the father's previously set** [time or situation]" (Gal. 4:2). We were all there, as described in Eph. 4:

> 13. **until we – the whole of mankind** (all people) **– can** (or: would) **come down to the goal** (or: attain; arrive at; meet accordingly; meet down face-to-face)**: into the state of oneness from, and which is, The Faithfulness** (or: the unity of, that belongs to and which characterizes that which is faith; or: the lack of division which has its source in trust, confidence and reliability, has the character of and is in reference to the loyalty and fidelity), **even which is the full, experiential and intimate knowledge** (or: and from recognition; and of discovery; as well as pertaining to insight) **which is** (or: of; from; in reference to) **the Son of God, [growing] into [the] purposed and destined adult man** (complete, finished, full-grown, perfect, goal-attained, mature

manhood) – **into** (or: unto) **[the] measure of [the] stature** (full age; prime of life) **of the entire content which comprises the Anointed One**

> (or: which is the result of the full number which is the Christ; of the effect of the fullness from the [Messiah]; from the effect of that which fills and completes that which refers to the Christ; of the result of the filling from, and which is, the Christ) –

14. **to the end that no longer would or should we exist being infants** (immature folks; not-yet-speaking ones), **continuously being tossed by [successive] waves and repeatedly being carried hither and thither by every wind of the teaching within the caprice** (the trickery) **of mankind, in readiness to do anything** (amoral craftiness; working everything; or: = while stopping at nothing) **with a view toward and leading to the methodical treatment** (or: the systematizing or technical procedure) **of The Wandering** (the straying; the deception; [A adds: of the thrusting-through; or: from the person who casts {divisiveness or harm} through the midst of folks]).

15. **But continuously being real and true** (living in accord with reality and the facts; holding to, speaking, pursuing and walking in Truth; truthing it) **within, and in union with, Love** (or: centered in unambiguous acceptance; a full giving of ourselves with an urge toward union), **we can grow up into Him – the ALL which is the Head: Christ** (or: [and] we would in love make all things grow up into Him Who is the head and source: [the] Anointed One)!

16. **– from out of Whom all the Body being continuously fitted and framed together** (made a common joint by a word; laid out and closely joined together) **and constantly being knit together and caused to mount up united through every fastening** (or: joint) **of the supply of rich furnishings** (or: through every assimilation of the full supply of funds; through every touch {kindling; setting on fire} of the completely supplied requirements) **in accord with** (or: down from; commensurate to; in the sphere and to the degree of) **the operation** (operative, effectual energy) **within [the] measure of each one part** [other MSS: member], **is itself continually making** (or: is for itself progressively producing and forming) **the growth and increase of the Body, [focused on and leading] into house-construction** (or: unto building [up] and edification) **of itself within the midst of, and in union with, love** (full self-giving in an unambiguous urge toward union or reunion; acceptance).

So, what was being **rendered useless and unproductive**? We are instructed about this in Heb. 8:

> 6. **But now He has hit the mark of a thoroughly carried-through public service, even by as much as He continues being a Medium** (an agency; an intervening substance; a middle state; one in a middle position; a go-between; an umpire; a Mediator) **of a superior** (stronger and better) **arrangement** (covenant; settlement; disposition) **which has been instituted** (set by custom; legally [= by/as Torah] established) **upon superior** (stronger and better) **promises!**
> 7. **For if that first one was being unblamable** (without ground for faultfinding; beyond criticism; satisfying), **a place of a second one would not have continued to be sought** (looked for)....
> 13. **In thus to be saying "new: different in kind and quality," He has made the first** (or: former) **"old," and that [which is] progressively growing old** (or: obsolete) **and decrepit** (failing of age; ageing into decay), **[is] near its disappearing** (vanishing away).

We also read in Heb. 7:12,

> "**For it follows that with the priesthood being presently place-changed** (or: progressively after-placed and transferred), **out of necessity** (or: compulsion) **even a change of law** [= Torah] **is being born** (or: also an after-placement transference of custom is coming into existence)."

Paul lived in this transition period that implemented the change from the old to the new. These quotes form the book of Hebrews indicated that the new had already come, and the old was being phased out. The Judaizers had come and had over-seeded the grain field with what was not the true Seed (Mat. 13:25), and would not produce the True Bread, but both plants we allowed to grow together until the harvest (Mat.13:30a). Mat. 13:30b explains what would then happen: "**First gather the weeds together and bind them into bundles for the purpose of burning them down**," and this happened in AD 70.

We read in 2 Cor. 5:17 that,
> "**[there is] a new creation** (or: [it is] a framing and founding of a different kind; [he or she is] an act of creation having a fresh character and a new quality)**: the original things** (the beginning [situations]; the archaic and primitive [arrangements]) **passed by** (or: went to the side). **Consider! New things have come into existence.**"

Furthermore, using himself as an illustration, Paul puts his infancy into the past (in the next verse), ending vs. 11 with, "**Yet when I had come to be an adult**," which was a then-present reality, at the time that he was writing this letter. This brings us to read vs. 10, with its "**whenever**," which is followed by the indefinite aorist subjunctive of the verb, "**comes** (arrives)," as indicating what he said in 15:23, below,
> "**each person within the result of his or her own set position [in line]** (or: effect of ordered placement; appointed class; arranged time and turn, or order of succession; = place in a harvest calendar, thus, due season of maturity)."

All agricultural crops reach their fruitful goal in their own seasons. Likewise with individuals and local communities. Paul was an adult, and had arrived at the goal for that season of his life. Although the community in Corinth had been "born into the kingdom," and were in this new sense "children of God," they were still immature and had not yet reached maturity. When Israel was delivered from Egypt, it was a "mixed multitude." Ever since the resurrection of Christ, the summoned communities have been "mixed groups," as Paul points this out in letter to Corinth. Most are simply immature – but as with all children, they would grow (Eph. 4:15, above).

11. **When I was an infant** (a baby; a non-speaking one), **I used to babble and make vocal utterances as a non-speaking infant. I used to habitually be in the frame of mind, take thought with the intellect and understand as a non-speaking infant** (baby). **I continued taking account, reasoning and logically considering things as a non-speaking infant. Yet when I had come to be an adult male, I had permanently made inactive** (idled-down so as to be no longer used and discarded) **the things which pertain to a non-speaking infant** (infantile things).

Paul referred to this same "infancy" in Gal. 4:
> 1. **Now I continue saying, for** (or: upon [the length of]) **as much time as the heir** (the apparent possessor of the distributed allotment) **is progressing from being an infant to a minor** (one having either no ability, or no right, to speak; = continues being under legal age) **he continues essentially differing nothing from a slave, [though] continuously being owner** (lord and master) **of everything** (of all)....
> 4. **Yet when the effect of the filling of the time came** (or: that which was filled up by time reached full term), **forth from out of a mission** (or: from out of the midst of [Himself]), **God sent-off His Son, being Himself come to be born from out of a woman, being Himself come to be born under [the rules, authority and influence of] Law,** [cf Ex. 19:17, LXX: "under {Sinai}"]
> 5. **to the end that He could** (or: would) **buy out** (release by purchase; redeem; reclaim [from slavery]) **those under [the] Law – so that we could and would receive and take away into possession the placing in the condition of a son** (or: the deposit of the Son; the setting in place which is the Son; the constituting as a son; the placing in the Son).

This, in Gal. 4, explains vs. 11, above: both passages refer to leaving the infancy of the Law (the old covenant) and coming into the maturity in Christ (with the new covenant). When Paul says that he "**permanently made inactive** (idled-down so as to be no longer used and discarded) **the things which pertain to a non-speaking infant** (infantile things)," he was talking about the Law of Moses and all of its requirements. But this also may be pointing back to 1:11-13, and the childish factions that were developing within their community, and then addresses their fleshly behavior and continued need of "milk" instead of solid food because of their "**existing being fleshly folks**" (3:1-3, above).

What Paul means in saying that he "idled-down, no longer used and discarded infantile things," was a reference to his previous "**frame of mind, taking thought, using intellect, and understanding**." He admonishes acting with a mature frame of mind, way of taking thought and use of "**the mind of Christ**" (2:16b, above; *cf* Phil. 2:5) in Phil. 4:

> 6. **Do not be habitually worried, anxious or overly concerned about anything! On the contrary, in everything** (and: within every situation), **by thinking and speaking toward having goodness and having things go well and with ease** (or: in prayer) **and in expression of need – together with thanksgiving – repeatedly let your requests be made known to** (toward; face to face with) **God,**
> 7. **and God's peace** ([shalom] from God; or: the harmonious joining, which is God), **which is continuously having a hold over** (habitually having sway over; or: constantly being superior and excelling over) **all mind and inner sense** (or: every intellect; all power of comprehension; or: all process of thinking), **will continue garrisoning** (guarding; keeping watch over; protecting) **your hearts and the results from directing your minds** (or: effects of your perceptions, concepts, thoughts, reasonings and understandings; or: dispositions; designs; purposes), **centered within, and in union with, Christ Jesus**.

Paul's letters are full of worthy admonitions, such as, while "**being real and true in union with Love, we can grow up** (enlarge; increase) **into Him – the ALL which is the Head: Christ**" (Eph. 4:15).

12. **For you see, at the present moment we continue seeing and observing through means of a metal mirror, within the midst of an enigma** (the result of something obscurely expressed, hinted or intimated, giving an indistinct image), **but at that point, face to face. Right now I am progressively coming to intimately and experientially know from out of a part** (gain insight from a piece; be acquainted with a portion of the whole), **but thereupon I shall continue accurately knowing and recognizing, from full intimate experience and added insight, correspondingly as I am also fully and accurately known, by intimate experience.**

Paul's metaphor of "a metal mirror" may be an allusion to Num. 12:8, where Yahweh had come down in a pillar of cloud to speak to Aaron and Miriam,

> "With [Moses] I speak face to face – clearly, not in riddles; and he beholds the form of the LORD" (NRSV).

The period of time within which Paul wrote this was the period of transition from the old into the new. Until AD 70 the Judeans were still doing sacrifices in the temple at Jerusalem. From the time of Paul being apprehended by Christ, he was being taught by the Spirit as he was viewing Christ "**through means of a metal mirror**" as he was "**being continuously and progressively transformed into the very same image, from glory into glory – in accord with and exactly as – from [the] Lord's Breath-effect**" (2 Cor. 3:18). He was being moved from the glory of the old into the glory of the new (2 Cor. 3:9). At this time, he was "**progressively coming to intimately and experientially know from out of a part** (gain insight from a piece; be acquainted with a portion of the whole)," as he and others were referencing the old covenant Scriptures (which we find him frequently quoting) as the Root out from which both the remaining branches and the newly engrafted branches were now growing (Rom. 11:17-18).

His present view, from the OT Scriptures, was still an intimate and experiential knowing "**within the midst of an enigma** (the result of something obscurely expressed, hinted or intimated, giving an indistinct image)" that the OT presented. But as he was being transformed by the Breath-effect, he was "**having a face that has been uncovered and remains unveiled – being [one] who by a mirror [was] continuously observing the Lord's glory**" (2 Cor. 3:18), so that he was now seeing "**face to face**," and thus knew that he would "**continue accurately knowing and recognizing, from full intimate experience and added insight**." In 2 Cor. 3:18 Paul was describing a present experience of everyone in the new covenant, and he had contrasted this with those remaining in Judaism, where "**until [that] very day the same head-covering** (veil) **continued remaining** (dwelling; abiding) **upon the reading of the**

old covenant.... [and] **a head-covering** (veil) **continued lying upon their heart** [until] **the time should be reached when it** [= the heart] **can** (or: would; may; should; or: shall at some point) **twist and turn upon, so as to face toward, [the] Lord** [and] **the head-covering** (veil) **is progressively taken from around [it]**" (2 Cor. 3:14-16). Paul was now face-to-face with the Lord, and was being transformed.

He wrote his letters from a position of humility, when it came to himself. We read him saying of himself, in Phil. 3:12-14,

> "**[Now this is] not because I already take it by the hand** (grasp, lay hold of it; or: obtained) **or even have been already brought to the purposed goal and destiny, but yet, I am consistently pursuing.... habitually forgetting, on the one hand, the things behind** (or: in the back; Phil. 3:4-8; = the old covenant), **and on the other hand constantly reaching and stretching myself out upon the things in front** (or: ahead), **I am continuously pressing forward, pursuing down toward** [the; or: an] **object in view**.... **God's invitation to an above place** (the upward calling)..."

So when writing to Corinth, he maintained this "forward perspective," using "now, at the present time... but then" language. He was writing to spiritual children, and so he put himself as being down, among them, in solidarity with them, as his Lord had done (Phil. 2:5-8). He was following the Pattern (Christ), even though he knew where he was presently sitting (Eph. 2:6), and where that "seat" was (Heb. 12:22-24).

13. **So at the present time trust** (or: faith; loyalty; trustworthiness), **expectation** (or: expectant hope) **[and] Love** (unrestricted acceptance which overcomes existential separation – Tillich) – **these three – continue remaining and habitually dwell [with us], yet the greatest of these [is] the Love** ([God's] urge toward unambiguous, accepting reunion – Tillich; self-giving – Rohr).
You folks make haste to progressively run after and continuously pursue this Love!

All that they needed – trust, expectation and Love – was already with them, and they would "**continue remaining and habitually dwell**" with them, and with us. The **trust** is in God; the **expectation** is God's "**expectation for all mankind**" (vs. 7, above), and the **Love** is God, Himself. And since God is this **Love**, it is the greatest of these Spirits. It (He/She) provides the other two for us. So it only follows that we should "**make haste to progressively run after and continuously pursue this Love!**" This is simply a pursuit of God Himself.

Where do we find this Love?

> "**The quality of being approved by testing [produces] expectation and hope. Now the expectation** (or: expectant hope) **does not habitually bring down shame** (disgrace; dishonor; thus: disappointment), **because God's Love** (the urge toward reunion and the unambiguous, uniting acceptance from God; God's giving of Himself to [us]) **has been poured out in a gush and shed forth so that it now floods within our hearts, permeating the core of our being, through the Set-apart Breath-effect** (or: Holy Spirit; Sacred Attitude) **being given to us** (in us; for us)" (Rom. 5:4b-5).

And then, we read from Rom. 8:

> 38. **For you see, I have been persuaded and now stand convinced that neither death, nor life** (or: living existence), **nor agents** (or: messengers), **nor sovereignties** (rulers; those in prime position; or: beginnings), **nor things being now here** (being placed within, at present), **nor things about to be** (impending, or about to consecutively come), **nor powers** (or: capabilities),
> 39. **nor height** (effect of being high), **nor depth** (or: deep places), **nor any other or different created thing** (or: founded thing; institution; = the Law; = old covenant; = adversaries) **will be having power or be able to separate, divide or part us from God's Love** (or: from the acceptance from God; from the urge toward reunion, which is God; God's full giving of Himself to us) **which is within Christ Jesus, our Owner** (Lord; Master; Possessor).

OOOOO ---------- OOOOO ---------- OOOOO ---------- OOOOO

Before we move on, we wish to introduce you to another 1st century Christian author's description of "the Way," from *The Epistle of Barnabas* (circa AD 75, per John A.T. Robinson), which was apparently written by a Jewish follower of Jesus, and written to a Jewish called-out community in Christ. In the early NT MS Codex Sinaiticus, this letter followed the book of Revelation. Where Paul has been speaking in more general terms, in 13:4-13, this teacher speaks more specifically in a manner that calls to mind Jesus' sermon in Mat. chs. 5 through 7. Here, we offer an excerpt from the *Epistle*, Chapter 19:

1. **Therefore, the Road** (Path; Way) **of the Light is THIS: should someone continue wanting, keep on intending and be repeatedly willing to progressively journey [the] Route and make one's way on to the Place** (or: region; position; space; location; occasion) **marked out and determined** (bounded, fixed and appointed), **he or she should urge on industriously, with eager haste, in** (with; for; to; by) **his or her works** (deeds; actions). **Consequently, the knowledge and insight being given to, for and in us, with a view to progressively walking about** (= living our lives) **within it, is such as** (or: like) **this:**

2. **You will continue urging toward reunion with, and will be progressively loving the One producing** (forming; creating; making) **you. You will be made to keep on revering and to continue respecting** (or: fearing) **the One fashioning and shaping you. You will continue giving a good reputation to** (glorifying; having a positive opinion of; producing a manifestation which calls forth praise to) **the One releasing you out of death. You will continue being single** (without folds; simple; noncomplex; open; sincere; guileless; straightforward) **in the heart, and yet wealthy in spirit and with Breath-effect. You will not continue being closely joined or glued or united with the folks habitually traveling in a road** (or: way) **of death** (or: a path from Death). **You will continue hating (regarding with ill-will) everything that is not pleasing to God or satisfying for God. You will continue hating (regarding with ill-will) all judging from a low position** (hypercriticism; hair-splitting legalistic nit-picking; pedantic behavior; or, a later meaning: hypocrisy). **You should by no means abandon** (leave down within the midst) **implanted goals from [the] Lord** (imparted, purposed-ends which pertain to [the] Lord; inner directives of, and from, [the] Master).

> [note: most of the verbs in this chapter are in the future indicative (a durative tense), not in the imperative; thus these are promises, not commands; comment: it is God working within us that produces these effects of His life and grace – the results of His Spirit]

3. **You will not keep on lifting** (exalting; elevating) **yourself up high, but you will continue being humble-minded in relation to all things** (oriented toward the lowly, with respect to all people). **You will not keep on lifting or taking up glory** (a reputation; credit; an appearance; a presumption; something imagined) **upon yourself. You will not continue taking or receiving a misery-gushed resolution** (a worthless design; an unsound decision; a bad plan) **against your associate** (neighbor; near one). **You will not keep on giving arrogance, insolent boldness or rashness to your soul.**

4. **You will not continue being sexually promiscuous, prostituting yourself, being unfaithful** (fornicating) **or participate in idolatry. You will not keep on committing adultery. You will not continue abusing or molesting children. Under no circumstances should the** *Logos* (Word; conveyance of the Message; patterned Information; Thought; Idea) **of, or from, God go forth from any folks centered in what is not lifted from having been down** (in union with uncleanness, defilement or un-lifted down-ness or contrariness; or: come out of any people within the midst of worthless waste or impureness [such as decayed flesh]). **You will not continue receiving the face** (showing favoritism or making a difference between people; using a double standard) **to reprove or correct someone, upon the result of a fall to the side** (on the effect of a false step or a stumbling aside; at an offense or a trespass). **You will continue being gentle and considerate. You will keep on being quiet, tranquil and at rest! You will habitually tremble with awe at the words** (*logoi*; conveyances of information; messages; thoughts; ideas) **which you heard. You will not continue remembering anything ugly, of bad**

quality, or as it ought not to be, about your brother (or: bearing a grudge about the one from the same Womb as you).

5. **Under no circumstance should you be two-souled** (double-minded; undecided; wavering; doubting) **whether a thing will proceed being** (something will continue existing), **or not. "Under no circumstance should you take the Name of [the] LORD** (= Yahweh) **on a meaningless, useless, fruitless or unprofitable [matter or situation]."** [Ex. 20:7] **You will progressively urge toward reunion with your associate** (continuously accept your neighbor; habitually love the one near you) **over** (or: more than) **your soul! You will not proceed** (or: keep on) **killing a child, in abortion** (or: in corruption, damage or deterioration), **nor even, again, after being born, kill it off. Under no circumstance should you remove, or take away, your hand from your son or your daughter, but to the contrary, you will, from [their] youth, progressively teach respect of God** (or: reverential fear, from God).

6. **"Under no circumstance should you come to be progressively rushing upon** (continuously overly-passionate about; constantly having strong impulse toward or over-desire for) **the things of, or belonging to, your associate** (neighbor; person near you)" [Ex. 20:17]. **Under no circumstance should you come to be a person who has more than another** (or: someone with more than his or her share; greedy; or: one who defrauds for the sake of gain). **Neither will you, from out of your soul, continue joined to, or glued with, proud or haughty people, or with folks of high cultic position, but in contrast, you will continue being turned back to engage with lowly folks and to be involved with just folks. You will continue receiving, accepting and welcoming the results of experiences** (the effects from inner operations and implanted workings) **repeatedly walking together with you** (or: constantly happening to you) **as good, fair and virtuous, from having seen, and thus knowing, that apart from God nothing comes to be** (or: that not even one thing is happening or transpiring without God).

7. **You will not continue being with divided-knowing or existing from a divided will** (or: decision), **nor [being] of a double tongue** (or: from deceit). **You will habitually station** (set; place) **under, to give submissive support to masters** (for owners; among lords; with employers), **as a copy of God** (a type and pattern from God; a beaten image, which reflects God): **centered in shame and respectful fear** (in union with modesty and respect). **Under no circumstance in bitterness set upon** (give instructions or orders centered in harshness or animosity to) **your slave or female servant – for those folks continually place expectation** (or: expectant hope) **upon the same God – lest in some way they will proceed not caused to fear or respect the God [that is] upon both parties, because He did not come to call with respect of persons** (corresponding to surface presentation; according to a face; with regard to reputation), **but to the contrary, [to call] upon those whom the Spirit prepared** (or: whom the Breath-effect made ready).

8. **You will progressively have common being and existence with your associate in all things** (or: will continue sharing, fellowshipping and being in alliance with your neighbor), **and so you will not continue saying things to continue being your own. For since you folks continue being partners of a common existence** (sharers of common being) **within the incorruptible and imperishable, how much more within the corruptible and perishable? You will not continue being talkative or quick to speak, for it follows that the mouth [is] a snare of death** (or: a trap from death, and which is death). **So far as you continue able and with power, you will progressively be clean and consistent over [situations; areas] of your soul** (or: will continue pure, on behalf of your inner person).

> [comment: the first two statements remind us of Acts 2:44-45; 4:34-37; they suggest a context of communal living, and thus point to an early period of Christ's movement, and to those following the Way, Acts 9:2; 19:23; perhaps it was because these were now given as general instructions, in this *Epistle*, that *Barnabas* was not included in the canon]

9. **"Do not continue becoming on the one hand a person constantly stretching out the hands to repeatedly receive** (or: take), **yet on the other hand a person constantly pulling back and drawing the hands together toward the [situation for] giving."** [Sirach (Ecclesiasticus) 4:31] **You will continue urging toward reunion with, and habitually accept with constant love – as an apple of your eye – all people continuing in speaking the** *Logos* **from [the] Lord to you** (or: constantly proclaiming the Word of [the] Lord for you; repeatedly telling the patterned Information of the Message with you).

10. **Night and day you will continue remembering** (calling to mind, thinking about, giving careful consideration to and mentioning) **a day of examining, deciding about, or judging** (or: a deciding day), **and so daily keep on seeking out and searching for the faces** (= personal presence) **of the set-apart folks. Or, through a word** (or: by means of a thought or a conveyance of patterned information), **after continuing tired and weary from laboring and then progressively journeying on into the midst of release from your failures** (mistakes; failures to hit the target), **you will not keep on hesitating from [receiving] a reward from an ideal Recompenser** (a beautiful One who gives away something instead; a fine Rewarder; an ideal One who gives back, in return or replacement).

> [note: in the second half of the verse, the text may be defective; Lightfoot reads: "Thou shall not hesitate to give, neither shalt thou murmur when giving, but thou shalt know who is the good paymaster of thy reward."]

11. **You will continue guarding, watching over and taking care of that which you take to your side, neither adding nor taking away. You will constantly hate the misery-gushed** (the unsound; the painful; the unprofitable; the bad condition; the unserviceable), **on unto maturity** (into the midst of [the] final act; unto an end; unto a finished product). **You will continually decide justly and in accord with the Way pointed out** (or: You will repeatedly evaluate from a rightwised paradigm; You will habitually be judging fairly and from being in covenant).

12. **You will not continue making an effect of tearing apart** (a result of splitting; a division; a schism), **but you will keep on joining and progressively bringing or making peace, while constantly bringing together those continually fighting, quarreling or disputing. You will go on making grateful acknowledgements upon your failures to hit the target** (or: admitting and giving thanks upon your mistakes, errors and sins; speaking from sameness with a view to your deviations). **You will not continue approaching upon a thought, word or act with a view toward having goodness, ease or well-being** (or: come to prayer) **in a misery-gushed** (unsound; unserviceable; painful; bad-conditioned) **conscience.**

THIS is, and continues being, the Road (Path; Way) **of the Light!** (JM)

ooooo ---------- ooooo ---------- ooooo ---------- ooooo

And now, back to Paul…

Chapter 14

1. **Now with boiling fervor and affection, be habitually welling-up and zealous in regard to the things of the spirit**

> (or, as an indicative: So, you folks are constantly with your hearts set on the matters pertaining to the Spirit; or, as a subjunctive: Now you should keep on being ardently devoted in aspects having the character of Breath-effect),

and especially (or: yet even more) **that you folks would be habitually prophesying**

> (or: would keep on speaking publicly before others, speaking Light ahead of time; or: = should on behalf of God, be repeatedly proclaiming His message),

2. for the person habitually speaking in a language is not speaking to or for humans, but rather, to, by and with God – for you see, no one continues listening so as to pay attention or obey. Yet for [the] Spirit (or: by Breath-effect; with attitude) **he goes on speaking secrets.**

  (or: for he or she that repeatedly speaks in a tongue is not speaking to people or for mankind, but to the contrary, in, to, for or with, God – for you see, no one continues listening [to him or her] – and yet in spirit he or she continues speaking mysteries!)

The first clause of vs. 1 takes Paul's listeners back to 12:1, above. The verb of this clause functions either as an imperative (the bold rendering), or as an indicative (the first parenthetical rendering) which would be an affirmation of what he discerns is their heart's desire. Or, it could be a subjunctive (the second parenthetical rendering) which would be an admonition. The renderings, "aspects having the character of Breath-effect" and the "matters pertaining to the Spirit," both point to the imperative of the last line of 13:13, above, To "**run after and continuously pursue this Love**" is to "**be habitually welling-up and zealous in regard to the things of the spirit/Spirit.**" Love is synonymous with the Spirit, in this context.

In the second clause of vs. 1, the conjunction with the adverb *mellon* can have a range of meanings. The two renderings that I selected, "**and especially**" and "yet even more," seem to best fit the context, of 13:13 on through 14:1a, and directs us to his point: the effect of grace, **prophesying**, that was discussed in 12:10a, above. He will develop his reasoning for the preeminence of prophesying, in vs. 2-3, below. Now 14:2 picks up another effect of grace, **speaking in a language**, of which Paul spoke in 12:10b, above. More will be said on this, as well.

Verse 2 gives Paul's first reason for preferring prophesying over "speaking in a language," and this is for the benefit of the corporate community, when it is gathered together. In such a meeting, "**no one continues listening so as to pay attention or obey**" when someone is "**speaking in a language.**" Nonetheless, he affirms that the person is speaking "**to, by and with** (or: in; for) **God,**" and "**for [the] Spirit** (or: by Breath-effect; with attitude) **he goes on speaking secrets.**" This last statement indicates a richness that is inherent in these spoken "secrets," but gives no understanding in regard to what these secrets (or, mysteries) might be. A clue to Paul's meaning might be found in 2 Cor. 12: 4 where he speaks of one who,

  "**heard inexpressible gush-effects and utterances** (unutterable sayings and results of a flow; unspeakable results of movement and flux; inexpressible matters and declarations) **which are not being from out of existence** (or: which are not continuing from within the midst of being; or: which it continues being not right; or: for which there is no privilege or authority; which are not being possible; which are not being allowed) **in a person** (to mankind; for a human) **to at any point speak.**"

There is obviously a sphere of the Spirit which is normally untapped by the majority of humans. This may also have been that to which he referred in Rom. 8:26b,

  "**the Spirit Himself** (the Breath-effect Itself; this Attitude itself) **from above constantly and repeatedly hits the target within us** (or: falls in on our behalf; instead of us hits within; falls in for and over us; or: makes hyper-intercession) **with unexpressed, unutterable or inexpressible groanings.**"

Or perhaps, he is referring to 2:10b, above,

  "**the spirit** (or: the Spirit; the Breath-effect; the Attitude) **constantly and progressively searches, examines and investigates all humanity, and everything – even the depths of, from, which pertain to, and which are, God.**"

And then in 2:11, above, Paul explains,

  "**For who, of humans, has seen so as to know the things of the human** (or: the [matters] pertaining to the person), **except the spirit of the human** (or: the person's spirit) **– the one within the midst of him? So, too, no one experientially or intimately knows the things of God** (God's matters), **except the Spirit of God** (or: God's spirit; the Breath-effect which is God).**"

So could we conclude that the person "speaking in a language" is speaking "secrets/mysteries" to his or her own spirit, and thus "**constantly upbuilds and edifies himself**" (vs. 4, below)?

We should also recall what Jesus said about the privilege that was given to disciples (students of Jesus),
> "**To** (or: For; With; In; Among) **you folks it has been given** (or: granted; gifted) **to intimately know from experience The Secrets** (or: mysteries) **of** (or: pertaining to; from and whose source is; or: which are) **God's reign** (or: kingdom; sovereign influence and activity)" (Lu. 8:10a).

The parenthetical expansion renders this person as "speaking TO God," in spiritual communion, or what we normally call prayer. This second translation also offers the rendering that the person is speaking IN spirit, referring to the spiritual realm of this activity, or to the state of being in union with the Spirit of God.

The dependent, subordinate clause, "**no one continues listening so as to pay attention or obey**," points to the character of the utterance as being unintelligible. In contrast, prophecy can be understood by the listeners.

Now he does not indicate whether the "speaking in a language" referred to a human language or to an ecstatic utterance that did not come from any human culture. The expanded teaching on the subjects of prophesying in the gatherings, and on speaking in a language, inform us that these were evidently prominent features of these gatherings, and in this chapter, Paul focuses mainly on these two effects of grace. Furthermore, center target is the focus of Love: **an act of building** (a construction; an edification), as we see in our next verse…

3. **Now the one habitually prophesying** (or: normally publicly speaking [God's message] and sharing Light ahead of time) **is constantly speaking an act of building** (a construction; an edification) **– even a calling to the side to give relief, aid and comfort and encouragement** (or: a speaking as, and doing the work of, a paraclete), **as well as a speech of stimulation, soothing and gentle influence or incentive – to people** (or: among humans; for mankind).

In the new covenant, prophesying has a positive character, and is described as having three functions:
> a) **speaking an act of building** (a construction; an edification);
> b) **calling to the side to give relief, aid and comfort and encouragement** (or: a speaking as, and doing the work of, a paraclete);
> c) **a speech of stimulation, soothing and gentle influence or incentive – to people** (or: among humans; for mankind).

Both b) and c) can be understood as existential examples of a), for a) is their aim. We find the same two Greek words – represented by b) and c) – in 1 Thes. 2:11-12,
> "**With reference to which you have seen and are aware of how [we treated] each one of you folks, continually calling you alongside to give assistance or relief and to exhort or encourage** (perform as a paraclete), **as well as speaking gentle influence and comfort at your side, as a father [to] his own children, even continuously giving evidence** (witnessing; confirming by testimony) **unto you folks to be continuously walking about worthily of the God** (= living your lives in a manner equal in value with regard to the God) **[Who is] continuously calling** (or: repeatedly inviting) **you people into His own royal activity** (or: reign; sovereign influence; kingdom) **and glory** (or: reputation; manifestation which calls forth praise; or: opinion and imagination; or: = manifest presence)."

The meanings of the Greek words that Paul used do not seem to indicate that the prophesying, in the new covenant communities, involves forecasting the future. They seem to be focused on building God's temple (3:9-17, above) and doing the work of a paraclete. We do not see in these words a sense of a prophecy giving any specific directing of the behavior for individuals, other than of abiding in Love, etc.

The focus seems to be on the corporate community, although general "**stimulation, soothing and gentle influence or incentive**," as well as "**relief, aid and comfort and encouragement**," would be accessible to individual members of the community. *Cf* 2 Cor. 1:4-7

4. **The person habitually speaking in a tongue** (or: language) **constantly upbuilds and edifies himself, yet the person constantly prophesying** (publicly speaking [God's message] before others) **continuously upbuilds, edifies and constructs the called-out community.**

Notice the contrast of these two grace-effects: the tongues/languages are for self-edification, while prophecy has the purpose of upbuilding the community. Both are for current, local situations. In God's new economy, it appears that with someone being given Light-ahead-of-time, this means that, like Paul, they receive knowledge through an unveiling of the Truth concerning Christ and the new creation – concerning what it means to be God's temple, body, wife, etc. – before the rest of the community receives that Light, and so the person who prophecies shares this Light (knowledge of or from God) with the others. Now all this seems to speak primarily to the functioning of grace-effects within local called-out groups.

Nonetheless, in the Unveiling (Revelation), John was given communications from the risen Christ to the called-out communities. The words of praise and warnings were to be sent to them, by John, in the form of letters which were included within a body of visions that pertained to present things and things that were imminent. The letter, as a whole, was called a prophecy. However, the apocalyptic imagery that referred to soon-happening events involving 1st century Jerusalem were focused on aspects that described the conjunction of the past Mosaic age and the present age of the Messiah. So that type of prophecy (a foretelling of future events) took the form of, and was significantly composed of, OT prophecies that pertained to a one-time event: the destruction of the physical temple, the physical Jerusalem and the end of the old covenant – as Jesus had prophesied in Mat. 24, Mk. 13 and Lu. 21. Revelation was the culmination of an old covenant genre of Jewish literature. It was brought to John through a symbolic manifestation of Jesus Christ, and then through various agents (folks with a message within the atmosphere, or in the realm of spirit). It does not seem to relate to what Paul is speaking of, here.

Can we apply the following statement by Jesus as speaking with a reference to the new covenant and the called-out communities?
> "**For you see, all the Prophets and the Law prophesy** (showed light ahead of time) **UNTIL** (to the point of time up to; till the time of) **John**" (Mat. 11:13).

In Mat. 11:11 Jesus had just said that up to that point there had been none greater than John, but the person in the reign/kingdom (the realm of the called-out communities) was greater than he was.

While we are on this question, let us jump ahead to vss. 29-32, below, to observe what Paul says there about prophesying within the communities:
> "**Now let two or three prophets be speaking, one after another, and let the other folks continue thoroughly sifting and sorting so as to fully EVALUATE and reach a decision. Yet if it may** (or: should) **be unveiled** (revealed; disclosed) **to another being seated, let the first hush, and keep silent, for you all continue able** (constantly have power) **to be repeatedly prophesying, one by one, to the end that everyone** (all) **can be learning, and everyone** (all) **can be called alongside to receive relief, aid, comfort and encouragement** (may receive the benefits of the Paraclete). **Also – [the] spirits and attitudes of the prophets are normally humbly aligned with [other] prophets, or, to [the] Prophets**
> > (or: breath-effects of those having fore-light are constantly subjected and subjoined to the arrangements [made] by [the] folks having fore-light)."

Notice the purpose of prophecy that is once more given in these verses: **to the end that everyone** (all) **can be learning, and everyone** (all) **can be called alongside to receive relief, aid, comfort and**

encouragement (may receive the benefits of the Paraclete)." We will, of course, visit these verses again, below, but notice the consistency of the purpose that Paul gives. What he speaks of does NOT appear to be a continuation of OT-type prophets in the new covenant. A word of knowledge is definitely a grace-effect, and the *Logos* was spreading through the proclamation by the sent-forth agents of Christ – but that *Logos* seemed to be about Christ, not about people and events. It was not that God was no longer speaking, but now "all were able to be repeatedly prophesying." Rom. 10:8 says something similar, but mark well WHAT is in their mouths:

> "**But rather, what is He** (or: it) **saying?**
>> '**The result of the flow** (the gush-effect; or: the saying; the declaration; that which is spoken; the speech) **is** (or: exists) **near you – within your mouth and within your heart!'** [Deut. 30:11-14]
>
> **– that is, the effect of the gush from The Faithfulness** (or: the result of the Flow which is the saying that pertains to the conviction of trust; the effect of the flux and movement of that Faith; or: that which is spoken which is trust; or: the speech and declaration which comes from [Christ's] Fidelity) **which we are habitually announcing publicly** (proclaiming extensively), **namely that whenever you can speak the same gush-effect** (or: because if you would agree with the result of the Flow) **within your mouth, that 'Jesus Christ [is] Lord'**" (Rom. 10:8-9a).

Also observe that what the prophets speak within the community is to be judged and decided about by the rest of the community (vs. 29, below, cited above). Their message did not stand alone, as did the messages of the OT prophets.

5. **Now I continue intending** (purposing; willing; wanting) **all you folks to be habitually speaking in tongues** (or: with languages), **yet preferably that you would be constantly prophesying** (or: should keep on speaking publicly before others [as God's spokesmen, proclaiming God's message]), **for the one repeatedly prophesying [is] of greater [importance; influence] than the one habitually speaking in tongues** (or: with languages) **– outside of this exception: [that] he should continue on to interpret** (or: translate), **so that the called-out assembly can receive an upbuilding** (or: may take hold of, and get, edification; would grasp [the] construction).

Notice his repeated emphasis on the purpose of prophecy, or languages that are interpreted: "**so that the called-out assembly can receive an upbuilding** (or: may take hold of, and get, edification; would grasp [the] construction)." Under 13:10, above, we cited Eph. 4:16, which also bears on our present verse:

> "**the operation** (operative, effectual energy) **within [the] measure of each one part** [other MSS: member], **is itself continually making** (or: is for itself progressively producing and forming) **the growth and increase of the Body, [focused on and leading] into house-construction** (or: unto building [up] and edification) **of itself within the midst of, and in union with, love.**"

It is about the construction of the House, the upbuilding of His Temple, as he brought up in 3:9-17, above. The focus of prophecy is the edification of the local community. In 1 Thes. 5:11 Paul admonished that community to, "**keep on performing as a paraclete by calling each other to [your] side** (to encourage, aid, urge, comfort or exhort), **and by habit let one person build up** (or: edify) **the [other] person** [comment: a one-on-one endeavor]..."

To the community in Rome, Paul wrote,

> "**Consequently, then, we are continuously pressing forward and pursuing the things pertaining to, belonging to and which are the peace and harmony from the joining, and the things pertaining to, belonging to and which are the act of building a house, pertaining to [input] into one another** (or: which [effect] edification [infusing] into each other)" (14:19).

In vs. 12, below, he repeats this same idea,

> "**In the same way also, since you, yourselves, are folks boiling with fervor and affection in regard to spirit things** (or: from attitudes; pertaining to spirits; [in matters] which are Breath-

effects), **be constantly and progressively seeking, [focused] toward the upbuilding, edification and construction of the called-out community**."

Then in vs. 26, we see this same theme:

"**Whenever you folks may at some point come together**... – **all things** (everything!) **and every person [directed] toward edification, upbuilding and construction – let it habitually happen** (normally come to be; constantly occur)**!**"

Upbuilding; construction of the community; edification: all the grace-effects have this one thing as the goal.

6. **So now, brothers** (= fellow believers), **if I should come to you repeatedly speaking in language after language** (or: continuously speaking in tongues), **what will I be benefiting, augmenting or furthering you folks – unless instead I speak either on an unveiling** (a revelation; a disclosure), **or in intimate knowledge based upon my experience and insight, or with a prophecy** (a proclamation of Light [from God]), **or by a teaching?**

Now even further, he speaks of benefiting, augmenting or furthering the people. How? By speaking to them "**an unveiling** (a revelation; a disclosure), **or in intimate knowledge based upon my experience and insight, or with a prophecy** (a proclamation [from God]), **or by a teaching**" – and he seems to put all these on a par with each other, because they will "**benefit the community!**" All of these examples are of intelligible communication – something the listeners can understand. Next, in vss. 7-11, he discusses examples of both intelligible and unintelligible sounds and languages...

7. **Likewise, [with] the inanimate** (soulless; = lifeless) **things [which] are normally giving a sound – whether a flute or lyre** (or: a wind instrument or a stringed instrument)**: how will it proceed being known [what] is being played on the flute or on the lyre unless it should give a distinction in the tones**

> (a set order throughout with a difference made through divisions in the arrangement or the sending of the sounds apart)**?**

The last clause in the meaning of *Logos* which is "a conveyance of patterned information." Musical instruments tell us a message, and the playing of them is meant to evoke a response, as the next verse indicates...

8. **For also, if a military trumpet should give an indistinct** (uncertain; dubious) **sound, who will proceed to prepare and make himself ready for battle or war?**

The military trumpet was used to communicate a command, a directive. Its sound gave forth a message, and we see this in the seven trumpets of the book of Revelation. So it is with "speaking" in the midst of the called-out community, as Paul now explains...

9. **In the same way also, unless you, yourselves, should give an easily understood word** (intelligible expression of patterned information; a *Logos* that gives clear meaning) **through the language, or by means of the tongue, how will the thing** (or: matter) **that proceeds in being spoken be personally understood and experientially known, with insight? So you will [just] proceed being a person continuing to speak or babble into [the] air.**

Paul's meaning is clear, and once again we see that his concern is for the listeners within the corporate gathering. Corporate understanding and insight is the goal of a corporate meeting – not individual self-interests or self-edification (vs. 4a, above). Babbling into the air gives no edification to the gathered community. It is a cause of confusion. A contrast to this unedifying behavior is expressed in 2 Cor. 2:17,

> "**You see, we are not – as the majority [are] – ones performing as hucksters in shameful traffic for unworthy gain, constantly peddling and marketing God's message** (God's thought

and idea; the Word of God; the *Logos* from God), **but to the contrary, we are constantly and habitually speaking as from out of the midst of that which is decided about when viewing in clear sunlight – and further, as from out of the midst of God; down within, in union with, and in the place of, God – within Christ!** (or: but in contrast, as out of clear integrity, we are progressively speaking in an Anointing – as [being] forth from God [and] in God's presence!)"

Another example is found in 2 Cor. 9:12,

> "**the attentive serving and dispensing of this public duty and service is not only repeatedly replenishing the needs** (results of defaults; the effects of shortcomings, lacks or deficiencies) **pertaining to the set-apart folks, but further is also progressively superabounding** (bringing excessive amounts) **through many expressions of gratitude to God**."

What a contrast to "**babbling into [the] air**."

10. **Since, as it happens to be, there are so many kinds of voices in [the] world** (or: sounds centered in the system of cultures, religions and societies, or in the midst of the aggregate of humanity) – **and not one of them voiceless** (= silent or without a language or meaning) –
11. **if then, I may not have seen so as to know the ability of the voice** (or: power of the sound; = force and meaning), **to the one presently speaking** (or: for the speaker [i.e., in his perception]) **I shall continue being a barbarian** (one who utters confused or unintelligible sounds; = a foreigner), **and in me** (or: in my case or view) **the one speaking [will be] a barbarian** (gibberish talker; = a foreigner).
12. **In the same way also, since you, yourselves, are folks boiling with fervor and affection in regard to spirit things** (or: from attitudes; pertaining to spirits; [in matters] which are Breath-effects), **be constantly and progressively seeking, [focused] toward the upbuilding, edification and construction of the called-out community – to the end that you folks can progressively surround yourselves with abundance** (or: be constantly superabounding).

Notice how he correlates "**spirit things** (or: from attitudes; pertaining to spirits; [in matters] which are Breath-effects)" with "**the upbuilding, edification and construction of the called-out community**." The fervor for "spirit things" does not translate into "having personal spiritual experiences," unless such experiences "**can progressively surround**" the community "**with abundance**." This "surrounding with abundance" should be in the realm of, and have the focus of, the upbuilding of the community. Paul uses the same term in 15:58, below,

> "**progressively come to be seated and settled folks – immovable and unswerving people – continuing to always be surrounded by more than enough** (or: superabounding) **within the midst of the Lord's work**."

In Rom. 15:13, the concept of surrounding abundance was set in a blessing:

> "**Now may the God of Expectation** (or: the God Who is the Expectant Hope) **make you full of all joy and peace of the joining, within the midst of constant trust and in union with continual operation of faith and believing, [leading] into the midst of continually surrounding you with abundance within The Expectation – within [the] power of a set-apart spirit** (or: within [the] Holy Spirit's ability; or: in union with a power which is, and whose source is, set-apart Breath-effect)."

He opens his second letter to Corinth speaking in similar terms,

> "**through the Christ, our calling [folks] to our side to give [them] help, relief, comfort and encouragement is also progressively superabounding so as to surround us in full quantity** (or: the work of the Paraclete constantly environs in abundance from us, by the Anointing)!" (2 Cor. 1:5b).

We find him again using this term in 2 Cor. 3:9b,

> "**the eschatological deliverance into fairness and equity in rightwised relationships progressively surrounds and continuously exceeds in glory**."

Then in 2 Cor. 4:15b, he speaks of "**the benefits of grace… surrounding in superabundance, [leading] into God's glory**."

We could list more places where he says similar things, but these quotes are sufficient to inform what he says here about "superabounding" with a view to corporate edification.

13. **Therefore, let the one constantly speaking in a language, or a tongue, habitually pray that** (or: focus his thoughts on having goodness and well-being [of the group] so) **he can presently continue on, to translate** (or: may proceed to interpret) **[it].**

Again, Paul's focus is on understanding and insights that build the community.

14. **So if I am habitually praying in a language** (or: speaking or thinking toward having goodness, with a tongue), **my spirit** (or: attitude; Breath-effect) **is continually praying, yet my mind continues being unfruitful** (or: my intellect is without fruit; = useless).

Paul restates his point by rhetorically using himself as an example. He brings his audience into a practical example, and demonstrates solidarity, indicating the he is on the same level of spiritual development as they are, yet he posits a deficiency of only "**habitually praying in a language**" – which is that the "**mind continues being unfruitful.**" Recall that he later wrote, in Rom. 12:2,
> "**be progressively transformed** (transfigured; changed in form and semblance) **by the renewing** (or: in the renewal; for the making-back-up-new again) **of your mind.**"
In the next verse, he presents a balanced approach to this topic…

15. **Which** (or: What) **is it, then? I will constantly pray** (or: focus my thoughts on having goodness and speak toward things going well; [other MSS: I should pray]) **in and by the spirit** (or: with the Spirit; to the Breath-effect; for the Attitude), **yet I will** [other MSS: should] **also repeatedly think and speak toward having good results in** (or: pray by and with) **the mind. I will continue striking the strings and sing** (or: making melody) **in and by the** (or: = my) **spirit** (or: attitude; or: the Breath-effect), **yet I will also habitually strike the strings and sing** (make melody) **in and by the** (or: = my) **mind.**

The songs may likely have been the singing of the Psalms, or extemporaneous lyrics of praise and worship.

16. **Else, if you may continue to speak a good word in spirit** (or: to utter eulogies within [the] Spirit; to be blessing in union with Breath-effect), **how will the one normally filling up the place of the private life of a non-specialist**
> [note: = one who occupies the ordinary position of the "average person," being unskilled, uneducated, uninitiated into the secrets of life in the kingdom or the mysteries of Christ] **normally say, "It is so!** (or: Amen; Make it so!)" **at your speaking of the ease and wholesomeness of grace, and your expression of gratitude – since he has not perceived and does not know what you are presently saying?**

The exclamation, "**It is so!** (or: Amen; Make it so!)," likely indicates Jewish or OT influence on this practice. This was still a period of transition, and familiar cultural norms would have likely carried-over into the new communities.

17. **For you yourself are indeed constantly expressing the ease and wholesomeness of grace and showing gratitude in a beautiful, fine and ideal way – but still the different person is not being progressively built up** (edified)!

Verse 15 expands upon his point in vs. 14, then vss. 16-17 bring his point back to the Corinthians and gives an example of a visitor attending their meeting. He presents this potential visitor as "one who occupies the ordinary position of the 'average person,' being unskilled, uneducated, uninitiated into the secrets of life in the kingdom or the mysteries of Christ." Then vs. 17 affirms that the called-out folks are doing something "**in a beautiful, fine and ideal way**," but Paul's concern is not about them, in this instance, but rather about the visitor. You see, Paul is addressing corporate behavior within the gatherings. Notice that he is not addressing any "leader" here, but the whole membership of the community.

Now consider the fact that Paul apparently expects them to have visits from those presently "outside" the specialized knowledge of the community. So if, as in vs. 16, they "**continue to speak a good word in spirit**," and the visitor "**has not perceived and does not know what you are presently saying**…. **the different person is not being progressively built up** (edified)" (vs. 17b). Paul expects the things that go on within the community meetings to be intelligible to folks from the surrounding Corinthian culture, or even from the Empire at large. This is not to be a secret cult with mysteries that need prior initiation in order to be able to understand what is being said.

18. **I am habitually speaking of the ease and wholesomeness of grace in** (or: by; with) **God, and giving thanks to God – I am habitually speaking in languages** (or: constantly babbling in tongues) **more than all of you folks!**

Keep in mind vs. 2, above, that "**speaking in languages** (or: constantly babbling in tongues)" is "**speaking to and with God**." We commonly call this "prayer." Now Kaplan has pointed us to what Jesus had to say about praying in Mat. 6:

> 6. "**Now as for you, individually, whenever you may by habit be thinking or speaking toward having goodness, ease and well-being** (or: praying), **enter into your storeroom** (or: barn; granary; chamber) **and, upon shutting** (locking; barring) **your door** (or: gate), **pray** (speak or think toward having goodness) **to your Father – the One within the hidden [realm; place]. So then your Father – the One continuously seeing within the secret [realm; place] – will continue giving back to and in you** (or: = giving in answer for your expectation; or: will habitually be paying you).
> 7. "**Now during speaking toward having goodness** (praying), **you folks should not babble** (or: make repetitious utterances; stack up meaningless phrases; or: stutter; speak without thinking; use empty words) **– even as those of the ethnic multitudes** (pagans; nations). **You see, they habitually imagine and continuously suppose that in their much speaking** (or: using many words; or: saying the same thing many times) **they will be fully heard and really listened to.**
> 8. "**So then, you folks should not be made to resemble them, for before the occasion for you to ask Him, God, your Father, has seen and thus knows** (is aware) **of what things you continue having need.**

The "storeroom (etc.)" can be a figure of the inner being – the "chambers of the heart." With these thoughts in mind, Paul's contrasting behavior within the assembly (vs. 19, below) is instructive for good form in group meetings. We wonder if Jesus' words in Mat. 6:7 might have had in mind the prophets of Baal, who Elijah confronted, in 1 Ki. 18:20-40. Many enthusiastic Christians have tended to drift into the thinking of "the ethnic multitudes," or have slipped back into old covenant paradigms. Kaplan has also pointed out that the manifestations of grace-effects, such as speaking in tongues or prophecy, have at times caused some to become proud of their supposed "spiritual elevation or elite status" within the congregations, even to the point of engendering arrogance. We are reminded of Jacob's words, in Jas. 4,

> 16. **Yet now you continue speaking loudly** (boasting; gloating) **in your empty, bragging speech and displays. All such boasting is misery-gushed** (harmful; painfully laborious; miserable; bad).
> 17. **So for and with one** (or: in a man; to a person) **having seen and thus knowing to be continually performing [the] beautiful** (doing [the] ideal; making [the] fine; producing [the] excellent), **and then not habitually performing** (doing) **[it], in him it is a failure** (for him it is error; to and with him it is sin; by him it is a missing of the target and a deviation from the goal).

19. **Nevertheless, within the called-out assembly I constantly intend to speak five words by my mind** (with my intellect and understanding) **– to the end that I may also sound-down instruction on others – rather than an innumerable number** (myriads) **of words** (the plural of "*logos*"; ideas; thoughts; patterned information) **within a language** (or: [ecstatic] tongue).

This topic is of such importance that Paul says it all again. Once again, what does he see as the purpose of the gathering? "**That I may also sound-down INSTRUCTION on others**." What is said in the meetings should teach, and in this way, build up those who have gathered together. Also, he explains that as being "**words by my mind** (with my intellect and understanding)." Rom. 12:2 is worth quoting, again,

> "**be progressively transformed** (transfigured; changed in form and semblance) **by the renewing** (or: in the renewal; for the making-back-up-new again) **of your mind** [with other MSS: from The Mind; of the intellect; pertaining to the faculties of perceiving and understanding; of the mindset, disposition, inner orientation and world view] **into the [situation and condition for] you folks to be habitually examining in order to be testing and, after scrutiny, distinguishing and approving what [is] God's will** (design; purpose; resolve; intent)**: the good and well-pleasing, even perfect** (finished, complete and destined)!
> (or: = the thing [that is] virtuous, satisfying and able to succeed in its purpose.)."

Notice the apparent normality of instruction, listed in the admonitions of Gal. 6, where vs. 6 instructs us,

> "**Now let the person being habitually orally-instructed** (being sounded down [from above] into the ears so that they ring) **in the Word** (the message) **constantly express common being to** (or: hold common partnership in and fellowship for; share equally with) **the one regularly giving the oral instruction** (sounding down and making the ears ring), **in all good things**."

Further observe the hyperbole (emphasis) of contrast between the "five words" (obviously, a short message) and the "**innumerable number** (myriads) **of words within a language**." With a view to the building up of the community, the contrasted values are extreme. We wonder if Paul had "wood, hay and stubble" (3:12, above) in mind with the latter comparison.

20. **Brothers** (= Fellow members of the community)! **Stop becoming little boys and girls in or by [your] way of thinking and use of intellect, but still be infants – non-speaking babies! – in the worthless, the ugly and the poor of quality or the evil. Yet progressively come to be mature as folks which manifest the purpose** (full-grown; perfect; ones having reached the goal and express the destiny; or: = adults) **in [your] way of thinking and use of intellect.**

In other words, "Grow up in your thoughts and way of thinking, but be harmless in your behavior." The idea of "**Stop becoming little boys and girls**" may be an allusion to what he said, above, in 13:11b. He wants them to "**progressively come to be mature as folks which manifest the purpose** (full-grown; perfect; ones having reached the goal and express the destiny; or: = adults) **in [your] way of thinking and use of intellect**." Jesus put it this way:

> "**Therefore, habitually come to be thoughtful, prudent, cautious and discreet** (or: = wary and on the alert; = observant, decisive and timely) **– as the snakes [are]; and yet [still] unmixed** (pure; = without negative characteristics added) **– as the doves [are]**" (Mat. 10:16).

21. **It has been written within the Law that,**
> "**In different** (= foreign) **languages** (tongues) **and with different** (= foreign) **lips shall I proceed in speaking to** (with; in) **this people – and not even in this manner will they proceed in paying attention to Me, or listen into and obey Me,**" **[the] LORD** [i.e., = Yahweh] **is saying.** [Isa. 28:11]

22. **Consequently the languages** (tongues) **are [pointing] unto and [leading] into a sign – not for believers** (or: to those constantly trusting)**, but rather for unbelievers** (or: to those without trust or faith) **– yet the prophecy** (the publicly spoken message [from God]; the speaking of light ahead of time) **[is]**

not for (or: to) **unbelievers, but rather for believers** (or: to those habitually trusting, progressively believing with conviction, and continuing loyal).

By quoting Isa. 28:11, in referencing the Law, Paul is most likely referring to Jews who are still "unbelievers." Also recall what he had said in 1:22, above, "**Jews constantly request** (habitually demand) **signs**." The first clause of vs. 22, here, may also be an allusion to Acts 2:6ff. But prophecy being for believers is simply restating what he has been saying about prophecy's intent being to build up the local congregation.

23. **Therefore, if the whole called-out community** (the entire local assembly) **should come together at the same [place], and everyone** (or: all) **should be speaking in languages** (or: with [ecstatic] tongues), **but then ordinary folks** (= unlearned people of the private sector) **or unbelievers should at some point enter, will they not proceed in saying that you folks are presently being crazy** (continuing to behave as insane people; now acting raving mad)**?**

He again brings up the "**ordinary folks** (= unlearned people of the private sector) **or unbelievers [who] should at some point enter**." Then he gives another reason for not speaking in languages during their meetings: the visitors would conclude that the community was crazy.

24. **Now if everyone may be prophesying, one after another, and some unbeliever** (person without faith) **or an ordinary uninstructed person may at some point enter, he is progressively being given the proof [of the situation], being exposed to convincing arguments, by everyone – [and] by everyone continues being sifted, sorted and held up so that a decision [regarding the situation] can come to him!**

In other words, if the visitors can understand what is being said, they will be "**progressively given the proof [of the situation], being exposed to convincing arguments, by everyone**." Furthermore, with everyone "**being sifted, sorted and held up**," before the visitors, "**a decision [regarding the situation] can come to him**." That is, the visitor will evaluate what the community is doing, and who they really are, as a group.

25. **The hidden things of his heart are now progressively coming to be set in clear light, and thus – falling upon [his] face – he will proceed to be doing obeisance to** (or: paying respect to; worshiping) **God, progressively proclaiming back [to you] that God is existentially within, essentially in union with, and is presently being among you folks!**

The "**doing obeisance**" was a normal cultural response to a manifestation of God, to an agent from the atmosphere, or even to a dignitary of high rank. Consider the response of women as they were leaving the tomb where Jesus had been lying:

> "**Jesus came suddenly and met them** [i.e., the women] **face to face, at that time saying, "Be constantly rejoicing!"** **Now they, upon approaching, took hold of His feet and, being prostrate, immediately gave homage and worship to Him**."

This is a remarkable statement about the effect that the gathered community should have upon the visitor. Through the words and behavior of the group, the visitor will clearly perceive the situation of his own heart, and he will respond to the influence of the Breath-effect, as it enters him and sheds the light of Christ within the core of his being. This is an example of the called-out being "the light of the aggregate of humanity" (Mat. 5:14a). The Corinthian community was "**a city located up on a mountain**" (Mat. 5:14b) – and this mountain was Mt. Zion (Heb. 12:22-24).

The last clause of this verse means that they would be reflecting the image and likeness of God, reflecting the glory of Christ (2 Cor. 3:18).

26. **What, then, is [the conclusion], brothers** (= fellow members)**? Whenever you folks may at some point come together: each one of you habitually has a psalm** (song; tune played on a stringed instrument, with a poem); **has a teaching; has an unveiling** (revelation; a disclosure); **has a language** (or: a tongue); **has a translation** (or: interpretation) **– all things** (everything!) **and every person [directed] toward edification, upbuilding and construction – let it habitually happen** (normally come to be; constantly occur)**!**

Paul instructed the folks in Colossae with similar advice for when they gathered together, or were by themselves:

"**Let Christ's Word** (or: the *Logos*, which is the Christ; the Idea which is the Anointing; or: the message of and from the Christ [other MSS: of God; of {the} Lord]) **be continuously making its home within you folks** (or: progressively indwelling and residing – centered in and in union with you) **richly, within the midst of and in union with all wisdom, habitually teaching [it] and placing [it] in the minds of yourselves by psalms, in hymns, by spiritual songs and odes, within grace and amidst favor constantly singing within your hearts to, for and with God**

(or: habitually singing in, by and to God [other MSS: to {the} Lord], in union with the grace resident within your hearts {= the core of your being})."

Take note of the emphasis on Christ's Word, on teaching and on "placing [it] within the mind." Such admonition was not just about getting good feelings from these activities, but about "wisdom" and "grace," and here in vs. 26b, about "**edification, upbuilding and construction.**"

They should all come with the purpose of blessing and edifying others, not on just getting a blessing FROM others. So the bottom line was that every person should be focused on edification, upbuilding and construction of God's Temple: the corporate Body of Christ. This was to be a habit, a constant occurrence. Furthermore, "**each one**" was to participate in the mutual edification by HAVING something to share with the group. It was not to be a "one-man-show" that was backed up by a choir, while the rest of the group remained as simply spectators.

27. **So if anyone is habitually speaking in a language** (or: with a tongue) **– let it be** (or: to the extent of) **two, or three, at the most – and then** (or: also) **let one be normally translating** (or: interpreting).
        [comment: 2 or 3 – the number of true witness]
28. **Now if there may be no translator within [this] assembly of the called-out, let him or her continue in silence** (or: Yet if he should not be an interpreter he must keep still in an assembly), **yet let him or her continue to speak to** (or: in) **himself, and to** (or: in; with) **God.**

As a good rhetor, Paul now begins a conclusion of the topic of the nature of corporate gathering by giving a restatement as a review of what he has said about "speaking in a language," above. No translator present? Keep quiet or speak in or to yourself. There is nothing ambiguous about this instruction. The potential language-speaker would have to know that a translator/interpreter was present before giving an ecstatic utterance. Paul is reining-in irresponsible behavior within the gatherings. He continues with more limitations for this context...

29. **Now let two or three prophets be speaking, one after another, and let the other folks continue thoroughly sifting and sorting so as to fully evaluate and reach a decision.**
30. **Yet if it may** (or: should) **be unveiled** (revealed; disclosed) **to another being seated, let the first hush, and keep silent,**
31. **for you all continue able** (constantly have power) **to be repeatedly prophesying, one by one, to the end that everyone** (all) **can be learning, and everyone** (all) **can be called alongside to receive relief, aid, comfort and encouragement** (may receive the benefits of the Paraclete).

Notice how vs. 29 limits the number of prophets that should speak in succession, before the group has a chance to "**continue thoroughly sifting and sorting so as to fully evaluate and reach a decision**" about what they had just said. Prophecy was not to be accepted out of hand, without the group first discerning whether what was said was correct and in line with the Good News of Christ, or was an anointed message. The members of the group were not to be left wondering whether any particular prophecy was from God, or not. Here, again, we can observe the difference of these community prophets from those of the old covenant. Can you imagine the folks in Isaiah's day hearing the Word of Yahweh through him, and then having a discussion about whether or not his message was from Yahweh? No, his words were written down, and then became a part of Israel's Scriptures. Not so the prophecies from the Corinthian community.

The Jerusalem leadership questioned the authority of John the immerser, and of Jesus, but they did not, as being their supporters, critique the messages or teachings. They were simply adversarial to both of them, with the System eventually killing both of them. Also, we have the bold contrast between the OT prophets, and the Son, in Heb. 1:1-2a,

> "**Long ago**... **God, having spoken to** (or: in talking with; when discoursing by; making vocal utterances for) **the fathers – in** (in union with; centered in; = through; in [the words of]) **the prophets – upon [the] last of these days spoke to** (or: speaks for and concerning; discourses in; makes conversation with) **us in a Son**..."

Each follower of Christ is "joined to the Vine" (Jn. 15:1ff) and receives direct input through His Spirit. This becomes the criterion for sifting, sorting and evaluating what other members of the body may proclaim. We are to listen to the Voice of the Spirit, within, and receive His judgment on the matter. In Mat. 17:5, the Voice from the Cloud told the disciples to listen to the Son, not to Moses (the Law) or Elijah (the Prophets). The new arrangement was being birthed!

Also, vs. 30 instructs us that anybody that was speaking did not keep control of the group. The speaker was to yield the floor to another person who received a revelation, an unveiling, and the person that had been speaking was to sit down and keep quiet. The group was to function as a democracy that was being on the spot led and guided by the Breath-effect. Thus did Paul explain that they "**all continued able** (constantly had power) **to be repeatedly prophesying, one by one**" (vs. 31). And what do you suppose was the purpose for all of this? It was "**to the end that everyone** (all) **can be learning, and everyone** (all) **can be called alongside to receive relief, aid, comfort and encouragement** (may receive the benefits of the Paraclete)." Yes, another restatement by Paul. In seeing this manner of teaching, we should not be surprised that Jesus taught the same way – saying the same thing over and over, varying it from time to time.

32. **Also – [the] spirits and attitudes of the prophets are normally humbly aligned with [other] prophets, or, to [the] Prophets**

> (or: breath-effects of those having fore-light are constantly subjected and subjoined to the arrangements [made] by [the] folks having fore-light),

The inserted brackets in the verse, and offering the double reading "**with [other] prophets, or, to [the] Prophets**," gives an interpretation that points in two directions: first to the other members of the local group – that there should be humble alignment among them – and second back to the Prophets, i.e., it should align with Christ that could be found in the OT (e.g., Lu. 24:27), as we repeatedly find in the writings of Paul who frequently cites the OT as the ground of his arguments and teachings. The parenthetical expansion gives both a localized, present time, rendering of this verse, but also speaks concerning other sent-forth folks who wrote to different communities. The message was to be One *Logos*, Christ, even if presented in different words or rhetoric by the different proclaimers and writers.

33. **for God is not the source of instability, but to the contrary, of peace** (or: for God does not exist being unrest, disorder or turbulence, but rather, [is] harmony and joining [= shalom]) **– as [He is] within**

all the called-out communities of the set-apart ones (or: as [it is] among all the called-out folks who are the sacred people that are different from what is common)....

This verse states the reason for vs. 32, which includes **all the called-out communities of the set-apart ones**. There was to be stability from the joining and peace of all these communities. This also is an allusion to 1:11-13 where Paul opened up the issues that he is addressing throughout these chapters. Where there are divisions, there is instability. Such things are not from God. From God comes a joining that creates peace.

The parenthetical rendering of the last clause could be seen as introductory remarks that lead to vss. 34-35, which due to MS variances have come into question as to their being original.

> [note: some scholars, e.g., Dr. Ann Nyland, have suggested that the following, vss. 34-35, is a quote from the letter sent from Corinth to Paul, not the position of Paul, himself]

34. **"Let the wives (or: women) habitually hush and continue silent [when] within the midst of the local assemblies of the called-out, for it continues not being allowed or permitted for them to be constantly babbling or habitually holding conversations, but rather, let them be habitually humbly aligned (or: be supportively attached and subordinate themselves) – correspondingly as also the Law (or: the custom; or: = [the Torah]) continues saying.**
35. **"Now if they are still desiring and intending to continue learning something, let them be habitually asking (inquiring of) their own husbands (or: adult males) at home (within [the] house), for it is, and continues being, bad form and shamefully offensive for a wife (or: woman) to be constantly babbling or habitually holding conversations within the midst of the local assembly of the called-out."**

> [note: D, F, G and other MSS place vss. 34-35 after vs. 40. Some scholars consider this as evidence of an early introduction into the text. If the author is referencing the Torah, in vs. 34, then this would have been a Jewish custom; if merely citing custom, he could have referred to the local custom in Corinth, or to the oral traditions of Second Temple Judaism; cf 11:5, above]

These two verses seem to be in conflict with the situation described in 11:5a and 13, above:

> "**Now every woman** (or: wife) **normally speaking to having well-being** (or: praying) **or prophesying [publicly] with the head uncovered** (or: [her] source not veiled down).... **Sift, sort-out and decide among yourselves: is it appropriate** (fitting and proper) **[for; in] a woman** (or: wife) **to [in public] be habitually praying uncovered** (not veiled down) **to God?**"

The question has also been raised, concerning the instruction in vs. 35, about unmarried adult women or widows who may live alone. Witherington suggests that these instructions may have been given to insure that the meetings would not "be turned into a question-and-answer session" (ibid p 287).

> "Paul affirms their right to learn, but suggests another context. In any case, Paul is correcting an abuse of a privilege... which he has already granted in ch. 11" (ibid).

Kugelman (ibid p 272) suggests that these verses come from the customs of the primitive Palestinian communities. This may be why vs. 34b references "the Law."

We will let the reader listen to the voice of the Spirit regarding these two verses.

36. **What? Or, really, did this "thought or message from God" come forth from you folks?** (or: Was it from YOU [that] this "word of God" came forth?) **Or into only you people did this reach down and attain?**

This verse opens with a disjunctive particle which I have rendered, "What?" or "Or, really." It also opens the second sentence where I simply rendered it, "Or." If the scholars who suggest that vss. 34-35 are a quote from the Corinthian letter that was written to Paul, then vs. 36 shows us Paul's amazed reaction to this position concerning women in the congregation. His response seems to be sarcasm. Nyland renders the disjunctive particle, "Utter rubbish!" One of the functions of this particle is the separating of opposites (*cf* Bauer, Arndt and Gingrich, *A Greek-English Lexicon of the NT*).

37. **If anyone habitually presumes** (continues in assuming; normally imagines [himself]) **to be a prophet or a 'spiritual one,' let him continue to fully know and acknowledge the things which I am now writing to you folks, because they are [the] Lord's implanted goals** (impartations of the finished product from [the] Master; inward, purposeful directives which are [the] Lord)**!**

We read Paul as referring to all that he has said, up to this point, in his gentle imperative in 37b, "**let him continue to fully know and acknowledge the things which I am now writing to you folks, because they are [the] Lord's**."

His opening, subordinate clause of vs. 37, "**If anyone habitually presumes** (continues in assuming; normally imagines [himself]) **to be a prophet or a 'spiritual one,'**" may be directed at those in Corinth who may have thought that God's word "**reaches down into only**" them. They may have been those who were "puffed up" (*cf* 4:6, 16, 19; 5:2; 8:1; 13:4, above). These "spiritual ones" may have been the prophetic source of vss. 34-35, and these verses may fit into the category of vs. 29, above, where we are enjoined to "**continue thoroughly sifting and sorting so as to fully evaluate and reach a decision**" about this "word of the Lord." The enthusiasts of earlier centuries, as well as the Pentecostals and Charismatics of more recent times, produced messages that the speakers believed were that word of the Lord, or prophecy. Since God lives within us and regularly communicates with us, these things may be valid, but it was Paul's advice that the hearers inquire of the Spirit within them as to the validity of each individual occurrence. Here is where the "grace-effect of discernment" comes into play.

38. **Yet if anyone continues being ignorant or mistaken [of this], let him or her continue without knowledge** [other MSS: he or she continues being left ignorant and mistaken].
> (or: Now if anyone is habitually without experiential understanding or insight, [this; it] continues being not known [by him], or he/she remains unknown.)

Paul is very likely using subtle rhetoric here, in speaking about those he just addressed in vss. 36-37. He is not bringing condemnation. He is leaving them with the Lord. This letter to them was intended to inform them, and remove the ignorance among them.

The second half of the verse has two different readings of the verb form, with each reading having multiple early MS witnesses. The bold reading, "**let him**…" renders the imperative form of the verb. Here Paul would be saying, "Let him be, it is not an issue, leave him/her with the Lord." The lightface, bracketed rendering gives the indicative form of the verb and simply states the fact, as though Paul is simply saying, "That's how it is… his/her condition continues that way until the Light shines in." It is remarkable that Paul does not say, "Instruct such a person." But being a member of the covenant community implies having been instructed. So perhaps Paul is alluding to there being a disconnect from the Vine (Jn. 15:1ff), which only the Spirit can repair.

The optional parenthetical rendering of the entire verse, "Now if anyone…," offers a neuter subject for the verb in the second half of the verse, "[this; it]," suggesting that Paul means that the person is unaware of his or her ignorance, or lack of "experiential understanding or insight." Following this, I conflated another rendering offering a different meaning of the verb: "or he/she remains unknown." This calls to mind 8:3, above, but suggesting that this person has not been "known by God" (as with Mat. 25:12). In any of these scenarios, Paul is referring to a person within the community who is apparently not abiding in the Vine. If he or she were living in intimate connection to the Vine, this person would not be ignorant of the "**Lord's implanted goals**" (vs. 37, above).

39. **Consequently, my brothers** (= fellow members and family), **with boiling fervor and affection, be habitually zealous for the prophesying** (the proclaiming [of God's message] before others; or: the having and/or speaking light ahead of time), **and do not be in the habit of cutting off, forbidding or hindering the habitual babbling in languages** (or: speaking or conversing in tongues).

So he strikes hard, again for his main point of the value of prophecy (i.e., intelligible words) within the corporate setting. But this does NOT mean that they should cut off or forbid members to speak or babble in languages – for this is a grace-effect from God's Spirit. Yet the situational conditions that he explained, above, would still hold.

40. **Yet let all things be progressively occurring** (or: coming to be) **with good form** (respectably; with good appearance and propriety) **and corresponding to an arranged order** (or: in the sphere of an aligned arrangement).

The reference to "**good form** (respectably; with good appearance and propriety)" was to support what he had said about the prophets speaking only two or three at a time, the group then seeking discernment about what was said, and the propriety of the meetings with respect to visitors. We do not think that he was placing any ritualistic form or solemnness upon them. Rather, we read him as admonishing respectability in their group meals and discussions. The "two or three at a time" would be part of the "**arranged order,**" so that everyone gets a chance to participate. The "sphere of an aligned arrangement" may be referencing "the spirits of the prophets," in vs. 32, above. There may also be a subtle allusion to the new arrangement/covenant in these words, as well. With all this discussion of thought, words and messages, his admonition in Phil. 4:8 seems an appropriate conclusion to this section of his letter:

> "**In conclusion, brothers** (= fellow believers; [my] family), **as much as is TRUE** (or: as many things as are genuine and real), **as many as [are] AWE-INSPIRING** (serious; respectable; noble; dignified by holiness), **as much as [is] RIGHTWISED** (put right; fair, equitable; just; in right relationship within the Way pointed out), **as many as [are] PURE and innocent, as much as [is] AFFECTION-INDUCING** (friendly; directed toward what is liked; lovable or lovely; agreeable; well-regarded; winsome; engendering fondness; attractive; kindly disposed; loveable), **as many as [are] WELL-SPOKEN-OF** (commendable; reputable; of good report; the effect of fair speaking; renowned), **if [there is] any EXCELLENCE and NOBLENESS** (virtues of braveness, courage, good character, quality, self-restraint, magnificence, benevolence, reliability) **[in them] and if [there is] any PRAISE applied** (expression of high evaluation; honor paid; approval or applause) **[to them], be habitually THINKING about these things in a logical way** (REPEATEDLY make these things the focus of careful CONSIDRATION and ANALYSIS; continuously take these things into account)!"

Chapter 15

This chapter introduces a new theme: the resurrection of the dead.

1. **Now I am progressively making known to you, brothers** (= fellow called-out folks; = Family, from the same Womb), **the good news** (the message of goodness, ease and well-being) **– which I myself announced as glad tidings for you** (or: the message of goodness to you; the directive of ease and well-being among you) **– which you also accepted and embraced, as well as within which you have taken a stand, and in union with which you now stand,**

In saying that he is "**progressively making known the good news**" to them, he is simply rehearsing to them that which he, himself had "**announced as glad tidings**" to them when he first met them. The very fact that he calls them "**brothers** (= fellow called-out folks; = Family, from the same Womb)" signifies their common existence as God's Family. He had announced "the directive of ease and well-being AMONG them," and now he affirms that they had "**accepted and embraced**" it, and more than that, in that very "message of goodness" they had "**taken a stand, and in union with which [they] now stand.**" There is no question of their "location" or "position" in Christ; they are God's Temple. He put it this way in Rom. 5:2,

> "**through Whom, also, we have had and now hold the conducted approach and access** (or: the act of bringing toward to gain entrée), **by [His] faithfulness** (or: in this trust; with that confidence; for loyalty), **into this grace and joyous favor within which we have stood and in union with which we now stand.**"

This prelude to his topic also serves as a reminder to his audience that what he will say is what they already know to be true. We find a similar affirmation in 1 Thes. 2:13,

> "**in receiving** (or: taking to [your] side; accepting) **God's Word and message, from a hearing from us at our side, you welcomingly accepted not a word of or from people** (or: a human message), **but rather, according as it really and truly is, a** *Logos* **of God** (God's Message; an idea from God; patterned information which is God), **Which** (or: Who) **also** (or: even) **is continuously in-working** (being active; operating; energizing) **within and among you folks…**"

The rendering of the last clause, "**have taken a stand, and in union with which you now stand,**" reflects the perfect tense of the verb: a past completed action (took a stand) with the effect of that action continuing of (you now stand). *Cf* 11:23, above

2. **[and] through means of which you folks are also progressively, and one after another, being rescued, delivered, and made whole** (saved, preserved and restored to your original state and condition) **– since you people are continuously keeping [it] in possession and retaining [it] – [even] by which, and in which, Word** (or: *Logos*; expressed message; laid-out idea) **I, myself, announced these glad tidings to you people: the message of goodness for you! [Now this is] outside of this exception: [that] you placed your trust randomly** (or: Unless, in fact, you folks did believe to no purpose and express conviction feignedly)**!**

It was "**through means of**" that same "announced glad tidings (message of goodness, ease and well-being)" that they "**are also progressively, and one after another, being rescued, delivered, and made whole.**" He goes on to tell them that the announcement of the Good News was, and is, *The Logos*, that was made flesh to become The Christ (Jn. 1:14). It was the creative power of **The Word** – which came in the expressed message and the laid-out idea about The Christ – that **rescued and delivered** them, that saved and preserved them, and that they were now "**continuously keeping in possession and retaining.**" This was the *Logos* that had made their community God's Temple, and that had made them "a new creation" (2 Cor. 5:17). It came as **glad tidings to** them, and was **the message of goodness for** them. This echoes what he had said in 1:21b, above,

> "**God delights and considers it profitable to deliver** (or: save; rescue; salvage and restore to wholeness) **the folks habitually trusting, repeatedly faithing, progressively believing and constantly being loyal, through the stupidity of the proclamation.**"

Now Paul recognizes that some of them might not have at that time been "good soil" (they may have been a trodden down path, or have had a rock in their heart, or have been overgrown with thorns and thistles – Lu. 8:5-8). So he adds provision for that fact: they may have placed their trust randomly (that is, on an idea that was not really the living Christ) and had believed to no purpose (the concept of the kingdom and discipleship had been plucked away by close friends who did not believe the message), or had expressed conviction feignedly (they went along with the crowd of the moment, but the Seed had taken no root in them). He made reference to such folks in 10:10, 12, above. Also, should some of these folks be influenced by Judaizers, and turn to the Law, his warning in Gal. 5:4 would be pertinent:

> "**You people who in union with** (or: centered in; [remaining] within) **Law continue being 'liberated, rightwised and placed in covenant,' were at once discharged** (made inactive, idle,

useless, unproductive and without effect; or: voided, nullified, exempted) **away from Christ** (or: [the] Anointing) – **you folks fell out from the grace** (or: fall from the midst of the favor)!"
All such folks would be in another class, or group (vs. 23, below).

3. **For I handed on** (or: give over as tradition; transmit and commit) **to** (or: among) **you folks, among [the] first** (or: primary) **things** (or: = above all things), **that which I also accepted and embraced: that Christ died over [the situation and circumstances of] our failures** (on behalf of our mistakes, deviations and sins) – **corresponding to the Scriptures –**

The first, primary and "above all" things, which Paul goes on to state, are an allusion to Isa. 53:12, which the LXX illuminates:

> "Because of this, He himself will continue inheriting [the] Many and will keep on causing [the] Many to inherit, and thus will progressively divide the spoils of the strong folks, because His soul was transmitted into (or: delivered unto and committed to; surrendered and entrusted into the midst of) death and He was considered and viewed (or: counted and reckoned as being) among the lawless folks. So He, Himself, took up and carried the failures (deviations; errors sins; etc.) of [the] Many, and through these acts of lawlessness (or: because of the constructs that were without a law, and the additions that had no law) He was transmitted, entrusted, committed, delivered, surrendered, handed over and given to [our] side" (JM).

Take note of the similarity of the structure of the first half of this verse with the structure and words of 11:23, above. Both verses are rehearsing virtually the same things, but instead of going on to describe the implications of Jesus' "last supper," here we have laid out what happened after that supper: the crucifixion of Jesus with an explanation of the purpose of His death. It was "**over [the situation and circumstances of] our failures** (on behalf of our mistakes, deviations and sins)," or as Eph. 2:1 explains, it was because WE were DEAD, "**by** (or: to; with; in) **the results and effects of your stumblings aside** (offenses; wrong steps) **and failures to hit the mark** (or: mistakes; errors; times of falling short; sins; deviations)." This is an allusion to the offense of Adam, in the Garden, which Paul cited in Rom. 5:12, where by Adam's failure (sin; disobedience; etc.) death passed throughout the midst of mankind. And upon that situation of death, now everybody sins – because they were severed from the Vine (that was in the Garden). Christ died OVER our dead existence in which all we could do was to fail, make mistakes, deviate from God's goal for us, and "sin."

This verse ends with a very important phrase, which is repeated at the end of vs. 4, below: "**corresponding to the Scriptures**." Paul is not just quoting a theological formula, but is stressing a crucial point: Christ's death and resurrection must be understood within the context of the OT. It must NOT be interpreted through the lens of pagan sacrificial theology as something that was done to satisfy a deity's anger, or to withhold its wrath from us. His death is embedded in Israel's story of God's deliverance from slavery, as was celebrated in the Passover festivals, and in His cleansing of this people and sending away their offences and deviations, as was celebrated on the Day of Atonement. It was about His placing a sheltering covering "**over**" the pitiful situation of this people. Ezk. 16 wrote of this in terms of Jerusalem:

> "You were flung onto the open field, with loathing for your soul, on the day you were born. And when I passed by you and saw you wallowing (or: flailing about) in your blood, I said to you, 'Live!' Yes, I said to you in your blood, 'Live!'…. Again I passed by you and saw you, and behold, your time was the time of affection; so I spread My hem over you and covered your nakedness; I swore an oath to you and entered into covenant with you… and you became Mine. Then I washed you with water… rubbed you with oil. I clothed you… sandaled you… bound you up… and I covered you…" (vss. 5-6, 8-10).

For an enlightening perspective on this phrase, "corresponding to the Scriptures," I recommend N.T. Wright's *The Day The Revolution Began, Reconsidering the Meaning of Jesus' Crucifixion*, HaprerOne 2016, pp 219-22).

Paul centered the work of Christ in the story of Adam (i.e., of humanity) in vss. 22, 45-49, below, and in Rom. 5:12-21 where he speaks of,

> "**the Grace of God** (God's Grace; favor which is God), **and the gift** (or: gratuitous benefit) **within Grace – a joy-producing act of Favor – by that of the One Man, Jesus Christ, surrounded** (or: encircles) **into encompassing superabundance** (extraordinary surplus and excess) **into THE MANY** (= the mass of humanity)" (Rom. 5:15).

Cf Gen. 3:15; Ps. 22:15; Isa. 53:5; Dan. 9:26; Rom. 5:6; 8:34; 1 Pet. 2:21-24

Paul makes an astounding conclusion regarding the death of Christ, in 2 Cor. 5:14,

> "**[We are] deciding** (discerning and concluding; judging) **this: that** [some MSS add: since] **One Person** (or: Man) **died over [the situation of] all people** (or: for the sake of all humans); **consequently all people died** (or: accordingly, then, all humans died)."

4. and that He was buried, and that He has been awakened and raised in (or: on) **the third day, and He remains thus – corresponding to the Scriptures –**

The verb, "has been awakened and raised," is in the perfect tense, therefore: "**and He remains thus**." Conzelmann quotes Ernst Kasemann, "The Saving Significance of the Death of Jesus," 1976:

> "Paul only spoke of the resurrection of Christ in connection with, and as the beginning of, the resurrection of the dead in general. It is not for him the individual event of the revivification of a dead person.... As the overcoming of death it is for him rather the beginning of the rule of the one with whom the kingdom of divine freedom begins..." (ibid p 251 n 21).

In 2 Tim. 2:8 we read:

> "**Be habitually keeping in mind** (or: remembering) **Jesus Christ** [= the Messiah], **from out of David's seed** (or: = [Who came] from David's descendants), **being the One having been aroused and raised, and now continuing risen, forth from out of the midst of dead folks – corresponding to and in the sphere of my message of goodness, ease and well-being** (or: in line with the good news that came through me; or: to the degree and realm of my glad tidings)."

Cf Ps. 2:7; Ps. 16:10; Is. 53:10; 1 Pet. 3:18

It should be noted that Paul specifically mentions, "**in** (or: on) **the third day**." This, of course is based upon the history of the tradition, but also may allude to Jesus, in Lu. 13:32,

> "**I continue throwing out demons** (Hellenistic concept and term: = animistic influences) **and finishing off** (or: completing) **healings today and tomorrow, and then on the third day I am proceeding in being brought to the purposed goal and destiny** (or: I am progressively being finished and made fully functional)."

This would happen, according to Jn. 19:28b, "**in order that the Scripture could be finished** (would be at once ended; should be brought to its purposed and destined goal and perfected)," and then in Jn. 19:30, on the cross He proclaims, "**It has been finished** (or: It has been brought to its goal and end), **and now stands complete** (having been accomplished, perfected, ended and now is at its destiny)!" All these references are allusions to Hos. 6:2,

> "After two days He will revive us; on the third day He will raise US up, that WE may live before Him."

It is interesting the Luke noted that Saul was "three days without sight" (Acts 9:9), until Ananias put his hands on him "that [he] would receive [his] sight and be filled with the set-apart Breath-effect" (vs. 17).

Recall Jesus teaching His disciples:

"**that it is necessary** (it remains binding) **for the Son of the Man** (or: the son of man; = the Human Being) **to experience** (or: to be affected by; to suffer) **many things, and after being put to the test, to be disapproved and rejected under and by the elders** (older men, perhaps signifying members of the Sanhedrin), **the head** (or: chief; ranking) **priests, and the scribes** (Torah-teachers; experts in the Law; theologians), **then to be killed-off – and yet, after three days, to stand back up again** (or: to rise up, again)" (Mk. 8:31). *Cf* Mk. 9:31; 10:32-34

Notice the association between Christ's death, His resurrection and our "rescue and deliverance" (vs. 2, above) in Paul's statement in Rom. 10:9,

"**Whenever you can speak the same gush-effect** (or: because if you would agree with the result of the Flow) **within your mouth, that 'Jesus Christ [is] Lord,'**

(or: because if at any time you should confess in your mouth the declaration that Jesus [is] Lord; [with other MSS: because if ever you should suddenly avow in your own mouth, "Lord Jesus!"]) **and then can trust, in union with your heart,** (or: could believe and have confidence within the core of your being) **that God raised Him forth from out of the midst of dead folks, you will proceed being healed and made whole** (or: will keep on being delivered, kept safe, rescued, saved, and will progressively be restored)."

Rom. 14:9 instructs us, "**For into this [situation] Christ not only died away, but also now lives, to the end that He would be Lord both of dead folks as well as of living people.**"

Paul shed light on the happy post-mortem situation in 1 Thes. 4:14,

"**For you see, since** (or: if) **we habitually believe that Jesus died and then arose** (or: stood up again), **thus** (in this manner) **also, through Jesus, God will continue** (or: be repeatedly and progressively) **leading together with Him the folks being made to sleep**."

We find further light, on our present passage, given in 2 Cor. 5:15,

"**And further, He died over all people** (over [the situation] of, and for the sake of all humans) **to the end that those living can** (or: may; could; would) **no longer live for themselves** (to themselves; in themselves; by themselves), **but rather for** (or: in; by; to; with) **the One dying and then being awakened and raised up over them** (over their [situation]; for their sakes),"

5. **and that He was seen by** (or: was caused to appear and made visible to) **Cephas – next** (or: later) **by** (or: to; among; within) **the Twelve.**
6. **After that He was seen by** (or: was caused to appear and made visible to, among or within) **over five hundred brothers** (= fellow believers) **at one time – of whom the majority continue remaining until right now** (the present), **yet some fell asleep** (= died; passed away).
7. **After that He was seen by** (or: was caused to appear and made visible to, or within) **Jacob** (= James), **next by all the sent-forth folks** (or: the representatives; the emissaries sent off with a mission).
8. **Yet last of all [these] folks, He was seen by** (or: was caused to appear and made visible to, or within) **me, also – as if it were** (or: just as if) **by one born prematurely**

(or: as though in a miscarriage; = born too soon, and thus weak and not fully developed, or, born dead, or, aborted; or: with that from out of a festering wound).

After rehearsing who all had seen the risen Christ, including Paul himself (presumably he is referring to the Damascus Road experience), why did he go on to describe his experience thus: "**as if it were** (or: just as if) **by one born prematurely**"? The parenthetical expansion gives the semantic range of that last term. I find "with that from out of a festering wound" to be fascinating, engaging the imagination. If this is the correct reading, was he referring to the spear wound in Christ's side (speaking metaphorically), or the wounding of Jesus' corporate body whom he, as Saul, had been wounding? Was he describing his past situation and activities, of persecuting the called-out folks, in these graphic terms? The word "one born prematurely" is found in Nu. 12:12, where Aaron pleads with Moses about their sister, "Let her not be as it were like death, as one born prematurely (an abortion) coming out of a mother's womb" (LXX). And in

Job 3:16 we read, "Or, as it were one born prematurely (an abortion) coming out of a mother's womb, or, as it were an infant who did not see light" (LXX). Eccl. 6:3 also uses this term:

> "If a man should give birth to a hundred… and his soul shall not continue filled full from The Goodness (The Virtue)… the premature birth (the abortion) [is] better than (or: over) him" (LXX, JM).

My friend Arthur Eedle sent me the following excerpts from the following commentaries:

> "**Ellicott, in his 1887 commentary** sees the definite article as important – '**the** abortion,' 'the one who, contrasted with the rest, was pre-eminently the abortion.' He also said that "the strong expression [EKTROMATI] is studiously softened by the HOSPEREI [as if it were], a form only occurring here in the N.T. but used in classical Greek.'
>
> **Barnes (Notes)** says, 'The word here used (*ektrōma*) properly means an abortion, one born prematurely. It is found nowhere else in the New Testament; and here it means, as the following verse shows, one that was exceedingly unworthy; that was not worth regard.'
>
> **Adam Clarke (Commentary)** says, 'it is likely that the apostle . . . refers to the original institution of the twelve apostles, in the rank of whom he never stood.'
>
> **John Gill** says, 'several learned interpreters think the apostle refers to a proverbial way of speaking among the common people at Rome, who used to call such supernumerary senators in the times of Augustus Caesar, who got into the senate house by favor or bribery, 'abortives,' they being generally very unworthy persons; and therefore calls himself by this name, as being in his own opinion a supernumerary apostle, and very unworthy of that office.'" (from a personal email)

Could Paul have been referring to his own inner death, that happened on the Damascus Road, and to which he later referred, in Gal. 2:20? Abortions, or miscarriages, normally die.

Or, was he identifying with the weak folks of the Body? A baby that is born too soon is usually "weak and not fully developed." Whatever he meant, he seems to be putting himself in the lowest category, as we see as he continues to describe himself in the next verse.

An important consideration is the aorist passive form of *horaō* that is used in each of these four verses. How we understand just what Paul meant depends upon how we render this verb, whose basic meaning is "to see" or "to observe." The ambiguity comes with the passive form, which can mean:

> a) was seen;
> b) was caused to appear and made visible.

The NRSV, and others, render it as if it were in the middle voice, "he appeared." The question has been raised whether Paul is saying that these were literal, physical experiences of "seeing," or were they visionary appearances? The Gospels and Acts 1 witness to physical appearances of the risen Jesus, but we cannot be certain about the experience to which Paul refers for himself. This list, in these four verses, lumps all the experiences together by using the same verb, in the same form – as it were placing them all on a par, which seems to be Paul's intent, so as to make his own experience equivalent to those of the others that he lists.

A second consideration is the form of all the nouns (from Cephas in vs. 5, to me in vs. 8). They are all in the dative case with no expressed preposition. My first, bold rendering is the instrumental, "**by**," with the passive verb, "**was seen**." Observe the parenthetical prepositional options on offer: to; among; within. Each of these, especially "among" or "within," present different potential situations. "Among" suggests a physical "appearance" that was "seen" by the group. "Within" suggests an inner, visionary experience. May the Spirit sort this out for each of us. The definitely visionary appearance to John, in Rev. 1, gives pause for consideration. That apocalyptic picture was intended to give a specific message to John. But what about what Jesus said about "seeing" the Father?

> "**The person having discerned and seen Me has seen, and now perceives, the Father!**" (Jn. 14:9)

Jesus used the same verb in this statement that Paul used in our present passage. The "sheep" used this same verb in Mat. 25:37 when questioning when they had "seen" the Lord in need, and responded in action. The Lord's response to them (vs. 40) was a statement of His solidarity with, and even identity in, those in need.

Whichever meaning Paul meant, in vss. 5-8, above, for those who have lived post-Acts chapter 1, the visionary and discerning aspect of "seeing" would seem to be the most important. Another important consideration is what we observe in Tit. 1:3,

"**Now He MANIFESTS** (or: brought into clear light) **His *Logos*** (His Word; the Thought from Him; the Reason, Idea, communication and expression from Him; the discourse pertaining to Him; and the message which is Him) **in Its** (or: His) **own seasons, fitting situations and fertile moments WITHIN a PROCLAMATION by a herald – which I, myself, was made to trust and believe – down from, in accord with and corresponding to a full arrangement of and from God, our Savior**." *Cf* 2 Cor. 3:18

9. **So it follows that I myself am the smallest** (thus: the least one) **of the sent-forth people** (envoys; representatives), **who am not adequate to reach [the stature] to be normally called a sent-off representative or emissary, because I pursued and persecuted God's called-out** (or: the community of the summoned-forth from God, which has the character of God).

In an honor/shame-based society such as that in which he lived, he is abasing himself, choosing shame rather than honor, before, or in the presence of, other people. His own path presents the grace and mercy of God in his life, and how God chooses the failures and deviants of the world – those in "**incompliance** (disobedience; stubbornness; lack of being convinced), **to the end that He could** (or: would; should) **mercy all mankind**" (Rom. 11:32). He referred to himself as "**the one far inferior to** (or: less than the least among) **all of those set apart** (or: the saints; the holy people)" in Eph. 3:8a. In 1 Tim. 1:15, he said,

"**Christ Jesus came into the ordered System** (or: the aggregate of humanity; the world of culture, religion, government and economy; or: the cosmos) **to rescue failures** (to deliver those missing the target; to save and make sinners healthy and whole; to restore outcasts to their rightful position), **of whom I myself exist being first** (or: am foremost)."

10. **Yet in** (or: by; for; with) **God's grace, and joyous favor which is God, I am what I am, and His [placed]-into-me grace** (or: [birthed]-into-me joyous favor) **was not birthed to be empty, but on the contrary, I toiled to exhaustion by hard labor in excess of them all – yet not I, but rather God's grace and favor** (or: the grace from God; the joyous favor, which is God) **together with me** [other MSS read: which {is} with me].

Now he gives credit (glory and honor) to Whom credit is due: God's grace – the joyous favor, which is God. In, by, for and with His grace, Paul was what he was. That grace was placed or birthed (there is an ellipse – the verb is missing) INTO him, and it "**was not birthed to be empty**." Paul goes on to explain how God's grace and favor labored together with him – he was a co-laborer with grace. In Phil. 2:15b-16, Paul gives a second witness to the fruitfulness of his ministry:

"**you folks are continuously shining** (giving light; or: appearing; made visible by light) **as illuminators** (sources of light; or: luminaries) **within [the] dominating, ordered System** (or: centered in a world of secular culture, religion, economics and government; or: **in union with the aggregate of mankind**), [*cf* Dan. 12:3] **constantly holding upon** (or: having added; keeping a good grip on and fully possessing) **Life's Word** (or: a *Logos* of Life; a message which is life; Reason and Patterned Information from Life; an idea with reference to Life; a laid-out thought that has the character of Life), **[leading you] into loud-tongued exulting-effects** (boasting; vaunting) **for me** (or: in me), **on into Christ's Day** (a day of [the] Anointed; or: a day which is anointed), **because I do not** (or: did not) **run into emptiness** (that which is without content; a void), **nor do I** (or: did I) **become weary or struggle in labor into emptiness** (unto that which is without content; into the midst of a void)."

Paul lays out more details of his "**toil to exhaustion by hard labor**," in 2 Cor. 11:21-33, where in vs. 23 he again asserts concerning his experiences, "**In toilsome labors and weariness more exceedingly; in prisons and jails more often; in blows** (stripes or beatings) **surpassingly; in deaths many times** (= in near-death situations often)." He lived the cruciform life.

11. Whether therefore I or those, in this way we are constantly proclaiming the message, and in this way you folks trusted, believed, experience loyalty and are faithful.

The antecedent of "**those**," in the opening phrase, is most likely the other "**sent-forth people** (envoys; representatives)" to whom he compare himself, in vs. 9, above. The whole point for him and for the other sent-forth folks was to "**constantly proclaim the message**." It was through this proclaiming that the Corinthian assembly "**trusted, believed, experience loyalty and [continued] faithful.**"

Notice Paul's use of contrasts to encompass the universal situations in life: "**whether – or**," here, as well as in 2 Cor. 5:9, "**whether staying at home** (dwelling within our district) **or being away from home and people** (out of our district)," and in Phil. 1:20, "**whether through life, or through death**," and in 1 Thes. 5:10, "**whether we can or would exist being continuously awake** (attentively watching) **or continuously falling asleep**." In other words, Paul is saying that situations and the people involved make no difference with regard to the calling and for life in God's reign. Everything was to focus on "**constantly proclaiming the message**," so that more and more people would be coming to "**trust, believe, experience loyalty and be faithful.**"

This verse concludes his foundation for the arguments which will follow, by recapping his opening statements in vss. 1-3, above. Verse 12 will now build on vs. 4, above, "**that He has been awakened and raised**"...

12. Now since (or: if) **Christ is habitually being publicly proclaimed** (heralded as a message) **that He has been, and remains, awakened and raised up from out of the midst of dead folks, how are some among you folks repeatedly saying that there is** (or: there presently exists and continues being) **no resurrection of dead people?**

Christ was, and is, "**the Faithful** (or: Trustworthy, Reliable) **and True Witness**" (Rev. 3:14). Furthermore, Paul had just cited both himself, and others, as witnesses of Christ having been raised, in vss.5-8, above. His resurrection was firmly established, so how are folks saying that "there presently exists and continues being" **no resurrection of dead people?**

Let us take note of Paul's first use of the present tense, when speaking about the "**resurrection of dead people**." I first rendered the verb as "**is**," for it is the 3rd person, singular of the verb "to be; to exist." The parenthetical expansion, "there presently exists and continues being" offers the full meaning of what Paul has said. He uses this same verb again, in the next verse...

13. Yet now if there is presently no resurrection of dead people (or: if there continues being no resurrection of dead ones; if a resurrection of dead ones does not constantly exist), **neither has Christ been awakened and raised up.**

Paul applies simple logic to the assumption that some folks in Corinth were "repeatedly saying." If it is true that "**if there is presently no resurrection of dead people**" – i.e., that "a resurrection of dead ones does not constantly exist," this means the Christ remains dead, and has not been "**awakened and raised up**." Paul maintains that you cannot have one without the other.

14. So if Christ has not been awakened and raised up, our message which we proclaim [is] consequently empty and without content – and your [other MSS: our] **faith and trust [is] empty and vacuous,**

Let us ponder Paul's reasoning here. The main message has been "Christ crucified." Why now does he maintain that faith and trust are empty if Christ has not been raised up? Because their trust and faith came from the faithfulness of Christ in drinking the cup that His Father had given Him to drink. If His death was the end of His existence, then His death was no different in its effects than were the effects of the animal sacrifices of the old covenant – and those were limited, because,

> "**For you see, blood from bulls and from he-goats [is] without ability [and is] powerless to be periodically carrying away sins** (or: lifting failures from; taking off misses of the target)" (Heb. 10:4).

This was because, "**the Law perfects nothing** (brought nothing to its goal or destiny; finishes nothing)" (Heb. 7:19). But Paul is only beginning, and he affirms in vs. 20, below: "**Yet now – at this present time! – Christ is roused and awake from having been raised up from out of the midst of dead people.**" Furthermore, we also have his witness in Col. 3:1, 3,

> "**Since, therefore, you folks were awakened and are raised up together in the Christ.... you folks died, and your life has been hidden so that it is now concealed together with the Christ, within the midst of God** (or: in union with God)."

The death and resurrection of Christ was not just His personal death and resurrection, but it was also ours, as well! Without His resurrection, there would be no new creation and the old things would not have passed away (2 Cor. 5:16-21). His death would have provided forgiveness of sins (Lu. 23:34), but if He was not raised to Life, we could not have His Life, nor be "in Christ." This Life was the new creation, the Second Humanity (vs. 47, below), the new covenant/arrangement. These things were the "**content**" of Paul's "**message**." But let us continue with Paul's present arguments…

15. and further, we [thus] continue to be found being false witnesses, from and concerning God, because we bring testimony and evidence down from God that He awakened and raised up the Christ – Whom, consequently, He did not raise up, if indeed (= as they say) **dead ones are not really being habitually** (or: periodically; one after another) **awakened and raised up!**

Notice Paul's affirmation: "**we bring testimony and evidence down from God.**" This was not just "hearsay" from people. Jesus told His followers,

> "**you will keep on being My witnesses** (those who testify and give evidence of what they have seen and experienced; = you will continue telling about Me), **both within Jerusalem and within all Judea and Samaria... even as far as [the] end of the Land** (or: an extremity of the region, or a farthest point of the earth)" (Acts 1:8b).

And now we see how this works, as given in Rom. 8:11,

> "**Now since the Breath-effect** (or: Spirit) **of the One arousing and raising Jesus forth from out of the midst of dead folks is continuously housing Itself** (making His abode; residing; making His home; by idiom: living together as husband and wife) **within, and in union with, you folks, the One raising Christ Jesus forth from out of dead ones will also continue progressively giving Life to** (or: will even habitually make alive) **the mortal bodies of you folks** (or: your mortal bodies) **through the constant indwelling of His Spirit** (or: the continual in-housing of His Breath-effect; the continuous internal residing of the Attitude, which is Him,) [other MSS: because of His habitually-indwelling Spirit] **within and among you folks.**" [cf 2 Cor. 4:14; 5:4-5]

God's witness and evidence is within us:

> "'**The result of the flow** (the gush-effect; or: the saying; the declaration; that which is spoken; the speech) **is** (or: exists) **near you – within your mouth and within your heart!'** [Deut. 30:11-14]
> – **that is, the effect of the gush from The Faithfulness** (or: the result of the Flow which is the saying that pertains to the conviction of trust; the effect of the flux and movement of that Faith; or: that which is spoken which is trust; or: the speech and declaration which comes from [Christ's] Fidelity) **which we are habitually announcing publicly** (proclaiming extensively)" (Rom. 10:8).

Paul turns the argument, relating Christ's resurrection to the truth of their witness, testimony and evidence, and then concludes that "**God did not raise [Christ] up, if indeed dead ones are not really being habitually** (or: periodically; one after another) **awakened and raised up!**" – His resurrection and our resurrection are tied together.

Observe the present tense of the verb, "awaken; raise up," in the final clause of the verse: "**being habitually** (or: periodically; one after another) **awakened and raised up**." For Paul, this was an ongoing event, or repeated, periodic events. He is not arguing from the position of some "end of time" final resurrection, but of a present reality. This "one after another" can be seen in vs. 23, below: "**each person within the result of his or her own set position**." This same thought of habitual, present, one-after-another happening is repeated in the next verse…

16. **For you see, if dead ones are not habitually** (or: presently, one after another; periodically) **being awakened and raised up, neither has Christ been awakened and raised up.**

Here he repeats the same argument of vs. 13, substituting "**dead ones are not habitually** (or: presently, one after another; periodically) **being awakened and raised up**" for "**there is presently no resurrection of dead people**." If either of these be true, then "**Christ [has not] been awakened and raised up**" – and yet he was seen to have been raised up, by many people (vs. 5-8, above).

17. **And if Christ has not been awakened and raised up, your faith, trust and loyalty exists being devoid of success and results – you are still within the midst of and in union with your mistakes, failures, deviations, failures to hit the target, and sins!**

This verse repeats the same ideas of vs. 14, above, but he pushes the argument farther: if this is the case concerning Christ, then their "**faith, trust and loyalty exists being devoid of success and results**," and, according to his reasoning, this means that they "**are still within the midst of and in union with [their] mistakes, failures, deviations, failures to hit the target, and sins!**" Trust, faith and loyalty are dependent upon Christ having been raised, which in turn was the outcome of His faithfulness. Release from their union with deviations and failures (being divorced from being in the midst of their mistakes; the flowing away of their sins) is tied to the trust and faith that they had received, the Source of which was the faithfulness of Christ which ended in His being raised up. All is dependent upon the plan being finished: Christ being raised up was the final act of the Devine play. He first represented "the whole house of Israel" (Ezk. 37:1-14). There Yahweh told Israel,

> "Behold O My people, I will open your graves and cause you to come up out of your graves, and then bring you into the land of Israel…. And I will put My Spirit in you folks, and you people will live…" (Ezk. 37:12b-14a).

But then the Gentiles were grafted into Israel's olive tree (Rom. 11:17), so Christ also represented the ethnic multitudes (the Gentiles; the nations; the non-Jews), as well. Paul addresses this same issue in 2 Cor. 5:14b-15,

> "**[We are] deciding** (discerning and concluding; judging) **this: that** [some MSS add: since] **One Person** (or: Man) **died over [the situation of] all people** (or: for the sake of all humans); **consequently all people died** (or: accordingly, then, all humans died). [*cf* Rom. 5:12, reversed] **And further, He died over all people** (over [the situation] of, and for the sake of all humans) **to**

the end that those living may (or: could; would) **no longer live for themselves** (to themselves; in themselves; by themselves), **but rather for** (or: in; by; to; with) **the One dying and then being awakened and raised up over them** (over their [situation]; for their sakes),"

Notice, here, the astounding statement: ALL PEOPLE DIED. This must be understood metaphorically. Paul spoke of himself in the same way:

"**You see, I myself through [the] Law died by [the] Law** (or: to [the] Law; in [the] Law; with [the] Law), **to the end that I could and would live by God, in God, for God, to God and with God!**" (Gal. 2:19).

But he continues:

"**I was crucified together with Christ** [= the Messiah], **and thus it remains... yet I continue living! [It is] no longer I, but it is Christ continuously living and alive within me! Now that which I, at the present moment, continue living within flesh** (= a physical body), **I am constantly living within [His] faithfulness – in and by that [faithfulness] which is the Son of God** (or: in union with the trust and confidence that is from God's Son)" (Gal. 2:20).

For Paul, the living to which he referred in Gal. 2:20 is, in fact, RESSURECTION life.

The death and resurrection of the One Person (Christ) included the death and resurrection of all people.

Paul would later write to the community in Rome, where in Rom. 6 we read:

3. **Or are you continuing to be ignorant** (are you remaining without experiential knowledge; do you continue not knowing) **that as many as are immersed** (or: were at one point soaked or baptized) **into Christ Jesus are immersed** (or: were then baptized) **into His death?**

4. **We, then** (or: consequently), **were buried together** (entombed together with funeral rites) **in Him** (or: by Him; with Him), **through the immersion** (baptism) **into the death, to the end that just as** (or: in the same manner as) **Christ was roused and raised forth from out of the midst of dead folks THROUGH** (through means of) **THE GLORY** (the glorious manifestation of splendor which calls forth praise; the notion; the renown; the reputation; the imagination) **of The Father** (or: which is the Father), **thus also we can walk around** (or: we also should likewise conduct ourselves and order our behavior) **within newness of life** (in union with life characterized by being new in kind and quality, and different from that which was former).

5. **For since** (or: You see, if) **we have been birthed** (have become; have come to be) **folks engrafted and produced together** (or: planted and made to grow together; brought forth together; congenital) **in, by, to and with the result of the likeness of** (or: the effect of the similar manner from) **His death, then certainly we shall also continue existing [in and with the effects of the likeness] of The Resurrection**

(or: which is the resurrection; or: from, and with qualities of, the resurrection)....

8. **Now since we died** (or: if we die) **together with Christ, we are continuously believing** (relying; trusting) **that we will also continue living together in Him** (by Him; for Him; to Him; with Him).

In this passage from Rom. 6, observe the metaphorical sense of our "death" into Christ's physical (and also spiritual/metaphorical) death. We were "buried together in Him," yet, like Paul, we still live. So now, we "can walk around within newness of life" (Rom. 6:4, here). You see, Jesus told Martha,

"**I am the Resurrection** (or: the standing back up again; the Arising) **and** (or: that is to say,) **the Life**" (Jn. 11:25).

In Rom. 6:8 we see the durative future tense in "**we will also continue living,**" which also means that we are presently living "in Him." We are presently in Christ, which means that we are presently within The Resurrection. But let us return to his present arguments...

18. **Consequently, also, those falling asleep within the midst of and in union with Christ lose themselves** (or: loose-away and destroy themselves).

But this is ONLY if Christ had not been raised up.

19. If we are folks having placed an expectation in Christ within this life only (or: If in this life only we are placing expectant hope centered in Christ), **we are, of all humanity** (or: mankind; people), **the ones most to be pitied and in need of mercy and compassion.**

You see, the implication is that our "**expectation in Christ**" reaches on forward to the "next life," as we saw in the quotes from Rom. 6, above. *2 Baruch (Syriac Apocalypse of Baruch)* is dated to the early 2nd cent. AD, but may have existed in Paul's day, perhaps in an earlier form. Here, in 21:13, we read,
> "For if only this life exists which everyone possesses here, nothing could be more bitter than this" (trans. by A.F.J. Klijn, *The OT Pseudepigrapha*, Vol. 2, Hendrickson Pub. 2013 p 628).

Dan Kaplan has observed another layer that can be seen in the phrase, "**within this life only**," which may perhaps be more easily seen in the parenthetical option for the first clause: "If in this life only we are placing expectant hope centered in Christ." What Dan opens for us here is the pity that results from having an expectation focused on the Adamic life, the life of the flesh. Or, as Paul puts it in vs. 46, below, "**the one having the qualities and characteristics of a soul** (the soulish; psychical)," or as he described it in vs. 47, "**The first human** (person; humanity) **[which was] forth from out of the earth** (land; ground; soil; dirt), **made of moist soil and mud** (or: having the quality and characteristics of moist dirt that can be poured; soilish)," Folks who have expectant hope in Christ only with regard to "the first humanity" are "in need of mercy and compassion." Those folks live in death, as seen in Rom. 8:6, cited below.

We find a cognate of the term "**ones most to be pitied and in need of mercy and compassion**" in Rev. 3:17,
> "**Because you are habitually saying, 'I am rich and have acquired wealth and continuously have need of nothing,' and yet you have not seen so as to know** (or: are not aware) **that you continue being wretched** (or: miserable; in hardship) **and pitiful and poor and blind and naked**."

Saying that one has something, when in fact one does not have it, seems to echo Paul's description of "**having placed an expectation in Christ within this life only**."

20. Yet now – at this present time! – Christ is roused and awake from having been raised up from out of the midst of dead people: a Firstfruit (= the first of the harvest; the Sheaf Offering, signally the beginning of the harvest [Lev. 23:10]) **of those having fallen asleep, and are yet sleeping** (reposing).

Paul spoke of Christ being "**aroused and raised**" in Rom. 8:11,
> "**Now since the Breath-effect** (or: Spirit) **of the One arousing and raising Jesus forth from out of the midst of dead folks is continuously housing Itself** (making His abode; residing; making His home; by idiom: living together as husband and wife) **within, and in union with, you folks, the One raising Christ Jesus forth from out of dead ones will also continue progressively giving Life to** (or: will even habitually make alive) **the mortal bodies of you folks** (or: your mortal bodies) **through the constant indwelling of His Spirit** (or: the continual in-housing of His Breath-effect; the continuous internal residing of the Attitude, which is Him,) [other MSS: because of His habitually-indwelling Spirit] **within and among you folks**."

Then in Rom. 8:23 he speaks of our having/hold "the firstfruit, which he defines as being the Spirit:
> "**Yet not only [this], but further, even we ourselves – constantly holding** (or: having; possessing) **the firstfruit of, and which is, the Spirit** (or: the Firstfruit from the Breath-effect; or: the first offering, or first portion, which is spirit and breath, and is from the Attitude)…"

Notice the interweaving and close association that Paul makes of the concepts "**arousing and raising** (= resurrection)," "Spirit/Breath-effect," and "firstfruit." It would seem that our having the Spirit (Breath-effect, which equals Life) means that we are part of the Resurrection (Christ). We find the term "Firstborn" used in a similar way in Col. 1:

17. **And He is before** (prior to; or: maintains precedence of) **all things and all people, and the whole has** (or: all things have) **been placed together and now continues to jointly-stand** (stands cohesively; is made to have a co-standing) **within the midst of and in union with Him,** 18. **and so He is the Head** (or: Source) **of the body – which is the called-out community** (the ecclesia; the summoned congregation) **– Who is the Beginning** (or: the Source, Origin and Ruling Principle; the Beginning Power and Ability of the process), **a Firstborn forth from out of the midst of dead folks, to the end that He would be birthed** (may come into existence; or: could come to be) **within all things and in all people: He continuously holding first place** (or: constantly being preeminent; or: habitually being the First One).

Peter shed further light in his sermon to the Judean leadership:

"**So you folks killed-off the Inaugurator of the Life** (or: Life's Originator; this Author, Founder, Leader, Prince and Initiator of the Life) **– Whom God raised up out from among the midst of dead folks, of which and of Whom we ourselves are witnesses, and continue being both evidence and testimony**" (Act. 3:15).

Paul had proclaimed Christ's resurrection when speaking before Agrippa:

"**that the Christ [would be] a suffering [Messiah, and]** (or: that the Anointed, [is] One subject to experience and suffering, [and]) **that He, [as] first forth from out of a resurrection of dead people, [would] continue about to be repeatedly and progressively announcing Light to the public, as a herald – both to and for the People** [= the Jews and Israel] **as well as to, for and among the ethnic multitudes** (the nations; the non-Jews; the Goyim; the Gentiles)" (Acts 26:23).

The basic idea of Christ being "**a Firstfruit**," is seen in these passages as meaning the He was "the Beginning," "the Inaugurator," or "the first forth from out of a resurrection of dead people." And being First means that He was the First in a series, as we will see in vss. 22-23, below. As time and the ages roll on, we can see no end to this series.

We need not worry about those who doubt the resurrection of Christ, and Paul concludes the discussion about those "nay-sayers" with this positive affirmation of the fact: Christ IS roused and awake. He was a Firstfruit, the beginning of the harvest, as noted within vs. 20. Now there is a subtle implication in Paul's having chosen the perfect tense for the verb "fallen asleep" in the last clause: some are "yet sleeping." But what is this sleep? Paul used this metaphor in Eph. 5:14,

Wherefore He is now (or: it keeps on) **saying,**

"**Let the sleeper** (the person continuously down and being fast asleep) **be waking up, continue rousing, and then stand up** (arise) **from out of the midst of the dead ones, and the Christ will continue shining upon you** (progressively enlightening you)**!**"

Notice that the Lord was NOW, and kept on, saying, "arise from out of the midst of dead ones!" This was spoken concerning those who were "dead," as stated in Eph. 2:1. *Cf* 11:30, above.

We can also see the metaphorical use of the "sleep" in 1 Thes. 5:

6. **Consequently, then, we may not continuously fall asleep [into death? in awareness?] even as the rest** (= as other folks), **but rather, we can and should continuously be aroused and stirred up from sleep** [comment: thus, awake to be alertly watchful; also a figure for being alive] **and sober** (or: clear-headed).

7. **For it follows that the folks continuously falling asleep** (or: drowsing) **are sleeping at** (or: from [the]) **night, and the ones continuously being made drunk are becoming drunk at** (or: from [the]) **night.**

8. **We, on the other hand, being of Day** (belonging to and having characteristics of [the] Day; having [the] Day as our source), **can and should continuously be sober** (clear-headed)…

Here, Paul is contrasting two ways of living in this present life: either being asleep to the Truth and Reality (Christ), and thus living in the "night" of the old covenant, or being "aroused and stirred up from sleep, and being clear-headed," because we now live in "the Day (Christ)." Paul shines his light on this in vss. 22b-23, below…

21. **For since through a person** (or: a human; or: humanity) **[came] death, through a Person** (or: a Human), **also, [comes] resurrection** (a standing back up again) **of dead people.**

The person referred to in the first phrase is Adam, as we see in the next verse (*cf* also Rom. 5:12), and the Person in the following phrase is, of course, Christ. Through Him is the "**resurrection of dead people**." We will see that Paul refers to these two people as "the first human Adam and the last Adam," in vs. 45, below, where the discussion of resurrection is continuing. Both of these "humans" fill the role of a kind of "primal man," each individual figure representing "the whole of humanity" in Paul's argument. We find similar reasoning in Ex. 4:22 where Yahweh terms corporate Israel as His "son."

The origin, or source, of the death of which Paul speaks in this verse is an allusion to the Garden story in Gen. 3. In Paul's day this same view is echoed in 4 Ezra 7:118,

> "O Adam, what have you done? For though it was you who sinned, the fall was not yours alone, but ours also who are your descendants" (trans. by B.M. Metzger, *The OT Pseudepigrapha*, Vol. 1, Hendrickson Pub. 2013 p 541).

In this verse, "death" is set off against "resurrection." In Scripture, both of these terms had both a literal and a figurative meaning. From here and on through the rest of the chapter we need to listen for the level of which Paul is speaking – whether it be the literal, or the figurative. We should keep in mind Paul's thinking on both of these topics as we consider what he presents from here on out. The traditional reading of Scripture, at least in the last two centuries, has been to take what is said literally, unless the literal interpretation seems implausible. With this in mind, let us review some NT statements that seem to be figurative, or metaphorical. We first of all saw this in 2 Cor. 5:14b, cited above. Here are others:

> "**And you folks – continuously being dead ones within** [other MSS: by] **the results and effects of falls to the side, and in** (or: by) **the uncircumcision of your flesh** (= physical bodies or national heritage; or: = estranged human nature and alienated self) **– He makes** (or: made) **alive together: you** [other MSS: us] **jointly together with Him**" (Col. 2:13). *Cf* Eph. 2:1, 5

Now being "made alive" from having been dead is just another way of saying "resurrected." Continuing on:

> "**and He jointly roused and raised** (or: suddenly awakens and raises) **[us] up, and caused [us] to sit** (or: seats [us]; = enthroned [us]) **together within the things situated upon** [thus, above] **the heavens**" (Eph. 2:6)

This affirmation is a metaphorical reference to resurrection: it is "Life in Christ." It corresponds to the metaphor that Jesus used: "abide in the Vine" (Jn. 15:1ff).

> "**Since** (or: If) **you folks died together with Christ, away from the world's system of elementary principles**" (Col. 2:20a).

This is the same as Paul said in 2 Cor. 5:14b. This is a metaphorical use of the word "died." It describes our present, existential reality in terms of the death of Christ.

> "**for you folks died, and your life has been hidden so that it is now concealed together with the Christ, within the midst of God** (or: in union with God)" (Col. 3:3).

Note Paul's repetition in this letter to Colossae, but with added insight to "where we are now."

> "**yet the woman continuously indulging herself in riotous luxury** (excessive comfort; sensual gratification), **while continuing being alive** (or: [though] living), **she is dead** (or: she has died)" (1 Tim. 5:6).

Here Paul uses the word "dead" to metaphorically describe a person who is not presently "living" in Christ.

> "**you folks at once place yourselves alongside for disposal to God** (or: stand yourselves with God, at [His] side; by and in God, present yourselves; set yourselves alongside [each other], for God) **as it were being folks continually alive forth from out of the midst of dead ones**" (Rom. 6:13).

He tells them to live like resurrected people, as people who are alive from the dead.

> "**Now I was at one time** (or: formerly) **habitually living apart from Law** (or: I was once alive, independent from custom and [Torah]); **yet, in connection with the coming of the implanted goal** (of the impartation of the finished product within; of the inward commandment and directive), **the Sin becomes alive again** (or: deviation, failure, error and the missing of the target revived and comes back to life), **but I die** (or: and I died)" (Rom. 7:9).

Paul is using the rhetorical device of "speaking in character," in Rom. 7. That character is first Adam, who was at one time "living" when he was independent from custom and Torah, or Law. But then the implanted goal of the Law came, and Adam (as Israel) died – because "the Sin came back to life" through the Law (*cf* vs.56, below). So here is another metaphorical use of death/dying.

> "**For the result of the thinking** (mindset; effect of the way of thinking; disposition; result of understanding and inclination; the minding; the opinion; the thought; the outlook) **of the flesh** (= from the human condition or the System of culture and cultus; or: = Torah keeping) **[is; brings] death, yet the result of the thinking** (mind-set; disposition; thought and way of thinking; outlook) **of the spirit** (or: from the Spirit; which is the Breath-effect) **[is; brings] Life and Peace** (joining)" (Rom. 8:6).

In this verse Paul opens for us his central concept of death as we find it in his writings: "the thinking, or mindset, etc., of the flesh." It is the "life" of the first humanity, personified in "Adam."

> "**You see, since** (or: if) **their casting away** (or: their rejection [of the good news]) **[is, means or brings the] conciliation of the aggregate of humanity** (the changing of the universal system to another level of existence; the complete change for the arranged order to be other than it was; the world's change from enmity to friendship), **what [will be] the receiving** (the acceptance; the taking or drawing toward one's self as a companion or associate) **[of them,** (or: the receiving of it)**] if not life forth from out of the midst of dead folks?!**" (Rom. 11:15).

Paul is speaking figuratively, in that chapter, of those Jews who were broken out of their olive tree (vs. 17) because of "**the lack of faith and trust** (or: unbelief)" (vs. 23), which was the result of a "**petrifying, from a part** (a stone-like hardening in some measure; a callousness [extending over] a part), **[that had] been birthed and come into existence in Israel** (or: has happened to Israel)" (vs. 25). Now "**if they should not persistently remain in the lack of faith and trust…God is able** (capable; is constantly powerful) **to graft them back in again**" (vs. 23). When this happens (vs. 26) it will metaphorically be "Life forth from out of the midst of dead folks." That would be a metaphorical "resurrection."

With these examples of "death" and "being raised up" seen as being metaphorical or figurative, let us resume our chapter here…

22. **For just as within Adam all humans keep on** (or: everyone continues) **dying, in the same way, also, within the Christ, all humans will keep on being made alive** (or: in union with the Anointed One, everyone will one-after-another be created and produced with Life)

Just who are the "**all humans**" of whom Paul speaks here, who he informs us "**will keep on being made alive** (or: in union with the Anointed One, everyone will one-after-another be created and produced with Life)"? The greater context of the chapter involves the topic of resurrection, and here, in vs. 21, above, the context is anthropological – Paul is speaking about the entirety of humanity. We find an echo of this verse in Paul's elaboration of this topic in Rom. 5:12-21.

Verse 22, here, continues Paul's anthropology, and "all humans" is the subject of each of the parallel clauses (*pantes* taken as a nominative, masculine). The topic under discussion is not "believers" or "the church," but rather, "humans." We see him expanding Christ's rule to "all the things..." below, in vs. 25, which vs. 26 instructs us as including "**the Death**."

Paul quotes Ps. 8:6 (vs. 27, below) and returns to speaking of "**all humanity**" (taking *panta* as masculine, in both uses, since this fits best his anthropological theme) as he focuses on "**the purposed goal and destiny**" (in vs. 24, *telos*). In vs. 28 he again expands to "**the whole**" (*ta panta*) which calls to mind Rom. 11:36a,

> "**Because, forth from out of the midst of Him, then through the midst of Him** (or: through means of Him), **and [finally] into the midst of Him, [is; will be] the whole** (everything; [are] all things; or: = Because He is the source, means and goal/destiny of all things – everything leads into Him)!"

But here, in 28b below, he uses the most inclusive term to express the final situation: "**to the end that** [a purpose clause introduced by *hina*] **God can be all things within the midst of and in union with all humanity** (*panta* taken as a masculine -- again in line with his anthropological theme)." Note that I also render this final *panta* as a neuter in the parenthetical expansion, ending with the offer of a simple inclusive/ambiguous "All in all," and then, "everything, within the midst of everyone (here rendering 'pasin' as a masculine, corporate noun)."

So it is within this "**all**" context that we must first exegete vs. 22. Here we find the rhetoric of parallelism with contrast as an extension of Paul's statement in vs. 21 of "**resurrection of dead people**" that has come "**through a Person** (or: a Human)," meaning, through Christ. The contrasts are between Adam and Christ, and between "**keep on dying**" and "**will keep on being made alive**." I have rendered this second clause as a durative future, to be in parallel with the durative present tense of the first clause. So the statements of the two clauses are:

> a) "**all humans keep on dying**" -- modified by the prepositional phrase, "**within Adam**"
> b) "**all humans keep on being made alive**" -- modified by the prepositional phrase, "**within the Christ**."

We must also consider the parallel functions of the contrasting conjunctions: "**just as**" -- "**in the same way, also**."

Turning again to Rom. 5, observe the parallelism in vs. 15:

> "**Yet to the contrary, [it is] not in the same way [with] the effect of grace** (result of favor; the thing graciously given) **as [it was with] the effect of the fall to the side** (or: = the result of the stumbling aside and the offence is not simply balanced out by the result of the joyful gift of grace – the gratuitous favor). **For you see, since** (or: if) **by** (or: in) **the effect of the fall to the side** (the result of the stumbling aside and the offense) **of the one THE MANY** (= the mass of humanity) **died, MUCH MORE** (= infinitely greater) **[is] the Grace of God** (God's Grace; favor which is God), **and the gift** (or: gratuitous benefit) **within Grace – a joy-producing act of Favor – by that of the One Man, Jesus Christ, surrounded** (or: encircles) **into encompassing superabundance** (extraordinary surplus and excess) **into THE MANY** (= the mass of humanity)."

Moving on in that passage, let us consider Rom. 5:18 as an interpretation of what he may have in mind here, in 15:22, in his phrase, "**will keep on being made alive**":

> "**Consequently, then, as [it was] through the effect of one fall to the side** (or: the result of one offense) **[coming] into all mankind** ([permeating] into all humanity; = [extending] into the whole race) **[bringing them] into a commensurate effect of a decision** (a corresponding result of a negative evaluation which fell in line with the decision and followed the pattern which divided [us] down), **THUS ALSO and in the same way, through one just-effect and the result of one right act which set [all humanity] right and in accord with the Way pointed out** (through the

result of one act of justice, equity and solidarity; through a single decree creating rightwised relationships; through one effect of rightwising which turns [people] in the right direction) **[it comes] into ALL MANKIND** (all humanity; all people; = the whole race) **[bringing them] into a setting right of Life and a liberating rightwising from Life [including them in covenant community]**

> (or: Life's turning [folks] in the right direction resulting in right relating, equity and justice which is in accord with the Way pointed out; a making of situations and conditions to be right, which pertain to Life; an expressing of fairness and equity, which IS LIFE; a rightly directed solidarity coming from Life; a just-acting deliverance having the qualities of life)."

"**One fall to the side**" brought "**all mankind into a commensurate effect of a decision.**" This was "**The Sin**" of Adam that Paul references in Rom. 5:12, which he calls "**the fall to the side**" in 5:15, and then refers to as "**the unwillingness to listen, or to pay attention, resulting in disobedience,**" in 5:19.

Now a fair reading of 15:22, here, presents us with an equation where on one side of the "equal sign" we have, "**as within Adam,**" and on the other side of the equation (the = sign being: "**in the same way**") we have "**also, within the Christ.**" Traditional interpretation of this equation inserts a proviso, "i.e., all those who are IN Christ." But we see that in this chapter, as in Rom. 5, Paul speaks of the two, Adam and Christ, as figures of two humanities: the 1st and the 2nd (vs. 47, below). But let us see how Paul handled the same topic, the same equation, in Rom. 5, and let it shed light on the inclusiveness of vs. 22, here:

> "**For you see, JUST AS through the unwillingness to listen, or to pay attention, resulting in disobedience** (or: the erroneous hearing leading to disobedience) **of the one person** [i.e., Adam] **THE MANY** (= the mass of humanity; note: cf Weymouth NT in Modern Speech, 1909 Edition) **were rendered** (established; constituted; placed down and made to be) **sinners** (failures; ones who diverge and miss the target), **THUS – in the same way – ALSO through the submissive listening and paying attention resulting in obedience of the One [i.e., Christ], THE MANY** (= the mass of humanity) **will continue being rendered 'set-right folks'**
>> (placed down and established [to be] just ones; constituted folks who have been rightwised to be people in the Way pointed out; made righteous ones who are guilt-free, fair, equitable, and rightly-turned in the solidarity of covenant relationships)" (Rom. 5:19).

This verse in Rom. 5 rightly interprets 15:22, here. A close reading of Rom. 5:12-21, especially noting the equations of "THE MANY... THE MANY" in that passage, will bear this out.

Here, 15:22 is anthropology; it is race-wide in its extent. The next question must be whether the second clause should be read in light of these two conjunctions, "**just as**" – "**in the same way, also.**" To introduce into this text "theological qualifiers" is to participate in "eisegesis." The text does not limit the first clause, nor does it limit the parallel second clause. An unbiased reading of this verse takes the subjects of both clauses (**all humans**) as being the same group of humans (**all**). The contrasting prepositional phrases inform us as to the reason for dying as opposed to the reason for being made alive.

If we move further into Paul's discussion of resurrection in this chapter, we find other sets of contrasting parallels that speak to this same topic: vss. 45 and 47. There Paul reintroduces Adam (first and last) and humanity (first and second). We should not miss the "divine passive" of vs. 44a,

> "**It is habitually** (continually; repeatedly; presently) **being sown a body having the qualities and characteristics of a soul** (a soulish body; or: = a body animated by soul; or: = a natural entity**); it is habitually** (repeatedly; constantly; presently; one after another) **being awakened and raised up a spiritual body** (a body having the qualities and characteristics of the Breath-effect; or: = a spiritual entity)."

This is all the work of God. God gives birth to us as a part of the first Adam, and also gives birth to us as a part of the *eschatos* (last) Adam. Again, there is no work of humans indicated in this later passage: no act of believing, receiving, assenting, etc. This passage is again anthropology: the old humanity; the new humanity. Adam was the "federal," or representative, head of the dead humanity; Christ is the "federal," or representative, head of the second humanity. In Paul's arguments we see no choice to be in Adam, and we observe no choice to be in Christ.

Verse 22 must be read in its context. Beginning with vs. 20 we read that, "**Christ is roused and awake from having been raised up from out of the midst of dead people: a Firstfruit**..." We can read *en* in vs. 22 as "**in union with**." Thus, we can understand the last clause of vs. 22 as speaking of being "in union with Christ" who is now "**raised up from out of the midst of dead people**." There is a connection, in the text, of Christ's resurrection with all humans being one after another (the durative future) made alive, because of the union that God has made between all humans and the Last Adam. But this comes about (as we have seen throughout history, since His resurrection), "**each person within the result and effect of his or her own class** (or: ordered place; appointed position [in line]; arranged time or order of succession; = place in a harvest calendar, thus, due season of maturity)," as we will see in vs. 23, below.

Before we move on, let us take note of the durative future tense in the verb, "**will keep on being made alive**." The parenthetical expansion gives further light: "everyone will one-after-another be created and produced with Life." Conzelmann admits, "It is true that a restitution of all could be read out of this," but he disagrees with this interpretation (ibid p 268 n 49). We see this as the only way of reading the text, considering the arguments and supporting passages from Rom. 5 that we have cited. So, keep in mind all that has been offered here, as we consider Paul's further explanation: the first clause of the next verse...

23. **– yet each person within the result of his or her own set position [in line]** (or: effect of ordered placement; appointed class; arranged time and turn, or order of succession; = place in a harvest calendar, thus, due season of maturity)**: Christ a Firstfruit** (a First of the harvest), **next after that, those belonging to the Christ** (or: the ones who have their source and origin in the Anointing; those who are [a part] of the Christ) **within the midst of, and in union with, His presence,**

The compound phrases that open this verse inform us that there is a situation, and from the metaphor used there is a time or turn, for **each person** to be made alive in Christ. This time and situation is dependent upon **the result** one's own **set position [in line]**. Now the semantic range of this Greek word can also be termed "the effect of ordered placement." Or, it could indicate an "appointed class." It was used of "a body of soldiers; a corps; a band." It can signify "an arranged time and turn," or, "an order of succession." Consider Paul's words in Gal. 4:2, "**the father's previously set** [time or situation]." I offered a paraphrase of this: "place in a harvest calendar, thus, due season of maturity." So what does all this suggest? First of all, perhaps that God does the arranging, the positioning, the ordering, the sequencing, etc. "For everything there is a season, and a time for every matter under heaven: a time to be born, and a time to die..." (Eccl. 3:1-2a).

Because Paul used an agricultural metaphor to classify Christ (a Firstfruit), I offered the paraphrase, "place in a harvest calendar, thus, due season of maturity." This suggests that "**those belonging to the Christ**" would be a harvest. But leaving the agricultural metaphor, that following phrase could read, "the ones who have their source and origin in the Anointing," or, "those who are [a part] of the Christ," i.e., His body, e.g., as incarnated in the local called-out community." These were also a part of the Firstfruit (Jas. 1:18). Paul adds a qualifier with the final phrase, "**within the midst of, and in union with, His presence**." But what does this mean?

We suggest that it is His presence that gives the person Life. It is His presence that enables one to be a branch in the Vine. It is His presence that makes a person His home, His Temple. It is His presence that creates the kind of existing where a person is "joined to the Lord" (6:17, above), and thus makes a person "one spirit" with God. In a normal birth, the head is born first, and then the other members of the body. There is a succession of emergence. John the immerser was set to come before Jesus, and was a part of the old covenant, and not a part of the kingdom. Jesus said, "**Wherever two or three are gathered together into His Name [He] was within the midst of them**" (Mat. 18:20). What Paul describes here was the situations that followed upon the Day of Pentecost, as recorded in Acts 2, and then written in the rest of the book of Acts, along with all the letters which compose the remainder of the NT. The risen Christ declares His presence among the called-out communities in Rev. 2:1b.

In Phil. 3:16, Paul said,

> "**Moreover, into that which we precede [others]** (or: into what we went before in; into what we come ahead so as to arrive at; = unto whatever stage we have reached) **in the very same thing [our goal is] to be habitually drawn into a straight line and consistently advance within our ranks**
>
>> [Aleph2 and other MSS add phrases to read as follows: Besides, into what we outstrip {others}, by the same standard (measuring rod; rule) {it is for us} to habitually advance in line (i.e., frame our conduct in an orderly routine; or: consider the elements and observe the rudimentary principles by the same standard) – to constantly be intent on and keep thinking of the same thing (or: be of the same frame of mind and attitude)]."

What Paul wrote to Philippi may give us insight to his metaphor here in 15:23. I have elsewhere commented on Phil. 3:16,

> "I suggest that Paul is continuing to use the racecourse metaphor here, especially in the first text. Wherever we are in this race, to whatever lap around the track we have attained, or mile marker we have reached, stay in your lane. Within whatever group you are moving, be consistent, stay with it and advance in your proper position.
>
> "In the Aleph 2 text he first seems to be advising competing by the rules, which include staying in your own line and be orderly while keeping in mind the elements of the game. The last part speaks to keeping your focus and being single-minded. Our thinking and our attitude, or frame of mind, are oft-repeated topics in Paul's writings. How we think, and what attitude we entertain is an important aspect of kingdom living." (Comments on Philippians, in *Peter, Paul & Jacob*, Harper Brown Pub., 2012, p 59)

We might also have further insights by reviewing Eccl. 3:1-2, again, from the Septuagint:

> "**For** (or: To; With; Among) **all the humans and all the things [there is, or will be] the time, and [there is, or will be] a season** (fertile moment; fitting situation; appointed arrangement) **for** (or: to; with; among) **all the results of positions set [in line]** (or: effects of ordered placements; appointed classes; arranged times and turns, or orders of succession; = the places in a harvest calendar, thus, due seasons of maturity) **by the heaven** (or: under the atmosphere): **a season** (fertile moment; fitting situation; appointed arrangement) **to at some point give birth** (bear children), **and a season** (moment, situation, appointed arrangement) **to die off; a season** (etc.) **to plant and a season** (etc.) **to pluck up what had been planted**" (LXX, JM).

24. **thereafter** (next, in order of sequence,) **the purposed goal and destiny** (the finished work; the embodiment of maturity and perfection; the fulfillment; the result; the outcome; the end and purpose attained; the realization of the perfect discharge; or: the end; the closing act; the consummation), **when He would continue passing on the sovereign influence and activities by God** (or: can progressively restore and continue transferring or returning the reign to God; may, with and in God, repeatedly transmit the kingdom; should keep on committing, handing over and relating the dominion, for God) **even [the] Father** (or: in [His] God and Father), **at the time that He would suddenly bring down to idleness** (make unemployed and ineffective; nullify; abolish; render useless and unproductive) **every rulership of government** (all headship and sovereignty), **even all authority and power** (or: every existing right, privilege and what comes out of being – as well as, able-ness and capability)!

So what is "**the purposed goal and destiny**"? The next four verses answer this question, ending in vs. 28 where he says, "**to the end that God can be all things within the midst of and in union with all humans**." That is the "finished work" of Christ. When God is "all, in all," it will be "the embodiment of maturity and perfection." Observe the other semantic uses of the word *telos*, that is normally rendered here as just "the end." But as we see, it can also mean, "the outcome; the realization of the perfect discharge."

If we were to put this in the historical context of 1ˢᵗ century Judea, vs. 23b, above, could be interpreted as Paul speaking of Jesus and the called-out communities within the generation of which Jesus said,
> "**I now say to you folks, that this generation can by no means pass by until all these things can happen** (should occur; may come to be)" (Mat. 24:34). *Cf* Lu. 21:32.

In Lu. 21:22 Jesus told His followers,
> "**these are days of executing justice** (or: from deciding the case, with a view to the maintenance of right: whether vindication or retribution) **– of bringing about what is fair and right and of establishing what accords with the Way pointed out – with a view to have fulfilled all the things having been written** (or: for all that is written to be fulfilled)!"

The contexts of Mat. 24 and Lu. 21 spoke of the destruction of Jerusalem in AD 70, which completed the end of the old covenant and the age of the Mosaic Law: that "old creation" passed away, and this is why Paul refers to our present time as a "new creation" in 2 Cor. 5:17. This was the time of which Paul spoke in 10:11b, above: those of Paul's day who were the "**ones unto whom the ends** (= conjunctions; or: consummations; goals) **of the** (or: these) **ages have come down to** (or: arrived at) **and are now face to face [with us]**." This would align with the Preterist view of eschatology.

Yet we must ask: To what purposed goal, destiny, end, fulfillment, closing act, finished work or maturity is Paul speaking? We see that in vs. 20 he was speaking of his own time (**Yet now – at this present time!**). There, calling Christ "**a Firstfruit**" presents the picture of the beginning of a process, or a progression into the fullness of the harvest. Yet we immediately see that the "harvest" is from the "field (which from Mat. 13:38a, we learn is' the aggregate of humanity,' or, the 'world')" which is "**of those having fallen asleep** (a euphemism for dying)." Verse 21 instructs us that Christ is the One who brings "**resurrection of dead people**" who had all died from being in Adam (Rom. 5:12). This brings us to vs. 22 which speaks of a "goal," i.e., "everyone produced with Life."

We need to pay attention to the durative future tense of the verb where in vs. 22 Paul instructs us that, "**all humans will keep on being made alive**," or, "everyone will one-after-another be created and produced with Life." We are dealing with what he speaks of in vs. 23: "the set positions in an ordered procession." So from this perspective, "the end" is a "time" that is progressively retreating into the future, until the last person to be born on earth will, in his or her "effect of ordered placement and appointed class," be made alive in Christ – thus making full the complete number of all that were ever a part of the corporate Adam, of which vs. 22a speaks, with all humans alive by being in union with the Anointed One.

Let us consider another approach to this verse, by reading 24a, "next, in order of sequence, **the maturity** [in Christ]…" What if the sequence, here, follows the metaphor of "Firstfruit… MATURITY… harvest"? What if Paul is not speaking of a time sequence but of a growth sequence – from Seed to harvest; from birth to maturity? We read of the "goal" of the edifying (building up) of the Body in Eph. 4:13-14a,
> "**[To go on] until we – the whole of mankind** (all people) **– can** (or: would) **come down to the goal** (or: attain; arrive at; meet accordingly; meet down face-to-face)**: into the state of oneness from, and which is, The Faithfulness** (or: the unity of, that belongs to and which characterizes that which is faith; or: the lack of division which has its source in trust, confidence and reliability, has the character of and is in reference to the loyalty and fidelity), **even which is the full, experiential and intimate knowledge** (or: and from recognition; and of discovery; as well as pertaining to insight) **which is** (or: of; from; in reference to) **the Son of God, [growing] into [the] purposed and destined adult man** (complete, finished, full-grown, perfect, goal-attained, mature

manhood) – **into** (or: unto) **[the] measure of [the] stature** (full age; prime of life) **of the entire content which comprises the Anointed One**

> (or: which is the result of the full number which is the Christ; of the effect of the fullness from the [Messiah]; from the effect of that which fills and completes that which refers to the Christ; of the result of the filling from, and which is, the Christ) – **to the end that no longer** (or: no more) **would or should we exist being infants** (immature folks; not-yet-speaking ones)…" [cf 13:10-11, above]

The "goal," or, "end in view," of this Eph. passage is reaching full, mature growth that is the measure of the effects from the fullness of Christ, so that we are no longer infants.

Perhaps moving to the rest of the verse 24 will come to our aid. This "**purposed goal/maturity**" is described as "**when He would continue passing on the sovereign influence and activities BY God, even [the] Father.**" I have begun with this option of the dative case, "**by,**" indication that God is leading us by His Spirit, which Paul describes as continuously "**passing on the sovereign influence and activities**" to His called-out communities. Is this not a central function of Christ's disciples, so that:

> "**the works** (actions; deeds) **which I Myself am constantly doing** (habitually performing; progressively making, constructing, creating, forming) **that person also will proceed doing** (performing; making; creating; producing), **and he will progressively be doing and producing greater than these, because I Myself am progressively journeying** (traveling; going from this place to another) **toward** (or: facing) **the Father**" (Jn. 14:11)?

He goes on to further explain his meaning:

"**at the time that He would suddenly bring down to idleness** (make unemployed and ineffective; nullify; abolish; render useless and unproductive) **every rulership of government** (all headship and sovereignty), **even all authority and power** (or: every existing right, privilege and what comes out of being – as well as, able-ness and capability)!**"

Let us look to the Writings to guide our understanding to what this means. To what "**authority and power**" is he pointing? Col. 1 should inform us:

> 13. **He who drags us out of danger** (or: rescued us) **forth from out of the midst of the authority of the Darkness** (from Darkness's jurisdiction and right; from existing out of gloomy shadows and obscure dimness; = the privilege of ignorance), **and changes [our] position** (or: transported [us], thus, giving [us] a change of standing, and transferred [us]) **into the midst of the kingdom and reign of the Son of His love**
>
> > (or: into the midst of the sovereign influence of the Son Who has the characteristics and qualities of His accepting love; into union with the sovereign activities of the Son Whose origin is His love; or: into the sphere of the reign of the Son of the Love which is Him; into the center of **the kingdom** of the Son, **which is His love and drive toward union**),
>
> 14. **in Whom** (or: in union with [which Son]) **we continuously have and hold the release into freedom from slavery or imprisonment** (the liberation from our predicament) **[which results in] the sending away of the failures** (or: the dismissal of the errors pertaining to falling short and straying to the side of the target; the flowing away of the sins; the divorce from mistakes).
>
> 15. **It is [this Son] Who is the Image of the not-seen God** (or: the unable to be seen God; the invisible God), **the Firstborn of all creation**
>
> > (or: of every creature; or: of every framing and founding; of every act of settling from a state of disorder and wildness; or: pertaining to the whole creation; or: = the Inheritor of all creation Who will also assume authority over and responsibility for every creature [note: this is the duty of the firstborn]),
>
> 16. **because within Him was created the whole** (or: in union with Him everything is founded and settled, is built and planted, is brought into being, is produced and established; or: within the midst of Him all things were brought from chaos into order) – **the things within the skies and atmospheres, and the things upon the earth** (or: those [situations, conditions and/or people] in

the heavens and on the land); **the visible things, and the unseen** (or: unable to be seen; invisible) **things: whether thrones** (seats of power) **or lordships** (ownership systems) **or governments** (rulers; leadership systems; sovereignties) **or authorities – the whole has been created and all things continue founded, put in order and stand framed through means of Him, and [proceeds, or were placed] into Him** (or: = He is the agent and goal of all creation). Col. 2:10 refers to Christ as "**Him, Who is** (or: exists being) [other MSS: the One being] **the Head of** (or: the Source of) **ALL government and authority**…" And in Col. 2:15 we read of,

> "**Himself causing the sinking out and away of** (or: stripping off and away [of power and abilities]; undressing [them of arms and glory]; putting off and laying away [of categories and classifications]; or: divesting Himself of) **the governments and the authorities** (or: the ruling folks or people of primacy, and the privileged folks). **And then He made a public exhibit, in a citizen's bold freedom of speaking the truth, leading them in a triumphal procession within it [i.e., the cross/suspension-pole]**."

All of this refers to the Christ Event, and now exists as His accomplished work. These do not speak of future events, but rather of past events. We find this same situation described in Rev. 11:15,

> "**Next the seventh agent sounded a trumpet, and great** (or: loud) **voices of themselves came to be** (birthed themselves; occurred of themselves) **within the sky** (or: atmosphere; heaven), **continuously saying, 'The reign of the dominating, ordered System** (of the world of religion, culture, government and economy; or: of the realm of the religious and secular; or: of the aggregate of humanity) **suddenly came to belong to our Lord** [= Yahweh or Christ] **and to the anointed of Him**
>
> > (or: The kingdom of the arranged system of our Lord and His Christ has come into existence; The sovereign influence pertaining to the aggregate of humanity, which belongs to our Lord and His Christ, is birthed!; The rule as King, concerning the world, has come to be the possession of, and now has reference to, [Yahweh], as well as of, and to, His Anointed),
>
> **and so He will continue reigning** (ruling as King) **on into the ages** (or: indefinite time periods) **of the ages** [other MSS add: So it is (Amen)].'"

The **7th trumpet** is the last message: Christ, and His Lordship, which is what the "**great voices**" were "**continuously saying**." These were the voices of the called-out and sent forth folks of the 1st century, and this is the message that they were proclaiming: "Christ rules! Jesus is Lord!" It is the continued witness of those who were slain by the little animal (beast), in Rev. 11:7, and then vss. 11-12 describe what Paul stated in Eph. 2:6. We read a parallel statement Rev. 12:10a, showing that these passages speak of the same Christ-event, from different viewpoints:

> "**Then I heard a great** (or: loud) **voice within the atmosphere** (or: sky; or: heaven) **repeatedly saying, "At the present moment** (or: Just now) **the deliverance** (the rescue; the return to the original state and condition; the health and wholeness; the salvation), **and the power** (or: ability), **and the kingdom** (or: reign; sovereign activities) **of our God was** (or: is) **birthed** (comes into existence; came to be), **also the authority** (privilege from Being) **of His Anointed** (or: which is His Christ; from His [Messiah])…"

The prophecy of this vision in Rev. 11 spoke to events that would happen in the 1st century AD. The proclamation of 11:15 applies to that time, and on into our present time. It is because of all of the above having been accomplished by the Christ Event that he could say in Rom. 8:

> 38. **For you see, I have been persuaded and now stand convinced that neither death, nor life** (or: living existence), **nor agents** (or: messengers), **nor sovereignties** (rulers; those in prime position; or: beginnings), **nor things being now here** (being placed within, at present), **nor things about to be** (impending, or about to consecutively come), **nor powers** (or: capabilities), 39. **nor height** (effect of being high), **nor depth** (or: deep places), **nor any other or different created thing** (or: founded thing; institution; = the Law; = old covenant; = adversaries) **will be having power or be able to separate, divide or part us from God's Love** (or: from the acceptance from God; from the urge toward reunion, which is God; God's full giving of Himself to us) **which is within Christ Jesus, our Owner** (Lord; Master; Possessor).

This list includes all realms of power, and all realms of existence.

What would it mean if we read the first clause, that explains "**the purposed goal and destiny,**" as in the parenthetical expansion: "**when He** may, with and in God, repeatedly transmit the kingdom"? Might this be an allusion to Jesus' words in Mat. 21:43,

> "**I am now saying to you men that God's reign** (or: the kingdom of God; the influence and activity of God's sovereignty) **will be progressively lifted up away from you folks, and it will proceed being given to an ethnic multitude** (or: nation; people group; swarm of people) **consistently producing its fruit**"?

We saw this taking place in the book of Acts, where the sent-forth folks were displaying God's influence and sovereign activities. Remember Jesus' words to His followers in Lu. 12:32,

> "**Stop fearing** (or: Do not continue being wary), **little flock, because it delights the Father** (or: because the Father thought it good, and thus, approved) **to give the reign** (rule; kingship; kingdom; sovereign influence and activities) **to you folks.**"

So WHO is doing the "giving" in this verse? God is. To whom is it given? To His disciples. We see the same picture in Mat. 25:34,

> "**At that time** (or: point), **the King** (or: Reigning One) **will proceed saying to the folks at [the places to] His right, 'Come here, you folks having received words of ease and wellness from** (or: having been spoken well of by; or: having received the blessing of; or: bearing thoughts, ideas, expressions and the Word of goodness from) **My Father! At once come into possession of the inheritance of, and enjoy the allotment of,** [the place of, or realm of] **the reign** (or: kingdom; influence and activity of sovereignty) **having been prepared and made ready from a founding** (a casting down [as of a foundation; or: of seed]) **of a system** (or: of [the] aggregate of humanity; of an arranged order; of [the] world).'"

The King passes on the inheritance of God's reign to His sheep. These passages and the renderings on offer in our present verse (15:24, above) display the picture given in Rev. 3:21, where Christ said that He,

> "**will continue giving** [to the overcomer] **to sit with Me within My throne, as I also conquer** (or: overcame and was victorious) **and sit with My Father within His throne.**"

The Son is in the same throne in which His Father is sitting, and He has accepted us into this same throne (Eph. 2:6). We are now a part of the Firstfruit, and through (by) God's Spirit we are passing on His sovereign influence (kingdom) into the oncoming generations. This has always been the goal, the end in view, i.e., the *telos*. We have been called to be together with God, on His throne – the throne that is in the holy of holies, i.e., within His Temple: which is US!

The bold rendering, "**when He would continue passing on the sovereign influence and activities BY God**" renders the dative case as instrumental, and would speak of Christ, through God's Spirit (i.e., BY God), passing His sovereign activities on to His communities. Note the "divine passive" (in Mat. 21:43, above) in the clause, "**will proceed being GIVEN to an ethnic multitude**…" It is God who transferred His kingdom functions away from the Judean leadership, as Jesus predicted in that statement.

The rendering "with and in God, repeatedly transmit the kingdom" would refer to the joint-participation of Christ and the called-out in spreading God's influence through the proclamation of the Message, and the sphere of this ongoing process would be "in God." The rendering "should keep on committing, handing over and relating the dominion, FOR God" pictures Christ's work in the world that He continues doing "for God" to bring His purposes to fruition.

The traditional dative rendering, "can progressively restore and continue transferring or returning the reign TO God," though grammatically viable, seems to make little sense for the context of what the rest of the NT shares about God's reign, the Good News, and the perceived Plan that threads from Genesis to Revelation. This reading comes from a mistaken futuristic reading of the text, and has no other witness in the NT. It has always been God's kingdom, and Jesus instructed His followers to pray:

"**Make Your reign and kingdom come. Make Your will** (the effect of Your intent and purpose) **come into existence** (happen; come to be; be birthed) – **as within heaven** (or: [the] atmosphere), **so also upon earth**" (Mat. 6:10).

But as it comes, He transfers His operations and sovereign activities to be shared by those who are seated with Him. Let us recall 3:9, above:

"**For we are God's fellow-workers** (or: we are co-workers of, and from, God, and are people who work together with God)."

Verse 25 sheds more light on all this…

25. **For it is binding and necessary for Him to be continuously reigning** (ruling as King; exercising sovereignty) **until which [time or situation]** (or: until where) **He would put** (or: may place; could set) **all the humans that have or hold ruin** (or: the enemies) **under His feet.**

Keep in mind what we just read in Rev. 3:21 – this includes the Body of Christ, as well. The last clause, "**until which** (etc.)," speaks to vs. 23, above, when having been put "**under His feet**" each one is made to be alive in Christ. In the first Adam, ALL humans "**have or hold ruin**," until He heals, reforms (as the pot in Jer. 18:2-4), transforms (Rom. 12:2) and resurrects them.

Now is this still waiting to be done? Let us consider what we read in Eph. 1:

19. **And further, [I pray that you may know] what [is] the continually surpassing greatness** (or: the constantly transcendent, huge extent) **of His ability and power [being given] unto, and into, us – the people continuously believing, progressively trusting and constantly loyal – in accord with** (or: down from and corresponding to) **the operation** (or: energizing; internal working) **of force** (or: might) **of His strength,**

20. **which is operative** (or: which He exerted and inwardly worked) **within the Christ, awakening and raising Him forth from out of the midst of dead folks and then seating Him within** (or: = at) **His right [hand], within the things** (or: among the folks, places or realms) **situated upon the heavens**

> (or: in the super-heavenlies; within the full, perfected heavenlies; in union with the celestials; among the folks [residing] upon the atmospheres),

21. **up over** (or: back above) **every primacy** (or: ruler; principality; government; controlling effect; or: beginning; origin) **and authority** (or: right and privilege from out of being) **and power** (or: ability) **and lordship** (or: ownership), **as well as every name being continually named – not only within this age, but also within the impending one** (the one being presently about to come) –

22. **and then placed and aligned all people in humbleness under His feet** [Ps. 8:6b; LXX]

> (or: and arranges everyone in a supportive position by His feet; or: then by the feet – which are Him – He subjects all things), **and yet gives** (or: gave) **Him, [as] a Head** (or:

Source; origin and beginning of a series; or: extreme and top part) **over all humanity and all things, for the called-out community** (or: and as a Head over all humanity, gave Him to the summoned and gathered assembly; or: and then by the called-forth congregation He gives Him [to be the] Source over [the situation] of, and for, all humanity),

23. **which [community] is His body, the result of the filling from, and which is, the One Who is constantly filling all things within all humanity** (or: humans)

> (or: which continues existing being His body: the resultant fullness, entire content and full measure of Him [Who is] progressively making full and completing all things in union with all things, as well as constantly filling the whole, in – and in union with – all people).

Take note of Eph. 1:23, here, and the description of Christ as being "**the One Who is constantly filling all things within all humanity** (or: humans)." Now let us read the last phrase in vs. 28, below:

"**to the end that God can be all things within the midst of and in union with all humans** (or: may be everything in all things; or: should exist being All in all; or: would exist being everything, within the midst of everyone)."

Can we see that this passage in Eph. 1 is parallel to our passage here in 1 Cor. 15?

26. **[The] last holder of ruin** (or: A final enemy or quality having ill-will) **being progressively brought down to idleness** (made unemployed and ineffective; rendered useless and unproductive) **[is] the Death** (or: Death, a last enemy, is being presently nullified and abolished).

Before we assume that this has not yet happened, let us quote vs. 54, below: "**The Death was drunk down and swallowed into Victory** (or: overcoming)!" And thus, in vs. 55: "**Where, O Death, [is] your victory** (or: overcoming)? **Where, O Death, [is] your stinger** (sharp point; sting; goad; spur)?" Now in vs. 56 we are informed that Paul has been speaking of "**the power and ability of the Sin [which is] the Law.**" It all depends upon the sphere from which we read vs. 26: from being seated with Him in the sphere of the heavens (Eph. 2:6), or from the viewpoint of minding the flesh. Here Rom. 8:6 instructs us:

"**You see, those continuously existing in accord with flesh** (or: = in correspondence to Torah-keeping and cultural boundaries; or: = the human condition) **habitually think about, have an understanding and outlook based upon, are inclined to, set their mind on and are disposed to the things of the flesh** (= the human condition with its cultural traditions, religious cultus and national boundary markers), **yet those in accord with spirit** (or: down from [the] Spirit; on the level of Breath-effect; in line with [His] Attitude) **[think about; have an outlook from] the things and matters of the spirit** (or: the Spirit; Breath-effect; the Attitude)."

Another writing to consider is Heb. 2:14-15,

"**He, nearly alongside as neighbor or lover, also partnered, took hold with, participated in, and shared theirs in common** (partook of the [ingredients] which comprise them), **in order that through means of death He might render useless** (or: deactivate; idle-down; discard) **the one normally having the strength** (or: the person presently holding the force) **of DEATH** (or: WHICH IS DEATH; or: whose source is death), **that is, the adversary** (that which throws folks into dualism with divided thinking and perceptions; or: the one That throws something through the midst and casts division; the one who thrusts things through folks; the slanderer who accuses and deceives) **and would set them free** (or: could fully change and transform these; or: should move them away to another [situation; existence]): **as many as were through all of life held within slavery by fear of death** (or: in fear, from death: or: with fear, which is death)!"

Now did He accomplish this, or not? We would answer that, Yes, He did! And who was it that had become "the adversary'? Paul answered that in Rom. 5:12. The Death came through Adam. And now we see that our next verse (27, below) focuses on "Adam," as "all humanity." The first Adam, of whom all of us are a part, is "the adversary" of humanity. This disconnected (i.e., from God and from other people), "dead" self is that which brings pain and gushes of misery to all of humanity and to all of creation (*cf* Isa. 14:16b; Ezk. 28:1-19).

During this morning's "table fellowship" on the phone with Dan Kaplan, the following thoughts arose from his contemplation on the "fear of death," cited in Heb. 2:15, above. Calling to mind that "The beginning of wisdom [is] fear of the LORD" (Prov. 9:10; Ps. 111:10), Dan brought up Adam's lack of "fear of the LORD." God had told Adam, and Eve had come to know, that the fruit from the tree of the knowledge of good and evil would bring death to them. As noted in Rom. 5:12, Adam's disobedience brought a metaphorical death (separation from the Vine that was in the Garden) that soon led to a physical death of one of their sons. They caused their own death, and from that, the metaphorical death of all humanity. They had rebelled against the "Garden rule," and took that spirit of rebellion with them as they left the Garden.

Verse 27, below, presents the needed remedy: the rebels must be humbled and aligned to His sovereignty. And how was this done? Well, Jacob shared an insight on this:

> "**You folks must consequently be made low** (humbled; demoted; brought to a low station), **in the Lord's sight** (= in [Yahweh's, or Christ's] presence), **and then He will progressively lift you up** (or: continue elevating you)" (Jas. 4:10).

And 1 Pet. 4:8 informs us that,

> "**Love** (the urge toward union; self-giving) **is constantly covering** (habitually throwing a veil over; progressively concealing; [and with other MSS: will be covering]) **a multitude of failures** (mistakes; errors; misses of the target; sins)." [*cf* Prov. 12:10]

Where the fear of death had brought them into slavery (Heb. 2:15), Christ came to set the captives free (Lu. 4:18), and 1 Jn. 4:18a informs us of what God's Love has done,

> "**Fear does not exist within the Love, but rather perfect love** (mature love; love having reached its goal) **repeatedly** (habitually; progressively) **throws the fear outside, because the fear constantly has and holds a pruning** (a curtailment; a checking; restraint; a lopping off – thus, a correction)."

And that is how He did it (Jn. 3:16). Alignment in, and sheltered subjoining to, His Love brings humanity into the liberty of His Life, as Paul said,

> "**For the freedom, Christ immediately set us free! Keep on standing firm, therefore, and do not again be habitually held within a yoke of slavery**" (Gal. 5:1).

Where Adam had transferred humanity into a realm of minding the flesh (being carnally minded), which is **DEATH** (Rom. 8:6), Christ brought us kingdom Love that instilled trust and confidence within us and removed the fear of submission from our hearts. We can now lovingly proclaim, "Jesus Christ is our Master." Where, later in the story, Moses was given the Law "**to the end that the effect of the fall to the side** (or: so that the result of the offense and the stumbling aside) **would increase to be more than enough** (should greatly abound and become more intense)" (Rom. 5:20), Christ became the goal and end of the Law, as we read in Rom. 10:4,

> "**for you see, Christ [is] an end of Law** (or: for Christ [is] Law's goal and destiny; for [the] Anointing [is] termination from [the] Law; for Christ [was the] final act of [the] Law) **[leading] into the Way pointed out in fair and equitable dealings, and rightwised [covenant] relationships of justice in eschatological liberation, to, for and in everyone habitually trusting and believing**
>> (or: because Christ [entering] into the pointed-out Way – in everyone normally exercising faith with conviction, and with each person remaining loyal – [is; brings] Law's climax)."

Before we leave Paul's thoughts in Romans, let us bring into our discussion what he said about Law, and the Commandment, in Rom. 7:

> 5. **You see, when we** [= Adam/Israel] **were existing within the flesh** (or: = in the old alienated Adamic existence, with the flesh sacrifices and markers of the Law), **the effects, impressions, emotions and impulses from the experiences, passions and suffering of the failures** (from the sins and deviations which caused misses of the target) – **the things through means of the Law** [the Torah] – **were continually operating** (working within; energizing and effecting) **within our members into the condition to produce fruit by Death** (in death; to death; for Death).
> 6. **But now** (at the present time), **we** [= Israel] **are** (or: were instantly) **rendered inactive** (brought down to living without labor, released from employment, made unproductive; discharged) **away from the Law** (= the Torah; [some MSS add: of Death]), **dying within that in which we were constantly being held down** (held in possession and detained), **so that it is [for] us to be habitually performing as slaves within newness of spirit** (a newness pertaining to spirit and has its source in the Breath-effect; freshness and new quality of attitude) **and not in oldness** (obsoleteness; outdatedness) **of Letter** (or: not in outwornness of written Scripture)....
> 9. **Now I was at one time** (or: formerly) **habitually living apart from Law** (or: I was once alive, independent from custom and [Torah]); **yet, in connection with the coming of the implanted**

goal (of the impartation of the finished product within; of the inward commandment and directive), **the Sin becomes alive again** (or: deviation, failure, error and the missing of the target revived and comes back to life), **but I die** (or: and I died; yet I die).

10. **Also, the implanted goal** (impartation of the finished product within; inward directive; commandment) – **the one [meant to lead] into Life – this was found by me** (for me; in me; to me) **[to be leading] into death.**

11. **For the Sin** (failure; error; the miss when shooting at a target; the deviation from the goal), **taking a starting point** (receiving an occasion and base of operation) **through the implanted goal** (impartation of the finished product within; inward directive; commandment [to Adam, then to Israel]), **completely makes me unable to walk the Path** (made me incapable to walk out [customs of the Law]; thoroughly cheats and deludes me, making me lose my Way; deceives me; [comment: reference to Eve in Gen. 3:13]) **and through it kills me off** (or: slaughtered me).

Now to see Paul describing the end of the Death, we need to look ahead to what he says, below, beginning in vs. 54b:

> **"The Death was drunk down and swallowed into Victory** (or: overcoming)**!"** [Isa. 25:8]
>
> 55. **"Where, O Death, [is] your victory** (or: overcoming)**?**
>
> **Where, O Death, [is] your stinger** (sharp point; sting; goad; spur)**?"** [Hos. 13:14; note: TR reads "O Unseen (Hades)" in the second line, following the LXX and Heb.]
>
> 56. **Now the sharp point and stinger of** (or: the sting, thus, the injection from) **the Death [is] the Sin** (the mistake; the error; the failure), **and the power and ability of the Sin [is] the Law.**
>
> 57. **But grace and joyous favor [is] in God** (or: by and with God) – **the One presently and progressively** (or: in the process of) **giving the Victory** (or: continuously bestowing the overcoming) **to us, in us and for us through our Lord.**

The death that came from partaking of the tree of the knowledge of good and evil (a figure of the Law) was the beginning of the Death to which Paul refers in Rom. 5:12, Rom. 7, and here in vs. 26. It was the Resurrection of Jesus Christ that brought the end to this metaphorical Death. In Christ, "Death, a last enemy, is being presently nullified and abolished." Death is nullified by resurrection (which is the topic of this present passage). The death of Christ was the second death of the first Adam. John saw a symbolic picture of this in Rev. 20:14,

> "**Next the Death and the Unseen** (or: = the grave) **are cast** (or: were thrown) **into the lake** (or: basin; artificial pool) **of the Fire** (or: the marshy area where there is fire). **This is the second death: the lake of the Fire** (or: the basin which is fire)."

Paul spoke of this as an immersion, a baptism into a "lake," in Rom. 6:

> 3. **Or are you continuing to be ignorant** (are you remaining without experiential knowledge; do you continue not knowing) **that as many as are immersed** (or: were at one point soaked or baptized) **into Christ Jesus are immersed** (or: were then baptized) **into His death?**
>
> 4. **We, then** (or: consequently), **were buried together** (entombed together with funeral rites) **in Him** (or: by Him; with Him), **through the immersion** (baptism) **into the death, to the end that just as** (or: in the same manner as) **Christ was roused and raised forth from out of the midst of dead folks THROUGH** (through means of) **THE GLORY** (the glorious manifestation of splendor which calls forth praise; the imagination; the assumed appearance) **of, from, and which is, The Father, thus also we can walk around** (or: we also should likewise conduct ourselves and order our behavior) **within newness of life** (in union with life characterized by being new in kind and quality, and different from that which was former).
>
> 5. **For since** (or: You see, if) **we have been birthed** (have become; have come to be) **folks engrafted and produced together** (or: planted and made to grow together; brought forth together; congenital) **in, by, to and with the result of the likeness of** (or: the effect of the similar manner from) **His death, then certainly we will also continue existing [in and with the effects of the likeness] of The Resurrection**
>
> > (or: which is the resurrection; or: from, and with qualities of, the resurrection)....

7. **for you see, the One at one point dying** (or: the person at some point experiencing death) **has been eschatologically released and rightwised away from the Sin**

> (or: set in the Way pointed out, away from the Failure; turned in the right direction, away from the deviation and missing of the target; placed into equity and right relationships, away from error; = has been delivered and moved away from The Sin, and has been brought into participation in covenant relationship).

8. **Now since we died** (or: if we die) **together with Christ, we are continuously believing** (relying; trusting) **that we will also continue living together in Him** (by Him; for Him; to Him; with Him),

9. **having seen and thus knowing and perceiving that Christ, being aroused and raised forth from out of the midst of dead folks, is no longer dying. His death is no longer exercising ownership** (or: Death is no longer being lord or exerting mastery pertaining to Him; or: From Him, DEATH is NO LONGER FUNCTIONING AS LORD/MASTER/OWNER),

10. **for it follows that what He died** (or: You see, [the death] which He died) **He died for the Sin** (or: by the Failure; in the deviation; to the Sin; with the Error) **at once and for all [time, and people]** (or: once and only once); **yet what He lives** (or: Yet [the life] which He continues to live), **He continues living in God** (for God; to God; by God; with God).

11. **Thus you folks, also, be logically considering** (reckoning, accounting and concluding) **yourselves to exist being dead ones, indeed, by the failure to hit the target** (or: in the Sin; or: to the deviation), **yet ones CONTINUOUSLY LIVING by God** (in God; for God; to God; with God), **within Christ Jesus, our Owner** (or: in union with [the] Anointed Jesus, our Lord and Master).

You see, in Christ (Who IS the Resurrection) the Death has already been abolished. We enter into this new existence, this new creation, this new Garden-City Jerusalem, when we are placed into the Vine, into Christ, into the immersion in Holy Spirit and Fire. Jesus also spoke of "**[The] last holder of ruin** (or: A final enemy or quality having ill-will) **being progressively brought down to idleness**" in terms of the Domination System (whether that be the Law, religion, or empire), when he said,

> "**be confident and take courage! I, Myself, have overcome and conquered the System** (dominating world; organized arrangement of religion and society; aggregate of humanity) **so that it stands a completed victory**!" (Jn. 16:33b)

27. **For you see,**
> "**He completely arranges, humbly aligns and then appends and puts under shelter all humanity** (or: subjoins, supportively arranges in subordination, and brings under full control, all things) **under His feet** (= as supporting forces in His kingdom)." [Ps. 8:6]

Now when He would say, "All humanity (or: everything) **has been completely aligned and arranged under full, subjected and sheltered control," [it is] evident** (clearly visible) **that [it is] with the exception of, and outside of, the One subjecting the whole** (or: arranging all things and situations in humble, subordinate, attached alignment) **in, by and for** (or: to) **Him.**

Paul first quotes Ps. 8:6 as the prophecy that foretold the work of Christ, and the subjection of ALL HUMANITY to be "supporting forces in His kingdom." Then he makes a statement about what he had just quoted, saying that when God would say such a thing, it is obvious that God is not subjecting Himself when He subjects all humanity and all things under Christ.

We should pause and reflect upon the semantic range of this verb that is usually only translated as "subjected." The first line of Ps. 8:6 is primarily an expanded rendering of this one term: **completely arranges, humbly aligns and then appends and puts under shelter**. With the meaning, "puts under shelter," we have an allusion to 13:7, above, "**[Love] continuously covers all mankind** (progressively puts a protecting roof over all things)."

241

Notice the meanings, "appends" and "subjoins." He makes them a part of His building, household, kingdom, flock, etc. He "arranges and humbly (Jas. 4:10) aligns" them and "puts them under shelter." Wow. This sounds like "having mercy upon all humanity" (Rom. 11:32b). He puts them in His sheepfold, where they have "sheltered control" (Rom. 11:32a).

Paul put the idea of this verse in different words in Phil. 2:

> 9. **For this reason, God also lifts Him up above** (or: highly exalted Him; elevates Him over) **and by grace gives to Him** (or: joyously favors on Him) **the Name – the one over and above every name! –**
> 10. **to the end that within The Name: Jesus!** (or: in union with the name of Jesus; in the midst of the Name belonging to [Yahweh-the-Savior]), **every knee** (= person) **– of the folks upon the heaven** (of those belonging to the super-heaven, or [situated] upon the atmosphere) **and of the people existing upon the earth and of the folks dwelling down under the ground** (or: on the level of or pertaining to subterranean ones; [comment: note the ancient science of the day – a three-tiered universe]) **– may bend** (or: would bow) **in prayer, submission and allegiance,**
> 11. **and then every tongue** (= person) **may speak out the same thing** (should and would openly agree, confess, avow and acclaim) **that Jesus Christ [is] Lord** (Master; Owner) **– [leading] into [the] glory of Father God** (or: unto Father God's good reputation; [progressing] into a manifestation which calls forth praise unto God [our] Father)!

Now this happens to everyone, within their appointed class – the result of having been set within that class (vs. 23, above).

28. **Now when the whole** (or: all things) **would be completely supportively-aligned in Him** (or: attached and appended to Him; subordinately sheltered and arranged by and for Him), **then the Son Himself will also continue being supportively aligned to, fully subjoined for and humbly attached under as an arranged shelter in, the One subjecting, appending and sheltering the whole in Him** (or: attaching all things to Him), **to the end that God can be all things within the midst of and in union with all humans** (or: may be everything in all things; or: should exist being All in all; or: would exist being everything, within the midst of everyone).

This verse is an expansion of what Paul said in Rom. 11:36, "**into the midst of Him, [is; will be] the whole** (everything; [are] all things)." The preposition *eis* (**into**) that is used in Rom. 11:36 prompted me to first choose the locative "**in Him**" as the first reading that ends the first clause, here. The parenthetical readings are equally valid, just presenting other views of what Paul meant in the statement. The universality and total inclusion of these two verses are really impossible to deny.

Consider the idea of being "attached or appended to Him." This is very much like 6:17, above, "being joined to the Lord," and pictures the closest intimacy possible. The reading, "subordinately sheltered and arranged BY and FOR Him" speaks to personal involvement and relationship, as well as to purpose. What this metaphorically "positional" relationship describes is what Jesus tells us in Jn. 17:21, 23, 26:

> "**to the end that all humans would** (or: all people can and should) **continuously exist being one, correspondingly as You, O Father, [are] within the midst of Me, and I [am] within the midst of You – so that they, themselves, may and would also continuously exist being within the midst of Us....** I **within the midst of and in union with them and You within the midst of and in union with Me, to the end that they would** (or: could; should; may; can) **continuously exist being folks having been perfected** (brought to the destined goal; finished; completed; matured and purposed) **into one – so that the human aggregate** (System; world of culture, religion, economics and government) **can** (or: could; would) **progressively come to know through experience that You commissioned and sent Me forth, and You love, accept, and urge toward reunion with, them correspondingly as** (or: just as; in the same sphere and to the same level as) **You love, accept, and give Yourself fully to, Me.... and I made Your Name intimately known to, for, in and among them – and I will continue making It**

experientially known, to the end that the love (acceptance; urge toward union with, and Self-giving to, [all]) **[in; with] which You love** (accept; give Yourself to) **Me can** (would; may; could) **continuously be** (or: progressively exist) **within the midst of and among them – and I Myself within the midst of, among, and in union with them**."

This is the goal, the destiny, the finished product of the Christ Event. It has been happening ever since the resurrection of Christ.

The middle section of the verse, describing the relationship of the Son to the Father, echoes Jesus' sayings:

"**I am progressively journeying toward the Father, because the Father is greater** (or: = more important) **than Me**" (Jn. 14:28).

"**I from Myself am habitually doing nothing** (not one thing), **but rather, according as the Father teaches** (or: taught) **Me, I continue speaking and uttering these things**" (Jn. 14:28b).

"**The Son continues unable to do anything from Himself** (or: the Son, from Himself, habitually has no power to be doing anything [independently]) **except He can** (or: unless He should) **continue seeing something the Father is in process of doing** (or: if not something He may presently observe the Father making, producing, constructing, or creating), **for what things That One may likely be progressively doing** (making; constructing; creating; producing), **these things, also, the Son is likewise habitually doing** (or: is in like manner constantly making, producing, creating, constructing)" (Jn. 5:19).

This is what is meant by what is said, above: "**the Son Himself will also CONTINUE being supportively aligned to, fully subjoined for and humbly attached under as an arranged shelter in, the One subjecting, appending and sheltering the whole in Him** (or: attaching all things to Him)." Christ was, and is the Pattern, as the Head of the body and the Leader of the Last Adam, as He lives out His union with humanity in being The Way, the Path, the Life and the Goal, or as Heb. 6: 20 puts it:

"**[The] Forerunner, Jesus, entered over us** (or: on our behalf; over our [situation]), **down from** (or: in accord with; in the line of [succession of]) **the station** (order; placement) **of Melchizedek, being born** (or: coming to be) **a Chief** (or: Ranking) **Priest on into the midst of the Age** (or: [proceeding] unto the Age [of Messiah])."

As we bring together what each joint of the Body has presented to us, the picture becomes clearer and more complete. It is as the risen Lord told John:

"**Consider this! I am presently making all things new** (or: habitually creating everything [to be] new and fresh; progressively forming [the] whole anew; or, reading *panta* as masculine: I am periodically making **all humanity** new, and progressively, one after another, producing and creating **every person** anew, while constantly constructing all people fresh and new, i.e., continuously renewing **everyone**)!" (Rev. 21:5; *cf* Isa. 43:19; 65:17-25; 2 Cor. 5:17)

Here, in vs. 28, Paul seems to be showing the Son as being in complete solidarity with the rest of humanity. It is as he says in Rom. 8:29b,

"**the [situation for] Him to be** (or: to continually exist being) **the Firstborn among, within the center of, and in union with many brothers** (= a vast family from the same womb; Gal. 4:26)!"

This is why He seats us beside Him (Eph. 2:6; Rev. 3:21). Also, let us keep in mind what Paul said about Christ in Rom. 9:5,

"**the Christ** (= the Messiah), **the [descendant] down the line of flesh** (or: on the level of the human realm) – **the One continuously being upon all mankind: God, worthy of praise and blessing on into the ages! It is so**

(or: – corresponding to natural descent – [is] the Anointed One [= the Messiah] who exists being God: One with a message of goodness, ease and well-being – superimposed on all things – on into the indefinite time periods! Amen – count on it)!"

Paul may be alluding to Zech. 14:9,

"And so [the] LORD (= Yahweh) will continue being King upon all the earth; in that Day there will continue being One Lord (or: one [Yahweh]), and His Name One" (LXX, JM).

Zech. 14:8 prefaced this statement with the proclamation: "Then in that day Living Water will continually and progressively flow forth from out of the midst of Jerusalem" (LXX, JM). Thus, we see that this passage spoke to the Christ Event.

The final clause affirms the message of vs. 22, above, as well as expanding the first clause of this verse. It bears repeating so that its magnitude and glory will not be missed:

"to the end that God can be all things within the midst of and in union with all humans (or: may be everything in all things; or: should exist being All in all; or: would exist being everything, within the midst of everyone)."

Nothing more needs to be said for the reader to see "the end," the goal and destiny of the ages. But we will let Paul speak, again, from Col. 3:9-11,

"[Be] folks at once stripping off from yourselves (undressing yourselves from; or: go out and away from) **the old humanity** (the old human; = the old Adam), **together with its practices, and then [be] suddenly clothing yourselves with** (or: entering within) **the new one, the one being continuously** (or: repeatedly; habitually; progressively) **renewed** (made back up new again, in kind and character) **into full, accurate, added, intimate and experiential knowledge and insight which is down from and corresponds to the image of its Creator, wherein there is no Greek** [figure of the multitudes who are non-Jews, and of those who are cultured and civilized] **and Jew** [figure of a covenant people of God], **circumcision and uncircumcision** [figure for religious in-groups and out-groups; there is no longer a covenant people versus non-covenant people], **barbarian** [foreigner who speaks a different language], **Scythian** [figure or example of wild, uncivilized groups], **slave, freeman, but to the contrary, Christ [is] all, and within all**
(or: Christ [is] all humanity, and within all mankind; or: Christ [is] everything or all things, and within everything and all things; [note: the Greek is plural, and is either masculine, ' signifying "mankind," or neuter, signifying all creation, in these phrases])."

29. **Otherwise, what will the folks now being baptized** (immersed) **continue doing – or what will they continue producing – concerning** (over [the situation] of; for the sake of) **the dead people? If dead folks are not altogether** (actually; absolutely; generally speaking) **being habitually awakened and presently raised up, then why are these folks even being repeatedly baptized** (or: presently immersed, as a normal practice) **concerning them** (over their [situation]; for their sake; in connection with them)**?** [Cf 6:14, above]

This verse has been a quandary for most scholars, but I suggest that it presents the perspective held by first century believers, and was a common practice, regarding their perceived relationship with those who died before coming to hear of the Christ, and thus be baptized – and it appears that their view was one of solidarity with those people. Paul's almost casual remark, with no further explanations, seems to indicate that baptism for the dead was not unusual. He does not criticize the custom, but simply uses it as a part of his argument. Now of course the "dead people" might have been physically living – assuming that those who performed this ritual understood the metaphorical sense of "dead" as Paul taught it. People may have done this to express their solidarity with friends or loved ones who were not yet born from above. It might have been like "praying" for them, and considering that their prayers were answered, even if the "result of having been set, or the appointed class" of those people had not yet arrived, and they were not yet being made alive in Christ (vs. 23, above).

Paul has used this ancient vicarious practice to bring his audience back to the topic of "**dead folks altogether** (actually; absolutely; generally speaking) **being habitually awakened and presently raised up**." His next rhetorical question is part of this same argument…

30. **And why are we constantly taking risks and being in danger all through every hour?**

Paul is now rehearsing the same topic (that there is presently an ongoing resurrection) that he raised in vs. 12, above, and labored on about through vs. 19. In fact, we suggest that he has never really left this topic, but he is here renewing the same kind of argumentation that he presented in those verses. And now he will use his own daily experiences, in the next two verses, to demonstrate how firmly he believes this affirmation, relating all that he goes through on behalf of the reality of this truth, sharing his total commitment to it…

31. **Daily I am repeatedly facing death** (or: progressively dying)! **Brothers, I swear** (or: strongly affirm) **by my reason for boasting!** [other MSS: Yes! On the basis of your own reason for boasting] – **which I continually possess** (hold), **centered in Christ Jesus, our Lord** (Owner; Master) –

Regarding the first clause, we have Paul's statement in 2 Cor. 4:10,
> "**at all times continuously carrying around** (or: bearing about), **among** (or: centered in) **the [corporate] body, Jesus' being put to death** (or: within [our] body the deadening, deadness and state of death, which comes from Jesus; or: within the midst of the body the dying associated with Jesus; or: the dying which is Jesus, in union with the body), **to the end that the life, also, of Jesus** (or: so that also the life which comes from and is Jesus; or: so that Jesus' Life) **can** (or: could; may; would) **be set in clear light and manifested, within our body** (or: in the midst of the body, which is us)!'
See the discussion of this verse in the Comments on 2 Cor., below.

Recall Paul's quote of Ps. 44:22, in Rom. 8:36,
> "**On Your account** (For Your sake; By reason of You) **we are progressively being put to death the whole day! We are logically considered** (accounted) **as sheep which belong to slaughter** (are associated with slaughter),"
But note the contrast of Rom. 8:37, "**But rather** (or: On the contrary), **within all these things we are habitually over-conquering** (we are remaining completely victorious) **through the One loving, urging toward reunion with, and giving Himself to, us**."

The MSS vary in the second statement, but in both textual readings we can assume that Christ is the "**reason**" for the boasting – as is affirmed by the final clause where he states the this boasting is possessed, or held, "**centered in Christ Jesus, our Lord**." We also have 2 Cor. 7:4 as another witness from Paul,
> "**[There is] much freedom of speech, frankness, outspokenness and boldness in me, toward you folks. [There is] much boasting in me, over** (in regard to) **you! I have been filled full so that I am stuffed with relief, encouragement and comfort – I continue overflowing from the progressive flood of superabundance which encircles me in joy – which tops all our pressure and tribulation** (or: by the joy upon every squeezing, ordeal, affliction and oppression)." *Cf* 2 Cor. 8:24

32. **if I fight** (or: fought) **in accord with human [means, methods or purposes] with wild beasts in Ephesus, what [is] the benefit for or to me** (or: how am I furthered by it)? **If dead people are not habitually** (or: continuously; periodically) **being awakened and raised up,**
> "**we should eat and drink, for tomorrow we continue dying away!**" [Isa. 22:13]

We can read about the "wild beasts in Ephesus" (he is speaking metaphorically, here) in Rev. 13, which shows them as an apocalyptic vision. If we consult Paul's list of ordeals that he had literally experienced, we do not find there any mention of literally fighting with wild animals (2 Cor. 11:23-29) – his Roman citizenship would not have allowed for this to happen. But we do see in 2 Cor. 1:8b that, "**we were weighted down** (burdened [with difficulty]) **so as to be without an exit** (with no way out) **for us, even to continue living!**"

Paul's quote of Isa. 22:13 may simply be a reasoned conclusion from observations of how life is. This can be understood in the sense of what we read in Wis. 2:6, 7,

> "Come on, therefore, let us enjoy good things from the continually existing things... let no flower of spring pass us by..."

This thinking came from Jewish wisdom literature, and was focused only on this present life. This is carnal reasoning, from a lack of spiritual insight. So what is the point? Verses 33 and 34 give us the answer...

33. **Stop being led astray** (or: Do not continue being deceived and caused to wander)! **"Worthless associations, conversations or interminglings in a crowd** (or: Companionships of corrupt quality [note: this can refer to sexual encounters]; Bad company or communication) **habitually and progressively corrupt, decay, spoil and ruin useful habits, kind customs and profitable characters."** [note: a quote from a play by the poet Menander]

Recall his directive and admonition in 6:9-10, above,

> "**Do not be repeatedly misled or constantly caused to wander** (or: be deceived). **Neither sexually licentious folks** (paramours; fornicators; [note: may also refer to men associating at idol temple-feasts]), **nor idolaters.... will proceed to inherit a kingdom from God.**"

Paul reaches out to the literature of which he was probably sure that they would be familiar, a known play. Who is he speaking about? Most likely those to whom he referred in 12b, above: "**some among you folks [are] repeatedly saying that there is** (or: there presently exists and continues being) **no resurrection of dead people.**" But, of course, this also serves as a general aphorism to admonish the Corinthians about a wide range of community relationships. A parallel admonition is found in Rom. 12:2, "**stop constantly conforming yourselves in fashion** (or: external show or appearance; guise; scheme) **to** (or, as passive: So then, quit being repeatedly molded by, fashioned for or patterned together with) **this age...**"

34. **Sober up by returning your senses into the Way pointed out, with fairness, equity and rightwised relationships, and stop sinning** (do not continue in error and failure by missing the target), **for some** (or: certain folks) **continue holding an absence of an intimate knowledge of God** (or: habitually possess an ignorance pertaining to God). **I am now saying this with a view toward a turning back within [the situation] by you people** (or: facing shame and humiliation for you folks).

The sharp imperatives that open both vs. 33 and vs. 34 are rhetorical devices to arouse his audience, within the midst of this long letter. But they also serve as stark contrasts to those who deny ongoing resurrection from among the dead folks, as related in vs. 32b, above. We read in *Corpus Hermeticum* 1:27, "O ye people, earth-born folk, ye who have given yourselves to drunkenness and sleep and ignorance of God, be sober now, cease from your surfeit, cease to be glamoured (allured) by irrational sleep!" (trans. by G.R.S. Mead, www.sacred-texts.com; expansion mine; dated from the early Christian era). Paul gave a similar admonition in 1 Thes. 5:6-8a,

> "**Consequently, then, we may not continuously fall asleep [into death? in awareness?] even as the rest** (= as other folks), **but rather, we can and should continuously be aroused and stirred up from sleep** [comment: thus, awake to be alertly watchful; also a figure for being alive] **and sober** (or: clear-headed). **For it follows that the folks continuously falling asleep** (or: drowsing) **are sleeping at** (or: from [the]) **night, and the ones continuously being made drunk are becoming drunk at** (or: from [the]) **night. We, on the other hand, being of Day** (belonging to and having characteristics of [the] Day; having [the] Day as our source), **can and should continuously be sober** (clear-headed)..."

He is bringing them back to the basics of their communal Life in Christ: **the Way** (Christ) **pointed out**... and **rightwised relationships**." By following or adhering to the teachings of those in vs. 12, above, they are in fact, **sinning** – they are continuing in error and failure by missing the target in regard to the importance of Paul's teaching that there continues being a resurrection out from among the dead. He goes on to characterize the situation of these folks as, "**some** (or: certain folks) **continue holding an absence of an intimate knowledge of God** (or: habitually possess an ignorance pertaining to God)." Peter spoke to this situation in 1 Pet. 2:15,

> "**Because thus is God's will** (or: For God's intent and purpose exists in this manner): **folks habitually doing good things** (constructing excellence; performing with virtues; creating goodness) **to repeatedly muzzle** (continuously gag; thus: progressively silence) **the ignorance of senseless and thoughtless people** (humans without intellect and prudence; unreasonable folks)."

We read in Wis. 13:1, "For all human beings who were ignorant of God were foolish by nature... nor, though paying attention to His works, did they recognize the Craftsman..." (NETS). Paul is telling them of their error "**with a view toward a turning back within [the situation] by you people** (or: facing shame and humiliation for you folks)."

There are obviously two nuances in the Greek noun found in this last clause. The first, bold, rendering offers the most literal meaning: **a turning back within**. This would be like saying, "I want you folks to look within yourselves and really think about what I've been saying." The parenthetical rendering would be Paul playing the "shame/humiliation" card on those who lived in an "honor/shame" society. Honor was the most prized thing to have; shame was the thing most to be avoided. Either rendering shows Paul being quite stern to them. Even the opening imperative of this verse is a strong admonition: "**Sober up by returning your senses into the Way pointed out**!" But enough of corrective admonitions... he returns to instruction on this all-important topic...

35. **But still someone will say, "How are the dead ones being habitually** (or: presently; periodically) **awakened and raised up? And in what sort of body** (or: with what kind of material organism) **are they continuing to come** (or: one-after-another going)**?"**

Note that there are two questions that Paul will be addressing: How are they raised; and In what sort of body? Notice that he employs the present tense in both questions. This was understood as a present and ongoing situation. Paul does not correct this view, but rather builds upon the assumption of the reality of it. So we will watch for his answer to how, and to "in what sort of body." His beginning, in vs. 36, appears to indicate that from simply observing nature they should know the answers...

36. **You idiot!** (or: You senseless and stupid fellow!) **What you are habitually sowing is not being progressively brought to life unless it should die off.**

Ah yes, Paul has such good manners; such gracious responses. Yes, he is following his Master, as we read in Jesus' parable in Lu. 12:20. But to the point: he answers with an agricultural metaphor. He did not choose this arbitrarily: Israel had an agricultural economy – there were at least three harvests per year; one for barley, one for wheat and one for grapes. In this argument, we are plants, so put on your gardening hat as you contemplate his word pictures.

Our first observation is that death seems to be the path toward resurrection. The idea of a seed being "**brought to life**" is Paul's picture of "resurrection." Each year there were repeated resurrections, and since this happened every year, we could say that resurrection was **continually**, repeatedly or habitually happening, if we follow Paul's metaphor of seeds and harvests representing resurrection.

Now, think back to the Garden, in Gen. 3. If Adam and Eve had not "died" on that day, through eating from the wrong tree, according to Paul's logic, here, there would be no resurrection. Can we extrapolate from this that there was no "resurrection life" in that Garden existence? Since Jesus proclaimed Himself as being the resurrection in Jn. 11:25 ("**I am the Resurrection, and** {or: that is to say,} **the Life**"), can we further conclude that they did not exist there with the Christ Life? In vs. 45, below, we will see that Paul makes a contrast between the First Adam and the Last Adam.

In Jn. 12:24, Jesus made a statement that says the same thing as Paul does here:
> "**Unless the grain of wheat** (or: kernel of corn; = seed of an agricultural crop), **upon falling into the earth** (the ground; the field), **should die, it by itself continues remaining alone. Yet if it should die, it proceeds to bear much fruit** (= it produces a harvest of many grains, or, seeds)."

If Adam and Eve had not "fallen into the 'ground/earth/wilderness/land' and DIED," by this metaphor they would have remained alone. There would be no 30, 60, 100-fold crops of humanity. Adam and Eve were set-up by God – or, you might say that they were "planted" through that Garden scenario. Adam was a type of Christ (Rom. 5:14). And so, like Jesus' teaching, Paul is teaching that in God's creation there is a necessity of death in order to then have life. In like manner it was necessary for the old covenant to die and pass away (2 Cor. 5:17) in order to bring in the new covenant of Life. Paul explained this in Rom. 8:2, "**For the principle and law of, from and which is the spirit and attitude of 'The Life within Christ Jesus' frees you away from the Law of the Sin and of the Death**." There had to be discontinuity between the old creation and the new creation that His resurrection brought into being. Furthermore...

Jesus also said, of Himself, in Jn. 16:7,
> "**It progressively bears together for you people** (It continues being advantageous and expedient in you; It is now for your benefit) **to the end that I should go away** [i.e., DIE]. **For if I should not go away** [read: DIE], **the One called alongside to aid, comfort, encourage and bring relief** (Helper; Paraclete) **will not come** [other MSS: may by no means come] **to you and be face to face with you folks. Yet if I should journey on** (or: would travel on to another place) [i.e., ascend into the realm of spirit as a Life-giving Spirit – vs. 45, below] **I will habitually send Him to you folks.**"

He knew the Pattern; He had to DIE to give humanity His Life and raise them up to live above the soil, with roots still in the earth. That is the agricultural picture. So, armed with this metaphorical equipment, let us proceed...

37. **And further, that which you continue sowing: you folks are not progressively sowing the body** [= the organism] **which shall be coming into being** (or: that will be developing), **but rather, a naked seed** (a bare kernel, or grain without clothing), **whether it may hit the target of wheat** (= perchance of wheat), **or any one of the rest [of the grains].**

The idea of "**naked seed**" could be an allusion to Gen. 3:10-11, before God made coverings for Adam and Eve, and Paul picks up this same idea of "naked" in 2 Cor. 5:1ff, where in vss. 3-4 he says,
> "**being folks at some point entering within and clothing ourselves** (or: being dressed, also), **we shall not continue** (or: proceed) **being found naked. For we also, being** (continually existing) **within the tent, are continuously groaning, being the ones constantly weighed down** (burdened). **Upon which [situation] we are not wanting to go out from** (to unclothe, strip or undress ourselves) **but rather to fully enter within and to add clothing upon ourselves...**"

But notice how vs. 4 ends: "**to the end that the mortal** (or: this mortal thing) **may be drunk down and swallowed under** (or: by) **The Life**," which corresponds to vss. 53-54, below. All of this speaks of existential realities that relate to us individually (in our own order, class and place in line – vs. 23, above) as we live out aspects of the ongoing story, from Genesis to Revelation.   But all of this is extrapolation from Paul's agricultural metaphor – which, of course, informs us about resurrection, the topic of his ongoing arguments. We may also detect an allusion to Gen. 1:11, since Paul elsewhere teaches in terms of creation (e.g., Rom. 8:19-23; 2 Cor. 5:17).

38. Yet God habitually gives a body to (or: for) **it, according as He wills** (intends; purposed), **and to** (or: for; with) **each of the seeds its own body.**

Now with this picture, Paul reminds folks that people do not "plant" wheat plants, but rather, wheat seeds. We take vs. 38 as speaking of God as the Creator: He created wheat seeds to produce wheat plants. He created olive seeds to produce olive trees. Paul is creating an analogy here. Remember that he is using plants to give us a picture about people being "planted" and then "germinated" (conceived) to be given birth ("sprouted") from out of the womb (i.e., the "earth") into the heaven outside the womb, where we walk "upon" the earth. In saying, "**to** (or: for; with) **each of the seeds its own body**," we read him as pointing to a correlation and a connection between the seed that is planted, and the plant (body) that is germinated and resurrected to live above the ground. He may also be giving a nod to our individuality, as well as to the corporate Seed/Second Humanity (vs. 47, below).

In this agricultural metaphor he is speaking of different seeds producing different plants. The picture is of "classes" or "kinds" of plants. Does this call to mind the appointed "classes" of vs. 23, above? But now he moves to another metaphor...

39. Not all flesh [is] the same flesh, but to the contrary, [there is] indeed one [flesh] of humans (of people; of mankind), **yet another flesh of tamed animals** (or: of livestock), **still another flesh of birds** (or: flyers), **and another of fishes.**

Here he is simply saying the same thing as vs. 38, but this time using the analogy of humans, animals, birds and fish, and this may be why he switches terms – from "body" in vs. 38, to "flesh," here. He is making the two terms synonymous, for his present argument. But the point is the same. An allusion may be to Gen. 1:20ff, and his later listing in Rom. 1:23 also comes to mind.

But why is he saying all this and giving all these metaphors? Is there a subtle significance to his choosing four categories of flesh? Could there be an underlying apocalyptic reference to the four directions, the four faces (which were of different kinds of flesh) of the living beings in the visions of both Ezekiel and John (in Revelation)? Those had human plus animal and bird faces. Paul often thought in apocalyptic pictures. But why not just clearly explain what he means by "resurrection"? Perhaps he is simply bringing the creation into his arguments, as he continues, with cosmological metaphors, below...

40. And then [there are] supra-heavenly bodies (bodies having the characteristics of that upon the dome of the sky, or the upper heavens, the celestial), **and earthly bodies** (bodies which exist upon the land; terrestrial bodies), **but [they are] indeed different: the glory of the supra-heavenly [is] one thing, while the glory** (assumed appearance) **of the earthly [is] different.**

Next, he expands the analogy of vs. 39 to a comparison between what can be seen in the sky and what can be seen on earth. For this part of his argument, he returns to the "body" metaphor, since this present analogy is not speaking of things composed of flesh. There are different "glories," or "assumed appearances," or, we could say, "manifested appearances," throughout the different realms and spheres of creation. Therefore, the topic of resurrection can receive light from, and be understood by, all of creation! This subject is the area of study that theologians call eschatology: the study about things of an end, a finished product, a goal or a destiny. Paul and his contemporaries were living in the end of the age of the Mosaic Law, and of one nation and people group being the focus of God's kingdom economy (cf Rom. 11:17; Eph. 2:15). One age came to an end and a new one began. One age was planted, and the new one was "resurrected."

The word "**glory**" (doxa) has a wide semantic range. It comes from the verb dokeō, which means "to think, imagine, suppose, presume," or, "to seem, to appear." So doxa can mean "a seeming, an appearance, a notion, imagination, an opinion, a supposition, an assumption, a reputation, a manifestation which calls forth praise, or, 'an assumed appearance.'" This analogy from cosmology is the first place where he introduces the idea of different "glories," and he associates these with different "bodies." If we go back to the seed/plant analogy (vs. 37, above) we see that "**God habitually gives a body to** (or: for) **it, according as He wills** (intends; purposed)" (vs. 38). We can thus conclude that in the same way, God gives each supra-heavenly body and each earthly body the "assumed appearance" (or, glory) according as He wills, intends and purposed. So in this analogy, each "body" that God creates has the "assumed appearance (etc.)" which God intends it to have – and we might conclude this to be a particular state of being.

Here, one begins to wonder what all this means, but we will consider this when we discuss vs. 42, because Paul is not yet finished with populating his analogy…

41. **[There is] one glory** (or: splendor) **of [the] sun, and another glory of [the] moon, and another glory of [the] stars, in fact star continues differing from star, in glory and splendor** (or: for you see, [one] star is progressively carrying through and bearing apart in excellence from [another] star).

His argument has moved from looking at a seed to looking at the skies, the universe. Everything has a different "body," and thus a different "glory (or, manifested appearance and state of being)." We should take note of Paul's emphasis on "glory," in vss.40 and 41, for this aspect of the different parts of the universe is a part of the resurrection, as we will see in vs. 42. We read in Col. 1:27 a statement about "the glory,"

> "**the riches of the glory of this Secret** (or: the wealth which has its source in this sacred mystery's manifestation which calls forth praise) **within the multitudes** (among the nations; in the Gentiles; IN UNION WITH the swarms of ethnic groups), **which is** (or: exists being) **Christ within you folks, the expectation of and from the glory**
>> (or: which is [the] Anointed in union with you people: the [realized] hope of the manifestation which called forth praise; or: which is [the] Anointing [and the Messiah] within the midst of you folks – the expectation which is the glory)."

In this particular analogy of vs. 41, we may see a subtle allusion to Joseph's dream in Gen. 37, where in vs. 10 Jacob interpreted the symbols of the sun, the moon and the stars as representing himself, Joseph's father, his mother, and his brothers. But we will not digress from Paul's line of reasoning, for you see…

42. **Thus also** (or: In this way too) **[is] the resurrection of the dead people. It is habitually** (repeatedly; presently; one after another) **being sown within corruption** (or: in union with decay and ruin; in perishability); **it is being habitually** (or: presently; repeatedly; one after another) **awakened and raised up within incorruption** (non-decayability; imperishableness).

So all that he has said from vs. 35 through vs. 41 was to give us pictures and analogies of **the resurrection of the dead people**! But all through those six verses he was speaking about the realities of creation, and in this verse we observe that "**It**" is not only "**habitually** (repeatedly; presently; one after another) **being sown**," but also, "**it is being habitually** (or: presently; repeatedly; one after another) **awakened and raised up**"! The immediate antecedent of "It" is Paul's topic: "**the resurrection**." The term has been personified and is now treated as though it were a seed, but it is in fact the Christ Life – for we see the Pattern in the Life-Death-Resurrection of Jesus. The Seed/seed contains "**the Spirit's law of life within Christ Jesus**" (Rom. 8:2). Now we must keep in mind that he has here returned to the agricultural metaphor of "**sowing [seed]**." At the same time, remember that this seed metaphor is speaking about people, or about people groups (as in Ezk. 37 – the "whole house of Israel"), or (going back to "being made alive in Christ" – vs. 22, above) about all of humanity. Paul is here answering the question of "How," in vs. 35, above.

In this seed analogy, where the seed is **sown within corruption** (the good soil that is full of decaying matter, manure, or things that are "perishable") and then, "**it is being habitually** (or: presently; repeatedly; one after another) **awakened and raised up within incorruption**," we observe what appears to be a recurring cycle, as noted above when we discussed the agriculture metaphors. Therefore, the resurrection is like the germinating and sprouting of a plant (no wonder Jesus and the OT writers used plants to talk about people). And so, life on earth, i.e., above the ground, is "resurrection life" – if a person is a sprouted seed. Now we need to keep in mind what Jesus said of Himself, and about seeds falling into the ground. We know that if there is Life in the Seed, there will be Life in the Plant (Christ's body).

Within any particular cycle, and especially when considering the cycle of an age in God's economy, we see in vs. 53, below, that regarding humanity, a person, a covenant, an age, a creation,

> "**it continues being necessary** (it is habitually binding) **for this perishable and corruptible to at some point plunge** (or: sink) **in and clothe itself with** (or: slip on; put on) **incorruption and imperishability, and for this mortal** (one that is subject to death) **to at some point plunge and sink in and clothe itself with** (or: put on; slip on as a garment) **immortality** (or: the absence of death; deathlessness; undyingness)."

That is always the goal, and this is "resurrection."

But let us consider another writing where Paul spoke of "sowing," in Gal. 6:

> 7. **Do not be continually led astray** (or: Stop being caused to wander and being deceived); **God is not one to be sneered at** (to have a nose turned up at; to be scorned, mocked or treated like a fool), for "**whatever a person is in the habit of sowing, this also he will reap,**"
> 8. **because the person continually sowing into the flesh of himself** (= his estranged inner being), **will progressively reap corruption** (spoil; ruin; decay) **forth from out of the flesh** (= the estranged inner being);
>> (or: the one habitually sowing into the flesh [system], of himself will continue to reap decay from out of the flesh [system];)
> **yet the one constantly sowing into the spirit** (or: the Breath) **will be progressively reaping eonian life** (life having the characteristics of the Age [of Messiah]; or: life from the Age that lasts on through the ages) **forth from out of the spirit** (or: the Spirit; the Breath; that attitude).
> 9. **So – not being people [who are] let loose out from** (or: set free from out of) **[the laboring]** (or: not being made unstrung or exhausted so as to be relaxing [from laboring]) – **we should not in worthlessness be remiss** (or: act badly by failing; be despondent; in bad quality, give up) **in habitually doing** (making; constructing; producing) **the beautiful** (the fine; the ideal; the noble), **for in our own appropriate situation** (or: in our own appointed season; or: to or by our own fitness and proportion) **we will progressively gather in a harvest** (or: will continue reaping).
> 10. **Consequently, then, as we are continuing to hold a fitting situation** [or, with other MSS: while we may continue having occasion or a fertile moment], **we can keep on actively working the good** [other MSS: we should habitually be performing the excellent; we can continue in the business of the virtuous] **toward all humans – and especially toward the families and the households of the Faithful One** (or: characterized by the faith-trust [arising] from [His] loyal act)!

If we sow our lives into the flesh of the first Adam, or into the flesh system of the old covenant, we will not "**progressively gather in a harvest** (or: continue reaping)," but rather "**will progressively reap corruption**." There is now a new place to sow, and be sown: into the spirit; into the new covenant; into Christ's reign. As we follow Christ, carrying our cross (Mat. 16:24), we will be planted into the Spirit of the Age of Messiah, and thus produce a harvest for "**the families and the households of the Faithful One**."

Now back to the sowing seeds: in Mat. 13:38, Jesus said that "the field" is "the world, or, **the aggregate of humanity**." In all of these metaphors, and in what Jesus said of Himself, "**resurrection**" has to do with something within this life here on earth. Resurrection is the life of a plant that ends in a harvest – a multiplication of seeds.

So if we see this metaphor of the seed planted, and then raised, as a cycle of life, a picture of the eonian purpose, we see the union of the two stages of a single cycle, as well as the transformation from stage one to stage two. Is this cycle, represented by the planting and germinating of the seed to a plant in the atmosphere, perhaps a picture of one complete life of a human – the one purposed by God? Is it also a picture of the journey of humanity, from corruption to incorruption? This goal, this "end," is God's "*eschaton*," His purposed Goal. The study of eschatology is about the whole purpose of God as it relates to creation and to humanity – it is about the end of a story that began with death, in Genesis, and "ends" in resurrection, in Christ. But because our end is in God (Rom. 11:36), it is a "never-ending story." Resurrection is always about a new beginning. But Paul has more to say about resurrection…

43. **It is constantly being sown within dishonor** (in union with lack of value; in the midst of worthlessness), **it is being habitually** (or: repeatedly; constantly; progressively; one after another) **awakened and raised up within, and in union with, glory** (a manifestation which calls forth praise; an assumed appearance of good repute). **It is constantly being sown within weakness** (in union with lack of strength), **it is being habitually** (or: repeatedly; constantly; one after another; progressively) **awakened and raised up within, and in union with, power and ability.**

Having read this verse, look back and observe the durative verbs: the "present tense" revealed in the terms "**constantly… habitually** (or: repeatedly; progressively; one after another)." He is talking about an ongoing process, using the metaphor of planting crops. Yet, strongly emphasized is the contrast and discontinuity between the two phases of the single process: **sown… awakened and raised**.

But what is the second layer of his meaning? A seed does not normally have "dishonor." It is not usually considered to be "weak." It's just a seed: good either for food, or to produce more seeds. However, the circumstance, environment and condition of the sphere into which it is sown does have "**dishonor** and **weakness**." In the following verses we will see that he is speaking of people, of humanity, and specifically of Adam and then of Christ.

Adam was the seed in the Garden that was sown into the field of the world (the Land outside the garden), and the context of the story was "**dishonor**." The reason for the sowing was his disobedience, and thus, his **dishonor**. It was a death into an environment of "lack of value" and "worthlessness." But keep in mind that the story of Adam is the story of every human – that is why, in this "earth" realm, there are constant plantings and constant harvests.

But Adam and Jesus are "two people" who represent two corporate humanities, as Paul will explain, below. So the original "planting" was when Adam was cast out of the Garden and into the Land. And time rolled on.

We have Adam's story acted out by Jesus, who entered Adam's story so that "**He might taste of** (or: eat from) **death over [the situation and condition of] all mankind** (or: for and on behalf of everyone)" (Heb. 2:9). He lived out the beginning of Adam's story, which was "death to the Garden environment" that He had with His Father, by submitting to the cross (the cross would have been a figure of the tree of the experiential knowledge of good and evil, a figure of "the Law," where He drank the cup of its fruit and died). But this was the Path to Resurrection. In Jesus, as we saw in 2 Cor. 5:14b, above, all humanity died a second death. Recall Eph. 2:1, that prior to the Christ Event we were all already dead in trespasses and sins. Then Paul informs us, in Rom. 6:2-4, that we were buried with Christ. And then comes the good news, in Rom. 6:5,

"**For since we have been birthed** (have become) **folks engrafted and produced together** (or: planted and made to grow together; brought forth together; congenital) **in, by, to and with the result of the likeness of** (or: the effect of the similar manner from) **His death, then certainly we shall also continue existing [in and with the effects of the likeness] of The Resurrection**

(or: which is the resurrection; or: from, and with qualities of, the resurrection)."
Notice the metaphors that Paul slipped into this verse: "**engrafted and produced together** (or: planted and made to grow together; brought forth together; congenital)." And now from the planting and raising up of One Seed, there is a "body" that is also raised up in the "last (*eschatos*) Adam" (vs. 45, below) that is producing many seeds that are "**within, and in union with, [His] glory**," and are "**awakened and raised up within, and in union with, [His] power and ability**" (vs. 43, here) – which speaks of His Spirit, the Breath-effect that gives humanity its Life. Take note of the word "glory" that he uses, once again. The concept of "glory" is tied to being raised up: **resurrection**! Dare we mention Eph. 2:6, again? Does Heb. 12:22-24 come to mind?

44. **It is habitually** (continually; repeatedly; presently) **being sown a body having the qualities and characteristics of a soul** (a body with the life of a soul and a consciousness of self; or: = a body animated by soul; or: = a natural, psychical entity); **it is habitually** (repeatedly; constantly; presently; one after another) **being awakened and raised up a spiritual body** (a body determined by the characteristics of the Breath-effect, or spirit; or: = a spiritual entity). **Since there is a soulish** (soul-animated) **body, there also is** (or: exists) **a spiritual** (spirit-animated) **one.**

Observe the subject "**It**" that Paul repeats. Resurrection is actually the Seed that is sown! It is "**sown a body having the qualities and characteristics of a soul**." Once it has died, "**it is habitually** (repeatedly; constantly; presently; one after another) **being awakened and raised up a spiritual body**." Think of Jesus' statement in Jn. 11, above: He IS the Resurrection. What is planted is one kind of life; what is resurrected is another kind of Life.

Note the germinal connection between the two "bodies" – they are a progression of the same body. There are two bodies because they each live in different creations. Taking them out of their metaphorical form, these two are the same person: this transformation we see happening now within ourselves and within others. At the end of the life of "**the first human, Adam**" (vs. 45), he "**is habitually being awakened and raised up**" in Christ (vs. 22b, above), or as our next verse puts it, as "**the Last Adam**."

Now in Paul's seed metaphor, the seed and the plant are one. The second grows out of the first (like Eve "growing out" of Adam when he was "put to sleep" – a figure of dying, in order for God to produce her). But the last instruction of this verse tells us that there are two bodies: "**Since there is a soulish** (soul-animated) **body, there also is** (or: exists) **a spiritual** (spirit-animated) **one**." There is a key here, which vs. 45 will explain. First of all, since we see that he is speaking of Adam, and keeping in mind what we learned in vs. 22, above, where it was, "**within Adam all humans keep on dying**" and where in Rom 5 Adam was really "The Many," we suggest that Paul is speaking of two CORPORATE bodies here, but neither of them is a "physical body." Next, in this last statement, Paul presents to his listeners two different realms of existence for the two Adams of vs. 45: the first was the "**soulish** (soul-animated); and last is the "**spiritual** (spirit-animated) **one**." These are figured by the two covenants, and the two houses:

> "**Moses [was] faithful and loyal in the midst of his whole house, as an attending therapeutic and medical care-provider** (or: trainer; cultivator; or: valet; squire; companion in arms)…. **Yet on the other hand, Christ [is faithful and loyal] as a Son upon His house**…" (Heb. 3:5, 6).

We also see the same picture in the sons of the two women in Gal. 4:22-31. In Gal. 4:26, Paul did not mean that "the Jerusalem which is above" is our "physical" mother. He teaches via metaphors. The last statement, "**Since there is a soulish** (soul-animated) **body, there also is** (or: exists) **a spiritual** (spirit-animated) **one**," refers to the two Adams of vs. 45, and is further explained by "**out of the earth/out of heaven**" in vs. 47.

45. **Thus also** (or: In this way also), **it has been written, "The first human** (or: man), **Adam, came for existence** (or: was birthed) **into [being] a living soul**" [Gen. 2:7]; **the Last Adam into [being] a continuously life-making** (life-producing; life-creating; life-forming) **Spirit** (or: Breath-effect; Attitude).

The **first Adam** is the "sowing;" the "**Last Adam**" is the Resurrection. We submit that Christ becoming "**a continuously life-making Spirit**" happened at His immersion by John, when the set-apart Breath-effect (Holy Spirit) descended upon Him (Jn. 1:32; Lu. 3:22), and thus, e.g., He could later call forth Lazarus from the dead (Jn. 11:43). But we also see this evidenced following His resurrection:

> "**He suddenly blows on, and says to, them** (or: He breathes within [them], so as to inflate them [note: same verb as used in Gen. 2:7, LXX], and is saying to them), **"Receive a set-apart spirit!** (or: Get [the] Holy Spirit!; take the Sacred Breath-effect!; or: Receive a sacred attitude)" (Jn. 20:22).

We have seen in Jesus, and now in us, that these two "humans" are the same Person, and are the two aspects of the one plan of the ages. Now Jesus was planted and died in one creation, and was resurrected in the new creation. Has not the Seed of God within us gone through the same journey?

Humanity began as a living soul, or a living being, a person. Now the first humanity was given the ability and the directive to "be fruitful and multiply" – i.e., give life to others, as children. But "**the Last Adam**" came into being (was birthed) "**a continuously life-making** (life-producing; life-creating; life-forming) **Spirit**." This is a remarkable statement. Let us not now suddenly divert from Paul's explanation about resurrection and try to fit this statement into an ontological concept about God, or Christ. Paul is contrasting two realms of existence: the realm and existence of the soul, versus the realm and existence of the Breath-effect/spirit. We saw this in Jesus, when He breathed upon His disciples:

> "**He suddenly blows on, and says to, them** (or: He breathes within [them], so as to inflate them [note: same verb as used in Gen. 2:7, LXX], and is saying to them), **"Receive a set-apart spirit!** (or: Get [the] Holy Spirit!; take the Sacred Breath-effect!; or: Receive a sacred attitude)" (Jn. 20:22).

Christ returned to the Father to continue doing the work of the Father: Breathing God's Breath into His new, Last Adam, body – the called-out communities. He is now being fruitful and multiplying in His new creation. Keep on track: Paul is still speaking about Resurrection.

46. **Nevertheless, the spiritual [is] not first, but rather the one having the qualities and characteristics of a soul** (the soulish; psychical), **then afterwards, the spiritual** (that pertaining to and having the qualities of Breath-effect and Attitude).

Again, two stages of one process, one person, one life. Also, two covenants; two ages; two realms of existence. We are resurrected into the "**afterwards**." In the next verse, Paul puts what he refers to in this verse as "**soulish**," and "**spiritual**," as two different "**humans**." We could also call these two temples, two priesthoods, two covenants, two creations or two **bodies**, for in vs. 44, above, we read "**being sown a BODY having the qualities and characteristics of a soul**... **being awakened and raised up a spiritual BODY**." The sowing represents death/planting, while the raising up represents resurrection. Verse 47 will designate these as TWO Humans/Humanities. In 2:14-15, above, he spoke of the "soulish person as contrasted to the spiritual person – both existing at the same time, in his day. Paul laid it out plainly in Rom. 8:6,

> "**For the result of the thinking** (mind-set; effect of the way of thinking; disposition; result of understanding and inclination; the minding; the opinion; the thought; the outlook) **of the flesh** (= from the human condition or the System of culture and cultus; or: = Torah keeping) **[is; brings] death, yet the result of the thinking** (mind-set; disposition; thought and way of thinking; outlook) **of the spirit** (or: from the Spirit; which is the Breath-effect) **[is; brings] Life and Peace** (joining)."

The difference between the two is determined by one's thinking, mindset, disposition, outlook and the result of understanding and inclination. This is why he said, "**be progressively transformed** (transfigured; changed in form and semblance) **by the renewing** (or: in the renewal; for the making-back-up-new again) **of your mind**" (Rom. 12:2).

What also comes to mind is the term and concept found in 1 Pet. 3:4,

> "**the hidden person** (concealed humanity; cloaked personality) **of the heart, within the incorruptible and imperishable quality of the gentle** (tender; mild; calm; kind; meek) **and still** (at ease; restful; tranquil; quiet) **spirit** (or: attitude; disposition; or: Breath-effect)…"

Furthermore, we have the "old humanity" contrasted to the "new one," in Col. 3:

> 9. **Do not keep on** (or: Stop) **lying unto one another! [Be] folks at once stripping off from yourselves** (undressing yourselves from; or: go out and away from) **the old humanity** (the old human; = the old Adam), **together with its practices,**
>
> 10. **and then [be] suddenly clothing yourselves with** (or: entering within) **the new one** (the fresh one which existed only recently), **the one being continuously** (or: repeatedly; habitually; progressively) **renewed** (made back up new again, in kind and character) **into full, accurate, added, intimate and experiential knowledge and insight which is down from and corresponds to the image** (an exactly formed visible likeness) **of its Creator** (of the One framing and founding it from a state of wildness and disorder).

The idea of "**the spiritual**" coming into being afterwards echoes Jesus' words in Jn. 3:7,

> "**It is necessary and binding for you folks to be born back up again to a higher place** (or: for you people to be given birth from above).'"

With these added insights, we can better understand Paul's contrasted ways of being; ways of living; ways of perceiving; ways of responding. But in vs. 47, Paul contrasts the very origins and substance of these two humanities.

47. **The first human** (person; humanity) **[was/is] forth from out of the earth** (Land; ground; soil), **made of moist soil and dust** (or: having the quality and characteristics of moist dirt that can be poured or mounded; soilish); **the Second Human** (Person; Humanity; [other MSS add: {is} the Lord]) **[is made] out of heaven** (or: [is] from atmosphere and sky; [p46 reads: {is} spiritual]).

First of all, let us remark that the phrases describing the materials, or the origins, of the two humans are grammatically parallel in the Greek MSS from which I have given the bold rendering. The repeated parallelism in this passage should be noted: it is a fundamental aspect of Paul's argument on this subject. Verse 47 is the second half of a two-verse couplet: vss. 46 and 47.

By introducing both the material and the origin of the first person/humanity, we see an allusion to Gen. 2:7, where Adam was formed out of the moist soil and dust of the earth. But keep in mind that Paul's topic is eschatology, as seen clearly in the second half of this verse. The Second humanity is the very incarnation of the *eschaton*, the time and realm of "the end; the goal." Paul may therefore also be drawing the listener's mind into another passage concerning both dust and resurrection: Dan 12:2, the main OT passage about resurrection. So let us rehearse this verse from Paul's Bible, the LXX. We should bear in mind that this passage is apocalyptic, in nature: figurative, symbolic language:

> 1. And then, in that season (fitting situation; fertile moment), Michael [He who is like God; *cf* Jude 9; Rev. 12:7], the Great Ruler (or: Prince; Originator), will proceed in standing back up again (or: in raising Himself up; [note the figure of resurrection] upon the sons of your People [i.e., Israel]. and next there will proceed being a season (fertile moment; appointed situation) of pressure and affliction – such pressure and affliction as has not occurred since an existence of a people-group within the earth (or: from [the] Nation having been birthed on the Land), until up to that season (fertile moment; appointed situation). Within the midst of (or: Centered in) that season (fertile moment) your People will proceed being delivered (rescued; saved; made whole; [Old Greek MS: exalted; lifted up) – all the humans having been written within the scroll.
>
> 2. Next (or: And so) many of those folks continuing sleeping within [the] dust of earth (or: in the middle of a mounded rubble heap of loose soil; or a sepulchral mound of [the] Land; or: centered in an embankment from [the] ground) will proceed being (or: will one-after-another be) raised up

forth from out of the midst: these into the midst of Life of, and pertaining to, the Age [of Messiah] (or: into a life of, for, and having the qualities of, the indefinite ages); and those into the midst of disgrace (reproach; insult; scorning; contempt) and into the midst of an indefinite period (or: age-long) embarrassed humiliation (or: shame, [during the Age of Messiah]. (Dan. 12:1-2; LXX, JM) *Cf* Mat. 25:34, 41, 46; Rev. 20:12, 15.

Another important OT passage to consider is Isa. 26:19,
> "Your dead shall come to life again – My dead body – they shall arise! Awake and shout for joy, you folks that dwell in dust [*cf* Gen. 2:7; 3:19 – same Heb. word], for 'a dew of lights' is your dew [LXX reads: the dew from you is healing to them], and the ground (or: Land) shall give birth to the inhabitants of the 'underworld'." (Rotherham; brackets, modifications, mine)

Don K. Preston, in his book, *The Resurrection of Daniel 12:2, Fulfilled or Future* (JaDon Management, 2016 p 63 n 73) offers these insights:
> "In Hebraic thought, to be 'in the dust' was metaphoric language for being alienated from God, covenantally dead. To be cut off from the land was to be 'dead.' When one follows Isaiah's discussion of Jerusalem, this is easily seen. However, in ch. 52:1f (and 62) Isaiah looks to the time of Jerusalem's redemption under Messiah and calls for Jerusalem to arise from the dust, put on her beautiful garments and rejoice that her days of mourning are over. Thus Jerusalem was 'in the dust' just as in Isa. 26 and in Daniel. She was cast off, separated, alienated from the presence of YHVH."

So we suggest that by Paul describing these two humanities, as he has, he is describing the death and resurrection of corporate humanity, as personified in the figures of the two Adams/two Humans. The resurrection that is described in Dan. 12:2 describes the metaphorical arising of the Second Humanity (as it is joined to Christ) from out of the "dust/sepulchral mound" of the first, "soil and dust" humanity. It is a picture of first Eph. 2:1, followed by Eph. 2:6. It is passing from the old and being raised up into the new.

A covenantal preterist view sees the completion of this in AD 70, on the physical level, in regard to those who went into the fire of Mat. 25:41, 46 and Rev. 20:15. It is pictured in Rom. 11:17 as some of the branches being broken out of the olive tree. It is the baptism in the Holy Spirit and Fire as spoken of by John the immerser, in Lu. 3:16, and in Mat. 3:11 (where John addressed this to the Pharisees and Sadducees – whom he characterized as a "generation of vipers" and told them that "**the ax is already continuing lying [being focused] toward** (or: facing toward) **the root of [their] trees**," in vs. 10).

Now let us consider the experience of Jesus. Again, we see that the two humans are one, the second one just being a transformed human, the New Being (as Paul Tillich calls it). The source of the Second is the same phrase that describes the source of the House from out of the midst of heaven, in 2 Cor. 5:2, our dwelling-house (habitation) – the one from out of the midst of heaven – and although it is a different metaphor, we think that they are parallel thoughts. Now we agree that the house (in 2 Cor. 5) and the person (here, in vs. 47b) are one and the same thing. We suggest that the Second Human was birthed from out of the midst of the First, as with Mary being the mother of Jesus, and "the Jerusalem that is above" (Gal. 4:26), or the "heavenly Jerusalem" (Heb. 12:22), being our mother. We read of Adam being put to sleep (a figure of death) in Gen. 2:21, and from out of him came his wife, his body (bone of his bone; flesh of his flesh). The types and figures are rehearsed and intertwined from Gen. to Rev. It is the story of God's great work: the New Humanity that is made of, and is birthed from out of, heaven (the atmosphere that covers, and shelters, the earth). What Paul sketches out here is more fully developed in Rom. 5.

48. **As [is] the person made of and having the character and quality of moist soil or dust** (mounded or poured dirt), **of such sort also [are] the people [who are] made of and have the character and quality of moist soil or dust** (soil-ish folks); **and likewise, as [is] the Heavenly Person** (or: the one

256

made of and having the quality and character of the supra-heaven), **of such sort also [are] the supra-heavenly people – those made of and having the quality and character of the supra-heaven** (or: the finished and perfected atmosphere, or the added sky).

Does this not describe us now? Are we not now seated with Christ among the celestials? If not, then we are ones who have only the character and quality of moist soil and dust. Because of being raised up, resurrected in Christ, we are NOW "**the supra-heavenly people – those made of and having the quality and character of the supra-heaven** (or: the finished and perfected atmosphere, or the added sky)." The term "supra-heavenly" gives the force of the term "heavenly" that has the preposition *epi-* prefixed to it. The "finished and perfected atmosphere, or the added sky" is an apocalyptic picture of the Anointing coming upon the human, who then becomes "clothed with Christ" (Rom. 13:14a; Gal. 3:27).

These two corporate people – the "soilish" and the "supra-heavenly" – are the same two groups with the contrasting functions and characteristics of which Paul speaks in 2 Cor. 3. Notice the comparisons, there:

> "**The attending service of the Death... a beaten impression of types and the outlines of patterns that exists as engravings within letters and the effects of written texts chiseled on stones... the glory... being progressively unemployed and nullified**" (vs.7). In contrast to...
> "**The attending service and dispensing of the provision of the Spirit... continues being in glory**" (vs. 8). And further...
> "**The attending service and dispensing of the corresponding evaluations and commensurate decisions which follow the pattern... to a much greater degree does the attending service and the dispensing of the eschatological deliverance into fairness and equity in rightwised relationships progressively surround and continuously exceed in glory**" (vs.9). And so...
> "**The transcending glory... is constantly surpassing [that one], and is progressively over-casting [us]**" (vs. 10). Now compared to the old, which was "**being made ineffective and nullified**"...
> "**to a much greater extent is the continuously remaining one** (the dwelling, abiding and enduring one) **[existing] within the midst of glory**" (vs. 11).

We see these contrasts in the teachings of Jesus, and all through Paul. They are all speaking of the same thing, and here Paul is speaking of two corporate persons: one earthly; one spiritual and pertaining to the heavens/atmosphere.

49. **And correspondingly as we bear and wear the image** (likeness; form) **of the mounded, dusty person,** [*p*46 adds: doubtless] **we can and should** [B reads: will continue to] **also bear and wear the image** (likeness; form) **of the supra-heavenly One** (or: belonging to the One having the quality and character of the finished, perfected atmosphere; or: from the fully-heaven [sphere]; of the added-sky person).

He says it almost matter-of-factly: as we have been in the image of the mounded, dusty person, we can, and of course should, "**also bear and wear the image of the supra-heavenly One**." That is our destiny, because as He took us all to the grave, he also raised us all up. That was the Father's plan, all along.

I follow the reading of Nestle-Aland text following Aleph, Alexandrinus, *p*46, Codex Bezae, and many others, which read the aorist subjunctive, not the future, as B and a few others do. The aorist suggests that we should now be wearing the image of the supra-heavenly One.

As to the word "**image** (likeness; form)," let us recall Rom. 8:29,

> "**because those whom He foreknew** (whom He knows from previous intimate experience), **He also marked out beforehand** (determined, defined and designed in advance) **[as] copies** (joint-forms) **of the image** (material likeness; portrait; form) **of His Son** (or: He previously divided, separated and bounded conformed patterns from the image/form of His Son) **into the [situation**

for] Him to be (or: to continually exist being) **the Firstborn among, within the center of, and in union with many brothers** (= a vast family from the same womb; Gal. 4:26)!"

That this is happening now, and how it happens, is given in 2 Cor. 3:18,

"**But we all, ourselves – having a face that has been uncovered and remains unveiled** [note: as with Moses, before the Lord, Ex. 34:34] **– being folks who by a mirror are continuously observing, as ourselves, the Lord's glory** (or: being those who progressively reflect – from ourselves as by a mirror – the assumed appearance and repute of, and from, [our] Owner), **are presently being continuously and progressively transformed into the very same image and form, from glory unto glory – in accord with and exactly as – from [the] Lord's Breath-effect** (or: from [the] Spirit and Attitude of, and which is, [the] Lord [= Christ, or, Yahweh])."

We find Paul saying something similar in Phil. 3:21,

"**Who will continue transfiguring** (progressively refashioning and remodeling; continuously changing the form of) **our body from the low condition and status** (or: the body of, and from, our humiliation; or: **the body which is us**, pertaining to this lowliness) **[to be] joint-formed in, and conformed by, to and with, the body of His glory** (or: from, and which is, His assumed appearance; [other MSS: into the {situation} for it to be brought into existence conformed to, and having the same form together with, His body, from that which calls forth praise and imagination for His character and good repute]), **down from** (or: in accord with; in the sphere of; to the level of; following the pattern of; in stepping with; commensurate with; as directed by) **the inwardly-centered operation** (functioning energy; inner-working) **of the [conditions, situation or sphere for] Him to be continuously able** (or: to progress with power) **also to humbly align The Whole to and in Himself** (or: to subject and subordinate all things for Himself; to arrange everything under so as to have full control and to support [it] by and with Himself)."

50. **Now I am saying this, brothers** (= fellow members and believers), **that flesh and blood** (= humans in their estranged condition; = people of dust who have not been resurrected) **have no power and continue unable to inherit or receive and participate in an allotted portion of God's reign** (kingdom or sovereign action) **– neither is corruption and decay** (the perishable) **continuing on to inherit** (participate in the allotment of) **the Incorruption** (Imperishability).

This statement is a summation, and a conclusion of what he has presented from vs. 42 through vs. 49. It is what follows from the first-Adam/Christ antithesis, and is what he was, or had been saying! It was not a new thought. Verses 51-54, which follow, simply describe the process of the transformation of the first Humanity into the Second Humanity. This transformation is, in fact, the Resurrection about which he is teaching. The first Adam, like the old covenant of Law, cannot "**inherit or receive and participate in an allotted portion of God's reign**," for the first Adam/Humanity was planted into corruption and decay – the result of the Death. Thus the need for Resurrection.

We see here that Paul is speaking of the natural, unregenerated person when he uses the term "flesh and blood," or, as elsewhere, "humans in their estranged condition." This would also apply to a person who was still living in the realm of the old covenant of Law. It is the resurrected Christ within us who inherits all things, and who shares this with us. The Plant receives the inheritance of the DNA of the Seed. It is that within one person, with earth (soil) and heaven (air) joined, and IN UNION, that the inheritance is received, resurrected into Life, and then bears the fruit.

And, as usual, there is a second layer of interpretation here. The "flesh and blood covenant" cannot "**inherit or receive and participate in an allotted portion of God's kingdom and sovereign activities**" – it "**has no power and continues unable**," for you see,

"[The] **preceding implanted goal** (impartation of the finished product and destiny within; inward directive) **is being born** (or: comes into existence) **because it [was] without strength and**

without increase (without help, profit, benefit or gain) – **for you see, the Law perfects nothing** (brought nothing to its goal or destiny; finishes nothing)" (Heb. 7:18-19a).

And as Paul said, in Rom. 8:3,

"**You see, [it was] the powerlessness and inability of the Law** (from the written code; = associated with Torah) – **within which it kept on making [folks] weak and feeble** ([note: the active voice]; but as an intransitive: in which [incapability] it was constantly falling sick and continued being without strength) **through the flesh**..."

Likewise, the corruption and decay of the old continues unable "**to inherit** (participate in the allotment of) **the Incorruption**" – on either layer of interpretation. Returning to Paul's agricultural metaphor, the new crop of grain grows in the air of the atmosphere, not in the soil with the roots. But the roots have their place, and bear up the new plant (Rom. 11:18). There is both continuity and contrast.

51. **See** (Look and consider)! **I am progressively telling you a secret** ([the] mystery)! **We, indeed, shall not all continue falling asleep, yet we all will continue being changed**

> (or: On the one hand, not all of us will continue [dying], but on the other hand, we all will be progressively altered;
> or: We all shall not continue being put to repose, and so we all shall keep on being transformed;
> or: All of us shall not continue sleeping, but we all will continue being rearranged to be another or made to be otherwise),

I suggest that here Paul was inserting a comforting promise to his first century readers: the Lord was soon to come in an event that would finalize the end of the old covenant, with the destruction of Jerusalem, and one event would happen to them all – they would all be changed and altered. But also, this was now the unveiling of a new **secret**/mystery.

On offer are four renderings of this secret, which Paul shares in typical Jewish parallelism. We will not quote these again, but simply point out the durative future tense, governed by the negative in the first clause, and the durative, or progressive future tense of the second clause – set in the positive proclamation. The MSS vary, slightly, in their texts. Of interest is A* which does not include the negative (not):

> "Indeed we – all people (the whole of humanity) – will one after another fall asleep, and we – all people (the whole of humanity) – will one after another be changed to be other than we were."

My last two alternative renderings suggest that "sleeping" or "reposing" was to end. Paul shared another "secret/mystery" in Rom. 11:25,

> "**You see, I am not willing for you folks to continue being ignorant of this secret** (or: mystery), **brothers** (= fellow believers; family) – **in order that you folks may not continue being prudent, thoughtful or discreet by** [other MSS: among or within; other MSS: beside] **yourselves** (or: = be conceited) – **that a petrifying, from a part** (a stone-like hardening in some measure; a callousness [extending over] a part), **has been birthed and come into existence in Israel** (or: has happened to Israel) **until which [time]** (or: to the point of which [situation]) **the effect of the full measure** (or: the result of the entire contents; or: = the full impact and full compliment of forces) **from the nations** (or: of the ethnic multitudes; or: – which are the Gentiles –) **may enter in.**"

It is obvious that this "secret" involves something that would happen here, in this life – at some time. For a discussion of this Rom. 11:25 verse, see my *Just Paul, Comments on Romans*, Harper Brown Pub. 2014. The "entering in" was a reference to entering the kingdom of God, symbolized in that chapter as being grafted back into their own olive tree (Rom. 11:17, 23). In Rom. 11:15b Paul made a revealing statement about the unbelieving of Israel being grafted in again:

> "**what [will be] the receiving** (the acceptance; the taking or drawing toward one's self as a companion or associate) **[of them be] if not life forth from out of the midst of dead folks?!**"

Now that is Resurrection language! Receiving them back into the "olive tree" is resurrection from among dead folks. You see, folks, it's all about being joined to the Vine (Jn. 15:1ff). Different metaphors; same truth.

52. **within the midst of an instant** (or: in union with what is uncut and indivisible), **in a rapid sweep, blink or glance of an eye, within, or in union with, the midst of the last or final trumpet. You see, the trumpet will continue sounding** (or: For He will proceed to be trumpeting; Indeed, it will keep on trumpeting), **and the dead people will one-after-another be awakened and raised up** [A, D and others: will keep on standing back up again; will continue being resurrected] **incorruptible** (imperishable). **And so we ourselves will keep on, one-after-another being changed** (or: progressively be made otherwise, altered and transformed).

If the "last trumpet" refers to the 7th trumpet in Rev., then what he just said already happened, at least with the preterist view. Another obvious connection is with 1 Thes. 4:16-17,
> 16. **because the Lord** [= Yahweh or Christ] **Himself will descend from heaven within a shout of command, within the midst of [the] Chief Agent's** (or: an original messenger's; or: a chief and ruling agent's; or: [the] beginning messenger's) **voice, and within** (or: in union with) **God's trumpet** [note: figure of a message or a directive for action], **and the dead people within Christ** (or: in union with [the] Anointed One) **will raise themselves up** (or: will stand up again) **first** (or: in first place)
> 17. **Thereupon** (or: After that; As a next step) **we, the living folks, the ones continuing to be left around, will at the same time be seized and snatched away** (carried off by force) **into the midst of air – together with them within clouds – into the Lord's meeting** ([Christ's or Yahweh's] encounter). **And thus** (in this way) **shall we always be** (or: exist at all times) **together with [the] Lord** [= Christ or Yahweh].

Note that the location of this meeting is in the air, among the clouds – two figures of the realm of spirit, or heaven (our atmosphere), and also the place of a plant which blossoms forth and bears its fruit in the heavens, while its roots sink deep into the earth. So connecting these two passages – if this indeed should be done – places the resurrection in the context of an upward call from the Lord, to have an encounter with Him. The language of both contexts is apocalyptic in nature, and should be understood as being figurative, not literal. Jesus used the figure of a trumpet in Mat. 24:31 when referring to the 1st century activities of His followers (which is recorded in the book of Acts):
> "**And then He will continue sending His agents** (messengers; folks with the message) **off on a mission 'with a great trumpet** (perhaps: = a large shofar; or: = a loud trumpet blast; [note: a figure of a publicly proclaimed message or instruction]),' [Isa. 27:13] **and they will progressively be fully** (or: additionally) **gathering together His picked out and chosen folks from out of the four winds – from [the] heavens'** (or: atmospheres') **extremities: until their farthest points** (= from the four quarters of the land, from one end of the sky to the other)!"

We find this apocalyptic imagery in Rev. 8:2-21, and in Rev. 11:15 we observe the "**last trumpet**" as being the 7th trumpet, in that vision.

The "**change**" is from being "**dead people**" to being "**one-after-another be awakened and raised up incorruptible.**" This word "incorruptible" picks up his thoughts in vs. 50, above, where "**inheriting or receiving and participating in an allotted portion of God's reign**" is related to "**inheriting** (or: participating in the allotment of) **the Incorruption.**" And now, in vs. 52, following the statement of "the dead people" continuing in being resurrected "incorruptible," Paul gives another explanation of what this means: "**And so we ourselves will keep on, one-after-another being changed** (or: progressively be made otherwise, altered and transformed)." Here, the conjunction "and so" connects the two thoughts "resurrected incorruptible" with "being changed and transformed." And Paul says that this referred to himself and his audience, just as he did with the audience in the 1 Thes. text, above. In both letters he says, "**we.**" He spoke of this "change" in Phil. 3:

20. **You see, our citizenship** (result of living in a free city; or: commonwealth-effects; political realm) **continues inherently existing resident within the midst of [the] atmospheres** (or: heavens), **from out of where we also continuously receive and take away in our hands from out of a Deliverer: [the] Lord** (or: a Master), **Jesus Christ,** [*cf* 2 Cor. 5:1, 4, 6, 8]

21. **Who will continue transfiguring** (progressively refashioning and remodeling) **our body** (or: **the body which is us**, pertaining to this lowliness) **from the low condition and status [to be] joint-formed in, and conformed by, to and with, the body of His glory** [*cf* 2 Cor. 3:18], **down from** (or: in accord with; in the sphere of; to the level of; following the pattern of; in stepping with; commensurate with; as directed by) **the inwardly-centered operation of the [conditions, situation or sphere for] Him to be continuously able also to humbly align The Whole to and in Himself** (or: to subject and subordinate all things for Himself; to arrange everything under so as to have full control and to support [it] by and with Himself).

In that passage, vs. 20 corresponds to Gal. 4:26, the "free city, Jerusalem," which is above. Notice that from this "atmosphere," or "realm of living," "**we also continuously receive and take away in our hands from out of a Deliverer: [the] Lord, Jesus Christ**." Then vs. 21 explains that He "**will continue transfiguring** (progressively refashioning and remodeling) **our body** (or: **the body which is us**, pertaining to this lowliness) **from the low condition and status [to be] joint-formed in, and conformed by, to and with, the body of His glory**." Reading the personal pronoun as in the genitive of apposition, it reads "the body which is us." His body is a corporate body (12:12, above) and this is the body of His glory (Christ in you the expectation of glory – Col. 1:27).

Now note the connection of resurrection with power, in vs. 43, above. Next, in vs. 44, we saw that it is "**being awakened and raised up A SPIRITUAL BODY**." In 45, above, Paul is relating both to resurrection and to the two bodies. We have the first human, Adam (the soulish person) and we have the Last Adam Who is a continuously life-making, life-creating, life-giving Spirit. The resurrected person is a spirit. This is the spiritual body (the "**afterwards**" person of vs. 46). The first Adam was corporate humanity, in this context; the Last Adam is the corporate spiritual body of Christ, with Jesus as its Head.

Verses 48-49 described humans transfigured to be conformed to His body of glory, and vs. 47 told us that they are "[**made] of heaven**/atmosphere," this latter being parallel to the "**made of moist soil and mud**" of the first clause. The "made of heaven" is a figure for the spiritual. Having the quality and character of the supra-heaven and wearing His image is equivalent to being conformed to the body of His glory.

What Paul describes here, in vs. 52, corresponds to what we read in Col. 3:4, but for its context, let us consider vss. 1-3, as well:

1. **Since, therefore, you folks WERE awakened and ARE raised up together in the Christ** (or: If, then, you are aroused and raised with the Anointed One), **be constantly seeking and trying to find the upward things** (or: the things being above), **where the Christ is** (exists being), **continuously sitting within the right [side]** (or: at the right [hand]; = at the place of receiving, and in the place of honor and the power) **of God.**

The verb "**raised**" is in the aorist tense, so could either be a simple past tense in English, or a simple present. – thus the two options. Either way, we are aroused and raised. When? When Christ was raised. It was "together with Him." We have been a part of the first resurrection (the Corporate Christ, the Firstfruit from among dead folks). Therefore we are seated with Him in the heavenlies (realms having authority upon the heavens, or the realm of spirit) – Eph. 2:6 – and we should seek out and try to find the "**upward things**," or the things being above, as opposed to the things below. Our focus and attentions should be on Christ and His position of reigning at God's right "hand." We are participating in the reign, or kingdom, of the heavens.

2. **Be constantly minding** (thinking about; setting your disposition and sentiments toward; paying regard to) **the upward things** (or: the things above), **not the things upon the earth,**

3. for you folks DIED, and your life has been hidden so that it is NOW concealed together with the Christ, within the midst of God (or: in union with God).

Verse 2 is a restatement of the admonition in vs. 1, expanding it, then vs. 3 restates the fact of the Christ event given in vs. 1, from the perspective of the past event of our dying "**together with the Christ,**" as well as referring back to 2:12 – "**buried together in Him** (jointly entombed with Him)," and 2:20, "**you folks died together.**" Then he explains that our life has now been hidden – concealed – together with the Christ. So Christ is also concealed. Where? Within His body, His house, which is at the same time both within the heavenlies and upon the earth. And all of this is "**within the midst of God, and in union with God!**" And so Paul tells those at Athens "**within the midst of and in union with Him we continuously live...**" (Acts. 17:28). Lightfoot reads, "All your thoughts must abide in heaven.... you *died* once for all to the world: you are living another life," and further on says, "You must not only *seek* heaven; you must also *think* heaven" (ibid, p. 206-7). Note the perfect tense of the verb in the second clause of vs. 3. It is a completed work.

The "**upward things** (or: the things above)" refer first to the realm "**in the Christ**" into which we were "**raised**" (vs. 1), but then to our life in "**the Jerusalem above**" (Gal. 4:26), which is a figure of the covenant community, and the "**invitation to an above place** (or: an upward call)" that Paul refers to in Phil. 3:14. The "atmosphere, or heaven," is what is above, and this is a metaphor for the realm of God and the realm of spirit, as contrasted to the earth, which is a figure to living in the natural realm: either realm can be lived in within this physical body, here on literal earth. Our "**expectation** (or: hope)" – ch. 1:5 – comes from living in and by these "**upward things.**" This is equivalent to 2 Cor. 3:18, "**continuously observing the Lord's glory**" so that we are "**progressively transformed into the very same image**" of Christ. It calls to mind Paul's words in Rom. 12:1, where we are called "**to stand [our] bodies alongside [the] Well-pleasing, Set-apart, Living Sacrifice by God.**" Our identification with Christ in His death is our "**sacred service.**" As Lohse says, "What was once, no longer applies. The old life has been put aside forever through the death which they died together with Christ" (ibid., p. 133). Now consider that this all happened before they had even heard of Christ.

4. Whenever the Christ, our life [other MSS: your life], **may be brought to light** (or: should be manifested), **you folks also will be brought to light** (will be manifested), **together with Him, within the midst of glory** (or: in union with a manifestation which calls forth praise; or: in a good reputation; or: = in His manifest presence)
> (or: When Christ, the Anointing, can be manifested, then your life – even you yourself, together with Him – will be manifested in His manifest presence).

So the entire Christ (Jesus and His body) have been hidden and concealed, but vs. 4 speaks of both Him and us being brought to light, manifested together. This manifestation comes within the midst of glory – i.e., in union with a manifestation which calls forth praise and establishes a good reputation. Note that Paul says, "**Whenever...**" This can be interpreted as saying, "At any time where Christ may be brought to light, we **also will be brought to light together with Him.**" This happens during the proclamation of the good news. The light is a figure of knowledge, of understanding. He is the Light of the ordered system (John 8:12); we are the light of the ordered system (Matt. 5:14) – we are now light in the Lord (Eph. 5:8), being "**living epistles.**" His glory is manifested when He is manifested, for His presence is the glory. When we manifest Him, bring Him to light, we bring Him glory and manifest His glory, or, His good reputation.

This transition has reminded the Colossians of what was then (and is now) the new reality of the new creation, while beginning the admonitions of where their thinking should be. The covenant community is a manifestation (the bringing to light) of Christ, and brings glory to the Father.

(Jonathan Mitchell, *Peter, Paul & Jacob, Comments on Colossians,* Harper Brown Pub. 2012 pp 98-99)

Now let us observe Paul's words in Rom. 8:11,

> "**Now SINCE the Breath-effect** (or: Spirit; Attitude) **of the One arousing and raising Jesus forth from out of the midst of dead folks IS continuously housing Itself** (making His abode; residing; making His home; by idiom: living together as husband and wife) **within, and in union with, you folks, the One raising Christ Jesus forth from out of dead ones will also CONTINUE progressively giving Life to** (or: will even habitually make alive) **the mortal bodies of you folks** (or: your mortal bodies) **through the constant indwelling of His Spirit** (or: the continual in-housing of His Breath-effect; the continuous internal residing of the Attitude, which is Him,) [other MSS: because of His habitually-indwelling Spirit] **within and among you folks.**"

This is an ongoing process that results from dwelling in the Vine.

Next he carries on with this theme of "**incorruption**" in the next verse, so before we come to a conclusion of what this means, let us read on…

53. **For it continues being necessary** (it is habitually binding) **for this perishable and corruptible to at some point plunge** (or: sink) **in and clothe itself with** (or: slip on; put on) **incorruption and imperishability, and for this mortal** (one that is subject to death) **to at some point plunge and sink in and clothe itself with** (or: put on; slip on as a garment) **immortality** (or: the absence of death; deathlessness; undyingness).

Where did Paul speak of something that was "**corruptible**"? Yes, just above, in vs. 42, where speaking of humanity being sown as a seed, he said it was, "**sown within corruption** (or: in union with decay and ruin; in perishability)," and like being clothed with "**incorruption and imperishability**" here, in vs. 53, back in vs. 42 he concludes with the seed's destiny of being "**awakened and raised up within incorruption.**" And all of this is still describing his theme of resurrection. Furthermore, this is all set within the agricultural metaphor of the planting of a seed and then receiving a harvest. Consider the fact that agricultural metaphors relate to existence here, in this life. Planting, sprouting, growing and then harvesting are all in this life. Likewise with death (that we experienced in the 1st Adam) and resurrection (that we experience in Christ).

And so when Paul speaks here about "**this perishable and corruptible**" and "**this mortal** (one that is subject to death)," he is speaking of we who have been planted in the earth (the place of death and corruption), as a part of the first Adam. Therefore, what is the "**incorruption, imperishability and immortality**"? Well…

This is the same thing as clothing ourselves with Christ, or "putting on Christ." The parallels of "**incorruption**" and "**immortality**" are synonymous – both are descriptions of Christ. Paul rehearses this same thought in 2 Cor. 5:4, "**to fully enter within and to add clothing upon ourselves, to the end that the mortal** (or: this mortal thing) **may be drunk down and swallowed under** (or: by) **The Life**" (*cf* vs. 54, below). It is one of Paul's imperatives, something that it is necessary to do, and the process is viewed as the instant act of a snapshot (the aorist tense). It is like what he says in Eph. 6, when we are told to put on "**the whole armor, which is God.**" Again, the language here does not suggest a future event, but an immediate necessity – plunging and sinking into the midst of Christ. Consider Peter's words in 1 Pet. 1:23,

> '**being folks having been born again** (been regenerated; been given birth back up again), **not from out of a corruptible** (or: perishable) **seed that was sown, but rather from an incorruptible** (imperishable; undecayable) **one: through God's continually living and permanently remaining *Logos*** (or: through a message or expressed thought of [the]

continuously living and constantly abiding God; or: through means of a living and dwelling Thought, Idea and Logically laid out Expression, Communication and Word, which is God)."
Notice the passive voice (this was the action of God) and the perfect tense (His action has been completed) of the verb "**born again (regenerated; given birth back up again)**" of the first clause, and now consider how this is done through an "**incorruptible seed**," i.e., God's *Logos* (Word; etc.). And how about 2 Tim. 1:10?

> "**and now** (at the present moment), **being set in clear light so as to become visible** (or: manifested) **through the bringing to full light** (or: the complete shining upon; the full appearance in light; the complete manifestation by light) **of our Deliverer** (Savior; Rescuer), **Christ Jesus – on the one hand, idling down death** (or: The Death) **so as to make it unproductive and useless, yet on the other hand, illuminating** (giving light to) **life and INCORRUPTIBILITY** (the absence of the ability to decay; un-ruinableness) **through means of the message of goodness, ease and well-being.**"

Can the present reality of all this be said more clearly? But there is more:

> "**Grace and favor, in union with INCORRUPTION** (or: within a state or condition of being unspoiled, and being incorruptible [note: see 1 Cor. 15:42]), **[are] with all the people continuously, unrestrictedly loving, fully giving themselves to, and experiencing the urge toward reunion with, our Lord** (or: Owner; Master), **Jesus Christ** ([the] Anointed Jesus). **Amen** (It is so; Count on it)!" (Eph. 6:24).

The late 1st century AD (or early 2nd cent.) *Odes of Solomon* makes an insightful statement in 15:8,
> "I have put on incorruption through His Name, and stripped off corruption by His Grace" (trans, by J.H. Charlesworth, *The OT Pseudepigrapha*, Vol. 2, ibid p 748).

In regard to what is "**perishable**," let us ponder Jesus' words in Mat. 16:25,
> "**You see, whoever may intend** (or: should purpose; might set his will; happens to want) **to keep his soul-life safe** (rescue himself; preserve the conscious life that he is living) **will continue loosing-it-away and destroying it. Yet whoever can loose-away and even destroy his soul-life** (the consciousness of self) **on My account, he will continue finding it!**"

Connecting these dots, we can now understand the "whenever" of our next verse...

54. **Now whenever** [other MSS add: this corruptible would (or: may) put on incorruption and] **this mortal would** (or: may) **plunge, sink in and clothe itself with** (or: slip on; put on) **the Immortality, then will continue taking place** (or: proceed being birthed; successively come into existence) **the word** (the thought; the message; the saying) **which has been written,**
> **"The Death was drunk down and swallowed into Victory** (or: overcoming)!" [Isa. 25:8]

Paul grounds his arguments about the change from mortal to immortality in a quote from Isaiah. Don Preston (ibid p 59ff) does a masterful job of connecting the dots between the prophecies of Isa. 24-27, the Dan. 12 passage, quoted above, and the NT prophecies such as Mat. 23 where Jesus reached back to the blood of Abel being shed (Gen. 4) and that of all the martyrs since him and up to Jesus' time, indicating that the judgment for all of that would come upon His own generation. He states that "virtually every OT prophecy of the resurrection posits the resurrection in the framework of the time of judgment of Old Covenant Israel" (ibid p 57). He further connects Dan. 12 to Rev. 11 and Rev. 20 (ibid p 69) as all speaking to a 1st century context.

Has not this prophecy of Isa. 25 been fulfilled in Christ? Have we not already taken the plunge into Him who alone is Immortal? We read in 1 Tim. 6:
> 16. **the Only One continuously holding and having possession of immortality** (deathlessness), **the One continuously making inaccessible** (or: unapproachable) **light His home** (or: dwelling), **Whom not one of mankind sees, saw or perceived, nor is able or has**

power to see or perceive, in Whom [is] honor (value; worth), **and eonian strength** (might having the qualities and characteristics of the Age; strength enduring through and pertaining to the eons). **It is so** (Amen)!

It is our being immersed into Christ that accomplishes this, and we saw above (in the verses cited from Rom. 6) that this has already happened. The only way there is a resurrection is by the Death (the Death spoken of in Rom. 5:12, which became "the disconnect" from the Garden covenant/arrangement in Gen. 3) being "drunk down" (the cup that the Father gave Jesus to drink) and swallowed INTO Victory (the resurrection of Christ),

55. **"Where, O Death, [is] your victory** (or: overcoming)**?**
     Where, O Death, [is] your stinger (sharp point; sting; drover's goad; spur)**?"** [Hos. 13:14; note: TR reads "O Unseen (Hades)" in the second line, following the LXX and Heb.]

56. **Now the sharp point and stinger of** (or: the sting, thus, the injection from) **the Death [is] the Sin** (the mistake; the error; the failure), **and the power and ability of the Sin [is] the Law.**

So why does Paul bring in the Law here? Because it is the realm of death of which he has been speaking (Rom. 7, quoted below). Christ's death brought an end to the Law, bringing it to its goal: "Christ in US, the expectation from the Glory" (Col. 1:27). It was the Law that brought death: the tree of the knowledge of good and evil in the garden; the Law in Israel, ever since.

We read in Rom. 7:

> 9. **Now I was at one time** (or: formerly) **habitually living apart from law** (or: I was once alive, independent from custom and [Torah]), **yet, in connection with the coming of the implanted goal** (impartation of the finished product within; inward directive; commandment), **the Sin becomes alive again** (or: deviation, failure, error and the missing of the target revived and comes back up to life), **but I die** (or: and I died; yet I die).
>
> 10. **Also, the implanted goal** (impartation of the finished product within; inward directive; commandment) **– the one [meant to lead] into Life – this was found by me** (for me; in me; to me) **[to be leading] into death.**
>
> 11. **For the Sin** (failure; error; the miss when shooting at a target; the deviation from the goal), **taking a starting point** (receiving an occasion and base of operation) **through the implanted goal** (impartation of the finished product within; inward directive; commandment), **completely makes me unable to walk the Path** (made me incapable to walk out; thoroughly cheats and deludes me, making me lose my Way; deceives me) **and through it kills me off** (or: slaughtered me).

The LXX offers an interesting reading of the first line of Hos. 13:14, "Where, O Death, [is] the way to which you point (or: the right Way)?"

In a conversation with Dan Kaplan, he offered a correlation between "**the Law,**" referred to here, in vs. 56, and the human will. It was Eve's will that came into play when she chose to listen to the serpent and to then eat of the tree of the knowledge of good and evil. It was Cain's will that led to him killing his brother. All through recorded Scripture, it is human will that led to rebellion against God. In choosing one's own will over "the Way pointed out," that person makes his or her will a law within himself or herself. This "law," this self-determination, will always give power and ability to sin: to deviate from the Path, to fail to live in Love, and to miss the target of union with Christ and others. And this always leads to some form of death. By following our Master, as His disciple, we are called to deny our "self" – our will – and walk the path of putting our soul (in this case, our will) to death as we carry our execution stake (a figure of the tree of the knowledge of good and evil) [Cf Mat. 16:24-25]. Jesus drank His cup in the garden, by saying to the Father,

> "**My Father, if it is possible** (or: since there is power; if it be able), **let this cup pass away** (or: go to the side, away) **from Me! Nevertheless, more than this, [let it be; it is] not as I**

continue willing (wanting; intending), **but to the contrary, as You [will and intend]**" (Mat. 26:39b).

Now Paul brings to a close his teaching about death and resurrection with a reference to the Law, and here, in vs. 56, we conclude that it was the Law that brought the death, and it was the resurrection from this old covenant, of which Jesus said, "I am the resurrection and the life" – John 11:25. So, thankfully, we learned from Paul that,

> "**Christ [is] an end of Law** (or: for Christ [is] Law's goal and destiny; for [the] Anointing [is] termination from [the] Law; for Christ [was the] final act of [the] Law) **[leading] into the Way pointed out in fair and equitable dealings, and rightwised [covenant] relationships of justice in eschatological liberation, to, for and in everyone habitually trusting and believing**
>
> > (or: because Christ [entering] into the pointed-out Way – in everyone normally exercising faith with conviction, and with each person remaining loyal – [is; brings] Law's climax)."

In vs. 56, we see that "**the sting, thus, the injection from the Death**" was "**the Sin** (the mistake; the error; the failure)" of Adam – as in Rom. 5:12, "**The Death thus also passed through in all directions into all mankind** (or: into the midst of humanity; or: to all people), **upon which [situation, condition, and with the result that] all people sin.**" If we read the Greek term as "**the sharp point,**" or "the drover's goad," (in relation to the Law), then we may have a clearer understanding of Acts 26:14b,

> "**To keep on kicking [your heel] toward [the] goads** (sharp points; e.g., as with an ox-goad; = futilely resisting) **[makes it] hard for you.**"

Saul had actually been kicking against the Law, by his persecution of the called-out folks. Thus did he become the foremost of sinners (vs. 9, above; 1 Tim. 1:15b).

The last clause, "**the power and ability of the Sin [is] the Law,**" calls to mind Rom. 5:

> 20. **Now Law and custom at one point entered in alongside** (or: intruded into the situation by the side) **to the end that the effect of the fall to the side** (or: so that RESULT of the OFFENSE and the stumbling aside) **would INCREASE to be more than enough** (should greatly abound and become more intense). **But where the Sin** (the failure; the divergence and missing of the target) **increases** (or: abounded to be more than enough; becomes more intense) **THE GRACE** ("the act producing happiness, which is granted as a favor" – Jim Coram) **at once super-exceeds** (or: hyper-exceeded) **over and above, surrounding to excessive abundance and overflow,**
>
> 21. **to the end that JUST AS the Sin** (the failure; the erroneous act; the deviation and digression which issued in missing the goal) **at one point reigned** (or: ruled as king; exercised sovereign sway) **within, and in union with, the Death, THUS SO** (or: in THIS way) **also the Grace and joyous favor would reign** (should rule as king; can exercise sovereign sway) **through an eschatological deliverance that created rightwisedness** (or: by means of being rightly-turned into an existence with equity in [covenantal] solidarity of right relationships which accord to the Way; through a liberating Justice-[expression]) **[which leads] into Life which belongs to, pertains to and has the characteristics of the Age** (or: eonian life; Life of the Age [of Messiah]; a life for the ages) **– through Jesus Christ, our Owner** (Lord; Master). *Cf* Rom. 6:23; 7:7-20

And so, look at what Paul proclaims in the next verse...

57. **But grace and joyous favor [is] in God** (or: by and with God) **– the One presently and progressively** (or: in the process of) **giving the Victory** (or: continuously bestowing the overcoming) **to us, in us and for us through our Lord** (Owner; Master), **Jesus, [the] Christ!**

God is "the One constantly giving **the Victory**" over death and the Law, through the Resurrection which is Jesus Christ, our Lord – what a gift! And take note of the present tense of the verb. Paul says that "**the Victory**" is over "**the Death**" (vs. 54b-55, above), and that God is "**presently and progressively** (or: in the process of) **giving the Victory** (or: continuously bestowing the overcoming) **to us, in us and for us**." Christ already gained the Victory, and now He was continuously giving it (as Himself) to us!

Let us consider Paul's statement on "raising the dead" when he was speaking to Agrippa, in Acts 26:

> 6. **"And yet now I stand being repeatedly** (or: constantly) **judged** (or: put on trial) **based upon [the] expectation** (or: hope) **of the promise having been birthed into our fathers** (= ancestors) **by God –**
> 7. **"unto which [promise] our twelve-tribed [people], constantly rendering sacred service in earnest perseverance night and day, is continuously hoping and expecting to attain. Concerning this expectation I am now being indicted** (or: charged) **by the Jews, O king.**
> 8. **"Why does it continue being judged unbelievable** (or: is it repeatedly decided [to be] incredible) **among** (or: by) **you folks – since God periodically** (or: habitually; constantly) **raises dead people?"**

Further, Paul said in vss. 13 and 16, above,

> 13. **Now if there is presently no resurrection of dead people** (or: if there continues being no resurrection of dead ones; if a resurrection of dead ones does not constantly exist), **neither has Christ been awakened and raised up.**
> 16. **For if dead ones are not habitually** (or: presently, one after another; periodically) **being awakened and raised up, neither has Christ been awakened and raised up.**

58. **Consequently, my beloved brothers, progressively come to be seated and settled folks – immovable and unswerving people – continuing to always be surrounded by more than enough** (or: superabounding) **within the midst of the Lord's work** (= [Yahweh's or Christ's] deed or act), **having seen and now knowing that your fatiguing labor** (or: toil) **does not exist without contents** (is not empty) **within and in union with [the] Lord** [= Christ or Yahweh].

As we think back over Paul's letter, we recall the upheavals within the community that came through factions being formed about this or that teacher. The community was unsettled, with some moving this way, and some moving that way. He touched on several issues, ending with this in-depth presentation about the resurrection. If they could receive his instruction that they were already seated together with Christ (Eph. 2:6), and thus had already been resurrected with, and in, Him, they would become settled and immovable – an unswerving temple of God that would be "**surrounded by more than enough**" as they continued "**within the midst of the Lord's work**." Yes, even though they had entered into the Lord's rest (Heb. 4:1), there remains the "fatiguing labor" of sowing the *Logos*, the Message of Christ, into the field of the world around them, and the work of the cross within their midst. There was the progressive building of the Temple (ch. 3, above), as God digs out the gold and silver from the group, and forms the precious stones within each member of the body. He picks up the theme he began in vss. 12-14, above, reminding them that because of Christ's (and our) resurrection, the labor "**does not exist without contents** (is not empty)." They are people "**having seen and now knowing**" the reality of the message – the Good News. He once again affirmed this to them in 2 Cor. 8:7,

> "**But further, even as you folks continuously superabound within everything and among everyone – in faith** (or: with trust; by loyalty) **and in word** (or: by thought, idea, reason, and message; with information) **and in experiential knowledge and by insight, as well as with all haste to earnest diligence, and in the Love** (with unrestricted acceptance; by self-giving) **from out of the midst of us in union with you** [other MSS: the love from you [that is] within us] **– that you may be progressively superabounding, centered in this grace** (amidst this favor), **also**."

And then, in 2 Cor. 9:8,

> "**Moreover, God is constantly able with continuous power to furnish all grace to surround and to make every favor superabound into** (or: into the midst of) **you folks, to the end that, continuously having every ability in yourselves to ward things off and constantly holding all self-sufficiency and complete contentment at all times [and] within every [situation] and**

in union with every person, you can (or: may; should; would) **continuously superabound into every good action, excellent deed and noble work**."

What a paraclete Paul was to Corinth!

Chapter 16

1. **Now concerning the collection [being gathered] into the midst of the set-apart folks** (or: for the holy ones; unto the saints), **just as I thoroughly arranged in** (or: for) **the communities of the called-out of [the province of] Galatia, you yourselves do** (perform; make) **the same:**

Now Paul turns to the practical matter of collecting donations for the Jerusalem community, and then speaks of his future traveling plans. In 2 Cor. 8:3-4 he made reference to the Macedonian community, and how:

> "**corresponding to [their] power and in accord with [their] ability, and even beyond [their] actual power and ability, [they are] those who act spontaneously and voluntarily from their own initiative, with much appeal and calling of us to their side to give us relief, assistance and encouragement** (performance of a paraclete), **repeatedly and constantly begging of us, and from us, the grace** (or: the favor) **and the common participation** (partnership and sharing from common existence) **of the attending service which pertains to the dispensing into the set-apart folks**." *Cf* 2 Cor. 9:1, 12.

We also read in Rom. 15:26,

> "**You see, Macedonia and Achaia take delight and were well-pleased to make some common sharing** (a certain participating contribution from partnership in common existence) **into the poor** (unto the destitute) **of the set-apart folks** (holy ones; saints) **in Jerusalem**."

The called-out communities lived in solidarity with other communities throughout that region. They lived in union with other members of Christ's body.

2. **on one day of the week** (or: on one of the sabbaths) **let each one of you have the habit of putting [something] beside himself** (= at home), **continually storing up that in which he may be repeatedly prospered** (or: has been led, along a good path; other MSS: can be well-guided along the way) **so that whenever I may come, no collections may continue to happen at that time.**

Notice that there was no "financial program" and no apparent organized system of the called-out in Corinth. Those were the days before religion sank in its claws.

3. **So whenever I should come to be at your side, whomsoever you folks may approve – after having examined and tested them – through letters [of introduction and recommendation] I will send these folks to bear** (carry) **off your grace into** (the favor from you folks [in the form of a gift] unto) **Jerusalem.** *Cf* Acts 20:1ff

4. **And if it should be appropriate** (or: worthwhile) **for me also to be traveling on [there], they will continue journeying [there] together with me.**

5. **Now I shall come to you folks whenever I can** (or: may; = should happen to) **pass through Macedonia, for you see, I am repeatedly passing through Macedonia.**

6. **So perhaps I shall aim toward you folks to temporarily lodge, or even spend the winter, so that you folks can yourselves send me forward** (= give me funds and supplies for my journey), **wherever I may continue traveling.**

7. **For I am not presently intending** (purposing; willing) **to see you right now, while passing by, for I continue expecting to stay on with you folks some time, if the Lord** [= Yahweh or Christ] **should turn [circumstances] upon [this plan]** (or: may turn [the outcome] upon [us to decide]; or: should instruct, or permit).

We should note, and consider for our own lives, how Paul sees the Lord as being both active and decisive concerning his plans. These were simply practical matters that Paul views as concerns of the Lord, for his daily life.

8. **Yet I am now continuing to remain on within Ephesus, until the [feast; festival] of Pentecost,**
9. **for a door, great and energetic** (working within; activated and operative), **has been opened for me, and stands wide open to me: even many men constantly lying in opposition**
> (or: for you see, a great and inwardly effectual entrance has been opened back up in me, and remains open again in me, and yet many folks [are] ones habitually lying in the opposite position).

We see the "divine passive" voice in the verb, indicating that Paul is saying that God is the One that has opened the door for him. The verb is in the perfect tense, telling us that the opening was done in the past, and that the door yet stands open. He does not further explain what he means, but it is normally assumed that he is using this metaphor to indicate that it is an opportunity, giving him access to the folks in Ephesus.

Now the final, subordinate clause can be taken in different ways, depending in part by how we render the conjunction – whether as "even," or as, "and yet." The bold translation reads "**even many men constantly lying in opposition**" as Paul viewing this situation as a "wide-open door" for God's kingdom to pass through with ease. The fact that the **door** is described as "**great and energetic**" calls to mind Jesus saying, "**I will progressively be constructing and building up My House – the called-out, covenant community. And even gates of [the] Unseen will not continue bringing strength down against it**" (Mat. 16:18), The parenthetical reading sees those who are "lying in the opposite position" as being in contrast to this open door, so that there is an open door, but there is still opposition.

10. **Now if Timothy can** (or: may; should) **come, be constantly seeing [to it] that he should come to be fearless toward you folks, for he continues actively working** (or: performing as a worker on/in) **the Lord's** [= Christ's or Yahweh's] **work** (deed; action), **as I also [do].**
11. **No one, then, should make nothing of him** (scorn, despise or treat him with contempt; slight him), **but should send him forward in peace from the joining** (= with shalom) **with funds and supplies, so that he can** (may; should) **come toward me, for I continue receiving [benefit] from out of him, together with the brothers** (folks of the same womb; = believers).
12. **Now concerning Apollos, the brother, I called him to my side many [times] to give aid, comfort and encouragement** (or: = I strongly urged him), **to the end that he should go to you folks with the brothers, and yet there was not altogether a purpose so that he should go now** (or: but it was not wholly [his] will {or: it was undoubtedly not [His] intent} that he should go at the present time), **yet he will proceed in going** (or: coming) **whenever there may be a good situation** (or: he may have an opportunity).

13. **You folks be habitually awake and constantly watching** (= be alert and with your wits about you)! **Continue standing fast in union with the Trust, and within the midst of The Faithfulness** (or: Constantly stand firm, centered in loyal confidence)! **Progressively come to Manhood** [= Adulthood] (or: = Be constantly courageous)! **Continue being strengthened.**

The first imperative "be habitually awake and constantly watching," echoes Mat. 24:42, 43; 25:13; Mk. 13:34-37 as well as Acts 20:31. We also find Paul using this same verb in Col. 4:2 and in 1 Thes. 5:6. Then this same admonition is in Rev. 3:2, and in Rev. 16:15 we read, "**The one continually watching** (or: in wakeful vigilance) **and keeping guard upon his garments [is; will be] blessed** (or: a happy person)," and this was in the context of a coming of Christ, as a thief! Jesus, Paul and the risen Christ all indicated His imminent activity within the lives of the called-out communities, as in Rev. 2 and 3, and what would turn out to be His judgment upon 1st century Jerusalem, within the time that they were living.

Both the first and second imperatives could also apply to their daily lives within Corinth. All followers of Jesus faced opposition in that time, and countless multitudes have also faced the same, ever since. As the first century opposition often came from the Jews who did not accept the idea of a crucified messiah, in later times the institutional churches would oppose those who held different views of Christ and of God. Paul put it this way, concerning the Judaizers who wanted to drag the communities of Galatia back into Law observance:

> "**For the freedom, Christ immediately set us free** (or: [The] Anointed One at once frees us in, to, for and with freedom)! **Keep on standing firm, therefore, and do not again be habitually held within a yoke of slavery** (or: a cross-lever [of a pair of scales] whose sphere is bondage)
>> (or: Continuously stand firm, then, in the freedom [to which the] Anointing sets us free, and let not yourselves be progressively confined again by a yoke pertaining to servitude)!
> (Gal. 5:1) *Cf* Phil. 4:1b

Paul calls them to grow up into the Manhood of Christ – i.e., be mature and not infants – and then gives both an imperative and an impartation in the form of the present tense, passive voice, "**Continue being strengthened**," (by God, is implied). He said it this way, in Eph. 6:10,

> "**be constantly empowering yourselves within** (or: finding or engendering ability within yourselves), **centered in and in union with [the] Lord – even within, and in union with, the force** (or: strength) **of His might**."

Paul may have also had Ps. 30:25 (LXX) in mind:

> "Take courage and let your heart be strong, all you who hope in the Lord" (NETS).

Or, as my sister, Rebecca, reminded us of Jesus' words to Peter,

> "**Don't you** [singular: = Peter] **let the heart of the group be continually shaken or concerned** (unsettled; agitated; troubled; disturbed)" (Jn. 13:38b [or: Jn. 14:1a, in the common versions]).

14. Let this continuously occur: all of you folks [be] in union with Love (Let it be repeatedly birthed: all centered in your unrestricted, self-giving urge toward reunion, with accepting solidarity; or: Let all from you folks happen, and come to be, in Love that participates in the other person as standing on the same ultimate ground, in spite of the distorted state of the other – Tillich)!

This is a one-sentence synopsis of chapter 13, above. The Love of which he speaks is, of course, God, who is the only One and place of "union with Love." The parenthetical expansions offer broadened views of what Paul meant, here, and Paul Tillich's insights into *agapē* color in the picture.

15. Now I continue calling you to my side to help and encourage you (or: So I am now performing as a paraclete), **brothers** (= my fellow believers; folks from the same Womb) **– you have seen and known the household of Stephanas and Fortunatus, that it is [the] firstfruit of Achaia, and they orderly arranged themselves into attending service for and among the set-apart folks** (holy ones; saints; sacred people) **–**

Here he points to folks that they know as examples for "orderly arranged themselves into attending service." The message is clear: do likewise. Note, again, that these "house-assemblies" (as noted in vs. 19, below) had no apparent organizational structure. The emphasis was on functions and services to people. And so he continues…

16. so that you folks can also be progressively aligned with humility to (or: habitually arranged under to give support for and among, and to be attached to) **such folks** (persons of that kind), **and for everyone habitually working together** (or: with all those constantly co-operating) **and exhaustively laboring** (toiling).

In other words, pull together with such as these. He was not promoting a life of "easy living," but rather of "exhaustively laboring and toiling" in the building of God's House (as in chapter 3, above).

17. **Now I continue rejoicing at the presence of Stephanas and Fortunatus and Achaicus, because these men fill up the deficiency belonging to you** (the result of your shortcoming; the effect of your being behind and in the rear; [other MSS: our deficiency]),

He is speaking as their father, noting that others had taken up the slack in order to "fill up the result of [their] shortcoming."

18. **for they rest, refresh and soothe my spirit – as well as yours. Therefore, come to progressively know and recognize such folks completely, by personal intimacy and continued experience with them.**

In other words, get to know these folks and imitate them – they are a blessing to the Body of Christ. Paul uses the term "spirit" in a generalized way, here. He is referring to his inner state of being and mental bent or attitude in regard to the situations in Corinth. Consider how he used this word in Gal. 6:18,
> **"The grace and favor of, and whose origin and source are, our Lord, Jesus Christ [are continually] with your spirit.**"
Compare this with Phil. 4:23,
> **"The grace of** (or: The joy-bringing favor belonging to and having its source in; The grace which is) **our Lord** [with other MSS: the Owner and Master], **Jesus Christ, [is] with the spirit of you folks** (or: [is] with your corporate breath-effect; or: [is] with the character and attitude manifested through you folks; [other MSS: {is} with all of you])."

19. **The called-out folks** (or: called-out communities) **of the [province of] Asia habitually greet and embrace you folks. Aquila and Prisca** [other MSS: Priscilla] **continue giving you many embraces and much greeting, within [the] Lord** [= Yahweh or Christ], **together with the called-out assembly down in their house.**

Kummel observes: "Since Paul sends greetings from the churches of Asia, he has, therefore, already worked a while in the province" (ibid p 205).

20. **All the brothers** (folks of the same Womb) **constantly greet and embrace you folks! Continue to greet and embrace one another with a set-apart** (holy; saintly; sacred) **expression of affection** (or: kiss).
21. **This greeting to embrace you [is] in** (or: by; with) **my own hand – Paul's.**
22. **If anyone continues having no fondness or affection for the Lord, let him constantly be a person placed up [in prayer to be consecrated before the Lord] – [you see,] our Lord is present** (has come).

Observe that I did not "transliterate" (supply English letters for Greek letters) the Greek word *anathema*, but actually translated it, in the imperative clause, "**let him constantly be a person placed up [in prayer to be consecrated before the Lord]**." The bracketed insertion is there to explain that *anathema* was a technical term for placing an offering on an altar of a deity. The prefix *ana-* in this term means "up." The stem *–thema* means "to set or place." It was the act of devoting an offering to a deity. In Rom. 12:14b Paul instructs us, "**be continuously blessing** (speaking well of [them] or thinking goodness for [them]) **and stop cursing**," so the KJV rendering, "let him be anathema," or the NASB rendering, "let him be accursed," are not appropriate here. Paul is saying, "Hold him up before the Lord, in prayer, and in the community."

The last phrase is variously rendered, in the translations. *Maran atha* is an Aramaic loan term that was brought into Greek. One of the meanings given in the lexicons is, "Our Lord is present (or: has come)," and I chose that rendering since it agrees with the concept of the Corinthian community being God's

Home (Temple). Another rendering, "May he come," is also viable, for Christ promised to repeatedly come to us, as He promises to the Asia Minor communities, in Rev. 2 and 3.

23. **The joyous favor and grace of the Lord Jesus, [the] Christ** (or: from [the] Anointed Master, Jesus,) **[continues] with you folks!**
24. **My love** (unambiguous acceptance and drive toward union) **[is] with all of you folks, centered in, and in union with, Christ Jesus. It is so** (Amen; Count on it)**!**

The grace-favor of, and from, the Lord continues with them, as does Paul's love (*agapē*: unambiguous acceptance and drive toward union). The last phrase, where I conflated two meanings of the common preposition, *en*, can refer back to his love (that is "**centered in, and in union with, Christ Jesus**"), or to the new creation existence of the community in Corinth that now lives "centered in Christ," and "in union with Christ." Both understandings of the text are true!

COMMENTS on 2 CORINTHIANS

Introduction

"2 Corinthians is one of the most difficult of Paul's letters for the interpreter because of the critical problems in regard to the letter's integrity and because some of the issues raised in the letter are so explosive" (Witherington, ibid p 327). "Indeed, many scholars are convinced that 2 Corinthians does not represent a solitary letter that Paul sat down one day and wrote, but a combination of two or more letters that he penned at different time for different occasions.... and possibly as many as four or five" (Bart D. Ehrman, *A Brief Introduction to the New Testament*, Second Edition, Oxford University Press, 2009 p 226, 231). Kummel views this letter "as an actual epistle out of the uniqueness of a developing historical situation..." and considers that, "the significance of 2 Cor. lies in the insight into Paul's apostolic consciousness of mission which the Epistle imparts to us" (ibid p 214, 215).

Witherington astutely points out:
> "When a letter has mixed rhetorical types, rhetorical form and function may be differently assessed. Different forms can serve the same ultimate aim" (ibid p 331 n 12).

He classifies the "compositional whole" of the letter as "forensic or judicial rhetoric.... [and] this forensic concentration on the past may help explain why 2 Cor. focuses so much on the past saving acts of God in Christ, and so little on what may be called future eschatology" (ibid pp 333-4; brackets added). Having laid out these varying opinions, we will investigate 2 Cor. as the text and MS variations present themselves to us.

The text suggests that Paul wrote this when he was in Macedonia, after having left Ephesus (*cf* Acts 20:1-2). Scholars place the date of the letter circa AD 55 or 56. As noted in 1:1, below, the letter was also for "the whole region of Achaia" (the whole territory of Greece south of Macedonia), with Corinth being the capital of this Roman province as well as having the principal called-out, covenant community. Paul was planning a third visit to Corinth. "The Epistle falls into three parts which are not clearly connected: 1-7; 8-9; 10-13" (Kummel, ibid p 206). Kummel also observes:
> "It is clear that the presence and agitation of [Paul's opponents] represent a different state of affairs in the life of the congregation from that discernible in 1 Corinthians" (ibid p 209).

Chapter 1

1. **Paul, one sent off as a representative from Jesus Christ** (or: an emissary of Jesus [the Messiah]; an envoy belonging to [the] Anointed Jesus) **through the effect of God's will and purpose, and Timothy, the brother** (Womb-mate). **To God's called-out, covenant community** (the congregation of God) **– the one being** (existing) **within the midst of Corinth – together with all those set apart** (the holy ones; the saints or sacred people) **being** (existing) **within [the] whole [region of] Achaia:**

The brother that was with Paul when he wrote 1 Cor. was Sosthenes; now it is Timothy. Paul presents his letters as coming from at least two witnesses – a pattern that reaches back to the Law of the old covenant. His remarks are sent to the entire called-out group in Corinth, as well as to those of the surrounding region of Achaia. Note that he refers to this group as "God's called-out, covenant community." This rendering reflects the use of the genitive case as showing possession: they belong to God. Another rendering is "the congregation of God," which can indicate that God is the source of this group. It designates them as those who pertain to God – that is why they have been "set apart." It is also possible to render the genitive as apposition, which would then read: the called-out community, which is God. Now that might seem presumptuous, in the least, but how is this different from them being called

"**Christ's body** (or: a body which is Anointed; or: a body whose source and character is Christ, and which is Christ)," in 1 Cor. 12:27? However we may view this phrase, the meaning is that this group of people have been called out of their normal social, political and religious affiliations to be specifically affiliated with God as His sacred people. They are to God what Israel, as a race and as a nation, were to God in the old arrangement that has now passed away (5:17, below). They are now God's representatives in the earth – to be the Light of the aggregate of humanity (Mat. 5:14a). They have been set-apart (made sacred, as is a temple: 6:16, below) to reflect the image of God (Gen. 1:26, and 3:18, below). So the identity, and the implied function, of this specialized community has been laid out in the first verse. They should know who they are, and what they are about. They were summoned to be the second humanity that would bear and reflect God's image, so that when folks saw them they would see God.

2. **Grace** (The act producing happiness, which is granted as a favor) **and peace from the Joining** (or: harmony; [= shalom]) [are] **with, in, and for you folks, from God, our Father and Lord, Jesus Christ** (or: from our Father, God, and Owner, Jesus, [the] Anointed [= Messiah]).

The parenthetical definition of "grace" I owe to Jim Coram, a featured author in the periodical, "Unsearchable Riches." Grace was the Christ Event that resulted in what is written in Mat. 5:3-11 – being blessed and made "happy" – the event that delivered us from the old covenant, from the old creation, and that inaugurated the new covenant and the new creation. Jesus, Israel's Messiah, also brought us "peace from the joining." Why have I added the phrase, "from the Joining"? First, the word "peace" is from the verb that means "to join;" there was an actual "joining" that happened. Second, the Act by Jesus happened "**that He may frame** (create; found and settle from a state of wildness and disorder) **The Two into One qualitatively New and Different** [*p*46 & others: common] **Humanity centered within the midst of, and in union with, Himself, continuously making** (progressively creating) **Peace and Harmony** (a Joining)" (Eph. 2:15b). The "Two" are the two groups of humanity in God's previous economy: circumcision and uncircumcision (Eph. 2:11). This peace/joining was not just "a peaceful, easy feeling," nor the prosperity implied by shalom, nor the lack of conflict. The cross joined all humanity into One, in Christ.

Observe that "grace and peace/joining" are "with us, in us, and for us." We are both the focus, the location and the purpose of the Christ Event, which imparted these gifts into us, among us, and to bring us to God's intended goal for humanity.

The final, compound phrases of this verse can be read and punctuated in the two ways that are on offer, here. We find the same collection of terms in 1 Cor. 1:3 (*cf* my comments there, in *Comments on 1 Corinthians*, above). Paul had already shared the Good News with those of Corinth, but in both letters he is led to remind them that Grace, and the peace from the Joining, are from God, and then he adds the rest of the formula. We know that it is purposeful, but what is his purpose? The bold rendering identifies the source of these gifts as God, "**our Father and Lord**," Jesus Christ. Mainline Christianity can accept Jesus as being God, our Lord, and the Christ. But applying the term Father to Jesus would be seen as heretical. And yet, Paul applied that function to himself, in 1 Cor. 4:15. Now the parenthetical rendering and punctuation offer the traditional distinction between the terms Father and Owner/Lord – and thus a distinction between God and Jesus. Note the absence of the term Spirit in Paul's formulation. In later centuries, theological theories are often read into functional phrases such as this one. We should keep in mind that Israel was termed God's son, in Ex. 4:22. Adam was "of, and from, God," in Lu. 3:38, and Jesus' genealogy begins right after He is identified as God's Son, in Lu. 3:22. It may be wise to refrain from adding theological constructs to Paul's words, here. Let us read the possible renderings, and let the Spirit speak to our hearts and understandings. The titles and relational words are there for a reason. How did Paul expect his listeners to understand them? Later centuries have seen continued division over these terms.

3. The God and Father of our Master, Jesus Christ (or: The God and Father, which is our Lord and Owner, Jesus [the] Anointed One [= Messiah]) **[is] One full of words of ease and thoughts of wellness** (or: [is] well-spoken of and blessed): **the Father of the compassions and sympathetic acts of pity, and God of every entreaty and of every calling to one's [or: His] side for aid, relief, comfort, consolation and encouragement** (or: a God who is ALL the functioning of a Paraclete),

The opening phrases of this verse seem to restate the last phrase of vs. 2 – the bold rendering here reflecting the distinctions as seen in the parenthetical, above; the lightface rendering here, expressing apposition, reflecting the bold rendering of vs. 2, above. [Cf Jn. 20:17; Rom. 15:6; Col. 1:3] But the message is that God is "**full of words of ease and thoughts of wellness**." He is **the Father**, the Source, of "**compassions** (etc.)." This is no doubt an allusion to Ex. 34:6,

"Yahweh… Yahweh, a God [Who is] compassionate and gracious, slow to anger, and abounding in lovingkindness and truth."

He is also a "God who is all the functioning of **a Paraclete**" – which is the role assigned to the Spirit (Breath-effect; cf Jn. 14:16, 26; 15:26; 16:7) and yet 1 Jn. 2:1 also informs us that, "**we constantly have One called alongside to help, give relief and guide us toward the Father** (or: we continuously possess **a Paraclete**, face to face with the Father): **Jesus Christ**." It would seem that any manifestation of, or encounter with, God presents us with the entirety of Who God is, and how He functions with, in and for, us. So we should focus on the beautiful descriptions that Paul attributes to God, the Father, Jesus and the Paraclete. Everything that Paul says of God, here, flies in the face of traditional Christian theology, with its doctrine of an "eternal hell/punishment." God is "well-spoken of and blessed" by humanity. He is full of words of ease (Mat. 11:29, 30) and thoughts of wellness.

He is a God of **ALL comfort**, relief, help, aid, consolation and encouragement. Why is it important for them (and us) to know this? From this verse and on through vs. 7, this noun, or its verb form, occurs nine times. In vss. 4-8 we find the term suffering four times and the word pressure/tribulation (etc.) used five times. Times were hard then, and have been hard ever since. Paul assures us that there is more than enough comfort and help from God to be sufficient for all the suffering and ordeals that confront us in our lives.

4. the One continuously calling us to receive aid, relief, comfort, consolation and encouragement at [His] side (or: the One habitually functioning as our Paraclete) **upon [the occurrence of] all our squeezing pressure** (or: our every affliction, tribulation and oppression), **[then] to progressively enable** (to constantly give power to) **us into the [sphere or situation] to keep on performing as paracletes in repeatedly giving aid, relief, comfort, consolation and encouragement for those within the midst of every** (or: all) **pressure** (oppression; squeezing, affliction and tribulation) **– [and this] through means of the [same] assistance with which we, ourselves, are being constantly called alongside by God to receive as aid, relief, comfort, consolation and encouragement [from Him]** (or: from which we, ourselves, are habitually being given the services of the Paraclete by God) –

Observe the present participle: He is CONTINUOUSLY calling us to His side in order for us to receive what we need to carry us through ALL the "squeezing pressure (etc.)." Paul put it this way in 2 Thes. 2:

16. **Now may our Lord, Jesus Christ Himself, even** (or: and) **our God and Father, the One loving** (accepting) **us and giving a calling alongside pertaining to the Age** (or: performance as a Paraclete with age-lasting aid; eonian relief, encouragement, consolation and admonition) **as well as a good expectation** (or: a virtuous and excellent hope) **in grace** (or: in union with favor),
17. **be at once calling your hearts alongside and establishing** (making to stand fast; making stable and firm) **you in every good** (or: excellent; virtuous) **work and word** (or: thought; idea; message).

He constantly gives power to us, which progressively enables us "**into the [sphere or situation] to keep on performing as paracletes**." How so? Well, we read in Phil. 2:13,

> "**for you see, God is the One habitually operating with inward activity, repeatedly working within, constantly causing function and progressively producing effects within, among and in union with you folks – both the [condition] to be habitually willing** (intending; purposing; resolving) **and the [situation] to be continuously effecting the action, repeatedly operating to cause function and habitually setting at work so as to produce – for the sake of and over the pleasing good form and the thinking of goodness in delightful imagination**."

We are God's instruments. Paul is functioning as a paraclete for the Corinthians. Recall how he was called to Jesus' side on the road to Damascus, and then we read Jesus speaking to Ananias about him:

> "**this one is** (exists being) **a vessel of choice to Me** (or: a picked-out and chosen instrument by and for Me)" (Acts 9:15).

Paul described us as "**containers of mercy** (instruments of mercy)" in Rom. 9:23. We are called to call others alongside so as to transmit God's mercy into them and into their situations. This suggests Paul's focus and intent in writing this letter. This kind of behavior defines both God and His "called-out."

5. **because correspondingly as the effects and results of** (or: from) **the Christ's experiences and sufferings are progressively superabounding into** (or: encompassing in full measure unto) **us, in the same way, through the Christ** (or: the Anointed One; [= the Messiah]; or: the Anointing), **our calling [folks] to our side to give [them] help, relief, comfort and encouragement is also progressively superabounding so as to surround us in full quantity** (or: the work of the Paraclete constantly environs in abundance from us, by the Anointing)**!**

The subject of the first clause is a plural noun with the *–ma* ending which indicates that what Paul is speaking about are "**the effects and results**" of "**Christ's experiences and sufferings**." They are the results and effects of the Christ Event that "**are progressively superabounding into us**." It is NOT His "sufferings" that are "encompassing in full measure unto us," but the effects of those sufferings – which we call Grace, His Deliverance and His Life. The awareness of these *–ma/mata* forms of Greek nouns make a huge difference, in many cases.

Now it is "**in the same way**" that Paul and his associates are "**calling [folks] to [their] side to give [them] help, relief, comfort and encouragement is also progressively superabounding so as to surround [Paul and his associates] in full quantity**" – and this is "**through the Christ** (or: the Anointing)." Christ, or, the Anointing, is the vehicle and the means for providing all this comfort and assistance. Reading "**us**" as an ablative, instead of a genitive (both cases have the same form/spelling), the last clause can read, "the work of the Paraclete constantly environs in abundance from us, by the Anointing." Notice Paul's intermingling of the terms/concepts of "the Anointing (or: Christ) and the Paraclete" with what we discern to be the functioning and operating of the Spirit, or we might say, God. Paul does not seem to want to put Christ or God in some theological box, as later theologians in fact did.

In regard to "**Christ's experiences and sufferings progressively superabounding into** (or: encompassing in full measure unto) **us**," we read in Col. 1:24,

> "**I am at this moment continuing to rejoice within the effects of experiences and the results of my sufferings over your [situation] and on your behalf, and I am progressively filling back up in turn – so as in [His] stead to replace, supply and balance out, within my flesh** (or: = with the means of my natural situation) **– the deficiencies** (or: results from what is lacking; effects from need) **with regard to the pressures** (or: from the squeezings, tribulations and tight spots) **that pertain to the Anointed One** (or: that belong to and affect Christ; or: from the [Messiah]) **over [the situation of] His body, which is the called-out, covenant community** (which exists being the summoned-forth congregation – the ecclesia)."

God is "**the Father of the compassions and sympathetic acts of pity**" (vs. 3, above). And since, "**God was existing within Christ** (God was and continued being centered in, and in union with [the] Anointed One) **progressively and completely transforming [the] aggregate of humanity**" (5:19, below), therefore, "**the effects and results of** (or: from) **the Christ's experiences and sufferings are progressively superabounding into** (or: encompassing in full measure unto) **us**." God's goodness comes from Himself, through Christ, then into us, so that we can be "**calling [folks] to our side to give [them] help, relief, comfort and encouragement, [which] is also progressively superabounding so as to surround us in full quantity**." This is what Jesus meant when He said in Mat. 10:8,

> "**Be constantly serving, curing and restoring to health** (or: giving attentive care to and treatment for) **those who are habitually weak, feeble and inadequate. Habitually be rousing and raising up dead people. Be continually cleansing lepers** (scabby folks). **Make it a habit to cast out demons** (Hellenistic concept and term: = animistic influences). **You folks receive** (or: received) **freely** (as a gift; = without cost), **[so] give freely** (as a gift; = without charge)."

6. **Now whether we are being continually squeezed and compressed, or oppressed in tribulation, over and on behalf of your assistance** (or: a calling to [His] side for relief, aid and comfort) **and deliverance** (salvation, rescue, health, wholeness and restoration), **or whether we are repeatedly being given relief, intimate assistance, comfort and encouragement over and because of your assistance and comfort – referring to [that aid and encouragement] which is continuously performing inward work and operation within the midst of [that] persistent remaining under in endurance of the very effects of experiences and results of sufferings which we, ourselves, also are habitually experiencing, or suffering –**

"For the Christian, therefore, distress and consolation are two sides of the same experience" (Harvey, ibid). In regard to the compound phrase, "**within the midst of [that] persistent remaining under in endurance of the very effects of experiences and results of sufferings**," Dan Kaplan brought to mind, here, the sufferings of God's faithful people in Israel's past, as recorded in Heb. 11:35b-38,

> "**Yet others were beaten to death with rods** (or: drummed upon), **not receiving** (or: accepting; taking) **toward** (or: with a view to) **themselves** (= refusing) **the releasing-away** (liberation; setting free from bondage or prison) **so that they may hit the target of** (or: attain) **a superior** (stronger and better) **resurrection** [comment: i.e., a spiritual resurrection]. [*cf* 1 Ki. 17:17-24; 2 Ki. 4:18-37; Acts 22:24-25; *cf* Phil. 3:8-15] **But different ones took a trial** (or: received a test) **of mockings** (scoffings), **and of scourgings, and further, of bonds and imprisonment** (= put in chains and thrown in jail). **They were stoned, they were cut in two with a saw, they were put to the proof** (tried; tested), **they passed away in a slaughter** (or: by murder) **with sword, they went around** (wandered) **in sheepskins, in goat skins, continuously being behind** (being in want; being in the rear), **being constantly pressed** (squeezed; afflicted), **habitually being held in the bad** (being maltreated; having it bad), **of whom the System** (the ordered arrangement; the world or culture, secular society, religions and government) **was not worthy** (was not of equal value) **– being continually deceived** (led astray; caused to wander) **in deserts and mountains and caves and the holes of the earth** (or: ground)."

Hard experiences and suffering are the common lot of humanity. Christ entered into our situation and experienced the same, and so do we.

The first clause of vs. 6 both expresses Paul's solidarity with them, and also instructs us about the connectedness that we have with one another. What Paul and his associates were experiencing in and among themselves effected the Corinthians. Their oppression was on behalf of the Corinthians having assistance, aid and comfort, and as he says in 4:15a, below, "**for you see, all things [are]** (the whole – everything – [is]) **because of you folks**." Their repeatedly being given relief, comfort and encouragement was because of, and over the situation of, the Corinthians receiving assistance and comfort. This latter is "**referring to [that aid and encouragement] which is continuously performing inward work and operation within the midst of [that] persistent remaining under in endurance**" within the called-out community. And their "remaining under in endurance" was connected to "**the very effects of experiences and results of sufferings which [Paul and his associates], [themselves], also [were] habitually experiencing, or suffering**." The union of Paul's current community with the community in Corinth and the surrounding area, could hardly be better expressed! What happened in one community affected other communities. This is an explicit result of "the peace of the Joining" (vs. 2, above). We saw this fact plainly stated in 1 Cor. 12:26,

> "**And further, whether one member is continuing to experience the effect of something, or constantly undergoes suffering, all the members continually experience the effect or the suffering together with [it; her; him]; or if a member is being constantly glorified, normally given an assumed appearance, or is progressively receiving a good reputation, all the members are continuously rejoicing together with [him; her; it]**."

But Paul continues his thoughts in the next verse...

7. **either way, our expectation** (or: expectant hope) **[stands] on good footing** (or: [is] stable, unwavering, with feet firmly planted; or: [stands] guaranteed as valid; [remains] a confirmation of a certification of the purchase) **over, and with regard to, you folks, having seen and continuing to know that just as you are – and continue to be – people of common existence** (partners, participants and sharers of Being) **from the effects of experiences and the results of sufferings, in the same way [are you] of the relief, aid and encouraging comfort, as well.**

Paul gives the following instruction, in Rom. 8:17,

> "**Now since children** (or: Yet if ones born by natural descent), **also heirs** (possessors and enjoyers of an allotted inheritance; those who hold sway over the allotted portion)**: on the one hand, God's heirs, on the other, Christ's joint-heirs**
>> (or: indeed possessors and enjoyers of an allotment pertaining to God and from God, yet possessors and enjoyers together in an allotment pertaining to Christ and belonging to Christ) **if so be** (or: provided) **that we are continually affected by sensible experiences together – feeling together; receiving impressions, undergoing passion or suffering together – to the end that we may also be glorified together**
>> (or: can be given a shared appearance; would together receive a manifestation of that which calls forth praise; should be given a joint-approval and a joint-reputation; may be thought of and imagined together [in covenant relationship])." *Cf* 2 Tim. 2:12

Observe that the "**good footing**," upon which Paul's **expectation** stands is on the Corinthians being "**people of common existence** (partners, participants and sharers of Being)" – both among themselves, as an organism of Christ, and together with Paul and his associates. But more than this, it was a common existence "**from the effects of experiences**," and from "**the results of sufferings**," as well as from "**the relief, aid and encouraging comfort**" that they had received through the Spirit – the God of "all comfort." Participating in common experiences – whether good or bad – knits us together in community. We see this demonstrated in everyday life, for God dwells with all of us. He evokes compassion from our hearts as we encounter human pain and tragedy.

We want to point out for your consideration the semantic range of the term first rendered, "**on good footing**," which expresses the root idea of the Greek word. Note the need to supply the ellipse, where on offer are the verbs "stands, is or remains." So the first alternate reading is "[is] stable, unwavering, with feet firmly planted." Next is "[stands] guaranteed as valid." This and the final rendering are extended applications of the term. The final application is a transactional function: "[remains] a confirmation of a certification of the purchase." So how was Paul using this term? Ambiguity is always a call for contemplation. Each meaning gives a slightly different nuance, or picture, of what Paul was saying, and we suggest the each one is equally valid.

8. **For we do not continue intending** (or: wanting; purposing) **for you folks to continue being ignorant** (unaware or without intimate knowledge), **brothers** (folks from the same Womb), **over** [other MSS: concerning] **our squeezing pressure** (tribulation; affliction; oppression) **– referring to [that] which happened** [other MSS add: to us] **in [the province of] Asia – that corresponding to an act of overshooting or throwing beyond the target** (= something extreme and excessive) **over and above [our] power and ability, we were weighted down** (burdened [with difficulty]) **so as to be without an exit** (with no way out) **for us, even to continue living!**

Observe that although he describes the effects that resulted, he does not go into detail, put blame on anyone, or even complain. He just states the fact that they had these experiences. He does not want them to be ignorant about this, because they, in Corinth, would likely experience the same. It is important to note that he does not describe this "**squeezing pressure** (etc.)" as having come from *satan* or the *devil*; neither does he refer to it as having been "an attack from the enemy," or as having been in "spiritual warfare." This tribulation, affliction and oppression was simply part of the cruciform life of following Jesus.

9. **Further yet, we ourselves had held and continued having, within ourselves, the result and effect from a decision of the Death** (or: from a judgment which meant death; or: the considered decision and insightful response in regard to death) **– to the end that we may not exist being ones having put trust and confidence upon ourselves, but to the contrary, upon the God Who is continually** (habitually; periodically; repeatedly; or: presently) **awakening and raising up the dead people!**

Paul now references his and his associates' past experience, in the province of Asia, which had seemed as though it would bring their end – from which there appeared to be "no way out." He does not say who, or what group, had made "**a decision of Death**" in regard to them. It may have been "a judgment which meant death" for them. But the Greek phrase can also be rendered a "considered decision and insightful response in regard to death," so it is possible that Paul is speaking of a spiritual or philosophical situation, for in Paul's writings, "death" is often metaphorical or symbolic. Recall, also, the metaphorical death of the soul to which Jesus referred in Mat. 16:24-26. Whichever the case, Paul saw God's purpose within it: it was "**to the end that we may not exist being ones having put trust and confidence upon ourselves, but to the contrary, upon God**." Such a statement can refer to either physical matters, or to things of the spirit and soul. Paul may be alluding to Jer. 17:5,

> "A correspondingly negative prayer (or: desired outcome) [is] upon a person who constantly holds the expectation (or: habitually has the hope) upon a human, and thus will continue supporting his arm of flesh (or: [the] flesh of his arm) upon him – and next his heart would (or: may) stand-off, away from [the] LORD (= Yahweh)." (LXX, JM)

But let us consider the final clause of vs. 9. O'Rourke points out: "the present participle expresses durative action" (ibid p 278). Was this continual (or: habitual, etc., i.e., "durative") "**awakening and raising up the dead people**" speaking of physical resurrection, or of spiritual resurrection? We saw in 1 Cor. 15 that much of what Paul said about "awakening" and "raising up" could be read as speaking of the raising up of the second humanity within the midst of the first humanity – an awakening from being "dead in trespasses and sins" (Eph. 2:1) to be spiritually raised up into the "heavenly realm" in Christ (Eph. 2:6). Paul's ambiguity, here, allows us to apply what he has said to any realm of our lives. God repeatedly awakens and raises folks in all dimensions of our existence.

10. **He Who snatched** (dragged so as to rescue) **us from out of the midst of the very prime** (or: peak) **of Death** (or: out of a death of such proportions) **will also repeatedly rescue and drag us to Himself – into Whom we have placed our hope and expectation so as to yet rely that He also will Himself continue still dragging us further toward Himself.**

Paul's expression in the first clause may be an allusion to Ps. 116:6b-8,

"I was impoverished (brought low), and He saved me. Return to your rest, my soul, for Yahweh, He has dealt bountifully with you. Indeed, You have extricated my soul from death, my eye from tears, my foot from foundering (stumbling)" (CVOT; expansions added).

We should first notice Who is doing all the action in this verse. God is very involved in human life. He not only rescued Israel from Egypt, but also Paul and his associates "from out of the midst of the very peak of Death." Physical death? Yes, probably so. But may it also have been the Death of the old covenant? Was it possibly the death of unhealthy relationships or atmospheres within the various towns and cities that they had visited? Our knowing which is not the point, but rather the point is that "**He also will Himself continue still dragging us further toward Himself**." The repetition of the two similar statements in this verse is for emphasis, and is characteristic of Asiatic rhetoric, with which his listeners would have been familiar.

We also recall Peter's words:
> "**[The] Lord** [=Yahweh], **having seen, thus knows to** (or: knows how to) **continuously drag out of danger** (or: rescue) **a reverent person** (one standing in devout goodness, in awe and in virtuous conduct with ease and well-being from relationship with God) **from out of the midst of a trial** (or: ordeal; [other MSS: trials])..." (2 Pet. 2:9a).

11. **Your habitually cooperating and working together in undergirding support over us** (on behalf of us, or, concerning our situation), **even in the need** (or: and by the [or: your] petition regarding [our] need), **[gives the result] that forth from out of** [other MSS: in] **many faces** (= people; or: = outward appearances) **[and] through** (or: by means of) **many folks, the effect and result of grace and favor can** (or: may; would) **be sent** (or: given) **unto us in the goodness, ease and well-being of grace** (or: from favor) **over our [situation]** (or: may be given in gratitude on our [other MSS: your] behalf).

The compound present participle rendered "**habitually cooperating and working together in undergirding support**" is found only here in the NT. It is from the verb that combines the elements *sun (with; together)* + *hupo (under)* + *ergon (work)*. *Sunupourgeō* means to render supportive service or aid, along with another person. Once again, we see the solidarity and interconnectedness of the body of Christ. In Rom. 15:30b-31a, Paul called for the Roman community to,
> "**through the Spirit's love** (or: and by means of the uniting and accepting love which is the Breath-effect; or: as well as through the full, unrestricted giving of yourselves in an urge toward reunion from this Attitude), **within the thoughts and words toward having goodness and well-being [directed] toward God over me** (or: in union with prayers, face to face with God, for my behalf), **to the end that I may be dragged out of danger from the habitually incompliant** (disobedient; stubborn; unconvinced) **folks within Judea**..."

The "working together" was obviously giving support in the realm of the spirit, and through the Spirit. Their "work" in this realm actually "**sent**" the "**effect and result of grace and favor**." We read in Jas. 5:16b,
> "**A binding need** (or: a petition and an entreaty out of need) **of a person within the Way pointed out** (of a fair and equitable person; of one in right relationship; of a rightwised and rightly aligned man; of a just one) – **which progressively works inwardly and itself continuously creates energy from union – constantly exerts much strength**."

The phrase "**over us even in the need**" is a literal rendering of what is often rendered idiomatically, such as is on offer in the interpretive, parenthetical expansion: "and by the [or: your] petition regarding [our] need." We observe rhetorical duplication in the parallel phrases, "**forth from out of** [other MSS: in] **many faces** (= people; or: = outward appearances) **[and] through** (or: by means of) **many folks**." In Phil.1:19 he said to them,

"**For I am aware** (have seen and thus know) **that this will continue stepping away into deliverance** (rescue; health and wholeness; salvation) **for me** (and: in me) **through your request and the supply** (support; provision) **of the Spirit of Jesus Christ**." *Cf* Philem. 22

The last clause begins with *charisma*, which is the noun "grace" with the *–ma* ending, which signifies "**the effect and result of grace and favor**." The common rendering, "gracious gift," misses the true meaning of the word. We find the word "grace" in the verb, where *charis* is prefixed by *eu-* together with a verbal ending. The common rendering is on offer in the parenthetical rendering, "may be given in gratitude." But the more literal rendering that is presented in "**can** (or: may; would) **be sent** (or: given) **unto us in the goodness, ease and well-being of grace** (or: from favor)," offers a more insightful understanding of the verb, letting the core idea of "grace" be seen.

12. **For you see, our boasting** (or: expression of a reason for being proud) **is this – [and it is] the witness and testimony of our conscience** (integrated inner knowing)**: that within the midst of the System** (dominating world of religion, culture, economy, and government; or: the aggregate of humanity), **and especially** (or: more exceedingly) **in our relationship with you folks, we were turned back and caused to live our lives and conduct ourselves centered within, and in union with, God's singleness** (single, uncompounded quality having no folds; [other MSS: quality of being set apart]) **and clearness from being judged** (discerned and evaluated) **in sunlight** (or: in a sincere and clear integrity from, and which, is God) **– and this not within fleshly wisdom or cleverness, but to the contrary, centered within the midst of and in union with God's grace** (or: the favor from, and which is, God).

The first point of this verse is the revealing statement, "**we were turned back and caused to live our lives and conduct ourselves**." The verb is in "the divine passive" – God is understood to be the Actor. But more than this, the modifying compound phrases unpack the realm and relationship in which we "live our lives and conduct ourselves." We are: "**centered within, and in union with, God's singleness** (single, uncompounded quality having no folds; [other MSS: quality of being set apart]) **and clearness from being judged** (discerned and evaluated) **in sunlight** (or: in a sincere and clear integrity from, and which, is God)." It is wonderful to be "centered in" this, and be "in union with" it, but what does the MS reading "**singleness**" tell us? The parenthetical definition is helpful: "single, uncompounded quality having no folds." This is the opposite of duplicity. He is One; He is Love. He is not "this AND that." The noun has been rendered "sincerity; simplicity," as the lexicons offer. But "having no folds" implies no shadows, and calls to mind Jas. 1:17b,

> "**beside Whom there is no otherness at [His] side** (or: in the presence of Whom is no parallel otherness; [other MSS: along with Whom is not one interchange, variation, shifting or mutation]),
> **nor a shadow cast by turning** [other MSS: an effect caused by the passing of shadows]."

Other MSS read: "quality of being set apart; or: holiness."

The next word is also worthy of note: God's "**clearness from being judged in sunlight** (or: in a sincere and clear integrity from, and which, is God)." The bold reading is the literal meaning. Ponder this quality of God, for it is GOD's clearness – a clearness from being "discerned, evaluated and judged." God put Himself in clear Light (Christ), and on the cross allowed Himself to be discerned, evaluated and judged. Now we can see God, for we are centered in His uncompounded pureness that has no hidden sides to it (no folds), and we are "in union with God's sunlight-revealing clearness. Yes, this is what it means to be within Him, and in union with Him. The contrast, "**fleshly wisdom or cleverness**" is an echo of 1 Cor. 2:4.

The second point is that we are "**centered within the midst of and in union with God's grace** (or: the favor from, and which is, God)." These are the central "keys to the kingdom." When we see this and know this, we can be active participants in the activities of His reign – right here on earth.

13. So then, we are not now writing other things to you, but rather either (or: other than) **what you continue reading and recognizing, or even what you folks continue progressing to full, intimate knowledge and insight about** (or: what you presently recognize and acknowledge as added knowledge and complete *gnosis*). **Yet I continue expecting and hoping that unto the purposed and destined goal** (until maturity and the finished product) **you will continue to additionally, accurately and intimately realize and know by experience,**

14. just as you recognized with added personal knowledge about us, partly, that we have as much cause to be proud of you, exactly as you also [have] of us – resident within and in union with this Day which pertains to, is from, and is, our Lord (Master; Owner), **Jesus.**

Paul is not writing new information to them, but is aware that their knowledge and insight is progressing, and he expects this process to continue on unto God's purpose and destined goal for them – which will bring added realization through their own experiences of this process. He also realizes that they are growing in their personal knowledge about him, and his associates, and that this mutual recognition is a cause from mutual pride such as parents have for children and children have for parents.

The last phrase of vs. 14 has often been rendered and understood as a reference to a future "day," but the context is all about present and ongoing knowledge and recognition of what was at that time happening within the called-out communities. This knowledge came from, and is resident within, the unveiling of the fact that Christ was within them and that they were at that time living within "**this Day which pertains to, is from, and is, our Lord** (Master; Owner), **Jesus.**" Christ is the Day. Paul wrote in 1 Thes. 5:5, 8-9,

> "**for you see, you all are** (or: exist being) **sons of** (from; associated with and having the qualities of; or: which are) **Light and sons of** (from; associated with and having qualities of; or: which are [the]) **Day! We are** (exist) **not of night, nor of darkness** (or: we do not belong to or have the characteristics of night, nor to or of dim obscurity from shadows and gloom).... **We, on the other hand, being of Day** (belonging to and having characteristics of [the] Day; having [the] Day as our source), **can and should continuously be sober** (clear-headed), **putting on** (or: clothing ourselves with; enveloping ourselves in; entering within) **a breastplate** (or: thorax) **of faith and love** (or: which is trust and acceptance urging toward union; from fidelity and a giving of self) **and, as a helmet, an expectation** (or: expectant hope) **from deliverance** (which is health and wholeness; of rescue and being kept safe; pertaining to salvation), **because God Himself did not** (or: does not) **place or set us into anger** (inherent fervor; violent emotion; wrath; or: teeming, passionate desire), **but rather, into an encompassing of deliverance** (or: unto establishing a perimeter of safety; into making health and wholeness encircle [us]; into the forming of an encompassing salvation around [us]) **through our Lord, Jesus Christ.**"

Cf 1 Cor. 1:8, above, and comments there.

In Phil. 2:16 Paul speaks of his "**loud-tongued exulting-effects** (boasting; vaunting) **for me** (or: in me), **on into Christ's Day** (a day of [the] Anointed; or: a day which is anointed)." In 1 Thes. 2:19 he says that those in Thessalonica "**continue being a crown** (victor's wreath) **of boasting and glorying in front of our Lord Jesus, in His presence** (or: in the place facing toward our Master, Jesus, within the midst of His being present alongside [us])." That was a present reality.

15. So, with (or: in; by) **this persuaded confidence, I had previously continued intending** (planning and purposing) **to come to you folks, so that you folks could have** (or: may hold) **a second grace** (influence and boon of joyous favor, kindness and goodwill; [other MSS: {occasion for} joy]),

In 1 Cor. 4:19 we read of his intent to visit them. His presence with them would indeed be an "influence and boon of joyous favor, kindness and goodwill."

Students of this letter have pondered Paul's meaning in the second clause of this verse, "**so that you folks could have** (or: may hold) **a second grace**." This would happen because of his intended visit to them. He had written to them twice before, but apparently only visited them once. Paul was a bearer of the grace of God, so his visit would allow them to have a "second helping" from the Messiah's banquet table. Like he said in vs. 13, above, it would be nothing new, but more of the same. Rom. 1:11 is most likely what he meant here:

> "**for I constantly long** (or: I am increasingly yearning) **to see you, to the end that I may share and exchange some spiritual effect of favor with you folks** (or: mutually partner in the impartation to you people, and among you, of some gift that is a result of grace and which has its source in the Breath-effect) **[leading] into the [situation for] you to be established** (firmly settled and made steadfast; stabilized)."

There is good MS support for reading "joy" (*charan*) instead of "grace" (*charin*) – a difference of only one letter. Grace and joy have the same root idea, and thus my parenthetical rendering "joyous favor" as one of the meanings of "grace." Paul's visit would bring them joy, as well as grace/favor. We need not read a strange doctrine into Paul's words, here.

16. **and then to pass on through you [i.e., through your city] into Macedonia, and to come back again to you from Macedonia, and [then] to be sent forward with funds and supplies** (perhaps: to be accompanied or escorted on part of the journey) **by you folks into** [other MSS: from you unto] **the Judean [area].**

Paul is simply laying out his travel plans for them, along with his intent to receive an offering of "funds and supplies" to pass along to the folks in the Judean area. The Greek term rendered "**sent forward with funds and supplies**" is an idiomatic translation of how the term was often used. However, the literal meaning of the verb (to be sent forward) could also simply mean that folks from Corinth would escort or accompany him on part of his journey, as he left Corinth that second time. The MS reading, "from you unto," suggests the first, bold, rendering that involved an offering for the Judeans.

17. **Therefore, continuing in determining, planning and intending this, surely I do not consequently engage in joking** (employ lightness; or: = resort to fickleness or irresponsibility), **do I? Or the things which I habitually plan and purpose, am I normally planning down from [the] flesh** (or: = in accord with estranged human nature; or: = on the level oriented to the System or the old covenant), **so that it may be with me, "Yes, yes," and "No, no!"?**

The rhetorical question, "**Or the things which I habitually plan and purpose, am I normally planning down from [the] flesh**...?" is answered by contrast in 10:2, below, when referring to,

> "**certain folks: those constantly considering and counting us as folks [who] are habitually walking around** (= living our lives; ordering our behavior) **in correspondence and accord to flesh** (= governed by principles of the human condition; or: = on the level of old covenant existence [T. Denton]; or: = in line with a self in bondage to the System)."

The verb variously rendered "**engage in joking**, employ lightness," or possibly, "resort to fickleness or irresponsibility," presents us with ambiguity as to Paul's meaning. But we can draw from the entire verse that he is serious about his plans to come to them, and that whether or not it may be that he would come, it will be a clear decision – and perhaps he means that they will hear which it will be. But he uses these expressions of a definite decision to transition into a point of teaching, in the next two verses...

18. **Now God [is] full of faith and reliable** (loyal; faithful; trustworthy)! **[With] that, our message** (or: Because the *Logos*, or Word, from us) **toward you folks is not** [other MSS: did not come to be] **"Yes," and then** [or, at the same time] **"No,"**

19. **for the Son of God, Jesus Christ** [= Jesus the Messiah] – **the One within the midst of, among, and in union with you folks – being heralded and publicly proclaimed through us, [i.e.,] through Silvanus** [this may = Silas], **Timothy and me, did not come to be** (or: was not birthed) **"Yes," and yet, "No," but to the contrary, [the divine] "Yes" has been birthed and remains in existence within Him** (or: in union with Him, "Yes" has happened and continues being; or: within the midst of Him, [the] "Yes" has come into being and remains)**!** Cf 1 Cor. 1:9; 10:13b; Acts 9:20; Mk. 1:1; Lu. 1:35

In vs. 18 Paul assures his listeners that his message to them was not fickle or ambiguous: not **"Yes," and then** [or, at the same time] **"No."** This is because "**the Son of God, Jesus Christ… did not come to be "Yes," and yet, "No."** Paul then affirms that to the contrary Christ's **"Yes" has been birthed and remains in existence within Him**. The next verse continues to explain that the Good News is a positive message; God's promises WILL be fulfilled. Paul is using the term "Yes" like the word "Amen." This is because it is all the work of God, and is not dependent upon human response or human works. The "Yes" that was birthed IS the Son of God. So God's YES to humanity is both within Jesus, and is "in union with Him." As the parenthetical alternative reads: "within the midst of Him, [the] 'Yes' has come into being and remains." That 'Yes' means eschatological deliverance, rescue, salvation and being place into the Christ. It means that everything is Good News. It means that,

> "**to the folks being called and invited according to [the] purpose He is constantly working all things together into good and is progressively working all humanity together into that which is advantageous, worthy of admiration, noble and of excellent qualities**" (Rom. 8:28).

The first clause of vs. 19 makes a profound statement, declaring the reality of the new creation (5:17, below) and the "whereabouts" of Jesus Christ, Whom most of Christianity has banished from our world, until He decides to come back. But consider Paul's words:

> "**the Son of God, Jesus Christ – the One within the midst of, among, and in union with you folks…**"

Where does Paul locate Jesus? Remember, we no longer know Him according to the flesh (5:16, below). For a second witness to where the risen Christ is, John reports to us in Rev. 2:1, "**the One continuously walking about within the midst of the seven golden lampstands**," and we are instructed in Rev. 1:20 that, "**the seven lampstands are the seven covenant communities** (or: summoned-forth congregations)." The risen Christ is here, among us and within us (as the Spirit). Remember Heb. 13:5b,

> "**I can** (or: could; would) **by no means let you go** (or: let up on you; send you back; release my grip on you), **neither by any means may** (or: could; would) **I leave you down within** (= forsake or fail you)," [Deut. 31:6; Josh. 1:5; cf Phil. 4:11]

Also, Jesus told His disciples,

> "**I will not be leaving you abandoned or be sending you off as orphaned ones** (or: folks without family). **I am repeatedly** (or: habitually) **and now progressively coming to** (or: face to face with; toward) **you people.**"

So here we have four witnesses to the fact that Christ is HERE, with us. We are not waiting for Him to return. He came with the Father, to make His home with us:

> "**If anyone continues** (or: may be habitually) **loving, accepting, fully giving himself to, and urging toward union with, Me, he WILL continue constantly watching over so as to observe, guard, preserve keep and maintain My word** (logos: thought, idea and message; laid-out, patterned information), **and My Father will continue loving, fully giving Himself to, and urging toward union with, him, AND, facing toward him, We will continue coming to him and will be progressively making** (constructing; forming; creating; producing) **a home** (an abode; a dwelling place; a place to stay) **with him** (or: at his side and in his presence)" (Jn. 14:23).

And thus, we see the existential reality of Paul's words to the covenant community in Corinth. The coming of the Spirit, on the Day of Pentecost (Acts 2) made it possible for folks to continually love Jesus.

The verb of the final clause of vs. 19, "has happened and continues being," or, "**has been birthed and remains in existence**," is in the perfect tense, which denotes an action that has happened in the past and yet continues in its effects after the action was completed. So the final word from the risen Christ is a positive one: "within the midst of Him, [the] 'Yes' has come into being and remains." This is why it is called "Good News."

20. **So you see, as many as [be] God's promises, [they are] the "Yes," within and in union with Him. Wherefore also, through Him [is] The Amen** (or: the affirmation; the "Count on it!;" the "It is so") **in** (or: by; with; or: to) **God with a view to** (or: face to face with) **glory** (an assumed appearance; a good opinion or reputation, and a manifestation which incites praise) – **through us.** [cf Rom. 15:8]

So, "**through Him [is] The Amen** (or: the affirmation; the "Count on it;" the "It is so") **in** (or: by; with; or: to) **God with a view to glory**," and this happens "**through us!**" The "Amen" seems to be a code word for "God's promises." This all came to be through Christ. Yet this Amen/promises is IN God, and BY God, and accompanies (is with) God – so God is involved in all that Christ did (cf 5:19, below) and was actually the instrument of Christ's work. Furthermore, the whole Christ Event happened IN God (cf Acts 17:28).

Now another reading of the dative case of the word "God" is that the Amen is "to God," yet it happens THROUGH Christ. This would say that Christ answers "Yes, Amen," TO God, on behalf of all humanity, and this recalls Phil. 2:10-11,

> "**that within The Name: Jesus!** (or: in union with the name [i.e., person] of Jesus), **every knee** (= person)... **would bow in prayer, submission and allegiance, and then every tongue** (= person) **may speak out the same thing** (should and would openly agree, confess, avow and acclaim) **that Jesus Christ [is] Lord – [leading] into [the] glory of Father God**."

All of this has a view "to glory." But this glory now appears THROUGH us! It is the glory of "Christ in us" (Col. 1:27), and this comes through beholding Him (3:18, below). This "glory" is an appearance of Christ that we, ourselves, assume (i.e., take on, or, are caused to appear as). We reflect His glory to the world about us. This happens in, and as, an unveiling of God's sons (Rom. 8:19). It brings God a good reputation, and incites praise to Him.

21. **Now God [is] the One repeatedly placing us on good, firm footing** (constantly stabilizing and establishing us; or: confirming, guaranteeing and validating us as possessed by a purchase) **and completely** (or: instantly, in one point in time) **anointing us, together with you folks, into Christ.** [cf 5:5, below; 1 Cor. 1:8]

Once again, our condition and situation is the work of God. This is similar to what Judah said,

> "**Now in and by** (or: with; to; for) **Him being powerful and able to keep and guard you folks from stumbling** (or: tripping) **and from harm, and then to stand you flawless and blameless** (or: unblemished; without defect or stain) **in the presence of His glory** (or: down in sight of the manifestation of Him which calls forth praise and yields a good opinion and reputation; or: down in the center of a view of the assumed appearance which is Him) **in extreme joy**" (Jude 24).

The verb of the first clause is also used in Rom. 15:8, in association with the promises of vs. 20, above:

> "**into the standing to confirm** (stabilize; make good; cause to stand by stepping in place on a good footing; or: to guarantee the validity of) **the promises from, which pertain to, and which belong to, the fathers** (or: the patriarchal promises)."

We find it again in Col. 2:7,

> "**being people having been rooted** (or: having been caused to take root) – **even ones being constantly and progressively built upon The House** (i.e., added to the structure) – **within Him; also being folks repeatedly made steadfast and progressively stabilized with good footing within the faith** (or: confirmed by the conviction; made secure for trust and loyalty)."

Then Heb. 13:9 instructs us, "**You see, [it is] beautiful** (fine; ideal; admirably proportionate) **for the heart** (= core of our being) **to be continuously made firm with a fixed footing by Grace, whose source is joy and which comes with favor.**"

The alternate use of the verb is given in the parenthetical expansion: "confirming, guaranteeing and validating us as possessed by a purchase." This is a different metaphor, but the message is the same. Our deliverance, release and salvation is all the work and action of God.

The last clause of vs. 21, here, speaks of God "**completely** (or: instantly, in one point in time) **anointing us… into Christ.**" A paraphrase of this could read: "Christing us into the Anointing," for the word *christos* means both Christ and Anointing. So in this same clause we have both the participle and the noun which in turn refer to the action, "anointing," and then to the noun, "the anointed one/the anointing." God anoints us (makes us a part of the Christ) with His Spirit. It is His Spirit that brings us "into Christ."

> "**And further, you folks continue having the effects** (or: constantly hold and progressively possess the results) **of an anointing from the set-apart One** (or: the Holy One), **and so you all have seen and are aware** (or: know; perceive; [other MSS: and you know all {those} folks])…. **and the effect of the anointing which you folks received** (or: receive) **from Him constantly remains** (abides; dwells; makes its home) **within you folks, and you continually have no use** (or: you are not constantly having a need) **that anyone should keep on teaching you** (or: be repeatedly giving you a course of lessons; coach you; instruct you), **but rather, just as the effect of His anointing is continuously and progressively teaching you about everything** (or: concerning all people), **and is continuously true, and real, and is not a lie, even according as it taught** (or: as He instructs) **you: you are continuously abiding** (remaining; dwelling; being at home) **within and in union with Him** (or, reading as an imperative: be constantly remaining, abiding, staying and dwelling within the midst of Him)" (1 Jn. 2: 20, 27).

22. **He [is] also the One completely** (or: instantly, in one point in time) **sealing us** (stamping us with an identity-mark; imprinting us for ownership; or: validating/guaranteeing our genuineness), **even** (or: and; or: and then) **completely** (instantly, in one point in time) **giving the advance transaction of the agreement** (or: the pledge and down payment guaranteeing full payment for purchase; or: a dowry) **of the Spirit** (or: which is the Spirit; or: from the Breath-effect; or: which belongs and pertains to the spirit; which pertains to the Attitude) **within the midst of our hearts.**

Here Paul uses Jewish parallelism, restating what he has just said in vs. 21 by using different metaphors to describe the results of the Christ Event. The first action by God is **sealing us**. We find this in the Unveiling, given to John, in Rev. 7:3ff and 13:16. The semantic range for this action is given in the parenthetical expansion. This metaphor is from legal or commercial life where the term can mean a "stamping with an identity-mark, or an imprinting that signifies ownership." The point of this usage is that we belong to God. The use for "validating/guaranteeing our genuineness" also comes from the realm of sales and trading. Paul, his associates, and the Corinthian community are all genuine representatives of Christ, and of God. We see in vs. 23, below, that Paul calls upon God to validate his actions.

The conjunction joining the first action to the second can be rendered "even," which would mean that the second action defines or describes the first action; or "and," which indicates that there are two actions; or, "and then," which describes a succession of actions. The "**advance transaction of the agreement**" has reference to "**the Spirit**" and can be read as the Spirit making the advance transaction, or, as apposition, can be read as a transaction, "which is the Spirit." But a reading as an ablative points us to its source, "from the Breath-effect (the meaning from the Greek elements of the word ordinarily rendered 'spirit')."

The rendering, "which belongs and pertains to the spirit," simply identifies this as a spiritual action that happens within our spirits, and belongs to the inner person of a human. We can especially see how this applies "**within the midst of our hearts**". The word "spirit" can also refer to a person's attitude, or in this case, to the Attitude of God. God no longer relates to humans with an Attitude from the Law of Moses, but with the Attitude of Grace (Jn. 1:17).

But further, this transaction of God's new agreement (in the new covenant/arrangement) takes place "**within the midst of our hearts.**" Paul uses this same expression, "advance transaction of an agreement," in 5:5, below, and we also find it in Eph. 1:13-14, where speaking of Christ it says,

> "**Whom also, upon trusting and believing, you people are stamped** (or: were sealed; marked for acceptance, or with a signet ring; = personally authorized) **by the set-apart Breath-effect of The Promise** (or: with the holy attitude of assurance; in the sacred essence from the promise; or: for the Holy Spirit which is the Promise) **– Which is continuously a pledge and guarantee of our inheritance** (or: Who remains being an advance transaction, an earnest deposit, a security and the first installment of our portion which was acquired by lot) **– [leading] unto a release into freedom** (liberation from slavery or imprisonment)…"

Putting these two verses together, we can infer that the "inheritance" of Eph. 1:14, i.e., "the set-apart Breath-effect of the Promise" (or: the Holy Spirit which is the Promise), is the Spirit of 2 Cor. 1:22, i.e., "the Spirit within the midst of our hearts." We have another description of God's reign in Eph. 4:30,

> "**Also, don't you folks have the habit of grieving** (distressing; giving sorrow or pain to; or: = troubling) **God's set-apart Spirit** (or: the Holy Breath-effect which is God), **within Whom** (or: in union with Which) **you folks were** (or: are) **sealed** (at one point stamped with a seal; suddenly marked; imprinted; = personally authorized) **into the midst of a Day associated with and arising from the liberation of a releasing-away from slavery or imprisonment** (or: a Day which is emancipation pertaining to a dismissal and a loosing-away into a freeing from bondage)."

We have another reference to a "**seal**" in 2 Tim. 2:19a,

> "**Nevertheless** (or: However), **God's firm and solid deposit which is placed down** (a deposit of money; treasure; or: a foundation; basis) **stands, continuing to hold** (or: have) **this seal:**
> > '**[The] Lord** [= Yahweh] **knows** (or: knew) **by intimate experience those being of Him** (or: the ones that belong to Him; those having Him as their source),'" [Num. 16:5; Nah. 1:7] *Cf* Rev. 7:3-8

Chapter 2

23. **Now I, myself, continue to call upon God [to be] a witness** (or: [as] evidence) **upon my own soul** (mind, will, emotions; inner life; self; or: = I stake my life on it!), **that in my continuing in holding back and sparing you folks, I no longer came** (or: I did not yet go) **into Corinth.**

As is obvious, I felt that these two verses better belong with the opening of chapter 2, where vs. 1 continues with the same subject about Paul's visit to Corinth. *Cf* 12:20-13:2, below.

In calling upon God to be his witness, we are reminded of both Elijah and Elisha calling upon Yahweh to back up their words. In 1 Ki. 17:1, Elijah uses the phrase, "As Yahweh lives, before whom I stand…" (*cf* 1 Ki. 18:18; 2 Ki. 3:14). Also, Jesus said in Jn. 5:37, "**Also, the One sending Me, that Father, has borne witness** (has testified) **about Me.**"

The last clause echoes 1 Cor. 4:21, "**Should I come to you people within [the realm of] a rod** (staff; = with corrective measures), **or within love** (solidarity), **and in a spirit of gentle friendliness and tender kindness** (or: meekness)**?**" But in both letters, he relates to them as a father to his children (1 Cor. 4:15). Witherington makes an astute observation here: "It was not an act of refraining from love, but an act of love" (ibid p 364 n 13).

24. **Not that we are constantly acting like your owners and exercising lordship with regard to the Faithfulness** (or: performing like masters over your loyalty, faith and trust), **but to the contrary, we exist**

being (or: we are) **fellow workers regarding and pertaining to your joy, for you folks have taken a stand and now stand firm by the Faithfulness** (or: in and for the Trust; or: with this faith and confident loyalty)**!**

In contrast to Christianity's "exercise of lordship" through pastors, bishops and archbishops, we see Paul declaring solidarity with the Corinthians, and affirming himself and his companions as being on the same level as his listeners: "**we exist being** (or: we are) **fellow workers regarding and pertaining to your joy.**"

The last clause echoes Rom. 11:20, "**you yourself stand in faith** (or: by trust; with confidence)." Then we hear the same thing in 1 Cor. 15:1,

> "**Now I am progressively making known to you, brothers** (= fellow called-out folks; = Family, from the same Womb), **the good news** (the message of goodness, ease and well-being) – **which I myself announced as glad tidings for you** (or: the message of goodness to you; the directive of ease and well-being among you) – **which you also accepted and embraced, as well as within which you have taken a stand, and in union with which you now stand.**"

The dative phrase, "**by the Faithfulness,**" refers to the faithfulness of Jesus to the Father, and to the work of the Spirit in the lives of the Corinthians. The renderings, "in and for the Trust" speak of the realm in which they live, and purpose for which they live. They trust Christ and their Father. Their trust is for the purposes of God. They now **stand firm** with this faith, and in confident loyalty to Christ. Paul's confidence in their stand calls to mind what he said of those in the province of Galatia,

> "**I myself have been convinced so as to be confident** (have come to a settled persuasion), **[with a view] into you folks – within [the] Lord** (or: I am confident in [the] Lord, [directing my thoughts] into you) – **that you will [in] nothing continue being disposed otherwise** (or: that you will have not [even] one other opinion or frame of mind)."

His constant encouragement identifies him as a paraclete. *Cf* vs. 3, below.

1. **So I decided this in** (or: for; by) **myself: not to come** (or: go) **to you folks again in anxiety** (or: grief; sorrow; sadness; = to make another painful visit).
2. **For since** (or: if) **I, myself, continually cause you anxiety** (sadness; sorrow; grief; pain), **who** (or: which one) **[is] the person constantly putting me in a good frame of mind** (habitually cheering me and putting my mind at ease), **if not** (or: except) **the one being constantly made sorrowful, sad, upset, anxious and caused painful grief by me?**

In vss. 1-2 we can observe Paul's sensitivity to their level of growth, and to their present situation. He wisely sets them in the position of being the only ones who can put him "**in a good frame of mind** (habitually cheering me and putting my mind at ease)." This is rhetoric to diffuse resistance and to draw-in his audience. We are aware that he had other communities to do this for him, but he is elevating their importance in what he sees as a reciprocal relationship.

3. **And so I write** (or: wrote) **this very thing, so that in coming I may** (or: should; would) **not have anxiety, sadness or grief from those concerning whom it was being necessary and binding for me to unceasingly rejoice, having been persuaded and now placing trust and confidence upon you all, because my joy has its source in all of you folks** (or: my joy exists being what pertains to all of your [situations]).

Witherington reads this section of the letter as Paul choosing "to build up goodwill and compassion" in his listeners; He "trusts that he and they will share a common joy" (ibid p 360, 364). This begs the question: Does our joy come from something that pertains to the benefit of others?

Notice the persuaded trust and confidence that Paul has in the entire community: he will not have anxiety, sadness or grief from them, but rather, unceasing joy. This must have made them feel good about their situation and condition. Such praise can evoke a positive response. Paul is a good father.

4. **You see, I write** (or: wrote) **to you from out of the midst of much pressure** (squeezing; affliction; tribulation; oppression) **and compression** (or: confinement) **of heart – through many tears – not so that you may be made anxious or sad, but rather to the end that you can** (or: may; should; would) **experience intimate knowledge and personal insight of the love** (the participating, self-giving, unrestricted, accepting drive toward reunion) **which I progressively possess and superabundantly hold [being directed] into the midst of you folks.**

Paul's very life is a living parable for the communities. He is experiencing difficult times and situations which weigh heavy on his heart – to the point of his heart's confinement! Such pathos is bringing many tears. He shares this not to make them sad or worried, but so that they can have experiential knowledge and personal insight into the love that he has for them.

The verb of the first clause, **write**, is in the fact tense (the aorist) and can be rendered as a simple present, which would have him referring to this present letter, or as a simple past (wrote) in which he would be referring to a previous letter. We cannot be certain, in this case, but in 7:8-9, below, he does refer to a previous letter, where in vs. 9a he says,

> "**Now I continue rejoicing – not just that you folks were at one point made sad or anxious** (pained or sorrowful) **– but rather, that you were made sad and anxious [leading you] into a change in thinking and frame of mind...**"

The last clause is often rendered such as, "the love I have for you in such abundance" (David Bentley Hart). This renders the preposition *eis* as "for," and this makes good sense in English, and rightly describes the surface meaning of the clause. However, the root idea of *eis* is that of something that is outside entering into the midst of something else. Human copulation is a perfect analogy for what the Greek terms portray. Paul is progressively possessing and superabundantly holding love for those folks. He is holding this "accepting drive toward reunion" focused, or directed, "**into the midst of**" them. The spiritual "participation and self-giving" is very real and existential. His unrestricted **love** (*agapē*) actually enters into them by the medium of the Holy Spirit that connects them.

5. **Now if anyone has been the cause of anxiety, pain, grief, distress, sorrow or sadness, he has not upset, caused grief or distressed me, but rather, to an extent, all of you – so then, I should not continue to be adding weight upon [you folks]** (or: but to the contrary, in part – not that I would now belabor [the point] – [it has been done to] you all).

The situations would have been different, but human nature is the same everywhere and what Paul says here calls to mind Gal. 4:12b-14a

> "**You did me no wrong** (or: You folks treat me unfairly in nothing). **Now you have seen and known that through weakness** (sickness; infirmity; feebleness) **of the flesh** (or: = pertaining to [my] imperfect human nature; = which is the deficient inner person) **I formerly brought and announced the message of goodness, ease and well-being to you folks, and yet you folks did not despise or treat as nothing your** [other MSS: my] **ordeal** (or: trial; testing) **– located within my flesh** (= in my human weaknesses)..."

But here he is referring to someone in their community, i.e., someone "**has been the cause of anxiety, pain, grief, distress, sorrow or sadness**." Paul is not specific about the issue, but assures them that the situation has not had a personal effect upon him, and in the next two verses he refers the issue back into their hands...

6. **This assessment** (or: added evaluation) – **the one [held; given] by the majority – [should be] sufficient** (or: enough) **for** (or: with; to) **such a person,**

In other words, their assessment of the situation and their evaluation of what should be done need not involve him and should be "**sufficient** (or: enough) **for** (or: with; to) **such a person**." We read in 1 Tim. 5:20,

> "**habitually put to the proof, test or expose** (or: lay bare and reprove) **the [folks] habitually missing the target or constantly being in error** (or: those repeatedly sinning; those continuously failing) **before all onlookers** (or: in the sight of all), **to the end that the rest, also, may continue holding reverence** (or: having respectful fear)."

But Gal. 6:1 explains how this should be done:

> "**Brothers! Even if a person may be at some point overtaken** (caught; laid hold of before; be surprised) **within the effect of some slip or falling to the side** (or: the result of some offense, lapse or mistake), **you folks – the spiritual ones** (the people influenced by the Breath-effect and Attitude) **– repeatedly** (or: continuously) **thoroughly restore, reconcile, adjust, align, mend or repair such a one so as to thoroughly prepare and equip him, within a spirit of gentle friendliness** (attitude of meekness; breath of mild kindness), **as you each are constantly keeping a watchful eye on yourself** (carefully noting yourself with regard to the goal), **and so you folks may not at some point be put to the proof** (or: and you, yourself, would not be tried, tested or harassed by some ordeal)."

And Heb. 12:12 adds,

> "'**straighten up** (or: build anew and restore) **those hands hanging down helplessly, and those knees having been paralyzed or loosened at the sides.**'" [Isa. 35:3]

Paul says the same thing in the next verse...

7. **so that in its place – and to a greater degree – you folks are to extend favor and grace, and then to perform as paracletes** (call him alongside giving aid, relief, encouragement, and comfort/consolation), **lest somehow such a person may be swallowed up by more excessive anxiety** (or: drunk down in, and to, more abundant sorrow, grief, pain, distress and sadness).

Now he advises them about what should happen "**in its** place," i.e., in the aftermath of the situation. Observe that the Corinthians are called "**to extend favor and grace, and then to perform as paracletes**." He is admonishing them to do the very same thing to this person that he, himself, is constantly doing to, and for, the community. Even though this person "**has been the cause of anxiety, pain, grief, distress, sorrow or sadness**," they are to "call him alongside giving aid, relief, encouragement, and comfort/consolation." They are to be Christ to him, or her.

8. **Therefore, I continue to call you folks alongside** (or: I am habitually being a paraclete, encouraging and entreating you) **to affirm** (make valid; ratify; authoritatively confirm) **love unto him** (unrestricted acceptance and urges toward reunion, into the midst of him),

And so Paul now metaphorically calls them to his side to encourage and entreat them "**to affirm** (make valid; ratify; authoritatively confirm) **love unto him** (unrestricted acceptance and urges toward reunion, into the midst of her)."

9. **for I write, also, into this [purpose], to the end that I can personally** (intimately and experientially) **come to know the proof** (evidence) **from your testing – whether you folks continue being those who submissively listen and pay attention unto all people** (or: hear and obey as you proceed into all situations; or: humbly pay attention, with a view to all [that has been said]).

Acting as a father to them, he seeks "**to know the proof** (evidence) **from [their] testing**." And what proof, or evidence, does he expect to see? That they "**continue being those who submissively listen

and pay attention unto all people." Why would this be important? We suggest that it would indicate that they are sheep, and not young kids (Mat. 25:31-46). This also describes gracious behavior toward people.

The parenthetical rendering offers a neuter reading of "all," suggesting that it may refer to "all that has been said" by Paul. Or, it can be applied as they proceed "into all situations." The cultural nuance of the verb "submissively listen and pay attention" communicates the notion of obedience to instruction. For historical Israel, to hear also meant to obey. The clause can also simply be rendered, "humbly pay attention, with a view to all." The qualifier "**submissively**" or "humbly" is indicated by the prefix *hupo-* (under) added to the verb.

10. **Now to whom you repeatedly extend grace or deal favorably [concerning] anything** (or: Now for whom you constantly deal graciously or give forgiveness [in] anything), **I also [do], for you see, in whatever I myself have also been extended grace, treated graciously or forgiven – since I have been extended grace, favor or forgiveness for something** (or, as a middle: for what I myself have extended grace – if I have extended grace for anything) – **[it is] on account of and for the sake of you folks, within the presence of Christ** (or: in union with the face of the Anointing; = in sync with what the anointing looks like),

Performing as a paraclete, as admonished in vs. 7, above, is defined here as "**extend grace or deal favorably**." Paul joins in solidarity with them in both their decisions and their actions, by saying, "**I also**." The reciprocity of this union between Paul and the community is seen is his explanation:

> "**for you see, in whatever I myself have also been extended grace, treated graciously or forgiven – since I have been extended grace, favor or forgiveness for something** (or, as a middle: for what I myself have extended grace – if I have extended grace for anything) – **[it is] on account of and for the sake of you folks**."

Take note of the repetition of the speaking about the giving and receiving of grace between people. We get the sense of the importance of a topic when he keeps speaking of it. Paul's **extending grace** is for the sake of the covenant community. But what about the final prepositional phrase?

We suggest that "**within the presence of Christ**" is another way of saying what he said in 1:14b, above, "**resident within and in union with the Day which pertains to, is from, and is, our Lord (Master), Jesus**." We saw there that it was speaking of the New Day of the Age of the Messiah – a present situation. Since Christ is within us, He is present, as we see in vs. 19, below. Since two or three are gathered together in His name, as a covenant community, He is among them (Mat. 18:20).

That phrase can also be rendered, "in union with the face (= focused presence which pays attention to us) of the Anointing." I have suggested an interpretive paraphrase, "in sync with what the anointing looks like," which is like saying, "aligned with what Christ looks like."

Observe that their "**repeatedly extending grace**" (first clause) winds up being "**on account of and for the sake of you folks**." The entire community benefits from extending grace and dealing favorably with "**anything**."

11. **to the end that we may** (or: can; would) **not at some point be held or possessed in more things or situations by the adversary** (or: be made, under "*satan*," to claim to have more than other folks; or: be overreached by [our] opponent, so as to desire personal advantage), **for we do not continue being without intimate and experiential knowledge of the effects from its directing people's perceptions, concepts and understanding** (or: we are not still ignorant, unaware or without *gnosis* about the results from directing one's mind from it).

This verse informed his listeners of the purpose for what he had just said in vs. 10. There is a purpose for every aspect of life in God's reign. There are purposes for living as a covenant community in Christ. One of those purposes is: "**to the end that we may** (or: can; would) **not at some point be held or possessed in more things or situations by the adversary**." The "adversary" (the word is *satan* in Greek) is different in each situation, and for each person, and at each moment or season in our lives. Paul had been an adversary to the body of Christ, before his conversion and transformation. The Jews who held to Judaism were adversaries of Paul, as well as of the Christ movement. The Law served as an adversary to make failure and sin increase (Rom. 5:20a; 7:9-11). The ethnic multitudes had been adversaries to ancient Israel. Job's friends were adversaries to him in his trials. Our inner, human wisdom can be adversarial to God's directions (e.g., the Garden of Eden affair). Any or all of these situations can come to possess us. We saw the Lord informing Paul that His grace was sufficient for the situation described in 12:7-10 (a "thorn" in his flesh), below. This grace is often administered through members of Christ's body, as they perform as paracletes.

Let us take a moment and consider what Peter said in 1 Pet. 5:8, and my comments on that verse, from *Pete, Paul & Jacob*, Harper Brown, 2012 pp 35-37:

8. **Be sober** (or: clear headed)! **Be awake, alert and watch! Your barrier in the Way pointed out** (your road hazard; your opponent at court; the one "in your face" opposing your fairness and equity), **one who casts or thrusts something through the midst of folks**
> (e.g., like a soldier casting a javelin or thrusting a sword through someone, or a person throwing an issue through the midst of a group, causing division; or: a slanderer), **as a constantly roaring lion, is continuously walking about, incessantly seeking to drink something or someone down** (or: searching to gulp and swallow [someone] down),
> [comment: this path-hazard and road barrier may have been local religions, cultural or political opposition, or a spirit of contrariness]

This verse should not be taken out of context and made to be a description of the works of "the devil," as has been the tradition. It flows out of vs. 6-7, describing the situation in which "**God's strong hand**" will humble us. Jacob/James 4:10 tell us, "**You must be made low** (humbled; demoted) **in the Lord's sight** (= in [Yahweh's, or Christ's] presence), **and then He will lift you up** (elevate you)." We see God's strong hand in Ex. 3:20 where Yahweh "put forth [His] hand" to smite Egypt. The "rod of God" (Moses' staff) brought victory to Israel in Ex. 17:9-12, but it had become a snake in Ex. 7:10-12, and brought plagues on Egypt in vs. 19-20. In ch. 10:3, Yahweh says to Pharaoh through Moses, "How long will you refuse to humble yourself before Me?"

Recall the story of Job, and how in ch. 40 and 42 he responded humbly to Yahweh. In ch. 2:10 he said, "Indeed, should we receive good from the One, Elohim, and should we not receive evil? In all this Job did not sin (err, miss the target) with his lips" (Concordant Version; my expansion). This last statement says that Job was right, that we should receive evil from God. But we see in the first two chapters that God used an adversary (the Sabeans; the Chaldeans), or adversarial situations (lightning; a great wind) and personal affliction (boils) – and Job was humbled. But later, Yahweh raised him up, as we see in ch. 42.

In Hos. 5:14-15 (LXX) we see Yahweh describing Himself:
> "**Because of this, I Myself am like** (or: exist being as) **a panther to** (or: for; in) **Ephraim, and like a lion to** (or: for; in) **the house of Judah: thus I Myself will tear, and then journey on; I will take** (grasp in [My] hand; seize), **and there will be no one to be rescuing and dragging [folks] out of [My grasp].**

I will journey on and return into My place until they will be caused to disappear, and then they will search for My face, and seek My presence."

Now in vs. 9, below, he tells us that "**these same experiences and suffering**," which they had observed as having come upon others in the brotherhood, were "**to repeatedly and progressively bring the goal**" that God had in mind, and in vs. 10-11 he says that it is God and His strength that will do this. These experiences are the same things that he spoke of in ch's. 1:6 and 4:12-14. Paul, in 2 Thes. 1:4-5 says,

> "... **all your pursuits** (or: chasings; or: persecutions; harassments) **and the pressures** (squeezings; constrictions; contractions; tribulations; oppressions; ordeals) **which you habitually have again** (or: sustain; hold up). **[This is] a display-effect** (result of pointing-out; demonstration) **of God's fair and equitable** (just; righteous; in accord with the Way pointed out) **decision** (separation for making a distinction and an evaluation or a judging), **unto your being accounted worthy** (of equal value) **of God's kingdom** (or: the sovereign reign which is God), **over** (or: on behalf of) **which you are also constantly having sensible experiences** (or: normally feeling emotions; or: repeatedly suffering)."

This being the case, they were nonetheless admonished to "**Be sober** (or: clear headed)! **Be awake, alert and watch!**" As the Messiah was delivered to the Romans "**by the specific, determined, bounded** (limited) **plan** (intended purpose, design and counsel) **and foreknowledge** (intimate knowledge which was experienced beforehand) **of God**" (Acts 2:23), so were they delivered into these tests and trials. As Jesus told His disciples to "watch" and "pray" in Gethsemane, so Peter advises these folks, and us. Paul in Eph. 6:10-18 told them to put on God's armor and to take a stand (as in vs. 9, below).

Dr. Ann Nyland (*The Source NT*, Smith and Stirling Publishing, 2004) points out that the Greek *diabolos* means "slanderer," and thus translates in a similar way the idea expressed by my expansion "opponent at court," seeing this as a legal metaphor. What I rendered "**Your barrier in the Way pointed out** (your road hazard; your opponent at court; the one 'in your face' opposing your fairness and equity)" she sees as a figure of a lawyer in a court of law, and a legal suit. The entire clause refers to opposition against the called-out community. There are folks or forces that are trying to thrust slander, legal suits, or whatever, to defame and discredit the community of faith, and as Saul did against the early church, these folks are operating as a roaring lion, wanting to devour this move of God. We face similar oppositions in our day, and history is replete with examples. Also see 2 Tim. 4:17c.

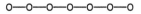

The verb of the first clause of vs. 11 is a compound of the comparative "more" with the verb *echō* that means both "to have, or possess," and "to hold." Here it is in the passive voice. The bold rendering offers the preposition *hupo* as "by," in the final phrase, "**by the adversary**." This identifies the adversary as the source and actor of the "things or situations" that can potentially "hold or possess" Paul or his listeners, as described in the previous paragraph. But *hupo* also, literally, means "under." Thus, the first parenthetical rendering offers, "be made, under 'satan,' to claim to have more than other folks." Again, "satan," here can be any of the things, attitudes or people discussed, above. And the verb can be understood to be speaking of "having more" than other people. The last rendering offers: "be overreached by [our] opponent, so as to desire personal advantage." Here, our opponent – in regard to the Way pointed out – may be a spirit of greed or an attitude of jealousy when thinking about, or observing, those who have more than we do. The temptation is to try to find some way of getting an advantage in whatever particular system that is attracting us. It is an inner attitude that is contrary to the Spirit of Christ: the Spirit of Generosity.

But now to the last half of the verse: "**for we do not continue being without intimate and experiential knowledge of the effects from its directing people's perceptions, concepts and understanding** (or: we are not still ignorant, unaware or without *gnosis* about the results from directing one's mind from it)." It has been a tradition, within Christianity, to personify the Greek term *satan* and thus render the possessive pronoun as "his," in modifying the noun "directing one's mind, perceptions, concepts, or understanding." But this possessive pronoun can also be neuter, or neutral. My choice, from consideration of the semantic range of the term *satan*, was to render it as the neutral genitive of possession, "**its**," in the bold offering, and as a neutral ablative, "from it," in the parenthetical option.

The religion of Second Temple Judaism was a source of "directing people's perceptions, concepts and understanding." Paul warns them about "the effects" (the *–ma* ending of the noun) of this. The culture of Hellenism, the politics of the Roman Empire, and the ego-centered distortion of the first Adam, all have correlating "results" if we direct our minds from the centers, or from the world views, of any or all of them. Paul and his listeners were not unaware of these sources of opposition, and of the effects of thinking or perceiving from those paradigms.

12. Now on coming (or: going) **into Troas – [continuing] on into the midst of Christ's good news** (the message of goodness, ease and well-being, which is the Anointing), **there also having been opened up, and still standing open, a door to and for me, within [the] Lord** [= Christ or Yahweh] (or: by and with me, in union with [the] Master and centered in [our] Owner) –

Here is more discussion of Paul's travels, but we can be instructed by his expressions and the metaphor of "a door standing open" to, or for, him. We suspect that he simply meant "an opportunity," as we still use this metaphor today. But notice that he perceives himself as coming or going... "**into the midst of Christ's good news**." The message of goodness, ease and well-being was seen as the realm of his life. It was open "**to** or **for**" him. The participle is in the perfect tense, so this door had already been opened up. It is in the passive voice, and so we may conclude that this is the "divine passive," i.e., that God has opened this door for Paul.

The dative case of "**me**" can also function so that it would read, "opened by or with me," and in this case he would be referring to the results of his ministry and the reputation that went before him. Furthermore, this "door of opportunity" was perceived as being "**within [the] Lord**." This can also be read as "in union with [the] Master," or, "centered in [our] Owner." The bold reading would be saying that, like Paul who was "in Christ," this opportunity was within the realm of Christ. The reading, "in union with [the] Master," signifies Paul being a co-laborer with Christ, and the solidarity that he had with our Master. The final reading, "centered in [our] Owner," suggests the nuance of Paul being Christ's slave (Rom. 1:1) and that his whole ministry had its center in Christ. It is amazing how much information can be unpacked from two Greek words!

13. **I had not had a release** (or: a relaxing; a letting flow; a relief) **in** (or: by; to; for; with) **my spirit** (or: inner breath-effect; attitude) **regarding my continuing not to find Titus, my brother, but instead, on sending off arrangements for myself among them and bidding them farewell, I went off into Macedonia.**

Observe Paul's being in touch with his own sprit (the inner "breath-effect," or "attitude"). "A **release**, a relaxing, a letting flow, a relief." If we ponder each expression of this semantic range, we can gain insight into how he viewed his "spirit," and how this "inner breath-effect" could function. The dative form of the phrase offers a variety of nuances of this functioning. Understanding the noun as "attitude," can bring his words into a slightly different place in his inner workings. The lack of an expressed preposition offers us latitude from this very ambiguity. We can identify with Paul on more than one level. All of this culminated in a decision, from his "**continuing not to find Titus**." He went off into Macedonia.

The beauty of these seemingly insignificant details instruct us by a snap-shot of what it meant, in Paul's life, to walk in the spirit/Spirit, or be "led by the Spirit" (Rom. 8:14).

14. **Now grace and favor [are] in, with and by God – in, by and with the One constantly celebrating us with a victory procession** (or: progressively exhibiting us in a triumphal procession) **at all times, within and in union with the Christ, and progressively** (or: habitually) **setting in clear light** (manifesting) **the fragrance** (aroma; odor; perfume) **of His intimate knowledge** (or: of the experience of intimacy and insight which has its source in knowing Him; or: the knowledge and *gnosis* from, and which, is Him) **through us in every place,**

I was pleased to find David Bentley Hart rendering *charis* correctly here, as "grace," instead of the common rendering, "thanks," that most other translations offer. As with many sentences in Greek, the English translation must add a copula. Since I have conflated the meanings of *charis* to read "grace and favor," I have supplied a plural copula, "[are]." The noun, "God," is in the dative case, so we have the usual options of functions which can fit this statement of fact: "**grace and favor [are] in, with and by God**." This assertion is followed by a subordinate participial clause, in the present (durative; lineal) tense, that modifies the previous prepositional phrase, about God, with another dative phrase that further describes God: "**in, by and with the One constantly causing us to triumph** (or: progressively leading us in a triumphal procession) **at all times**." Observe how the construction of this clause modifies "God," in the same way that a similar construction modified "Jesus Christ," in 1:19, above: "**the Son of God, Jesus Christ – the One within the midst of, among, and in union with you folks**."

The meaning of the participle has been debated by scholars, so I have on offer two competing renderings. The parenthetical interpretation comes from the practice of a returning triumphant Roman army leading an exhibit of its conquered captives in a parade back into the city of Rome. But Paul's reference (if this is the actual source of his metaphor) could point to the army, led by its general, that heads up the parade. So the "**us**" in this clause could be either a part of God's team (*cf* Rev. 19:11-16), or a part of those that He has conquered. Paul may have seen himself as one of this latter group, since as Saul he was a part of the opposing forces. In either scenario, we could be "**Christ's sweet fragrance**" (vs. 15, below). Now since Paul has elsewhere used the metaphor of the games, perhaps this should simply be understood as "**celebrating us with a victory procession**." He leads us, He exhibits us, He celebrates us with His victory over Death. Observe the qualifier that modifies this activity: "**at all times**." This is not speaking of a one-time event. Changing metaphors, this could be the celebration of the Messianic banquet, or the celebratory marriage procession of Mat. 25:10.

This verse seems to display parallelism. The first clause ends with, "at all times;" the second clause ends with, "**in every place**." So this second clause says the same thing as the first clause, but using a different metaphor: "**progressively** (or: habitually) **setting in clear light** (manifesting) **the fragrance** (aroma; odor; perfume) **of His intimate knowledge** (or: of the experience of intimacy and insight which has its source in knowing Him; or: the knowledge and *gnosis* from, and which is, Him)." This metaphor of "fragrance" is an allusion to Israel's offerings, and especially the altar of incense that is centered in the holy place of the Temple (*cf* Rev. 8:3, 4). Or, it could be an allusion to Song 3:6; 4:6.

Both of these things happen, "**within and in union with the Christ**," which Paul sets in the middle of the verse, pointing in both directions, and yet also, it all takes place, "**through us**" – which harks back to 1:20, above. He continuously works through His body, which is the Vine's cluster of branches (Jn. 15:1ff).

15. **because within** (or: by) **God, we continuously exist being Christ's sweet fragrance** (or: because, with God, we are an aroma of well-being from an Anointing; or: because for God we continue being an odor of ease, and a smell of goodness, which is Christ) **within and among those being progressively delivered** (habitually rescued; continuously made whole and restored; repeatedly saved; constantly kept

safe) **– yet also within and among those being progressively loosed-away** (or: habitually destroying themselves; or: repeatedly being lost)**:**

Observe that the dative form of the term "God" is used again, but this time the copula is supplied, "**we continuously exist being**." In and by Him, we are "**Christ's sweet fragrance** (or: because, with God, we are an aroma of well-being from an Anointing; or: because for God we continue being an odor of ease, and a smell of goodness, which is Christ)." What a magnificent function we serve. We recognize and remember through fragrances. This is another metaphor of our bringing Christ's sweetness to the world. But this is tied to "the Anointing," which calls to mind Mat. 26:7-12 and Lu. 23:56. We are also called back to Ps. 23:5; 45:7; 92:10; 133:2; Eccl. 7:1; Song. 1:3; Isa. 61:3.

"**Those being progressively delivered** (habitually rescued; continuously made whole and restored; repeatedly saved; constantly kept safe)" is a description of the called-out communities. They recognize this perfume and rejoice at its fragrance – the fragrance of Christ in and among them, the expectation of His glory. But "**within and among those being progressively loosed-away**" – those who hold to the old covenant and the former age of the Law, and thus are "repeatedly lost" – these communities were something else, as the next verse explains...

16. **to** (in; for; with) **these [latter ones], a stench from out of Death, [leading] into death** (or: from the midst of [one] death on into [another, or, more] death); **yet to** (in; for; with) **those [former ones] a fragrance from out of Life, [leading] into life** (or: from out of the midst of [one Life] on into [another, or, more] life). **So who [is] adequate, sufficient or qualified [in facing or approaching] toward these matters?**

This verse finishes vs. 15. Why were these other folks "**a stench from out of Death**"? Because they were going "**into death**" in AD 70. It was a stench from the spiritual (and metaphorical) death in which they were dwelling, being full of dead men's bones (Mat. 23:27); they were carnally minded (Rom. 8:6).

The sweet fragrance of those of 15a was "**a fragrance from out of Life, [leading] into life**." They were the fragrance of the Christ Life, which lead into the Life of the Age of the Messiah. They were the fragrance of resurrection Life, from out of the death of the first Adam (Rom. 5:12) and into the Life that is the Last Adam, which is the Life that is the Light of humanity (Jn. 1:4). With the parenthetical expansion, "from out of the midst of [one Life] on into [another, or, more] life," we have a preview of 3:18, below:

> "**presently being continuously and progressively transformed into the very same image and form, from glory unto glory – in accord with and exactly as – from [the] Lord's Breath-effect.**"

After all this building up, his question brings everyone to humility. "**So who [is] adequate...?**" "What is man that you are mindful of him, and the son of man that you care for him?" (Ps. 8:4). But the next verse really gives the answer, and 17b lays out the qualifications...

17. **You see, we are not – as the majority [are] – ones performing as hucksters in shameful traffic for unworthy gain, constantly peddling and marketing God's message** (God's thought and idea; the Word of God; the *Logos* from God), **but to the contrary, we are constantly and habitually speaking as from out of the midst of that which is decided about when viewing in clear sunlight – and further, as from out of the midst of God; down within, in union with, and in the place of, God – within Christ!** (or: but in contrast, as out of clear integrity, we are progressively speaking in an Anointing – as [being] forth from God [and] in God's presence!)

This affirmation is the direct answer to the rhetorical question that ends vs. 16, and in the Greek text there is no separation between the question and this response. Hucksters and peddlers are NOT "adequate, sufficient or qualified" with regard to the matters that Paul is discussing. Sadly, in Paul's day and also in ours, "**the majority**" are **hucksters** and **peddlers**. There is money to be made, in religion.

The qualification for presenting the Good News must be compared to people who "**are constantly and habitually speaking as from out of the midst of that which is decided about when viewing in clear sunlight**." Now what Light might this be? We think that Paul explains this in 4:6, below:

> "**the God suddenly saying, 'Light will shine forth** (give light as from a torch; gleam) **from out of the midst of darkness** (dimness and shadiness; gloom and the absence of daylight),' [is] the One who shines forth within the midst of our hearts, with a view to illumination of the intimate and experiential knowledge of God's glory – in a face of Christ**."

It is the Light of the new creation (5:17, below). There must be no deceit or trickery; no subterfuge; no hidden motive of gain. A common rendering of the preposition phrase is, "from (or: out of) sincerity," which is given in the lexicons. But the noun literally means, "that which is being judged or decided about from viewing it in sunshine," so I have offered this as the first rendering, for the best picture of Paul's meaning. They, and their message, can be clearly seen to be pure, and the Light of Christ is the standard of purity. From this, one of the lexical meanings is "purity" (i.e., of substance – i.e., no mixture of other ingredients). They are "the real deal." The parenthetical rendering gives, "as out of clear integrity." In our current culture, the word "sincerity" has been watered-down.

But more than this, Paul and his associates obtain their "adequacy" by speaking "**as from out of the midst of God**." So we see how Paul perceives the realm in which he and his companions live, and speak. They spoke *ex cathedra*: from out of the Temple, which they were; from out of being seated with Christ, in the heavenly realm of God's atmosphere (Eph. 2:6). They spoke from out of the holy of holies, i.e., from out of the presence of God, Who dwells among and within us (we are His temple, i.e., His home). They know the realm from which they minister: the realm of God's sovereign influence – the realm of the Spirit. The coordinating conjunction, "**as**," occurs three times in this verse. Each use introduces how people are functioning. The first is negative; the next two set Paul and his friends on solid ground – as being trustworthy and dependable.

He goes on to color-in the picture of the place of where they stand, and the realm from which they speak: "**down within, in union with, and in the place of, God**." This phrase is from *kata* (down) + *en* (within/in union with/centered in) + *anti* (in the place of), modifying the noun, God. This phrase is parallel to being "**within the midst of God**" (*cf* Acts 17:28), and expands our understanding of what it means to be "**joined to the Lord**" (1 Cor. 6:17).   The optional rendering is, "in God's presence." Paul is straining to have them get the picture of "being in Christ" – and so he adds-on the phrase: "**within Christ!**" What a picture he paints!

However, the syntax can be read in a different order, but saying essentially the same thing: "but in contrast, as out of clear integrity, we are progressively speaking in an Anointing – as [being] forth from God [and] in God's presence!" This is closer to the common renderings, but think about it: it is simply the other side of the same coin – a different view of the same existential situation. Being in God's presence was what Moses experienced when, in the holy of holies, he spoke with God "face-to-face" (Ex. 33:11).

And furthermore, there is no shameful trafficking here (Ezk. 28:5). No religion here. No Babylon here (Rev. 17-18).

Chapter 3

1. **Are we beginning again to continue commending ourselves** (giving ourselves a standing together with [you folks]) **as if we, like some, now need letters of recommendation to you, or from you?**

It seems that likely the "**hucksters [who] shamefully traffic for unworthy gain,**" of 2:17, above, are behind Paul's forensic rhetoric that we find here in chapters 3-4. He gives a direct, negative answer to this rhetorical question in 5:12, below. He is making a defense against such folks who probably resided in Corinth. "Letters of introduction or recommendation... were exceedingly common in antiquity" (Witherington, ibid p 377; cf Acts 18:27). Paul's tactic is asking if he and his companions are like strangers who need others to recommend them to the Corinthians. We can sense a bit of sarcasm by feigning insecurity toward them, yet ironically shooting these words towards his opponents, who were in fact false representatives of Christ.

2. **You yourselves are and continue being our letter – being one having been written** (inscribed; imprinted; engraved) **within your hearts** [other MSS: our hearts]; **one progressively being experientially known and continuously read** (or: periodically recognized and experienced again) **by all people** (human beings) **–**

But he quickly turns to the facts of the case. THEY are their letter of recommendation! Paul had written, even engraved, this letter **in the hearts** of the Corinthians. Perhaps that letter had also been "**sealed**" (1:22, above). Perhaps that letter was the "**the advance transaction of the agreement of the Spirit within the midst of [their] hearts**" (1:22). It was a letter "**progressively being experientially known and continuously read** (or: periodically recognized) **by all people!**" People were reading the Word of God in the lives of these Corinthians! This letter had been written by Paul's group by being "**fellow workers regarding and pertaining to [their] joy**" (1:24, above).

Recall his words in 1 Cor. 9:2b,
> "**you, yourselves, are my seal of the expedition** (or: = the validated document of my sent-off mission), **within, and in union with, the Lord** (or: centered in the Master)."

3. **because you are and continue being those continuously set in clear light and progressively manifested: Christ's letter** (a letter whose source is Christ, and which is Christ), **being one dispensed in attending service by us, being one having been written** (inscribed; imprinted; engraved), **not in black** (= not with ink), **but rather, by** (or: in; with) **God's Spirit: One continuously living** (or: in a Breath-effect which has its origin in God, Who is constantly living); **not in stone tablets** (or: on tablets composed of stone), **but rather within tablets which are hearts made of flesh** (or: on tablets in hearts composed of flesh). [cf 1 Cor. 3:5; Rom. 8:26-27]

The old, Mosaic covenant originated with STONE tablets, which had the arrangements, instructions and commands that God had written on them, laying out how Israel, as a society and as individuals, should live and behave. But within this arrangement there was provision for a more intimate, organic relationship with Yahweh. Some, in Israel's history, came to know Him on this more personal relationship. In Ps. 40:8b we read, "Your law is in the midst of my internal parts" (CVOT). That was the prelude to what comprised the promise of the new covenant, spoken of in Jer. 31:33. Then Ezekiel announced,
> "And so I will give them [i.e., all the house of corporate Israel] one heart, and I will put a new spirit within you; and I will take the stony heart out of their flesh and will give them a heart of flesh" (Ezk. 11:19).

Ezk. 36:26 said the almost the same thing, but there speaking of "a new heart."

The first clause, here, puts his listeners in the same category as described about himself in the first clause of 1:17b, above. They stand on the same ground, in Christ. In fact, they themselves are "**Christ's letter,**" a "**letter whose source is Christ,**" which was "**dispensed in attending service by [Paul and his companions].**" He is basically repeating the first clause of vs. 2, above. Then he further explains that it was not a letter written in ink on a parchment, "**but rather, by** (or: in; with) **God's Spirit.**" Next he takes them deeper: God's Spirit is "**One continuously living not in stone tablets** [note: a reference to the Law] **but rather within tablets which are hearts made of flesh.**" This could alternately be read, "in, or with, a Breath-effect which has its origin in God, Who is constantly living." In Heb. 8:10, we find it put this way:

> "**Because this is the arrangement** (covenant; disposition) **which I shall continue arranging for the house of Israel, after those days,' says the Lord: 'progressively giving My Laws into their thought** (into that which goes through their mind; into their perception and comprehension), **and I shall progressively imprint them** (write or inscribe marks) **upon their hearts, and I shall continue being in and among them** ([in relation] to them; for them), **into** [the position of] **a God, and they shall continue being** (exist being) **in Me** ([in relation] to Me; for Me), **into** [the position of] **a people.'"**

This is the "letter" of which Paul now speaks, in regard to the Corinthians.

We should note that the term "**flesh**," in this context, does not have a negative sense; rather it indicates people. The contrast is between something outside of a person (something "written in stone"; a legal construct; a civil or religious law) and that which is within a person – something of one's nature that has been written in the core of his or her being, by the Spirit of God. This is a classic contrast between the old covenant and the new covenant. The old involved outward observance and compliance; the new pertained to the heart of a person (cf vs. 16, below). A classic example of this was given by Jesus, in Mat. 5:27-28,

> "**You folks hear** (or: heard) **that it was declared,**
> **'You will not continue committing adultery!'** [Ex. 20:13]
> **Yet I, Myself, am now saying to you people that every man who is continuing in, or, repeatedly looking at and observing** (constantly watching or leering at; = fantasizing over) **a [married] woman, with a view toward the [situation, or, condition] to crave her** (to experience strong passion for her, or, to desire to rush in a heat of emotion upon her), **has already committed adultery with her, within his heart!**"

O'Rourke defines the following, vss. 4-18, as a comparison of the old and new covenants (ibid).

4. **Now through the Christ we continuously possess** (or: So, by means of the Anointing we progressively have and hold) **this sort of persuaded trust and faith-based confidence [directed and leading] toward God** (or: face to face with God)

This is a very straightforward statement that having "**persuaded trust and faith-based confidence [directed and leading] toward God** (or: face to face with God)" is "through the Christ," or, "by means of the Anointing." Apart from Him, faith and trust do not reside in us. But now, Paul is beginning his argument…

5. **– not that we are competent** (adequately enough; sufficiently qualified) **from ourselves to logically evaluate or count anything as it were forth from out of ourselves – but to the contrary, our competency** (adequacy; sufficiency; qualification) **[is] forth from out of the midst of** (having its source in) **God,**

Here, vs. 5 is reaching back to 2:16b-17, with Paul reiterating about himself and his associates what he had just said, above, by saying: "**our competency** (adequacy; sufficiency; qualification) **[is] forth from out of the midst of** (having its source in) **God.**" He once again re-affirms that God is the validation for them, and for what they teach. God is the source of their competency and qualification – not some human organization or tradition. Paul was probably aware that Jesus had said to His disciples, "**apart from** (or: separated from) **Me you folks continue having ability and power to do** (make; construct; create; form; perform; produce) **nothing!**" (Jn. 15:5b) Cf 1 Cor. 15:10, above.

6. **Who also adequately qualifies us** (or: made us fit, competent and sufficient) **[to be] attending servants and dispensers of an arrangement that is new in quality** (or: pertaining to a new kind of

covenant that has a different, innovative character and is fresh and effective) – **not of [the] letter** (or: not from Scripture, or pertaining to the result of that which is written down; not having its source in Scripture or the effect of a written text), **but in contrast, of a Breath-effect** (or: pertaining to the result of [the] Spirit; having its source in and being the effect of spirit and attitude), **for the effect of letter habitually kills** (or: Scripture, the result of writing something into a text, repeatedly puts away in death), **yet the Spirit** (or: the spirit; the Breath-effect; the Attitude) **continuously produces Life** (or: repeatedly makes alive; progressively forms life; habitually creates Life)! [*cf* Rom. 8:2, 6]

As a good rhetor, he repeats his point, this time adding that God "**adequately qualifies**" them, and this is so that they can function as "**attending servants and dispensers of an arrangement that is new in quality**." The last phrase can also be rendered, "pertaining to a new kind of covenant that has a different, innovative character and is fresh and effective." As he will say in 5:17, below, the old has passed and the new has come. He is early-on preparing them for the astonishing presentations in chapter 5.

In vs. 3, above, he stated that THEY were a letter that was written by the Spirit. But now he makes it clear that this new arrangement (covenant) was "**NOT of [the] letter**," i.e., something that was written down, "**but in contrast, of a Breath-effect**." Not only was it not written on tablets of stone, as was the former covenant, but this new covenant is "pertaining to the result of [the] Spirit; having its source in and being the effect of spirit and attitude." It had to do with the kingdom and reign of God that is within us, where we are joined to the Lord and are one Spirit/spirit (1 Cor. 6:17).

The next clause makes a bold statement: "**the effect of letter habitually kills** (or: Scripture, the result of writing something into a text, repeatedly puts away in death)." Now this echoes what Paul said in Rom. 7:
> 9. **Now I was at one time** (or: formerly) **habitually living apart from Law** (or: I was once alive, independent from custom and [Torah]); **yet, in connection with the coming of the implanted goal** (of the impartation of the finished product within; of the inward commandment and directive), **the Sin becomes alive again** (or: deviation, failure, error and the missing of the target revived and comes back to life), **but I die** (or: and I died; yet I die).
> 10. **Also, the implanted goal** (impartation of the finished product within; inward directive; commandment) – **the one [meant to lead] into Life – this was found by me** (for me; in me; to me) **[to be leading] into death.**

Paul made this clear in Gal. 3:10,
> "**You see, however many people continue their existence from the midst of observances and works of Law** (= Everyone who lives by deeds and actions based upon the Torah) **are continuously under a curse** (a negative, down-focused or adversarial prayer; an imprecation), **for it has been and now stands written, namely that,**
> > '**A curse** (or: an adversarial prayer; imprecation) **[is settled] upon all** (or: [is] added to everyone) **not constantly remaining within all the things having been and standing written within the scroll of the Law** [= Torah], **in order to do them.**'" [Deut. 27:26]

We should not take this statement, here in the middle of vs. 6, apart from the following, contrasting clause: "**yet the Spirit** (or: the spirit; the Breath-effect; the Attitude) **continuously produces Life** (or: repeatedly makes alive; progressively forms life; habitually creates Life)." Paul is contrasting two covenants, two arrangements for relating to God, and for God dealing with humans. He put it this way, in Rom. 7:6,
> "**But now** (at the present time), **we** [= Israel] **are** (or: were instantly) **rendered inactive** (brought down to living without labor, released from employment, made unproductive; discharged) **away from the Law** (= the Torah; [some MSS add: of Death]), **dying within that in which we were constantly being held down** (held in possession and detained), **so that it is [for] us to be habitually performing as slaves within newness of spirit** (a newness pertaining to spirit and

has its source in the Breath-effect; freshness and new quality of attitude) **and not in oldness** (obsoleteness; outdatedness) **of Letter** (or: not in outwornness of written Scripture)."

That "oldness, outdatedness, outwornness" was put this way in Heb. 8:13, when speaking of the covenants: "**In thus to be saying 'new: different in kind and quality, He has made the first** (or: former) **'old,' and that [which is] progressively growing old** (or: obsolete) **and decrepit** (failing of age; ageing into decay), **[is] near its disappearing** (vanishing away)." Its time of direct application had passed. But we need to keep all of Paul's arguments of Rom. 7 in mind here, for,

> "**For you see, we have seen and are aware** (or: on the one hand I recognize and know) **that the Law** (= Torah; or: law; custom; principle) **constantly exists being spiritual** (is pertaining to spirit; is having the qualities of a Breath-effect; is relating to attitude)..." (Rom. 7:14).

Paul may be alluding to what Jesus had said, as recorded in Jn. 6:63,

> "**The Spirit** (or: Breath-effect; or: spirit; Breath; Attitude) **is** (or: continues being) **the One continuously creating Life** (or: repeatedly making alive; habitually forming life)... **The declarations** (gush-effects; spoken words; sayings; results of the Flow) **which I, Myself, have spoken to you folks are** (or: continue to be) **Spirit** (or: spirit; Breath-effect; attitude) **and they are** (or: continue being) **Life**."

The contrasts of "**letter**" and "**Breath-effect/Spirit**" are also explained in Rom. 8:2,

> "**For the principle and law of, from and which is the spirit and attitude of 'The Life within Christ Jesus'**
>> (or: For you see, the Law of Life's spirit, joined with [the] Anointing of Jesus; or: For the Spirit's law of life within Christ Jesus; or: the Law [= Torah] from the Breath-effect, which is Life in union with [the] Anointed Jesus)
> **frees you away from the Law of the Sin and of the Death**."

Paul goes on to speak of this Law of the Sin and of the Death as being "the attending service" and "the dispensing which is the Death" in the next verse...

7. Now since (or: if) **the attending service of the Death** (or: the dispensing of provision from death; the serving of provisions and support, which is the Death) – **being one that has been formed by a beaten impression of types and the outlines of patterns that exists as engravings within letters and the effects of written texts** (Scriptures) **chiseled on stones – was birthed and came into existence within glory** (in a manifestation which called forth praise and with a good reputation; in union with an assumed appearance), **so that the sons of Israel came to be continuously unable** (or: habitually having no power) **to intently gaze into the face of Moses, because of the glory and manifestation which came from his face – which [glory] was being progressively unemployed so as to be brought down to having no work, to be ineffective and nullified –**

In the first clause, "the attending service; the dispensing of provision" is the singular of a different form of the same word that we saw in vs. 6a, as a plural. There it is "attending servants and dispensers;" here it is what those servants/dispersers do: service; the dispensing of provision. Paul and his associates correspond to the functions of the Levites and the priests of the old covenant, but there is where the similarity ends, for they (and we) now function in the new covenant, the new arrangement: in Spirit and in Truth (Jn. 4:23-24). So to what is he referring as "the attending service of the Death"? We saw in the citations from Heb. and Rom., in the previous verse, that this refers to the Law, the Torah, the Jewish priesthood and the temple cultus of physical offerings and sacrifices. See the whole books of Hebrews and Romans for the detailed pictures and explanations on this topic. All of the old arrangement revolved around the Death that came through Adam (Rom. 5:12).

Now observe the fuller description of this "attending service of the Death" that is set off by dashes:
"**formed by a beaten impression of types and the outlines of patterns that exists as engravings**

within letters and the effects of written texts (Scriptures) **chiseled on stones.**" This leaves us with no doubt as to what he was referring: the Law; the Torah; the old arrangement.

He affirms that the Law came into existence at Sinai and, "**was birthed and came into existence within glory** (in a manifestation which called forth praise and with a good reputation; in union with an assumed appearance)." The "assumed appearance" was in the altar of sacrifice, the priesthood and the tabernacle-temple. But there was also "a manifestation which called for praise" when they saw the radiance of God's Spirit on Moses' face [Ex. 34:29].

But Paul is quick to note that the glory and assumed appearance of the old, "**was being progressively unemployed so as to be brought down to having no work, to be ineffective and nullified.**" Not only was the Law being done away, but even its glory, and its assumed appearance as a religion no longer had any work to do, was ineffective, and in fact, was nullified! This fact can hardly be stated more clearly, but religions die hard, and this one went on to infect Christianity, bringing with it another dispensing of the Death, once more.

8. **how shall not rather the attending service and dispensing of the provision of the Spirit** (or: which has its source in the Breath-effect; marked by, pertaining to and being the effect of the spirit and attitude) **continue being within glory** (existing in the midst of a manifestation eliciting praise; centered on and in union with a good reputation and with an assumed appearance)**?**

Here he simply points out the superiority of the new covenant, the new arrangement, over the former covenant, the old arrangement of a physical religion with its literal temple, literal priests and lesser glory. The Spirit of Life is always better and greater than the service that attended the Death. The "assumed appearance" of the "dispensing of the provision of the Spirit" is that of a called-out, covenant community.

This verse calls to mind Gal. 3:5,
> "**The One, therefore, continuously furnishing and supplying to** (or: for; in) **you folks the Spirit** (or: the spirit; the breath; or: = attitude and vitality), **and constantly and effectively energizing, being active, working and producing abilities and powers within you people – [is its source] from out of works of Law, or out of a hearing of a report of faithfulness,**
>> (or: The one, then, constantly supplying the Breath-effect for you folks, and repeatedly working powers among you – [does he do it] from out of deeds based on [the] Law and of observances of [Torah], or from out of faith's attentive listening or a hearing from trust,)**?**"

9. **For since** (or: if) **the attending service and dispensing of the corresponding evaluations and commensurate decisions which follow the pattern** (or: separations for condemnation; judgments which are down-decisions against folks) **[had] glory, to a much greater degree does the attending service and the dispensing of the eschatological deliverance into fairness and equity in rightwised relationships** (or: righteousness from covenantal inclusion: that which corresponds to the Way pointed out, and which turns us in the right direction) **progressively surround and continuously exceed in glory** (or: habitually overflow with a manifestation which calls forth praise and brings a good reputation for and by its assumed appearance)**!**
> [comment: it would seem that Paul is casting the Law as a dispenser of condemnation, and is contrasting that to the Good News – casting this latter as a dispenser of "righteousness" and a servant for folks being turned in the right direction]

So now he spells out the "**much greater degree**" of glory inherent in the service from the Spirit: "**the dispensing of the eschatological deliverance into fairness and equity in rightwised relationships** (or: righteousness from covenantal inclusion: that which corresponds to the Way pointed out, and which turns us in the right direction)." The old covenant dispensed "**corresponding evaluations and commensurate decisions which follow the pattern** (or: separations for condemnation; judgments which are down-decisions against folks)." As we saw in Rom. 7, this latter simply left folks dead, while the new brings deliverance and points and turns folks in the right direction and "**into fairness and equity in rightwised relationships**." The old covenant pointed TO Christ; the new covenant IS Christ. The "attending" is actually God's Spirit attending us as we walk through the valley under the shadow (Law) of the Death. It is God "serving" us, as we are called to serve others as we bear Him to them.

Finally, let us take note that this work of the Spirit "**progressively surrounds and continuously exceeds in glory** (or: habitually overflows with a manifestation which calls forth praise and brings a good reputation for and by its assumed appearance)!" The NEW is better than the Old (cf Jn. 2:10).

10. **In fact, even that which had been made glorious, [by comparison] has not been glorified so as to now be glorious – in this respect: on account of the transcending glory which is constantly surpassing [that one], and is progressively over-casting [us].**

His comment about "**that which had been made glorious**" refers back to "**the attending service of the Death**" (vs. 7, above) and to "**dispensing of the corresponding evaluations and commensurate decisions which follow the pattern**" (vs. 9, above) – both of which describe the Law (judgments which are down-decisions against folks, which are chiseled on stones), and "**which was being progressively unemployed and brought down to doing no work**" (vs. 11a, below). But in Light of the new, which "is the continuously remaining" attending service, that of the old, i.e., the Mosaic Law, had "not been glorified so as [still] **to now be glorious**." How so? "**On account of the transcending glory which is constantly surpassing [that one], and is progressively over-casting [everyone]**." You see,
> "**If that first one was being unblamable** (without ground for faultfinding; beyond criticism; satisfying), **a place of a second one would not have continued to be sought** (looked for)" (Heb. 8:7).

11. **You see, since that which was being progressively unemployed and brought down to doing no work – even being made ineffective and nullified – [came] through glory, to a much greater extent is the continuously remaining one** (the dwelling, abiding and enduring one) **[existing] within the midst of glory, and in union with [greater] imagination** (repute).

We can look ahead to vs. 18, below, and see where we all, "**are presently being continuously and progressively transformed into the very same image, from** [one] **glory unto** [another] **glory**." That is why the former was "**being made ineffective and nullified**." Christ moved us into the "**much greater extent**" which continues remaining – dwelling and enduring. Like Israel following the movement of the cloud, in the wilderness, Paul was calling his listeners to move on, because the Spirit had moved on – out of the old, and into the New! Now since the new, "**continuously remaining**" attending service (vs. 9) is "**the transcending glory which is constantly surpassing [that one], and is progressively over-casting [us]**" (vs. 10), it functions "**within the midst of glory, and in union with [greater] imagination** (repute)." If it transcends and over-casts, then it is GREATER than the former. Keep in mind that Paul is speaking of the ATTENDING SERVICE of the new arrangement, and that its GLORY transcends the former arrangement. It presents us with a greater imagination than was presented at Mt. Sinai, and the shining face of Moses. This was foretold in the transformation of the appearance of Jesus on the mount, where Moses and Elijah (figuring the Law and the Prophets) appeared with Him (Mat. 17:2), and where it was not just His face, but all of Him, including His clothing, that "**radiated light, like a lamp, and shone like the sun… turned white – bright as the light**." At that time, the three disciples attending that experience were told that now they were no longer to listen to Moses or Elijah, but rather were to "**Make it a habit to listen, to continue paying attention, and then to [really] hear [the Son]**" (vs. 5b). This also calls to mind Heb. 1:1-2a. And because of all this…

12. **Therefore, in progressively possessing** (while continuously having and holding) **an expectation** (or: expectant hope) **such as this, we habitually use much freedom of speech and bold lack of**

reserve (or: are constantly telling it all with absolute unreservedness, based upon our citizenship), **unlike Moses.**

Paul and his listeners continued having and holding **an expectation**. Since the present tense can also refer to progressive action, I have offered the rendering "**in progressively possessing**" an expectation of goodness from God. The more we learn of, and from, God, the more our expectations concerning Him grow.

Note the contrasting comparison between the new situation, and that of Moses. Observe that Christ's representatives have "**much freedom of speech and bold lack of reserve**" in performing this new attending service. That freedom and boldness is "based upon our citizenship" in the Jerusalem that is above (Gal. 4:26), which sits upon a different mountain: Mt. Zion (Heb. 12:22ff), which is an allegory of the new covenant/arrangement (Gal. 4:24). But returning to Moses, in our text...

13. **He kept on putting a head-covering** (veil) **upon his face so that the sons of Israel were not to gaze intently into the purposed and destined goal** (the end; the result; the termination; the fruition) **of that which was being progressively unemployed and brought down to doing no work and being made ineffective, nullified and abolished.** [Ex. 34:29; 33-35]

We see that he "**kept on putting a head-covering** (veil) **upon his face**." Now this is in direct contrast to vs. 18a, below, where "**we all, ourselves [are] having a face that has been uncovered and remains unveiled.**" It is now a greater glory, but also a glory that does not have to be veiled. Why? Well, Moses' face was veiled "**so that the sons of Israel were not to gaze intently into the purposed and destined goal** (the end; the result; the termination; the fruition)" of the Mosaic arrangement, because it "**was being progressively unemployed and brought down to doing no work and being made ineffective, nullified and abolished.**" Even from the time of its inception, it represented the "dying you will die" of Gen. 2:17b. It was destined to come to an end (to die), so Moses veiled His face so that Israel of his day would not observe the fading glory of that arrangement (figured in the fading radiance from His face). We find this clearly explained in Rom. 10:4,

> "**for you see, Christ [is] an end of Law** (or: for Christ [is] Law's goal and destiny; for [the] Anointing [is] termination from [the] Law; for Christ [was the] final act of [the] Law) **[leading] into the Way pointed out in fair and equitable dealings, and rightwised [covenant] relationships of justice in eschatological liberation, to, for and in everyone habitually trusting and believing.**"

That past situation, during the time of Moses, is given more detail (along with the contrast to the present situation under the new arrangement in Christ) in Gal. 3:

> 23. **So before the [time, or, event for] the Faithful One to come** (or: prior to the coming of this faith, trust, assurance, conviction and loyalty), **we were being continuously restrained, confined and held in custody under the watch of a guard, being folks constantly encircled, enclosed, shut up and locked together by and under Law, [with a view to, aimed and moving] into the Faithfulness** (or: the Act of Trust) **being about to be unveiled** (or: revealed; disclosed), [*cf* Ex. 19:17 (LXX)]
> 24. **so that, consequently, the Law** (= Torah) **had come to be** (had been birthed into existence) **and continued being our supervising guardian and attending, custodial escort unto, with a view to, and [pointing] into Christ, to the end that we could** (or: would) **be delivered by the just act and then rightwised to be in the new covenant of right relationships with justice and fairness that characterize the liberty in the Way pointed out, from out of Faithfulness** (or: an act of loyalty, trust and faith).
> 25. **So now with the coming of the Faithful One, we no longer continuously exist** (or: are) **under [the] supervising guardian or an attending escort** [comment: = the Law; Torah]!

26. **For you folks are all** [i.e., Jew and non-Jew; male and female; slave and freeman] **God's sons, through the faithfulness located and resident within Christ Jesus** (or: by means of the trust in union with an Anointing from Jesus; [*p46*: through Jesus Christ's faithfulness])!

(or: You see, all you folks [who are] located and centered in Christ Jesus exist being sons of God, by means of that Faithful One!)

27. **For you see** (or: It follows that) **as many of you folks as were immersed into Christ, at once clothed yourselves with Christ** (or: were plunged into so as to be enveloped by then saturated and permeated with Anointing – or, the Anointed One – instantly entered within and put on [the/an] Anointing)!

14. **But further, the results of their perceptions, concepts and understanding** (effects of directing the mind and thought processes) **were petrified** (were hardened into a stony concretion and made callous [note: a medical term for being covered with thick skin]), **for until this very day the same head-covering** (veil) **continues remaining** (dwelling; abiding) **upon the reading of the old covenant** (arrangement; thorough placement) – **it** [i.e., the reading of the old, or the old covenant itself] **continues not being uncovered or unveiled – because it** [i.e., the old covenant and arrangement] **continues being progressively and fully unemployed and brought down to doing no work and being made useless, ineffective and nullified within Christ** (or: [the old arrangement and covenant] is abolished in union with an Anointing, and in the midst of Christ).

The plural subject *noēmata*, in the first clause, is a form of the noun for "mind, *nous* (mind), and refers to what is produced by the activity of the mind. Hence we read, above, "**the results of their perceptions, concepts and understanding** (effects of directing the mind and thought processes)" – due to the –*mata* ending of this plural noun. The singular ending has been noted, in passages above, the –*ma* endings.

This first clause is an allusion to Isa. 6:10, quoted in Jn. 12:40,

"**He has blinded their eyes with the present result that they are still blind, and He hardened** (or: petrified) **their heart, to the end that they could** (or: should; would) **not see with [their] eyes nor could they direct [their] mind so as to perceive and get the thought in** (or: with) **the heart and be turned, so I, Myself, will proceed to heal** (or: will progressively cure) **them.**" *Cf* Mat. 13:14

Now consider how Paul shifts his argument from the veil on the face of Moses (who is a figure of the Law, here) to the present state of that unbelieving part of Israel (*cf* Rom. 11:17) and to the fact that "**until this very day the same head-covering** (veil) **continues remaining** (dwelling; abiding) **upon the reading of the old covenant** (arrangement; thorough placement)." That means that they cannot see the glory of the old covenant (which pointed to, as was, Christ). Christ is hidden to them. They cannot see what the resurrected Jesus unveiled to the disciples in Lu. 24:27. Therefore, for them, "**it** [i.e., the reading of the old, or the old covenant itself] **continues not being uncovered or unveiled**" to, or for, them. Why? Well, it is like Moses' face, "**because it** [i.e., the old covenant and arrangement] **continues being progressively and fully unemployed and brought down to doing no work and being made useless, ineffective and nullified within Christ**." Now he has stated it plainly. In Christ we have a transcending glory that abolished the previous, lesser glory.

Take note that this last phrase can be rendered, "in union with an Anointing, and in the midst of Christ" – where we now exist "joined to the Lord" (1 Cor. 6:17).

But we skipped over the first clause of this verse. Not only was the previous attending service of the Law "**brought down to doing no work and being made ineffective**" (13b, above), but Paul instructs us that, "**the results of their perceptions, concepts and understanding** (effects of directing the mind and thought processes) **were petrified** (were hardened into a stony concretion and made callous [note: a medical term for being covered with thick skin])." A "calloused" heart is an insensitive heart – one that is neither sensitive to impressions from the Holy Spirit, nor sensitive to the feelings and needs of others. The reading of **the old covenant** (the OT, the Tanakh) is veiled, and "the effects of directing [their] minds – of [their] perceptions" were turned to stone or covered with thick skin. "Scripture is not self-explanatory…" (Harvey, ibid p 580). To understand its spiritual meaning requires the service of the Holy Spirit (*cf* Lu. 24:27). The minds of the Jews in Paul's day had become petrified (corresponding to the stone of the old attending service, vs. 7, above), and in the next verse we see that their corporate heart was affected.

15. **Still furthermore, until today, whenever Moses should be habitually read** [e.g., in the synagogue], **a head-covering** (veil) **continues lying upon their heart** (= the innermost being of the group).

This is the rhetoric of re-statement, or redundancy, so that they really can get the point. This verse virtually repeats the central part of vs. 14. It makes clear the spiritual state of the unbelieving Jews who continue to stay with Moses, instead of their Messiah. But there is hope for them – an expectation…

16. **Yet whenever the time should be reached when it** [= the heart] **can** (or: would; may; should; or: shall at some point) **twist and turn upon, so as to face toward, [the] Lord** [= Christ], **"the head-covering** (veil) **is progressively taken from around [it]."**
>   [note: an allusion to Ex. 34:34, LXX, where Moses would enter in to speak with Yahweh; the same act was performed by the husband, on the bride, after the wedding ceremony]

Paul may be alluding to Isa. 25:7-8a and the promise of what Yahweh would do:
>   "And He will swallow up on this mountain the presence of the wrap which is wrapped over all the peoples, and the blanket which is blanketing over all the nations. He will swallow up death permanently…" (CVOT) *Cf* 1 Cor. 15:54b

We find this same thought of vs. 16 echoed in Rom. 11:23,
>   "**Now they also, if they should not persistently remain in the lack of faith and trust** (or: unbelief), **they will proceed in being grafted in, for God is able** (capable; is constantly powerful) **to graft them back in again!**"

All it takes is for them to "**twist and turn upon, so as to face toward, [the] Lord** [= Christ]." This is the same picture that is given in Nu. 21:8-9, which Jesus allegorically applied to Himself in Jn. 3:14-15. There, in the wilderness, all they had to do was "look upon" the serpent upon the pole – i.e., "turn toward" it and just look. So, "**whenever the time should be reached when it** [= the heart] **can** (or: would; may; should; or: shall at some point) **twist and turn upon**" so as to face (look at) the Lord, "**the head-covering** (veil) **is progressively taken from around [it]**." This will also, of course, affect "**their perceptions, concepts and understanding**" (vs. 14). The common modern translations, such as NRSV and ESV, give the subject of the verb "turn; twist" as "one" (= a person) instead of "it." This seems reasonable, but it misses the nuance intended by Paul. The referential subject is "**their heart**," in the last clause of the previous verse. Paul is saying that "their heart" must turn – an inner action of the core of one's being. The KJV, CLNT and David Bentley Hart correctly read the Greek and render the subject "it."

Now, turning again to Rom. 11, we find Paul giving a fuller explanation:
>   25. **You see, I am not willing for you folks to continue being ignorant of this secret** (or: mystery), **brothers** (= fellow believers; family) **– in order that you folks may not continue being prudent, thoughtful or discreet by** [other MSS: among or within; other MSS: beside] **yourselves** (or: = be conceited) **– that a petrifying, from a part** (a stone-like hardening in some measure; a callousness [extending over] a part), **has been birthed and come into existence in Israel** (or: has happened to Israel) **until which [time]** (or: to the point of which [situation]) **the effect of the full measure** (or: the result of the entire contents; or: = the full impact and full

compliment of forces) **from the nations** (or: of the ethnic multitudes; or: – which are the Gentiles –) **may enter in.**

> [comment: Does the last clause refer to the entrance of the Roman legions into Jerusalem? Or, is this referring to the fullness of all ethnic multitudes, which now includes Israel, entering into the kingdom, since vs. 32, below, says that God has locked up all mankind in disobedience, etc., so as to have mercy upon all?]

26. **So then, thus, in this manner and with this result: all Israel will progressively be delivered** (rescued, saved, made whole and restored to their original position [in the olive tree]), **according as it has been written,**

> **"The One continuously dragging out of danger and drawing to Himself** (The Rescuer; The Deliverer) **will repeatedly arrive and be present from out of Zion; He will continue turning irreverence away from Jacob.**

27. > **"And this [is] the arrangement for them from beside Me** (or: And this [will be] My covenant in, to and for them) **when I take away their failures** (deviations; sins; mistakes; misses of the target; shooting amiss of the goal)." [Isa. 59:20-21; 27:9]

17. **Now the Lord** [= Christ or Yahweh] **continuously exists being the Spirit** (or: Yet the Breath-effect is the LORD), **so where [the] Lord's Breath-effect** (Spirit; Attitude) **[blows, there is] freedom** (or: and so in the place in which the Breath-effect – the Spirit – which is [the] Lord [= Christ or Yahweh] [blows; exists], liberty [comes; arises]).

Paul has not changed the subject, here. "**The Lord**" of this verse is the same "Lord" of the previous verse. Paul has been contrasting the two covenants, the two attending services. What was it that ignited Christ's followers? Was it His resurrection, or, was it the coming of the Spirit (Acts 2:1-4)? This was "**the Father's promise** (or: the promise pertaining to, and from, the Father; or, as a genitive of apposition: the promise which is the Father)" – Acts 1:4. We do not think that Paul is making an ontological statement about the identity of Godness, or Yahweh, or Christ, or the Anointing, in this verse. More likely Paul is pointing out the union of function between the Lord (or: Master?) and the Breath-effect. The unbelieving Jews need to turn to "the Lord" in, and as, Christ, and in, and as, the coming of His Spirit – which created the called-out communities, the body of Christ. This connection may be an allusion to creation in Gen. 1:2b, and, perhaps, Lu. 1:35. The Greek phrase, *ho kurios* frequently refers to Jesus, in Paul's writings. If this is its meaning here, then Jesus himself is **the Spirit**. Another interpretation is that Paul is following the LXX usage, where *ho kurios* is used to represent the name Yahweh. God is spirit (Jn. 4:24). Paul may be referring to the presence of God – the Holy Spirit (sacred Breath-effect) – among us, which bring us freedom and liberty. This verse may also be a restatements of vs. 6b, above, "**yet the Spirit** (or: the spirit; the Breath-effect; the Attitude) **continuously produces Life** (or: repeatedly makes alive; progressively forms life; habitually creates Life)."

Added to all this we have Paul elsewhere speaking of, "**the Spirit of Jesus Christ** (or: the attitude pertaining to and having the characteristics of Jesus Christ; the Breath-effect which is Jesus, [the] Anointed)" (Phil. 1:19b).

Now here, he goes on to explain, "**where [the] Lord's Breath-effect** (Spirit; Attitude) **[blows, there is] freedom.**" This corresponds to our being a part of "**the Jerusalem above, [which] is free.... brothers** (= fellow believers; family), **we are... of the freewoman**" (Gal. 4:26, 31). Paul explains the results of these situations in Rom. 8:1-2,

> "**Nothing, consequently, [is] now a result of condemnation in** (or: a commensurate effect of a decision for; a corresponding result of a negative evaluation which falls in line with a decision or follows the pattern which divides [folks] down, with) **those within Christ Jesus**
>> (or: In that case, therefore, [there is] now not one thing [that is] really an effect of a downward-judging to, in or with the folks in union with or centered in [the] Anointing of Jesus)! [A, D & later MSS here add: {They} are not habitually walking around (= living

> their lives) in accord with (or: corresponding to) flesh] [Aleph2, D2 & later MSS here add:
> but to the contrary, in the sphere of spirit and attitude (or: Breath-effect; or: {the} Spirit).]
> **For the principle and law of, from and which is the spirit and attitude of 'The Life within Christ Jesus'**
>> (or: For you see, the Law of Life's spirit, joined with [the] Anointing of Jesus; or: For the Spirit's law of life within Christ Jesus; or: the Law [= Torah] from the Breath-effect, which is Life in union with [the] Anointed Jesus)
> **FREES you away from the Law of the Sin and of the Death** (or: immediately set you [other MSS: me] at LIBERTY from the principle of the failure, or of the missing of the target, and from the death; exempts you from this code involved with error and deviation from the goal, as well as from the death; emancipated you from this law from the mistake, and which is, the Death)."
>> [comment: This law from sin and from death refers both to the principle of the old Adamic life and to Israel's Torah; *cf* 1 Cor. 15:53-54; 2 Cor. 3:6; 5: 4]

This verse describes the Life in Christ, the Life of the called-out folks. It is freedom from the Law, and from religion. It is liberty in eschatological release from our failures and sins. It is freedom from the slavery of, and which is, the Death. The Spirit brought the Jubilee of Lev. 25 and 27. It is the incarnation, the inspiration, the filling of, and from, the Spirit that brings people freedom, and Life from out of the Death.

18. **But we all, ourselves – having a face that has been uncovered and remains unveiled** [note: as with Moses, before the Lord, Ex. 34:34] **– being folks who by a mirror are continuously observing, as ourselves, the Lord's glory** (or: being those who progressively reflect – from ourselves as by a mirror – the assumed appearance and repute of, and from, [our] Owner), **are presently being continuously and progressively transformed into the very same image, from glory unto glory – in accord with and exactly as – from [the] Lord's Breath-effect** (or: from [the] Spirit and Attitude of, and which is, [the] Lord [= Christ or Yahweh]).
>> [comment: considering the context of this chapter, this may refer to the transformation from glory of Moses, into the glory of Christ; or, it may be speaking of a from-time-to-time transfiguration from the glory of humanity into the "**glory, imagination and assumed appearance**" of the Anointing, on an individual and/or corporate basis; *cf* Mat. 17:1-8]

When discussing with Dan Kaplan the picture that is described by Paul in this verse, we came to the conclusion that Paul may have had in mind the cherubim that were a part of the mercy seat, the lid of the "ark of the covenant," which was positioned in the holy of holies of the Tabernacle. They both faced the space that was between them, and when Yahweh would meet with Moses they would always (figuratively) behold His glory. In the description of their construction, Ex. 25:20 (and 37:9) reads "and their faces [shall be] one to a brother," in the Hebrew. Then it continues, "… toward the mercy seat shall the faces of the cherubim be."

In vs. 13, above, Paul referred to Moses using a veil (head-covering) over his face after meeting with Yahweh within the holy of holies in the Tabernacle. Ex. 33:8 tells us that Moses entered the Tabernacle to meet with Him, and Ex. 33:11 instructs us that "Yahweh spoke to Moses face to face, just as a man speaks to his associate." A second witness is Deut. 34:10 where we read of "Moses, whom Yahweh knew face to face." Again, speaking of Moses, Yahweh said, "Mouth to mouth am I speaking with him, and by an appearance, not in enigmas…" (Num. 12:8; CVOT). In Ex. 25:22, Moses was told,
> "I will keep appointment with you there, and I will speak with you above the mercy seat, from between the two cherubim which are over the ark of the testimony…"

The purpose of relating all this from Israel's story is to point out that the setting for those specific meetings was within the holy of holies, the innermost chamber of the Tabernacle, which later was reproduced in the Temple. So now, in the new creation of the new covenant, what is the Temple? Yes, it is US, as Paul instructs us in 6:16, below: "**For you see, we ourselves continuously exist being a temple of [the]**

living God." It is within us, and among us, that "**we all, ourselves – having a face that has been uncovered and remains unveiled are continuously observing… the Lord's glory**." This need not happen in some far-off place or distant realm. It happened with Moses right there in the wilderness, during the journeys of Israel. Paul indicates that we should be observing this here, and now.

Now Paul returns to the "us" of vs. 6, and the "we" of vs. 12 – i.e., the context of the new covenant. The **face** of the new creation (5:17, below) and of the Second Humanity (1 Cor. 15:47) "**has been uncovered and remains unveiled**." We suggest that this is, in fact, "**a face of Christ**," Who is, "**the One who shines forth within the midst of our hearts, with a view to illumination of the intimate and experiential knowledge of God's glory – in a face of Christ**" (4:6b, below).

This verse echoes a present reality of what Paul alluded to in 1 Cor. 13:12, "**but at that point, face to face**," and is what we find in Rev. 22:4, "**and [they] will constantly see His face, and His Name [is; or: will be] upon their foreheads**." We are, by a mirror, "**continuously observing, as ourselves, the Lord's glory**." This clause can also be read that we all are "being those who progressively reflect – from ourselves as by a mirror – the assumed appearance and repute of, and from, [our] Owner." We are His image-bearers (Gen. 1:26). The plural personal pronoun, "ourselves," reflects the middle voice of the verb in this clause. And, if we are a mirror that reflects the Lord's "assumed appearance," then when He looks as us, He sees Himself. This calls to mind Mat. 25:35-40.

Can we see in this verse what Jesus said in Mat. 5:8?
> "**Those who are clean in the heart [are] happy and blessed, because they, themselves, will progressively see God!**
> > (or: = The folks that have had the core of their beings made clean [are] happy people, in that they will continue to see God [in everything]!)."

As the transformation proceeds, we progressively see Him more clearly. But do Jesus' words, here in His sermon, put a requirement upon us? Do we have to clean ourselves, or endeavor to keep ourselves clean? No… Remember the words of 1 Jn. 1:7b, 9,
> "**the blood of, from, and which is Jesus, His Son, keeps continually and repeatedly cleansing us** (or: is progressively rendering us pure) **from every sin** (or: from all error, failure, deviation, mistake, and from every shot that is off target [when it occurs]).... **to the end that He would at once send away for us** (or: dismiss or pardon and cause to flow away in us) **the errors** ([some MSS add: our] failures, mistakes and deviations) **and then would cleanse** [other MSS: He will cleanse] **us from all injustice**."

Notice the "divine passive" of the continuous, progressive action of the verb "**transformed**." This is the work of God, done upon and within us. This is the reason for His giving us His Spirit: it makes our "ground holy." Now His words are Spirit, and they are Life (Jn. 6:63). In Eph. 5:26 we read of another metaphor of His cleansing us,
> "**that He may set [the called-out community] apart** (separate her; consecrate and make her holy), **cleansing** (purging) **[her] by the bath of the Water [that is] within a result of a flow** (or: in union with a gush-effect; or: in the midst of a spoken word, a declaration, or an utterance)."

And in Tit. 3:5b, he put it this way:
> "**down from and corresponding to His mercy, He delivered us** (or: He saves, rescues and restores us to the wholeness and health of our original condition) **through a bath of and from a birth-back-again** (or: [the] bathing of a regeneration; note: can = a ritual immersion pool of rebirth) **and a making back-up-new** (of a different kind and quality)-**again from a set-apart Breath-effect**
> > (or: of a renewal and renovation whose source is [the] Holy Spirit; or: a set-apart spirit's creating or birthing [us] back-up-new-again; a renewal which is a holy attitude)."

Now being "transformed" also calls to mind his admonition in Rom. 12:2, "**be progressively transformed** (transfigured; changed in form and semblance) **by the renewing** (or: in the renewal; for the making-back-up-new again) **of your mind** [with other MSS: from The Mind; of the intellect; pertaining to the faculties of perceiving and understanding; of the mindset, disposition, inner orientation and world view] **into the [situation and condition for] you folks to be habitually examining in order to be testing and, after scrutiny, distinguishing and approving what [is] God's will** (design; purpose; resolve; intent)**: the good and well-pleasing, even perfect** (finished, complete and destined)**!**"

He used different imagery in Col. 3:9-10, but the results are the same:

"**[Be] folks at once stripping off from yourselves the old humanity** (the old human; = the old Adam), **together with its practices, and then [be] suddenly clothing yourselves with** (or: entering within) **the new one** (the fresh one which existed only recently), **the one being continuously** (or: repeatedly; habitually; progressively) **renewed** (made back up new again, in kind and character) **into full, accurate, added, intimate and experiential knowledge and insight which is down from and corresponds to the image** (an exactly formed visible likeness) **of its Creator** (of the One framing and founding it from a state of wildness and disorder)."

And in Rom. 8:29 we read:

"**because those whom He foreknew** (whom He knows from previous intimate experience), **He also marked out beforehand** (determined, defined and designed in advance) **[as] copies** (joint-forms) **of the image** (material likeness; portrait; form) **of His Son** (or: He previously divided, separated and bounded conformed patterns from the image/form of His Son)…"

Paul used a variety of pictures and processes to describe the work of the Spirit of Christ within us. We may want to think of these as pieces of a puzzle: any one piece, by itself, does not present the whole picture, and each piece needs to be seen in its proper place (context) so that it has the proper relationship with the other pieces, and tells the whole story.

All this from "**continuously observing the Lord's glory**," and then, "progressively reflecting the assumed appearance and repute of, and from, [our] Owner."

Chapter 4

1. **Because of this – while continuously possessing** (having and holding) **this attending service and dispensing of provision – correspondingly as we were mercied** (shown mercy), **we do not habitually behave with a bad attitude, or perform in a worthless manner, or act from out of a mood or motive that is poor in quality, or, become discouraged.**

Paul is continuing the same subject matter of chapter 3: "**this attending service and dispensing of provision**." So he continues speaking to the Corinthians about this, and how he and his companions behave while functioning as dispensers of Christ. I conflated the potential renderings of *egkakeō*: **behave with a bad attitude, or perform in a worthless manner, or act from out of a mood or motive that is poor in quality, or, become discouraged**. That final offering, "become discouraged," is the most remote use of the verb whose root idea (*kakos*) is the opposite of something fine, ideal or beautiful. In his oft-used parallelism, or re-statement, take note in the following verse of how they were NOT living their lives: craftiness, guile, etc. In other words they did not "walk around" in a worthless manner, or with a bad attitude.

2. **To the contrary, we speak-away from ourselves** (or: spurn; renounced; disowned) **the hidden things pertaining to the shame** (or: whose source is [our] shame; that result in dishonorable conduct or bring disgrace), **not habitually walking around** (= living our lives) **in craftiness or guile** (or: in union with a capability for every work; within readiness to do anything), **neither constantly distorting, diluting or adulterating God's message** (the Word, thought and idea of God; the *Logos* from, and which is, God), **but rather, in a manifestation of the Truth and by a setting of the Reality in clear Light, we**

are progressively placing ourselves together in addressing every conscience of mankind (or: commending ourselves toward every human awareness), **in God's sight and presence** (or: before, or, in front of, God; in the midst of a viewing from God).

Paul wrote similarly in 1 Thes. 2:3, 5,

> "**You see, our calling alongside to assist** (our admonition and encouragement; our work as paracletes) **[is] not out of wandering** (from being led astray; from deception), **neither out of uncleanness, nor yet within a bait for entrapping or with guile or craftiness.... For neither did we at any time come to be flattering in word, according as you saw and are aware, neither within pretense** (held-forward specious cloak) **from greed: God is witness!**"

Corresponding to 2b, above, we have 1 Thes. 2:4, 7,

> "**but rather, to the degree that and according as we have been approved by testing under God to be entrusted [with] the message of goodness, ease and well-being, thus we are continuously speaking: not as constantly pleasing to people, but rather [as] to the God [Who is] repeatedly testing** (or: giving proof of) **our hearts.... But rather, we were birthed babes** (or: became infants; [other MSS: we were made to become gentle and kind ones]) **within the midst of you folks, as whenever a nursing mother would constantly or repeatedly cuddle to impart warmth to her own children.**"

In contrast to behaving from "**a motive that is poor in quality**" (vs. 1), Paul and his associates "**speak-away, spurn, renounce and disowned**" things that are shameful or that bring disgrace. Examples of those "hidden things pertaining to the shame" are: **craftiness, guile**, readiness to do anything, or **distorting, diluting or adulterating God's message**. This last phrase can refer to "God's thought and idea," or, to "the Word (*Logos*) of, from, and which is, God." Later theological scholarship and theory has at times been guilty of diluting **God's message** by adding philosophical constructs to the simplicity of the Good News as found in the NT. The adulterating of God's thought and idea (which has been manifested in Christ) happened when the Christian religion added the Law, and various arrangements from the old covenant, into the new covenant by mixing into God's gift of grace (as well as into His mercy, deliverance, rescue and resurrection) requirements that people had to meet.

In contrast to such things, these slaves of Christ (Rom. 1:1) lived their lives "**in a manifestation of the Truth and by a setting of the Reality in clear Light.**" Substitute the word "Christ" for the words "Truth" and "Reality" and we can see the central point that he is making. How were they doing this? By "**progressively placing [themselves] together in addressing every conscience of mankind, in God's sight and presence.**" In other words, they operated and functioned in a manner that acknowledged that God was present among them, and that He saw all that was happening. Rendering the participle in accord with other common usages, they were constantly "commending [themselves] toward every human conscience before, or, in front of, God, and, in the midst of a viewing from God." Again, they knew that God was present, among them and among those to whom they brought the Good News, as we see next...

3. **Now if the good news coming from us** (or: our message of goodness, ease and well-being) **continues being covered from having been veiled with a head-covering, it continues being thus covered in union with, within the midst of, and centered in, those on their way to ruin** (being progressively lost; repeatedly loosing-away, undoing, and thus, destroying themselves),

Notice here that Paul is equating "**the good news** (etc.)," here, to "**the attending service and dispensing of the provision of the Spirit within glory**" (3:8, 9, above) and relating the second half of this verse to 3:14-15, above. Therefore, "**those on their way to ruin**," here, is a reference to the unbelieving Jews who continued with "**the attending service of the Death... the effects of written texts** (Scriptures) **chiseled on stones**" (3:7, above). Paul referenced these folks in 1 Cor. 1:18a (*cf* Isa. 6:9).

But those of the Corinthian community were NOT "being progressively lost; repeatedly loosing-away so as to be undone; or: destroying themselves" – because THEIR faces were unveiled (3:18, above).

We want to point out implications of the perfect tense of the same participle, used twice, together with the present tense of the verb, "to be," in the clause, "**if the good news**... **continues being covered from having been veiled with a head-covering, it continues being thus covered**..." Two perfect participles (that show a completed action in the past that has continuing and present results) are used to rhetorically emphasize the sad condition of those Second Temple Jews who rejected Christ.

Paul may have in mind Jesus' words in Mat. 24 and Lu. 21 (prophesies about the destruction of Jerusalem, which happened in AD 70) when he chose the terms "**those on their way to ruin**." But his ambiguity can also be understood as a reference to "the lost sheep of the house of Israel" (Mat. 15:24), or to the parables of "the lost" in Lu. 15:4-9. The participle used for these phrases is in the middle voice: the action is self-inflicted, or involves their actions in the outcome. Observe the semantic range of the preposition that modifies this phrase: **in union with, within the midst of, and centered in**. We can see from the context that was begun in chapter 3 that this description only applies directly to the Jews of 1st century, Second Temple Judaism. We may extrapolate Paul's thinking, and the principle involved, to other similar or parallel situations, but it is distorting the text to make a blanket application of Paul's words to humanity at large. The context does not support such a use of the text.

4. **within and among which folks the God of this age** (or: the God [ruling] this indefinite time-period; the God Who is in relationship with this eon) **blinds** (or: deprived of the ability to see) **the effects of the perceptions, concepts and understanding** (or: the results of directing the mind to something) **of those without faith** (of the un-trusting ones; of the unbelieving and disloyal), **[leading them] into the [situation that] the shining forth of light and the illumination of** (or: the beaming forth of enlightenment from) **the good news of the glory of the Christ** (or: of the message of goodness, ease and well-being from the assumed appearance which is the Anointed One; from the glad tidings pertaining to the manifestation which calls forth praise of the [Messiah]) – **Who continuously exists being God's image** (a resemblance and likeness of [Concordant Text adds: the unseen; the invisible] God) – **would not shine forth as the dawn to irradiate them.** [cf Mat. 13:11-15; Jn. 12:40; Rom. 11:7-12, 25]

Take note of the bracketed references to Mat. 13, Jn. 12 and Rom. 11. All of these concerned Israel and the Jews. They applied to situations involving the old covenant, up to the final destruction of that covenant in AD 70. Again, this verse applied to the preceding context. I will here insert an excursus that investigates the meaning of the first clause of this verse:

THE GOD of THIS AGE

Who is the God (or: god) of this age? Most Christians will without hesitation answer, "Satan." Why do we think this to be true?

First of all, you can see my take on this passage, in that I capitalized the word "God" in vs. 4, so right up front you have a hint of where I am going with this study. But please don't cry "Heresy!" yet, and read on, with an open (un-blinded) mind. Now in the second place, keep in mind that our verses, above, follow the context of ch. 3 where it speaks of Israel's minds being blinded, there being a "veil upon their hearts" (vs. 10-11). This is talking about when they are reading Moses (i.e., God's Word). So who put the veil there, and thus blinded them?

In Isa. 6:10, Yahweh says, "**Stouten the heart of this people, and make its ears heavy, and make its eyes squint, lest it may see with its eyes, and with its ears it may hear, and with**

its heart it may understand, and it gets healing again for itself" (CVOT). So this was the work of Yahweh, just as where, in another place, He said, "Let there be light." Now John quotes this text, in his gospel, in ch. 12:40.

> "**He has blinded their eyes with the present result that they are still blind, and He hardened** (or: petrified) **their heart, to the end that they could** (or: should; would) **not see with [their] eyes nor could they direct [their] mind so as to perceive and get the thought in** (or: with) **the heart and be turned, so I, Myself, will heal** (or: cure) **them.**" [Isa. 6:10]

Notice that in vs. 39 of this chapter, John says, "**On account of this they were unable** (or: they had no power) **to be trusting or believing**" and this was because of what Isaiah said.

Do you notice that there is no mention of satan in these passages? It was God who did this. Paul takes up this theme in Rom. 11:7-12 and 25.

> 7. **What, then? That which Israel is constantly searching for** (or: seeking out), **this it did not encounter** (or: did not hit upon the mark, and thus, obtain), **yet The Selected One** (the Picked-out and Chosen One; or: the choice collection; the elect - that which is chosen out) **hit upon the mark, encountered and obtained it. But the rest** (the folks remaining) **were petrified** (were turned into stone; were made calloused and were hardened),
> 8. **just as it has been and stands written, "God gives** (or: at one point gave) **to them a spirit** (breath-effect and attitude) **of stupor, from receiving a piercing blow** (or: deep sleep; a senseless mental condition), **eyes of the [condition] to not see, ears of the [condition] to not hear, until this very day** (or: until today's day).**"** [Deut. 29:4; Isa. 29:10]
> 9. **And David is saying, "Let their table be birthed into a snare** (a trap) **and into a wild beast trap-net and into a trap-stick, even into a repayment to them** (for them; in them).
> 10. "**Let their eyes be darkened, to not see, and let them bend** (or: bow) **their back together [in bondage] through all** (or: every [situation]).**"** [Ps. 69:23-24]

But lest we feel saddened by God's actions to Israel, Paul tells us His purpose in Rom. 11:12,

> "**Now since** (or: if) **their fall to the side [brings, or, is] enrichment of the world** (universe; the ordered system outside of Israel) **and their lessened condition** (their lapse; their diminishing; their loss; = their defeat) **[brings, or, is] enrichment of the nations** (the ethnic multitudes; the non-Jews; the Gentiles), **how much exceedingly more their filled-full condition** (their full measure with the entire contents)!"

If you have eyes to see, you will realize that this was also the same purpose of the "fall" of humanity, and the expulsion from Eden. It was for enrichment. Paul continues this theme in Rom. 11:25, where he speaks of God's actions as "a secret," or, "a mystery,"

> "**For I am not willing for you folks to continue being ignorant of this secret** (or: mystery), **brothers, in order that you folks may not continue being thoughtful, prudent or discreet by yourselves** [other MSS: among yourselves (or: within yourselves)], **that a petrifying, from a part** (a stone-like hardening in some measure; a callousness [extending over] a part), **has been birthed and come into existence in Israel** (or: has happened to Israel) **until which [time; situation] the full measure** (or: the entire content; = full number) **from the nations** (or: of the ethnic multitudes who are non-Jews) **may enter in.**"

Now reread our text, above - and note the action of the God of this age. It is the same as what we have read in these other passages. There is only one God who has any power. All other gods are imaginary, and are not gods at all. Sadly, orthodox Christianity participates in dualism.

313

They have a good God, and a bad god (satan). But this view is false. The God of this age is the same God of every age. The writer of Hebrews gives insight into the origins of the ages. In ch. 1 we see,

> 2. **upon [the] last of these days spoke to us in a Son whom He placed** (or: sets) **[as; to be] Heir of all** (or: One who receives all men as an allotment; or: heir of all things; or: One who received everything as his allotted inheritance) **through Whom He also made** (or: formed; constructed) **the ages** (or: various designated periods of time).

The One who constructed the ages is the God of the ages, the Creator. Again, the thought expressed above is seen in Heb. 11:3,

> "**In faith and by trust, with the mind we constantly perceive** (with the intellect understand) **the ages to have been completely equipped by** (and, or: thoroughly adjusted to; knit together and put in order in) **God's declaration** (that which flowed in speech that had the source, character and qualities of God; or: a spoken word which was God)."

Again, the One who completely equipped the ages did it through His declaration. Yet someone may ask, "Well what about Gal. 1:4, where Paul speaks of 'the present wicked (or: evil) age'?" My expanded version reads thus:

> 4. - **the One at one point giving Himself, over the situation of** (or: on behalf of; for the sake of; [p46, Aleph*, A, D & other MSS read: concerning]) **our failures** (situations and occasions of falling short or to the side of the target; deviations; mistakes; errors; sins) **so that He could carry us out from the midst of the present misery-gushing and worthless age** (or: bear us forth from the indefinite period of time - characterized by toil, grievous plights and bad situations - having taken a stand in [our] midst; or: extricate us from the space of time having been inserted and now standing in union with base qualities), **corresponding to** (or: down from; in accord with; in line with; in the sphere and to the level of) **the effect of the will** (or: intent; purpose; design) **of our God and Father.**

The question implied is, "Did God construct this 'misery-gushing, worthless age'?" Let us see who creates evil:

> "Former of light and Creator of darkness,
> Maker of good and Creator of evil,
> I, Yahweh, make all these things!" (Isa. 45:7, CVOT)

The God of this present age of bad situations and grievous plights made this age this way! Yahweh said in Amos 3:6, "Would there come to be evil in a city and Yahweh NOT have done it?" (CVOT) Only faith, trust, and loyalty to God can answer, "No." For you see, there is only One God. When Adam and Eve left the Garden of Eden, they entered into the first "evil age," and Cain killed Abel. In Gen. 6 we are told the story of Noah, and in vs. 5, "Yahweh saw that the evil of humanity was multiplying on the Land (or: earth), and every form of the devising of its heart was surely evil all the day." We later read of the evil that Joseph's brothers did to him. Through Adam, "**The Death thus also passed through in all directions** (or: came through the midst causing division and duality; went throughout) **into all mankind** (or: into the midst of humanity; or: to all people)..." (Rom. 5:12). In Exodus we have the story of Israel's slavery in Egypt, and later we read of God's judgment of Israel in the exiles of first the northern tribes, and then of the southern tribes. Every exile is an "evil age."

In the days of Jeremiah, Yahweh said,

> "When backsliding (rebel) Israel committed adultery, I sent her off and gave her the scroll of her divorce. Yet treacherous Judah, her sister, did not fear, and she also went forth and committed prostitution" (Jer. 3:8).

That was an evil age, and Yahweh was dealing with His people. But then in vss. 12-17 He says,

> "Return, backsliding Israel, averring is Yahweh; I shall not cast My face down upon you, for I am benign (compassionate, merciful and full of kindness), averring is Yahweh; I shall

not hold resentment (bear a grudge) for the eon (age).... I will take you, one from a city and two from a family, and I will bring you to Zion. Then I will give you shepherds according to My own heart.... In that era they shall call Jerusalem the throne of Yahweh, and all the nations will be expectant toward her, for the Name of Yahweh, at Jerusalem, and they shall no longer walk after the obduracy (willful or stubborn promptings) of their evil heart" (CVOT; additions mine).

In the 1st century AD the Jews were still in exile, under the dominion of Rome. If we look at this situation through the lens of Second Temple Judaism – that had the paradigm of two ages: the present one, and then the Age of the Messiah – that present age that led up to the coming of Christ was an evil age from which they hoped to be delivered. Jesus described the character of that age by a reference to the Judean leadership and their followers, in Mat. 15:14,

"**Abandon them at once!** (other choices: Divorce them; Let them flow away; Leave them; Leave them [alone]; Send them away; Let them go; Forgive them) **They exist being blind guides of the Path** (or: blind leaders of the Way). **Now if a blind person should ever lead or guide [another] blind person, both people will proceed to be falling into a pit!**"

He was describing a misery-gushed, worthless age.

Although Judean leadership could not accept it, that age fully ended in AD 70. Paul was living in the conjunction of those two ages (while the temple and Jerusalem still were standing), where the end of the evil age of the old covenant/creation was overlapping with the beginning of the new age/covenant/creation. But keep in mind Heb. 1:2, quoted above, that the Son "**made** (or: formed; constructed) **the ages** (or: various designated periods of time)." This was all a part of what Paul termed,

"**a purpose of the ages** (a fore-designed aim, plan and object of the unspecified time-periods) **which He formed** (forms; made; constructs; creates; produced) **within the Christ by our Lord and Owner, Jesus**" (Eph. 3:11).

Those previous ages were the Darkness and the Night before the coming of the Light and the Day!

o—o—o—o—o—o--o

And now back to our text in 2 Cor. 4: observe this illuminating phrase,

"**the shining forth of light and the illumination of** (or: the beaming forth of enlightenment from) **the good news of the glory of the Christ** (or: of the message of goodness, ease and well-being from the glory which is the Anointed One; from the glad tidings pertaining to the manifestation which calls forth praise of the [Messiah]) **– Who continuously exists being God's image** (a resemblance and likeness of [Concordant Text adds: the unseen; the invisible] God)..."

That it is a "shining forth of light" echoes Jn. 1:4-5,

"**Within It** (or: Him), **life was continuing and progressively existing. And the life was continuing being, and began progressively existing as, the Light of mankind** (or: Furthermore, the Light progressively came to be the life known as "humanity," and was for human beings; or: Then later the life was existing being the light from the humans). **And the Light is constantly shining in the dim and shadowed places, and keeps on progressively giving light within the gloomy darkness where there is no light** (or: within the midst of the obscurity of The Darkness where there is no light of The Day; or: = in the ignorant condition or system). **And yet the darkness does not grasp or receive it on the same level.**"

Our present context, of "**the attending service of the Death**" informs our understanding of "the Darkness" of which John spoke in his prologue. It was the darkness of their blindness from their veiled hearts and minds.

We find this "**the illumination of** (or: the beaming forth of enlightenment from) **the good news**" referred to as "**illumination of the intimate and experiential knowledge of God's glory,**" in vs. 6, below. But observe that this is also, "**of the glory of the Christ.**" Or, the whole phrase can read: "of the message of goodness, ease and well-being from the assumed appearance which is the Anointed One; or: from the glad tidings pertaining to the manifestation which calls forth praise of the [Messiah]." This glorious phrase that Paul uses to speak of Christ recalls his similar phrase in Phil. 2:11b,

> "**into the midst of a praise-inducing manifestation and assumed appearance which is God: a Father!**"

Word, Light, Message, Good News, Glory, Christ, God, Messiah – Paul's parallel statements display the unification of all these terms into "**the One**" of vs. 6, below.

The next phrase, that describes Christ, presents Him as the Last Adam (1 Cor. 15:45; Gen. 1:26), "**Who continuously exists being God's image** (a resemblance and likeness of [Concordant Text adds: the unseen; the invisible] God)." In Jn. 12:45, Jesus said, "**the person continuing in attentively gazing at and contemplatively watching Me continues looking at** (contemplatively viewing; watching, discerning and seeing) **the One sending Me.**" And then there is Jn. 14:9b,

> "**The person having discerned and seen Me has seen, and now perceives, the Father!**"

Col. 1:15 affirms that the Son "**is the Image** (portrait; the Exact Formed Likeness; the Figure and Representation; visible likeness and manifestation) **of the not-seen God** (or: the unable to be seen God; the invisible God), **the Firstborn of all creation.**"

But this Light and Illumination (*cf* Heb. 1:3), "**would not shine forth as the dawn to irradiate them**" (vs. 3, above; 3:14-16, above), since they remained under a "head covering" that veiled their ability to see Him. However, Paul gave further explanation of God's purpose for this in Rom. 11:17, 22, 24b, 26a,

> "**Now since some of the branches are broken off, yet you yourself, being a wild olive tree of the field or forest, you are grafted in within** (or: among) **them, you also came to a joint-participant** (a co-partaker) **of the Root and of the Fatness** (= sap) **of The Olive Tree**.... **Observe, perceive and consider, then, God's useful kindness** (benevolent utility) **and abruptness** (sheer cutting-off; rigorous severity) **– on the one hand upon those falling: abruptness** (sheer cutting-off); **on the other hand** (or: yet) **upon you: God's useful kindness** (benign, profitable utility), **provided you should persistently remain in** (or: with; by) **the useful kindness. Otherwise you, also, will proceed in being cut out!**.... **To how much greater an extent will these, the ones in accord with nature, proceed in being engrafted into their own olive tree!**.... **So then, thus, in this manner and with this result: all Israel will progressively be delivered** (rescued, saved, made whole and restored to their original position [in the olive tree])..."

You see, in all of the ages, "**He is constantly working all things together into good and is progressively working all humanity together into that which is advantageous, worthy of admiration, noble and of excellent qualities**" (Rom. 8:28).

5. **For you see, we are not constantly preaching** (proclaiming; heralding) **ourselves, but rather, Christ Jesus [as] Lord** (or: [the] Anointed Jesus, [the] Lord, Master and Owner; or: = [the] Lord Jesus [as the] Messiah), **yet ourselves [as] your slaves, because of Jesus,**

This last complex phrase reminds them of how he had presented himself to them, in 1 Cor. 9:19, "**I enslave myself to all people** (or: to everything and for everyone), **to the end that I can** (may; would) **gain [all] the more folks.**" What a mindset! What a personal vision of one's purpose and destiny!

6. **because the God suddenly saying** (or: the God Who once was saying), **"Light will shine forth** (give light as from a torch; gleam) **from out of the midst of darkness** (dimness and shadiness; gloom and the absence of daylight)," **[is] the One who shines forth within the midst of our hearts, with a view to illumination of the intimate and experiential knowledge of God's glory – in a face of Christ

(or: [is] He Who gives light in union with our hearts, [while] facing toward an effulgence and a shining forth which is an intimate knowing of the praise-inducing manifestation and assumed appearance whose source and origin is God, and which is God, [while] in union with face to face presence of Christ [other MSS: Jesus Christ]).

Wow! "**Christ Jesus [as] Lord**... **shines forth within the midst of our hearts**!" This "knowledge of God's glory" is the same "glory" that he spoke of in 3:18, above. And it shines forth "**in a face of Christ**" which we present to the world.

The alternate parenthetical rendering is worth careful pondering. Read it slowly, savoring each phrase, so that the picture can sink deep into your spirit. Consider, "a shining forth... which is God." And, "in union with face to face presence of Christ." This is a rich verse. This is the reality of the "new creation" (5:17, below), which Paul here set in an allusion to Gen. 1:3-4. The present application was to "**the Light of mankind**" (Jn. 1:4), Christ, the Incarnate *Logos* of God. Light was a symbol of deliverance and salvation, for Israel, e.g., Isa. 9:2,

"O people who continue traveling within the midst of darkness, look and consider: a Great Light! O you folks presently settling down and continuing in dwelling within a region (or: country) [that is] in a shadow of death (or: which is Death), a Light will progressively and continuously shine upon you!" (LXX, JM).

We find a description of the process of this new creation, which happens both within us and among us, in 2 Pet. 1:19,

"**And so, we continue having** (or: constantly hold) **the Idea which was spoken ahead of time in and as Light** (or: the prior-enlightened Thought and Reason; or: the Prophetic Word) **more confirmed** (validated; established; certain), **by which** (or: in which) **you folks continue doing beautifully** (performing ideally; producing finely), **while continuously holding toward** (= playing close attention to) **[it] as to a lamp continually shining within a parched place – until which [time or occasion] the Day may shine through and a light bearer** [= a morning star] **may rise within your hearts**."

Perhaps both Peter and Paul had Ps. 27:1 in mind as they wrote:

"Yahweh [is] my Light and my Salvation; whom should I fear? Yahweh [is] a stronghold and refuge; of whom should I be afraid?"

Or, perhaps Ps. 36:9,

"For with You [is] a Fountain of Life; in and through Your Light do we see Light."

Or, Isa. 2:5b, "Let us walk in [the] Light of Yahweh."
Making this more personal, we have Eph. 5:8,

"**for you folks were once existing being darkness** (dimness; obscurity; gloom; shadiness), **yet** (or: but) **now [you are] Light, within and in union with [the] Lord** [= Christ or Yahweh]."

And further, he explains and admonishes (or: calls forth from the dead!) in Eph. 5:14,

"**for you see, all that is continuously being manifested** (clearly displayed, made apparent and is progressively shown for what it is) **is, and continually exists being, Light. Wherefore He is now** (or: it keeps on) **saying,**

'**Let the sleeper** (the person continuously down and being fast asleep) **be waking up, continue rousing, and then stand up** (arise) **from out of the midst of the dead ones, and the Christ will continue shining upon you** (progressively enlightening you)!'"

What a statement of the present reality of the Resurrection! In 1 Pet. 2:9b we read of:

"**the One calling you out of darkness** (gloomy dimness; the realm of shadows and obscurity) **into the midst of His wonderful** (marvelous; amazing) **Light**."

Much could be said about each of these references, but we have already commented on them in previous commentaries (cf jonathanmitchellnewtestament.com). They are all pieces of the same puzzle. Verse 6, here, may reach back to Paul's experience on the road to Damascus. Cf Gal. 1:16; 1 Thes. 5:5; Jn. 1:9; 8:12; 12:46; Mat. 5:14.

7. **Now we presently and continuously hold** (have and possess) **this treasure within containers** (jars; pots; vessels; equipment) **made of baked clay** [e.g., pottery; bone ware] **so that the transcendence of the power may habitually originate its existence in God – and not from out of us** (or: the over-cast of ability can be that which is God – and not of us; or: the overwhelming which comes from the Power would exist with the character and quality of God – and not from what characterizes us)!

Please take note! "**We presently and continuously hold** (have and possess) **this treasure**." It is "**within the midst of our hearts**" (vs. 6), i.e., "**within containers** (jars; pots; vessels; equipment) **made of baked clay**" – that's US! In Col. 2:3 we read about Christ,

> "**within Whom** (or: in which) **are** (continually exist) **all the hidden-away** (or: concealed) **treasures** (or: treasure chests or vaults; storehouses) **of the wisdom and experiential, intimate knowledge and insight**."

Then we recall Jesus speaking about treasures:

> "**be continuously accumulating and storing up for yourselves treasures within heaven** (or: [your] atmosphere).... **You see, where your treasure is, there also will be your heart**" (Mat. 6:20, 21).

And in Mat. 13:44 He made this analogy:

> "**The reign** (or: kingdom; sovereignty; dominion) **of the heavens and atmospheres exists being** (or: is) **like a treasure – having been hidden** (or: being concealed) **within the midst of a field**..."

But in Mat. 13:38 He had explained the previous parable by saying,

> "**Now the field is the organized System** (the ordered arrangement; the world of religion, economy, culture and government; = the realm of society; or: **the aggregate of humanity**)."

When God breathed into the human being (Gen. 2:7), He breathed into him His treasure: the Breath of Life. [In Gen. 2:11-12, the earth/land is associated with gold, precious stones and an aromatic tree resin (Heb.: *bedolach*; NRSV renders this "bdellium"; CVOT has "pearl," and Wikipedia attributes this meaning to Rabbi Saadiah Gaon)]. With that Life came treasures of wisdom (Ex. 35:31; Ezk. 28:3-17). God breathed the atmospheres, the heavens, into humanity and this is why His dwelling place (the Tabernacle/Temple, and now the body of Christ) was to be among people (Lev. 26:11-12; Rev. 21:3), and the Tabernacle-Temple-People were, and now are, both a symbol and an existential manifestation, and assumed appearance, of heaven: God's dwelling place (note the cherubim in its décor as a figure of it being a heavenly, or spiritual, realm).

Paul instructs us of the reason for God putting His treasure (Himself and His kingdom/reign) in "jars of clay." It is, "**so that the transcendence of the power may habitually originate its existence in God**." Apart from God, there is no "transcendence of power." Said otherwise, it is so that "the over-cast of ability can be that which is God." Or, this clause can be rendered, "the overwhelming which comes from the Power would exist with the character and quality of God." Paul expressed this same thought in 1 Cor. 2:5,

> "**to the end that your trust would not be in human wisdom** (your faith and reliance would not exist in cleverness of people), **but rather in God's power, means, influence and ability**."

All this is so that God will get the glory, the reputation, and not us, and it would "not [be] from what characterizes us," since we are His creation. The reign of God was to be within and among ordinary people, and would NOT be presented to folks through "super-beings" like the heroes of pagan mythologies who supposedly had arisen from the union of some god with a human woman. "**This treasure within containers** (jars; pots; vessels; equipment) **made of baked clay**" pictures God's program and economy among people: "**so that no flesh [nature, government or religious system] – [including, or at] all – could boast in God's sight or presence** (or: before God)" (1 Cor. 1:29). Paul picks up the "**clay**" metaphor in 5:1, below:

"our house, which is this tent upon the earth;" or: "**our House – from the Tabernacle which was pitched on the Land**."

The Tabernacle in the wilderness journeys of Israel was a symbol of corporate Israel within and among whom Yahweh took up residence – on the Land.

The next three verses lay out for us the weakness and humanness of these "clay vessels,' to emphasize Paul's point. He made this same point in 1 Cor. 1:26,

> "**take a comprehensive look at** (or: as an indicative: To be sure, you folks are progressively seeing and observing) **your calling** (or: vocation; social role, position or station) **brothers, that [there are] not many wise folks – according to flesh**."

8. **We are people being constantly pressed [as grapes] on every [side]** (or: squeezed and constricted within the midst of everything; given affliction, oppression and tribulation by everyone), **but yet not constantly confined by a narrow space or a tight place so as to be restricted or hemmed in** (or: = not cramped beyond movement); **we are those being repeatedly made to be without resources, a place to walk or a means for conveyance** (or, as a middle: we are habitually at a loss about things, in doubt and perplexed), **but yet not continuously caused to be living utterly without resources or absolutely with no way out or place to walk or means for conveyance** (or, middle voice: but still, we are not continually living at a total loss, being in complete doubt, being greatly perplexed or in utmost despair);

Paul did not lead a life of a "name-it-and-claim-it," prosperity "gospel" – which is "another gospel" that is not the Good News. But he here gives testimony of God's faithfulness to bring them through hard times.

> "**Within the System** (dominating and controlling world of culture, religion, economy and government; or: among and in union with the aggregate of humanity) **you normally have pressure and stress** (or: continually have squeezing; repeatedly have tribulation and oppression), **but nonetheless, be confident and take courage! I, Myself, have overcome and conquered the System**" (Jn. 16:33).

In the first clause, I inserted "**[as grapes]**" to give the picture that resulted in what he said in 2 Tim. 4:6a,

> "**You see, I, myself, am already being progressively poured out as a drink offering**."

But let us take time to note the other optional renderings, to get a complete picture:

> a) squeezed and constricted within the midst of everything;
> b) given affliction, oppression and tribulation by everyone.

Does this not describe the cruciform life? In following His Master, Paul probably related to Ps. 22:12-17. But he does not end there: "**but yet not constantly confined by a narrow space or a tight place so as to be restricted or hemmed in** (or: = not cramped beyond movement)."

Now in good rhetorical parallelism, he continues:

> a) **we are those being repeatedly made to be without resources, a place to walk or a means for conveyance** (or, as a middle: we are habitually at a loss about things, in doubt and perplexed);
> b) **but yet not continuously caused to be living utterly without resources or absolutely with no way out or place to walk or means for conveyance**.

The verb of this last refrain can be either passive, or the middle voice. The bold rendering is the former, and parenthetical expansion "(but still, we are not…)" renders the latter. Pause to consider the semantic range on offer in both of these conflated translations. They were blessed, but perhaps not always "happy" – as we use this word. But note vs. 16, below!

9. **we are folks being constantly pursued and persecuted, but yet not habitually left in the lurch, being forsaken down within some situation; we are those being repeatedly thrown down, but yet not continuously caused to fall apart** (be loosed-away into ruin; be undone so as to be destroyed) –

He expands their contrasting realities in rhetorical redundancy as he continues describing their situations: "**we are**... **but yet not**...; **we are**... **but yet not**...!" They were "**constantly pursued and persecuted**" and were "**repeatedly thrown down**." Can we relate to these situations? But let us focus on the positives that he projects to us: "**not habitually left in the lurch, being forsaken down within some situation**," and "**not continuously caused to fall apart** (be loosed-away into ruin; be undone so as to be destroyed)." What assurance!

We call to mind Rom. 8:18,

> "**You see, I have come to a reasoned conclusion** (or: I am reckoning and logically considering) **that the effects of the sensible experiences – sufferings, impressions, passions or feelings – of the current season** (or: of the situation fitted to the present time) **[are] not equivalent** (do not balance the scales; are not of equal value or worth), **[being] face to face with the glory** (or: [are] of insufficient weight when put in balance to the manifestation which calls forth praise as well as the reputation and good opinion) **which is progressively about to be disclosed unto us, and for us** (or: unveiled into our midst; revealed to and [enter] into us)."

10. **at all times continuously carrying around** (or: bearing about), **among** (or: centered in) **the [corporate] body, Jesus' being put to death** (or: within [our] body the deadening, deadness and state of death, which comes from Jesus; or: within the midst of the body the dying associated with Jesus; or: the dying which is Jesus, in union with the body), **to the end that the Life, also, of Jesus** (or: so that also the life which comes from and is Jesus; or: so that Jesus' Life) **can** (or: could; may; would) **be set in clear light and manifested, within our body** (or: in the midst of the body, which is us)!

The first clause is a continuation of vs. 9, and so should be read in its light. However, this assertion is still enigmatic. I have rendered it four different ways, and we will consider each of these. But there is, first of all, a possible allusion to Gen. 50:25 and Ex. 13:19 where we have first Joseph, and then Moses rehearsing Joseph's request, speaking for them to be "carrying up [Joseph's] bones" away from Egypt, when Israel left that country (i.e., their **Exodus**). In Lu. 9:28-36 Moses and Elijah were seen with Jesus, and in vs. 31 we are informed that "They kept on talking [about] **His exodus**..." – a reference to His soon coming execution and death. Was Paul saying that their lives were living out a parable that pointed to the new Exodus from Second Temple Judaism and its collusion with Rome? Joseph had been a savior in Egypt, but he pointed ahead to Israel's deliverance through Moses. Paul is possibly taking up the next chapter of that narrative.

Now vs. 11, below, gives a literal explanation of his words, here, in the form of a restatement. But why did he frame it with these words in our present verse? Let us now examine them to see why he said that they were "**at all times continuously carrying around** (or: bearing about),"

> a) **among** (or: centered in) **the [corporate] body Jesus' being put to death**
> b) within [our] body the deadening, deadness and state of death, which comes from Jesus
> c) within the midst of the body the dying associated with Jesus
> d) the dying which is Jesus, in union with the body.

The variations arise from the possible functions of the genitive/ablative case of these two prepositional phrases. The first option (a) calls to mind Paul's words in 1 Cor. 2:2,

> "**for I decided not to see, perceive or know anything within or among you folks, except Jesus Christ – and this One being one having been crucified** (suspended from a pole)!"

This would mostly be a reference to living a cruciform life (Mat. 16:24-25). The second option (b) may be related to what he said in Gal. 2:20,

> "**I was crucified together with Christ** [= the Messiah], **and thus it remains** (or: I have been jointly put on the execution stake in [the] Anointed One, and continue in this state)... **yet I continue living! [It is] no longer I, but it is Christ continuously living and alive within me.**"

The third option (c) may simply be what vs. 11, below, describes, and what all followers of the Way were told would happen, from the persecution by the Jews of that day, as we read about in the book of Acts. Paul carried this persecution as he moved among the various called-out communities. We read in 1 Cor. 15:21, "**Daily I am repeatedly facing death** (or: progressively dying)!" And in Gal. 6:17b Paul said,

> "**I myself continuously carry the brand marks [of a slave or a soldier, showing ownership] of Jesus, within** (or: the effects of being stuck by a point from Jesus, on) **my body!**"

Then. Phil. 3:10b speaks of,

> "**being a person that is being continuously conformed by** (being progressively brought together with the form of; being habitually configured to) **His death**."

Option (c) may also refer to the purification process (*cf* Mal. 3:2-3) or the "child-training" referred to in Heb. 12:3-17. Consider, also, the admonitions from the risen Christ in Rev. 2 and 3.

The final parenthetical rendering (d) is in apposition, "the dying which is Jesus, in union with the body," and may signify the union of Jesus with the corporate body of Christ, and may be echoing Rom. 8:17, "**if so be** (or: provided) **that we are continually affected by sensible experiences together – feeling together; receiving impressions, undergoing passion or suffering together – to the end that we may also be glorified together**." There is a mystery in this Romans verse that speaks of our union with Christ in all that He went through, and now goes through, in us. Alternate renderings of the last clause of 8:17 may open our understanding a little more:

> "**that we... by suffering together**... can be given a shared appearance; would together receive a manifestation of that which calls forth praise; should be given a joint-approval and a joint-reputation; may be thought of and imagined together [in covenant relationship]."

Peter gives us insight which parallels Paul's statement, here:

> "**But on the contrary, keep on rejoicing and being glad to the extent or degree that you folks are continually participating with a common share and common existence in the effects of the experiences, along with the results of the sufferings, of the Christ, to the end that, while continuously exulting and celebrating exceedingly, you folks can** (or: should; would) **also rejoice within this unveiling of His glory** (or: in union with the disclosure of His reputation; or: in the midst of this praise-inducing manifestation which is Him)!" (1 Pet. 4:13)

11. **For we, ourselves – the continuously living ones – are ever being repeatedly handed over and committed into death** (or: = continuously delivered into life-threatening experiences) **– because of Jesus – to the end that the Life, also, of Jesus** (or: so that also the life which comes from and is Jesus; or: so that Jesus' life) **can** (may; could; would) **be set in clear light and manifested – within our mortal flesh!**

And now Paul presents the purpose for all of the above "death and dying." It is "**to the end that the Life, also, of Jesus** (or: so that also the life which comes from and is Jesus; or: so that Jesus' life) **can** (may; could; would) **be set in clear light and manifested – within our mortal flesh!**" This is that to which all disciples (students; followers) are called. THIS is what reflects the image of God: He was "**handed over and committed into death**," and this is why He said that His disciples must follow Him in this way. This is the kind of Love that God IS, and so this kind of Love is needed to reflect the glory (3:18, above), image and likeness of God. The "**mortal flesh**" is what he meant, above, by clay pots. The cruciform life sets the Life of Jesus into clear Light, and manifests God's Love for humanity, and thus, "**the creation is constantly receiving and taking away from out of the unveiling of, and the disclosure from, God's sons**" (Rom. 8:19). And as a result...

12. **So then** (or: Consequently), **the Death is repeatedly and progressively operating and inwardly working within us, yet that Life [is constantly operative] within you folks.**

Paul spoke similarly in Phil. 2:17,

> "**But even more, since** (or: if) **I am also repeatedly poured out as a drink offering upon the sacrificial offering and public service pertaining to your faith** (or: which comes from your trust; in regard to the faithful loyalty which comprises you people), **I am constantly rejoicing** (or: glad) – **even continually rejoicing** (glad) **together with all of you!**" Cf Rev. 11:7-8

We have, here, a clear statement that affirms the solidarity of the body of Christ. It reminds us of 1 Cor. 12:26,

> "**whether one member is continuing to experience the effect of something, or constantly undergoes suffering, all the members continually experience the effect or the suffering together with [it; her; him]; or if a member is being constantly glorified, normally given an assumed appearance, or is progressively receiving a good reputation, all the members are continuously rejoicing together with [him; her; it].**"

It also shows us how Paul understood the words of Jesus:

> "**No one continues holding** (or: having) **greater love** (full giving of oneself; urge toward reunion) **than this: that someone should place** (set; lay; lay down) **his soul** (or: soul-life; inner being; self; person) **over [the situation or circumstances of]** (or: on behalf of) **his friends**" (Jn. 15:13).

13. **Now continuously possessing** (having and holding) **that faith's very Breath-effect and the same Spirit of fidelity** (or: the Spirit which itself is the Trust; or: the spirit and attitude which itself comes from the Faithfulness [of Christ]), **corresponding to that which has been written,**

> "**I trust and am faithful, therefore I speak** (or: I believed and was loyal, [and] for this reason I spoke)," [Ps. 116:10]

we ourselves, also, are constantly faithful and loyal, habitually trusting and progressively believing; therefore we also keep on speaking,

Paul's rhetorical move is now to anchor his arguments in an OT quote, affirming that he and his friends are speaking from the same trust, belief and faithfulness that is found in the Scriptures. The sent-forth representatives of Christ continuously possessed "**that faith's very Breath-effect and the same Spirit of fidelity** (or: the Spirit which itself is the Trust; or: the spirit and attitude which itself comes from the Faithfulness [of Christ])" as that which was seen to be in the fathers of the past age. It is the same Spirit that also keeps them speaking, and so…

14. **having seen, and now knowing, that the One at one point arousing and raising Jesus** [other MSS: the Lord Jesus] **will also continue arousing and raising us up together with** [other MSS: through] **Jesus and will CONTINUE making us stand alongside** (placing us beside; positioning us parallel, [for disposal]; setting us by, [for support]), **together with you folks,**

Now he reminds them that "**One at one point arousing and raising Jesus**" is the One that is operating within all of Christ's body – both Paul with his group, and also the Corinthians. Traditional eschatology has read this verse as speaking to a future event. But the context of both vs. 13 and vs. 15 speaks to the present situations of both Paul and his audience. The future tense of the verbs in the second and third clauses indicates durative, ongoing action. So God (the One), Who has already aroused and raised Jesus, "**will also continue arousing and raising us up together with Jesus and will continue making us stand alongside, together with you folks.**" Now Eph. 2:6 affirms that,

> "**He jointly roused and raised [us] up, and caused [us] to sit together in union with, and among, the heavenly people, and within the things situated upon** [thus, above] **the heavens within and in union with Christ Jesus.**"

This was continually happening, as individuals kept on being born again, from above, and were one-by-one entering into God's reign. We find another witness to this in Heb. 12:

> 22. **But to the contrary, you folks have approached so that you ARE NOW at Mount Zion – even in a city of a continuously living God; in "Jerusalem upon heaven"** [cf 11:16, above]

(or: in a Jerusalem pertaining to and having the character and qualities of a superior, or added, heaven and atmosphere; or: in Jerusalem [situated] upon, and comparable to, the atmosphere; centered in a heavenly-imposed Jerusalem) – **also among ten-thousands** (or: myriads) **of agents and messengers** (people with a/the message)**:**

23. **[that is] in** (or: to) **an assembly of an entire people** (or: an assembly of all; a universal convocation) **and in** (or: to) **a summoning forth** (or: a called-out and gathered community) **of firstborn folks having been copied** (from-written, as from a pattern; or: enrolled; registered) **within [the; or: various] atmospheres** (or: heavens), **and in** (or: to; with) **God, a Judge** (an Evaluator and Decider) **of all mankind, even among** (or: to; with) **spirits of just folks** (or: breath-effects from those who are fair and equitable and in right relationship within the Way pointed out) **having been brought to the destined goal** (perfected; finished; matured; made complete), [cf Rev. 3:12; 21:1-2; Eph. 2:6; Phil. 3:20; Rev. 14:1-5; Ex. 4:22; Gal. 3:19]

24. **and in** (or: to) **Jesus, a Medium** (or: an agency; an intervening substance; a middle state; one in a middle position; a go-between; an Umpire; a Mediator) **of a new and fresh** (young; recently-born) **arrangement** (covenant; settlement; a deposit which moves throughout in every direction; a placing through the midst; a will and testament), **and to and in blood of sprinkling, and to One continuously speaking something superior to** (or: stronger and better than) **Abel.** [cf Mat. 17:1-5; Gal. 4:22-26; Rev. 21:1-2; 9b-22:5; Jn. 4:21; Ps. 46:4; 132:13; Isa. 28:16; 33:5]

Take note of the first clause of 12:22, quoted here: the verb is in the perfect tense. His audience "had approached" in the past, so that they were NOW at Mt. Zion. This states what was said in Eph. 2:6 but using a different metaphor. We HAVE BEEN born from the Jerusalem which is above (in the atmosphere of God; in the Spirit; in the heavenly realm), and this is why SHE IS our mother (Gal. 4:26).

We also read in Rom. 8:

11. **Now since the Breath-effect** (or: Spirit; Attitude) **of the One arousing and raising Jesus forth from out of the midst of dead folks is continuously housing Itself** (making His abode; residing; making His home; by idiom: living together as husband and wife) **within, and in union with, you folks, the One raising Christ Jesus forth from out of dead ones will also CONTINUE PROGRESSIVELY giving Life to** (or: will even habitually make alive) **the mortal bodies of you folks** (or: your mortal bodies) **through the CONSTANT INDWELLING of His Spirit** (or: the continual in-housing of His Breath-effect; the continuous internal residing of the Attitude, which is Him,) [other MSS: because of His habitually-indwelling Spirit] **within and among you folks.** [cf 5:4-5, below; Acts 1:8]

The optional renderings of the phrase, "positioning us parallel, [for disposal]; setting us by, [for support]," also suggest a current setting in regard to the needs of situations among the Corinthian community. They would be there to perform as paracletes among them.

15. **for you see, all things [are]** (the whole – everything – [is]) **because of you folks, to the end that the grace and favor – increasing and becoming more than enough through the greater part** (the majority) **of the people – can** (should; would) **cause the benefits of grace** (or: the goodness, ease and wellbeing from grace; or: this attitude of gratitude; or: the expression of thanksgiving) **to be surrounding in superabundance, unto God's glory** (or: [proceeding] into the praise-inducing manifestation of, and assumed appearance from, God)**!**

The first clause, "**all things [are]…**," echoes the idea in 1 Cor. 3:22b-23,

"**all things [are] yours** (or: everything pertains to you, belongs to you, and [is] from you folks), **yet you folks [are] Christ's – yet Christ [is] God's!**"

Here he builds upon the last, preceding phrase, "**together with you folks**" (vs. 14), bringing their importance to God, and to Paul's group, to the forefront by affirming that it follows that "**all things**" are because of them. How would you feel if someone said that to you? What Paul and the other sent-forth representatives were going through was so that, with "**the grace and favor increasing and becoming more than enough**" for everyone, this grace would "**cause the benefits of grace to be surrounding [everyone] in superabundance**" – and this would bring glory to God.

The dependent participial clause, set off by dashes, "**increasing and becoming more than enough...**," modifies the conflated term "**the grace and favor**." But let us take note of the predicate that follows the participle. Grace increases (to be more than enough) "**through the greater part** (the majority) **of the people**." The preposition, "**through**," with the genitive "**the greater part**," can signify immediate agency, causation or instrumentality. In other words, with "the majority of the people" functioning as a source of grace (for Christ is within them, filling them with grace), they "**can** (should; would) **cause the benefits of grace to be surrounding in superabundance**." Put another way, they are "the Light" of the community. This, of course leads "**unto God's glory**," or "into the praise-inducing manifestation of, and assumed appearance from, God." This is why "**all things [are] because of**" the majority of the community. They are Corinth's lampstand: the oil of the Anointing is in them and they shine the Light of Christ upon the rest of the community (recall that the lampstand was within the temple – and represented the covenant group, as in Rev. 1:20).

But also, the primary idea of the word "**through**," speaks of something passing through the midst of something else. In this case it would be "**the grace and favor... passing through the midst of the greater part of the people**." Both readings present the correct picture – each one giving a different emphasis. And this "**grace**" is "**increasing**." It is the increase of the kingdom of God. The increase of His reign (in more and more people) brings a superabundance of "the goodness, ease and wellbeing from grace." "A little leaven, leavens the whole lump" (Gal. 5:9; Mat. 13:33) – in a positive way, or in a negative way. Here, in vs. 15, it is the leaven of grace and the kingdom. What passes through the midst of the majority will also radiate through the midst of the minority. (*Cf* his reference to "the majority" in 2:6, above, and its significance in that situation.)

Think of it! All that Paul had been saying, above, as well as all their pressures and trials, would cause a surrounding of the superabundance of the **benefits of, and from,** God's **grace**. My first two renderings of *eu-charis-tian* are based on the root of this word being "grace (*charis*)," and the prefix, *eu-*, signifying "benefits," or, "goodness, ease and wellbeing." This seems to better fit both Paul's theology of the central role of grace, as well as the context. I have also acknowledged the more common renderings of this word in, "this attitude of gratitude," and "the expression of thanksgiving," which of course would attend grace's benefits, which are, "the Spirit of grace" (Zech. 12:10; Heb. 10:29b)

If we view the Corinthian community as a type, a symbol, a figure, or as representative, of the aggregate of humanity, we can read the first clause as saying "all things [are] for humanity." To this we would say, "Yes, it is so."

16. **For this reason we do not habitually behave with a bad attitude, or perform in a worthless manner, or act from out of a mood that is poor in quality, or become discouraged. But to the contrary, even if** (or: since also) **our outside person** (or: outer humanity; = body of flesh) **is being progressively wasted away** (is constantly being decayed and brought to ruin and corruption), **certainly our inside [person]** (= inner humanity; Eph. 2:15) **is day by day** (or: from day to day; on a daily basis) **being progressively made new again** (or: renewed) **in kind and quality so as to have a different character that is fresh and effective.**

"**For this reason**" refers directly back to what he just said in vs. 15. This is a restatement of vs. 1, above. Grace is increasing to be more than enough, so there is no reason for worthless behavior. Furthermore, that which is "**poor in quality**" can likewise permeate the community as negative leaven (Gal. 5:9). So Paul is being the paraclete, admonishing them not to "**act from out of a mood that is poor in quality, or**

become discouraged," because he and his associates had not given them that kind of example to follow.

With the first clause being a summation of his arguments in this passage, he then makes a summation of vss. 8-12a, stating that even if all that is the case, nevertheless, the "**inside [person]** (= inner humanity; Eph. 2:15)" of him and his associates "**is day by day** (or: from day to day; on a daily basis) **being progressively made new again** (or: renewed) **in kind and quality so as to have a different character that is fresh and effective**." So, once again he presents his own life, and those of the other representatives, as a parable set in clear light that reveals the purpose of "**being progressively wasted away**." They are like the seed that falls into the ground in order to produce much fruit in their lives (Jn. 12:24). Of course, the parable of Paul's life is there to apply to our lives, as well. We can take heart as we observe our own progressive "wasting away."

Paul presents a view of humanity as having two parts, here: "**our outside person**," and "**our inside [person]**." He has moved away from the traditional Jewish view of humanity as being just "a person." This may be because he is writing to a predominantly Hellenistic community, and this dualism comports with the Hellenistic view. Witherington observes, "Paradoxically, it is the new person or the new creation, the spiritual part, which is constantly being renewed in the life of the Christian" (ibid p 389). Paul spoke of "the renewing of the mind" in Rom. 12:2. This contrast, combined with transformation, may be alluding to 3:18, above.

We want to point out that there is a process that is involved in renewal, i.e., "**being progressively made new again in kind and quality so as to have a different character that is fresh and effective**." This expanded conflation of *anakainountai* presents a full expression of the present passive verb that is based upon the elements *ana-* (re- or, again) and *kainos* (new in kind and character that is fresh and effective). The passive voice again points us to the fact that God was, in all the situations, working everything into goodness (Rom. 8:28). Paul's life gave witness to his theology.

Witherington (ibid) views the passage from vs. 16, here, through 5:10, below, as a section that should be read and interpreted together, noting as one reason that the conjunction *gar* (for; so you see; because, it follows that) is used repeatedly throughout these verses (7 times). It would be wisdom to read this whole section before proceeding with the commentary, to see if his observation holds true.

17. **So you see, the momentary light [aspect or character]** (or: lightness) **of the pressure and squeezing** (the affliction, oppression and tribulation) **is progressively working down in us a corresponding** (commensurate) **and consecutively transcending eonian weight of glory**
> (or: is repeatedly producing for us a heavy burden of glory, down from one over-casting on into another over-cast, each of which pertains to the Age; or: is now accomplishing with us an according, age-lasting weight of a good reputation – [each] a transcending one [leading] into [another] transcending one; or: is continuously effecting in us – on the level of "surpassing leading into surpassing" – a weight which has the quality of the realm of [Messiah's] Age, and which belongs to a praise-inducing, assumed manifestation),

The **upgrading renewal** of which he spoke in 16b he now describes as "**progressively working down in us a corresponding** (commensurate) **and consecutively transcending eonian weight of glory**." This clause is so pregnant with meaning that we need to list the alternative ways of rendering it – lest the reader pass over its richness to quickly:
> a) is repeatedly producing for us a heavy burden of glory, down from one over-casting on into another over-cast, each of which pertains to the Age;
> b) is now accomplishing with us an according, age-lasting weight of a good reputation – [each] a transcending one [leading] into [another] transcending one;

c) is continuously effecting in us – on the level of "surpassing leading into surpassing" – a weight which has the quality of the realm of [Messiah's] Age, and which belongs to a praise-inducing, assumed manifestation.

Paul is saying that all the pressure, squeezing, affliction, oppression or tribulation – is worth it! In vs. 9, above, we quoted Rom. 8:18, and it applies here, as well. The final rendering of *doxa*, commonly rendered "glory," that is on offer is the conflation: "a praise-inducing assumed manifestation." What is manifested is what other folks are able to see, observe and contemplate. When what is being observed is the image of God (as in Gen. 1:26; *eikōn*: resemblance; representation; appearance; manifestation; form), what folks will see will be a manifestation of God, which by His Spirit we have assumed, and it will call forth praise to God. We will in this form of existence and behavior become an instrument to reflect Who and What He is – we will be a reflection of His glory (1 Cor. 11:7). When they see us, they will see the Father (Jn. 14:7-9). It is the "**pressure and squeezing** – the affliction, oppression and tribulation" that produces His image in us.

18. **while we are not constantly fixing our gaze on or carefully noting the things that are being constantly seen or repeatedly observed, but rather, [we are continuously looking at] those things not being constantly seen or repeatedly observed, because the things being constantly seen and observed [are] for a season** (temporary; set toward a certain situation; transient), **but those things not being habitually seen or observed pertain to and have their source in the Age** ([are] eonian; [continue] age-lasting). [*cf* 5:7, below; Eph. 2:7]

Paul uses two different verbs for looking-at, or seeing, in this verse. The first one – and note the present tense (constant, continued or repeated action) in both of these verbs – in participle form, is *skopeō*: to keep a watchful eye fixed on a distant object; notice carefully; survey; view attentively; watch. In other words, we see, but we are not focusing our constant attention on seasonal or transient things. Jesus instructed us about what we should "*skopeō*": "**Continue alert and be habitually watchful, continually taking careful notice, therefore, [that] the light within you is not darkness** (does not continue being dimness from shadows)" (Lu. 11:35). Paul also used this verb in Gal. 6:1b,

> "**as you each are constantly keeping a watchful eye on yourself** (carefully noting yourself with regard to the goal), **and so you folks may not at some point be put to the proof** (or: and you, yourself, would not be tried, tested or harassed by some ordeal)."

The second word is the more commonly used verb, *blepō*: to cast a glance at; to look at; to exercise sight; to see; to regard; to observe – and things that can be observed by exercising physical sight are NOT the things that Paul, and those being led by the Spirit, are "**constantly fixing our gaze on or carefully noting.**" No, Paul wanted people, having unveiled faces, to be fixing their gaze on and carefully noting the glory of the Lord (3:18, above). In Eph. 3, he described his mission as being:

> "**to illuminate all people** (give light to everyone) **[as to] what [is] the execution of the detailed plan and household administration of the secret** (or: mystery) **pertaining to that having been hidden** (concealed) **away, apart from the ages** (or: disassociated from the [past] periods of time), **within the midst of God – in the One forming and founding** (framing, building and settling from a state of disorder and wildness; creating) **all things** (the Whole; everything) **– to the end that now** (at this present time), **in union with the heavenly people, God's greatly diversified wisdom** (the exceedingly varied in colors [as in a tapestry or the Veil] wisdom which is God; or: the many-phased wisdom from God) **could be made known – through the called-out community – to the governments** (or: rulers; sovereignties; chief ones) **as well as to the authorities and folks with privilege among those situated upon elevated positions**
>> (or: made known by the agency of the summoned and gathered congregation: by the original members and the folks who have the right, that is, among the imposed-heaven folks; or: made known by means of the ecclesia with the founders and people having the privilege – in union with these celestial people, within the midst of the things situated upon the atmospheres and among the folks [residing] in the added atmospheres), **in**

accord with (or: down from; corresponding to) **a purpose of the ages** (a fore-designed aim, plan and object of the unspecified time-periods) **which He formed** (forms; made; constructs; creates; produced) **within the Christ by our Lord and Owner, Jesus**" (vss. 9-11).

Now THIS is something to "scope" out and, by the indwelling Spirit, be folks who are "**having organs of perception trained as in gymnastic exercise and thus being skilled, because of practice, and [being] disciplined, with a view to a discerning**" (Heb. 5:14).

As well as the recommended references in the brackets, above, recall Jesus' words which say the same thing, but in a different way:

> "**So you folks be continuously accumulating and storing up for yourselves treasures within heaven** (or: [your] atmosphere) **– where neither moth nor corrosion causes [things] to disappear, and where thieves do not constantly dig through nor are they repeatedly stealing** (Mat. 6:20).

We find a similar statement in Col. 3:2-3,

> "**Be constantly minding** (thinking about; setting your disposition and sentiments toward; paying regard to) **the upward things** (or: the things above), **not the things upon the earth, for you folks died, and your life has been hidden so that it is now concealed together with the Christ, within the midst of God** (or: in union with God)."

These three verses are all speaking of the same thing: focus on God's reign (kingdom. Sovereign activities and influences), not on human culture, politics, economy, religion or mind sets. It does not mean that we ignore these or don't participate in them, but we focus on the glory of the Lord (3:18, above). We see Him in the naked, the hungry, the sick, the imprisoned (Mat. 25:35-36) – and we give them our "attending service and dispensing of provision." It is like what we read in Heb. 2:9, "**But yet, we are continuously seeing Jesus**…" And as Heb. 12:1b-2a instructs us,

> "**we can and should through persistent remaining-under** (or: relentless patient endurance and giving of support) **keep on running the racecourse** [Gal. 5:7] **continuously lying before us** (or: lying in the forefront within us; or: lying ahead, among us), **turning [our] eyes away from other things and fixing them** (or: looking away) **into Jesus, the Inaugurator** (First Leader; Prime Author) **and Perfecter** (Finisher; the Bringer-to-maturity and fruition; He who purposes and accomplishes the destiny) **of the faith, trust, confidence and loyal allegiance**…"

As regards "**the Age**," Paul expands upon this in Eph. 3:21,

> "**by Him** (to Him; for Him; in Him; with Him) **[is] the glory** (the manifestation which calls forth praise) **within the called-out community** (the summoned-forth congregation) **as well as within Christ Jesus: unto** (or: [proceeding] into) **all the generations** (births; progenies) **of the Age of the ages** (= the most significant, or crowning, Age of all the ages)!"

Chapter 5

1. You see, we have seen, perceived and know that if our House – from the Tabernacle which was pitched on the Land – would at some point be dismantled (or: that whenever our house, which is this tent upon the earth, should be loosed down), **we constantly have** (continuously hold; presently possess) **a dwelling structure or place** (a building for an abode; or: a household; = a family or a possession) **forth from out of the midst of God: an eonian act of building a roofed house** (or: a covered building for dwelling having qualities and character which pertain to the Age [of the Messiah]; a structure of edification for, and pertaining to, the ages) **– not made by hands – resident within the atmospheres** (or: in union with the heavens).

The first thing to observe is that this verse is a continuation of 4:18, above: this chapter division is an artificial break in Paul's thinking. He is still speaking of "**fixing our gaze on or carefully noting… those things not being constantly seen or repeatedly observed.**" One of those things that is "not being seen" is "**a dwelling from out of the midst of God:** a covered building for dwelling having qualities and character which pertain to the Age [of the Messiah]."

So we must first ask: What does he mean by the term "**House**" which he then calls "**the Tabernacle**, or, tent"? This qualifier, "**Tabernacle**," or "tent," signifies that which is not permanent – and to put it in the words of 4:18, above, it refers to something that was "**for a season** (temporary; set toward a certain situation; transient)." Tony Everett Denton (*Pertinent Parousia Passages, Second-Coming Scripture Studies*, 2016 p 148) has pointed us to Phil. 3:19b where Paul warned about,

> "**people continually thinking about** (habitually being intent on; constantly minding) **the things existing upon the EARTH** (or: upon the Land; or: = folks whose minds are earthbound). [Rom. 8:6-8; Hos. 4:7; 7:13]

Such folks were still living as being a part of the earthly Tabernacle – most likely the Judaizers – who were constantly "**walking about** (i.e., are living their lives) **as enemies of the cross of the Christ**" (Phil. 3:18).

Paul goes on to contrast this with "**a dwelling structure or place** (a building for an abode) **forth from out of the midst of God**... **resident within the atmospheres** (in union with the heavens)." The terms "House" and "Tabernacle" were traditionally applied to corporate structures [cf Rev. 21:3] that were also referred to as "the Temple." We are reminded of Jesus' words in Jn. 14:2-3a,

> "**Within My Father's HOUSE** (or: household) **are many abodes** (staying places; dwelling places; homes; rooms). **Now if not, I would at once tell you folks, because I am progressively passing** (or: traveling) **along to prepare and make ready a place in you** (or: for you; with and among you folks). **Even if I should journey on and prepare** (make suitable, fit and appropriate) **a place** (or: a spot; a position; a role) **in you folks** (or: with, among and for you)..."

So when Paul says, "**OUR House**," is he speaking of the temple (whether speaking of the literal temple that was destroyed in AD 70, or of their corporate community), or of our individual bodies? We should note here the qualifying clause "**not made by hands**," which may be a contrast that has reference to the physical Tabernacle, or Temple. Those were "made by hands." Our physical bodies were not "made by hands." Where else do we find this phrase "not made by hands"?

The "**the set-apart** (or: holy) **place pertaining to that system** (suited to that ordered arrangement)," that is, of the old covenant (cf Heb. 9:1), was the type of this new, "heavenly" Temple (as we read of in Heb. 9:1-8). But notice Heb. 9:11,

> "**So Christ** ([the] Anointed One; [Messiah]), **after suddenly coming to be present at [our] side [as] a Chief** (or: Ruling; Ranking) **Priest of the good things happening** (or: of virtuous people being birthed; [with other MSS: pertaining to impending excellent things]), **by means of the greater and more perfect** (more matured, complete and destined) **Tabernacle NOT MADE BY HANDS – that is, not of this creation – and not by means of blood from he-goats and calves, but by means of and through His own blood.**" [cf Heb. 6:19-20; 8:2]

Now observe that the author uses the same expression as our verse here: "**not made by hands**." But in this Heb. 9 text, it goes on to explain that this term was "**not of this creation**." In vss. 1-10, the author had been speaking of the physical tabernacle and the cultic rituals of the old covenant, i.e., of the old creation that was formed at Mt. Sinai. Furthermore, we read in Heb. 10:19b, 20, 22 that we are admonished to draw near, "**within and in union with the blood of Jesus, a Way** (Path; Road) **which was done anew** (or: which He innovates and makes new in species, character or mode, within and in the midst) **for us and in us**," with our "**hearts having been sprinkled from a misery-gushed consciousness of what is evil or unserviceable** (or: a joint-knowledge full of annoying labor; a conscience in a bad condition)." So now WE are the Temple (cf 6:16, below) of the Atmospheres (the **new creation**, of verse 17, below) into which Jesus entered, **sprinkling OUR hearts** (the new holy of holies) with His blood/Life. Let us now look at Heb. 9: 24, with the above in mind:

"**For Christ did not enter into set-apart places made by hands** (= by humans) – **representations** (things formed after a pattern) **of the true and real things – but rather into the atmosphere and heaven itself, now to be manifested** (exhibited to view; caused to appear in clear light; made apparent) **by the presence of God over us** (or: in God's face and countenance [being] on our behalf)."

The body of Christ is the new heavens, the new atmosphere that presents the new arrangement (covenant) to the world.

Now observe: "**we constantly HAVE** (continuously hold; presently possess) **a dwelling structure or place** (a building for an abode; or: a household; = a family or a possession) **forth from out of the midst of God.**" [*cf* Rev. 21:2, 10b] Consider that this term, *oikia*, can also be rendered "a household." By extension this can refer to "a family or a possession (that is associated with one's household)." He is not speaking about something that we will have when we die, or that we will have in the future, or that is somewhere off in space! It is something that we "**presently possess.**" If they destroy the temple in Jerusalem, it would not affect either Paul or his listeners (nor us, nor anyone). We continuously hold this "House" each time we hold a person within the community.

The word *oikodomē* can refer either to an action, or to the result of that action: **an eonian act of building a roofed house**, or, "a covered building for dwelling having qualities and character which pertain to the Age [of the Messiah]; a structure of edification for, and pertaining to, the ages." Next, he locates this "act of building," and "the structure of edification," and it is: "**resident within the atmospheres** (or: in union with the heavens)." In other words, it is not in literal Jerusalem, nor in Judea, or any other location on the physical earth. But in Gal. 4:26 we read that it is in "**the Jerusalem above.**" We find a description of it in Heb. 12:22, "**you folks HAVE approached so that you are NOW at Mount Zion – even in a city of a continuously living God; in 'Jerusalem upon heaven.'**" It is in the "atmosphere (or: heaven) of the kingdom of the atmospheres (or: kingdom of the heavens)."

Paul put it this way in 1 Tim. 3:15,
> "**[I am writing this] to the end that you may see and thus know how it is necessary and binding to be twisted and turned back up again within God's household** (or: to be treated, conducted or caused to behave in God's **HOUSE**), **which is** (or: exists being) **a called-out community of [the] Living God** (or: whose source is a living God; which has the qualities and character of [the] living God; or: which is a living god), **a pillar and foundational seat of The Truth** (or: a base from and an effect of a settling of reality)."

In Eph. 2:11 we find Paul using the phrase "**made by hand**" in a reference to circumcision – which related to the Tabernacle and the House of the old covenant:
> "**On which account** (or: Wherefore; So then), **you folks must continuously call to mind** (or: keep in mind; remember) **that once you, the nations** (multitudes; ethnic groups; Gentiles; non-Israelites) **in flesh** (= in your physical beings and cultural heritages) **– the ones habitually termed** (spoken of as; called; said to be) **"uncircumcision" by the one** (or: that) **habitually being termed "circumcision," in flesh** (= body, culture and religion), **[i.e.], made BY HAND.**"

Now observe how he uses the metaphor of the "body" in Col. 2:11, 12a, and how it refers to the work of Christ that has already happened with us:
> "**within Whom you folks were also circumcised** (or: in union with Whom you are cut around and off) **by** (or: in; to; with) **a circumcision NOT done BY HANDS** (not handmade)**: in the sinking out and away from** (or: the stripping off and undressing of; the going out and away from) **the BODY of the flesh**
>> (= the corporate body of the Jewish religion and national heritage; or: = the natural the body pertaining to the natural realm; or: = the estranged human nature and alienated self) **– in the circumcision of the Christ** (in Christ's circumcision; in the

circumcision which was done to Christ; or: in the circumcision which is the Anointing), **being buried together in Him** (jointly entombed with Him)."

The phrase "without hands" may also be an allusion to the new kingdom spoken of in Dan. 2:44-45 which was "cut out of the mountain **without hands**." This spiritual kingdom is associated with the New Jerusalem of Rev. 21-22, which is composed of His people, His eonian House, which is a "**dwelling structure or place** (a building for an abode; or: a household; = a family or a possession) **forth from out of the midst of God**" (*cf* Rev. 21:10b, where we read that this City, His Bride, is "**progressively** {or: habitually; or: presently} **descending out of the atmosphere** {or: heaven}, **from God**"). And just what was it that Abraham was wanting? Was it another physical body? No, for we read in Heb. 11:10,

> "**For he continued taking with the hand from out of** (or: reaching in and receiving, then taking away from within) **the city** [i.e., the New Jerusalem] **continuously having the foundations – whose Craftsman** (or: Technician; Artisan) **and skilled Worker for the people** (or: Producer of a People; Architect of a public corporate entity) **[is] God**."

A verse that has been associated with 5:1, here, is found in Phil. 3. We will examine this verse from the comments on it found in my commentary, *Peter, Paul & Jacob*, Harper Brown Pub. 2012 p 60-63:

> 21. **Who will be actively transfiguring** (progressively refashioning and remodeling; continuously changing the form of) **our body from the low condition and status** (or: the body of our humiliation; or: the body which is us, pertaining to this lowliness) **into the [situation] for it to be birthed conformed to the body of His glory** (or: be brought into existence having the same form together with His body, from that which calls forth praise; [with other MSS: joint-formed by and with the body of His good reputation]), **down from** (or: in accord with; in the sphere of; along the lines of; to the level of; following the pattern of; stepping along with; commensurate with; following the bidding of; as directed by) **the inward operation** (energy; in-working) **of the [conditions or situation for] Him to be continuously able** (or: with power) **also to humbly align The Whole to and in Himself** (or: to subject and subordinate all things for Himself; to arrange everything under so as to have full control and to support [it] by and with Himself).

Christ, by His Spirit (Who/Which also dwells within His called-out folks) and by His Word, will be progressively refashioning, remodeling and transfiguring our body from the humiliation, to be conformed to the body of His glory. This is what happens as we walk the Path within Him who is the Way. We have much to anticipate as we live our lives here. Now the first question that we need to ask is: What body is it to which he is referring? Is it our individual physical body, or is it the corporate body of Christ? Reading the personal pronoun as in the genitive of apposition, it reads "the body which is us." His body is a corporate body (1 Cor. 12:12) and this is the body of His glory (Christ in you the expectation of glory – Col. 1:27). Recall John 17:22,

> "**And I, Myself, have given to them** (or: in them), **and they now possess, the glory** (the notion; the opinion; the imagination; the reputation; the manifestation which calls forth praise) **which You have given to Me, and which I now possess, to the end that they may continuously exist being one correspondingly as** (just as; according as; on the same level as; in the same sphere as) **We [are] one**."

That glory was not an outward glory, but an inward one, just as His working is an inward one. It was the glory that the Father had given to Him, which He then possessed, but could not be seen outwardly.

The words "**down from**" is the Greek *kata*, which as you see has a broad semantic range. If we use the meaning of "in the sphere of," this corresponds to His inward working – where the transfiguration and remodeling takes place. The meaning "along the lines of" says the same thing. It is not an outward, physical transformation, but an inward one – of which he is here speaking.

In vs. 10, above, Paul made reference to having the power of His resurrection. Let us look in 1 Cor. 15 where he also speaks of bodies, resurrection and Christ:

> 42. **Thus also** (or: In this way too) **[is] the resurrection of the dead people. It is habitually** (repeatedly; presently; one after another) **being sown within corruption** (or: in union with decay and ruin; in perishability); **it is being habitually** (or: presently; repeatedly; one after another) **awakened and raised up within incorruption** (non-decayability; imperishableness).
>
> 43. **It is constantly being sown within dishonor** (in union with lack of value; in the midst of worthlessness), **it is being habitually** (or: repeatedly; constantly; one after another; progressively) **awakened and raised up within, and in union with, power and ability.**
>
> 44. **It is habitually** (continually; repeatedly; presently) **being sown a body having the qualities and characteristics of a soul** (a soulish body; or: = a body animated by soul); **it is habitually** (repeatedly; constantly; presently; one after another) **being awakened and raised up a spiritual body** (a body having the qualities and characteristics of the Breath-effect). **Since there is a soulish body** (or: = body animated by soul), **there also is** (or: exists) **a spiritual one** (or: = one animated by spirit).
> [comment: note the germinal connection between the two – they are a progression of the same body]
>
> 45. **Thus also** (or: In this way also), **it has been written, "The first human** (or: man), **Adam, came for existence** (or: was birthed) **into [being] a living soul"** [Gen. 2:7]; **the Last Adam into [being] a continuously life-making** (life-engendering; life-creating; life-giving) **Spirit** (or: Breath-effect).

Now note the connection of resurrection with power, in vs. 43. Next, in vs. 44, we see that it is **"being awakened and raised up A SPIRITUAL BODY."** Then he tells us that there is a natural body that pertains to the soul – the one which is sown – and there is a spiritual one – the one that is resurrected, and consider my note that this is a progression of the same body. It is like the seed that fell into the ground that I referred to, above (vs. 11 comments). Note also the present tense of the verbs: habitually, repeatedly, constantly, presently, one-after-another. This, again, is an ongoing process that was happening in Paul's day, as it has ever since the resurrection of Jesus.

Now note vs. 45 which Paul is relating both to resurrection and to the two bodies. We have the first human, Adam (the soulish person) and we have the Last Adam Who is a continuously life-making, life-creating, life-giving Spirit. The resurrected person is a spirit. This is the spiritual body (the **"afterwards"** person of vs. 46). The first Adam was corporate humanity, in this context; the Last Adam is the corporate spiritual body of Christ, with Jesus as its Head.

Now let us look further in 1 Cor. 15,

> 47. **The first human** (person; man) **[was/is] forth from out of the earth** (land; ground; soil; dirt), **made of moist soil and mud** (or: having the quality and characteristics of moist dirt that can be poured; soilish), **the Second Human** (Person; Man) **[is made] of heaven** (or: sky; atmosphere).
>
> 48. **As [is] the person made of and having the character and quality of moist soil or mud** (pourable dirt; soil), **of such sort also [are] the people [who are] made of and have the character and quality of moist soil or mud** (soilish folks); **and likewise, as [is] the Heavenly Person** (or: the one made of and having the quality and character of the supra-heaven), **of such sort also [are] the supra-heavenly people – those made of and having the quality and character of the supra-heaven** (or: finished and perfected atmosphere).

49. **And correspondingly as we bear and wear the image of the dusty person,** [p46 adds: doubtless] **we can and should** [B reads: will] **also bear and wear the image of the supra-heavenly One** (or: the One having the quality and character of the finished and perfected atmosphere).

Vs. 48-49 describe humans transfigured to be conformed to His body of glory, and vs. 47 tells us that they are "**[made] of heaven**/atmosphere," this latter being parallel to the "**made of moist soil and mud**" of the first clause. The "made of heaven" is a figure for the spiritual. Having the quality and character of the supra-heaven and wearing His image is equivalent to being conformed to the body of His glory.

And then there is 1 Cor. 15:51,

51. **See (Look and consider)! I am progressively telling you a secret** ([the] mystery)! **We, indeed, shall not all be laid to sleep [in death], yet we all will be changed**
>> (or: On the one hand, not all of us will be made to [die], but on the other hand, we all will be altered; or: We all shall not be put to repose, and so we all shall be transformed; or: All of us shall not sleep, but we all will be rearranged to be another or made to be otherwise),

And then,

53. **For it continues being necessary** (it is habitually binding) **for this perishable and corruptible to instantly plunge** (or: sink) **in and clothe itself with** (or: slip on; put on) **incorruption and imperishability, and for this mortal** (one that is subject to death) **to instantly plunge and sink in and clothe itself with** (or: put on; slip on as a garment) **immortality** (deathlessness; undyingness).

This sounds very much like 2 Cor. 5:1-2, but looking at a couple more verses in 1 Cor. 15, we see another interesting aspect of what we now possess.

54. **Now whenever this mortal instantly plunges and sinks in and then clothes itself with** (or: slips on; puts on) **the Immortality, then will come into existence** (will be birthed; will take place) **the word** (the thought; the idea; the message; the saying) **which has been written,**
"The Death was drunk down and swallowed into Victory (or: overcoming)!" [Isa. 25:8]

And then,

57. **But grace and joyous favor [is] in God** (or: by God) **– the One presently and progressively giving the Victory** (or: the overcoming) **to us, in us and for us through our Lord** (Owner; Master), **Jesus, [the] Christ!**

So we now have and possess the Victory – God has given it to us – and it is the Victory that drank down and swallowed the Death (vs. 54b). Jesus drank the cup that the Father had given to him (Jn. 18:11; Mat. 20:22). This is the final way (Mat. 20:23a) of being conformed to His death (Phil. 3:10), which ended in victory (the "out-resurrection" of vs. 11, above). Now this was a corporate event that coincided with His resurrection – and this was all the result of "**the inward operation** (energy; in-working) **of the [conditions or situation for] Him to continuously be able** (or: have power) **also to humbly align** (or: to subject; to subordinate; to arrange under so as to have full control of and support) **The Whole** (or: all things; everything) **in Himself** (to Himself; for Himself; by and with Himself)."

He is able to align the whole of humanity – as well as the whole universe – "in Himself, to Himself, for Himself, by Himself, and with Himself!" He refashions the whole body of humanity, as well as the universe (the new creation in Christ), to be birthed conformed to the body of His glory.

2. It follows that also, in union with (or: centered in) **this, we are continuously groaning, utterly longing and constantly yearning to fully enter within and to completely clothe upon ourselves our dwelling-house** (habitation) **– the one [made] out of heaven** (or: the one from, or of, atmosphere; the [inhabited or settled place] from the midst of [the] sky) **–** [Heb. 10:34]
3. since, in fact, also being folks at some point entering within and clothing ourselves we shall not continue (or: proceed) **being found naked.**

Ps. 84:1-4 spoke of this "**dwelling-house** (habitation)."
> "How endearing [is] Your tabernacle, O Yahweh of hosts.… Even the sparrow finds a home, and the swallow a nest for herself... [So also] Your altars, O Yahweh of hosts, My King and my Elohim. Happy [are those] dwelling in Your house…" (CVOT).

It spoke of Yahweh's temple, His House, as Israel's dwelling place.

The traditional reading of this verse, together with the next verse, has understood Paul to be speaking of the physical body. However, considering what we have just shared on vs. 1, is there also a more probable corporate reading, as well as the metaphor of "**clothe upon ourselves**" being a figure of something different?

Paul also speaks about "**continuously groaning**" in Rom. 8:23,
> "**Yet not only [this], but further, even we ourselves – constantly holding** (or: having; possessing) **the firstfruit of, and which is, the Spirit** (or: the Firstfruit whose source is the Breath-effect; or: the first offering, or first portion, which is spirit and breath, and is from the Attitude) **– we ourselves also continually sigh and groan within** (in the center of) **ourselves, continuously accepting and with our hands taking away from out of a placing in the condition of a son** (or: [the] deposit of the Son; a setting in place which is the Son; a constituting as a son; a placing in the Son)**: the process of the release of our body from slavery**
>> (or: [and] the loosing from destruction pertaining to the [corporate, old covenant] body, which is us; or: = the unbinding and release of the body [of Adam; of humanity], which belongs to us)."

Here we again see Paul affirming that we are "**constantly holding** (or: having; possessing)" something: "**the firstfruit of, and which is, the Spirit**." While now having this, "**we ourselves also continually sigh and groan within ourselves**." So we have two things: **a dwelling structure or place** (or: a household), in vs. 1, above, and "**the Spirit**" – or, are these two things actually the same thing? Was the "place" to which Jesus referred in Jn. 14:3a, above, the "**placing in the condition of a son**" or "a placing in the Son" of our Romans text, as well as the "dwelling place" to which Paul refers in our present Corinthian text?

Paul used the metaphor of "clothing" elsewhere. In Rom. 13:12b, 14 we read:
> "**CLOTHE ourselves with the instruments** (tools; weapons; implements; [some MSS: works; deeds]) **of Light** (or: The Light).… **you folks must CLOTHE yourselves with** (or: enter within and put on) **the Lord, Jesus Christ, and stop** (or: do not continue) **making forethought** (constructing provision; planning ahead; performing provident care) **into excessive desires of the flesh** (= old covenant system and cultus)."

Then in Gal. 3:27 he put it this way:
> "**For you see, as many of you folks as were immersed into Christ, at once CLOTHED yourselves with Christ** (or: were plunged into so as to be enveloped by then saturated and permeated with Anointing – or, the Anointed One – instantly entered within and put on [the/an] Anointing)!"

Now in Eph. 4:23-24 he expresses it differently:
> "**be continuously renewed** (or: from time to time, or, progressively made young again) **by** (or: in; with) **the spirit** (or: attitude; breath-effect) **of your mind** (or: from the mind which is you folks; or: by the Spirit which is your [collective] mind), **and to enter within** (or: CLOTHE YOURSELVES

with) **the new humanity** (or: **the Person** that is different and innovative in kind and quality; *cf* 1 Cor. 15:44-57) – **the one in accord with and corresponding to God** (or: the person at the Divine level) – **being formed** (framed, built, founded and settled from a state of disorder and wildness; created) **within the Way pointed out** (or: in union with fair and equitable dealings with rightwised relationships, justice, righteousness and covenant participation; centered in [His] eschatological deliverance) **and reverent dedication** (or: benign relationship with nature) **pertaining to the Truth** (or: in intrinsic alignment with reality, which is the Truth)." *Cf* Col. 3:10.

We find this same word "put on/clothe" used in a different metaphor in Eph. 6:11, 14,

"**you folks must at some point, for yourselves, enter within** (or: CLOTHE yourselves with) **the full suit of armor and implements of war** (panoply; the complete equipment for men-at-arms) **which is God** (or: which comes from and belongs to God), **in order for you to be continuously able and powerful to stand**.... **then, after girding yourselves around your waist** (or: loins) **in union with Truth and within the midst of Reality, and then, entering within** (putting on; CLOTHING yourself with) **the breastplate armor** (cuirass; corslet) **of fair and equitable dealing of the eschatological deliverance**..." *Cf* 1 Thes. 5:8.

Notice the kind of "clothing" that we observe in Col. 3:12,

"**Therefore, as God's chosen, set-apart and beloved ones** (or: God's sacred, loved and chosen people; or: as elect... ones from God), **CLOTHE yourselves with** (or: enter within) **bowels** (internal organs; = the tender parts; seat of deep feelings) **of compassion, kindness** (adaptable usefulness), **humility** (the minding and disposition of things of lowness or of low station), **gentleness** (meekness; mildness), **waiting long before rushing with emotions** (even-temperedness; long-suffering; putting up with people/situations; pushing anger far away)."

We suggest that all of this variety of "clothing" is speaking of the same thing: Christ, our dwelling-place from God, our House from heaven. *Cf* Rev. 1:13; 4:4; 7:9; 15:6; 19:14 for clothing as a symbol. In His promises to the overcomers within the called-out communities in Rev. 3, we observe "white garments" being used symbolically in 3:4-5, and then in 3:18 we read:

"**I continue advising you** [singular] **to buy from Me gold having been refined** (set ablaze) **forth from out of fire, to the end that you may become rich; and white garments, to the end that you may CLOTHE yourself and the shame** (disgrace) **of your nakedness may not be manifested** (brought to light; caused to appear); **and eye-salve to anoint** (rub in) **your eyes, to the end that you may be continuously observing** (or: progressively seeing)."

In Rev. 3:17, the risen Christ told the community in Laodicea that they were "naked." He was not saying that they did not have bodies; He was saying that they had not been living in His robe, as the Lamb's bride, corporate covenant community, is described in Rev. 19:8,

"**Then it was** (or: is) **granted** (or: given) **to her to the end that she may CLOTHE herself with bright and clean fine cotton** (or: she may cast bright, pure, fine linen around her) **– for the fine cotton** (or: linen) **represents the effects of right relationship and equity in the life of the Way pointed out**

(or: the results of being rightwised; the actualizations of justice; consequences of justice rendered from being turned in the right direction; the effects of having been eschatologically delivered and placed in the Path pointed out; or: the just acts or awards)

of the set-apart folks."

We might say that being "**naked**" is being "**posterior to, falling short of, inferior to and wanting of, God's glory**," which is Christ.

Instead of being "found naked" referring to being nude, or "without a body," is Paul then possibly alluding to his previous letter where in 1 Cor. 15:37 he spoke of "**a naked seed**"? In that analogy, he was speaking about a seed that was planted in the earth, as compared to the plant (i.e., its "clothing") that would grow up into the atmosphere. His analogy was speaking about **resurrection** in that context. We recall Jesus drawing on a farming analogy in Jn. 12:24,

> "**unless the grain of wheat** (or: kernel of corn; = seed of an agricultural crop), **upon falling into the earth** (the ground; the field), **should die, it by itself continues remaining alone. Yet if it should die, it proceeds to bear much fruit.**"

There, Jesus was speaking in the context of His upcoming death. Is Paul saying something similar here, in reference to not being found to have lived a cruciform life?

4. For we also, being (continually existing) **within the tent, are continuously groaning, being the ones constantly weighed down** (burdened). **Upon which [situation] we are not wanting to go out from** (to unclothe, strip or undress ourselves) **but rather to fully enter within and to add CLOTHING upon ourselves, to the end that the mortal** (or: this mortal thing) **may be drunk down and swallowed under** (or: by) **The Life.** [cf Isa. 25:6-9; Rom. 13:14]

Paul spoke of the corporate "**groaning**" in Rom. 8:22-23,

> "**You see, we have seen, and thus know and are aware, that all the creation** [note: = Old Covenant Israel] **keeps on sighing, groaning or querulously moaning together, and yet progressively travailing together as in childbirth** (continues suffering common birthing pains) **until now** (to the point of the present moment). **Yet not only [this], but further, even we ourselves – constantly holding** (or: having; possessing) **the firstfruit of, and which is, the Spirit** (or: the Firstfruit whose source is the Breath-effect) **– we ourselves also continually sigh and groan within ourselves, continuously accepting and with our hands taking away from out of a placing in the condition of a son** (or: [the] deposit of the Son; a setting in place which is the Son; a constituting as a son; a placing in the Son): **the process of the release of our body from slavery** (or: [and] the loosing from destruction pertaining to the [corporate, old covenant] body, which is us; or: = the unbinding and release of the body [of Adam; of humanity], which belongs to us)."

Kaplan has pointed out that "groaning" can also be done in a positive sense – from the experiences of what is good.

Following the reasoning laid out regarding vss. 1-3, might Paul have in mind his views of the two Adams, the two Humanities, of which he had spoken in 1 Cor. 15:42-50? There, in vs. 49 we read:

> "**And correspondingly as we bear and wear the image of the mounded, dusty person,** [p46 adds: doubtless] **we can and should** [B reads: will continue to] **also bear and wear the image of the Added, Imposed, Heavenly One** (or: belonging to the One having the quality and character of the finished, perfected atmosphere; or: from the fully-heaven [sphere]; of the added-sky person)."

Now we should note that here he is speaking of "**bearing and wearing the IMAGE of the Added, Imposed, Heavenly One**." This is not speaking of having a different kind of body, but is saying the same thing as 3:18, above, "**being continuously and progressively transformed into the very same IMAGE**." Remember that Paul spoke of being, "**progressively transformed** (transfigured; changed in form and semblance) **by the renewing** (or: in the renewal; for the making-back-up-new again) **of your mind**" (Rom. 12:2). And thus, we have Paul explaining this in 1 Cor. 15:48,

> "**As [is] the person made of and having the character and quality of moist soil or dust** (mounded or poured dirt), **of such sort also [are] the people [who are] made of and have the character and quality of moist soil or dust** (soil-ish folks); **and likewise, as [is] the Added, Imposed, Heavenly Person** (or: the one made of and having the quality and character of the added-heaven), **of such sort also [are] the added, imposed, heavenly people – those made of and having the quality and character of the added, imposed, heaven** (or: the finished and perfected atmosphere, or the added sky)."

This "**Added,** Imposed Heavenly **Person**" is what Paul is speaking of when here he refers, in vs. 4 above, "**to fully enter within and to add clothing upon ourselves, to the end that the mortal** (or: this mortal thing) **may be drunk down and swallowed under** (or: by) **The Life**." It is putting on Christ. It is not physically having another body put upon us. Paul is using apocalyptic imagery here. Look anew at what Jesus said in Jn. 10:11 about what would be put on us (i.e., added to us):

"**The Ideal** (Fine; Beautiful) **Shepherd continually places His soul over the sheep**."

When we dwell in the Vine (Jn. 15:1ff) we are enveloped by His soul – we are immersed into His Spirit. He becomes our "white garment," our building/temple that is made of His atmosphere/Spirit. The Anointing comes upon us, and His Spirit fills us.

Returning again to 1 Cor. 15, we see in vs. 53 that,

"**it continues being necessary** (it is habitually binding) **for this perishable and corruptible to at some point plunge** (or: sink) **in and clothe itself with** (or: slip on; put on) **incorruption and imperishability, and for this mortal** (one that is subject to death) **to at some point plunge and sink in and CLOTHE itself with** (or: put on; slip on as a garment) **IMMORTALITY** (or: the absence of death; deathlessness; undyingness)."

Now consider the instruction presented in 1 Tim. 6:14b-16a:

"**until the shining-upon from** (or: the display in clear light of) **our Lord, Jesus Christ, which, in its own fitting situations** (appropriate seasons; appointed occasions; fertile moments), **will proceed to exhibit and point out The Happy and Only Able One** (only Powerful One; alone Potent One)**: The King of those reigning as kings, and Lord of those ruling as lords, the Only One continuously holding and having possession of IMMORTALITY** (the absence or privation of death; deathlessness), **the One continuously making inaccessible** (or: unapproachable) **light His home** (or: dwelling)…"

Putting the insight of 1 Cor. 15:53 together with 1 Tim. 6:16, we see that our being clothed with immortality is simply being clothed with Jesus Christ. THAT is what gives us the Victory: "**The Death was drunk down and swallowed into Victory** (or: overcoming)!" (1 Cor. 15:54), and now this very **Victory** has been given to us (1 Cor. 15:57) through Jesus Christ. This is what is meant in 5:4b, above, "**the mortal** (or: this mortal thing) **may be drunk down and swallowed under** (or: by) **The Life**." It is The Life that is The Victory. Paul spoke of this same thing in Rom. 8:11,

"**Now since the Breath-effect** (or: Spirit; Attitude) **of the One arousing and raising Jesus forth from out of the midst of dead folks is continuously housing Itself** (making His abode; residing; making His home; by idiom: living together as husband and wife) **within, and in union with, you folks, the One raising Christ Jesus forth from out of dead ones will also continue progressively giving Life to** (or: will even habitually make alive) **the mortal bodies of you folks** (or: your mortal bodies) **through the constant indwelling of His Spirit** (or: the continual in-housing of His Breath-effect; the continuous internal residing of the Attitude, which is Him,) [other MSS: because of His habitually-indwelling Spirit] **within and among you folks**."

His Spirit, which is God Himself, is the Life and Immortality that has already been given to us. In Jn. 10:10b Jesus said,

"**I, Myself, come so that they** [i.e., His sheep] **can progressively possess** (would continuously have; could habitually hold) **Life, and may continue possessing [it] in superabundance** (or: and may have a surplus surrounding them in excessive amounts)."

The Life of Christ, within us individually and corporately, swallowed down The Death that spread through the first Adam (Rom. 5:12) and drinks down "**the mortal**" – the temporary of which Paul spoke in 4:18, above, and which is figured by "**being** (continually existing) **within the tent**" here in 5:4a. That tent first refers to the Tabernacle of the old covenant, as we discussed in vs. 1, above, and can be discerned from this metaphor. But the metaphor can also apply to us as individual members of His permanent Temple, as we live in the atmosphere of His presence, and yet in time lay aside our individual, physical tents. Paul was living and writing this letter when the physical temple in Jerusalem was still standing. They were still suffering under Second Temple Judaism (the tent), and were "**continuously groaning, being the ones constantly weighed down** (burdened)" by persecution from that temporary "tent" of the Jewish leadership. But in reality, that was like the tent of the old creation: it was soon to pass away. Paul understood that,

> **"the effects of the sensible experiences – sufferings, impressions, passions or feelings – of the current season [were] not equivalent [being] face to face with the glory…. of the creation constantly receiving and taking away from out of the unveiling of God's sons**
>> (or: = the uncovering and revealing of folks who have the character and qualities of God; or: the disclosure pertaining to the sons of God; or: the unveiling and revelation which belongs to God's sons; or, as an ablative: **the disclosure from God's sons**)" (Rom. 8:18-19).

5. Now the One working this down, commensurately producing and correspondingly fashioning US into this very thing (situation and condition) **[is] God, the One giving to us the pledge and guarantee** (earnest deposit; security; first installment) **which is the Breath-effect** (or: of the Spirit; from the Attitude). [*cf* 1:22; 4:10ff, Ex. 15:16b]

Paul may be offering an allusion to Isa. 29:23a, "For when [Jacob/Israel] sees his children, the work of MY hands…" Here he makes it very clear that this is not a "self-works," or a "self-improvement" program. The One doing the working is God, and His work is on, and within, US. But to what work is Paul referring? The closest antecedent is the aorist passive verb of vs. 4: "**may be drunk down and swallowed under.**" God, in Christ (vs. 19, below), does the drinking (the Cup that the Father gave to Jesus to drink) and the swallowing of the Death: "**the mortal thing.**" Again, keep in mind that it is drunk down and swallowed, "**under** (or: **by**) **The Life.**" You see, the Life is now within US, and that LIFE (Christ) swallows the mortal under Itself, or, by the Spirit. The aorist tense is used in these verbs, accommodating their application to any existential time within the existence of a group or of an individual, on through the ages.

Accordingly, the participle of the first clause of this verse is also in the aorist tense. And the "**working this down, commensurately producing and correspondingly fashioning**" of this new creation (vs. 17, below) is the producing of the Body of Christ, and of us as members of this Body. Paul used the same verb in 4:17, above, where "**the momentary light [aspect or character]** (or: lightness) **of the pressure and squeezing** (the affliction, oppression and tribulation) **is progressively working down in US a corresponding** (commensurate) **and consecutively transcending eonian weight of glory.**" God is producing **US.** This can be seen as an allusion to Ex. 15:17 where it speak of Israel being planted in the Lord's prepared dwelling place, which He "adjusted-down and fully prepared" (LXX).

Denton (ibid) astutely points us to Phil. 3:20-4:1,

> "**You see, our citizenship** (result of living in a free city; or: commonwealth-effects; political realm) **continues inherently existing resident within the midst of [the] atmospheres** (or: heavens), **from out of where we also continuously receive and take away in our hands from out of a Deliverer** (a Savior)**: [the] Lord, Jesus Christ, Who will continue transfiguring our body from the low condition and status** (or: **the body which is us**, pertaining to this lowliness) **[to be] joint-formed in, and conformed by, to and with, the body of His glory** (or: from, and which is, His assumed appearance; *cf* 2 Cor. 3:18), **down from** (or: in accord with; in the sphere of; to the level of; following the pattern of; in stepping with; commensurate with; as directed by) **the inwardly-centered operation** (functioning energy; inner-working) **of the [conditions, situation or sphere for] Him to be continuously able** (or: to progress with power) **also to humbly align The Whole to and in Himself** (or: to subject and subordinate all things for Himself; to arrange everything under so as to have full control and to support [it] by and with Himself). **Consequently, my brothers – loved ones and longed-for folks, my joy and winner's wreath – thus** (in this way) **you constantly stand within [the] Lord: [as or being] loved ones!**"

This "heavenly Temple" has been the topic of Paul's discussion, ever since 4:18, above. And what is the focus of His **work**, i.e., His **drinking down and swallowing fo**r, and in, US (4b, above)? The next phrase gives us the answer: "**into this very thing** (situation and condition)." So what is the antecedent of this phrase? Well, the phrase is neuter, and thus it corresponds to the previous neuter "thing" which we find in vs. 4: "**the mortal** (or: this mortal thing)," Now that which is **mortal** is temporary (4:18, above), and it is expressed in all the death and dying that we SEE, or observe, in this transient life. But here, the thing that was mortal and dying was also the old covenant and the old age that was passing away in Paul's day. We do not fix our gaze or focus upon these temporary things, but rather upon "**those things [not] habitually seen or observed, [which] pertain to and have their source in the Age** ([are] eonian; [continue] age-lasting)." That refers to,

> "**a dwelling structure or place** (a building for an abode; or: **a household**; = a family or a possession) **forth from out of the midst of God: an eonian act of building a roofed house** (or: a covered building for dwelling having qualities and character which pertain to the Age [of the Messiah]; a structure of edification for, and pertaining to, the ages)" (vs. 1, above).

This building (temple) of the new arrangement (covenant) is the household of God. Now this **work**, this swallowing down **by the Life** (vs. 4b), has something that **the Life** produces. Tony Denton appropriately observes that it is "the clothing of 5:2-4, the heavenly habitation/house of 5:2, the building from God in 5:1, and that which was of great weight of glory in 4:17" (ibid p 137).

The last half of this verse informs us that God is "**the One giving to us the pledge and guarantee** (earnest deposit; security; first installment)." This is a metaphor from the world of buying and selling, often used for buying property, or a house. Notice that this down-payment is given to US. God is buying US. Does not this call to mind Paul saying,

> "**for you people were bought, as at a marketplace: [there was] value and honor involved in the price** (or: [you are] of value)
>> (or: = you see, you folks were bought and paid for; or: it follows that from a valuable price you folks were bought at market)" (1 Cor. 6:20).

And what was His security deposit to, among, and within, US? "**The Breath-effect** (or: the Spirit)." This clause of His giving the first installment implies that the remainder of the price is yet to come. We have an expectation for more, from the Spirit. He spoke of expectation in Rom. 8:24-25,

> "**For in the expectation and with hope we are suddenly made whole and healthy…. Yet since** (or: even if) **we continue expecting what we are not seeing** (or: observing), **we continue taking away and accepting from out of it through remaining under [our present situation and circumstances]** (or: through patient, humble, persistent, supportive endurance)."

This expectation is for the rest of the purchase price to be paid to us (on monthly installments? Ha!). He bought us (to be His property, His Land – which was an OT figure of Israel); and He bought us out of slavery – as when Israel was in slavery to Egypt (where Ex. 15:16b informs us that Yahweh purchased Israel). He released us, and then paid us the purchase price.

We saw this term "pledge; guarantee; advance transaction; earnest deposit, (etc.)" in chapter 1, above:

> 21. **Now God [is] the One repeatedly… anointing us, together with you folks, into Christ,**
> 22. **He [is] also the One completely sealing us… completely giving the advance transaction of the agreement** (or: the pledge and down payment guaranteeing full payment for purchase; or: a dowry) **of the Spirit** (or: which is the Spirit; or: from the Breath-effect; or: which belongs and pertains to the spirit; which pertains to the Attitude) **within the midst of our hearts.**

Once again, the "down payment" is given to US! And remember: "**we all… are presently being continuously and progressively transformed into the very same image, from glory unto glory – in accord with and exactly as – from [the] Lord's Spirit**" (3:18, above). This same "advance transaction" is also referenced in Eph. 1:13b-14a,

> "**you people are stamped** (or: were sealed; marked for acceptance, or with a signet ring; = personally authorized) **by the set-apart Breath-effect of The Promise** (or: with the holy attitude of assurance; in the sacred essence from the promise; or: for the Holy Spirit which is the

Promise) – **Which is continuously a pledge and guarantee of our inheritance** (or: Who remains being an earnest deposit, a security and the first installment of our portion which was acquired by lot) – **[leading] unto a release into freedom** (liberation from slavery or imprisonment) **from that which was made to surround [us/you]** (or: of the encircling acquisition; or: which is that which has been constructed as a perimeter around [us])…"

6. Being, then, at all times and always courageous and of cheerful confidence, and having seen, perceived, and thus knowing, that continuously staying at home (dwelling within the district of our own People), **in union with, and centered in, that body, we are continuing being exiles, away from the Lord's home** (we are out of the Lord's district) [Heb. 11:14; 12:22-24; Gal. 4:26]
7. – for we are habitually walking about (= living our lives) **through faithfulness and trust** (or: faith; [His] loyalty) **not through perception of the appearance of external form –** [cf 4:18, above]

Paul now moves to a new aspect of the topic which he has been discussing. He opens vs. 6 with a dependent clause that is composed of three participles (Being courageous… having seen and knowing… staying at home). These lead into a prepositional phrase that I have rendered, "**in union with, and centered in, that body**." Previously I had rendered this phrase in the traditional manner, "within the body." Why did I make this change? The answer is: context. The rendering of *en* as "in union with" emphasizes the preposition's nuance of relationship (like being "in union with Christ"). The rendering "centered in" suggests and corresponds to his home, the district of his People (the Jews). After considering our understanding of Paul's topic from 4:18 through vs. 5, above, the idea that Paul was now suddenly speaking of his physical body did not align with either the immediate context or the greater context to which he will return, in vs. 10, below. The central theme has been the corporate: the Tabernacle of the old covenant, and then the new Temple (House/dwelling place/household) of the new arrangement.

Also, it seems appropriate to render the definite article as its original use, as a demonstrative, "**that**" in pointing to the term "**body**" in vss. 6, and in 8, below. Furthermore, the participle "**staying at home**" has the central meaning of "dwelling within the district of our own People." We do not think that Paul was suddenly speaking about being "disembodied" into a spirit realm in order to be "**staying at home** (to be dwelling in the district of our new home and people) **[with orientation] toward, and face to face with, the Lord**" (vs. 8, below). This is contrary to his obvious teachings, elsewhere, of the Lord being within and among us. It would also contradict Rev. 21:3, that "**God's tent** (the Tabernacle of God) **[is] with mankind** (the humans)." Denton (ibid p 148) points us to Rom. 7:24b,

> "**What will be progressively rescuing me from out of the body of this death** (or: from out of this body of the death; out of this body which pertains to death and which has its origin, character and qualities in death)**?**"

He then bids us consider this in light of Rom. 8:2, 6, 7,

> "**For the principle and law of, from and which is the spirit and attitude of 'The Life within Christ Jesus' frees you away from the Law of the Sin and of the Death…. For the result of the thinking** (mind-set; effect of the way of thinking; disposition; result of understanding and inclination; the minding; the opinion; the thought; the outlook) **of the flesh** (= from the human condition or the System of culture and cultus; or: = Torah keeping) **[is; brings] death, yet the result of the thinking** (mind-set; disposition; thought and way of thinking; outlook) **of the spirit** (or: from the Spirit; which is the Breath-effect) **[is; brings] Life and Peace** (joining). **Because of that, the result of the thinking** (disposition; thought processes; mind-set, outlook) **of the flesh** (= attention to Torah boundary-markers, custom and cultus; or: = from the human condition) **[is; brings] enmity, alienation and discord [streaming] into God** (or: hostility unto, or active hatred with a view to, God), **for it continues not being humbly aligned and supportive** (habitually placed under and submitted; or, as a middle: subjecting, humbly arranging or marshaling itself) **to the principle and law which is God** (or: in God's principle; by the Law from God), **for neither is it able nor does it have power**."

The death that Paul is speaking of in this Romans passage is metaphorical (or: figurative; symbolic) in that Rom. 8:6 defines it as being "**the result of the thinking** (mind-set; effect of the way of thinking; disposition; result of understanding and inclination; the minding; the opinion; the thought; the outlook) **of the flesh** (= from the human condition or the System of culture and cultus; or: = Torah keeping)." The system of the old covenant brought death (Rom. 7:9-10). The law of "**the spirit and attitude of 'The Life within Christ Jesus' frees [those in the new covenant] away from the Law of the Sin and of the Death**" that was the "body" of the old covenant (the Law of Moses).

Now observe in Rom. 8:7, above, that "**the result of the thinking** (disposition; thought processes; mind-set, outlook) **of the flesh** (= attention to Torah boundary-markers, custom and cultus; or: = from the human condition) **[is; brings] enmity, alienation and discord [streaming] into God** (or: hostility unto, or active hatred with a view to, God)," Staying within "**that body**" of Laws, culture and mindset would keep folks "**away from the Lord's [new] home**," the Temple: i.e., the called-out communities that live in Christ's Law of the Spirit of Life, the culture of love and acceptance of others, and the mindset of Christ.

Because of the Roman occupation of Judea, scholars have concluded that the Jews of the 1st century AD considered themselves still to be in exile, as they last were in Babylon/Persia, Greece and then under the Seleucids. They were looking for a messiah to be a new Moses, to lead them out from under the dominion of the Roman Empire. We suggest here that Paul is continuing to identify himself with, "**[his] brothers, [his] relatives** (kinsmen; joint or commonly born ones; fellow countrymen) **according to flesh** (= in the sphere of natural human birth), **the very ones who are Israelites**" (Rom. 9:3b-4a). Therefore, by remaining "**in union with, and centered in, that body**" (Second Temple Judaism) he and his Jewish companions were "**continuing being exiles, away from the Lord's home**." Where was "the Lord's home"? It was within the called-out communities – they were now "the Lord's district," i.e., His Temple. The Jerusalem that was located in Judea (the physical city) was still "**in slavery** (i.e., exile) **with her children**" (Gal. 4:25). But Paul and his communities were no longer there. They were, "**habitually walking about** (= living our lives) **through faithfulness and trust** (or: faith; [His] loyalty) **NOT through perception of the appearance of external form**" (i.e., not by the temple cultus and with old covenant identity markers – purity codes; dietary codes; animal sacrifices; circumcision; etc.). Here we need to review Gal. 3:

> 23. **So before the [time, or, event for] the Faithful One to come** (or: prior to the coming of this faith, trust, assurance, conviction and loyalty), **we were being continuously restrained, confined and held in custody under the watch of a guard, being folks constantly encircled, enclosed, shut up and locked together by and under Law, [with a view to, aimed and moving] into the Faithfulness** (or: the Act of Trust) **being about to be unveiled** (or: revealed; disclosed),
> 24. **so that, consequently, the Law** (= Torah) **had come to be** (had been birthed into existence) **and continued being our supervising guardian and attending, custodial escort unto, with a view to, and [pointing] into Christ, to the end that we could** (or: would) **be delivered by the just act and then rightwised to be in the new covenant of right relationships with justice and fairness that characterize the liberty in the Way pointed out, from out of Faithfulness** (or: an act of loyalty, trust and faith).
> 25. **So now with the coming of the Faithful One, we no longer continuously exist** (or: are) **under [the] supervising guardian or an attending escort** [comment: = the Law; Torah]!
> 26. **For you folks are all** [i.e., Jew and non-Jew; male and female; slave and freeman] **God's sons, through the faithfulness located and resident within Christ Jesus** (or: by means of the trust in union with an Anointing from Jesus; [p46: through Jesus Christ's faithfulness])!
> (or: You see, all you folks [who are] located and centered in Christ Jesus exist being sons of God, by means of that Faithful One!)
> 27. **For you see** (or: It follows that) **as many of you folks as were immersed into Christ, at once clothed yourselves with Christ** (or: were plunged into so as to be enveloped by then

saturated and permeated with Anointing – or, the Anointed One – instantly entered within and put on [the/an] Anointing)!

That last verse echoes 5:2, above, by referring to immersion into Christ, and then he says that they "CLOTHED [themselves] with Christ." I just could not help repeating that! Good rhetorical redundancy!

The last phrase of vs. 7, "**through perception of the appearance of external form**" is often rendered simply, "by sight," which is often understood to mean the "faculty of sight." However, the main thought of this noun is "what is visible to the eye," i.e., the object that is seen, or perception of that object. Paul may have been referencing what he was speaking of in 4:18b, above (although there, a different word is used). And what comes to mind is Paul's reference to being "**led by the Spirit**" (Rom. 8:14), which may be an allusion to Israel being led by the pillar of cloud (a manifestation of God's Spirit) during their wilderness journeys, but now we are not led by "**an external form**," so this would be in CONTRAST to the old covenant. Examples may be Jesus saying, "**I am habitually speaking things which I, Myself, have seen, [being] at the side of** (or: present with) **the** [other MSS: My] **Father**" (Jn. 8:38) – which was NOT the perception of an appearance of external form. Or, "**And I have seen and know... His implanted goal** (purposed impartation of the finished product within; inward directive of destiny)" (Jn. 12:50) – which is a spiritual perception. Paul's idea, here, may be parallel to what was said of Moses, "**he was strong and stout as continually seeing the invisible** (or: the Unseen One)" (Heb. 11:27b). Moses fled Egypt "**by, and in, faith**" (Heb. 11:27a). The whole of Heb. 11 speaks of living in and by trust and faith.

Now some will ask: What about 1 Thes. 4:17? Let us examine this text:

> "**Thereupon** (or: After that; As a next step) **we, the presently living folks, the ones presently continuing to be left around, will – at the same time, together with them – proceed being seized and snatched away* within clouds**** (or: carried off by force, in union with clouds,) **into the midst of [the] air** (the air that we breathe in; the mist; the haze; the atmosphere around us; [note: this would be in the earth's lower atmosphere, the place where there is air]) **– into the Lord's meeting** ([Christ's or Yahweh's] encounter; an encountering which is the Lord). **And thus** (in this way and such a manner) **shall we always continue being** (or: continue existing at all times) **together with [the] Lord** [= Christ or Yahweh]." [* cf 2 Cor. 12:2; ** Heb. 12:1]

We suggest that this is one of Paul's apocalyptic texts, and thus should be interpreted symbolically, not literally. I will quote my commentary on this verse, as found in *Peter, Paul and Jacob*, under the section, *comments on First Thessalonians*:

> "Paul here is speaking of an event that those then living, 'we,' would experience: being '**seized and snatched away within clouds into the midst of [the] air**.' Much of Christianity believes this to be a future event, and some have considered Paul to have been misguided to have expected it to happen in the then near future. But others, among them those of the full preterist paradigm, believe that this happened when the Lord returned to Jerusalem in judgment, both through the agency of the Romans and in a literal 'snatching away' and resurrection during the period of AD 66-70.

> "It should be noted that Paul did not say that the Lord would take everyone off to heaven, but that they would be with Him 'in [the] air.' Thus would they be in our atmosphere – close enough to touch. That, of course, is putting a literal spin on the interpretation of his words. A figurative interpretation – since he spoke in apocalyptic terms of a shout, the blowing of a trumpet, and descending – would speak of the joining of the heavens and the earth in the realm of spirit, and thus catching folks up into the realm of spirit, similar to the descending of the New Jerusalem as symbolically pictured in Rev. 21:2, and its existence upon earth in ch. 22. This, of course, was a figurative description of the Lamb's wife (21:9), the bride of Christ, God's tabernacle (= His temple, His body) dwelling with humanity (21:3).

> "I should also point out that this same word '**seized and snatched away**' is used in Matt. 11:12 in the context of the reign of the heavens, where I render it as 'grasping it and drawing it up,'

> '**Now from the days of John the Immerser until right now, the reign of the heavens** (or: sovereign rule of the kingdom of the atmospheres) **is itself continuously pressing** (or: is progressively pressing and forcing itself) **forward with urgency, and those urging and pressing forward [toward the goal] are constantly grasping it and drawing it up [to themselves].**'"

The realm of "clouds" is the realm of our atmosphere, and our atmosphere (heaven) is a figure of the realm of spirit and mind. This is why both John the Immerse and Jesus proclaimed a "change of mind and thinking into a new state of consciousness" (*cf* Mat. 3:2; 4:17; 11:20, 21, *et al*) where our perceptions and perspectives are on the level of God's reign – i.e., "seated in the heavenlies" (Eph. 2:6, e.g.).

8. yet we are constantly courageous and of cheerful confidence, even continuously delighting and thinking it good to a greater extent (with exceeding preference) **to be away from home** (to be out of the district of our normal home and people), **forth from out of that body, and to be staying at home** (to be dwelling in the district of our new home and people) **[with orientation] toward, and face to face with, the Lord** [= Christ or Yahweh].

Now he opens this verse with the verb form of the participle that opened vs. 6, above, so he is bringing his audience back to their present condition of being "**constantly courageous and of cheerful confidence**." Then he adds to this that they are, "**even continuously delighting and thinking it good to a greater extent** (with exceeding preference) **to be away from home** (to be out of the district of our normal home and people)." Not only are they physically away from Judea (this letter was apparently written from Macedonia – *cf* 2:13 and 7:5), but more importantly, they were away from their "home" of Second Temple Judaism. They had come "**forth from out of that body**," and were now, "**staying at home** (to be dwelling in the district of our new home and people) **[with orientation] toward, and face to face with, the Lord**." Being "face to face with the Lord" is a reprise of 3:18, above. It is "staying at home" in the New Jerusalem, which is where they now are: they are in "the Jerusalem which is above" (Gal. 4:26) and had come to Mount Zion (Heb. 12:22-24). In this heavenly City, they "**constantly see His face, and His Name [is] upon their foreheads**" (Rev. 22:4). Also remember where God now dwells:

> "**God's tent** (the Tabernacle of God) **[is] WITH MANKIND** (the humans), '**and He will continue living in a tent** (dwell in a Tabernacle) **with them, and they will continue being** (will constantly exist being) **His peoples, and God Himself will continue being with them**'" (Rev. 21:3).

Neither Paul nor the Word of the Lord to John, in the proclamation just quoted, mean being out of our physical bodies or being off-world in another physical location. The new creation (5:17, below) refers to "being in Christ." It means belonging to a different "corporate" body. We are instructed concerning our new home, in Eph.. 2:

> 11. **On which account, you folks must continuously call to mind that once you, the nations** (multitudes; ethnic groups; Gentiles; non-Israelites) **in flesh** (= in your physical beings and cultural heritages) **– the ones habitually termed "uncircumcision" by the one habitually being termed "circumcision," in flesh** (= body, culture and religion), **[i.e.], made by hand –**
> 12. **that** (or: because) **you were, and continued on being for that season apart from Christ: people having been alienated from the state of being a citizen** (or: estranged from citizenship in the commonwealth and society) **of, and which is, Israel and [being] strangers pertaining to the arrangements of** (or: foreigners from covenants and testamentary dispositions whose origin is) **The Promise and the assurance, continually having no expectation, and [were] folks without God within the ordered System** (centered in the world of culture, religion and governments; or: in union with the aggregate of humanity).
> 13. **But now, within, in union with and centered in Christ Jesus, you – the folks once being far off** (or: at a distance) **– came to be** (are suddenly become) **near, immersed within and in union with the blood of the Christ**....
> 19. **Consequently then, you folks no longer continuously exist being strangers** (foreigners) **and sojourners** (folks being or living beside a house; temporary residents in a foreign land), **but in contrast, you continually exist being fellow-citizens of those set apart to be sacred**

people (or: folks residing together in a City belonging to, and composed of, the holy ones)**: even God's family** (members of God's household),

20. **being fully built as a house upon the foundation from the sent-forth representatives** (or: emissaries) **and prophets** (folks who had light ahead of time), **Jesus Christ continuously being a corner-foundation [stone] of it,**

21. **within, and in union with, Whom all the home-building** (all the construction of the house; or: the entire building), **being continuously fitted [and] progressively framed together, is continuously and progressively growing into a set-apart temple within [the] Lord:**

22. **within the midst of Whom you folks, also, are continuously and progressively being formed a constituent part of the structure** (or: being built together into a house) **– into God's down-home place (place of settling down to dwell; abode; permanent dwelling) within [the] Spirit.**

We are "out of the district of our normal home and people," and are "**staying at home, face to face with the Lord,**" with our faces unveiled (3:18, above). We are now in the place where we can see Him in the homeless, the naked, the hungry, the thirsty, the imprisoned, the sick (Mat. 25:35-36). You see, we presently have and possess and are a part of the "**dwelling structure or place** (a building for an abode; or: **a household**; = a family or a possession) **forth from out of the midst of God: an eonian act of building a roofed house** (or: a covered building for dwelling) **– not made by hands – resident within the atmospheres**" (5:1, above).

We live our individual lives as well as our corporate lives. As with many of Paul's sayings, this verse can be interpreted in both levels of existence. Although his main focus has been on the corporate level, it may be that he also had in mind the end of his course, as seems most apparent in Phil. 1:23-24,

"**So I am being continuously held together** (or: caught; squeezed) **from out of the two: constantly having the craving** (holding the strong desire and impulse) **into the [situation] to untie and loose back up again** [as in loosing tent pins and ropes when striking camp, or loosing moorings to set sail], **and to be** (to exist being) **together with Christ – for [that is] rather to a much higher rank** (a more advantageous situation; a more profitable thing; [it is] much better)! **Yet the [situation] to be staying** (remaining-on) **in the flesh [is] more necessary** (indispensable; a more forced constraint) **because of you folks**."

Love, and being a paraclete for the sheep, always ruled in his heart. Christ is here in this life, and also in the next life. We view our graduation (our exodus from this life) as being to "a much higher rank," but we value what our Father selects as being "more necessary" for His plans.

9. Therefore we are constantly loving the value (or: ambitious for the honor), **also – whether staying at home** (dwelling within our district) **or being away from home and people** (out of our district) **– to constantly be folks [who are] well-pleasing to Him** (who give satisfaction for Him),

The verb in the first clause is also found in Rom. 15:20, and 1 Thes. 4:11. It is from the joining of *philos* (affection, fondness, "brotherly" love and friendship) and *timē* (value; honor; worth; price). The lexicons give the basic meaning as being "ambitious for honor." So Paul could be saying that he is ambitious for the honor **to constantly be well-pleasing to** GOD. The following verse would instruct us about his reasons, if this is what he meant by this verb.

However, Paul may have been thinking of the value of the **pledge and guarantee** (earnest deposit; security; first installment) that was given to us (vs. 5b, above), and **the value** of the purchase of us, of which he spoke in 1 Cor. 6:20, cited above. It seems most likely to us that he was loving the value of "**being away from home and people** (out of our district) **– [so as] to constantly be folks [who are] well-pleasing to Him**." But whichever the case – staying within their district, or being away from their district – they could constantly be people who gave satisfaction to God. It seems that, following his conversion, he spent most of his life away from his home, and away from his People. As he had said in 1 Cor. 9:20ff,

"**So I come to be** (or: became) **as a Jew for** (or: to; with; among) **the Jews**.... **as without law**... **to those without law**.... **to the end that I can** (would; may) **by every means** (in every way; under all circumstances; entirely; everywhere) **save** (rescue; deliver; restore to health) **anybody!**"

10. for it continues (or: is repeatedly) **necessary for us – the all-people** (the whole of humanity) **– to be manifested in front of Christ's elevated place** (a step, platform, stage, or place ascended by steps to speak in public assembly in the center of a city; or: = an official bench of a judge or public official), **to the end that each one may himself take into kindly keeping, for care and provision** (= be responsible for), **the things [done] through** (or: by means of; or: [during our passing] through the midst of) **the Body – [oriented] toward, and facing, what things he practices** (or: she accomplishes), **whether good or bad, whether serviceable or inefficient, whether fair or foul, whether capable or careless.**

> (or: for you see that it continues binding for us all to be set in light so as to be clearly seen in the presence of the judgment seat which is Christ, so that each should keep and provide for the things performed throughout [His] body, with a view to, and face to face with, what things [were practiced], whether virtuous or vile).

This verse is a continuation of vs. 9, and however we read that verse, there is a continued, or repeated, necessity (the present tense of the verb) "**for us**." Now Paul qualifies this accusative plural pronoun by the accusative plural adjective, *tous pantas*: **the all-people**. Another way to say this, since the term is masculine (referring to people) is: "the whole of humanity." And just what is this continued necessity? "**To be manifested in front of Christ's elevated place**." The parenthetical expansion shows that this could be "a step, a platform, a stage, or a place ascended by steps to speak in public assembly in the center of a city." It can also refer to the official bench of a judge or a public official. Since Christ is also the King, this might be an allusion to Mat. 25:31-32ff. It might also be an allusion to Rev. 7:9.

Before we continue, we should take note that Paul uses the same word "**manifested**" about himself and his companions in the next verse: "**So we HAVE BEEN, and thus remain, manifested** (set in the light so as to be clearly seen) **in God** (by God; for God; to God; with God)," so this is not speaking about some so-called end of time judgment, or even a judgment after this life. It is speaking about a repeated necessity – in this life. God does not wait until our life is over to make corrective decisions about people, or, to give them awards. Read the OT to observe this, and read Jesus' teachings and parables, as well. We have seen that Jesus' predictions of judgment upon Jerusalem and Second Temple Judaism happened in AD 70 – as set forth in Mat. 24 and Lu. 21.

Now the reason for this manifestation is "**to the end that each one may himself take into kindly keeping, for care and provision** (= be responsible for), **the things [done] through** (or: by means of; or: [during our passing] through the midst of) **the Body**." In keeping with our corporate reading of this text, I capitalized the term "Body," to suggest that Paul is speaking of the Body of Christ, the called-out communities. A larger reading might be to see this as referring to the Body of Adam – humanity at large, but most likely he has the covenant communities in mind with the term **the Body**, as we saw in 1 Cor. 3:9-17. But what does he mean by "take into kindly keeping for care and provision"? My suggested paraphrase for this is "be responsible for," but these results seem to place a personal effect upon the person, or the group. They must now care for something, or someone. They must now maintain provision for something or someone. This judgment sounds like now having to do something they had failed to do – perhaps such as "care for the sick" or "visit the imprisoned" of "provide clothing for the naked" or "feed the hungry." Yes, this rather reminds us of the kids (immature goats) of Mat. 25:41-46a.

The basis for Christ's decision is: "**[oriented] toward, and facing, what things he practices** (or: she accomplishes), **whether good or bad, whether serviceable or inefficient, whether fair or foul, whether capable or careless**." This sounds very much like reaping what one has sown. Yes, harvests happen throughout the year, and throughout our lives. This sounds a lot like 9:6, below, and like Gal. 6:7b-8,

> "'**whatever a person is in the habit of sowing, this also he will reap,' because the person continually sowing into the flesh of himself** (= his estranged inner being), **will progressively reap corruption** (spoil; ruin; decay) **forth from out of the flesh** (= the estranged inner being);
>> (or: the one habitually sowing into the flesh [system], of himself will continue to reap decay from out of the flesh [system];)
>
> **yet the one constantly sowing into the spirit** (or: the Breath) **will be progressively reaping eonian life** (life having the characteristics of the Age [of Messiah]; or: life from the Age that lasts on through the ages) **forth from out of the spirit** (or: the Spirit; the Breath; that attitude)."

Paul made a similar statement in Rom. 14:10, "**For you see, we will all continue** [take note of the durative aspect of the future tense: we stand before Him now: the OT is full of example of people living their lives before God, and of His making decisions regarding them] **standing in attendance alongside on God's elevated place**." Saul "stood" before Jesus on the road to Damascus and was judged (a decision was made by Christ that changed his life). Jesus was watching what Saul had been doing. We find a promise of Him making decisions about people, in Rev. 22:12,

> "**Consider this! I am continuously** (or: habitually; progressively; repeatedly) **coming quickly** (swiftly), **and My wage** (reward for work; compensation; recompense) **[is] with Me, to give back** (give away; render; pay) **to each one as his work** (accomplishment) **is** (= what he deserves)."

Rev. 20:11-15 does not necessarily speak of some "end of time" or "end of life" situation. This was simply a vision that John saw: it is a picture of God judging folks based upon "**their works**." Another picture is found in the parable of the sheep and the kids, in Mat. 25:31-46. He appeared "in His glory" to John in Rev. 1:12-16 – when John was "**within spirit** (or: in union with [the] Spirit; in the midst of a Breath-effect)" (vs. 10). In Rev. 1:8 it was proclaimed to John,

> "**I am continuously the Alpha and the Omega,**" says the Lord God, '**the One continuously being, even the One Who was and continued being, and the One presently and continuously** (or: progressively) **coming and going, the Almighty.**'"

He is constantly active, among us.

11. Being, then, folks having seen, perceived, and thus knowing, the Lord's respect (or: the reverence from, and which is, the Owner and Master [= Christ]; the reverential fear*, regard and recognition pertaining to or coming from [Yahweh]), **we are constantly persuading people** (habitually convincing people; one after another making humans confident). **So we have been, and thus remain, manifested** (set in the light so as to be clearly seen) **in God** (by God; for God; to God; with God), **yet I am also continually expecting** (or: hoping expectantly) **to have been manifested** (set in clear light) **within** (centered in; in union with) **your consciences.** [* cf Deut. 6:5, 13]

The opening, dependent clause is referencing vs. 10, above: **Christ's elevated place**. We must not forget that Christ bought us – He owns us; we are His possession. Paul was so aware of this that he opened his letter to the community in Rome by introducing himself as, "**Paul, Jesus Christ's slave!**" This does not usually sit well, in our post-modern, independent-minded societies. We find it hard to relate to our Savior in a slave/Lord relationship. But just what do we think it means to call Him "Lord"? Slavery was a universal fact of life, in Paul's day, for a large part of the society in the Roman Empire. Slaves understood the authority and power that their owners had over them. Today, it may be hard for us to relate. We believe that we are free, and have our cherished "free will" – at least until we come to understand that only God has true "free will," and that we are actually slaves to our governments that continue imposing new restrictions upon us, and to our economic societies that demand most of our earnings. And since Paul has just affirmed that it continues being a binding necessity that we continue living our lives before God's "official bench," we may better be able to understand that they were "**folks having seen, perceived, and thus knowing, the Lord's respect** (or: the reverence from, and which is, the Owner and Master [= Christ]; the reverential fear, regard and recognition pertaining to or coming from [Yahweh])." Do we still have doubts? Let us turn to Heb. 10:

> 30. **For we have perceived, and thus know, the One saying,**
> **"Execution of right in fairness out of the Way pointed out [is] by Me** (or: Maintaining justice and equity [is] in Me). **I will continue giving back** (repaying) **in its place,"**
> **says the Lord** [= Yahweh], **and again,**
> > **"The Lord** [= Yahweh] **will continue separating and making a decision about** (or: judging) **His people."** [Ex. 32:35-36; cf Rom. 12:19-21]
> 31. **[It is] fearful** (a fear-inspiring [experience]) **to suddenly fall-in – into hands of a continuously living God!**

And then the same author continues, in Heb. 12:

> 25. **Continue looking, and see! You folks should not at any point ask to the side for yourselves** (or: beg for release; decline; refuse; or: = turn your back on) **the One continuously speaking** (or: the Speaker)! **For since** (or: if) **those asking aside for themselves** (begging off; refusing; or: = turning their backs) **did not by flight escape** (or: flee out from) **the one constantly managing** (conducting business and instructing) **upon earth** (or: [the] land), **much more we [will not escape], that is those habitually turning ourselves away from the One from [the] atmospheres and heavens,**
> 26. **Whose voice shook the land** (or: earth) **at that time. Yet now it has been promised** (or: He has promised for Himself), **saying,**
> > **"Still once [more; or: for all] I am shaking not only the land** (or: earth), **but also the heaven** (or: atmosphere; sky)." [Hag. 2:6; cf vs. 19, above; Ex. 19:18; Joel 3:16-17]
> 27. **Now the "Still once [more; or: for all]" constantly points to and makes clearly visible the transposition** (transference; changeover; change of setting or place) **of the things being repeatedly shaken, to the end that the things not being repeatedly** (or: continuously) **shaken may remain.** [cf 2 Cor. 3:7-13]
> 28. **Therefore** (or: Because of which), **continuously taking to our sides** (or: progressively receiving alongside) **an unshaken Reign** (or: Kingdom; Sovereign influence), **we are constantly holding** (or: progressively having; [other MSS: can be now having]) **grace and joyous favor, through which we are** [other MSS: can be] **continually serving, well-pleasingly, in God** (or: for God; by God; to God), **with modesty** (an unseen behavior and manner) **in taking hold easily of goodness and well-being, as well as discretion and awe as to what is proper,** [cf Jn. 1:17]
> 29. **for you see, "even our God [is] a continuously all-consuming Fire** (or: our God [is] also a progressively fully-devouring fire)." [Deut. 4:24; 9:3; Isa. 33:14]

Paul was simply aware of who God is; Jesus had stopped him dead in his tracks on the road to Damascus, and so he and the called-out communities had a healthy, respectful fear of their Creator and Lord. To John had been revealed the judgments that were going to come upon Jerusalem (AD 70), and the corrective measures that might come to the called-out communities in Asia Minor (Rev. 2 and 3). I have a healthy respect for His force of gravity, and had a wise element of fear when walking walls, as a carpenter! OK, I think I've made my point. But it was because of all this, and for this present life, that he and the other representatives "**[were] constantly persuading people** (habitually convincing people; one after another making humans confident)."

There is another element of fear which we might not ordinarily recognize as being fear. This is in relationships of deep love and respect. Heb. 12:5-11 discusses the child-training discipline in the relationship between a father and a son and vss. 5b-6 cites to Prov. 3:11-12 when we are instructed,

> "'**My son, do not be neglecting** (giving little care to) **the Lord's discipline** (education; child-training), **neither be exhausted** (dissolved; = fall apart) **while being continually scrutinized or convicted** (exposed and put to the test; or: reproved) **by** (or: under) **Him, for whom the Lord is loving** (urging toward reunion and acceptance), **He is continuously and progressively educating** (or: disciplining; child-training), **and He is periodically scourging every son whom He is taking alongside with His hands** (accepting; receiving).'"

Then vs. 9b admonishes us "**shall we not be continually placed under and humbly arranged and aligned by the Father of the spirits** (or: the Progenitor of breath-effects and Mentor of attitudes)**? And then we shall proceed living** (or: progressively live)**!**" [cf Nu. 27:16]

Paul addressed this same topic in Eph. 6:

> 1. **You children make it a habit to humbly listen and pay attention to, and thus submissively obey, your parents** (begetters; those who birthed you into existence) **in union with the Lord** [= Christ or Yahweh], **for this is the Way pointed out** (is fair, right and just).
> 2. **"Be continuously honoring** (holding in respect; valuing; reverencing; treating as precious and with dignity) **your father and mother,"** which very one is a foremost implanted goal (impartation of the finished product within; inward directive) **within an act of promising** (or: in [the] promise; or: = that embodies assurance),
> 3. **"to the end that it may come to be well and easy for** (or: to; in; with) **you and you will continue existing a long time upon the land** (or: earth).**"** [Ex. 20:12; Deut. 5:16]

We have had parents, grandparents, teachers and mentors who we respected so much that we would "fear" disappointing them, or having them in any way think less of us. How much more so should we fear God in this way.

Now the final alternate rendering, in the parenthetical expansion, gives us a positive perception of Christ's "judgment seat," for we also know that it is a mercy seat. Knowing that we belong to the Lord gives us confidence that He will take care of us and provide for us (vs. 10, above), for He is also the Good Shepherd for His sheep. And He will often do this through His sheep (Mat. 25:35-36).

But as noted, above, Paul was aware that "**we have been, and thus remain, manifested** (set in the light so as to be clearly seen)," in front of Christ's city platform. The object of this verb "manifested (etc.)" – which is in the perfect tense (a past event that continues with lasting effects) – is the term **God** that is in the dative case, with no expressed preposition. Because of this, we find that Paul may have intended the location function of the dative: they had been manifested "**in God**." Sound strange? Well, remember Acts 17:28?

> "**within the midst of and in union with Him we continuously live** (or, as a subjunctive: could be constantly living), **and are constantly moved about and put into motion, and continue existing** (experiencing Being)."

But the other dative functions also make sense to this context. We all continue manifested before His tribunal, "by God; for God; to God; with God." The NEB offers a helpful paraphrase, here: "To God our lives lie open…" But we keep in mind that this is His work, it is FOR Him, and He presents us TO Himself, and WITH Himself. Remember: we are joined to the Lord (1 Cor. 6:17), so wherever we are, He is there, too (think Ps. 23)! Ah, this is wonderful!

All the same, let us keep a balanced perspective about the fear of and from the Lord, which we learned as children: that it was the beginning of Wisdom. Keep in mind that God is our Father. Respect does not mean that we are to be afraid of God. I'm not afraid of gravity, either. We know that God is Love, and that:

> "**Fear does not exist within the Love, but rather perfect love** (mature love; love having reached its goal) **repeatedly** (habitually; progressively) **throws the fear outside, because the fear constantly has and holds a pruning** (a curtailment; a checking; restraint; a lopping off – thus, a correction). **But the one habitually fearing or dreading has not been perfected within the Love** (has not been brought to the destined goal of maturity – in union with love)" (1 Jn. 1:18).

The balance comes when we simply "abide in the Vine" (Jn. 15:1ff). His abiding presence automatically perfects His love, and we move beyond fear to respect and admiration.

Next Paul returns to his theme of solidarity with his called-out communities, and he tells them: "**yet I am also continually expecting** (or: hoping expectantly) **to have been manifested** (set in clear light) **within** (centered in; in union with) **your consciences**." He wants them to clearly see him, see his motives, and see his love for them. He wants his teachings to be implanted within their very consciences, so that they too will "**constantly be folks [that are] well-pleasing to Him**" (vs. 9, above).

12. We are not again recommending ourselves to you (or: making ourselves stand together for you), **but rather, continue giving you a starting point and an occasion** (a base of operations and an incentive) **from the effect of boasting over and being proud of us** [other MSS: you] **– to the end that you folks may constantly possess** (have and hold) **[a position; a response; a defense] toward those continuously boasting in a face** (in presentation; in personal appearance; in a surface facade) **and not in [the] heart.**

Paul is saying that this is not a "letter of introduction" to them. He and his associates are not promoting themselves, but rather is wanting to turn their thinking so as to "**continue giving [them] a starting point and an occasion** (a base of operations and an incentive) **from the effect of boasting over and being proud of [him and his associates].**" As elsewhere, Paul is having to warn them about, and to prepare them to take a stand against, other members or teachers within their community that either incite division or preach a different "gospel" that is based upon "presentation, personal appearance or surface facades." He wants them rather to be living from their hearts.

13. For whether we are beside ourselves (standing without; = out of our minds), **[it is] for God** (in God; to God; by God; with God); **or whether we remain sane** (of sound mind; reasonable), **[it is] for you** (to you; with you) **folks,**

Regardless of Paul's or his friends' situations or conditions, it is all for (i.e., on behalf of) the community in Corinth (and of course it would be the same for all of his communities). And in this, it is also, of course, "**for God**." Observe, once more, the dative form of the term "**God**," and the pronoun, "**you**." Read, and contemplate, the parenthetical functions on offer: in, to, by, with. All of these make sense to these respective terms, as noted. It is God, all the way, and in every conceivable way.

This verse may be an example of Paul's irony.

14. for you see, Christ's love (urge toward accepting reunion; full giving of Himself to [us]) **continuously holds us together. [We are] deciding** (discerning and concluding; judging) **this: that** [some MSS add: since] **One Person** (or: Man) **died over [the situation of] all people** (or: for the sake of all humans); **consequently all people died** (or: accordingly, then, all humans died). [cf Rom. 5:12, reversed]

This verse continues vs. 13, amplifying and defining the statement, "[it is] for God (etc.)." What "**continuously holds [them] together**" is "**Christ's love**" – even if they "stand without," that is, "outside of being accepted in the group," or are, "beside themselves." This applies to us, as well. "Christ's urge toward accepting reunion and full giving of Himself to [us]" is what constantly **holds us together**. Once again, the NEB offers an interpretation of this verb that suggests another insight: the situation described in vs. 13 is for the Corinthians, and so Paul is seen as saying that "the love of Christ leaves us no choice…" Although this may be true, the literal rendering, "**holds us together**" seems to give a better explanation of how Paul and his associates survive what he just described in vs. 13.

Paul now begins another teaching which continues on through vs. 19. We suggest that he is referring to both Adams, here, by alluding to the first Adam of which he wrote in Rom. 5:12, through whom the Death passed throughout the whole of humanity, but then here he is now pointing us to the Last, or *eschatos*, Adam which he described as being the Second Humanity, in 1 Cor. 15:47, the One that is "**[is made] out of heaven** (or: [is] from [the] atmosphere)." It is this Last One that reverses what the first one did. He explained this reversal of humanity's situation in Rom. 5:15b,

"**For you see, since** (or: if) **by** (or: in) **the effect of the fall to the side** (the result of the stumbling aside and the offense) **of the one THE MANY** (= the mass of humanity) **died, MUCH MORE** (= infinitely greater) **[is] the Grace of God** (God's Grace; favor which is God), **and the gift** (or: gratuitous benefit) **within Grace – a joy-producing act of Favor – by that of the One Man, Jesus Christ, surrounded** (or: encircles) **into encompassing superabundance** (extraordinary surplus and excess) **into THE MANY** (= the mass of humanity)."

This Last One, the *eschatos* Adam, of course, is Christ, and now we read this astounding statement about what Paul "discerned, concluded, judged and decided":

"**that One Person** (or: Man) **died over [the situation of] all people** (or: for the sake of all humans); **consequently all people died** (or: accordingly, then, all humans died)."

Don't read on, just yet. Read that statement again, and just contemplate its import! That "**One Person (or: Man)**" is Christ, as vs. 15 explains.

ALL HUMANITY DIED... IN CHRIST! This is the key that unlocks the rest of what he informs us in vss. 15-19.

The symbol of immersion (baptism) gives us a physical picture and is an acted-out parable for what Paul tells us in Rom. 6:3-4,

"**as many as are immersed into Christ Jesus are immersed into His death? We, then** (or: consequently), **were buried together in Him** (or: by Him; with Him), **through the immersion into the death, to the end that just as** (or: in the same manner as) **Christ was roused and raised forth from out of the midst of dead folks THROUGH** (through means of) **THE GLORY** (the glorious manifestation of splendor which calls forth praise; the assumed appearance) **of, from, and which is, The Father, thus also we can walk around** (or: order our behavior) **within newness of life**."

Paul goes on to say this last part, again, in Rom. 6:5b, "**then certainly we will also continue existing [in and with the effects of the likeness] of The** [or: His] **Resurrection**." David Bentley Hart's recent translation of the NT affirms the need of the inserted brackets, due to Paul's condensed Greek, here in Rom. 6. (*Cf* his footnote "u" p 299)

So here we can recall how Paul put it so plainly in 1 Cor. 15:22,

"**For just as within Adam all humans keep on** (or: everyone continues) **dying, in the same way, also, within the Christ, all humans will keep on being made alive** (or: in union with the Anointed One, everyone will one-after-another be created and produced with Life)." [*cf* Rom. 5:18]

15. And further, He died over all people (over [the situation] of, and for the sake of all humans) **to the end that those living can** (or: may; could; would) **no longer live for themselves** (to themselves; in themselves; by themselves), **but rather for** (or: in; by; to; with) **the One dying and then being awakened and raised up over them** (over their [situation]; for their sakes),

We find a parallel expression of this verse in Rom. 4:25,

"**[He] who was handed over** (or: transmitted; delivered; passed along; or: given to [our] side) **through and because of the effects of our falls to the side** (or: with a view to and for the sake of the results of our stumblings aside, transgressions and offenses), **and yet was roused and raised up through and because of our eschatological deliverance, being placed in the Way pointed out and turned in the right direction**

(or: for the benefit of our being made to be just; or: on behalf of our justifying, leading to freedom from guilt; or: for the purpose of our being brought into equity and right relationship: a rightwising of solidarity in covenant inclusion and participation).

Cf Rom. 5:9; Gal. 2:17; Phil. 3:9.

His death made all this possible, for all of humanity. But as in 4:18, above, "**[we are continuously looking at] those things not being constantly seen or repeatedly observed**," and he explained this in 1 Cor. 15:23,

> "**yet each person within the result of his or her own set position [in line]** (or: effect of ordered placement; appointed class; arranged time and turn, or order of succession; = place in a harvest calendar, thus, due season of maturity)…"

We do not observe all people now living "**for** (or: in; by; to; with) **the One dying and then being awakened and raised up over them**," But we know that Christ is both the Alpha and the Omega, the First and the Last (Rev. 1:11), of all humanity, and that each one, in his or her own time, will journey on "**into the midst of Him**" (Rom. 11:36).

Note AGAIN the dative case, without an expressed preposition, of "**the One**" – IN the One, FOR the One, BY the One, TO the One, and WITH the One. He is the sphere in which we live, the One for whom we live, the One by whom we live, the One to whom our lives are directed, and the One WITH whom we can now live our lives. He is the Path which we all follow: **dying and then being awakened and raised up.** THIS is the Good News! THIS is the glory of God! THIS is our patterned destiny!

The dependent clause, "**can** (or: may; could; would) **no longer live for themselves** (to themselves; in themselves; by themselves)," should make us aware of our ontological oneness within this resurrected realm of the new creation (vs. 17, below). We no longer live by ourselves, we are joined into one body, in the One New Humanity (Eph. 2:15). This is the Peace – the Joining – that He has given to us. 1 Pet. 4:1-2 gives us another view of not living for ourselves:

> 1. **Christ, then, having undergone experiences and suffering IN FLESH** (or: being physically and emotionally affected to the point of suffering) **over us** (or: over our [situation] and for our sakes), **you folks also arm and equip yourselves with the same mental inclination** (idea; thought; way of thinking; frame of mind; attitude), **because the person [thus] suffering or going through physical or emotional experiences which affect him IN [the] FLESH has in and for himself put a stop to failures, errors and mistakes** (or: sins) [or, with other MSS: has been caused to cease from sin],
>
>> "This is a word for the disciple, the follower of the Messiah. In Matt. 16:24-25 Jesus speaks of denying ourselves, taking up our execution stake and following Him. Peter here points to His suffering and then tells us to expect the same, but then goes on to give a reason for it: to put a stop to failures, errors and mistakes. This may refer to our own times of missing the target (as the other MSS state), or, as in laying down your life for another, we may by such experiences do the works that Christ did, and bring life to others. Paul said in 2 Cor. 4:
>>
>>> 11. **For we, ourselves – the continuously living ones – are ever being repeatedly handed over and committed into death** (or: = continuously delivered into life-threatening experiences) – **because of Jesus – to the end that the Life, also, of Jesus** (or: so that also the life which comes from and is Jesus; or: so that Jesus' life) **can** (may; could; would) **be set in clear light and manifested – within our mortal flesh!**
>>> 12. **So then** (or: Consequently), **the Death is repeatedly and progressively operating and inwardly working within us, yet that Life [is constantly operative] within you folks.**"
>>
>> (*Peter, Paul & Jacob*, Jonathan Mitchell, Harper Brown Pub., 2012 p 27).
>
> 2. **[and comes] into the [condition or situation] to NO LONGER live out the additional remaining course [of his] time within [the] FLESH** (= in the natural realm) **in the midst of** (or: in union with) **[the] full passions** (or: for [the] over-desires; to [the] rushings of emotions upon things) **of humans** (or: pertaining to or originating in mankind), **but to the contrary, in God's will** (or: for God's intent; to God's purpose).

16. so that we, from the present time (or: from now) **[on], have seen and thus know** (or: perceive; or: are acquainted [with]) **no one on the level of flesh** (= in the sphere of the estranged human nature; = in correspondence to the self that is enslaved to the System; = according to the old covenant), **if even we have intimately, by experience, known Christ** ([the] Anointed One) **on the level of flesh** (or: = in the sphere of estranged humanity; or: = in correspondence to a self that is oriented to the System; or: = according to the old covenant), **nevertheless we now** (in the present moment) **no longer continue [thus] knowing [Him or anyone].**

This verse continues his thought that was presented, beginning in vs. 14b, "**all people died,**" together with the result of that death of the One, together with everyone else, along with the thought (vs. 15): **that those living can no longer live for themselves** (to themselves; in themselves; by themselves), **but rather for** (or: in; by; to; with) **the One dying and then being awakened and raised up**. It is for this reason that from **that present time** (the generation of the Resurrection) "**we have seen and thus know (or: perceive; or: are acquainted [with]) no one on the level of flesh!**" This shift in perspective and perception signals the change of the ages: the inauguration of Age of the Messiah, together with its new arrangement (or: covenant) and its "new creation" (vs. 17, below). This was begun, and embodied, in Jesus – as we see from His statement in Mat. 12:50,

> "**You see, whoever may be doing the will, intent, purpose and desire of My Father – the One within and in union with [the] heavens** (or: in the midst of [the] atmospheres) **– that very person is My brother and sister and mother!**"

This is also why Paul could posit in Rom. 8:29b,

> "**the [situation for] Him to be** (or: to continually exist being) **the Firstborn among, within the center of, and in union with many brothers** (= a vast family from the same womb; Gal. 4:26)!"

Not only that, **even Christ**, the Anointed One, the Messiah, "**we now** (in the present moment) **no longer continue [thus] knowing on the level of flesh**" – or, "according to the old covenant," with its Law that pertained to the life in the flesh and all the codes and ordinances. Paul's statement is an outgrowth of Jesus' words in Jn. 6:63a,

> "**The Spirit** (or: Breath-effect; or: spirit; Breath; Attitude) **is** (or: continues being) **the One continuously creating Life** (or: repeatedly making alive; habitually forming life). **The flesh continues being of no help or benefit to anything** (furthers or augments not one thing)."

We no longer know Christ in relation to the prophecies of the OT, for within the Christ Event – which we suggest extended from His crucifixion and resurrection on through that generation until the end of Second Temple Judaism in AD 70 – it was,

> "**to have fulfilled all the things having been written** (or: for all that is written to be fulfilled)!" (Lu. 21:22).

So we no longer know Christ in relation to Second Temple Judaism, or the Law. We no longer know other physical races according to their blood lines or genetic heritage. There is no more separate classifications of "Jew/Gentile." Paul made this clear in Gal. 3:28,

> "**Within** [Him; us], **there is not** (there does not exist) **Jew nor Greek** (or: Hellenist); **within, there is not** (does not exist) **slave nor freeman; within, there is not** (does not exist) **'male and female'; for it follows that, you folks all exist being one within Christ Jesus** (or: for you see, all you people are one person, centered in, and in union with, an Anointing from Jesus)."

We might take note that in this new existence where there is not the separation of "male and female," he is speaking of a new creation (Christ; the realm of spirit) that has no gender and no separation into "Adam and Eve." It is the sphere of Christ joined to humanity (the Bride) to now be One Spirit (1 Cor. 6:17).

He said it this way in Col. 3:

> 9. **Do not keep on** (or: Stop) **lying unto one another! [Be] folks at once stripping off from yourselves** (undressing yourselves from; or: go out and away from) **the OLD HUMANITY** (the old human; = the old Adam), **together with its practices,**

10. **and then [be] suddenly CLOTHING yourselves with** (or: entering within) **the NEW one** (the fresh one which existed only recently), **the one being continuously** (or: repeatedly; habitually; progressively) **renewed** (made back up new again, in kind and character) **into full, accurate, added, intimate and experiential knowledge and insight which is down from and corresponds to the image** (an exactly formed visible likeness) **of its Creator** (of the One framing and founding it from a state of wildness and disorder),

11. **wherein** (or: in which place [i.e., within the New Humanity]) **there is no Greek** [figure of the multitudes who are non-Jews, and of those who are cultured and civilized] **and Jew** [figure of a covenant people of God], **circumcision and uncircumcision** [figure for religious in-groups and out-groups; there is no longer a covenant people versus non-covenant people], **barbarian** [foreigner who speaks a different language], **Scythian** [figure or example of wild, uncivilized groups], **slave, freeman, but to the contrary, Christ [is] all, and within all**
>   (or: Christ [is] all humanity, and within all mankind; or: Christ [is] everything or all things, and within everything and all things; [note: the Greek is plural, and is either masculine, signifying "mankind," or neuter, signifying all creation, in these phrases]).

17. **Consequently, since someone [is] within Christ** (or: So that if anyone [is] in union with [the] Anointed One; or: And as since a Certain One [was] in Christ), **[there is] a new creation** (or: [it is] a framing and founding of an essentially different kind; [he or she is] an act of creation having a fresh character, a new quality)**: the original things** (the beginning [situations]; the archaic and primitive [arrangements]) **passed by** (or: went to the side). **Consider! New, essentially different things have come into existence** (have occurred and been birthed; or: It has become new things that are essentially different from what was habitual, before; or: He has been birthed and now exists being ones of a different kind, character and quality). [Rev. 21:5]

This opening word, "**Consequently** (or: So that)," refers back to all that Paul has just been saying, and now presents us with a concluding result: **since someone** (or: if anyone) **[is] within Christ** (or: in union with [the] Anointed One), **[there is] a new creation**." As you can observe from the inserted brackets, there are ellipses in Paul's Greek: there are no verbs in these clauses. This is common in ancient Greek, but in English we must insert a verb, and that is normally some form of the verb "to be; to exist." In the first clause, "[is]" is the normal copula that is used. But in the second clause, translators have chosen different forms. Following the sense of the first clause, most all translators choose a third person singular of the copula, "is." But with the second clause, a subject needs to be inserted, along with the verb – and for a third person singular verb we have the choices: he, she, it or there. So how are we to choose? The KJV used italics, instead of brackets, to indicate that the subject and the verb are missing, and has: *he is*. Now this fits with the subject of the first clause: someone; anyone (KJV gave us: any man). But the antecedent of "**a new creation**" need not be "someone" or "anyone." I, and other translators, have read Paul as referencing what preceded his opening word, "**Consequently** (or: So that)," i.e., vss.14b-16, and "someone/anyone" is merely a marker that indicates that those things have already occurred, and that a new situation now exists. The existential reality of this "**new creation**" and of the "**original things**" having "**passed by**," is affirmed by what Paul says in 12:2a, below:
>   "**I have known, and am acquainted with, a person** (or: a man; a human being) **in Christ** (or: within the midst of Christ; in union with [the] Anointed) **more than fourteen years ago...**"
And so...

Looking at the explanation that follows "a new creation," we find that "**the original things** (the beginning [situations]; the archaic and primitive [arrangements])" – note the plural subject – "**passed by** (or: went to the side). **Consider! New, essentially different things have come into existence**." We suggest that Paul is speaking about the new age, the new arrangement (or: covenant) and the new sphere of existence (Christ; the Spirit; the atmosphere/heaven) that HAVE COME, and it is that the old age, the old arrangement, the old sphere of existence (the Law; the flesh; the earth realm) is what **passed by**." This is why "**from the present moment** (or: from now) **[on], have seen and thus know** (or: perceive; or: are acquainted [with]) **no one on the level of flesh**" and therefore no longer participate in the temple cultus and codes of the Law, nor the divisions between circumcision and uncircumcision or Jew and Gentile. The One New Humanity (Eph. 2:15) has come into existence that corresponds to the new Age of the Messiah. Paul may have been alluding to Isa. 65:17,

> "For behold Me creating new heavens (atmospheres) and a new earth (or: Land), and the former shall not be remembered, nor shall they [come] up on [the] heart" (CVOT; additions mine).

It is not that the choice to render the subject/noun of this second clause, "he/she," is grammatically wrong, it is that it is missing the larger picture of the corporate, the new covenant and the new age. It brings the focus on the individual, instead of on the corporate Christ, the Second Humanity of Paul's eschatology. The NEB seems to blend these views:

> "When anyone is united to Christ, there is a new world (or, f b: a new act of creation); the old order has gone, and a new order has already begun."

It also offers f c: "he is a new creature." Our reading of the scope of Paul's words will color which rendering that we will prefer.

Before moving on, let us take a moment to focus on the alternative renderings of the last clause:
a) New, essentially different things have occurred and been birthed;
b) He has been birthed and now exists being ones of a different kind, character and quality;

> In other words, we are His corporate body and He, being the Head, was birthed in resurrection as the New Being (Tillich) -- no longer separate, but joined to us so that now we are (corporately) Him. "A body you have prepared for Me" (Heb. 10:5b).

c) It has become new things that are essentially different from what was habitual, before.

These last two renderings offer two potential subjects (He; It) for the third person which could be referring to either Christ (He), or the new age, etc. (It). A very literal rendering could be, "Look! He has come into existence: [there are] new things (or: situations; etc.)!" Now we find the same ambiguity in the rendering of *panta* (all humanity, or, all things) in Rev. 21, which we suggest is speaking of the same thing as Paul is speaking of here, in 1 Cor. 5:17. Rev. 21:5,

> **"Consider this! I am presently making all things new** (or: habitually creating everything [to be] new and fresh; progressively forming [the] whole anew; or, reading *panta* as masculine: I am periodically making **all humanity** new, and progressively, one after another, producing and creating **every person** anew, while constantly constructing all people fresh and new, i.e., continuously renewing **everyone**)!" [Isa. 43:19; 65:17-25]

Seeing that *panta* functions as a corporate masculine, singular, or as a neuter plural, both the corporate and the individual are included in Rev. 21:5, and so both readings of vs. 17, here, can be seen. The greater includes the lesser. The first Person to be "in Christ," was Jesus: **the Firstborn among, within the center of, and in union with many brothers** (= a vast family from the same womb; Gal. 4:26)!" (Rom. 8:29b).

We see the idea of the terms, "**a new creation**," and the whole of the rest of this verse, said differently in Rev. 21:1,

> "Then I saw '**a new** (new in nature; different from the usual; better than the old; superior in value and attraction; new in quality) **atmosphere** (or: sky; or: heaven) **and a new Land** (or: earth)' [Isa. 66:22], **for you see, actually, the first** (former; preceding; earlier) **atmosphere** (or: heaven) **and the first** (former, preceding) **Land** (or: earth; soil; ground) **went away** (or: moved off, and passed away)…"

Paul wrote using a cognate of this "new" in Rom. 6:4b,

> "**thus also we can walk around** (or: we also should likewise conduct ourselves and order our behavior) **within newness of life** (in union with life characterized by being essentially new in kind and quality, and different from that which was former)." *Cf* Rom. 8:10

He also wrote of this same topic, as his closing argument, in Gal. 6:

14. **Now may it not happen to me** (or: in me) **to take up the practice of boasting, except within the cross of our Lord, Jesus Christ, through Whom** (or: through which [i.e., the cross]) **the organized System** (or: the world of culture, economy, government and religion) **has been, and continues being, crucified in me** (or: to me; for me; by me; or: through Whom the aggregate of humanity has been, and is now, crucified with me), **and I by** (to; in; with; for) **the domination System** (the world; = their culture, secular society, religion, and government).

15. **For you see** [some MSS add: within Christ Jesus], **neither circumcision nor uncircumcision continues being anything, but rather: a NEW and different CREATION** (a founding and settling [as a village] with a new character and quality, in a place that was wild and without order; an innovative, new act of framing and building [or: = constructing a covenant]).

16. **So as many as are habitually** (or: are one-after-another) **advancing in line by ranks, corresponding to this measuring rod**
> (or: continue belonging to the rank living in conformity to this rule; or: shall in this
>> standard progressively observe the rudimentary elements or elementary principles and

walk in line with them), **Peace** (Harmony of the Joining) **and Mercy [are continually] upon them – even** (or: that is) **upon the Israel of, and from, God** (or: God's Israel).

This answers to his opening lines, in Gal. 1:4,
> "**the One at one point giving Himself, over [the situation of]** (or: on behalf of; for the sake of; [p46, Aleph*, A, D & other MSS read: concerning]) **our failures** (situations and occasions of falling short or to the side of the target; deviations; mistakes; errors; sins) **so that He could carry us out from the midst of the present misery-gushing and worthless age**
>> (or: bear us forth from the indefinite period of time – characterized by toil, grievous plights
>> and bad situations – having taken a stand in [our] midst; or: extricate us from the space of
>> time having been inserted and now standing in union with base qualities)…"

The picture created by this terminology in Gal. 1:4 is an allusion to Israel's Exodus from Egypt, anchoring the work of Christ within Israel's story – which is most likely the reason for mentioning Israel in Gal. 6:16, above.

We see another picture in Eph. 4:
> 22. **to put off from yourselves** [as clothing or habits] **what accords to the former entangled manner of living** (or: twisted up behavior)**: the old humanity** (or: the past, worn-out person) **– the one continuously in process of being corrupted** (spoiled; ruined) **down from and in accord with the passionate desires** (the full-covering, swelling emotions) **of the deceptions** (or: seductive desires) **–**
> 23. **and then to be continuously renewed** (or: from time to time, or, progressively made young again) **by** (or: in; with) **the spirit** (or: attitude; breath-effect) **of your mind** (or: from the mind which is you folks; or: by the Spirit which is your [collective] mind),
> 24. **and to enter within** (or: clothe yourselves with) **the new humanity** (or: the Person that is different and innovative in kind and quality) **– the one in accord with and corresponding to God** (or: the person at the Divine level) **– being formed** (framed, built, founded and settled from a state of disorder and wildness; created) **within the Way pointed out**…

Similarly, we have Col. 3:10,
> "**and then [be] suddenly clothing yourselves with** (or: entering within) **the new one** (the fresh one which existed only recently), **the one being continuously** (or: repeatedly; habitually; progressively) **renewed** (made back up essentially new again – different in kind and character) **into full, accurate, added, intimate and experiential knowledge and insight which is down from and corresponds to the image** (an exactly formed visible likeness) **of its Creator** (of the One framing and founding it from a state of wildness and disorder)."

In God's economy of the new covenant, "**the original things passed by** (or: went to the side). **Consider! New, essentially different things have come into existence**." These new things are the glory of God: manifestations which call forth praise, in newly assumed appearances.

18. Yet further, all things [are] (or: the Whole [is]; = all the things that exist [are]) **forth from out of the midst of God – the One transforming us to be completely other [than we were]**
> (or: bringing us into another place or state of being; changing us to correspond with other [perceptions and conceptions]; altering us to be conformed to another [person]; changing us from enmity to friendship; reconciling us) **in Himself** (or: with Himself; by Himself; to Himself; for Himself), **through Christ, and giving to us the attending service of, and the dispensing from, the complete transformation [for folks] to be other [than before]**
> (or: the change into another [position]; the changing to correspond with other [situations; perceptions]; the alteration to be another [person]; the change from enmity to friendship; the reconciliation), [*cf* Rom. 8:19-21]

The first clause could not be a more inclusive statement. Paul is restating what he said in Rom. 11:36,
> "**Because, forth from out of the midst of Him, then through the midst of Him** (or: through means of Him), **and [finally] into the midst of Him, [is; will be] the whole** (everything; [are] all things)."

This leaves nothing out; it also leaves no one out. The final destiny of all humanity is clearly stated in both of these witnesses.

But now Paul goes on to tell us what God (i.e., humanity's final destination) is like, and what He does:
> "**the One transforming US to be completely OTHER [than we were]**."

Because this is a work of God, Paul uses the verb tense that can be seen as either timeless, or without reference to process or duration. This is simply what God does... and in this He remains the same. God transforms people. The extent of this work, its scope, is clearly stated in the next verse: **[the] aggregate of humanity** (etc.).

What I have rendered as "transforming... to be completely other" is commonly rendered "reconciling." Now the idea of reconciliation is contained in the extended semantic range of the participle, but it falls far short of the explicit meanings of the elements of the compound verb *katallassō*. The root, *allassō*, means: to make other than it is; to change; to alter; (by extension) to exchange something for something else. In this verse, the addition of the prefix, *kata-*, can be understood as an intensifier, thus my rendering, "**completely other**," with the participle, and "**complete transformation**," with the noun that follows.

Now the preposition *kata* has a semantic range, and so in rendering these compound words, the meanings of this prefix can enter into the resultant meaning of the verb and of the noun. So let us consider these other optional renderings:
a) bringing us into another place or state of being; -- God's reign and sovereign activities/the heavens;
b) changing us to correspond with other [perceptions and conceptions]; – i.e., the new arrangement;
c) altering us to be conformed to another [person]; -- i.e., conformed to Christ;
d) changing us from enmity to friendship; -- with God and with one another; and thus...
e) reconciling us.

Next we observe that God does this "**in Himself**." Pause, and think about what this can imply... Well, we do exist within the midst of Him (Acts. 17:28). But wait, there's more... This phrase can also read, "with Himself, by Himself, to Himself, or/and for Himself." Each of these options is a thought worth contemplating. Paul used this same verb, *katallassō*, in Rom. 5:10,
> "**For you see, since** (or: if) **WHILE continuously existing being actively HOSTILE ones** (or: enemies [of people, or of God]) **we WERE suddenly CHANGED from enmity to friendship by God** (or: conciliated to God; or: **CHANGED to be WHOLLY OTHER** and to be in line, consistent and compatible **IN God**) **through His Son's death, much more** (or: all the more, then) **we will continue being kept safe and will be progressively delivered** (rescued; saved; cured and restored to the health and wholeness of our original state and condition) **– being folks that were**

conciliated (fully changed from enmity to friendship and made totally other than we were) **within His Life** (or: in union with the life which is Him)."

How can Paul be any more explicit about the unilateral work of Christ? He used another word for "transformation" in 3:18, above, but he is speaking here about the same things that he was speaking about there.

Then, we see that this all happens "**through Christ.**" This is laid out more fully, in Eph. 2:8,

"**For you see, by** (or: to; in; for; with) **the grace and joyous favor you are** (you continuously exist being) **folks having been delivered** (rescued; kept safe; saved; made whole; restored to your original state and condition) **so as to now be enjoying salvation through** [some MSS add: the] **faithfulness** (or: loyalty; trust; faith; confidence), **and even this not forth from out of you folks, [it is] the gift of and from God** (or: the gift which is God; or: the gift pertains to God)."

But now the baton is passed on to US, for Paul continues, "**and giving to us the attending service of, and the dispensing from, the complete transformation [for folks] to be other [than before]**." Here, again, we have some optional renderings:

　　　a) the change into another [position]; -- from "earth" to "the atmosphere of the spirit;"
　　　b) the changing to correspond with other [situations; perceptions];
　　　c) the alteration to be another [person];
　　　d) the change from enmity to friendship; -- the Peace of the Joining (Eph. 2:15);
　　　e) the reconciliation; -- between heaven and earth.

This third rendering, c, that means that we are to be "another person," suggests the idea of being born back from above – which also is completely the work of our Father. Opting for the rendering "reconciliation," and offering what I give as "**attending service**" as the performance of an "ambassador," we can imagine the reconciliation a beings set in motion by a representative from the other party. That "other party" is God, in Christ. The NEB reads: "We come, therefore, as Christ's ambassadors. It is as if God were appealing to you through us: in Christ's name... be reconciled to God!" Reconciliation is good, but "**the complete transformation [for folks] to be other [than before]**" is better. Keep in mind: this announcement is intended for the whole aggregate of humanity.

This "**attending service of**" and "**the dispensing from,**" is what the sent-forth representatives (Paul and his associates; Peter; etc.) were doing by birthing (Gal. 4:26 – they became a part of the Jerusalem which is above) the called-out communities, and then by caring for them – as through the very letter that we are presently reading. This service has continued ever since it began.

19. as that God was existing within Christ (God was and continued being centered in, and in union with [the] Anointed One) **progressively and completely transforming [the] aggregate of humanity** (or: world) **to be other [than it is]**

　　　(or: progressively bringing [the] ordered System into another level or state; repeatedly changing [the] universe to correspond with other [conditions; perceptions]; progressively altering [the] ordered arrangement of culture, religions, economy and government to be in line with another one; habitually and progressively changing [the] secular realm [of humanity] from enmity to friendship; reconciling [the] world [of mankind]) **in Himself, to Himself, for Himself, by Himself, and with Himself, not accounting to them** (not putting to their account; not logically considering for them; not reasoning in them) **the results and effects of their falls to the side** (their trespasses and offenses), **even placing within us the Word** (the *Logos*; the Idea; the Reason; the message; the pattern-forming information) **of the corresponding transformation to** otherness (or: the full alteration; the change from enmity to friendship; the conciliation).

And so Paul goes on to expand the message of Goodness, Ease and Well-being, which he had just told them was this complete transformation. He points out that it was **God** that **was existing within Christ**. Rendered differently, "God was, and continued being" – here the verb is in the imperfect tense: a state of being that was begun in the past (either in the Incarnation, or at Jesus' immersion by John in the Jordan River, and the Anointing by the Spirit) and continued in existence, on into the present. **God was CENTERED in**, and **IN UNION with** [the] **Anointed One**." Christ's work on the cross was NOT to appease an offended god; Oh NO! God was **WITHIN** Him experiencing the beating and the death, on the cross. God and Jesus were together in this Act of giving Their Life to humanity. The mystery of this cannot really be explained, other than it was an Act of Love that completely covered humanity's pain and death, and in Their resurrection (remember Jesus and His Father were/are One) They brought Humanity into Resurrection Life – each one to experience this in their own time and re-birth (1 Cor. 15:23).

"God was... **progressively and completely transforming [the] aggregate of humanity to be other [than it is]**." The participle in this clause is in the present tense. As you observe, we have alternate renderings on offer:

a) progressively bringing [the] ordered System into another level or state; -- the term rendered "aggregate of humanity" and "ordered System" is the Greek *kosmos*. This is the same word used by John in Jn. 3:16, "**For thus God loves the aggregate of** humanity (ordered System)..." God loves everything that He made (Gen. 1:31), and He cares for all of it; here, the "ordered System" may be speaking of the "new creation" of vs. 17, above;

b) repeatedly changing [the] universe to correspond with other [conditions; perceptions]; -- this may seem to be an extreme rendering, but it is legitimate; this could be seen as an allusion to Gen. 1:2-3ff, i.e., to God in His ongoing acts of creation, such as referenced in Rev. 21:5;

c) progressively altering [the] ordered arrangement of culture, religions, economy and government to be in line with another one; -- God repeatedly invades history and makes changes;

d) habitually and progressively changing [the] secular realm [of humanity] from enmity to friendship; -- as we see in the last clause, He has us participate in this; this extended use of the word calls to mind Jas. 2:23, where Abraham "**was called 'God's friend,'**" and so here we can see "the world" being changed in order to be a part of what Abraham signifies in Paul's teachings; we even see this change of relationship evidenced in what Jesus said to His disciples (Jn. 15:15b):

"**now I have declared you folks friends, because I make intimately and experientially known to you everything** (or: all things) **which I heard and hear at My Father's side and in His presence**;"

e) reconciling [the] world [of mankind]; -- this is completely inclusive.

Now He did, and continues doing this: **in Himself, to Himself, for Himself, by Himself and with Himself**. Regarding the last phrase, "with Himself," let us call to mind Paul's words in Gal. 2:20a,

"**I was crucified together with Christ [= the Messiah], and thus it remains** (or: I have been jointly put on the execution stake in [the] Anointed One, and continue in this state)**... yet I continue living! [It is] no longer I, but it is Christ continuously living and alive within me!**"

Putting Himself within us is what changes us – completely transforms US!

The next statement flies in the face of the old covenant arrangement (the old *kosmos*). This new covenant swallowed up the old, and now – to our great joy we find that God is "**NOT accounting to them** (not putting to their account; not logically considering for them; not reasoning in them) **the results and effects of their falls to the side** (their trespasses and offenses)." What grace; what mercy! Here, Paul may be reaching back to Isa. 43:25,

"I! I [am] He [Who] wipes out your transgressions on My [own] account; and your sins I shall not remember further" (CVOT).

Unfortunately, much of Christianity did not get the memo – they have completely overlooked this. They not only (unlike God) hold people's trespasses against them, they threaten folks with their imaginary "endless torment" if they don't comply with religion's demands. But in contrast to this, Paul instructs us that God was "**even placing within us the Word** (the *Logos*; the Idea; the Reason; the message; the pattern-forming information) **of the corresponding transformation to** otherness (or: the full alteration;

357

the change from enmity to friendship; the conciliation)." Through His body, the *Logos* is repeatedly becoming flesh (Jn. 1:14), so that others can continue to behold His glory (3:18, above; Jn. 1:14b). What an honor; what a privilege.

20. Over [the situation] in regard to Christ, then (or: Therefore, on behalf of Christ), **we are elders of God, performing as ambassadors from God, as [Him] continually calling alongside to give comfort and relief** (performing as a Paraclete) **through us. We are constantly begging and urgently asking, on behalf of Christ** (or: for Christ's sake)**: "Be fully transformed in, be correspondingly altered by, be changed from an enemy to be a friend with, be reconciled to, and be altered to be another [person] in, by, and with, God!"** [*cf* 6:1, below]
> (or: "You folks be completely exchanged with God; or: Be conciliated to, and for, God!"),

Next, Paul explains how they were conducting "**the attending service**" and performing "**the dispensing**" (vs. 18, above), by functioning as "**elders of God**" and serving "**as ambassadors from God**." Paul also used this same description in Eph. 6:20,
> "**I am an old man in a manacle** (or: on behalf of which I continue performing the duties of an elder and an ambassador – in a chain!) **– to the end that within Him** (or: it) **I may speak freely** (or: openly in public, boldly as a citizen."

In Mal. 2:7 we read,
> "For the lips of a priest should preserve knowledge, and instruction should they seek at his mouth, for he is the messenger of the LORD of hosts" (J.M. Powis Smith).

They were indeed representing Him: "**continually calling [people] alongside to give comfort and relief** (or: performing as paracletes)." They were "**constantly begging and urgently asking [people], on behalf of Christ**," and this was the empowering proclamation: "**Be fully transformed in God**." We all live "in God" (Acts 17:28), and are transformed **BY** Him.

My rendering has conflated the other ways that Paul repeats what he has just said, above: "**be correspondingly altered by, be changed from an enemy to be a friend with, be reconciled to, and be altered to be another [person] in, by, and with, God**." This is the reason for what he said in Eph. 5:18b,
> "**be continuously or repeatedly filled full in spirit** (within [the] Spirit; within the midst of [the] Breath-effect; in the sphere of attitude; in union with [the] Breath)."

Peter referred to this realm of spirit/Spirit as,
> "**the hidden person** (concealed humanity; cloaked personality) **of the heart, within the incorruptible and imperishable quality of the gentle** (tender; mild; calm; kind; meek) **and still** (at ease; restful; tranquil; quiet) **spirit** (or: attitude; disposition; or: Breath-effect), **which is** (or: continually exists being) **of great value and very costly in God's sight** (= God's view, or, perspective)" (1 Pet. 3:4).

It was symbolized by the holy place and the holy of holies in the tabernacle – which may pertain to the soul and the spirit of the inner, hidden person, while the outer court with its flesh sacrifices and washings symbolized the outer person, the body of flesh. Yet all of those three realms were set apart within the camp of Israel during their wilderness journeys for 40 years (a symbol of Israel's testing period). Since the Tabernacle was a type of heaven (the atmosphere in which God was dwelling among Israel during that period), review the decorations of its constructions, with the presence of cherubim in the vail and on the ark. We wonder if the realm of spirit (the holy of holies within us, His tabernacle/temple) was the "third heaven" of which Paul speaks, in 12:2, below.

This statement, "Be fully transformed...," is an impartation from Paul, and it becomes in us an incarnation of the "**giving to us the pledge and guarantee** (earnest deposit; security; first installment) **which is the Breath-effect** (or: of the Spirit; from the Attitude)" of vs. 5, above.

On offer are two alternate renderings of this announcement:

a) "You folks be completely exchanged with God;"
b) "Be conciliated to, and for, God!"
The "for God" may imply "being conciliated to and reconciled with" one another.

Paul used a strengthened form of *katallassō, apo-katallassō*, in Eph. 2:16. In that passage, he was speaking of two covenantal categories of humanity, in vs. 11: the "circumcision" (i.e., the Jews), and the "uncircumcision" (i.e., the Gentiles). Then in vs. 15 he spoke of these two groups,

> **"to the end that He may frame** (create; found and settle from a state of wildness and disorder) **The Two into One qualitatively New and Different** [*p46* & others: common] **Humanity centered within the midst of, and in union with, Himself, continuously making** (progressively creating) **Peace and Harmony** (a **joining**); **and then should fully transfer, FROM a certain state to another which is quite different, The Both – centered in, and within the midst of, One Body in God** (or: make completely other, while MOVING AWAY FROM what had existed, and fully reconcile The Both, in one Body, **by**, **to**, with and for **God**), **through the cross** (execution stake) **– while in the midst of Himself killing the enmity and discordant hatred** (or: killing-off the characteristics of enemies within it)." (Eph. 2:15b-16).

Take note of where I emphasized the force of *apo-* by using all upper case: "FROM," and "MOVING AWAY FROM." Paul is stressing how God moved humanity from divided categories into a single category of "One qualitatively New and Different (or: common) Humanity." He used this same, strengthened form of the verb in Col. 1:20-22,

> 20. **and THROUGH Him at once to transfer the all** (the whole; = all of existential creation), **AWAY FROM a certain state to the level of another which is quite different**
> > (or: to change all things, bringing movement away from being down; to reconcile all things; to change everything from estrangement and alienation to friendship and harmony and move all), **INTO Him – making** (constructing; forming; creating) **peace** (harmonious joining) **through the blood of His cross** (execution stake/pole): **through Him, whether the things upon the earth** (or: land) **or the things within the atmospheres and heavens!**
> 21. **And so you folks, being at one time people having been alienated away** (being estranged; being rendered as belonging to another; = having been put out of the family) **and enemies** (or: hated ones) **by the divided thoughts** (in the dualistic perceptions and things going through the mind in every direction) **within** (or: in the midst of; in union with; or: = in the performance of) **the miserable deeds** (gushes of wicked actions; laborious and painful works) –
> 22. **yet now He at once reconciled** (or: changed and transferred to a different state) **within the body of His flesh, through His death, to place you folks alongside, down before Him and in His sight: set-apart** (holy) **folks and flawless** (unblemished; blameless) **ones, even people not accused, with nothing laid to your charge** (or: unaccusable ones; unimpeachable ones; folks without reproach).

Dan Kaplan insightfully termed this work of Christ as the "*cross-over*," calling to mind Israel's "crossing over" the Red Sea (a picture of baptism into His death) from the bondage in Egypt into the wilderness experience, and then another "crossing over" of the Jordan River (a picture of resurrection), into the Promised Land (a figure that pointed to our present life in the kingdom of God). "Bringing [them/us] into another place or state of being" (vs. 18, above) involved the wilderness journey (for them: the death of the old generation; for us: the cruciform life). He also pointed us to the "crossing over" from the "old man" – through the One Man that died on the "cross" (vs. 14, above) – and being transferred into the "new man" in Christ. It is the "crossing-over" which is a transfer from the old covenant and old age into the new covenant and new age, or as Paul said in Col. 1:13,

> "**He who drags us out of danger** (or: rescued us) **forth from out of the midst of the authority of the Darkness** (from Darkness's jurisdiction and right; from existing out of gloomy shadows and obscure dimness; = the privilege of ignorance), **and changes [our] position** (or: transported [us], thus, giving [us] a change of standing, and transferred [us]) **into the midst of the kingdom and reign of the Son of His love**."

A different compound term, *ana-kata-stasis,* which Luke used in Acts 3:21, tells a similar story: Peter, speaking of Jesus:

> "**Whom indeed it continues necessary and binding for heaven to welcome, accept and embrace** (or: for [the] atmosphere to grant access, admit, receive and take to itself) **until times of a movement away from all things that have been firmly put down, set and established and until the periods of successive events which occur in passing moments, moving all mankind** away **from having been placed and positioned down as well as from the state or condition of all things that had been determined from an indefinite period of time** (or: from a [particular] age)..."

So where was humanity? Exiled from the Garden of God's intimate presence, being "dead in trespasses and sin" (Eph. 2:1; Rom. 5:12). And in Adam's story, Israel was selected to portray another act of God's Play, and present the picture of "having been placed down, set and established" by being positioned under the Law. What Peter announces, here in Acts 3, is the "movement away from" those flesh-focused situations, and INTO the "**seasons of cooling again, as well as fitting situations and fertile moments of refreshing could, should and would come from [the] face** (= personal presence) **of the Lord**" (Acts 3:19), i.e., INTO the NEW creation. Peter was speaking of the same thing that Paul stated, in vs. 17, above: "**the original things** (the beginning [situations]; the archaic and primitive [arrangements]) **passed by** (or: went to the side). **Consider! New things have come into existence.**"

We read of those "the original things," that pertained to the "uncircumcision," or, the "Gentiles," in Eph. 2:12, where they:

> "**were, and continued on being for that season** (or: in that appointed situation), **apart from Christ** ([the] Anointed One; = [the] Messiah)**: people having been alienated from the state of being a citizen** (or: estranged from citizenship in the commonwealth and society) **of, and which is, Israel and [being] strangers pertaining to the arrangements of** (or: foreigners from covenants and testamentary dispositions whose origin is) **The Promise and the assurance, continually having no expectation** (or: hope), **and [were] folks without God** (or: godless; atheists) **within the ordered System.**"

That describes the situation for the ethnic multitudes (the "nations") during the age of the old covenant and the Law of Moses. And then in the next verses, we read of the "new things" that pertain to them:

> 13. **But NOW, within, in union with and centered in Christ Jesus, you – the folks once being** (continuously existing) **far off** (or: at a distance) [i.e., the Gentiles; the "nations"] **– came to be** (were birthed; are generated; are suddenly become) **near, immersed within and in union with the blood of the Christ** (the Anointed One; = the Messiah).
> 14. **You see, He Himself is our Peace** (or: continuously exists being our JOINING) **– the One making** (forming; constructing; creating; producing) **The Both [to be] ONE, and within His flesh** (= physical being; or: = System-caused crucifixion) **is instantly destroying** (unbinding; unfastening; loosing; causing to collapse) **the middle wall of the fenced enclosure** (or: the partition or barrier wall – [i.e., the LAW])**: the enmity** (cause of hate, alienation, discord and hostility; characteristics of an enemy; -- [Israel's Law caused the division, and the hostility]),
> 15. **rendering useless** (nullifying; rendering down in accord with inactivity and unemployment) **the Law** (or: the custom; = the Torah) **of the implanted goals** (or: concerning impartations; from commandments; which was inward directives) **consisting in decrees** (or: prescribed ordinances)...

In Rom. 11:17 he described this NEW situation as the Gentiles being grafted into Israel's olive tree.

What this looks like is described as God's reign, which is His sovereign influence and activities in the world – which are:

> "**eschatological deliverance into fair and equitable dealing which brings justice and right relationship in the Way pointed out** (being turned in the right direction; rightwisedness; also = covenant inclusion and participation), **peace and harmony from the joining and joy** (or:

happiness; rejoicing) **within set-apart Breath-effect** (or: in union with and amidst a dedicated spirit and a sacred attitude; or: in [the] Holy Spirit)" (Rom. 14:17b).

Paul described an organic growth of God's reign that would first happen within the growth of the branches of the Vine (Jn. 15:1ff). Christ first sent out representatives:

> "**for the preparation** (mending; knitting together; adjusting; fitting; repairing; perfectly adjusting adaptation; equipping; completely furnishing) **of the set-apart folks unto a work** (or: into an action; into the midst of a deed or task) **of ATTENDING SERVICE and DISPENSING, [leading] unto** (or: into) **construction** (house-building) **of the body which is the Christ, [to go on] until we – the whole of mankind** (all people) **– can** (or: would) **come down to the goal** (or: attain; arrive at; meet accordingly; meet down face-to-face)**: into the state of oneness from, and which is, The Faithfulness** (or: the unity of, that belongs to and which characterizes that which is faith; or: the lack of division which has its source in trust, confidence and reliability, has the character of and is in reference to the loyalty and fidelity), **even which is the full, experiential and intimate knowledge** (or: and from recognition; and of discovery; as well as pertaining to insight) **which is** (or: of; from; in reference to) **the Son of God, [growing] into [the] purposed and destined adult man** (complete, finished, full-grown, perfect, goal-attained, mature manhood) **– into** (or: unto) **[the] measure of [the] stature** (full age; prime of life) **of the entire content which comprises the Anointed One**
>
>> (or: which is the result of the full number which is the Christ; of the effect of the fullness from the [Messiah]; from the effect of that which fills and completes that which refers to the Christ; of the result of the filling from, and which is, the Christ) – [cf 1 Cor. 13:10-11]
>
> **to the end that no longer** (or: no more) **would or should we exist being infants** (immature folks; not-yet-speaking ones)..." (Eph. 4:12-14a).

But now let us observe how Paul informs us that God inaugurated all this...

21. **for you see, He made** (or: formed) **the One not at any point knowing failure** (sin; error; mistake) **by intimate experience [to take the place of; to be] failure over us and our [situation]** (or: He constructed and produced a sin [offering], for our sake, the Person who was not having an experiential knowledge of missing the target or making a mistake), **to the end that we may be birthed God's just and rightwising act of eschatological deliverance** (or: would come to exist in righted, liberated relationships of equitable fairness; would become God's justice, the Way pointed out; could become participants in the new covenant from God: expressions of well-ordered living of the way it should be, which is God), **within Him and in union with Him.***

Paul now describes a part of what Jesus referred to as "**the Way** (or: Path), **the Truth** (the Reality) **and the Life**" (Jn. 14:6). In Phil. 2, he put it this way:

> 7. **but to the contrary, He empties Himself** (or: removed the contents of Himself; made Himself empty), **receiving** (or: taking; accepting) **a slave's form** (external shape; outward mold), **coming to be** (or: birthing Himself) **within an effect of humanity's** (mankind's; people's) **likeness.**
> 8. **And so, being found in an outward fashion, mode of circumstance, condition, form-appearance** (or: character, role, phase, configuration, manner) **as a human** (a person; a man), **He lowers Himself** (or: humbled Himself; made Himself low; degrades Himself; levels Himself off), **coming to be** (or: birthing Himself) **a submissive, obedient One** (one who gives the ear and listens) **as far as** (or: to the point of; until) **death – but death of a cross** (torture stake)!

Keep in mind that God "**made, formed, constructed and produced**" what follows as the direct object of this verb. I have offered two theological lines of thought in what God "made (etc.)" of "**the One not at any point knowing failure** (sin; error; mistake) **by intimate experience.**" By supplying two optional verbs, representing two pictures that suggest two possible understandings of what Paul is saying in this ambiguous statement, the first rendering tells us that God made, formed or constructed Christ either "**to

take the place of failure," or, "**to be** (personify?)" **failure** (sin, etc.)… **over us and our [situation]**. Now we can see one picture of this in the statement from Phil. 2 that we just quoted. This picture does not necessarily imply the idea of Christ being a sacrifice for us, for in this first reading we would have to insert the idea of sacrifice into the text. This, together with the added light from Phil. 2, simply says that He entered into solidarity with the human predicament. Humanity was personifying and living out the entire complex of what the term "**failure** (error; sin; mistake)" actually means. The first Adam missed the mark, as is easily seen. That mistake brought death (the human predicament) as Paul explains in Rom. 5:12. This, of course, was not speaking of physical death, as we can see from Paul's instruction in Rom. 7:9-10.

This line of thought points to the very Incarnation of the Son of God as the Seed of what would come about that is described in vss. 16-19, above. He came into our situation in order to lead us (Rom. 8:14) out of slavery to death and into our inheritance of the Spirit. Jn. 10:10 further explains the purpose of the Incarnation and of the coming of the Messiah: "**I, Myself, come so that they can progressively possess** (would continuously have; could habitually hold) **Life, and may continue possessing [it] in superabundance**." Mark 2:10 informs us of Jesus saying that,

> "**the Son of Man** (or: mankind's adult son; or: the Son who is human; or: = a human being) **continuously holds authority** (or: from out of his being possesses [the] right) **to repeatedly send away** (to habitually release and dismiss; to constantly forgive) **mistakes** (failures to hit the target; errors; sins) **upon the earth**."

This was before His death on the cross. The very gift of the Spirit (the down-payment of the purchase, stated above) accomplishes humanity's full transformation. In light of this, we might view the death of Jesus as the rejection of Him by both religion and empire. Is this not what His followers have experienced, down through the centuries? So in this first line of thinking, He (God) entered into our situation in order to lead us out from the slavery to corruption and into the freedom of the children of God (Rom. 8:21).

On offer in the parenthetical rendering is the second theological thought: that of Christ as a sacrifice. You will note that, with the more common rendering of what I first give as "failure," we see that God "constructed and produced a **sin** [offering], for our sake…" I have followed the *Concordant Literal NT*, by supplying (here in brackets) the word "offering." Now the rational and basis for this addition is that the OT reference to a "sin offering" was sometimes indicated by simply using the word "sin; the missing of the target; the failure." Due to this precedence, I have also offered this potential understanding of Paul's meaning here. We find a similar picture in the vision of Christ as "**a little Lamb standing, as one having been slaughtered**" (Rev. 5:7). Also, in reference to Jesus, we read of John the Immerser saying, in Jn. 1:29,

> "**Look!** (Pay attention, see and perceive)! **God's Lamb** (or: the Lamb from God; the Lamb having the character and qualities of God; or, in apposition: the Lamb which is God), **the One continuously lifting up and progressively carrying away the Sin of the world, and removing the sin which belongs to and is a part of the System**
>> (or: habitually picking up and taking away the failure and error brought on by system and in the cosmos; progressively removing the falling short and the missing of the goal from the world of culture, religion, economy, government, society, and from the aggregate of humanity)!"

Now this would have been a reference to the Jewish Festival, during the Feast of Tabernacles, which was called the Day of Atonement. That Day was an annual day for cleansing the altar and tabernacle furniture, and for ritually removing all the sin of all of Israel that had been committed in the prior year. Part of this day was the scapegoat ritually taking those sins (that were symbolically placed upon its head) and carrying all the Sin of Israel outside of the camp of Israel. We read about how Christ fulfilled this type in Heb. 9, and then how the cleansing of the tabernacle (which was done by sprinkling the blood of the sacrifice on the furniture) was fulfilled by Christ's blood (a figure of His Life) being sprinkled on our hearts

(Heb. 10:22). So there is some merit to this second reading of Paul here in 5:21. We also have the instruction from Heb. 7:26, 27b,

> "**For you see, a Chief Priest such as this One was, and continues to be, fitting** (appropriate; proper) **for us: loyal and dedicated, benign** (without bad quality; harmless; without bad form; not ugly), **unstained** (undefiled), **having been parted** (severed; separated) **away from those failing to hit the target** (those deviating or making errors; the sinners), **even being birthed** (coming into existence) **higher than the atmospheres and heavens... For this He performed just once and once for all [times and people], offering up Himself** [other MSS: bringing Himself toward {God, or, us} (or: **presenting Himself**); *cf* 9:25-28]."

I will leave it to our readers to hear from the Lord on which thought Paul had in mind – and as with numerous cases (we suggest), probably both. Perhaps we can gain insight by reading from Isa. 53, in the LXX:

> 8. Within the midst of the low status and the experience of being abased and humiliated, His justice and equity (or: the opportunity for a fair trial; or: the chance or ability to divide, separate and make decisions; or: the judging) was lifted up and taken away. So who will continue fully taking over the lead of His generation (or: will proceed conducting a thorough narration to recount His generation), because His life is now being taken up, away from the earth (or: taken away from the Land)? From (= on account of) the acts of lawlessness of my (or: My [?]) people, He was led into (or: unto; to) death.
>
> 9. And so I will continue giving and entrusting (or: proceed appointing, assigning or surrendering) the useless, unprofitable and unsound people (the bad, malicious, unserviceable folks) in the place of and corresponding to (or: instead of; in exchange for) His burial, and the rich folks in place of and corresponding to (or: instead of; in exchange for) His death, because He committed and produced no lawlessness (neither practiced nor built that which is without a law) – nor yet [was there] bait, fraud, guile, treachery or deceit within His mouth.
>
> 10. So [the] Lord (= Yahweh), from desire, continued intending and purposing to cleanse and purify Him from the blow (the beating; the calamity; the plague): If you would give, around and concerning [those] failures (deviations; sins; etc.), the soul (consciousness; inner being) of you folks will see and perceive a long-lived Seed (or: offspring).
>
> 11. And yet with desire [the] Lord kept on purposing to take away from the trouble (or: hard, distressful labor; bodily exertion) of His soul (the consciousness which is Him) and then to point out and demonstrate Light in and by Him, and thus to shape and mold understanding.
>
> And so He himself will continue taking and bearing-up (or: keep on bringing-back [from them] so as to carry-up) their failures (deviations; errors; mistakes; sins) [in order] to bring eschatological deliverance and turn folks in the right direction (or: to institute the Way pointed out; to demonstrate fairness and equity; to establish righted relationships) in and by [the] Just One ([the] Fair Person; [the] One who is pointed in the right direction) – the One continuously slaving well for and among [the] Many (or: within many people; by many [groups]).
>
> 12. Because of this, He himself will continue inheriting [the] Many and will keep on causing [the] Many to inherit, and thus will progressively divide the spoils of the strong folks, because His soul was transmitted into (or: delivered unto and committed to; surrendered and entrusted into the midst of) death and He was considered and viewed (or: counted and reckoned as being) among the lawless folks. So He, Himself, took up and carried the failures (deviations; errors sins; etc.) of [the] Many, and through these acts of lawlessness (or: because of the constructs that were without a law, and the additions that had no law) He was transmitted, entrusted, committed, delivered, surrendered, handed over and given to [our] side.

With either reading, we see that what God had in mind is: "**to the end that we may be birthed God's just and rightwising act of eschatological deliverance**." The Christ was produced by God for this purpose. But in producing Christ, He also produced us, IN Him. We are God's great opus, in Christ. But we should also take note of what Paul did NOT give as the end in view, from this great Production: he did not tell us that God's purpose in this was to "forgive our sins," or, "to take us to heaven." Paul gave us the purpose, said differently, in 3:18, above: so that we would reflect His glory and His image (through being transformed!).

We will, as usual, point to the other optional, expanded renderings:
> a) come to exist in righted and liberated relationships of equitable fairness;

This presents us as existing in a transformed existence – from out of death, into the Life of Christ.
> b) would become God's justice, the Way pointed out;

This presents us as representative of God's character (He is just and merciful; His removal of human guilt, and the transformation of humanity, are the right things to do), an embodiment of His justice (reconciliation, on His part, and His changing of humanity to be His friends), and also, a picture of Christ, the Way.
> c) could become participants in the new covenant from God: expressions of well-ordered living of the way it should be, which is God.

This third option gives the concept of *dikaiosunē* in its common, cultural use: well-ordered living, in the way it should be. The last prepositional phrase is rendered here in apposition: this new existence in well-ordered living "is God" living in US.

And now, which is not surprising, Paul tells us that this new, transformed existence is "**within Him and in union with Him**." It is the result of, "**the Word** (the *Logos*; the Idea; the Reason; the message; the pattern-forming information) **of the corresponding transformation to otherness** (or: the full alteration; the change from enmity to friendship; the conciliation)." We see in the book of Acts how the *Logos* of God increased (Acts 6:7; 12:24; 16:5; 19:20), and now in vs. 19, above, we read that this same *Logos* was given to His representatives: God is doing what He told humans to do; He is being fruitful and is multiplying and is filling the earth with Himself – as an ever-increasing Family of God (Acts 17:28, 29).

Notice how Paul says virtually the same the about God's Act in three different ways, as I have rendered thus:
> 1) "**giving to us the attending service of, and the dispensing from, the complete transformation [for folks] to be other [than before]** (etc.)" (vs. 18b, above);
> 2) "**placing within us the Word** (the *Logos*; the Idea; the Reason; the message; the pattern-forming information) **of the corresponding transformation to otherness** (or: the full alteration; the change from enmity to friendship; the conciliation)" (vs. 19b, above);
> 3) "**that we may be birthed God's just and rightwising act of eschatological deliverance** (or: would come to exist in righted and liberated relationships of equity, fairness and justice in the Way pointed out, and be participants in the new covenant from God...)" (vs. 21, here).

Let us compare this, with Gal. 3:13-14,
> "**Christ bought us [back] out** (or: redeems and reclaims us out [of slavery] and liberates us) **from the midst of the curse** (or: adversarial prayer; imprecation) **of and from the Law, while becoming** (or: birthing Himself to be) **a curse** (or: an accursed One; an [embodied] adversarial prayer) **for our sakes** (or: over our [situation]) – **for it has been and now stands written:**
>> '**A curse** (an adversarial prayer) **[is settled] upon all** (or: [is] added to everyone) **continuing hanging upon a tree** (or: wood; a stake or pole)' [Deut. 21:23, omitting the phrase "by God," after the word "curse"] –
> **to the end that the Good Word** (the Blessing; the Word of wellness and goodness) **pertaining to Abraham** (belonging to and possessed by Abraham; whose intermediary source is Abraham) **could within Jesus Christ suddenly birth Itself** (or: may from Itself, within Anointed Jesus, at once come into being [and be dispersed]) **into the multitudes** (the nations; the ethnic groups;

the Gentiles), **so that we** [note: "we" = the new "one" mankind; *cf* Eph. 2:11-16] **could receive the Spirit's promise through the Faithfulness [of Christ]**

> (or: to the end that we [all] may take in hand the Promise from the Breath-effect, through faith and trust; or: in order that we [Jew and Gentile] can lay hold of and receive the Promise – which is the Spirit – through that loyalty; [*cf* Isa. 44:3]).

In 1 Cor. 15:3, Paul wrote,

> "**For I handed on** (or: give over as tradition; transmit and commit) **to you folks, among [the] first** (or: primary) **things, that which I also accepted and embraced: that Christ died over [the situation and circumstances of] our failures** (on behalf of our mistakes, deviations and sins) – **corresponding to the Scriptures**."

This last phrase, "corresponding to the Scriptures," points to Israel's story in relation to the New Testament images in which Christ's death is variously portrayed, such as "made [to be] sin," found here in vs. 21, above. Concerning the OT stories, they can be read as consecutively interpreting one another. For example, Adam and Eve's story is a preview of Israel's story, and Israel fleshes-out the story of Adam and Eve (which is a figure of the human predicament). In between those is the story of Abraham and Sarah who were chosen as vehicles within which to plant a Seed that would in time solve humanity's predicament. Mankind's story began in a garden, and its journey ends in a garden city (Rev. 22). From Adam to Christ, Israel was frequently figured as a garden, a fruitful field or an orchard. They carried God's plans in the design and symbols of the Tabernacle.

Consider the picture given in Joshua 3 and the story of Israel leaving the desert and entering into "the promised Land." There, the priests were instructed to take the Ark of the Covenant and be the first ones to step into the Jordan River, while carrying the ark. Once their feet were dipped into the brim of the water, the river stopped flowing and the people passed over into the Land. Now recall what is on the top of the Ark: the cherubim. And what do we read was placed at the entrance of the Garden of Eden, in Gen. 3:24? Cherubim. So the priests were living out a parable of humanity returning into paradise, a bountiful Land flowing with milk and honey, and the Presence of God. Recall how Jesus used the story from Nu. 21:9, the serpent on the pole, to describe His upcoming death (Jn. 3:14), and how in another place He said that His being "lifted up" (on the cross; Jn. 12:32) would drag all humanity to Himself.

In Phil. 3:9, we observe that Paul's constant, expressed desire was always to "**be found within Him** (or: in union with Him; centered in Him)." In this same verse, he proclaims that this condition comes,

> "**through means of Christ's faithfulness** (or: the trust-conviction which is Christ; the faith of and from [the Messiah]): **the rightwising, eschatological deliverance into the new covenant fairness and equity of righted relationships within the Way pointed out [which is] forth from out of the midst of God as a source** (or: the just Act from the midst of God) **[and based] upon that Faithfulness** (or: [Christ's/God's] loyal allegiance; or: the Trust and confident faith)."

This "rightwising" is what is often translated "righteousness," and calls to mind Jer. 23:6b, "His Name by which one shall call Him: Yahweh, our Righteousness" (CVOT, the Heb. text; LXX reads differently). Rom. 1:17a instructs us,

> "**for by Him God's justice** (solidarity in fair conduct; equity; righteousness; [covenantal] qualities of the Way pointed out; way of righting what is wrong; right relationship [with us]; or: a means of turning us in the right direction by an eschatological deliverance, which is God,) **is continuously and progressively being unveiled** (revealed; disclosed), **from out of faithfulness** (or: forth from the midst of faith, trust, conviction and loyalty), **[reciprocally proceeding] into faith, trust, conviction and loyalty**."

Paul gives us another view of this passage of vss. 14-21, above, and this is found in Rom. 8:

> 3. **You see, [because of] the powerlessness and inability of the Law** (from the written code; = associated with Torah) – **within which it kept on making [folks] weak and feeble** ([note: the active voice]; but as an intransitive: in which [incapability] it was constantly falling sick and

continued being without strength) **through the flesh** (= the alienated self that is oriented toward the System; or: = Torah culture and cultus, with boundary-marker observances) **– in sending His own Son** (or: by sending the Son, Who is Himself) **within a result of a likeness of flesh that is connected with sin** (or: in an effect of being made similar to sin's flesh; = in union with a result from being made like the alienated existence that came from failure), **and concerning sin**

> (or: encircling failure and error; to address a missed target; surrounding deviation; [note: or, as a technical term for the sin offering: = to be the sin-offering; see: Lev. 4:32; 5:6-9; 2 Chron. 29:24; Ps. 40:6; Ezk. 42:13, LXX]), **God gives a commensurate decision from a corresponding negative evaluation which falls in line with and follows the pattern which divides down** (or: condemned; gives a down-oriented verdict; passed down a sentence on and gave judgment against) **the Sin within the flesh [system]**

> > (or: the failure, the error, the miss of the target and the deviation [which is] in union with the human condition; or: = the mistake of the estranged, System-dominated self),

4. to the end that the effect of the just Deed of deliverance in which wrong was set right, resulting from being liberated and turned in the right direction within the Way pointed out, which is the principle, (or: so that the effect of the fair relationships which come from [His] law and custom; or: in order that the result of the equity and rightness of the Law) **can** (would; could; may) **be fulfilled and become full within us – in those habitually walking about** (or: = for the folks ordering their behavior/living their lives) **not in accord with flesh** (or: = not corresponding to the human condition; or: = on the level of Torah-keeping boundary-markers), **but rather in accord with spirit** (or: down from [the] Spirit; corresponding to [His] Attitude; on the level of and in the sphere of Breath-effect). [cf 2 Cor. 3:3]

Let us keep in view that all of which we have been discussing happened, or happens, "**within Him and in union with Him**." What He did in vs. 21a was done to create the result that is described in vs. 21b. If we render *dikaiosunē* as "justice," then we see that "we have BECOME the justice of God" – our being reconciled and changed, to be different than we were, is the embodiment of God's justice!

Chapter 6

1. Now we, habitually (or: continuously) **working together [with Him], are constantly calling you folks alongside to aid, comfort, direct and urge/encourage you not to accept/receive God's grace into a void** (or: an empty or vain [situation; way of life]; or: = for no purpose),

The dependent participial clause modifying the subject "**we**," of the main clause, echoes what Paul said in 1 Cor. 3:9, "**we are God's fellow-workers**," and their "**calling folks alongside to aid (etc.),**" here in vs. 1, repeats what he described as the work of their being "**elders of God, performing as ambassadors from God**" (5:20, above).

Paul goes on to explain that "**the attending service and the dispensing**" given to them (5:18, above) – in order to bring "**the complete transformation**" to people (5:18, above) – by saying again that this comes through "**constantly calling [them] alongside to aid, comfort, direct and encourage [them] to accept [and] receive God's grace.**" But... they should "**NOT accept or receive [it] into a void**" – or into an **EMPTY** or vain situation or way of life. They are called into Adam's purpose, Abraham's promise, Israel's covenant, and into the narrative "in all the Scriptures" from which the risen Jesus revealed, to the disciples in Lu. 24:27, that which was God's vocation for Him.

But what, specifically, might Paul be referring to with this word "**void, empty, vain**"? In Col. 2:8 he spoke of.

> "**the philosophy and EMPTY seduction** (or: a deceitful trick having no content) **being handed down from and being in line with the tradition of the people** (or: corresponding to the thing handed along from humans), **down from** (or: in line with and corresponding to) **the elementary**

principles (or: rudimentary teachings and fundamental assumptions) **of the organized System** (the world of culture, religion, government, secular society or economy)."

Corresponding to this is Eph. 5:6, "**Let no one keep on deceiving** (or: seducing) **you folks by EMPTY words** (or: messages; reasons; thoughts; ideas)." These statements remind us of what Jesus said to the scribes and Pharisees, in Mat. 15:6b,

> "**thus you people at once invalidate** (make **VOID** of authority; cancel and make of no effect) **God's idea, word and message through your tradition!**"

Then He goes on, in vss. 8-9, to quote Isaiah to them:

> "'**This people habitually honor Me with [their] lips, yet it constantly holds their heart far away from Me** (or: yet their heart continuously holds [itself] off, distant from Me).
> '**So they habitually revere Me and commit acts of devotion to Me in VAIN** (to no profit; fruitlessly), **repeatedly giving instruction concerning teachings [that are] directions coming from mankind** (or: constantly teaching for "[the] teachings" [the] results of inner goals and commands of humans {or: man-made rules})."'" [Isa. 29:13]

Paul used this same word "**void, empty, vain**" in 1 Cor. 15:10,

> "**Yet in** (or: by; for; with) **God's grace, and joyous favor which is God, I am what I am, and His [placed]-into-me grace** (or: [birthed]-into-me joyous favor) **was not birthed to be EMPTY**."

Paul's idea, here in vs. 1b, may be parallel to his thoughts in 2 Tim. 3:

> 4. **pre-committers** (or: ones who give-over in advance, or who abandon), **rash** (reckless), **folks having been inflated with the fumes of conceit** (or: ones being beclouded in smoke), **pleasure-lovers** (ones fond of self-gratification) **rather than friends of God** (ones fond of God),
> 5. **continuously holding** (having) **a form of reverence** (virtue and pious awe) **yet being folks having refused, contradicted and now denying** (saying, "No," to) **its power and ability!**...

We find another witness in Acts 4:25, concerning the ethnic multitudes,

> "**To what end or purpose did** (or: do) **the ethnic multitudes** (or: nations) **snort, neigh and stomp around [as a high-spirited horse]** (or: behave arrogantly or with insolent and haughty airs) **and peoples show care for and take interest in EMPTY things** (or: concern themselves over meaningless [activities]; or: mumble **empty** [phrases]; or: practice useless [rituals]; or: meditate on, give careful thought and attention to and then devise futile [schemes] or hollow [projects])**?**" [Ps. 2:1]

In this situation, the followers of Jesus were requesting God to give them boldness to speak the *Logos* despite the persecution by the Judean leadership in Jerusalem.

Another possible allusion of the term "void" may be the emptiness of the old covenant and the Law of fleshly ordinances. The Anointing had moved on, the new creation had arrived and the "old things" had passed on by (5:17, above). The tomb where Israel and that past arrangement had been buried (in Christ's death and burial) was now "empty." Consider, also, the admonition in Heb. 12:15

> "**overseeing** (looking diligently and carefully watching upon and seeing to it) **[that] no one be lacking** (be falling short; be living behind or in the rear; = misses out), **[by wandering] away from God's grace and joyous favor; [that] not any "root of bitterness"** [Deut. 29:18], **progressively sprouting upward, would be crowding in to cause disturbance like the spirit of a mob, and then, through means of it, many folks may be stained** (polluted; defiled; = the whole community could be contaminated)."

Dan Kaplan has pointed us to Jesus' words on the cross,

> "**O Father, let it flow away in them** (or: send it away for them; forgive them), **for they have not seen, so they do not know or perceive, what they are now doing**" (Lu. 23:34).

Dan went on to say, "they were empty and void in their minds: they did not know what they were doing." This calls to mind what Paul said in 3:15, above, "**Still furthermore, until today, whenever Moses should be habitually read** [e.g., in the synagogue], **a head-covering** (veil) **continues lying upon their heart**."

2. for He continues saying,

> **"At an acceptable season** (or: In an appropriate situation; For an agreeable *kairos*) **I fully hear and respond in regard to you, and within a day of deliverance** (on a day of health, restoration and salvation), **at your cry for help, I run to give aid to you** (I run with help for you)." [Isa. 49:8]

Consider (Look)! **[It is] now** (at this moment) **an especially acceptable season** (a fitting situation well-directed toward acceptance; a fertile moment of ease and face-to-face reception)!

Consider (Look)! **[It is] now** (at this moment) **a day of deliverance** (of health, rescue, safety, salvation and restoration to the wholeness of the original state and condition)!

Yes, God fully heard and responded in accord to His timetable. The "run with help for [us], and **to give aid to** [us]" was God functioning as the Paraclete. Jesus was the first Paraclete, and the Holy Spirit was the next Paraclete, as Jesus said in Jn. 14:16-17a,

> "**I Myself will continue asking** (making a request of) **the Father, and He will proceed to be giving another Helper** (One called alongside to give assistance, relief, comfort and encouragement; Paraclete), **of like kind, to you folks – to the end that He** (or: It) **can continue being** [other MSS: would be constantly remaining and dwelling] **with you folks on into the midst of the Age – the Spirit of the Truth** (or: the spirit and breath of reality; the Breath-effect and Attitude which is this Reality)..." *Cf* Jn. 14:17-28; Lu. 24:49; Acts 1:8; 2:4

Paul's next two, parallel statements are both revealing and decisive: "**[It is] now** (at this moment)…" That is, all that he has been speaking of pertained to his day, in the 1st century AD. He was not, nor had he been, speaking about things in the distant future. They all existed in Paul's present day, and as Jesus said in Jn. 14, above, They would be present with THEM, "**on into the midst of the Age**" in which we are still now living.

So we see that he emphasized the "NOW" aspect of all this, but what did he mean by it being "**an especially acceptable season**"? The Greek phrase picks up two words from the quote of Isa. 49:8, "**acceptable season**," *kairos* and *dektos* (in their dative forms, in the quote). Paul is saying that he was living in the "season" (*kairos*) of which Isaiah spoke. But with the second term, in his usual emphatic style, he adds a preposition and an adjective to the word *dektos* (acceptable), to make it *eu-pros-dektos*. So he is not just saying "this is a good time" for God to act, but it is an "especially acceptable season; a fitting situation well-directed toward acceptance; a fertile moment of ease and face-to-face reception!" It is the season of God's grace and eschatological deliverance through the advent of the Messiah and the giving of the Holy Spirit which is the Father's promise! The same adjective, *dektos*, is found in Lu. 4:19,

> "**to publicly and loudly proclaim [the] Lord's** [= Yahweh's] **year which is characterized by being welcomed, favorably received, approved and acceptable...!**" [Isa. 61:1-2a; 58:6; note: some see this as a reference to the 'year of Jubilee,' Lev. 25:10]

Paul also used this word in Phil. 4:18b, in reference to attending service:

> "**I have been filled full, receiving from beside Epaphroditus the things from your side: an odor of a sweet fragrance** (a fragrant aroma), **an acceptable sacrifice, well-pleasing to God** (or: with God; for God; in God)."

But a most telling use of the adjective is by Peter, in Acts 10:35,

> "**within every nation and ethnic group the person habitually reverencing and fearing Him, as well as repeatedly doing works and performing acts of fairness, equity, justice, deliverance, or rightwised relationships which accord with the way pointed out** (= covenant principles) **is and continues being welcome and acceptable to Him.**"

This was the Day of the Gentiles (ethnic multitudes) being accepted into the new covenant, as Peter witnessed in the house of Cornelius, and as Paul wrote of in Rom. 11:17ff.

In the parallel statement, he uses the term *sōtērias*: "**of deliverance** (of health, rescue, safety, salvation and restoration to the wholeness of the original state and condition)," and now says that this DAY has arrived – they were living in the very Day of which Isaiah prophesied. We want to also point out that their Day was "A Day." It was not limited to their time or their situation. It was the inaugural "season" of God's kingdom and reign being present among humans. The Jerusalem which is above (Gal. 4:26) had descended to bring the River of Life to humanity (Rev. 21:10; 22:1). Paul spoke of this Day in Eph. 4:30,

"**don't you folks have the habit of grieving** (distressing; giving sorrow or pain to; or: = troubling) **God's set-apart Spirit** (or: the Holy Breath-effect which is God), **within Whom** (or: in union with Which) **you folks were** (or: are) **sealed** (at one point stamped with a seal; suddenly marked; imprinted; = personally authorized) **into the midst of a Day associated with and arising from the liberation of a releasing-away from slavery or imprisonment** (or: a Day which is emancipation pertaining to a dismissal and a loosing-away into a freeing from bondage)."

There, Paul was invoking the story of Israel's Exodus from Egypt. And in 1 Thes. 5:5 he affirmed:

"**you all are** (or: exist being) **sons of** (from; associated with and having the qualities of; or: which are) **Light and sons of** (from; associated with and having qualities of; or: which are [the]) **Day!**'

Then he went on, in 1 Thes. 5:8, to admonish them:

"**We, on the other hand, being of Day** (belonging to and having characteristics of [the] Day; having [the] Day as our source), **can and should continuously be sober** (clear-headed), **putting on** (or: clothing ourselves with; enveloping ourselves in; entering within) **a breastplate** (or: thorax) **of faith and love** (or: which is trust and acceptance urging toward union; from fidelity and a giving of self) **and, as a helmet, an expectation** (or: expectant hope) **from deliverance** (which is health and wholeness; of rescue and being kept safe; pertaining to salvation)."

This verse presents "realized," or "fulfilled," eschatology." "**Now** (at this moment) **an especially acceptable season**… **now** (at this moment) **a day of deliverance**."

3. [We are] normally giving no one a cause for striking [a foot] against something so as to stumble (or: a reason or occasion for making a cutting attack toward someone) **– not in even one thing – so that the attending service and dispensing of provision would not at any point be found flawed so as to be discredited or censured,**

Having in vs. 2 inserted the quote from Isaiah, with the attending explanation as to how the present situation was anything but "**a void**" (vs. 1), Paul now continues with the subject of calling-urging, begun in the first part of vs. 1, by expanding upon what they are "**normally giving**." This echoes a refrain from 1 Cor. 9:12b: "**so that we should not GIVE any hindrance to the progress of Christ's good news**."

In good rhetorical form, Paul keeps his audience awake and focused by returning to speaking about how he and his friends normally present their "**attending service and dispensing of provision**." They are careful not to cause people to stumble, or to give them "a reason or occasion for making a cutting attack toward someone." He does not want Christ's followers to think of others as enemies – "**not in even one thing**." He and his friends are attentive that their ministry to others "**would not at any point be found flawed so as to be discredited or censured**." And so…

4. but to the contrary, in the midst of every [situation] and in every [way], [we are] continuously placing and standing ourselves together, and recommending ourselves, as God's attending servants who dispense provisions: within the midst of much patient endurance and steadfast remaining under [the situation] for support; in compressed squeezings, pressures, afflictions and tribulations; within the midst of constraining necessities and compulsions; within tight spots that cramp, restrict and hem us in;

From vs. 4b on through vs. 10, Paul presents a series of paradoxes in regard to what one might expect in regard to "**attending servants**" of, and from **God**. But when we read what may be considered as being negative circumstances, look back to Christ's crucifixion, and what He said that His followers would encounter (e.g., Mat. 10:24-25a; Jn. 16:2).

369

Referencing the work described in vs. 1, above, he now terms their functions as being "**God's attending servants who dispense provisions**," where in 1 Cor. 4:1 he described their functions as being "**God's subordinates** (God's deputies; those under God's orders; God's under-rowers) **and house-managers** (or: administrators) **of God's secrets**." Connecting the dots of these descriptions of their "ministries" gives us a more comprehensive picture of all that the sent-forth representatives did for the called-out, covenant communities. Add to these what he said in 1 Cor. 3:10,

> "**Corresponding to, in accord with and to the level of, God's grace and favor [which are] being given to** (or: by) **me, as [being] a skillful master-carpenter** (wise chief-builder; clever head-artisan; learned, competent leading-stonemason; like a wise architect, engineer, foreman or director of works) **I lay** [other MSS: have laid] **a foundation** (or: laid a foundation [Stone]), **yet another is progressively building a house upon [it]**."

For the next ten verses Paul gives detailed descriptions of how he and his friends have behaved in the vocations given to them by the Lord. Remember, they all lived in honor/shame-based societies. Personal decorum was of great importance. He begins by telling them that they do not have ulterior motives, but are "**continuously placing and standing ourselves together, and recommending [themselves] as God's attending servants who dispense provisions**." They do this everywhere they go, and under all circumstances. Next he describes what this should look like:

> "**within the midst of much patient endurance and steadfast remaining under [the situation] for support;**
> **in compressed squeezings, pressures, afflictions and tribulations;**
> **within the midst of constraining necessities and compulsions;**
> **within tight spots that cramp, restrict and hem us in**."

This does not sound like a pleasant vocation, does it? It is exactly what Jesus told his followers in Mat. 16:24-25,

> "**If anyone continues intending** (purposing; willing; wanting) **to come on behind Me, let him at once completely say, 'No,' to, deny and disown himself, and then in one move lift up his execution stake** (pole for suspending a corpse; cross), **and after that proceed to be by habit continuously following after Me! You see, whoever may intend** (or: should purpose; might set his will; happens to want) **to keep his soul-life safe** (to rescue himself; to preserve the interior life that he is living) **will continue loosing-it-away and destroying it. Yet whoever can loose-away and even destroy his soul-life** (the interior self) **on My account, he will continue finding it!**"

Paul and his associates were REPRESENTATIVES of Christ; their lives were to look like Him, and their message was to announce what the Father was doing. So here, Kaplan reminds us of what Paul wrote in Rom. 8:28,

> "**Now [look], we have seen, and thus know and are aware, that to those habitually or progressively loving and giving themselves to God – to the folks being called and invited according to [the] purpose – He is constantly working all things together into good and is progressively working all humanity together into that which is advantageous, worthy of admiration, noble and of excellent qualities**."

This is how God's reign appears "To US," because this is what we have seen, and thus know of, and about, God. What Paul describes Him doing, in the second half of Rom. 8:28, gives us a summation of God's ongoing work. What a beautiful picture and purpose these words describe!

5. in [the receiving of] blows or beatings [as with a rod] or lashings; within prisons (or: times of being in custody); **in the midst of unsettled situations** (conditions of disorder; turbulences; political instabilities; riots); **within toilsome, vexing and exhausting labors; in sleepless nights** (or: vigils); **within times without food** (or: fasts; times of hunger). *Cf* Acts 13:30; 14:5, 19; 16:22-23; 17:5; 18:12; 19:23

So… Do you "feel called to the ministry"? Paul is not bragging, but is letting those in Corinth know what at least he, himself, had gone through in order to give them "attending service and spiritual provision." Few of us normally go through these extremes, although some have and some presently are.

Let us hear from one of Paul's fellow-slaves who gives a beautiful picture of our calling, in 2 Pet. 1, as we contemplate the hard times that we may be experiencing:

1. **Simon Peter, a slave and sent-off representative of Jesus Christ, to** (or: for; with; among) **the folks obtaining by lot an equally valuable** (precious; honorable) **faith, conviction, trust and loyalty, along with us, within the midst of an eschatological deliverance, in union with fair and equitable treatment in rightwised relationships in the Way pointed out, and centered in covenant inclusion-and-membership, which come from and characterize our God and Savior** (Deliverer; Rescuer; Source of health and wholeness), **Jesus Christ:**

2. **May grace and peace** (or: favor from **the Joining**) **be multiplied to you folks** (or: by you; in you; for you) **within full** (or: accurate; complete; added) **intimate and experiential knowledge and insight of God, even Jesus, our Lord** (or: from God as well as from Jesus, Who is our Master; or: of God, and of our Owner, Jesus),

3. **just as all those things [leading] toward life and reverence [are] being now available for us from having been freely given to us from His divine power and ability through the full** (accurate; complete; added) **intimate and experiential knowledge of the One CALLING us to His own** (or: by His own; for His own; in His own) **glory and excellence in nobleness**.

4. **[It is] through means of which things – the precious** (valuable; honorable) **and greatest effects of the promises – [that] He has freely given to us, to the end that through these [gifts], you folks would come to be people of common-being from a divine essence and nature** (or: folks having a partnered share that is based upon a common existence from a divine born-instinct and native condition; or: fellow participants of a germination which is divine), **while fleeing from the corruption** (ruin; decay) **within the domination System** (or: that is united with the secular realm; or: centered in the ordered world of society, religion, culture, economy and government; or: in the center of the aggregate of mankind), **[which is] in the midst of passionate cravings** (rushing emotions; lusts; over-desires).

Remember, it was for the joy that had been set before Christ that He endured His cross (Heb. 12:2). Peter has described the joy that is set before us, despite the cruciform life that we are called to live – if we expect to function as a representative of Christ. As to the "**labors**" that Paul mentions, cf Acts 18:3; 1 Cor. 4:12; 1 Thes. 2:9 and 2 Thes. 3:8. He spoke of "**sleepless nights** (vigils)" in 11:27, below, and in 2 Thes. 3:8. As to the "**times without food** (or: fasts; times of hunger)," this was his way of life.

Verses 4 and 5 have described the hard times, but vs. 6 begins setting forth the positive aspects of being "**God's attending servants who dispense provisions**" (vs. 4)…

6. **[We have served and dispensed] with pureness** (or: centered in [a life of] purity); **in personally experienced knowledge; with forbearing patience** (in taking a long time before becoming emotional or rushing with passion); **with useful kindness; in a set-apart** (holy) **spirit** (or: within the midst of [the] Holy Spirit; within a hallowed breath-effect; in a set-apart attitude); **centered in, and with, uncritical love** (or: acceptance that is free from prejudice and from a separating for evaluation; love that is not based on making distinctions, fault-finding or judging)

Now he explains how God's sent-forth folks should live and behave, and this is a beautiful picture. These are high qualifications, but they are the Beauty of the Lord, the "beauty (or: adornment) of holiness" (Ps. 96:9). We must remember that we who serve Christ represent His kingdom and reign: we are called to bear His image and reflect Him to the world (3:18, above). We are called to have a "**set-apart** (holy) **spirit**." That means that we are not supposed to have the spirit of the world (of our religion or culture; of our culture's economic mindset or the idea of getting ahead of others, or of domination). Serving with "**useful kindness**" is such a beautiful picture. This noun "useful kindness" is part of the word family that has the root idea of "making use" of something with a view to a "need." So this is not just a "kind smile," or "a kind word" – although those, of course, have a positive impact on the recipient – but rather it is a kindness that provides something useful to the person in need (food; drink; clothing; care; etc.).

It will be to our advantage to consider what Paul means by being "**centered in, and with, uncritical love**." The Greek adjective used here, to characterize a kind of love, is *an-upokritos*. I have followed the research, conclusion and rendering (**uncritical love**) of Dr. Ann Nyland (*The Source New Testament*, Smith and Stirling Pub., 2007, pp 26, 341) on this word, which she maintains is normally mistranslated as "sincere" or "genuine." This is due to the common mistranslation of *hupokritēs* as virtually a simple transliteration, "hypocrite," but a *kritēs* is a "judge," i.e., one who separates out the issues, makes distinctions, evaluates and makes a decision. The prefix *hupo-* has the primary meaning "under," and thus can signify "judging from a low position," or from not seeing clearly. It can also be an intensifier, so that when combined with the noun it would mean to be hyper-critical, nit-picky or pedantic. According to Nyland, this word did not come to refer to an "actor" until the 2nd century AD. So, based upon the Greek elements of the word in this verse, on offer are alternate renderings of the adjective, in the complete phrase:
> a) acceptance that is free from prejudice and from a separating for evaluation;
> b) love that is not based on making distinctions, fault-finding or judging.

Such love would indeed be sincere, genuine and unfeigned, but with the three renderings given here, we see a greater depth to what Paul is saying.

But, we might ask: What were some of the aspects that the sent-forth folks were providing and "**dispensing**"? Here Kaplan points us to 2 Pet. 1:
> 5. **Yet, also, this same** (or: And yet for this very cause)**: while bringing into and alongside** (i.e., making full use of) **all diligent haste, you folks at once fully lead the chorus of** (or: completely choreograph and outfit) **the excellence and nobleness** (virtues of braveness, courage, good character, quality, self-restraint, magnificence, benevolence, reliability and valor [of 1 Pet. 1:3, above]) **[being inherent] within your faith and trust; along with the intimate, experiential knowledge and insight [being] within the excellence and nobleness;**
> 6. **also the inner strength and self-restraint [which is inherent] within the intimate, experiential knowledge, as well as the persistent remaining under in humble support** (or: steadfast, patient endurance) **[being inherently] within the inner strength and self-restraint; and then the reverence** (ease of virtuous conduct from true relation to God) **[inherent] within the persistent remaining under in humble support** (or: steadfast, patient endurance);
> 7. **and further, the brotherly affection [resident] within the reverence, and then finally, the love** (uniting acceptance) **within the brotherly affection.**
> 8. **You see, these things are constantly subsisting** (or: supportively sub-governing; humbly ruling; beginning from below) **as a possession in you folks and are repeatedly being more than enough** (abounding) **– neither [being] inactive** (or: ineffective) **nor unfruitful** (or: unproductive). **He is continually setting [these] down and causing [them] to stand in accord [in you] unto the accurate, additional** (or: full), **experiential and intimate knowledge of our Lord** (or: Owner; Master), **Jesus Christ.**

Look back over this passage from 2 Pet., and notice that each virtue that is listed is resident "**within**" the next virtue that is listed. This means that each virtue is encapsulated within and so is provided by the virtue that is next given, in this list. So their origins all come from "**the love** (uniting acceptance) **within the brotherly affection**" (vs. 7b). "**The Love** (uniting acceptance)" is the Source of all other virtues, and this Love is "**uncritical.**"

7. with a *Logos* and in a message of Truth (or: centered in a thought, idea and Word of Reality; in union with pattern-forming information from Reality); **within God's power and ability; through means of the tools and instruments** (or: weapons; utensils; implements) **of and from the liberating deliverance,**

rightwised relationships and with the justice and equity of the Way pointed out in new covenant participation – on the right hand and on the left;

Now Paul inserts into this passage a short teaching which ties this all together, for you see, all the "dispensing" comes "**with a *Logos* and in a message of Truth**." (*Cf* 2:17; 4:2, above) Of course, this "message" is Christ, Himself, that becomes incarnated – via the message – within the listener whose heart has been prepared to be good soil for this Seed. On offer are two other ways to render Paul's statement:

> a) centered in a thought, idea and Word of Reality; -- this Reality is the "new creation" of 5:17, above;

> b) in union with pattern-forming information from Reality; -- this picture of "pattern-forming information" presents us with the means of "the transformation to be other than we were" of 5:19, above. We can also call to mind 3:18, above, and Rom. 12:2b, "**be progressively transformed** (transfigured; changed in form and semblance) **by the renewing** (or: in the renewal; for the making-back-up-new again) **of your mind**."

But next, Paul gives further explanation of how this all works: "**within God's power and ability** [*cf* 1 Cor. 2:4]**; through means of the tools and instruments** (or: weapons; utensils; implements) **of and from the liberating deliverance** (etc.)." Now the first phrase is a common thought, in Paul, and we can wrap our minds around "God's power and ability." But what about "**through means of the tools and instruments** (or: weapons; utensils; implements)" of, and from, "**rightwised relationships and with the justice and equity of the Way pointed out in new covenant participation**"? I have taken the meaning of *dikaiosunē* as being "covenant participation" from the writings of N.T. Wright. Combining this thought with Paul's metaphor of "the body of Christ" (found elsewhere), gives us at least one layer of perceiving what he means here by the metaphor "**tools and instruments** (etc.)." We can also see that the expanded rendering of "**liberating deliverance**," by "**rightwised relationships**" (which I took from Douglas A. Campbell and William Barclay, respectively), dovetails with Paul's metaphor of a "body" (used elsewhere) and "covenant participation," here. The picture that Jesus presented in Jn. 15:1ff (the Vine and its branches) also expresses the organic aspect of Paul's multi-metaphorical tapestry.

The renderings "weapons and implements" call to mind Paul's metaphor in Eph. 6:13, "**take in hand and receive back** (or: at once take up) **the full suit of armor** (panoply; implements of war) **which is God** (or: which belongs to and has its source in God)." He uses his same term "tools, instruments, weapons, etc." in 10:4-5, below,

> "**the tools and weapons of our military service and warfare [are] not fleshly** (= do not pertain to our human condition; ["are not the weapons of the Domination System" – Walter Wink]), **but rather, [are] powerful ones and capable ones in God** (or: by God), **[focused] toward [the] pulling down** (demolition) **of effects of fortifications** (or: strongholds; strongly entrenched positions [of the "Domination System" – Walter Wink, *Engaging the Powers*]), **progressively tearing down and demolishing conceptions** (concepts; the effects of thoughts, calculations, imaginations, reasonings and reflections) **and every height** (or: high position; high-effect) **and lofty [attitude, purpose or obstacle] that is habitually lifting itself up against** (or: elevating itself up on so as to put down) **the intimate and experiential knowledge of God, and then taking captive every effect of perception, concept and understanding** (result from directing one's mind) **– one after another – and leading them prisoner into the hearing obedience of the Christ**."

At a time that was apparently what Paul felt might be the end of his life, he said,

> "**I have contended the beautiful contest in the racecourse** (or: I have with agony struggled, wrestling in the ideal combat {the fine fight} in the public games)" (2 Tim. 4:7a).

Peter used the verb form of this word family (tool; weapon) in 1 Pet. 4:1-2 (quoted under 5:15, above), then in Rom. 13:12 we find Paul instructing us, "**clothe ourselves with the instruments** (tools; weapons;

implements; [some MSS: works; deeds]) **of Light** (or: The Light)," which as pointed out, above, equates to "**clothe yourselves with** (or: enter within and put on) **the Lord, Jesus Christ**" (Rom. 13:14).

The rendering "utensils" reflects the idea of "**USEFUL kindness**," above. He inserts a phrase to show the scope of what he has been saying: "**on the right hand and on the left**," which is to say: "everywhere." This refers to the Message of Truth/Reality, to God's power/ability, and to the tools and instruments that he just described. All of this encompasses Paul and his associates. O'Rourke makes a cogent observation: "[The] attacks of his adversaries were at least part of the reason for Paul's writing this letter..." (ibid). But Paul continues...

8. through a good reputation, and [by means of] dishonor (or: through means of glory and a praise-inducing manifestation, as well as [by] absence of value or respect); **through means of words of ill omen and [by] words of good omen** (or: through bad reports and defamation, and [through] good reports and praise); **as wanderers and yet real** (or: as [considered being] men who deceive and lead astray, and yet [being] true);

These next three verses reveal the contrasts of their experiences: from what seem to be very **good**, to the extremes of what are very bad. This verse refers to how they are regarded, spoken about, treated, and assessed by various individuals or groups, "**on the right hand and on the left**" (7b). The varied regions and social climates through which Paul traveled tells us that he did not keep his message to just a small niche; he apparently spread the Good News of God's reign and kingdom to everyone.

In the final couplet, Paul begins a series of antitheses: "**as**... **and yet** (or: as well as)." The rendering of the nouns in this first antithesis determines whether he is simply stating a "neutral" fact about their lives (the bold rendering), or whether it has a negative/positive contrast: the former speaking of a false report, the latter stating what is true. With this ambiguity before us, let us consider this first word...

The first term of the last couplet is the word *planos* (from which we get our word "planet") and the verb form literally means to "wander about," or "go astray." Due to that second meaning it came to also indicate "to lead astray," and thus, likely, "to deceive." Paul and his friends may have been accused of being such people (a charge that was likely made by either the Jewish leaders, or by the Judaizers), and Paul himself characterizes such people as being "**false emissaries** {pseudo-representatives} – **fraudulent and deceitful workers**" in 11:13, below. But how was he using this term here? An expanded form of this noun, *planētēs*, is found in the celestial metaphor of Judah (Jude) 13,

> "**Wandering and deceived stars, for whom the gloom of darkness** (shadowy dimness; obscurity void of Daylight) **has been maintained** (guarded; kept and watched-over) **unto an indefinite time period** (or: into the midst of [the] Age; or: for a life-time)."

In 1 Tim. 4:1-2a, Paul used the word *planos* to describe "spirits."

> "**Now the Spirit is explicitly saying that within subsequent seasons some of the faith will proceed standing off and away [from the Path, or from the Community], habitually holding toward wandering and deceptive spirits** (or: straying and seducing breath-effects and attitudes) **and to teachings of, or about, demons, within perverse scholarship of false words...**"

John's second letter defines such folks: "**this is the PERSON wandering astray, even the one in opposition to Christ**" (2 Jn. 7b).

Such a use of this term would have set Paul in "**dishonor**, as well as [having] an absence of value or respect." But other folks might have simply meant that they were "wanderers," with no particular connotation of either good or bad. Itinerant teachers were a common occurrence in that time and culture. With either meaning, Paul assures the Corinthians that he and his co-workers were both "**real**" and "true."

9. as continuing being unknown (nonentities) **and yet constantly being ones fully known, recognized; as being those continually or progressively withering and dying, and yet look and consider: we continue living; as being those progressively being disciplined, trained and educated as young boys, and yet not being ones regularly delivered** (put) **to death;**

The contrasts continue. Here, "**yet constantly being ones fully known, recognized**" may be a reference to 5:11, above – a reference to their relationship with the Corinthian group. It could also refer to those who oppose Paul and his associates. But the most important referent in 5:11 would be that they were "**manifested** (set in the light so as to be clearly seen) **in God** (by God; for God; to God; with God)." Being "**fully known**" by God is of supreme value; being "**fully recognized**" by others is but a temporal thing. The root of this word is *ginōskō*: to know and thus have insight by intimate experience. Paul may have had in mind what he wrote in 1 Cor. 8:3,

> "**Yet if anyone is continuously or habitually loving** (urging toward union with; fully giving oneself to) **God, this person has been personally and intimately known by God and continues under the experience of His knowledge.**"

How many of us normally see ourselves as "**continually or progressively withering and dying**"? Some of us, of course, can certainly relate to this, physically or spiritually. This could describe a cruciform life. In 1 Cor. 4:9 he termed it, "**as men condemned to die in the public arena.**" This passage calls to mind Isa. 53, cited above. He wrote something similar to this in his previous letter to them:

> "**Daily I am repeatedly facing death** (or: progressively dying)! **Brothers, I swear** (or: strongly affirm) **by our boasting!** [other MSS: Yes! On the basis of your own boasting] – **which I continually possess, and hold within Christ Jesus, our Lord** (Owner; Master) **– if I fight** (or: fought) **in accord with human [means, methods or purposes] with wild beasts in Ephesus…**" (1 Cor. 15:31-32a).

We see it as very likely that what he refers to in these three verses may be the same kind of thing that he ambiguously describes in 12:7, below:

> "**And now, in the excess of the unveilings** (or: with the transcendence of the revelations; by the extraordinary amount and surpassing nature of the disclosures), **through this [situation] and for this reason – so that I could not be progressively exalted** (or: would not continue being overly lifted up [in myself or by others]) **– something with [its] point in [my] flesh is given in me** (or: an impaling-stake for the human nature was given for me; or: a thorn to the natural realm, and a splinter by alienated humanity, was assigned to me)**: an agent of** (or: a messenger from) **the adversary, to the end that he** (or: it) **could** (or: should; would) **repeatedly beat me in the face** (or: slap me on the ear) **with his** (or: its) **fist.**"

This personification of the irritation may well be metaphorical and may refer to his social or cultural-religious situation. Nonetheless, let us keep in mind how he ended this couplet, here in vs. 9: "**and yet look and consider: we continue living.**"

Observe that he considered himself, and his friends, "**as being those progressively being disciplined, trained and educated as young boys.**" Even though being Christ's representatives, they regarded themselves as still being in that which is described as "education" in Heb. 12:2-11. Today many of us think of ourselves as "life-long learners." It is often what my mother used to say with a smile, in the colloquial wisdom heard in her early childhood: "hurtin' will learn ya." Oh, how true! Paul may have been alluding to Ps. 118:18,

> "Yah has disciplined, [yea] disciplined me; yet He has not given me [over] to death." (CVOT)

In Phil. 1:21, Paul said,

> "**For you see, to me, to be living [is] Christ** (or: For the [situation] in me and for me, life [is the] Anointed One), **and to be dying [is] gain** (advantage; profit)" (Phil. 1:21).

This is an expression of what he later said in Phil. 2:5,

> "**You see, this way of thinking** (this attitude and disposition) **is continuously within and among you folks** (or, as an imperative: So let this minding be habitually within you folks) – **which [is] also within Christ Jesus**,"

and then he goes on to describe that attitude and mindset in Phil. 2:6-8. But here he gives the balancing contrast to the "child-training" with the qualification, "**and yet NOT being ones regularly delivered** (put) **to death.**"

10. as those being repeatedly made anxious, sad, vexed, distressed or in pain, but yet ever rejoicing; as constantly being people that are poor, destitute and living as beggars, but yet repeatedly making many rich (or: enriching many folks); **as those possessing** (having or holding) **nothing, and yet continuously possessing all things to the full** (or: habitually having and retaining everything in a firm grasp; or: repeatedly holding fast to all folks)**!**

Look at the range of emotions and experiences that he lists in this first clause – and they are "**ever rejoicing**" as they go through them. They address what appears to be their "constant" physical situations: "**being people that are poor, destitute and living as beggars**... **possessing** (having or holding) **nothing.**" Yet, we suspect that the positive contrasts refer to aspects of God's reign, their ministry, and their life in the Spirit: "**repeatedly making many rich** (or: enriching many folks)... **continuously possessing all things to the full** (or: habitually having and retaining everything in a firm grasp)." Now since "all" in this phrase is either neuter (things) or masculine (referring to people), the final phrase can also be rendered, "repeatedly holding fast to all folks," which is a beautiful expression. They threw nobody away! They loved everyone, as God (within them) does (Jn. 3:16).

Now if they were "**possessing all things to the full**," and we know that he was not speaking of material things, does this not suggest that he was not waiting for any further fulfillment of the promises? If you have Christ, the Spirit, the Father, you have it all. He perceived that he had all of creation and the cosmos to enjoy. This does not mean that he didn't expect that in time more developments of, and growth from, God's reign would continue to flow into humanity, and specifically into himself. Some MSS have him saying, "I will continue moving on to sights, apparitions and appearances, as well as revelations and disclosures" (12:1, below). But most likely, this in vs. 10 was a statement of his contentment with what he had and his gratitude for what God had given him. What an example!

11. Our mouth has been opened up and continues open toward you, O Corinthians: our heart has been broadened and is now enlarged.

The figure of speech, "**our mouth has been opened up toward you**," is saying that they had been straightforward and had shared everything with them. There were no "speaking out of the side of the mouth," or saying things "under their breath," or slick subtleties, or asides spoken obscurely. They had not been "tight-lipped." They had been completely open with the Corinthians. Not only that, they had been completely receptive to the community – their "**heart has been broadened and is now enlarged**," which is to say that they had made room for these folks, both in their daily living and their emotions (down to the core of their beings). In fact, these folks had increased their capacity to love!

12. You folks are not being constantly restricted into some limited place within us (= in our hearts), **but you are being repeatedly squeezed into restrictions in your own inner sensitivities and deep feelings** (within your interior organs).

He says first that they do not have a limited place in their lives, or in their feelings. They are not "second-class relatives in his family." But now, he has observed, or discerned, that THEY are experiencing an inner "squeezing" and "restriction" in their "**sensitivities and deep feelings.**" He does not say with regard to whom these restrictions apply – perhaps toward everyone; perhaps toward other members of the community; perhaps just toward "outsiders." So what does he advise? Witherington suggests that here Paul is seeking "reciprocity" (ibid p 400). In 12:15, below, he gives this refrain:

> "**So I myself most gladly shall spend** (pay the expenses) – **even be completely spent** (exhausted; bankrupted) – **over** (on behalf of) **your souls. Even if I am constantly loving you excessively, I am habitually being loved or accepted less.** (or: And since I am continuously loving you and seeking union with you more abundantly {or: too much}, am I being loved less?)"

It would seem that there was a definite lack of equity between the two parties, in the realm of love and acceptance. Paul is pointing out this contrast – he is aware that there is something amiss in their relationship. He addresses the need for change on their part, as we see in this next verse…

13. **Now I am speaking as to children: [let's have] the same fair exchange of recompense. You folks also be broadened and enlarged!**

This first clause sounds a lot like his previous letter (1 Cor. 3:1-2). He opened that letter by pointing to the division that was among them. Here, he is again addressing relational issues. Asking for a "**fair exchange of recompense**," is suggesting that they are not living their lives in "the Way pointed out," which includes "rightwised relationships." They are not acting like a "called-out covenant community," and so he is once more functioning as their father, reasoning with them, so that as they live their lives, they would not stray from the Path of Christ and become "wandering stars." He ends his arguments, of vss. 11-13, with an admonition – actually an imperative – to them: "**You folks also be broadened and enlarged!**" Translate: Open your hearts to others! But keep in mind that with the *Logos*, the Word of the Lord, comes empowerment, not Law!

14. **Do not of yourself continue** (or: Stop) **becoming yoked differently** (or: unevenly yoked; yoked with ones of a different sort) **with folks without faith** (or: by those without trust; to unbelievers; with disloyal people), **for, what mutual holding** (having-with: sharing; partnership; communion; membership) **[have] rightwised living and lawlessness** (or: fairness/equity, and a lack of following rules; deliverance to right relationship which accords with the Way pointed out, and [the] inequity or wrong which come from violation of law), **or what common existing** (participation; partnership; sharing of Being) **[is] in Light [directed] toward, or face to face with, darkness** (or: [is there] for light with dimness from murky obscurity in the realm of shadows)**?**

This verse begins a new argument (6:14-7:1), which Witherington classifies as a "digression" that addresses the topic of what he calls, "entangling alliances" (ibid. p 402). This is clearly seen in the metaphor of a "yoke" such as joins two oxen in pulling one plow. They are side-by-side, going in the same direction, and laboring in the same work. But different kinds of animals were never yoked together.

For members of the covenant community to be so closely involved with folks outside the community, who were not following the Lord or engaged in kingdom work, would either lead to dissention and division in the relationship, or the community member may likely be led astray, away from walking in the Way pointed out. Paul instructs them not to continue in such an "**uneven yoke**," or, put more bluntly, "Stop being yoked with ones of a different sort," for the reasons laid out above. This may be an allusion to Deut. 7:2-3 where Israel was instructed not to make covenants or arrangements with the cultures and religions that they would encounter. The Corinthian situation is put in a contrast between "**rightwised living**" (i.e., in the Life of Christ) and "**lawlessness**" which would be the kind of living that was the norm for those who were not living as having Christ as their Lord and Master – which he describes as being in close relationships "**with folks without faith** (or: by those without trust; to unbelievers; with disloyal people)." On offer are other ways of terming this lifestyle: a lack of following rules; inequity or wrong which come from violation of law. These are in sharp contrast to: fairness/equity and their deliverance to right relationship which accords with the Way pointed out. The called-out community had been "rightwised: turned in the right direction" to focus on and follow Christ. This contrast, between living in union with God's reign and living in accord to the domination System, was set forth by Jesus in Mat. 11:29-20,

> "**At once lift up My crossbeam** (or: the yoke which is Me; the balance beam that comes from and pertains to Me) **upon you people, and instantly learn from Me, because I am** (or: I continuously exist being) **mild-tempered** (gentle, kind and considerate) **and humble** (low) **in the heart, and 'you folks will continue finding refreshment and discovering rest in and for your souls** (the consciousness and whole inner person; the mind, emotions and nerves).' [Jer. 6:16] **You see, My crossbeam** (or: the yoke which is Me; the balance beam that comes from and pertains to Me) **is useful, well-fitting and kindly obliging, and My load** (the burden that is Me and which pertains to Me) **continues being light** (not heavy)."

What Jesus said, there, was such a contrast to Second Temple Judaism. Here, Paul was speaking about not being yoked either to Judaism (and the Law), nor to Hellenism (or the Empire).

The last contrast in the verse speaks to their sphere of being and level of existence. He describes their new realm of living (as the body of Christ; as being in the kingdom of God) as a "**common existing in Light.**" This first term is rooted in a present participle, *ōn*: "being or existing," joined to the adjective that means "common" in the sense of "shared." It can be rendered a "sharing of Being (capitalized as referring to Christ or God)." We share His Life, His very Being. In human or spiritual relationships this can be termed "participation" (which implies personal, mutual interaction), or, "partnership" (which can imply an agreed arrangement for a venture, or the creation of a social entity). These terms lend insight into what it means to be a member of Christ's called-out, covenant community. It is like being a branch in the Vine – the extension of the Vine is an existential part of the Vine. The branches are its "body."

So, Paul asks, "**What common existing does Light** (the Christ Life; vision and understanding) **mutually hold** (have; share; be a membership; have communion) **toward, or face to face with, darkness?**" (*cf* 1 Sam. 5:2-5) Or, put another way, "What partnership [is there] for light with dimness from murky obscurity in the realm of shadows [a figure of the Law, or of pagan ways and religions]?" We find a similar thought in Eph. 5:7-8,

> "**Stop, therefore, becoming** (or: Therefore you folks are not to continuously come to be) **their joint partakers** (their joint members or partners; ones sharing together with them), **for you folks were once existing being darkness** (dimness; obscurity; gloom; shadiness), **yet** (or: but) **now [you are] Light, within and in union with [the] Lord.**"

Paul is calling those who are wandering (away from the Way pointed out) back into the Path that follows Christ. Putting it this way calls to mind Prov. 4:18-19,

> "The path of the just (rightwised) person is like the light of dawn, which shines brighter and brighter until full Day; the way of the wicked (or: worthless person) is like deep darkness: they do not know over what they stumble" (ESV, modified).

15. **And what joining of voice** (concord, agreement and harmony of sound) **has Christ [when faced] toward** *belial* [Hebrew word for "worthlessness"]**? Or what part for one full of faith and trust** (or: portion in a loyal believer) **[corresponds] with one who lacks faith** (an unbeliever; one who is not trustworthy or loyal)**?**

Christ came to bring us into the Way, the Truth and the Life (Jn. 14:6) – which was the Path to the Father. He came to rescue us from a worthless existence. How can these two spheres of existence "join in a harmony of voice"? The Greek word used here is where we get our English transliteration of it: "symphony." It is literally "a sounding together," and thus implies a concord and "agreement" of **voice.** The metaphor is a good parallel to the concept of a "common existence," as we saw in vs. 14. The contrasts between a loyal person that is "**full of faith and trust,**" and "**one who lacks faith** (is not trustworthy or is unbelieving)" is a restatement of the contrasts between "**rightwised living and lawlessness,**" above. The differences of ethics between these two ways of living reach back to those found throughout the Psalms, Proverbs and Jewish wisdom literature. The "freedom" referred to in Gal.

5:1 implies freedom from old covenant temple cultus and from the legal purity codes that separated Israel from the nations of ethnic multitudes and brought that "wall of separation" of which Eph. spoke, dividing humanity into different categories in relationship to God. But this freedom did not imply a freedom from common ethical behavior:

> "**For you folks were called upon the foundation of** (on the basis of; for the purpose of) **freedom, [my] brothers. Only not** (or: Just not) **the freedom [which is leading] into a starting point** (or: unto an opportunity, occasion or incentive; to a base of operation) **for** (to; in; by; with) **the flesh** [comment: = circumcision with the flesh ordinances and ceremonial laws of Judaism; or: = personal license for the estranged human nature], **but to the contrary, through the Love** [agapē: unrestricted acceptance; the urge toward reunion] **be continuously slaving for one another** (serving and performing the duties of a slave to each other)" (Gal. 5:13).

Or as Peter said,

> "**as free folks** (those not bound) **– and not continually holding** (or: having) **the freedom as a covering** (or: a veil) **of worthlessness** (bad quality; evil; poorness of situation) **– but still, as God's slaves**" (1 Pet. 2:16).

The second clause of this verse echoes the "yoke" metaphor of vs. 14, above. *Cf* 1 Cor. 8:9. We should mark Paul's emphasis on trust, faithfulness, loyalty and being full of faith, in these two verses. This was a central theme in Israel's story, and we find Paul rooting his argument about faithfulness in OT passages, in the next three verses. It was Israel's unfaithfulness to Yahweh, and their straying from the ethical behavior that He set out for them, that brought exile upon them.

Apparently Paul expected his audience to understand the Hebrew loan-word, *belial*. Robert Young (*Analytical Concordance* p 86) instructs us:

> "This should not be regarded as a proper name. It is generally associated with the words 'man,' 'son,' 'daughter,' or 'children.' Hence, 'son' or 'man' of belial simply means 'a worthless person.'"

In 1 Sam. 2:12 we read that "the sons of Eli were sons of *belial*." In Deut. 13:13 we read of the potential of, "[Certain] men, the sons of *belial* (= base or worthless men) [who might go out]... and serve other gods..." Also *cf* Jud. 19:22. This word is only found here, in the NT. It has been found in the Dead Sea Scrolls in 1QS 1:18, 24; 2:5, 19. "The term *belial* appears frequently in Jewish texts of the Second Temple period (texts classified by Christians as the OT pseudeipgrapha and apocrypha)" (Wikipedia). Once again, Paul is drawing upon OT examples for what constitutes being "set-apart," for God's service and to bear His image. What was to be done physically, in the old covenant, was instructional for understanding the Life in the Spirit of the new covenant:

> "**All Scripture [is] God-breathed and beneficial-to-furtherance toward instruction toward** (with a view to) **testing unto proof** (or: exposure; laying bare), **toward full restoration to straightness** (or: straightening-up upon; = improvement), **toward child-training** (education; discipline) **of the person within the Way pointed out**" (2 Tim. 3:16).

16. **Now what mutual deposit** (or: concurrence or agreement arrived by group decision) **[does] God's Temple [have] with idols** (or: external forms or appearances; or: phantoms of the mind; unsubstantial images or forms)? **For you see, we ourselves** [other MSS: you folks] **continuously exist being** (indeed we/you are) **a temple of [the] living God, just as God said,**

> "**I will proceed to make My home and will continue walking about within and among them** (or: I will habitually reside {dwell}, as in a house, and live My life within and among them), **and I will continue existing being their God, and they will continue existing being My people.**" [Lev. 26:12]

Paul uses another "together" term, "**mutual deposit** (etc.)," that he stacks up upon the pictures evoked from "yoke," "common existence," and "joining of voice" in the previous two verses. This latest term literally means "something that is set down, or placed, together" with something else. Yahweh's covenant could not be "placed together" with the religions of the idols of the nations. God's temple was His home among the tribes of Israel. His tabernacle was constructed so that He would, "**continue walking about within and among them**," and be their God... and they His people. We see the resurrected Christ doing exactly this, in Rev. 2:1. Peter also viewed the called-out folks as God's temple:

"**You yourselves are, as living stones, continuously being erected** (or: progressively constructed and built up), **[being] a spiritual house** (a building with its source being the Spirit, with the characteristics of a Breath-effect)..." (1 Pet. 2:5a).

We recall, from Paul's previous letter to Corinth, that this community was having issues regarding some of its members eating meals at banquets in the local idol temples. Paul may be alluding to this topic, in the first clause of this verse. For discussions about these issues, see the comments in 1 Cor. 8:1-10 and 10:19-28, above, in this volume.

To help us perceive "idols" as more than a carved piece of word or stone, let us note other renderings of the Greek term:

a) external forms or appearances – the very addictions of our modern cultures – both religious and secular; human self-images;

b) phantoms of the mind – theories, doctrines, philosophies, and vain imaginations about "heaven or hell," and mental or psychic visions;

c) unsubstantial images or forms – the pagan concepts of demons, or gods; spiritual "warfare."

The great majority of Christians do not believe that God or Christ are actually within us or our atmosphere. They have images of God being off in some other "place," that is "up there;" again, these are "visions and dreams" from the mental imaginations of the first Adam.

Let us take a closer look at this quote of Lev. 26:12, "**I will proceed to make My home, and will continue walking about, within and among them** (or: I will habitually reside {dwell}, as in a house, and live My life within and among them)." Paul brings the life of historical Israel, and God's "down-home" arrangement of His living among them, into its spiritual fulfillment in the new covenant (new creation; new arrangement). Ezk 37:26-27a spoke of this future situation:

"I will contract with them a covenant of peace [LXX: an arrangement of joining]... I will put My Sanctuary in [their] midst [LXX: My holy things within the midst of them] for [the] eon, and My Tabernacle will be over them..." (CVOT; LXX, JM).

If His Tabernacle is "over them," then they live in His home, and His home is here, "**within and among**" US. *Cf* Jer. 31:33; 32:38; Ezk. 36:28; Zech. 8:8 – and Rev. 21:3. We ARE the fulfillment of all those prophecies. Take note of how the next verse brings more prophecies into present application...

17. **On which account [the] Lord** [= Yahweh] **says,**

"**Instantly go forth from out of their midst and be instantly marked off by boundaries so as to be defined and restricted – and do not continue** (or: stop) **touching what is unclean** (= ceremonially defiled), [Isa. 52:11; Jer. 51:45] **and then I, Myself, will constantly admit you folks and receive you into [Myself; My family]**, [*cf* Ezk. 20:41]

Paul admonishes the Corinthians to model their outward behavior based upon the words of the Prophets. Each person is to draw from these examples the spiritual counterparts of the old covenant, as they live "seated together" with Christ (Eph. 2:6) in the heavenly atmospheres of Mt. Zion (Heb. 12:22-24). Paul is not taking them, or us, back into the old age, but is grounding his arguments in the Christ that is within that old covenant (Lu. 24:27). He is following the example of the teachings of Jesus... doing the things that He did. These quotes are no different from his reaching back to Adam or Abraham to found this covenant community solidly upon the Rock. The building (1 Cor. 3) is built upon Christ, who was founded upon the ground, earth, of the old covenant. Christ is not just some ethereal Being, but is the One who inhabits the New Jerusalem that descends, bringing His kingdom into the earth (Rev. 21-22).

Rev. 18:4 (written to the seven called-out communities – Christ's body) is another witness to Paul's message:

> "**Come out of her** (or: Go forth from out of her midst) **My people, so that you may not jointly participate with** (be a partner with; fellowship together with) **her sins** (failures; occasions of missing the mark), **and so that you may not receive from out of her plagues** (blows; impacts)."

This is the same message that Paul has been presenting in vss.14-17.

18.   **"and so I will proceed into being a Father for you, and you will proceed in being** (or: will continue being) **sons and daughters in Me** (by Me; to Me; for Me), **says [the] Lord** [= Yahweh] **the All-strong** (Almighty)." [2 Sam. 7:14; Isa. 43:6]

We read in Jer. 31:9b, "for I am a Father to Israel, and Ephraim is My firstborn." Then in Rev. 21:7 we have:

> "**The one habitually being victorious** (or: progressively overcoming) **will proceed inheriting** (acquiring by lot) **these things, and I will continue being a God for him** (in him; to him) **and he will continue being a son** [Griesbach reads: the son] **for Me** (in Me; to Me; with Me; by Me)."

It was a Way of Life that characterized Israel as being Yahweh's "**sons and daughters**." Paul has strung together unrelated texts outside of their contexts – and now he is applying these to the body of Christ! How we live reflects an image to the "world" about us. Do we bear the image of the "beasts" of Rev. 13, or the image of God? When the *Logos* was made "flesh," folks beheld "**Its** (or: His) **glory and assumed appearance as of an only-begotten person** (or: like One that is an only kin, of a solitary race, in a by-itself-class) **at a father's side** (or: in the presence of, and next to, [the] Father), **full of grace and truth** (filled and replete with joy-producing favor, as well as reality and genuineness)" (Jn. 1:14). We should, with confidence in the Spirit that indwells us, project to others that reality of His abiding presence so that we will know (even if we do not say it) that if they have seen us, they have seen the Father. This is the vocation described in 3:18, above. This is why He incarnates within us, identifies with us (Mat. 25:40b, 45b). Solidarity in the Spirit goes both ways. This is what "BEING in Christ" means.

1. **Therefore, beloved ones, continuing in possessing** (having and holding) **these – the [aforementioned] promises – we can and should cleanse ourselves off from every stain, pollution or ceremonial defilement of flesh** (= the estranged human nature; = a self that is oriented to the System) **and of spirit** (or: from flesh as well as from a spirit or attitude; or: pertaining to an alienated persona or an attitude bound to a domination System), **while progressively bringing the state and condition of being set-apart** (sacredness) **to a successful completion** (or: in continuing to perform dedicated consecration amidst its destined goal), **centered in a reverence from God** (or: in union with respect, with regard to God; in God's fear; [p46 reads: in God's love]).

The first clause calls to mind 1 Jn. 3:2-3,

> "**Beloved ones, now** (at the present time) **we continuously exist being God's children.... So everyone, who** (or: all mankind, which) **in continuously having** (or: habitually holding) **this expectation [placed; resting; based] upon Him is [by this] constantly** (repeatedly; progressively) **purifying himself, just as** (according as; in the way that) **That One is** (or: exists being) **pure**."

Because of all that Paul has said, from chapter 1 to this present verse – which all express what we are "**continuing in possessing** (having and holding)" – he admonishes us to "**cleanse ourselves off from every stain, pollution or ceremonial defilement of flesh**." Remember what Jesus told His disciples:

> "**Jesus in turn says to him, 'The person being one having bathed himself or herself** (or, as a passive: being one having been washed and cleansed) **does not continue having a need to wash himself or herself – except the feet.... If I Myself, then, the Lord and the Teacher,**

wash your feet, you men also are constantly indebted (obliged; continuously owe it) **to be habitually washing one another's feet** [= their way of life and daily living on the Path]" (Jn. 13:10, 14).

To what was Paul referring by "**every stain, pollution or ceremonial defilement of flesh and of spirit**"? The parenthetical expansions of Paul's concept of "flesh" are based upon the insights from various scholars. Witherington suggests:

> "The social function of this passage was the same as its predecessors in 1 Cor. 8 and 10, namely to create a stronger sense of what the proper moral and social boundaries were for the Christian community in Corinth" (ibid p 406).

Involvements with, or attachments to, the first Adam (within us, or within others) or the dominations' Systems of the old religions, the old mindsets, the old ways of dealing with people, the old ways of doing business, aspects of the spirit of the Empire, or anything that is not Love, are the minding of the flesh, and that bring death (Rom. 8:6).. We must be cleansed from prior worldviews of "us and them," which ignore the fact that Christ has made of "the circumcision and the uncircumcision" One New Humanity (Eph. 2:15). We must be cleansed of any attitude of "better-than-them" or "separate-from-them." Jesus was all about solidarity. The concept of "ceremonial defilement" is a religious/spiritual concept – Paul's words must be spiritually discerned. Even under the old covenant, the main sense of prostitution was that of turning to idolatry. Infidelity to Yahweh involved leaving Him and turning to idolizing something of His creation. A domination System is anti-Christ (be it a church, a business or a government). Paul is also speaking to our spirits – the attitudes of our hearts. Being spiritually cleansed from these things and these thoughts is what sets us apart from the realm and mindset of the System. So how is this done? We have one answer in 1 Jn. 1:7,

> "**If we keep on walking about** (= continue living our life) **within the midst of and in union with the Light, as He exists** (or: is) **within the Light, we constantly have common being and existence** (or: hold common fellowship, participation and enjoy partnership) **with one another, and the blood of, from, and which is Jesus, His Son, keeps continually and repeatedly cleansing us** (or: is progressively rendering us pure) **from every sin** (or: from all error, failure, deviation, mistake, and from every shot that is off target [when it occurs])."

Or, there is Eph. 5:18b, "**be continuously or repeatedly filled full in spirit** (within [the] Spirit; within the midst of [the] Breath-effect; in the sphere of attitude; in union with [the] Breath)." Breathe in and drink in God. Jesus said, "Abide in Me" (Jn. 15:1ff). It's really very simple: see Him everywhere and in everything, and in everyone. With your focus on Him, you will behold His glory and be transformed (3:18, above).

The second half of vs. 1 speaks of "**progressively bringing the state and condition of being set-apart** (sacredness) **to a successful completion**." How are they to do this? Recall 1 Cor. 5:9, 11,

> "**I wrote to you folks, in the letter: not to keep on mixing yourselves together again with men who make a practice of whoring**.... **not to continue mixing yourselves back together with anyone being regularly recognized as a 'brother,' if he should continue being a prostitute, or a covetous and greedy person, or an idolater, or a verbally abusive one, or a drunkard, or a snatching one** (or: an extortioner) **– not even to be habitually eating with such a person.**"

Now this admonition from Paul is based upon what follows: "**WHILE... centered in a reverence from God.**" This is their new state of being – their condition of "**BEING** set-apart" by God, and all that was described in 5:18-20, above. They are now "in union with respect, with regard to God," and they are, "in God's fear; [*p*46 reads: in God's love]." You see,

> "**the One inwardly beginning** (making an inward start; inciting; inwardly originating [note: in the context of sacrifices, this word meant "to begin the offering"]) **a good work, a virtuous action or an excellent deed within you people** (or: among you folks; or: in union with you [all]), **will progressively bring it to the completed goal** (will keep on bringing perfection upon it; shall

continue upon it to the final act and finished product: its completion; will continue bring upon its destiny])..." (Phil. 1:6).

Also, Paul instructs us:

> "**for you see, God is the One habitually operating with inward activity, repeatedly working within, constantly causing function and progressively producing effects within, among and in union with you folks – both the [condition] to be habitually willing** (intending; purposing; resolving) **and the [situation] to be continuously effecting the action, repeatedly operating to cause function and habitually setting at work so as to produce – for the sake of and over the pleasing good form and the thinking of goodness in delightful imagination**" (Phil. 2:13).

Chapter 7

2. **You folks make room** (create space; set up an environment) **for us! We wrong no one** (We at no point related to anyone unfairly or contrary to the Way pointed out; We act unjustly to no one). **We spoil no one** (We caused no one to decay or be corrupted). **We have more than no one** (or: We overreached no one so as to have an advantage over him or her; We exploit none).

Having completed his arguments in the above diversion (6:14-7:1), he resumes the thoughts that he had presented in 6:13, "**You folks also be broadened and enlarged!**" Now he goes on to explain what he meant by that directive: "**make room** (create space; set up an environment) **for US!**" And this was because Paul's and his fellow workers' "**heart had been broadened and is now enlarged**" toward, and concerning, the Corinthians (6:11, above). So we see that Paul goes on to assure them that abuse was not their practice, in fact, they "wrong no one," "spoil no one," and indeed "have more than no one." Notice the repetition of the phrase, "**no one.**" Paul does not want them to miss the point, and at the same time he is leveling the playing field. They are not getting rich by giving attending service and dispensing from the Spirit of God. As a background to this verse, visit again 2:14-3:6a, then 4:2, 15-17, and then 6:1-10, above. These prior remarks should have worked to open the hearts of the Corinthian community so as to "make room for THEM." Paul's letter is being sent to heal and repair the damage done by "false apostles" and those seeking personal gain.

Notice that he says "**no one**" three times: they had "exploited none." 12:17-18, below, again affirms that neither he nor Titus took advantage of anyone. From these strong denials we may surmise that Paul's opponents had, in fact, been taking advantage of the Corinthian community – exploiting them in some way.

3. **I am not now speaking with a view toward condemnation** (a decision to bring [you] down), **for I have said before that you folks continuously exist** (or: are) **within our hearts – into the [situations of both] to die together and to be continuously living together!**

He puts no blame on the members of the community, but rather assures them of what he and his comrades feel toward Christ's body in Corinth. The feeling of solidarity is expressed in his words, "**you folks continuously exist** (or: are) **within our hearts**" – whatever the case or situation might be, even if that means "**to die together**" with them, it would still mean "**to be continuously living together**." Recall our quote of Phil. 1:21, above: **to be living [is] Christ**, and, **to be dying [is] gain** (advantage; profit). This is the greater Love of which Jesus spoke in Jn. 15:13. Paul is ready to do this for the Corinthians.

Another affirmation of solidarity is presented in the final two infinitive phrases: "to die together... to continue living together." The subject of these infinitives would seem to be Paul and his associates, but grammatically, the subject-verb "**you folks continuously exist/are**" is followed by the infinitive phrases. Thus Paul could be understood as saying that the subject of these infinitives is the Corinthians. With either reading, the emphasis is "**together**" – solidarity. They are one with the Corinthians. The same sentiment is found in Ruth 1:16-17a, "Wherever you go I shall go, and wherever you lodge I shall lodge… Where you die, I shall die…"

4. **[There is] much freedom of speech, frankness, outspokenness and boldness in me, toward you folks. [There is] much boasting in me, over** (in regard to) **you! I have been filled full so that I am stuffed with relief, encouragement and comfort – I continue overflowing from the progressive flood of superabundance which encircles me in joy – which tops all our pressure and tribulation** (or: by the joy upon every squeezing, ordeal, affliction and oppression).

Paul has been so enriched by the Spirit of God that any rejection from the Corinthians, or even death, could not out-weigh what he has been given. Here, again, we are reminded of Christ's attitude, as expressed in Heb. 12:2,

"**instead of and in place of the joy** (or: in the position on the opposite side from the happiness) **continuously lying before Him** (or: lying in the forefront within Him; lying ahead for Him), **remained under a cross** (an execution pole for suspending a body) **– despising shame** (or: thinking nothing of [the] disgrace)."

To more clearly see what Paul is expressing, here, let us examine the parts of his statement:
a) **[There is] much freedom of speech, frankness, outspokenness and boldness in me, toward you folks**;
b) **[There is] much boasting in me, over** (in regard to) **you**; *Cf* 1 Cor. 1:4
c) **I have been filled full so that I am stuffed with relief, encouragement and comfort**;
d) **I continue overflowing from the progressive flood of superabundance which encircles me in joy**;

And now he concludes, regarding these spiritual riches: "**which tops all our pressure and tribulation** (or: by the joy upon every squeezing, ordeal, affliction and oppression)." He put it this way in Phil. 2:17,

"**But even more, since** (or: if) **I am also repeatedly poured out as a drink offering upon the sacrificial offering and public service pertaining to your faith** (or: which comes from your trust; in regard to the faithful loyalty which comprises you people), **I am constantly rejoicing** (or: glad) **– even continually rejoicing** (glad) **together with all of you!**" *Cf* 4:12, above.

This is the attitude, the mindset, the horizon and mental focus that was in Christ (Phil. 2:5). Paul could only say this by his actually living in the realm of Eph. 2:6, and in the reality of Gal. 2:20,

"**I was crucified together with Christ** [= the Messiah], **and thus it remains** (or: I have been jointly put on the execution stake in [the] Anointed One, and continue in this state)**… yet I continue living! [It is] no longer I, but it is Christ continuously living and alive within me!**"

If we do not live in this realm or in the awareness of the reality of this statement, we will have great difficulty in giving attending service, or in dispensing the Word, Life and Spirit of Christ. Jesus gave this testimony of Himself, and set the pattern of the Way pointed out:

"**I, Myself, am continually unable** (or: As for Me, I habitually have no power or ability) **to be doing anything from Myself: correspondingly as I am continuously hearing, I am habitually sifting, separating, evaluating and deciding** (or: judging), **and My deciding** (separating and evaluating; judging) **is right and just (continues being in accord with the Way pointed out and is turned in the right direction of fairness, equity, justice and right relationship), because I am not seeking my own will** (intent; purpose), **but rather the purpose** (intent; will) **of the One sending Me**" (Jn. 5:30).

This is one of the keys of kingdom living. Paul obviously used this key. It gave him so much joy that he had no need of financial, or any other kind of, gain from his spiritual children. He only wanted to give, just like his Master. Being a part of Christ's body, Paul functioned like Christ:

"**You see, even the Son of the Man** (or: For it follows that the Human's son, as well,) **did not come** (or: does not go) **to be given attending service, but to the contrary, to give attending service, and further, to give His soul** (or: the consciousness from Him; the conscious life, which is him) **[as] a ransom payment – a loosener for unbinding and release – for, as, in the place of, and thus on behalf of and which corresponds to, many people**" (Mk. 10:45).

5. **For even upon our coming into Macedonia, our flesh** (= physical selves, or inner natural beings) **had not had a let-up or slackening** (a release so as to be at ease; relief), **but to the contrary, among all people and in every situation and manner [we were] ones being continuously pressed, rubbed together, afflicted and oppressed: outside, fights and battles; inside, fears!**

We want to point out that here it is their "**flesh**" that has no rest from stress and ordeals, while in 2:13, above, he uses the same term, but in reference to his spirit: "**I had not had a release** (or: a relaxing; a letting flow; a relief) **in** (or: by; to; for; with) **my spirit** (or: inner breath-effect; attitude)." Two different spheres of experiences, and both spheres can wear us out. Here, their flesh was suffering harsh opposition.

Paul was a kingdom priest who could sympathize with the lack of strength of other people, because like his Master, he was a person "**having been put to the proof – in accord with all things** (or: down with all men; corresponding to all people) **[and] in corresponding likeness**" (Heb. 4:15). What he describes of his experiences in this verse is simply the cruciform life, as described by Jesus in Mat. 16:24-25. Paul himself had preached,

> "**It continues binding and necessary for us to enter into the reign of God** (or: God's kingdom; the sovereign activities which are God) **through the midst of many pressures, squeezings, tribulations, afflictions and oppressions**" (Acts 14:22b).

Now it is possible that he is listing all these ordeals to explain the extent of what he almost casually described in vs. 4 as, "**all our pressure and tribulation.**" Recall 4:8, above, "**constantly pressed [as grapes] on every [side]** (etc.)." This then strengthens his argument that the "**progressive flood of superabundance which encircles me in joy**" – along with the other blessings listed in vs. 4 – tops even the serious pressures and afflictions mentioned here in vs. 5. He seems to be following the Path that is described in the Servant passages of Isaiah (e.g., Isa. 53). He is following our Lord. He is being led by the Spirit (Rom. 8:14), and now see what this looks like! Does it remind us of the "valley of the shadow of death" (Ps. 23)? Perhaps he is alluding to his previous letter, where in 1 Cor. 15:32 he said, "**if I fight** (or: fought) **in accord with human [means, methods or purposes] with wild beasts in Ephesus…**" Yes, it seems that he experienced what John saw by a vision (Rev. 13:6-18). In vs, 10b of that chapter we read,

> "**The patient and persistent endurance** (or: the steadfast, humble and supportive remaining-under) **and the reliability and faith of the set-apart ones** (or: trust and loyal confidence of the holy folks) **continually exists here**" (Rev. 13:10b).

Paul's last phrase in this verse, "inside, fears," could be understood corporately of his dispensing team, as well as individually, of each member. Everyone has to face inner fears when adversarial situations suddenly loom against us. We again point to what he described in 12:7, below: "**something with [its] point in [my] flesh is given IN me: an agent of** (or: a messenger from) **the adversary.**" Perhaps it was this to which he referred in Gal. 6:17, "**for I myself continuously carry the brand marks of Jesus, within** (or: the effects of being stuck by a point from Jesus, on) **my body!**" For more details of his ordeals, read ahead in 11:25-29, below. The last two phrases, here, that parallel Deut. 32:25a, may have been on Paul's mind:
> "The sword shall deal death without, as shall the terror within" (Tanakh).

These were not easy times. Both **fears**, above, and "terror," here, are in the realm of the **flesh**, but we have vs. 6, below: "**Nevertheless God…**" This passage in Deut. 32 spoke of God's judgment upon Israel for their idolatry. Was Paul perhaps not simply recounting the hard times that they had gone through, but also alluding to Jesus' words in Lu. 23:28-31, on His way to be crucified? This letter was written circa AD 56, some ten years before the Jewish rebellion against Rome. Was Paul discerning the political scene? Did Paul sense that, due mostly to their personal persecutions from the Jews, that fulfillment of Jesus' prophecies in Mat. 24 and Lu. 21 was near, and that his oppressions were a prelude to an episode of "Jacob's troubles" (Jer. 30:6-9)?

6. Nevertheless God, the One continuously performing as a Paraclete for the low ones (i.e., repeatedly calling the humbled and downhearted to [His] side to give them aid, relief, ease, comfort and encouragement), **paracleted** (comforted, assisted and encouraged) **us in the arrival and presence** (*parousia*) **of Titus,**

We who have followed the Way for any length of time can certainly relate to the first two words of this verse, "**Nevertheless God** (often rendered: But God...)." These opening words call to mind Eph. 2:4, "**But God, continuously being rich in mercy, because of His vast Love**." Because of His vast Love, He continuously performs as a Paraclete. Many a woe besets us during our journey through this life. Our consistent witness has always been, "Nevertheless God." Many were the times, during my childhood, that I would hear my mother quote 1 Sam. 7:12, which she simplified to, "Ebenezer, Hitherto hath the LORD helped us." That was her, "Nevertheless God." It is amazing how one short sentence can be embedded into a child's heart to bear fruit in many seasons over a person's life – and that statement of faith by my mother is one such example. The old saying, "Through thick and thin" seems for the majority of folks to be "through thin." But for those of us of whom this has been the case, if we were blessed to have had planted within us a "Nevertheless God," at some point, we value the thin times more than the thick. The Celtic tradition of "thin places" – although describing something different than that of which I have been speaking – refers to places or encounters where we experience the divine, the sacred. Well, both traditions of "the thin" intersect at the same point. And this is that to which Paul was referring, here in vs. 6. Consider how Paul described one such encounter: "**the One continuously performing as a Paraclete for the low ones paracleted us!**"

Because of the theological reference to the Holy Spirit as the Paraclete (KJV renders it as "Comforter" in Jn. 14:16) my rendering is a transliteration of first the participle, and then the verb – and elsewhere as a noun. The dependent clause that follows the subject, "God," is set off by commas and functions as a description of God. He is "**the One continuously performing as a Paraclete for the low ones** (i.e., repeatedly calling the humbled and downhearted to [His] side to give them aid, relief, ease, comfort and encouragement)." What a beautiful description. "Ebenezer!" The parenthetical expansion gives us the definition of the term with the semantic range of the word included). This is what God does "**for the low ones**." Kinda' like what Jesus did, during His ministry, eh? Paul put so much into four Greek words!

Now we get to the verb, that tells us what God did for Paul and his comrades: He "**paracleted**" them! He comforted, assisted and encouraged them. All this came about simply "**in the arrival and presence of Titus**." And today, we find that there are so many who believe in God, and yet who do not think that God is working through such a simple thing as the arrival of a friend who will help us. Well, as has happened in the past, many a time, things today are changing. When hard times come, many who profess that God does not enter into history or act personally in peoples' lives, begin to ask God for help. Like Israel in Egypt, they begin to groan under their burdens, and God hears them and responds. This is too large a topic to cover in this work, but let us just point our readers to the witness of the OT, the witness of the Gospels, the witness of Acts, the witness of the Epistles, and finally the witness of Revelation. If you believe in the God of these Scriptures, how can you doubt that He/She, etc., is involved in His creation? Paul believed that it was God who was comforting and assisting him through the *parousia* (**the arrival and presence**) of Titus. May we receive his instruction, and be blessed.

> "**Now may our Lord, Jesus Christ Himself, even** (or: and) **our God and Father, the One loving** (accepting) **us and giving a calling alongside pertaining to the Age** (or: performance as a Paraclete with age-lasting aid; eonian relief, encouragement, consolation and admonition)... **be at once calling your hearts alongside and establishing** (making to stand fast; making stable and firm) **you**..." (2 Thes. 2:16-17a).

7. **yet, not only in his presence** (*parousia*), **but further, also within the relief, comfort and encouragement** (the influence of a paraclete) **in which he was paracleted** (comforted and encouraged) **upon you folks [i.e., over your situation], repeatedly reporting back to us your longing** (strong and anxious love with fond regret), **your grievous expression of anguish and remorse, your fiery zeal** (ardor) **over me – with result that it caused me rather to rejoice –**

Here we see the flow of the Spirit (the Paraclete) flowing back and forth between members of Christ's body. Where one group or member is comforted or encouraged, a similar effect happens to other members of the body. This demonstrates the UNION and CONNECTEDNESS between the members of the body. We have all experienced such things. Just hearing a good report concerning others can cause us "**to rejoice.**" This beauty of solidarity brings life to our spirits. How far better is it than divisions that arise over doctrines, or over various allegiances to groups (or factions).

"**Your grievous expression of anguish and remorse, your fiery zeal over me**" is explained in the next verse: "**the letter.**" The phrase, "**over me**" would refer to what he had said in that letter. Now, through Titus, he received the report of their reaction to the letter, and this reaction was what he had hoped that the letter would invoke. The hyperbole, expressed in the terms "**fiery zeal**" that describes their response to his message, suggests both that Titus' report was vivid and that the Corinthian community was noticeably stirred to a reformation of their behavior – at least at that time! The three-fold repetition of the personal pronoun "**your**" is in each case in the emphatic position in the Greek. This emphasis tells us that what the Corinthians had shown in their "strong and anxious love," their "anguish and remorse," and their "ardor," had impacted and comforted Paul.

8. **because even if I made you sad and anxious** (or: cause you grief, pain and sorrow) **in the letter, I am now not regretting or changing my purpose of conduct – even if I had been regretting and altering my purpose of conduct – for I see** (observe) **that that letter made you sad and anxious** (grieved, pained and sorrowful), **even if for an hour.**

Paul does not regret what he had said to them in a previous (lost to us) letter, because he sees that it had its intended effect upon the Corinthians. Any sadness or anxiety that it may have caused would be temporary. It is obvious that his intent was for them to be "made sad, anxious, pained, sorrowful," and that they would be grieved, because of what he had said in that letter.

As regards to Paul "**not regretting or changing [his] purpose of conduct,**" the Greek verb is *metamelomai*: to change one's judgment on past points of conduct; to change one's purpose; to regret. It is unfortunate that the KJV rendered this as "repent," as though it were the verb *metanoeō*: to change one's mode of thought, way of thinking or perspective. Rendering it "repent" omits the sense of regret, or a change of purpose. Paul had a definite purpose for writing the previous letter to which he refers. He is saying that he neither has a regret from writing it, nor has he changed the purpose of his conduct in this matter. In all of his letters, Paul uses the verb *metanoeō* only once: in 12:21, below. He uses the noun *metanoia* (a change in thinking and frame of mind) in vss. 9 and 10, below, but nowhere else in these two letters to Corinth. It does not seem to be a central part of his theology, or of great significance for his presentation of the Good News to the Gentiles (Acts 15:19-30; Gal. 2:7). He seems to focus more on the work of God, in and through Christ, which brings a complete change for people to be other than they were (to be a part of the Second, One new Humanity) in the new age of the new covenant, which he terms "a new creation." *Cf* 5:14-21, above. Furthermore, he uses the verb *metamelomai* only here, in all of his writings. Let us further consider these things…

How should we understand this development in Paul? When John the Immerser came on the scene, he called the Judeans to *metanoeō*:
> "**You folks be continuously and progressively changing your THINKING – change your perceptions, attitudes, frame of mind, mode of thought and understanding, and turn back**

[to God, in a new direction], **because the reign and dominion of the heavens is now near at hand and is close enough to touch** (= has arrived and is now accessible)!" (Mat. 3:2).

Then, in vs. 11, John explains to his listeners,

"**I myself, on the one hand, continue immersing you folks in water, [which proceeds] into the midst of a change in THINKING...** '

Then, in vs. 13, Jesus comes to be immersed by John, and in vs. 14 John objects, saying that he is the one who should be immersed by Jesus, but Jesus replies,

"**Let this situation flow its course and send [Me] off, right now** (at present), **for it is in this way proper and fitting for us to fulfill all that accords with eschatological deliverance from the Way pointed out, making full being TURNED in the RIGHT DIRECTION; righting covenantal relationship**" (Mat. 3:15).

We might ask, Did Jesus need to change His own thinking? Well, He was raised a Jew, and as Paul explains, Jesus was "**being Himself come to be born under [the rules, authority and influence of] Law,** [*cf* Ex. 19:17, LXX: 'under {Sinai}']" (Gal. 4:4). But His vocation was to be the Messiah, the Deliverer. He would have had to change His frame of mind from being just a Judean craftsman, and like John, to confront the Judean leadership – because He was bringing the kingdom of God. He would have to change His thinking about the temple (*cf* Jn. 4:21-24), and would later predict its destruction (Mat. 24).

Later, in Mat. 4:17 we read,

"**From that time on, Jesus began to be repeatedly making loud public proclamations** (performing as a herald), **and to be continually saying, "You folks be progressively changing your thinking** (change your frame of mind, mode of thought, perceptions and understanding and turn your focus to [Yahweh]), **BECAUSE the sovereign reign, dominion and activity of exercising the sovereignty of the heavens** (or: kingdom from the sky and the atmosphere) **has drawn near and now continues being at hand and is close enough to touch** (= has arrived and is now accessible)."

This was the key to *metanoeō*: the change in thinking was necessary because of the advent of God's reign imposing itself upon the world, through the advent of Israel's Messiah. As we saw in 5:17, new things had come.

On the Day of Pentecost, with the coming of the Spirit, Peter told the citizens of Jerusalem and those who had come for the Feast,

"**At once change your way of thinking** (your frame of mind and point of view; [by customary use this implies: and turn in a different direction, to Yahweh]). **Then at once let each one of you folks be immersed** (baptized) **within the Name** (= in union with the identity, the character, the authority, the essence) **of Jesus Christ** (or: of [the] Anointed Jesus; which is Jesus [the Messiah]) – **into the midst of a release and sending away, a divorce and an abandonment, a cancellation and a forgiveness: of your failures, your mistakes, your times of missing the target, your errors, your deviations and your sins – and then you will proceed receiving and continue taking in hand the free gift** (the gratuity) **of the Set-apart Breath-effect** (or: which is the Holy Spirit; or: which is from, and has the character of, the Sacred Attitude)" (Acts 2:38).

What is the common thread, from John the Immerser, on through the ministry and death of Jesus, and into the book of Acts? Like Jesus told the Samaritan woman, "**the deliverance** (the rescue and being restored; the health and wholeness; the salvation) **continues being** (habitually is; constantly exists being) **from out of the Judeans** (or: from among those of Judah {or: from the Jews})" (Jn. 4:22). It was the Judeans, and the Samaritans (who also claimed Jacob as their father – Jn. 4:12), who lived by the Torah, the old covenant, who during the ministry of Jesus needed to change their thinking into the reality that the promises to Abraham, Isaac and Jacob were being fulfilled in Jesus, that the Messiah had come. Dan Kaplan pointed us to how Peter emphasized the distinction between these folks who lived under the Law, and the Gentiles who were later to receive the Good News:

"To YOU folks FIRST, God, in raising up His Servant (or: Boy), **sent Him forth continually blessing you people and repeatedly speaking words of goodness, ease and well-being within the [situation for] constantly and progressively TURNING each one away from your misery-gushed situation of worthless conditions, laborious works, painful relationships, malicious deeds** (or: from these wicked ways, as well as from the evil thoughts, plans and dispositions of you people)" (Acts 3:26).

Notice the subtle change from Peter's first response in Acts 2:38, to now explaining that, through the resurrection of Jesus, God was "**constantly and progressively TURNING each one...**" The understanding of what was being accomplished by the work of Christ was being expanded into a perception of the ongoing work of the Holy Spirit in people's lives.

Paul would later explain how the promise to Abraham had included the ethnic multitudes (the Gentiles). But these new branches (Rom. 11:17ff) would not need to change their thinking away from Israel's old covenant. So *metanoia* did not need to have the same prominence to the Gentiles as it needed to have for the Israelites. The Gentiles were now included because the new covenant had been inaugurated in the blood of Jesus (Mat. 26:28; 1 Cor. 11:25). This would indeed create a change in their thinking, but Paul did not use this verb in regard to them in the way that John, Jesus or Peter had used it, in regard to Israel.

Now it seems to us that, at least with John and Jesus, there were imperatives that were given before the empowerment had happened, via Jesus' resurrection and the coming of the Spirit in the new arrangement. Their imperatives ("Change your thinking") were based upon the nearness, and the accessibility, of the kingdom ("because the kingdom/reign has drawn near and is close enough to touch"). When Paul admonished the Roman community to "be transformed by the RENEWING of your mind" (Rom. 12:2), we see him as encouraging them to live out of the mind of Christ that had been given to them (1 Cor. 2:16b), the presence of which was ongoingly renewing their minds (their perceptions; their way of thinking). This is the working of the Spirit, within us. This renewing produces transformation. While being rightwised implies an action of God upon the individual, once they are "pointed in a different direction (i.e., the Way pointed out)," it results in a new horizon and a different way of thinking (Christ).

During the ministries of John the immerser, and Jesus, the Seed was being planted, and It had Life within It, but once It sprouted (resurrection) that new Life was being manifested in His body -- those firstfruit folks. In the same way, Jesus was forgiving sins before the cross. This was the heralding of Israel's deliverance from exile -- for their sins were what took them into exile, and even though some had returned in the days of Ezra & Nehemiah, they were still under Persian rule, and now in the 1st century AD, they were still under the thumb of Rome. They were still under a political state of domination, and that equaled to being in exile. The Atonement, the cleansing away of Israel's sins, needed to happen (through Christ's blood), and this would also cleanse all the temple furniture. But with the event of His resurrection, there was a new temple, a heavenly one: His body, the called-out folks. And with this resurrection, new terms came into view -- like *apokatastasis* which we find in Acts 3:21. That new term described a movement away from what had been "put down and established" (i.e., the Sinai covenant, and behind that, the exile of Adam from the Garden of Eden). We noted the new term, *katallassō* in 5:18-19, above. The new age brought new terms and a new emphasis.

Heb. 6 also comes to mind (the field of good soil that had become overgrown with weeds and brambles, which needed to be burned off so that a new crop could be sown -- lest the Seed would fall among the weeds and thorns and be choked off) and tied to this was John the Immerser's proclamation that the Messiah would thoroughly purge His threshing floor (for it was harvest time for Israel), which he characterized as an immersion into Fire and Holy Spirit. God was still operating through His prophets (John and Jesus) within the closing days of the old age, the Mosaic covenant. But He was in process of making all things new (Rev. 21:5) -- a "new creation," as Paul termed it in 5:17, above. Jesus spoke of this as "the resurrection," in Mat. 22:30, and "the rebirth" in Mat. 19:28 -- which we read as being synonymous – and these we understand as being references to our being placed into Christ, and to the realm of the new covenant (e.g., Eph. 2:5-6). Of course all of this was the work of Christ and the Holy Spirit, and specifically what was about to happen in the conjunction of the ages (the change from the old covenant to the new) although, like the cross itself, it continues applicable on throughout the ages as people continue being born. All that we have discussed on the topic of Paul's little use of the verb *metanoeō* may seem like very fine points of interpretation, but as these observations soak in, we find that they are important aspects of the Christ Event, and what followed as the "new creation" came into being.

9. **Now I continue rejoicing – not just that you folks were at one point made sad or anxious** (pained or sorrowful) **– but rather, that you were made sad and anxious [leading you] into a change in thinking and frame of mind, for you were saddened and made anxious down from, in the sphere of, in line with, and in correspondence to, God, to the end that you could in nothing be disadvantaged through loss, injury or damage due to** (or: from) **us.**

Here we see that the intent of the previous letter was "**a change in thinking and frame of mind**" with regard to the subject matter of the letter. Then he makes an important point about the existential realm of what was most likely a "child-training and corrective" content of that letter: it was "**in the sphere of, in line with, and in correspondence to, God**" and in fact it had, through Paul, come "**down from God.**" This expanded conflation expresses the semantic range of the preposition *kata*. A common rendering of the phrase is a rather ambiguous, "godly grief," and Nyland paraphrases it, "you were made sad, as God would have it." So Paul assures them that their sadness and anxiety was not merely human sadness or anxiety, but that these feelings, or moods, came from the realm of God, through the *Logos* of Paul's previous letter. Might we be well advised to view any sadness or anxiety as something that God has sent us, for our training – especially if it comes through a member of Christ's body? Should we examine our situation and ask our Father if He is prompting us to a change in our thinking or our frame of mind?

The first thing that we should discern is whether or not our sadness or anxiety has God as its source. If we perceive that it does (especially if our normal horizon is that "**all things are from out of God**" – 5:18, above), keep in mind what Paul goes on to explain in this next verse…

10. **For you see, the anxiety, sadness and pain down from** (or: in the sphere of; in line with; in correspondence to) **God continuously works, habitually effects and progressively produces a change in thinking and frame of mind: [in turn, leading] into a deliverance and wholeness of health** (a rescue and restoration to the original state and realm; salvation) **void of regret and without change in purpose. Yet the anxiety, sadness, pain and sorrow which belongs to the world** (or: from the dominating, organized System of religion, culture, or government; which pertains to the aggregate of humanity) **is continuously working down the production of death** (or: is in line with repeatedly and progressively bringing about death).

We might see in the first clause an allusion to Jer. 31:18-20,
> "You have disciplined me, and I am disciplined… Restore me, and let me return… Indeed, after my captivity, I repented (was filled with regret), and after I [was] informed (came to know myself), I slapped [my] thigh [in grief]; I am ashamed and mortified…. Therefore My internal [parts] clamor for him; I (must) have compassion upon him, averring [is] Yahweh" (CVOT; parenthetical additions: Rotherham). *Cf* Mat. 26:75

Since Paul is now speaking about potential situations or experiences that are beyond the specific situation of his letter, I added the semantic meaning of "**pain**" for this Greek word, *lupē*. Here, he explains that if is from God, or if it is in the sphere of God, or if it is in line with God, or corresponds to God, then there will be a positive result. Anxiety, sadness or pain that have this relation to God,
> "**continuously works, habitually effects and progressively produces a change in thinking and frame of mind: [in turn, leading] into a deliverance and wholeness of health** (a rescue

and restoration to the original state and realm; salvation) **void of regret and without change in purpose**."

For many people this will be hard to swallow. But let us consider the horizon from which Paul has been speaking all through his letters to Corinth. First of all, would we not say that the "**anxiety, sadness and pain**" which Christ experienced had this very effect? Paul experienced the same thing, as we read in his various letters. Christ's experiences "continuously work, habitually effect and progressively produce" these things for, and in us. Paul is saying that these negative experiences – when they are associated with God – produce the same things in us, and then through us, in and for others. This very sort of thing was a central ingredient that enabled Paul to be an attending servant, and a dispenser, to the called-out communities. These Corinthians were already those who had been given trust and were already in Christ – this is what made them a called-out, covenant community. So here he is speaking about their ethical behavior, and the ongoing work of the Spirit which progressively brings a change in their thinking about certain behavioral issues. The deliverance and wholeness would be in the sphere of their ongoing transformation, from glory to glory (and: from opinion to opinion), as he said in 3:18, above. His thrust involves their becoming God's image-bearers, reflecting the glory of Christ, living worthy of their calling, their vocation (*cf* Eph. 4:1).

The term rendered "**void of regret and without change in purpose**" can modify either "**a deliverance (etc.)**" or "**a change in thinking and frame of mind**" – both make sense, and this may be why Paul said it this way in the text.

Now in contrast to this are the negative experiences "**which belongs to the world** (or: from the dominating, organized System of religion, culture, or government; which pertains to the aggregate of humanity)." Paul is contrasting two existential, although simultaneous, realms of existence. This latter realm "**is continuously working down the production of death** (or: is in line with repeatedly and progressively bringing about death)." *Cf* Mat. 27:4-5

If we continue "joined to the Vine" (Jn. 15:1ff), and if we continue beholding Him with unveiled faces and hearts (3:18, above) we will not fall into the world's negative feelings or moods. This does not put any burden upon us, but is simply the way it is. We may have experiences where we might say, "Father, if it is possible, take this cup from me." But the very fact of bringing this situation to the Father, in such a request, will assure us that this pain, anxiety, sadness or sorrow is in the realm of God, and He will work it into good (Rom. 8:28). We will also know that this is the case of the matter when we observe the results, as Paul goes on to explain…

11. **For consider** (or: look)! **This very thing – the [experience for] you to be made sad and anxious down from and in accord with God – to what extent it accomplished** (produces; worked down and effects) **[qualities] of haste to earnest diligence in you folks; but further, verbal defense** (apologetics); **but still further, indignant displeasure [with the whole situation]; yet further, fear and respect!; but then, longing** (strong and anxious love with fond regret); **on the other hand, fiery zeal and enthusiasm; yes, in fact, righting of what is wrong** (maintaining equity out of rightwised relationships from the fairness of the Way pointed out; awarding of justice [to all parties]) **– within the midst of everything, in every respect, in union with every situation, as well as among all people, while placing yourselves, and standing, together to continuously exist being pure in this practice-effect** (or: results of the matter).

The first clause, together with its accomplishments, calls to mind Jer. 50:4-6a.
> "'In those days and at that time,' declares the LORD, 'the sons of Israel will come… they will go along weeping… and it will be the LORD their God they will seek. They will ask for the Way to Zion… they will come that they may join themselves to the LORD…. My people have become lost sheep; their shepherds have led them astray…'" (NASB) *Cf* Zech. 12:10

The rest of this verse presents the fruit of the cruciform Life, and so let us observe what it produces:

  a) **it accomplished** (produces; worked down and effects) **[qualities] of haste to earnest diligence in [them]**; -- this is just the opposite of sloth and slumber; it speaks of vitality of Life;

  b) **verbal defense** (apologetics); -- concerning the message of goodness, ease and well-being;

  c) **indignant displeasure [with the whole situation]**; -- the negative aspect of our environment;

  d) **fear and respect!**; -- in all appropriate situations;

  e) **longing** (strong and anxious love with fond regret); -- in regard to the sorrows of others;

  f) **fiery zeal and enthusiasm**; -- as conduits of the Spirit;

  g) **righting of what is wrong** (maintaining equity out of rightwised relationships from the fairness of the Way pointed out; awarding of justice [to all parties]); -- being instruments of dispensing;

  h) **placing yourselves, and standing, together to continuously exist being pure in this practice-effect** (or: results of the matter); -- "standing in the gap" with the standard of Victory!

And all of this was "**within the midst of everything, in every respect, in union with every situation, as well as among all people.**" So the results of "**the anxiety, sadness and pain down from** (or: in the sphere of; in line with; in correspondence to) **God**" are both practical and effective for our vocation (calling) of bringing God's reign (kingdom, sovereign activities and influences) to the world around us.

12. **Consequently, even if I write** (or: although I wrote) **to you, [it is] not on account of the one doing wrong** (or: the person behaving contrary to the Way pointed, acting unjustly or being injurious; the offender), **nor either on account of the one being wronged** (the person being treated unfairly or unjustly; the one being injured; the victim), **but rather on account of the [opportunity] to set in clear light and manifest to you folks your haste to earnest and diligent care – that which [was] over us and on our behalf – in God's sight and presence. Because of this we have been, and remain, encouraged and comforted** (we have received the influence of a paraclete).

His opening remark in this verse, "**Consequently,**" is a reference to the previous verse and all the good results that had happened due to his writing to them. The verb which follows is in the aorist tense, and so can be construed as either a simple present, "**I write**," which could refer to this present letter, or, as a simple past tense, "I wrote," which would refer to the previous, "lost" letter. In either case, the purpose for the letter was neither because of the offender (in the matter which he does not bring up again) nor on account of the victim of the offense. He was not writing to bring condemnation to anyone (Rom. 8:1-2), "**but rather on account of the [opportunity] to set in clear light and manifest to you folks your haste to earnest and diligent care.**" He brings (or had brought) up the whole issue in order to let them see and perceive the image of God that they would reflect within that situation. He is wanting to encourage them by letting their behavior be set in clear light – so that they would realize their own growth in Christ's Love. They had manifested "**haste to earnest and diligent care over us, and on our behalf,**" and this was one more thing to add to the list of benefits in vs. 11.

But more than this, their loving response toward Paul and his associates was "**in God's sight and presence.**" God was not absent, somewhere off in the universe making new stars (although of course He may also have been doing that, too!) but was PRESENT, there among them. This meant that they were living in the heavens – the realm and atmosphere of God – corresponding to Eph. 2:6. And so, because of all of this, Paul's group had been, and remained (the perfect tense of the verb), "**encouraged and comforted** (we have received the influence of a paraclete)." THIS is exactly Paul's goal: for THEM to be paracletes for other people. Their behavior, in a difficult situation, was the work of The Paraclete (the Holy Spirit) ministering back to Paul's group, doing the same work of the Spirit that the sent-forth representatives were doing for the called-out communities. Paul had multiplied himself (thus multiplying Christ) in them. He had been a seed that was planted in Corinth, and now he was encouraged to see a harvest of that Seed. They were being co-laborers with Christ! (1 Cor. 3:9)

13. Yet, in addition to our encouragement and comfort, we rejoice still more abundantly due to the joy of Titus, because his spirit has been rested up and continues refreshed by all of you folks (or: from you all),

This is a second witness for them: another example of how their behavior was being a paraclete. Paul does not elaborate about just how Titus was refreshed by the Corinthian community, other than the situation had brought him joy, and "**his spirit [had] been rested up and [continued] refreshed**" by the entire called-out group. They were manifesting the fruit of the Spirit; they were living as sons of God (Rom. 8:19), and "**the creation [was] constantly receiving and taking away from out of this unveiling**" of them, and from their "disclosure." We have, for our consideration on this verse, Paul's request for prayer, in Rom. 15:31b-32,

> "**that my attending service of dispensing which is directed into Jerusalem may come to be well-received by, and acceptable to, the set-apart people** (holy ones; saints; sacred folks) **in order that, in coming to you in joy through God's will and purpose, I myself will proceed to be taking rest, repose and refreshing in company with you folks.**"

14. because if I have made any boast to him, over you folks, I have not been brought down in shame or disgrace, but to the contrary, as we speak all things to you folks in truth and reality, thus also our boasting on Titus came to be truth (produced reality)

How good Paul's listeners must have felt as they heard this letter read to them: they had not let Paul or his associates down, in the matters corresponding to Titus' arrival among them. They had lived up to all of Paul's boasts to Titus about them. Paul had been confident in doing this because he and his fellows "**speak all things to you folks in truth and reality**" – there was no false praise in their words. They had not tried to manipulate the folks in Corinth.

15. and so his innermost feelings and compassions (literally: internal organs; intestines) **are progressing more abundantly unto you folks, while progressively calling back to mind the submissive hearing and humble obedience of you all – as with fear and trembling** (or: respect and attentive concern) **you received him.**

The result of Titus experiencing the fruit of the Spirit from the called-out in Corinth made "**his innermost feelings and compassions [to be] progressing more abundantly unto [them].**" The results from Paul's letter had caused the folks in Corinth to be even more endeared to him. What a beautiful testimony of the purposes of God in our lives, even when our experiences are "**the anxiety, sadness and pain**" (vs. 10, above).

And more than that, Titus was "**calling back to mind [their] submissive hearing and humble obedience**" – more fruit of the Spirit – as they "**received him**" with "respect and attentive concern," while trembling with fear that they would fail to do enough for him, or would let him down. Paul spoke of concern about their "humble obedience" in 2:9, above. They must have taken to heart the 13th chapter of Paul's first letter to them. In line with these things, we have what Paul affirmed and admonished in Phil. 2:12,

> "**Consequently, my loved ones, according as at all times** (or: as always) **you folks submissively listened, paid attention and humbly obeyed, not as only in my presence, but further, now** (at this moment) **much more in my absence – in company with reverent fear and trembling** (or: = earnestness and concern) **– be habitually working commensurately with the deliverance** (or: be constantly producing on the level and sphere of the wholeness and well-being which are the outcome of the rescue and salvation) **of, or pertaining to, yourselves.**"

16. I continue rejoicing, that in everything I am constantly with good courage and confidence in you – that I can keep on depending and relying on you folks.

Nothing needs to be said about Paul's words here. They sum up all that he has just been saying to them. But we observe that he spoke similarly to those in Thessalonica:

> "**Yet we have been persuaded and so place confidence on you, in [the] Lord** [= Christ or Yahweh], **that the things which we are repeatedly passing along as an announcement to you people, you folks both habitually do and will continue doing** (or: normally produce and will keep on producing)" (2 Thes. 3:4; *cf* Philemon 21).

Chapter 8

Chapters 8 and 9 have traditionally been interpreted as Paul bringing up, again, the topic of the collection of money which he was in the process of raising from all the called-out communities, which would then be given to the poor in Jerusalem. He had previously presented this project to them in 1 Cor. 16:1ff. Now, it is felt, that he is subtly reminding them of their financial commitment to this cause. *The New Bible Commentary: Revised* (Wm. B. Eerdmans, 1970) gives the following chapter headings: "8:1-24 the Collection" and "9:1-15 Principles of Christian giving" (pp 1082, 1083). Now we grant some merit to this reading of the text, but if we only read these chapters from the window of this general categorization, or from what we may discern as a rhetorical construct in which Paul would then be seen as manipulating his audience, we might miss some of the fine points of what he is saying and misconstrue his actual intent. So let us read the text, keeping in mind that in 9:7, below, he does in fact broach the topic of giving. But we question whether these two chapters have contributing money to a cause as their main content. So let us see…

1. **Now, brothers** (folks from the same Womb; = family), **we are progressively making known to you God's grace** (the joyous favor from, and which has the character and quality of, God; the GRACE which is God), **which has been given and now continues as a gift among the called-out folks** (or: in union with the called-out communities) **of Macedonia,**

The covenant communities in the province of Macedonia were in Thessalonica, Philippi and Beroea.

This first passage, from vs. 1 through vs. 7, opens with "**grace**/favor" and ends with the phrase, "**centered in this grace** (amidst this favor)." We also find the term "grace" in vss. 4, and 6, along with the topic of which Paul has been repeatedly speaking, above, brought into the discussion about grace, in vs. 4: "**the attending service**," and "**the dispensing**." Now in vs. 2, below, where I have first chosen the semantic meaning of the Greek term as "**singleness and simplicity**," the KJV chose the meaning "liberality," and others have chosen the meaning "generosity." Which meaning we choose (if we offer only one from among others) can influence the reading of the text. Furthermore, the KJV renders the word "grace/favor" as "gift" in vs. 4, planting a particular interpretation into the mind of the reader. The NRSV renders the word as "generous undertaking," at the end of vs. 6, but to their credit it footnotes the fact that the Greek is the word "grace," and in this same place the ESV gives us "this ACT of grace," again slightly tweaking the text to a presumed interpretation. But before we move from this overview, take note of what Paul said that those in Macedonia were giving, in vs. 5: **they gave themselves**. Our point is that Paul is speaking about much more than money in this opening passage.

Paul's opening words are relational and conciliatory: "Now brothers (etc.)…" Next he affirms that God's **grace** was being progressively known to them. But they are not the only ones who are learning about "the joyous favor from, and which has the character and quality of, God." No, there are others included in this: he affirms that "**the GRACE which is** [actually] **God**" has also been given to the called-out folks in Macedonia. The perfect tense of the verb in the last clause, "has been given," tells us that they now have

GRACE as a "gift." As noted, about vs. 5, the gift of grace to them compelled them to now give themselves to others. That is what God is like. That is what is meant by the appositional rendering, "the GRACE which is God." When they were given **grace,** they were given God, as the Gift of Himself, to them. This is the Good News. This is about transformed lives. The next verse explains more, from the JOY that resulted from the gift of GRACE...

2. **how that within the midst of much testing and proving which came through pressure** (or: tribulation, oppression and affliction), **the superabundance of their joy – also contrasted with the depth of their destitution** (poverty, and/or life as beggars) **– superabounds into the wealth** (or: riches) **of their singleness [of heart and purpose] and the simplicity** (un-complexity; integrity; or: openness and sincerity in generous sharing with others) **from them,**

He spoke of the "**pressures** (etc.)" in Acts 16:20 (at Philippi) and 17:5 (Thessalonica) and in 1 Thes. 1:6; 2:14. So, even amidst all the testing and proving that came from pressure, tribulation, oppression and affliction, there also came this **grace** (vs. 1), which was the presence and manifestation of "**The Happy God**" (1 Tim. 1:11 – JMNT; or: "the blissful God" – David Bentley Hart). No wonder they had "**the superabundance of their joy!**" – one aspect of the Fruit of the Spirit (Gal. 5:22). It is the presence of God within, and among, us that gives the Christian "♪joy unspeakable and full of glory♪." In Jn. 15:11, Jesus told His followers, "**I have spoken these things to you to the end that MY joy would** (or: can; should) **remain and continuously exist within the midst of you people, and that your joy may be filled full** (or: fulfilled)."

And that JOY "**superabounded**" – even "**with the depth of their destitution** (poverty, and/or life as beggars)!" – and it came to be "**the wealth** (or: riches) **of their singleness [of heart and purpose] and simplicity.**" As noted above, this last term, "**singleness/simplicity,**" also means: "un-complexity; or: openness and sincerity in generous sharing with others." The first meanings – which arise out of the JOY of the Lord – quite naturally lead into the latter meanings, within the new creation Life of the new covenant. What we have within, we share with others. Jesus also told His followers, "**You folks receive** (or: received) **freely** (as a gift; = without cost), **[so] give freely** (as a gift; = without charge)" (Mt. 10:8b), but notice to what this was referring, in Mat. 10:8a,

> "**Be constantly serving, curing and restoring to health** (or: giving attentive care to and treatment for) **those who are habitually weak, feeble and inadequate. Habitually be rousing and raising up dead people. Be continually cleansing lepers** (scabby folks). **Make it a habit to cast out demons** (Hellenistic concept and term: = animistic influences)."

He was not speaking of freely giving money. Then in the next verse Jesus told them, "**You should not be procuring or acquiring gold, nor yet silver, nor even copper** [i.e., no pocket money] **into your belts or girdle purses.**" Having little or no money, these Macedonians "**gave themselves**" (vs. 5, below). They would have been giving "**singleness [of heart and purpose] and simplicity** (un-complexity)," which was their wealth and riches. But Paul continues, for there is more...

3. **because – I continue bearing witness and testifying that – corresponding to [their] power and in accord with [their] ability, and even beyond [their] actual power and ability, [they are] those who act spontaneously and voluntarily from their own initiative,**

Each person within those Macedonian communities had some degree of "**power,**" and some level of "**ability.**" Now Paul would have included in his meaning whatever sustenance or money that they had – for this is what we do, when we hear of a need among others: this is kingdom living. He leaves it ambiguous when he said, "**and even beyond [their] actual power and ability.**" Did he mean that some may have taken out a loan against their property, or sold an animal, in order to contribute to the need? Or did they "**act spontaneously and voluntarily from their own initiative**" by sending people along with Paul, to give physical help? Could this have been a part of "giving themselves"? Or was it sending along food and supplies to support the needs of everyone traveling with Paul? It may simply have been giving "**the attending service**" to Paul and the rest, in the "performance of a paraclete" – as noted in the next verse…

4. **with much appeal and calling of us to their side to give us relief, assistance and encouragement** (the performance of a paraclete), **repeatedly and constantly begging of us, and from us, the grace** (or: the favor) **and the common participation** (partnership and sharing from common existence) **of the attending service which pertains to the dispensing into the set-apart folks** (the holy ones; the saints; the sacred people).

What Paul is emphasizing here is an expansion of the Macedonians' extreme desire to be a living part of God's reign as it was being expressed through "**the attending service which pertains to the dispensing into the set-apart folks.**" He is saying that they were "**repeatedly and constantly begging of us, and from us, the grace** (or: the favor) **and the common participation** (partnership and sharing from common existence)" – in all of its existential aspects. They had received, and they wanted to be a part of dispensing the Life of Christ to others. Their "begging" for the "favor" – and the necessary supply from God's grace – was accompanied by their "**calling of us to their side to give us relief, assistance and encouragement**" – as they performed as paracletes for Paul and his associates.

Now even though "**the dispensing into the set-apart folks**" may have partially been a reference to a collection of money for the folks in Jerusalem (scholars often narrow the term "the saints, etc.," to the Jewish Christians in Jerusalem), as is traditionally taught, Paul may have been referring to the Macedonians being stirred up to supply more help within their own, local community. We do have Paul arriving in Jerusalem "**to make gifts of mercy and offerings unto [his] nation** (or: ethnic group)" (Acts 24:17), and his references to the same, in Acts. 11:29-30, Rom. 15:14-32 and 1 Cor. 16:1-4, may have been a region-wide response to the Judean famine of AD 46-47. But Paul also seemed to be making a general reference to the Galatians, for them to, "**habitually be mindful of the poor ones** (or: should keep on remembering the destitute folks)" (Gal. 2:10). So we should not box-up Paul's words as referring to just one issue. Keep in mind how he referred to, and addressed, the Corinthians in 1 Cor. 1:2,

> "**to those having been set-apart within Christ Jesus** (or: made holy, sacred, different from the normal and sanctified, in union with an Anointing of, and from, Jesus)**; to called** (or: summoned) **folks [and] to set-apart people** (holy ones; saints; sanctified folks; sacred ones)."

5. **And not according as we expected, but rather they gave themselves first to the Lord** [= Christ or Yahweh; p46 & others read: God], **and next even** (or: also) **to and for us, through the effect of God's will and a result of purpose, which is God,**

Paul is not speaking about the Macedonians giving money to help the poor in Jerusalem (often referred to as "the collection"). Instead, vs. 5 explains that "**the set-apart folks**" of vs. 4 are actually Paul and his associates – to whom the Macedonians "**gave themselves first to the Lord, and next even** (or: also) **to and for us.**" This explains how they wanted to partnership with Paul, *et al*, in "**the attending service and dispensing**" which Paul and his fellows were at that very time giving to the called-out communities. The "sacred people; the set-apart folks" were now all those who were both alive and active in Christ. They are what Paul called the "new creation" in 5:17, above. There was no more Jew/Gentile dichotomy in God's economy. The term "the saints" simply referred to the living branches of Israel's olive tree (Rom. 11:17) that was made up of former Jews and former Gentiles, but had now become a part of a tree of life whose fruit produced the oil of the anointing – they were the body of the Anointed One.

The final prepositional phrase, which I expanded in order to offer two renderings of the terms involved, modifies and thus governs what has come before it. The giving of themselves, by the Macedonians, not only exceeded Paul's expectations, but this happened, "**through the effect of God's will,**" or stated otherwise, through "**a result of purpose, which is God.**" Paul makes it quite clear that God is intimately involved in our lives. He used the preposition *dia* in this phrase, to express the agency and instrumentality of the "will and purpose of God, or which was God" in regard to the self-giving action of the Macedonians. This is why Paul would elsewhere say, "**[It is] no longer I, but it is Christ continuously living and alive within me... in and by that which is the Son of God**" (Gal. 2:20). You see, Christ is not somewhere off in the skies, far away, but rather He is within us. In 1 Cor. 6:17 Paul instructed us that the person who is "joined to the Lord" is "One Spirit," and thus also, is "One Attitude" – that of self-giving Love.

6. **[leading] us to assist and encourage** (to paraclete) **Titus, so that, just as he did before in the beginning, thus, as well, he should fully finish and complete also this favor unto you folks** (or: he should bring this GRACE to its goal, even into the midst of you people).

The assistance and encouragement (the results of the Macedonians functioning as paracletes) was passed from Paul, and his fellows, on to Titus. This is reciprocal body ministry that exemplifies new covenant life in the realm of God's reign. Titus receives the flow of Life, from the Macedonians, on through Paul, *et al*, so that he is energized to pass it on to the folks in Corinth. Thus do we see "**the common participation** (partnership and sharing from common existence) **of the attending service and dispensing**" moving through the joined covenant groups, like blood flowing through the various members of a person's body.

This "**favor**" that Titus will "**fully finish and complete**" unto the Corinthian community is the same GRACE for which the Macedonians begged of Paul, that they would be a part of, in vs. 4, above. Most commentators read the verb "fully finish and complete" as a reference to the Corinthian community keeping their commitment to donate money unto "the collection" that was to go to the Jerusalem called-out. Although that may have been a part of what Paul meant, here, in observing the thread of the theme of "aid and encouragement – performing as a paraclete" that Paul has woven into this tapestry, a more generalized picture comes into view: that of passing on from what we receive; that of being paracletes and joining in with the Father's purpose of giving to others the Spirit's attending service and its dispensing of the Love and the Life of Christ. With these thoughts in mind, let us observe how Paul ties these threads together into an inclusive picture of multiplied virtues, in vs. 7...

7. **But further, even as you folks continuously superabound within everything and among everyone – in faith** (or: with trust; by loyalty) **and in word** (or: by thought, idea, reason, and message; with information) **and in experiential knowledge and by insight, as well as with all haste to earnest diligence, and in the Love** (with unrestricted acceptance; by self-giving) **from out of the midst of us in union with you** [other MSS: the love from you [that is] within us] **– that you may be progressively superabounding, centered in this grace** (amidst this favor), **also.**

He alerts his listeners that he will be saying more on this same topic by the conjunction, "**But further**," and then points them to their "**continuous superabundance within everything and among everyone.**" He is obviously appealing to their sense of how blessed they are, but notice the sphere of this "superabundance":

> "**in faith** (or: with trust; by loyalty) **and in word** (or: by thought, idea, reason, and message; with information) **and in experiential knowledge and by insight, as well as with all haste to earnest diligence, and in the Love** (with unrestricted acceptance; by self-giving)."

These are all spiritual wealth that is topped off by the all-inclusive fruit of the Spirit: Love, which is unrestricted acceptance and self-giving – and also the drive toward reunion with those who have become estranged from us, or from God (the driving force of the ministry of reconciliation).

Observe our thread, again, where Paul informs them that they are joined with him, for all this abundance comes "**from out of the midst of us in union with you.**" The same communion of flow is stated in other MSS as, "the love from you [that is] within us." This flow of life and love provides both the environment and the agency/instrumentality so that THEY "**may be progressively superabounding, centered in this**

397

grace (amidst this favor), **also**." This grace, this favor, is the Grace of God that is incarnated within them by the gift of His Spirit into them. Paul is speaking of so much more than a financial offering. He is speaking about their spiritual superabundance. That kind of wealth will produce the "giving of themselves," which is so much more than money. He reminds them that their "**center**" is this grace and favor that comes from Christ and progressively moves through His body. Observe the sphere of "**the grace of Jesus Christ**," in vs. 9, below. Also, *cf* 9:8, below.

8. I am not now saying [this] down from some arrangement added or put upon [you], but still [I am] also continuing in testing and proving the legitimacy of the birth (or: the genuineness) **of the Love** (self-giving urge toward unrestricted acceptance and union), **which belongs to, and pertains to, you folks, through means of the haste to earnest and diligent care about** (or: pertaining to; or: from; of) **different folks.**

He assures them that he is not acting like the Judean scribes and the Pharisees that were in this way described by Jesus:

> "**they habitually tie up and bind heavy loads** (or: burdensome cargos), **and then constantly place [these] as an addition upon the shoulders of people** (or: mankind) **– yet they, themselves, are not willing to budge or put them in motion with their finger** (or: = to 'lift a finger' to help carry them)!" (Mat. 23:4).

That is the way of religion, but Paul did not operate this way. However, his letter was "**testing and proving the legitimacy of the birth** (or: the genuineness) **of the Love** (self-giving urge toward unrestricted acceptance and union) **which belonged to, and pertained to, [them]**." In other words, was the love, that they felt that they had, really the Fruit of the Spirit? How they responded to Titus and his work among them would be the proof in the pudding. It would be shown "**through means of the haste to earnest and diligent care about** (or: pertaining to; or: from; of) **different folks**." This last word is commonly rendered "others," and it has this general meaning, but this word has the basic meaning of "different." Offering diligent, earnest care to folks who are "different" asks more of us than just making haste to help others of our own group or our own kind. With this term being in the genitive case, on offer are functions expressed by the English "about" or "pertaining to." But rendering it with the function expressed as, "of different folks," would mean that the action of haste may be coming to the Corinthian community, from these different folks – and this describes a different situation with which to deal. The same situation is seen from rendering the form of this word as an ablative: "from different folks." This apparent ambiguity allows for application to multiple or varied situations.

9. For in fact, you people continue knowing by experience and insight the grace of Jesus Christ (or: the favor from, and which is, Jesus [the] Anointed), **our Lord** (Master; Owner), **that although continuously existing being rich** (wealthy), **because of, and for the sake of, you folks He became destitute and led the life of a beggar, to the end that by, in and with the destitution and poverty of That One, you yourselves could** (or: should; may; would) **come to be rich** (wealthy).

An important point to note, here, is that Paul is accessing the personal story of Jesus for founding the message and argument that would follow. The Lord – His origin, life and ministry – is the Pattern for His body of followers: His family of many brothers (Rom. 8:29). He is the Path, the Way, the Reality and the Life. He is the Alpha, and the Omega (Rev. 1:11). Paul enlarges Jesus' primary story in Phil. 2:5-11:

> 5. **You see, this way of thinking** (this attitude and disposition) **is continuously within and among you folks** (or, as an imperative: So let this minding be habitually within you folks) – **which [is] also within Christ Jesus,**
> 6. **Who, starting and continuing as inherently existing** (or: beginning under; subsisting) **within God's form** (or: in an outward mold which is God), **He does not consider the [situation] to be equals in and by God a plunder** (or: a pillaging; a robbery; a snatching; or: a thing or situation seized and held),

(or: Who, [although] constantly humbly and supportively ruling in union with an external shape and an outward appearance from God, did not give consideration to a seizure: the [situation] to continuously exist being the same things with God, even on the same levels in God, or equal [things; aspects] to God,)

7. **but to the contrary, He empties Himself** (or: removed the contents of Himself; made Himself empty), **receiving** (or: taking; accepting) **a slave's form** (external shape; outward mold), **coming to be** (or: birthing Himself) **within an effect of humanity's** (mankind's; people's) **likeness.**

8. **And so, being found in an outward fashion, mode of circumstance, condition, form-appearance** (or: character, role, phase, configuration, manner) **as a human** (a person; a man), **He lowers Himself** (or: humbled Himself; made Himself low; degrades Himself; levels Himself off), **coming to be** (or: birthing Himself) **a submissive, obedient One** (one who gives the ear and listens) **as far as** (or: to the point of; until) **death – but death of a cross** (torture stake)!

9. **For this reason, God also lifts Him up above** (or: highly exalted Him; elevates Him over) **and by grace gives to Him** (or: joyously favors on Him) **the Name – the one over and above every name! –**

10. **to the end that within The Name: Jesus!** (or: in union with the name of Jesus; in the midst of the Name belonging to [Yahweh-the-Savior]), **every knee** (= person) **– of the folks upon the heaven** (of those belonging to an imposed heaven, or [situated] upon the atmosphere) **and of the people existing upon the earth and of the folks dwelling down under the ground** (or: on the level of or pertaining to subterranean ones; [comment: note the ancient science of the day – a three-tiered universe]) **– may bend** (or: would bow) **in prayer, submission and allegiance,**

11. **and then every tongue** (= person) **may speak out the same thing** (should and would openly agree, confess, avow and acclaim) **that Jesus Christ [is] Lord** (Master; Owner) **– [leading] into [the] glory of Father God** (or: unto Father God's good reputation; into the midst of a praise-inducing manifestation and assumed appearance which is God: a Father)**!**

When in vs. 9, above, Paul refers to Him as "**continuously existing being rich**," he was not referring to material wealth, but rather such as what we find in Col. 2:9,

> "**within Him all the effect of the fullness of the Deity** (the result of the filling from the Godship and feminine aspect of the Divine Nature) **is repeatedly corporeally** (or: bodily, as a whole; embodied; as a body) **settling down and progressively taking up permanent residence** (or: is continuously dwelling in person)."

And so it also follows that:

> "**because WITHIN Him all – the entire contents** (the result of that which fills everything; all the effect of the full measure [of things]) **– delights to settle down and dwell as in a house** (or: because He approved all the fullness [of all existence] to permanently reside within Him)" (Col. 1:19).

But let us not miss what characterized Christ's life as a human, here on earth in the 1st century AD: "**because of, and for the sake of, you folks He became destitute and led the life of a beggar.**" Take note of the reason for Him becoming destitute, or, for taking the form of a slave: it was "**because of, and for the sake of, you folks** (also, read: US)." His incarnation was for Humanity, in order to return Adam to the Garden of Eden (Rev. 22). But there is more. The plan and purpose is here revealed: "**to the end that by, in and with the destitution and poverty of That One, you yourselves** [and all humanity] **could** (or: should; may; would) **come to be rich.**"

What is the referent of US becoming "**rich**"? It refers back to Christ having been "**rich**" before becoming destitute. Well, what were Christ's previous "riches"? How about, "**inherently existing** (or: beginning under; subsisting) **within God's form**"? How about:

> "**continuously accepting and with our hands taking away from out of a placing in the condition of a son** (or: [the] deposit of the Son; a setting in place which is the Son; a constituting

as a son; a placing in the Son): **the process of the release of our body from slavery**" (Rom. 8:23b).

How about:

> "**by** (with; in) **the Grace and joyous favor you continually exist, being folks having been delivered** (rescued and saved, so that you are now safe; made whole)**! – and He jointly roused and raised** (or: suddenly awakens and raises) **[us] up, and caused [us] to sit** (or: seats [us]; = enthroned [us]) **together in union with, and among, the heavenly people, and within the things situated upon** [thus, above] **the heavens**" (Eph. 2:5b-6).

How about: the promises to the overcomers (those in union with The Overcomer) set down in Rev. 2 and 3!

10. And so, in this [testing and proving], I am now offering an effect of knowledge and insight gained from my experience (conclusion from *gnosis*), **for this [effect] is progressing to bring things together for you, to your benefit and expedience – you who from a year ago were first in making a beginning not only to do, but even to desire and purpose [it],**

Again, this is about more than just money (giving an offering, as most commentators interpret Paul's inference). Just as those in Macedonia "**gave themselves**" (vs. 5, above), we read Paul as urging those in Corinth to do the same – first of all to the folks within Corinth, whether they are part of the called-out group, or not! Paul is speaking to them about "**an effect of knowledge and insight gained from my experience** (conclusion from *gnosis*)." Religion has been so focused on raising money that they are reading Paul through that lens. Giving aid to others, and providing for others is basic to the Life in the kingdom. But the called-out group in Corinth has had divisiveness and factions to the point that in 1 Cor. he had to teach them about the basics of *Agapē* Love (1 Cor. 13). Christ was divided (1 Cor. 1:13). In 1 Cor. 2:10 he was pointing them to "**the depths of, from, which pertain to, and which are, God,**" because they were still "**fleshly folks… infants in Christ**" (1 Cor. 3:1). In vs. 6, above, he was speaking about Titus "should bring this GRACE to its goal." Then in the next verse his topic was faith, the word, knowledge and Love. So now is his focus on a collection of money? That topic may attend his visit, for the Path of Christ is a path of giving to others. But it is also about feeding folks in their own area; about clothing the naked in their area; about visiting those in prison and about tending the sick (Mat. 25:35-36). All of these activities also had their spiritual (or: metaphorical) counterparts, as well. Christ preached a full gospel that was for the spirit, soul and body.

Here, he goes on to say, "**this [effect] is progressing to bring things together for you, to your benefit and expedience – you who from a year ago were first in making a beginning not only to do, but even to desire and purpose [it],**" which calls to mind Paul's words to the province of Galatia:

> "**You folks have been running beautifully** (finely; ideally; with good form)**! Who** (or: What) **cut in on you folks, to hinder or thwart you, [for you] not to continue to be persuaded** (convinced) **by** (or: in; with) **the Truth and this reality?**" (Gal. 5:7).

Paul's letters to Corinth seem to indicate that they had problems similar to those in Galatia.

11. even so now – bring the doing to its goal (fully accomplish the performing and the producing), **so that, even as the eagerness to will** (or: the propensity to rush ahead from the purposing), **thus also [may be] the accomplishing of the goal** ([situation] to fully complete), **from out of [your] possessions and holdings** (or: from the [situations] to normally have).

Bring what "**doing**" to its goal? We would answer "The entirety of a cruciform life." We would add to that all the imperatives from Eph. 4:1, "**exhorting, admonishing, imploring and entreating you to walk [your path]** (= behave; = live your life) **worthily pertaining to** (or: in a manner suitable to the value of) **the calling and invitation in regard to which you folks are called** (or: from which you were summoned)," on through Eph. 6:18. Sure, supply folks' basic needs, but the called-out communities were called to support their local community – as well as missionary or humanitarian efforts, abroad – "**from**

out of [their] possessions and holdings (or: from the [situations] to normally have)." Their entire lives were to be lived with the worldview that:

> "[Their] **citizenship** (result of living in a free city; or: commonwealth-effects; political realm) **continues inherently existing** (or: continues humbly ruling; continuously subsists; repeatedly has its under-beginning) **resident within the midst of [the] atmospheres** (or: heavens), **from out of where** (or: which place) **we also continuously receive and take away in our hands from out of a Deliverer**" (Phil. 3:20).

God was their supply.

12. You see it follows that, since (or: if) **the eagerness continues lying before [a person], [it is] well-embraced and very acceptable – in proportion to whatever one may normally possess** (have and hold), **not corresponding to what he does not normally have.**

This is an expression of common existence and joint-participation in the new covenant. Paul is here expressing the general equity of rightwised existence in the reign of God. His words apply to all areas of our lives, not just to "giving offerings." Older folks may not "normally possess" the strength or energy to assist in some community needs, even though they might have "**the eagerness continues lying before [them].**" Others may not have the necessary skills to give aid in particular cases. It's not just about money.

13. For, you see, [the situation is] not that to (or: for; in; with) **other folks [there is] a letting up with relief and ease, yet to** (or: for; in; with) **you folks [there is] pressure with tribulation, oppression and affliction** (or: = hardship),

He is speaking of fairness and equity (principle elements of "the Way pointed out" – Life in the kingdom). Of course this applies to financial issues, but not ONLY to financial issues: to everything! He can be speaking about division of labor within the covenant community. Those who have worked as volunteers in humanitarian or social efforts know very well how things can become unbalanced.

14. but to the contrary, out of the fairness and equity of equality within the present season (or: from an equalization in the current occasion and situation), **your superabundance** (or: your encompassing surplus-result) **[can flow] into the lack resulting from the shortcoming of those folks** (= offset their deficiency), **keeping in mind that the superabundance** (or: surplus-effect) **of those folks could also at some point birth itself into the lack resulting from your shortcoming** (= offset your deficiency), **so that an equalizing can occur** (or: by that means there would come to be equality).
15. [This is] just as it has been written,
> **"the person [who gathered] the great quantity did not have too much, and the person [who gathered] the small amount did not have too little."** [Ex. 16:18]

This is an allusion to Israel's corporate situation with Moses in the wilderness journeys. The analogy is to the gathering of manna (food) in the wilderness. Its application is to all areas of "**fairness and equity of equality within the present season,**" and it applies to everyday life within all the communities – not just about how, if you have a superabundance, it can be turned into cash for a particular offering. He is speaking about an ongoing flow from out of "**superabundance into the lack resulting from the shortcoming**" of others – both within the community, and between communities. It may be supplying food for a neighbor, or helping them with their rent, or participating in a "barn-raising" (a community endeavor) to help those who need that kind of help. It's about Love lived out.

Notice that this is supposed to flow both ways: "**keeping in mind that the superabundance** (or: surplus-effect) **of those folks could also at some point birth itself into the lack resulting from your shortcoming.**" The idea is an ongoing, healthy community of shared, common existence (*koinōnia*).

16. **Now grace [is] in and with God** (or: Yet favor [is] by God; or, perhaps: But thanks [be] to God) **– in** (or: by; with) **the One constantly imparting within the heart of Titus this very same haste and earnest, diligent care over you folks,**
17. **because [Titus] indeed embraced and responded to the comfort, relief, assistance and encouragement** (the influence of the Paraclete), **and being inherently quicker to earnest diligence, spontaneously and of his own accord went forth to you folks.**

As is characteristic of Paul, he brings his audience back to the basics of the reality that "**grace [is] in and with God.**" This is a literal reading of the Greek. "Yet favor [is] by God" is another literal rendering. The reading of *charis* as "thanks" is a secondary use of this word in Paul's writings. I have included it here because it makes sense to the text, even though it need not be what Paul was saying. It is merely a conventional reading, since the dative form of "God" can be rendered, "to God."

As has been the constant message that Paul has trumpeted in this letter, performing as a paraclete is the topic of this chapter. A paraclete gives "**earnest, diligent care over folks,**" and gives "**comfort, relief, assistance and encouragement**" in whatever area of life where there is a need. It involves "**embrace and response**" of, and to, people. Titus displayed this to, and for, those in Corinth.

18. **So we sent together with him the** (or: his) **brother whose full approval** (praise and added applause) **in connection with the good news** (the message of goodness, ease and well-being) **[has spread] in every direction through all the called-out folks** (or: called-out communities)
19. **– yet not only [this], but further, [he is] also one having had hands extended, spread wide and pulled tight** [note: either, in love, or in "selecting" him] **by the called-out folks, [being] our traveling companion within this grace and favor** [other MSS: together with this grace] **which is being progressively dispensed and constantly given in attending service by us [moving with a view] toward the Lord's glory** (to the good reputation and manifestation which calls forth praise of Christ and Yahweh; or: face-to-face with the Master's assumed appearance), **and [to] a rushing forward with strong emotion and eagerness which pertains to us** (or: toward our Owner's glory and propensity to eagerly rushing with strong feelings) **–**

Observe the subject matter of this passage that is specifically laid out by Paul in vs. 19: "**this GRACE and favor** [other MSS: together with this grace] **which is being progressively DISPENSED and constantly given in attending SERVICE by us.**" Paul is speaking about the message of, and from, Christ that they were constantly giving out to people.

Here, in vs. 19, and below, in vs. 20, Paul speaks of their ministry as that which is "**being progressively dispensed and constantly given in attending service**" by them. That expresses the present participle form. In Eph. 3:6b-7a, he uses the noun form, and observe what it was that he became an attendant, a server, and a dispenser:

> "**the GOOD NEWS of which I came to be** (was birthed; became) **an attendant** (a server; one who renders service and dispenses)."

He dispensed, and gave attending service of, the GOOD NEWS: the *Logos* that is Christ! He used this same noun to express the same thing in Col. 1:23, as well, where he spoke of:

> "**the message of ease, goodness and well-being of which you hear** (or: heard)**: the [message] being heralded** (announced; publicly proclaimed and preached) **within all creation which is under the sky** (or: heaven) **– of which I, Paul, am myself come to be a herald, an emissary, and an attending servant** (or: a dispenser)."

20. **[we] being those progressively ordering and arranging this for ourselves: [that] no one can find fault with us** (or: may find flaws or defects in us) **in connection with this ripe maturity which is being progressively dispensed in attending service by us.**

He spoke of the same thing in Rom. 15:

> 15. **Yet I more daringly write to you partly as habitually calling you back to full recollection because of the grace and favor being given to me from** [other MSS: by; under] **God,**
> 16. **into the [arranged ability for] me to be Christ Jesus' public servant into the nations** (a public worker of Jesus Christ unto the ethnic multitudes and pagans), **constantly doing the work of a priest for God's good news** (or: habitually functioning as the Temple for the message of the goodness, which is God), **to the end that the offering composed of the ethnic multitudes** (or: the approaching of the nations as an offering) **can become well-received and pleasingly acceptable, it being [an offering; a carrying toward] having been set-apart and remaining sacred within the midst of holy spirit and a sacred attitude** (or: in union with a set-apart Breath-effect; within [the] Holy Spirit)....
> 18. **You see, I will not venture to speak anything of which Christ does not** (or: did not) **work down, produce and bring into effect through me [leading] into a submissive giving of the ear** (or: humble, obedient hearing and paying attention) **from [the] ethnic multitudes** (or: of non-Jews, nations and pagans) **by an arranged speech and message as well as by a work** (or: in word and in action or deed) **– in a power of signs and of miracles, [that is], in [the] power of God's Spirit** (or: in union with an ability from God's Breath; in an ability from an Attitude which is God [other MSS: in the midst of set-apart Breath-effect]) –
> 19. **with a view for** (in the purpose for) **me to have filled [the region] from Jerusalem even, around in a circuit, as far as Illyricum [with] the good news of, from, and concerning the Anointed One** (or: the message of goodness, ease and well-being – which is Christ).

This is what he meant in vs. 20, above, when he spoke of "**this ripe maturity which is being progressively dispensed in attending service by us**." They were "**progressively ordering and arranging this for ourselves: [that] no one can find fault with us** (or: may find flaws or defects in us)" in connection with this mission. They were attentive to their behavior (7:2, above), for they were quite aware that, "**it is constantly being looked for and sought after, in house-managers** (administrators), **that this person may be found [to be] full of faith** (loyal; reliable; trustworthy; faithful)" (1 Cor. 4:2).

21. **For you see, we**
> "**habitually give forethought for providing beautiful things, ideal [situations] and fine [insights] – not only in [the] Lord's** [= Yahweh's] **sight and presence, but also in the sight and presence of people** (humans)." [Prov. 3:4 LXX]

Notice the broad, inclusive, potential application of these words. Forethought is necessary for the general maintenance of all areas of community life, and especially for those who are "**progressively dispensing of, and constantly giving attending service**" for the message of Goodness (God in Christ)!

22. **Now we send** (or: sent) **our brother** (person from the same Womb), **together with them, whom we often tested and proved as continually being quick to be earnest and diligent in many things, yet now much more quickly and with more earnest diligence, but with great confidence, which [he imparts] into** (or: that [he brings] unto) **you folks.**

They were sending only "**tested and proved**" folks to be paracletes to the covenant community of Corinth. These folks were also "**continually being quick to be earnest and diligent in many things,**" so they would be of useful service to the group, in many areas of their common existence among the called-out folks. This brother that they were sending was "**much more quickly and with more earnest diligence, but with great confidence, which [he would impart] into** (or: that [he brings] unto) **[them].**"

23. **So whether concerning Titus – my partner** (person of common being and existence) **and co-worker [dispensing] into you people – or whether our brothers** (= fellow believers), **[they are] those sent forth pertaining to the called-out folks: Christ's glory**

(or: [these are] delegates, emissaries and representatives who belong to, and are from, the called-out communities – a good reputation and assumed appearance of the Anointed One, and a manifestation which brings Him praise).

Paul continues giving high recommendations concerning Titus and their brothers who would be coming to the called-out folks in Corinth. Notice how he characterizes these emissaries (sent-forth folks): they are **Christ's glory** – or, "a good reputation and assumed appearance of the Anointed One." This is our calling, as well, my friends! We are called to be "**God's image** (resemblance; likeness; portrait) **and glory**" (1 Cor. 11:7).

24. **Therefore, show within** [other MSS: be continuously being ones showing within] **the display and demonstration of your love** (selfless solidarity) **– and of our boasting over you – into the face** (= presence, or persons) **of those called-out folks** (or: the called-out communities).

Now he admonishes them how to respond to these folks, and what to show them: "**the display and demonstration of your love** (selfless solidarity)."

Take note that nowhere in this chapter did Paul speak specifically about taking an offering (or: a collection) for the folks in Jerusalem.

Chapter 9

1. **So indeed it follows that it is superfluous for me to be writing to you folks concerning this attending service and dispensing of this into the set-apart folks** (unto the sacred folks/communities).

This chapter opens as a continuation of the previous passage, and we see from his repeated reference to their ministry (**concerning this attending service and dispensing of this**) that he is still on the same topic of which we read in chapter 8. Since they are aware of this, and he has made repeated references to this, above, "**it follows that it is superfluous for [him] to be writing to [them]**" about it – and yet he does, as a good rhetor who redundantly repeats his message. This service and dispensing (*diakonia*), which he references again, in vs. 12 below, is described there as "**public duty and service [that] is not only repeatedly replenishing** (aiming toward filling back up again) **the needs** (results of defaults; the effects of shortcomings; lacks; deficiencies) **pertaining to the set-apart folks** (the holy ones; the saints; or: the sacred [communities])," and is also manifested in "**expressions of gratitude to God.**"

Recall 5:20, above where he defined their roles as being "**elders of God, performing as ambassadors from God, as [Him] continually calling alongside to give comfort and relief** (performing as a Paraclete)." In 8:1, above, he related that they were "**progressively making known to [them] God's grace.**" In 3:6, above, he said that they were "**servants and dispensers of an arrangement that is new in quality.**" Paul's intent was for them to do and be the same. Jesus expected His followers to do the works/deeds that He was doing (Jn. 14:12). So "**this attending service and dispensing**" is the main subject of this chapter, as well.

2. **For I have seen, and thus know, your eagerness** (fore-spiritedness; forward bent in passions and emotions) **– concerning which I am constantly boasting over you folks to [the] Macedonians – that "Achaia has prepared itself and stands ready since last year** (from a year ago)**," and your zeal stimulates the majority [of them].**

The common interpretation of the quote, "**Achaia has prepared itself and stands ready,**" is that Paul was speaking of their preparation and readiness to contribute to "the collection." But if this was Paul's main point, he could have been more explicit. The lens of "the collection" reads this interpretation into Paul's words. But his central point has been for them to be paracletes – for everyone, and in all areas of life, especially in dispensing the knowledge of God's grace, and giving of attending service to the expansion of God's reign.

3. **Yet I send the brothers** (= fellow members of the Family), **so that the effect of our boasting over you may not be made void** (empty; to no purpose) **in this respect** (or: on this part), **so that you may be folks who have prepared yourselves – just as I have been saying –**
4. **lest by any means, if Macedonians should come with me and they should find you folks unprepared, we ourselves – not that we should proceed to mention you folks! – should be completely brought down in disgrace and be embarrassed in this underlying assumption** (or: substructure) **of boasting.**

In 1 Cor. 2:2, he wrote to them,
> "**I decided not to see, perceive or know anything within or among you folks, except Jesus Christ – and this One being one having been crucified** (suspended from a pole)!"

We suggest that this is still paramount for him, in regard to them, that they would have "**prepared themselves**" to continue manifesting the cruciform life in Christ. In 6:1, above, his concern for them was that they would "**not to accept/receive God's grace into a void** (or: an empty or vain [situation; way of life])."

What would bring the Corinthians "**down in disgrace**" if "**Macedonians should come with me and they should find you folks unprepared**"? We find Paul giving forethought to avert this by sending the brothers to help them prepare, in the next verse...

5. **Therefore I considered it compelling to call the brothers alongside and to urge them so that they would come** (or: go) **unto you folks in advance and then that they could thoroughly adjust, prepare and arrange in advance "the blessing"** (or: idea and word of goodness, ease and well-being; reasonable goodness; plausible act of giving) **from you folks** (or: your bountiful yield), **which had been previously promised and was being fore-announced, [and for] this to continually be ready, thus: as a blessing** (or: bountiful gift; or: word of goodness/act of generosity) **and not as one who has advantage in having more** (or: not grudgingly, from greed; possibly: not as the result of a scheme of extortion).

Now it may well be that part of "**the blessing**" to which he referred was the collecting of money for an offering to others – as is the traditional interpretation of this term. But let us dig a bit deeper and consider the semantic range of *eulogia*. It literally means a "word of goodness, ease and well-being." Our English word eulogy is a transliteration of the Greek word. Because *logos* also means an idea or a thought, this can also nuance the meaning. The lexicons offer the idea of "reasonable goodness," or, a "plausible act of giving." From this, an extended meaning had developed as it representing a "bountiful gift" or "an act of generosity." The central idea of "bounty" (which some translations offer) is an agricultural term for a good yield.

Now if Paul was referring to a financial offering, and if those in Corinth had not over the past year set-aside money on a regular basis, how would the coming of the brothers help them produce a large sum so that they would not be disgraced or embarrassed? Few were rich, in those days. Would the brothers "lean on" the rich of the community to come up with the offering? The last clause of vs. 5 would seem to point toward the "blessing" being of something that those in the community had. And he does not want this "blessing" to be offered grudgingly, or from greed, and certainly not come across as extortion – whether the offering were of money or of agricultural goods. Could this perhaps refer to appropriate hospitality for those who might come to visit? For the needy among them, this could be a burden, but with preparation by the whole group the need could be met. Whatever Paul's central idea was, the idea of generosity and blessing was standard fare among God's sacred people.

Before moving on, let us consider other passages where Paul, and others, use the term *eulogia*:

"**Now I have seen and thus know** (or: am aware) **that when coming** (or: going) **to you I will continue coming** (or: going) **in an effect of the fullness of Christ's message of Goodness** (or: within that which fills up pertaining to [the] good word {*Logos*} about Christ; in a result of the entire contents of well-speech from [the] Anointing; in union with an effect of the filling of [the] Blessing, which is [the] Anointed One)" (Rom. 15:29)

"**for such folks are not habitually performing as slaves for our Lord Christ, but rather for their own belly and through the useful smooth talk** (profitable words) **and complimentary speech** (blessings!) **they continuously deceive** (mislead; seduce)…" (Rom. 16:18).

"**the Good Word** (the Blessing; the Word of wellness and goodness) **pertaining to Abraham** (belonging to and possessed by Abraham) **could within Jesus Christ suddenly birth Itself into the multitudes** (the nations; the ethnic groups; the Gentiles)" (Gal. 3:14).

"**Characterized by and full of thoughts of well-being, good words and messages of ease** (or: Worthy of being spoken well of) **[is] the God and Father of our Lord, Jesus Christ – the One speaking Good to** (or: blessing; expressing thoughts of well-being to) **us within every spiritual good word**" (Eph. 1:3).

"**The cup of The Blessing** (or: The cup which is the Word of Goodness, ease and well-being; the cup of the Idea from Goodness) **which we are habitually blessing** (speaking well of; speaking of with reference to goodness, ease and wellness), **is it not** (does it not exist being) **the common existing and sharing with, participation in, fellowship of, communion…?**" (1 Cor. 10:16)

"**For you see, a piece of land which is drinking the rain often coming upon it, and… sharing in and partaking of a blessing from God**" (Heb. 6:7).

"**For you know that even afterwards, continuously purposing** (intending; wanting; willing) **to inherit the blessing** (the words of goodness and well-being)…" (Heb. 12:17a).

"**that you folks may inherit a word embodying wellness** (a blessing; a message of goodness; a thought bringing ease)" (1 Pet. 3:9b).

In vs. 4 Paul again mentioned the Macedonians. In 8:2, above, he spoke of their "**destitution.**" So what was it that they gave? In 8:5 he informs us that, "**they gave themselves… to and for us, through the effect of God's will and a result of purpose, which is God.**" Paul's overall teachings would suggest that this is what he would expect, and encourage, from those in Corinth, as well. They had "**The cup of The Blessing**" to share with those who came to visit.

6. Now this [is the reality]: the person who is habitually sowing sparingly (thriftily; in a limited way) **will also continue reaping** (or: harvesting) **sparingly; and the person who is habitually sowing on [the basis of] good thoughts and words** (or: with or for added blessings; or: bountifully; with things well and fully laid out and arranged for ease and a reasonable yield) **will also continue reaping upon [those] good thoughts and words** (or: with added blessings; or: bountifully; with things well laid out and arranged for added ease and a reasonable yield) –

Yes, we are used to preachers quoting this verse – right before taking an offering. But Paul also used this verb, "sow" in Gal 6:7, and in vs. 8 used it again:

"**because the person continually sowing into the flesh of himself will progressively reap corruption** (spoil; ruin; decay) **forth from out of the flesh** (= the estranged inner being);
(or: the one habitually sowing into the flesh [system], of himself will continue to reap decay from out of the flesh [system];)
yet the one constantly sowing into the spirit (or: the Breath) **will be progressively reaping eonian life** (life having the characteristics of the Age [of Messiah]; or: life from the Age that lasts on through the ages) **forth from out of the spirit** (or: the Spirit; the Breath; that attitude)."

Jacob also used this verb, in Jas. 3:18,

"**Now the fruit of fair and equitable dealing** (eschatological deliverance which brings justice and right relationship in accord with the Way pointed out; the condition of being rightwised, or turned in the right direction; also: = covenant participation) **is continuously being sown in peace and harmonious joining by and for those habitually performing** (making; doing; producing) **peace and harmonious joining.**"

Now, as always, there is a balance that emerges from the joining of the natural with the spiritual, and Paul pointed this out in 1 Cor. 9:11,

"**Since, upon [the ground of] an expectation, we ourselves sowed the spiritual things in** (to; for; with; among) **you folks, [is it] a great thing if we ourselves shall reap a harvest of your fleshly things** (= natural or material goods pertaining to the material life)**?**"

We should also keep in mind Jesus' use of the metaphor of sowing in his parables – e.g., in Mat. 13, and in Mk. 4:14 He said, "**The one habitually sowing** (The sower) **is continually sowing the Word** (the *Logos*; the idea; the thought; the meaning and reason; the message; the patterned Information)." And in Jn. 4:37 He observed that, "**The one is habitually sowing, and another is habitually reaping** (or: One is the sower, and another the harvester)." All these metaphors apply to all areas of our lives.

7. **each one [doing; giving] correspondingly** (or: accordingly; to the level) **as he has before chosen in** (or: by) **the heart, not from out of anxiety** (sorrow; pain; distress) **nor compulsion, for**
"**God habitually loves** (seeks reunion with) **a cheerful** (merry) **giver.**" [Prov. 22:8 LXX]

Those who teach, herald the message, give hospitality, or any other area of self-giving, know the effect of the flowing-out of virtue, and the consumption of energy that is involved in all of these efforts. It can be exhausting. As folks get older they must "**correspondingly** (or: accordingly; to the level) **[beforehand] chose in** (or: by) **the heart**" with regard to their energy and ability. This can facilitate an attitude of "**cheerful giving.**" The giving of one's time to another is the giving of one's life. Paul was not being evasive or using euphemisms about contributing money; he was speaking on broader categories of application.

Now if there is a cause to which a person is led to contribute, the same applies. Choosing in, and by, the heart means to consult the Spirit within us, and proceed accordingly. Paul informed those at Philippi,
"**So my God will continue and progressively be filling to the full your every need** (or: will keep on making full all lack which pertains to you folks) **down from His wealth [being] within [the] glory [that resides] within Christ Jesus**" (Phil. 4:19).
In Phil. 4:16 he gave recognition of what they had done: "**in Thessalonica both once, and even twice!, you folks sent [provision] into my need**." Generosity characterizes those who abide in the Vine.

8. **Moreover, God is constantly able with continuous power to furnish all grace to surround and to make every favor superabound unto** (or: into the midst of) **you folks, to the end that, continuously having every ability in yourselves to ward things off and constantly holding all self-sufficiency and complete contentment at all times [and] within every [situation] and in union with every person, you can** (or: may; should; would) **continuously superabound into every good action, excellent deed and noble work,**

Notice the focus of the last clause: **every good action, excellent deed and noble work**. It is for these purposes that **all grace** and **every favor** are abundantly furnished, by God. But this is not all: because of the grace and favor, while engaged in these good works, etc., we can "**continuously have every ability in ourselves to ward things off and constantly hold all self-sufficiency and complete contentment – at all times [and] within every [situation], and in union with every person.**" Paul is not just speaking about donating money; this instruction applies to the whole of the life of the community.

9. **just as it stands written,**

> **"He scattered abroad and widely disperses; He gives to the ones who work hard for their bread, and yet are poor; His eschatological deliverance** (rightwised dealings and relationship which correspond to the Way pointed out, in covenantal faithfulness) **continuously remains and constantly dwells, on into the Age."** [Ps. 112:9]

The reference to God "**scattering**" and "**dispersing**" calls to mind Jesus' metaphors of sowing seeds to grow a crop, cited in vs. 6, above. My father used to sing a song about "scattering seeds of kindness." Paul's choosing a Psalm that affirms that "**He gives to the ones who work hard**" recalls the reality of kingdom living, and:

> "**the fact is, we are** (continually exist being) **the effect of what He did** (or: His creation; the thing He has constructed; the result of His work; His achievement; His opus; the effect of His Deed)**: people being founded from a state of disorder and wildness** (being framed, built, settled and created; being changed from chaos to order), **within and in union with Christ Jesus; [founded and built] upon GOOD WORKS** (virtuous actions; excellent deeds) **which God made ready** (prepared; or: prepares) **beforehand, to the end that we may, could, should and would walk about** (= LIVE our LIVES) **centered within and in union with them**" (Eph. 2:10).

This declaration about the faithfulness of God is drawn from the old covenant economy, but Paul affirms that God still provides for humanity. The reference to the "**poor**" reminds us of the Beatitudes:

> "**Happy and blessed [are you] poor and destitute folks! – because God's reign** (or: sovereign influence and activity; kingdom) **is now yours** (or: belongs to you, as a group). **Happy and blessed folks [are] those at the present time being constantly hungry! – because you folks will be progressively fed until satisfied**" (Lu. 6:20b-21a).

His "**eschatological deliverance** (rightwised dealings and relationship which correspond to the Way pointed out, in covenantal faithfulness) **continuously remains!**" We can count on Him. Paul's citing an OT text that points to "**the Age** [of Messiah]" should not go unnoticed. Paul and the Corinthians were living in that (and now, this) Age.

10. **Now the One habitually adding further supply and fully furnishing "seed to** (or: for) **the one habitually sowing** (the constant sower) **and bread unto eating** (= for food),**"** [Isa. 55:10b] **will continue supplying and furnishing – He will even continue to multiply and give increase to fullness – your seed, and He will continue causing the offspring and produce** (or: product; yield) **of, and from, your eschatological deliverance** (justice in rightwised relationships of the Way pointed out, in covenant participation) **to grow and increase** (be enlarged and amplified),

We hear an echo, here, of Hos. 10:12,

> "Sow in, for, among and with yourselves with a view to eschatological deliverance tor rightwised relationships in the Way pointed out (or: into the justice and equity of a covenant community); gather unto [the] fruit of Life. Shine and give Light for, among and with yourselves [the] Light of intimate, experiential knowledge and insight. Seek out the LORD until effects of the birth of eschatological deliverance for rightwised living in the Way pointed out (or: the produce and offspring of Justice and Equity) come upon you (or: to and in you folks)" (LXX, JM). Cf Mat. 6:1

Here Paul begins one of his long sentences, and it continues on through vs. 14a, below. So this is a paragraph that holds one train of thought, as you will see by his use of a participle opening vs. 11; a conjunction joining vs. 12 to vs. 11; then vs. 13 opening with a preposition, with vs. 14a joined to vs. 13 by a conjunction. We advise reading straight through the text a few times before reading the comments.

Here, he builds upon the quotation of this Psalm and brings it to an immediate application for the covenant community in Corinth. Now observe where he goes with this: "**He will continue causing the**

offspring and produce (or: product; yield) **of, and from, your eschatological deliverance** (etc.)." He wants their "justice in rightwised relationships of the Way pointed out, in covenant participation, **to grow and increase**." This will include sharing of their "**produce** (or: product; yield)" with others. That is what "rightwised relationships" are all about. But he is accessing one aspect of the core of the good news in the new creation: **deliverance** and being **rightwised**, so his references encompass the totality of the new covenant – everything involved with being "in Christ." He affirms that God "**will even continue to multiply and give increase to fullness [their] seed**" – and, as we just mentioned, this is a metaphor for God's reign and sovereign influence/activities.

11. being progressively enriched unto abundance within every person* (or: in union with everything) **[leading] into complete singleness [of purpose] and simplicity [of being] for all generosity** (liberality), **which constantly produces** (works down; accomplishes) **thanksgiving to and for God through us, and through our midst** [or, with B: which repeatedly works in accord with God's ease of grace, instilling gratitude through the midst of us], [* cf 1 Cor. 1:5]

This is a continuation of vs. 10, as he weaves another strand into his tapestry: "**complete singleness [of purpose] and simplicity [of being] for all generosity** (liberality)." And he builds on what he said about "**to multiply and give increase to fullness**," in vs. 10, by describing the "**growth and increase**" as "**being progressively enriched unto abundance within every person** (or: in union with everything)." Paul's vision of the kingdom is so much greater than a one-time collection of money to help the poor. As we unpack his words we see a worldview of universal proportions. This, of course, does not exclude providing for very real and present needs that folks have.

The singleness of purpose and simplicity that embodies "**all generosity** (liberality)" is God's purpose for humanity and creation. All of this "**constantly produces** (works down; accomplishes) **thanksgiving to and for God through us, and through our midst**." It transforms our inner and outer environments, as we are changed "from glory to glory" (3:18, above). Recall 4:15, above,

> "**that the grace and favor – increasing and becoming more than enough through the greater part of the people – can cause the benefits of grace to be surrounding in superabundance, unto God's glory**."

The reading of MS B is a beautiful, early variation of this picture: "which repeatedly works in accord with God's ease of grace, instilling gratitude through the midst of us." He goes on to expand these thoughts, in the next verse…

12. because the attentive serving and dispensing of this public duty and service is not only repeatedly replenishing (aiming toward filling back up again) **the needs** (results of defaults; the effects of shortcomings, lacks or deficiencies) **pertaining to the set-apart folks** (the holy ones; the saints; or: the sacred [communities]), **but further is also progressively superabounding** (bringing excessive amounts that overflow) **through many expressions of gratitude to God** (or: by means of many examples of the goodness of grace in God)

Once again, note what he is talking about: "**the attentive serving and dispensing**." You see, this thread is his main topic, along with functioning as a paraclete, that we have been unpacking over the last few chapters. Paul is still on the same track. Here, he adds the outreach to the community: **this public duty and service**. Yes, all of their "good works" are "**repeatedly replenishing** (aiming toward filling back up again) **the needs** (results of defaults; the effects of shortcomings, lacks or deficiencies) **pertaining to the set-apart folks**," but that is only a beginning. It is "**also progressively superabounding** (bringing excessive amounts that overflow)." Now from where should we suppose that the "**many expressions of gratitude to God**" arise? Would it not be from all the recipients of those who have had their needs, the effects of their shortcomings, or their lacks and deficiencies, MET? This happened both through, and to, the public service performed or supplied by "**the set-apart folks** (the holy ones; the saints; or: the sacred [communities])." Some of those set-apart were local receivers of attentive care; other "holy ones" were those who gave the care. This social outreach (Mat. 25:35-36) will "bring excessive amounts... **of gratitude to God**."

By removing conjunctions, modifiers and parenthetical expansions, the main clause of this verb reads: "**the attentive serving and dispensing of this public duty and service is**... **replenishing the needs**... **is also progressively superabounding through many expressions of gratitude to God**." But Paul continues by further explaining "through what" these expressions came...

13. **through the evidence which is shown by** (or: the proof of) **this attending service and dispensing: [they are] folks constantly glorifying God and praising His reputation because of** (or: based upon) **the subjoined, humble alignment, supportive arrangement and subjection in appended shelter – which is your accordance to the message and agreement in thought** (and thus: your profession of saying the same thing), **[showing] assent unto Christ's message of goodness, ease and well-being, as well as by [the] simplicity and generosity from this partnership of common-existence sharing unto them, and into the midst of all people,**

The action of the people (**glorifying God**) points us back to the teaching of Jesus:
> "**Let the Light, which you folks possess** (or: which has a source in you folks; or: which you people are), **shine in front of mankind** (before humans), **so that people can see your fine works** (or: the beautiful works that you are; the ideal acts which come from you folks) **and they can give glory to** (or: and [these deeds; or: these works of beauty] will bring a good reputation for) **your Father – the One in union with the atmospheres [that surround you folks]**" (Mat. 5:16).

This verse is complex, and is lacking an expressed subject for the participle. Paul gave us no verbs: the verse is composed of prepositional phrases stacked upon each other – all related to the one present participle, conflated as, "**folks constantly glorifying**... **praising reputation**." Therefore, a subject is inserted, "**[they are]**," which ties the last phrase of vs. 12, "**expressions of gratitude**," to the plural participle, "**folks constantly glorifying**..." To give the semantic range of the noun, *homologia*, I inserted a verb, "**[showing]**," to facilitate readability in English: "**which is your accordance to the message and agreement in thought** (and thus: your profession of saying the same thing), **[showing] assent**..."

We trust that these grammatical explanations are helpful. Other translations have simply added verbs, a subject, and render the participle as a finite verb. I want to stay closer to the text and then indicate my insertions by brackets.

The object of the first preposition, "**through**" (which answers to the same, final preposition in 12b), is the noun "the proof" (offered parenthetically) which I first render as "**the evidence which is shown by**." The next phrase, "**this attending service and dispensing**," modifies and explains the source of the "proof/**evidence**," and these two phrases, together, give the source of the "**many expressions of gratitude to God**" (12b, above).

Now we come to the participial clause that defines those "**expressions of gratitude**," and it is "**folks constantly glorifying God and praising His reputation**." Why are they doing this? Paul explains: "**because of** (or: based upon) **the subjoined, humble alignment, supportive arrangement and subjection in appended shelter**." All of this is a conflation of the potential meanings of the noun that some render as "obedience" (Hart; NASB), "subjection" (CLNT; KJV), "support" (Nyland). The root meaning is: "an arranged alignment," prefixed by the preposition, "under." Now this term refers to a characteristic, or attribute, or situation that other people see in the Corinthian community. Consider the semantic range of what Paul could be indicating:
> a) **subjoined** (to Christ), **humble alignment** – this is a beautiful picture

410

b) **supportive arrangement** – also beautiful;

c) **subjection in appended shelter** – this pictures their relationship to Christ as Lord, and the meaning "appended shelter" says that they are attached to Him and are sheltered by Him.

Next Paul describes this "subjoined humble alignment (etc.)" with the explanation: "**which is your accordance to the message**... **[showing] assent unto Christ's message of goodness, ease and well-being**." He can't say enough about what is causing the "**many expressions of gratitude to God**" (12b, above). This is typical Asiatic rhetoric of Paul's time and culture. And we get to benefit from all the facets of the gems that he presents to us. But there is more: "**as well as by [the] simplicity and generosity from this partnership of common-existence sharing unto them, and into the midst of all people**." Paul used this word, "**simplicity and generosity**," in 1:12, in 8:2, and in vs. 11, above. He also uses it in 11:3, below, as a contrast to Eve being deceived by the serpent, in the Garden. The term *koinōnia* (**partnership of common-existence sharing**) refers to a core element of the kingdom Life of the called-out community. It and Love are the source of "simplicity and generosity." Paul is simply describing a covenant community with all of these prepositional phrases. This "common-existence sharing" was "**unto them**," i.e., to those who were expressing gratitude to God and glorifying God. This was a communal cause-and-effect. The lives of those who were both observing and receiving from these things were being positively affected by it, and saw its source as being God.

But further, all of what has been described in this verse was being observed as going "**into the midst of all people**." God's reign was expanding through these folks (Mat. 28:19-20), and we are instructed by Heb. 13:16,

> "**Now be not forgetful of well-doing** (performing well; producing or constructing goodness; doing good deeds of ease; creating well-being) **and of partnership** (common-being/existence; community; participation; having things in common; fellowship; sharing and contributing), **for by** (or: in) **such sacrifices God is continuously well pleased**."

But Paul's thoughts along this line are not quite finished...

14. **even by their request over [the situation of]** (or: on behalf of) **you folks – from people constantly longing and yearning for you. [It is] because of God's transcendent favor and surpassing grace [resting] upon you people –**

This participial clause that opens the verse is a continuation of vs. 13. Paul's immediate thought began with, "**through the evidence which is shown by this attending service and dispensing**" (13a), and continued with, "**folks**... **[showing] assent unto Christ's message**... **by [the] simplicity and generosity from this partnership of common-existence sharing**," and now (in 14a) adds, "**even by their request over [the situation of]** (or: on behalf of) **you folks – from people constantly longing and yearning for you**." You see, it was through these means and these folks that "**thanksgiving to and for God**" (vs. 11) was "**constantly [being] produced**."

I decided to make 14b into a statement (by inserting "**[It is]**... **[resting]**") that would flow into vs. 15 which, by restatement, affirms the source of "**God's transcendent favor and surpassing grace**."

15. **grace and joyous favor, in and by God, [resting; based] upon His free gift** (the gift which is Him) **– a wonder beyond description** (or: added to His indescribable gratuity)**!**

Where vs. 14 ends with "**grace [resting] upon you people**," vs. 15 begins with "**grace**... **[resting; based] upon His free gift**." For emphasis, I set off the adjective that modifies "**the free gift**" with a dash, and rendered the genitive form "of Him" as a possessive, "**His**." Grace and joyous favor are both "**in and by God**." This shows how, "**thus God loves** (or: You see God, in this manner, fully gives Himself to and urges toward reunion with) **the aggregate of humanity**" (Jn. 3:16a) – through "**transcendent favor and**

surpassing grace." Before we move on, notice what the rendering as a genitive of apposition the final phrase offers us: "the gift which is Him."

Here, we are reminded of Jas. 1:17a,

> "**Every good leaving of a legacy, profitable contributing or excellent dosing, as well as all virtuous giving, and** (or: All giving [is] beneficial, and yet), **every perfect gift** (finished, complete or mature result of giving) **is from above, descending from the Father of the lights**…"

Chapter 10

Norman Hillyer observes:

> "Recently scholars have been more ready to accept the unity of 2 Cor., a unity which can be observed, despite the variations in subject and tone, in the common theme of Paul's intended third visit" (*The New Bible Commentary, Revised*, Wm. B. Eerdmans Pub., 1973 p 1050).

1. **Now I myself, Paul, am making a personal appeal in continuing to call you to my side to encourage and entreat you folks through Christ's gentle friendliness** (mild kindness; tender meekness) **and abundant, lenient reasonableness and fairness** (or: considerate suitableness) **– I, who indeed [am] humble and lowly when face to face** (= in person) **among you, yet, being absent, am constantly showing bold, cheerful courage and confidence unto you –**

Here Paul appeals to two attributes of Christ that should not be overlooked. The first is His "**gentle friendliness** (mild kindness; tender meekness)." This sounds like "Someone" that is approachable, the kind of Person that you would like to have as a Friend. Yes, Jesus is the same today as He was with the little children (Mat. 19:14). He also expects us to be the same (Mat. 19:14)! So Paul is presenting his entreaty to them on the basis of the character of Christ that is within both himself and them. But just as God has both "**useful kindness** (benign, profitable utility)" but also "**abruptness** (sheer cutting-off)" (Rom. 11:22), so Paul has "**bold, cheerful courage and confidence**," with which he can "**be with resolved daring**" (vs. 2, below), if need be. Some commentators have suggested that the final statement of this verse, set off by dashes, is a charge made by Paul's adversaries that he repeats here, using the rhetorical devise of sarcasm. The NEB inserts "(you say)" before the final statement of this verse. The rational for this is seen in vs. 10, below.

Paul also characterized Christ by the term rendered here as "**abundant, lenient reasonableness and fairness**" when addressing the governor, Felix, in Acts 24:4, "**I am now entreating you, in your abundant, lenient reasonableness and fairness**." These are the only two places where this noun is used in the NT, but the adjective form is used elsewhere, such as in Phil. 4:5, where I conflate the semantic range:

> "**Let your gentle fairness, lenience, considerateness and suitable reasonableness be intimately and experientially known to all mankind** (or: by and for all humans). **The Lord** [= Christ or Yahweh] **is near** (close by – at hand, close enough to touch, and available)!"

Jacob also used the adjective to describe "**the Wisdom from above**," in Jas. 1:17.

2. **and am normally requesting, [that] when being present, not to have a situation where I need to be bold or courageous with** (or: in; by) **the assured confidence in** (by; with) **which I am reasonably considering** (or: counting on) **to be with resolved daring upon certain folks: those constantly counting or considering us as folks [who] are habitually walking around** (= living and behaving) **in the sphere of, or corresponding to, flesh** (= governed by human principles or conditions; or: = on the level of old covenant existence [T. Denton]; or: = in line with a self in bondage to the System).

Following the inserted statement, Paul now returns to state the appeal that was begun in vs. 1a. He is requesting that there not be a situation that involves those of their group that are putting-down Paul and his associates. He does not want to have a need for being "**bold**" with "**resolved daring**" in opposition to those folks.

Observe that his boldness and courage is "**with** (or: in; by) **the assured confidence in** (by; with) **which I am reasonably considering** (or: counting on) **to be**." He was far from being unsure about his authority from out of his place and function in Christ. By stating this, he was instilling this same confidence in his listeners. Those "**certain folks**" were probably trying to elevate their own position, in the eyes of the community, by putting Paul down through insinuations that he lacked spiritual insights, or was still living in the old covenant. Perhaps these folks were Gnostics who saw themselves as "spiritual" and others, such as Paul and his comrades, as being on a level below them. They may have accused Paul of being of the old age of Law, while they themselves were a part of the new age of Spirit. Paul spends no more time on them, here, but proceeds to affirm to the called-out listeners just how he and his friends lived their lives…

3. **For though habitually walking about** (ordering our behavior) **within flesh** (= in the physical, human condition), **we are not now serving as a soldier** (or: continuing in military service) **in correspondence and accord to flesh** (= on the level of estranged/enslaved humanity, or in line with the human condition; or: = in the sphere/mode of old covenant Jewish reasonings),

The first clause sets the contrast: living and ordering their behavior in the physical, human condition and situations. This being the case for everyone, it was not the realm from which they served Christ, in the kingdom. He uses a military analogy to counter the accusations of those "**certain folks**," describing their attentive service and dispensing as **NOT** "**serving as a soldier** (or: continuing in military service) **in correspondence and accord to flesh**." He expands this analogy in the next verse, and goes on to explain the characteristics of their service. But let us expand the phrase, **in correspondence and accord to flesh**:
> a) this can mean "on the level of estranged/enslaved humanity, or in line with the human condition," or,
> b) "in the sphere/mode of old covenant Jewish reasonings."

They were "**jointly roused and raised** (or: suddenly awakens and raises) **[us] up, and caused [us] to sit** (or: seats [us]; = enthroned [us]) **together in union with, and among, the heavenly people, and within the things situated upon** [thus, above] **the heavens**" (Eph. 2:6). They operated in the "**new creation**" (5:17, above). And so he explains…

4. **for you see, the tools and weapons of our military service** (campaign) **[are] not fleshly** (= do not pertain to our human condition; ["are not the weapons of the Domination System" – Walter Wink]), **but rather, [are] powerful and capable ones in God** (or: by and with God), **[focused] toward [the] pulling down** (demolition) **of effects of fortifications** (or: strongholds; strongly entrenched positions [of the "Domination System" – W. Wink, *Engaging the Powers*]),

Their "**tools and weapons**" were not those of either the old covenant, nor of the Domination System (or religion and empire), both of which operated in the flesh realm of natural humanity – the earthly realm. No, their tools and weapons (two meanings of the same Greek word) were spiritual. They were "**powerful and capable ones in God** (or: by and with God)." Note the nuances of the three functions of the dative case, on offer: in, by or with. God is the object of all these potential prepositions. These tell us the realm of these tools (in God), or the One actually using these tools (by God), or that God is participating in their use of the tools – and for all these reasons, they are "**powerful and capable**."

Are these tools and weapons to be used against people? NO! Well what, then is their function? Their use is "**[focused] toward [the] pulling down** (demolition) **of effects of fortifications**." But, since these are not used in the realm of flesh, what are the "**effects of fortifications**"? Another term for them is "strongholds" – the results (the –*ma* ending of the noun, in its plural form) of fortifying something in the realm of "spirit." Walter Wink suggested that these were "strongly entrenched positions [of the

413

Domination System]" – in whatever form they were encountered: religious, political, economic, social, racial, personal mindsets or addictions, etc. One of the main strongholds that Paul was working to demolish was Second Temple Judaism, or the remnants of that which continued on within the Judaizers who were fortified with the Law of Moses. We find the same things in our day. In Christianity it is the creeds, dogmas and doctrines of theologians and churchmen. They are "organizational positions" or rulings meant to control the citizens or members, or to defend the hierarchal structures of Domination Systems. These are the products of human minds or deranged spirits (within individuals or centered in corporate entities). They come from hearts that have not yet been made alive by the Love and Life of God.

To expand on the subject which he touches on here, Paul again used the "soldier and defensive equipment" metaphor in Eph. 6. So let us let him speak from that chapter:

> 10. **Of the remainder** (or: Concerning the rest; Finally), **be constantly empowering yourselves within** (or: finding or engendering ability within yourselves), **centered in and in union with [the] Lord** [= Christ or Yahweh] **– even within, and in union with, the force** (or: strength) **of His might** (or: the mightiness of His strength and forcefulness)**:**
> 11. **you folks must at some point, for yourselves, enter within** (or: clothe yourselves with) **the full suit of armor and implements of war** (panoply; the complete equipment for men-at-arms) **which is God** (or: which comes from and belongs to God), **in order for you to be continuously able and powerful to stand** (or: to make a stand) **facing toward the crafty methods** (stratagems; schemes; intrigues) **of the adversary**
>> (or: = which throw folks into dualism with divided thinking and perceptions; or: from the person that throws something through the midst and casts division; or: which is the person who thrusts things through folks; or: from the slanderer who accuses and deceives; or: that have the quality of [what is commonly called] the "devil"),
> 12. **because for us the wrestling is not against** (toward; with a view to) **blood and flesh** (= physical bodies), **but rather against** (toward; i.e., "face to face" with) **the beginning controls and rules**
>> (or: original rulings; or: rulers and controllers; governments; those things or people in first position; the beginning things or people; the original ones; the princes) **and face to face with the rights and privileges** (or: liberties to do as one pleases; or: authorities; or: aspects from out of existence), **with a view to the strengths of the System** (or: strengths of the ordered arrangement; or: universal powers of domination; the world's strong-ones; or: the strengths from the aggregate of humanity) **of this darkness** (realm of shadows, gloom and dimness; [comment: = ignorance]), **facing** (toward; or: with a view to) **the spiritual aspects** (or: breath-effected attitudes; or: conditions and qualities of a spirit) **of the worthlessness**
>> (the badness of conditions; the unsoundness and miserableness; the wickedness and depravity; the evil and malice; the disadvantageousness; the unprofitableness; the thing that brings toilsome labor and a gush of misery) **among those situated upon imposed, elevated positions and centered among the imposed "heavenly people"**
>> (or: situated within the heavenly positions or places; among the imposed "heavenly" realms; positioned in union with the "celestials and heavenly ones"; resident within the midst of added atmospheres; among the folks [residing] in the imposed atmospheres).
>>> [note: this verse could be speaking about the ruling authorities of the religious world of ignorance, with its now worthless sacrifices, or, about the political system of darkened strength which was currently in power, bringing bad situations; Walter Wink, in *Engaging the Powers*, uses the phrase "against suprahuman systems and forces" for part of this verse]
> 13. **On account of this, you folks are to again take in hand and receive back** (or: at once take up) **the full suit of armor** (panoply; implements of war) **which is God** (or: which belongs to and has its source in God), **to the end that you would have power and be able to withstand**

414

and resist (to stand opposite, over against as facing an opponent; or: stand in [other folks'] place, instead of [them]) **within the harmful and misery-gushed day** (or: this day of bad conditions), **and then accomplishing all** (achieving and effecting everything [the whole]), **to stand firm.**
14. **You folks must** (or, as a subjunctive: can; should) **stand** (or: at once take your stand), **then, after girding yourselves around your waist** (or: loins) **in union with Truth and within the midst of Reality, and then, entering within** (putting on; clothing yourself with) **the breastplate armor** (cuirass; corslet) **of fair and equitable dealing of the eschatological deliverance**
> (or: which is the rightwised relationships of the Way pointed out; the Righteousness; the Justice; also = covenant inclusion and participation),

15. **and next, sandaling** (or: binding under) **the feet in readiness and in union with preparedness which comes from, has the character of and which belongs to the good news** (or: message of goodness, ease and well-being) **of the Peace** (or: which are peace and harmony [= shalom]; from the Joining) –
16. **within all things and situations** (or: in union with **all people**) – **[be] at once receiving again** (or: taking back up) **the large oblong shield which is the Faithfulness** (or: of Trust; which has the quality of Faith; that belongs to Confidence and Assurance; from the Loyalty), **within which you will continue having power and be progressively able to extinguish all the fiery arrows of and from the worthless person**
> (or: evil one; unsound and miserable situation; disadvantageous and unprofitable condition; malicious and depraved attitude; toilsome labor that is gushed with misery).

17. **And at once accept** (or: receive and retain) **for yourselves the helmet of the Deliverance** (or: which comes from the Salvation; that belongs to health and wholeness; which is the restoration to the original realm and condition) **and the Spirit's sword** (the short sword from the Attitude; or: the dagger which is spirit; the dirk which is the Breath-effect) – **the one being God's gush-effect**
> (or: which is the result of the flow from God; the one existing [as] a result of a flux or an effect of a continuous movement, the source of which is God; or: which is a spoken Word of God; or: that being an utterance or declaration which is God).

18. **By means of all thought, desire, imparted message or action toward having things be well** (or: Through every prayer) **and request** (or: declaration) **regarding need, [be] folks continuously thinking, speaking and acting toward goodness and well-being** (or: praying) **within every season** (in union with every fitting situation; on every occasion; in the midst of every fertile moment) **within and in union with [the] Spirit** (Breath-effect; Attitude), **while maintaining a constant alertness** (or: in spirit being constantly vigilant and abstaining from sleep), **also, to that end, in all focus to unremitting and stout continuance** (or: in union with every view to resolute, potent perseverance which brings control) **and request regarding need concerning** (or: surrounding) **all of the set-apart folks** (holy ones; saints; sacredly different people).

Let us now return to the offensive actions that he expands upon in our present passage…

5. **progressively tearing down and demolishing conceptions** (concepts; the effects of thoughts, calculations, imaginations, reasonings and reflections) **and every height** (or: high position; high-effect) **and lofty [attitude, purpose or obstacle] that is habitually lifting itself up against** (or: elevating itself up on so as to put down) **the intimate and experiential knowledge of God, and then taking captive every effect of perception, concept and understanding** (result from directing one's mind) **– one after another – and leading them prisoner into the hearing obedience of the Christ** (or: the humble attentive listening, which comes from the Anointed One; or: the submissive paying attention, which is the Anointing),

This is a continuation of vs. 4, above, where he was speaking about "**pulling down** (demolition) **of effects of fortifications** (or: strongholds; strongly entrenched positions)." Now he explains what he meant by this:

a) "**progressively tearing down and demolishing conceptions** (concepts; the effects of thoughts, calculations, imaginations, reasonings and reflections)." These are "spiritual" aspects that are the results of human thinking or of indoctrination or of brainwashing. They are false narratives held in the mind; they are products of disoriented imaginations or illogical reasonings or worthless calculations or vile reflections. In 1 Cor. 1:19, Paul cited Isa. 29:14,

"**I will undo** (untie and loose away; destroy) **the wisdom and cleverness of the wise ones, and I will set aside** (or: displace; invalidate) **the intelligence** (comprehension; understanding) **of the intellectual** (intelligent; comprehending) **people.**"

This is what he is speaking of, here. *Cf* 1 Cor. 3:19. Jer. 17 opens with a description of the tribe of Judah, in that day: "Judah's sin [is] written with an iron pen... on the tablet of their heart." Yahweh goes on to pronounce judgments upon them. Then, in 17:5 He explains:

"A negative wish, or a downward prayer, [comes] upon the person (human) who constantly holds (habitually has) the expectant hope (or: expectation) upon a person (a human), and thus will continue leaning (supporting) his flesh arm (or: strength) upon him, and then at some point his heart would stand off, and away from [the] LORD (= Yahweh)" (LXX, JM).

Such is the situation, or the heart condition, which Paul addresses in this participial clause of vs. 5a. In Jer. 1:10, Jeremiah was given the commission from Yahweh: "To pluck up and to break down and to destroy and to demolish – [and then] to build and to plant" (CVOT). As a prophet, himself, Paul may have been alluding to a "prophet's work" in Israel's history. All of it had the correction of God's people in view.

b) "**and every height** (or: high position; high-effect) **and lofty [attitude, purpose or obstacle] that is habitually lifting itself up against** (or: elevating itself up on so as to put down) **the intimate and experiential knowledge of God.**" On offer in the text are the inserted potential examples of the "height; high position; or, high-effect; and, lofty [thing]." Paul left this ambiguous, giving no specifics, so that it could apply to anything that is "habitually lifting itself up against, or elevating itself up so as to put down, **the intimate and experiential knowledge of God.**" Now what in the world does that? Surely, I jest. It is "the wisdom and cleverness of the wise ones," as cited above. It is the pride of a human, the elevation of human intellect as an opponent to what has been revealed about, and from, God. In Jesus' day it was the attitudes and argument that assaulted Him from the scribes and Pharisees. In Paul's day it was those of the Jewish religion, those Christians who were Judaizers, and his opponents from the other religions. The followers of Jesus, upon receiving the Holy Spirit, had thereby received "**the intimate and experiential knowledge of God.**" It is possible that Paul had Ezk. 28:2 in mind:

"Because your heart is haughty, and you are saying, 'I [am] a god! I sit on the seat of God in the heart of the seas (figure of humanity, at large)!,' yet you [are] human [Heb. Adam] and not a god, although you are deeming your heart like the heart of God..."

The main thing that lifts itself up is the human ego.

c) "**and then taking captive every effect of perception, concept and understanding** (result from directing one's mind) **– one after another.**" So we break down the fort of the mind, and then make "**every effect of perception, concept and understanding**" our prisoner – i.e., we halt and take control of every "result from directing one's mind." The realm of activity of which Paul is speaking is very clear. It is the realm of "**the result of the thinking** (disposition; thought processes; mind-set, outlook) **of the flesh**" (Rom. 8:7).

d) "**leading them prisoner into the hearing obedience of the Christ.**" We read of one way that folks can do this in 3:18, above: "**being folks who by a mirror are continuously observing, as ourselves, the Lord's glory.**" Paul set forth another way in Rom. 12:2,

"**be progressively transformed** (transfigured; changed in form and semblance) **by the renewing** (or: in the renewal; for the making-back-up-new again) **of your mind** [with other MSS: from The Mind] **into the [situation and condition for] you folks to be habitually examining in order to be testing and, after scrutiny, distinguishing and approving what [is] God's will** (design; purpose; resolve; intent)**: the good and well-pleasing, even perfect** (finished, complete and destined)**!**"

This is done "**in God** (or: by and with God)," (vs. 4, above). Recall, again, Phil. 2:13,

"God is the One habitually operating with inward activity, repeatedly working within, constantly causing function and progressively producing effects within, among and in union with you folks – both the [condition] to be habitually willing (intending; purposing; resolving) **and the [situation] to be continuously effecting the action, repeatedly operating to cause function and habitually setting at work so as to produce – for the sake of and over the pleasing good form and the thinking of goodness in delightful imagination."**

He does not leave it up to us. In fact, the last phrase is instructive when read as an ablative (with the preposition "from"): "the humble attentive listening, which comes FROM the Anointed One." And more light comes from rendering this phrase as apposition: "the submissive paying attention, which is the Anointing." You see, this is why we were given the Spirit. In 1 Jn. 2:20 we are informed:

> **"you folks continue having the effects** (or: constantly hold and progressively possess the results) **of an anointing from the set-apart One** (or: the Holy One)."

And that settles it! But Paul has more to say about all this, in the next verse...

6. **even continuously holding [them] in a ready state and prepared condition to support justice and equity, while maintaining rightwised relationships from out of the Way pointed out, for every mishearing** (or: hearing-aside; setting of our attention to the side; or: disobedience) **– whenever your hearing obedience may be made full** (or: as soon as the humble attentive listening and submissive paying attention can be brought to full measure, would be completed and thus fulfilled, from, and with regard to, you folks)!

So we take captive every "**effect of perception, concept and understanding**" and then we are expected to "**continuously holding [them].**" You see, perceptions, concepts and understandings are not bad in or of themselves, they just need to be submitted unto the direction of the Holy Spirit for building up God's temple (His people – ch. 3, above) and for spreading the *Logos* and expanding His reign in human hearts and minds. Therefore, our perceptions (etc.) are to be held "**in a ready state and prepared condition to support justice and equity.**" This has both a social application, and an informational/transformational application – since we are talking about the "**justice and equity**" of God. This is His entire program, as we read in 5:18-21, above. My semantic conflation of the optional rendering of the verb in this clause offers: "**while maintaining rightwised relationships from out of the Way pointed out.**" It is sad that, considering that Christ has brought us Good News, the KJV rendered this verb "revenge," the NWT offers "avenge/inflict punishment," Nyland gives "take vengeance," the NRSV and ESV both give "punish." The verb is *ekdikeō*: to operate from what is right, just and fair; to maintain what is right, just and fair. The original idea in the root, *dikē* is: to point the Way, or the Way pointed-out; the right Way. For the body of Christ this can only mean: to support Christ, the Way, as they live their lives; to show folks "the Way pointed out in Christ. To maintain lives that are rightwised: turned in the Right Direction!

So this enlightened understanding is to be continuously held – why? It is to be used "**for every mishearing** (or: hearing-aside; setting of our attention to the side; or: disobedience)." Now this is for evangelizing folk, for instructing folks and for being a tool to open their ears to hear the Good News. And what about those who are in disobedience (part of the semantic range of "mishearing; hearing aside")? Well, recall what Paul said in Rom. 11:32,

> **"God encloses, shuts up and locks all mankind** (everyone; the entire lot of folks) **into incompliance** (disobedience; stubbornness; lack of being convinced), **to the end that He could** (or: would; should) **mercy all mankind** (may make everyone, the all, recipients of mercy)!"

So everyone is included in what Paul is saying in this verse.

Now, perhaps, the final clause makes sense: "**whenever your hearing obedience may be made full.**" You see, before we can help people get a splinter out of their eye, we first must have the log/timber removed from our own eye. Before we can be a vessel for the Master's use, we must be purified (Mal. 3:2-30; we must be child-trained; we must be reflecting His image to others. Paul is simply saying that we should be spiritually mature in order to be a proper "attending servant and dispenser." The final parenthetical expansion in this verse is instructive. When this latter is fulfilled, then we can be used for the former, which has been prepared and made ready.

7. **You folks constantly look at things according to external appearances!** (or: Are you now regarding things in the sphere of surface meanings?; or: Keep on seeing the things that face [you]!) **If anyone has trusted and now continues persuaded for himself to exist belonging to Christ** (or: with himself to be from Christ; or: in himself to be with the qualities of the Anointing), **let him continue considering and reckoning this again upon himself: that just as he belongs to Christ, with the qualities of the Anointing, in this same way [do] we, also.**

The first sentence is offered in three forms: the first reads the verb in the indicative, as a statement of fact; the second offers the sentence as a question; the third takes the verb as an imperative (the verb form functions either as an indicative, or an imperative). Obviously, Paul can be read as potentially saying three different things. The first two renderings say virtually the same thing, but just in different expressions, pointing out how they are perceiving "**according to external appearances**" or regarding, and thus judging things "in the sphere of surface meanings." Both of these phrases render the extended use of the term which is literally, "face." Hart renders the verb as an imperative, and (similar to my rendering) renders the noun literally: "See the things right before your face." The imperative rendering is therefore saying something quite different than the indicative rendering. May we let the Spirit speak to us as to which Paul was meaning. Remember, these letters would have been written hearing Paul's tone of voice and inflection, and then they would have been read aloud to his audience in Corinth, where the rhetor would give the appropriate emphasis. We do not have this advantage.

Any of these three renderings are appropriate to the challenge that Paul next sets before them: "**If anyone has trusted and now continues persuaded for himself to exist belonging to Christ** (or: with himself to be from Christ; or: in himself to be with the qualities of the Anointing)…" The operative terms, here, are "has trusted and now continues persuaded for himself." These words seem intended for those in Corinth who oppose him, and have an opinion of their place within the community. The alternative renderings of the infinitive clause are worth noting:
> a) **persuaded** "with himself to be from Christ;"
> b) **persuaded** "in himself to be with the qualities of the Anointing."

Paul has just set the bar for those to whom he then proceeds to lay out the qualifications for a person being "**persuaded for himself**" as this relates to Paul and his associates: "**let him continue considering and reckoning this again upon himself: that just as he belongs to Christ, with the qualities of the Anointing, in this same way [do] we, also.**" Notice that Paul does not set himself above his opponents. He graciously grants them equal status, but requires that they likewise reciprocate with this same attitude and "reckoning."

It may be helpful at this point to insert Kummel's assessment of the identity of Paul's opponents in Corinth:
> "[It] is clear that Jewish Christians have come into the Corinthian church who boast of their indubitable apostolic dignity, their Palestinian origin, their contact with the earthly Jesus, their irreproachable Jewish descent, and also their spiritual gifts; they have letters of recommendation and deny all of these advantages to Paul. The intruders, who originated from Palestine, are therefore, not 'Judaizers,' but Palestinian opponents… Paul in 2 Cor. polemizes… against a definite Gnostic, Palestinian, Jewish-Christian opposition created by new additional opponents" (ibid pp 209-10).

And now Paul continues with his argument to them…

8. **For besides, if I should boast somewhat more excessively concerning our privilege from out of Being** (or: right and authority) – **which the Lord** [= Christ or Yahweh] **gives us with a view unto**

edification and up-building (construction into being a house), **and not unto your tearing down or demolition – I shall not be put to shame or be disgraced,**

He begins by referring to himself, "**if I should boast somewhat more excessively**," but then deftly includes his companions, "**concerning OUR privilege from out of Being** (or: right and authority)... **gives US**." The phrase "privilege from out of Being" is a conflation of an extended meaning, and then a literal rendering, of the noun *ex-ousia*. *Ousia* is a present participle of the verb "to be." *Ex-* is a preposition that is prefixed to the participle, and is here rendered "from out of." I capitalized the word "**Being**" to intimate that their "right, authority and privilege" comes from God. But this could also be understood as "privilege from being [sent-forth folks; representatives {of God}]."

Next, note that he proceeds to say specifically that it is "**the Lord**" that "**gives**" them this "privilege from out of Being." And to what end is this given to them? "**With a view unto edification and up-building** (construction into being a house)." The root of the noun "edification/up-building/construction" is the word "**house**." We miss this nuance, and Paul's corporate application (God's House, i.e., His Temple – the people) if we only render the word "edification" or "up-building." These are good renderings, but are often only taken to refer to individuals. Paul normally has as his first priority the corporate. Recall 1 Cor. 3:9-17, where in vs. 10 Paul refers to himself as a "master builder."

And now he bolsters his point by a negating contrast: "**and NOT unto YOUR tearing down or demolition**." Observe that he uses the same word, "tearing down/demolition" that he used in vs. 4, above, with regard to "strongholds (etc.)," there. They demolish false concepts, not people. To make this point I put "YOUR" in all caps, here. Their attending service and dispensing was never to tear people down.

If we remove Paul's parenthetical statement, which I set off by dashes, his statement reads: "**if I should boast somewhat more excessively concerning our privilege from out of Being... I shall not be put to shame or be disgraced**." This helps us follow his thought, which is completed in the next verse...

9. in that I would not seem, as it were, constantly to be completely intimidating you folks (or: as if to be repeatedly making you really alarmed or afraid) **through the** (or: [my]) **letters.**

This verse explains his reference to the potential of being "put to shame or disgraced." It could be construed as shame or disgrace if, via his letters, he was "**constantly, completely intimidating [them]**" or "repeatedly making [them] really alarmed or afraid." But he would NOT be put to shame, because his letters were NOT really intimidating them or bringing them alarm or fear. Would that more "preachers" or "teachers" would take this to heart – that intimidation, alarm and fear are disgraceful ways to share the teachings of Christ.

10. "Because," one person is [other MSS: they are] **constantly saying, "the letters [are] indeed weighty and strong** (or: = severe and violent), **but the presence of the body [is] weak, and the *Logos*** (Word; idea; information; message) **has been collected from out of nothing** (or: and [his] expression continues being scorned, despised and disregarded)**!"**

First there is sarcasm about his letters (**indeed weighty and strong**), or it can be read as the criticism of these works (severe and violent), then it moves to an *ad hominin* attack against his person (**the body is weak**), and finally a criticism of **the *Logos***, which may refer to the content of his message, his idea or the information that he brings.

The reference to "the body" is uncertain in its meaning. I have given a literal rendering. Hillyer suggests, "The allegation concerns character rather than physique" (ibid). The CLNT and ESV render the phrase, "bodily presence." Hart stretches this even more, with: "his bodily presentation." Nyland paraphrases: "in person he's unimpressive." NASB is similar to Nyland. Rotherham sticks to the literal, "the presence of the body is weak." The "presence of the body" is set in contrast to "the letters," in the Greek text. Now in the next verse, Paul emphasizes "**the kind of person we are in *Logos*,**" so this should inform our understanding of the phrase, here. Hillyer seems to be on target.

11. **Let such a person take this into account, that the kind of person we are in *Logos*** (word, etc.) **through letters, being absent, such also [are we], being present, in action.**

This statement contrasts "**in *Logos*** (word, etc.)" with "**in action,**" while at the same time using the contrasts of their opponents (**through letters**... **being present**). Paul neatly sums all four elements as being equivalent: "**such also.**" They are the same kind of person: in *Logos*, through letters, being absent and being present.

> "**Beside Whom there is no otherness at [His] side** (or: in the presence of Whom is no parallel otherness; [other MSS: along with Whom is not one interchange, variation, shifting or mutation]), **nor a shadow cast by turning** [other MSS: an effect caused by the passing of shadows]" (Jas. 1:17b)!

12. **Of course we are not daring to classify ourselves among, nor compare or explain ourselves with, some of those setting themselves together for commendation. But in fact they, themselves, are constantly measuring themselves among** (or: within) **themselves, and are repeatedly comparing themselves with themselves – they continue not comprehending or understanding!**

Recall 5:12, above, in regard to the first statement. This can be taken as sarcasm, but without hearing the tone of voice, it seems presumptuous to assume this. Hillyer calls this "heavy irony [that] clothes an important principle" (ibid; brackets mine). It could also simply be a statement of "extreme wisdom." The second statement characterizes such behavior as an absence of "**comprehending or understanding.**" To make any human to be a standard for "**measuring [oneself]**" is foolishness.

> "The only true comparison must be with a standard which is external and unchanging. Paul knows this can only be Christ" (Hillyer, ibid).

Paul spoke of:

> "**The Faithfulness** (or: the loyalty and fidelity), **even which is the full, experiential and intimate knowledge** (or: and from recognition; and of discovery; as well as pertaining to insight) **which is** (or: of; from; in reference to) **the Son of God, [growing] into [the] purposed and destined adult man** (complete, finished, full-grown, perfect, goal-attained, mature manhood) – **into** (or: unto) **[the] measure of [the] stature** (full age; prime of life) **of the entire content which comprises the Anointed One**" (Eph. 4:13).

In Rev. 11:1, John was told to, "Rise, and measure the temple of God..." God can have us measured by others within the body – but this is not "**measuring themselves among** (or: within) **themselves.**" Observe that this phrase is followed directly by "**repeatedly comparing themselves with themselves.**" These actions reveal pride within the ones that are doing it. It reveals the heart of Eve, in the Garden: a desire to be more – and within Corinth, a desire to be seen a superior to others.

13. **Now we ourselves will not boast into what is not measured** (or: about the things that cannot be measured), **but rather, corresponding to the measure of the measuring rod** (rule; standard; canon; = sphere of allocated influence) **which God divided and gives as a part to** (in; for) **us – of a measure** (or: = sphere of influence) **to reach even as far as upon you folks.**

IF Paul and his associates should boast (vs. 8, above), it will be based upon what God manifests in those who they serve. It will not be upon personal attainment or subjective standards. But to what is he referring, when he says, "**into what is not measured**"? Is he speaking about something that God "measures out" to, or for, them? What he says in contrast is in reference to that "**which God divided and** gives as a part to (in; for) us." So the "measure" refers to what God has given to them. Then he further explains that this is "a measure (or: = sphere of influence) to reach even as far as upon you folks." The parenthetical paraphrase suggests that he is referring to "a measured sphere of influence." The Spirit directed him and his associates into specific places, or physical areas, of ministry. Verse 15, below, instructs us that they did not venture beyond where the Spirit led, or had given to, them. In our day it is common for folks to think of "world-wide" ministries. Through modern transportation and technology, we have the abilities to easily go almost anywhere. But, do we stop to seek the Lord's direction about this?

Another thought on this, based upon the rendering, "about the things that cannot be measured," may have been meant to point his listeners to the realm of kingdom influence: the realm of the Spirit, which cannot be measured. In both interpretations, God had obviously measured out their influence as far as the Corinthian community. "Paul is 'in the lane' (athletics metaphor) of service marked out by God" (Hillyer, ibid).

14. **Certainly we are not progressively overspreading** (or: overstretching) **ourselves – as if not being repeatedly reaching-on into you folks – for we advanced beforehand as far as even you people in the declaring of Christ's good news** (or: the message of goodness, ease and well-being pertaining to and having its source in the Anointed One).

Paul and his associates had through original visit, and then previous letters, been "**repeatedly reaching-on into you folks.**" Therefore, they were "**certainly not progressively overspreading** (or: overstretching) **[themselves].**" Then he reminds them (and the opponents within Corinth) that "**[they] advanced beforehand as far as even you people in the declaring of Christ's good news.**" Corinth has been "measured out" and "given" to Paul and his group, for attending service, dispensing, and to "be a father" to them (1 Cor. 4:15b). In 1 Cor. 9:1b he had asked them: "**Are you folks not my work within the Lord** (or: = in union with Christ or centered in Yahweh)**?**"

15. **No, we are not men habitually boasting into what is not measured [off for us] – in labors** (toils) **belonging to other folks – but are continuously holding an expectation and having expectant hope of a progressively growing increase of your faith, trust and loyalty to be made great and enlarged within you** (or: among and in union with you folks) **– in line with and corresponding to our measured-out range and area** (= sphere of allocated influence) **– [leading] into abundance** (being surrounded with overflowing excess),

The first clause is similar to Rom. 15:20,
> "**Now thus** (or: in this manner) **am I constantly loving the honor, which is my driving ambition, to habitually be proclaiming the message of goodness and well-being where Christ is** (or: was) **not named, to the end that I should not be building upon another person's foundation.**"

So no, they had not trespassed into someone else's field of spiritual **labors**, they came into what had been "**measured [off for them].**" Therefore, they were "**continuously holding an expectation and having expectant hope of a progressively growing increase of [their] faith, trust and loyalty to be made great and enlarged within [them]** (or: among and in union with [them])." And both territorially and spiritually, they were laboring "**in line with and corresponding to our measured-out range and area** (= sphere of allocated influence)."

They had previously planted the Seed, and now they had an expectation of its "**growing increase [in] faith, trust and loyalty,**" so that IT would "**be made great and enlarged within [them].**" This would lead to their having "**abundance** (being surrounded with overflowing excess)" of the Seed (i.e., the *Logos*, Christ) both to feed themselves and to share with others – planting in new fields!

16. **[increasing] into the [regions] beyond those of your area, to yourselves** (or: to ourselves) **cause the good news to be proclaimed – not in the midst of a measured-out range and area** (= sphere of allocated influence) **belonging to another – [and] to boast into things [that have been] prepared and made ready,**

Yes! That **abundance** and overflow would increase "**into the [regions] beyond those of [their] area**," so that the Corinthian called-out folks would themselves "**cause the good news to be proclaimed**" into areas not yet given to other sent-forth folks. This would mean that they, too, could "**boast into things [that have been] prepared and made ready**," just as Paul and his associates had been given to do, as they were, by God, sent into "**the midst of a measured-out range and area** (= sphere of allocated influence) **NOT belonging to another**."

So who makes the field, or the area, "**prepared and made ready**"? The answer is God, Who first burns-off the field (Heb. 6:8), or the person who he sends to plow the ground (Lu. 9:62). In Jesus' time, one of them was John the Immerser and those who responded to his message: "**you folks at once prepare and make ready the road of [the] Lord**" (Mk. 1:3).

17. **so, "the one [among you] that is habitually boasting is to be habitually boasting in the Lord** [= Christ or Yahweh]**."** [Jer. 9:24]

Paul knows that the "**growing increase**," among folks who have been sown with Christ, is the work of the Lord, within them. He laid this out in 1 Cor. 3:7,

> "**So that neither is the one habitually planting anything [special]** (anyone [of importance]), **nor the one habitually irrigating** (watering; giving drink), **but rather God: the One habitually and progressively causing growth and increase**."

And thus, the boast must be "**in the Lord**." Paul's use of this quote from Jer. 9 calls to mind Isa. 65:16-17,

> "So he who blesses himself in the land (or: earth) will bless himself in the God of [the] Amen [LXX: the true and real God]; and he who swears in the land (earth) will swear by the God of [the] Amen – because the former troubles have been forgotten, and because they are hidden from My eyes. For behold me, creating new heavens (atmospheres) and a new earth (land), and the former shall not be mentioned, neither shall they come up on the heart." *Cf* 1:20, above; 1 Cor. 1:31; 2:9

18. **Now it follows that, the person constantly placing himself with others – so as to be commended – is not that one who is qualified or approved, but rather, he whom the Lord** [= Christ or Yahweh] **consistently includes and commends.**

Here, Paul draws an obvious conclusion of his arguments that were begun in vs. 7, above, and then brought into focus in vs. 12. Seeking commendation from one's peers leave a person **unqualified, unapproved, and** "**not comprehending or understanding!**" Thus, Paul has, by his arguments, placed his opponents in this latter category. It is only the Lord's inclusion (in the ministry) and commendation (as a faithful servant) that counts:

> "**whose praise** (applause; full recommendation; [note play on words: Jew is a derivative of "Judah," which means "praise"]) **[is] not from out of mankind** (humanity), **but rather from out of God**" (Rom. 2:29b), and recall Paul's instruction in 1 Cor. 4:5,
> "**Hence, do not be constantly evaluating** (or: stop judging, making decisions about or critiquing) **anything before [its] season** (before a fitting, due or appointed situation; prior to a fertile moment)**: until the Lord would come – Who will continue giving light to the hidden things of the Darkness, and will progressively set in clear light** (or: keep on manifesting) **the intentions and purposes** (designs, dispositions, motives and counsels) **of the hearts – and**

then the praise and applause from God will repeatedly be birthed (happen; come into being) **in each human** (or: for every person)!"

Chapter 11

Witherington contends: "The material in ch. 11 should be grouped with at least the first ten verses of ch. 12" (ibid p 442).

1. **I wish that you folks were continuing to put up with a little something of my thoughtlessness** (or: unreasonableness; lack of common sense; foolishness; imprudence). **But in fact, you are also always patiently tolerant of me** (or, as an imperative: Still further, be also patiently tolerant of me),

It is difficult to determine the tone or mood or rhetorical device of Paul's first statement, since we cannot observe the body language or hear the voice of the person reading it to the audience. Added to this is the semantic range of "**thoughtlessness** (or: unreasonableness; lack of common sense; foolishness; imprudence)." Was he speaking "tongue in cheek"? Or, was this sarcasm, meant to sting just a bit?

Next is the question of whether the second statement is in the indicative, or is an imperative. The form of the verb serves both functions, and either reading serves the context. We might say that Paul is asking his audience to patiently indulge him in what he is about to say.

2. **for I continue with hot zeal** (ardor; eager vehement passion) **concerning you in, with and by God's fervent zeal** (ardent, passionate affection from, and which is, God), **because I myself joined you folks in marriage to one Husband** (or: Man), **to make** (place) **a pure virgin** (= unmarried girl) **to stand alongside in and with the Christ** (or: by the Anointed One; as the Anointed [body])

We should observe that Paul's "**hot zeal** (ardor; eager vehement passion)" that is being experienced and expressed by Paul is, in fact, "**in, with and by God's fervent zeal**." Paul's zeal is God's zeal (same word in both cases). Having rendered this last phrase first as a genitive of possession (God's), consider also the parenthetical expansion, where "God" is rendered first as an ablative, and then as a genitive of apposition: "ardent, passionate affection from, and which is, God." If the Holy Spirit is the source (and not our old Adamic, or human, emotions being the source), then as we "walk in the Spirit" (Gal. 5:16) and He incites ardor and vehement passion within us, we are actually experiencing and/or expressing feelings and emotions that are God, Who, of course, is indwelling us. Remember 1 Cor. 6:17? If we are joined to the Lord, WE are One Spirit. Therefore, Paul is not just using hyperbole, but is speaking forth a reality that he was living – a reality of being seated as "one grasped" (literal meaning of cherub; cf Phil. 3:12b, "**taken down by hand** (fully seized; forcefully grasped and taken possession of) **by, and under [the control of], Christ Jesus**") on the Mercy Seat (Eph. 2:6), with the Lord.

Next, we see that he functioned as a priest, or a father/mother (Gal. 4:19; 1 Cor. 4:15): "**I myself joined you folks in marriage to one Husband**." Here we have an allusion to Yahweh's relationship with Israel:
> "And so, I Myself will proceed betrothing you to Myself, on unto the Age [of Messiah]. I will also proceed betrothing you to Myself, centered in eschatological deliverance and in union with the Way pointed out, as well as in and for the result of justice (fairness of a right decision for equity), and centered in compassionate mercy, as well as in pity that is enacted to relieve sorrow. I will also proceed betrothing you to Myself in faithfulness (centered in loyalty; in union with trust). And then you will progress to fully know the Lord (= Yahweh) by intimate, experiential insight and discovery" (Hos. 2:19-20; LXX, JM).

In Eph. 5, Paul has been giving instruction to husbands and wives and, near the end of this discourse, vs. 32 informs us:

"**This secret** (or: mystery) **is great** (= important), **but I am speaking unto** (or: into; with a view to) **Christ, even** (or: and; as well as) **unto** (or: into; with a view to) **the called-out community** (or: the called-out person; or: the summoned-forth covenant assembly)."

But Paul continues in his descriptive metaphor of the covenant community in Corinth, saying, "**to make** (place) **a pure virgin** (= unmarried girl) **to stand alongside in and with the Christ**." This may be an allusion to Lev. 21:13, concerning who a priest should marry. The verb in this clause is an infinitive. Paul "joined" them to Christ, and the intended result was for them "to stand alongside "by the Anointed One." Recall his admonition about not joining members of Christ with a prostitute, as discussed in 1 Cor. 6:15-16, above (that possibly being an allusion to Lev. 21:7). It was the joining to Christ that made them "a pure virgin (a girl that had not been married)." Joining them to the Lord was what enabled them "**to stand alongside, with Christ**," as the Anointed [body] of Christ. Paul described this same idea in Col. 1:28b,

"**to the intent that we may place every person** (or: human) **finished** (mature; perfect with respect to purpose; complete; as having reached the goal of destiny) **by [our] side, within the midst of, centered in, and in union with, Christ**."

3. **Yet I continue fearing lest somehow, as the serpent thoroughly deceived** (or: seduces; fully deludes; cheats) **Eve within its capability for every work** (its cunning ability in all crafts and actions; its readiness to do anything), **the results of directing your minds** (or: effects of your perceptions, concepts and understanding) **should be decayed** (could be ruined; would be spoiled or corrupted) **away from the singleness [of commitment] and simplicity [of being] – even the purity – which [focuses us] into the Christ** (or: with a view to the Anointing).

From noting this reference to Eve, we may conclude that the Paul's listeners were instructed in the content of the OT. This allusion to the deception of Eve by the serpent recalls a part of the origin story in Gen. 3:4, and Paul may also have had in mind Jesus' teaching in Jn. 8:44. In that passage Jesus was speaking to the Judean leadership in Jerusalem and He cast them in the role of the serpent: folks that "**not stood and does not now stand within the Truth**" and are "**speaking the lie**." Paul is, like Jesus, casting the false teachers in this same role: as deceptive serpents.

Observe how Paul crafts a description of an adversary's methods: "**within its capability for every work** (its cunning ability in all crafts and actions; its readiness to do anything), [and] **the results of directing your minds** (or: effects of your perceptions, concepts and understanding)." Deception is a mental game. It involves "the effects of perceptions, concepts and understanding."

Paul is concerned lest somehow those results "**should be decayed,** (could be ruined; would be spoiled or corrupted) **away**." Think about what happened when Eve was deceived! With Adam's disobedience, the Death "**passed through in all directions, into all mankind**" (Rom. 5:12). Paul does not want this to happen again, now in Corinth, because of the "**false emissaries – fraudulent and deceitful workers**" who are "**attending servants and dispensers**... [of] **the adversary** (opponent; *satan*)" are deceiving folks in Corinth by "**repeatedly change their form and outward fashion** (or: are habitually transformed) **as attending servants of eschatological deliverance, justice and equity** (dispensers of the rightwised way pointed out; = ministers of the new covenant)," as we read in vss. 13, 15, below. These false emissaries bring decay, ruin, spoilage and corruption to the life of the community to the end that folks turn "**away from the singleness [of commitment] and simplicity [of being] – even the purity – which [focuses us] into the Christ** (or: with a view to the Anointing)."

What would corrupt the purity of their minds? How about yesterday's manna (Ex. 16:20)? We suggest that it was the Judaizing practices that the deceitful workers were bringing into the community – old manna from the old covenant or the previous Day of Moses, with the Law. It could also be the wisdom of humans or the imagined philosophies that would have tainted the pure Word given by Paul and the true emissaries. Such folks, and the Jews, were the primary adversaries of Paul. The dualism taken from the tree of the knowledge of good and evil (either the Law, or the dualistic religion of Zoroastrianism that had corrupted the Jews when they were under Persian influence) would also have spoiled the Message of the Christ. It would be like a wife taking another lover – as Israel brought in idols, in the previous age.

In 1 Tim. 1:3, Paul encouraged Timothy "**that you should pass on an announcement** (could notify; would bring along a message) **to certain folks** (or: for some) **not to continue teaching different things**." Timothy was in Ephesus at the time. In that same letter, in chapter 4 we read Paul predicting:

1. **Now the Spirit** (or: Breath-effect) **is explicitly saying that within subsequent seasons** (in fitting situations and on appropriate occasions which will be afterwards) **some of the faith** (or: certain folks belonging to this trust) **will proceed standing off and away [from the Path, or from the Community]** (or: some people will progressively withdraw from this conviction and loyalty), **habitually holding toward** (having a propensity to) **wandering and deceptive spirits** (or: straying and seducing breath-effects and attitudes) **and to teachings of demons**

    (to teachings about and pertaining to, or which are, demons [note: a Hellenistic concept and term: = animistic influences]; or: to instructions and training which come from animistic influences [= pagan religions]),

    [comment: this prophesied about the future institutionalization of the called-out community, and the introduction of pagan teachings, all of which later came to be called "orthodox"]

2. **within perverse scholarship of false words**

    (or: in association with overly critical hairsplitting of false messages; in the midst of gradually separated interpretations of false expressions; or: in union with deceptive decisions by speakers of lies), **from folks having their own consciences cauterized**
    (seared; branded) **as with a hot iron.**

The author of Hebrews instructed his listeners, in chapter 13:

8. **Jesus Christ [is] the same yesterday and today and on into the ages,**

    (or: Jesus [is and continues being] Christ [= the Messiah] – the Man Himself {or: the Very One}: yesterday as well as today, and even into the midst of the ages,) [*cf* 1:12b, above]

9. **[so] do not be carried aside** (or: swept away) **by various and strange** (or: with many-colored [as in tapestries], intricate and foreign) **teachings. You see, [it is] beautiful** (fine; ideal; admirably proportionate) **for the heart** (= core of our being) **to be continuously made firm with a fixed footing by Grace, whose source is joy and which comes with favor – not by** (or: in; with) **foods** (= rules and regulations pertaining to eating or what is edible), **in which those [thus] walking about** (= occupying themselves) **were not increased** (or: = which have not helped or benefited those who follow this way of life). [*cf* Eph. 4:14; 1 Tim. 4:1b; Rom. 14:17; Col. 2:16]

The potential for deception was widespread. 2 Pet. 3:17 advises:

"**You, then, beloved and accepted ones, being ones by repeated experiences previously acquainted [with this]** (or: knowing beforehand by experiences), **be constantly on watch, guard, maintain and keep yourselves in custody, lest – at some point being carried** (or: led) **away together by the deception** (or: in straying; or: to deceit) **of the unestablished** (or: from unprincipled, inordinate or lawless) **folks – you could fall out from your own state of fixed firmness** (or: steadfastness)."

In a similar vein, Judah informs his audience:

"**You see, some people came in unobserved, from the side – those having been previously written of old into this judgment** (or: people having from long ago been written into the effects and result of this decision): **[to exist being] impious ones, people continuously changing the grace and favor of God into licentiousness, as well as repeatedly contradicting, saying, "No," to or about, disclaiming, denying and disowning our only Sovereign and Lord** (or: Supreme Ruler and Owner), **Jesus Christ [= Messiah]**" (Jude 4).

The Spirit had alerted Christ's agents about these potential hazards for the called-out communities, and they were faithful to give these warnings.

4. **For if, indeed, the person periodically** (or: presently) **coming is habitually preaching** (normally heralding or proclaiming) **another Jesus – whom we do not preach** (or: did not herald and proclaim) – **or, [if] you folks are continuously receiving a different breath-effect** (or: are repeatedly laying hold of a spirit or attitude that is different in kind and nature) **which you did not receive, or a different "good-news"** (a message of ease and well-being which is different in kind and character) **which you did not welcome and accept, are you repeatedly holding back from [him] in an ideal way?** (or: you folks are beautifully putting up with and tolerant of [it]! [other MSS: were you finely holding back from {him; it}?]).

The ongoing action signified by the present tense of the verb "**coming**" can be viewed either as periodic action (someone who occasionally visited the group), or action that was then presently taking place – referring to someone within the community that was presently coming to their gatherings on a regular basis. The present tense of the verb "**preaching** (etc.)" indicates repeated or habitual activity of heralding a gospel. This fits either scenario indicated in the first verb. So Paul is not speaking of someone presenting a one-time teaching that differed from what he had taught in Corinth. He is speaking of a person with an agenda to sidetrack the community away from the Way pointed out and into a divergent path that was NOT good news.

Now his first topic of concern is someone who preaches "**another Jesus – whom we do not preach**." O'Rourke suggests that this refers to, "Not another historic personage, but one who differs doctrinally from him whom Paul preached" (ibid). We've had the same problem, both in the organized, institutional churches, as well as in independent splinter groups. They preach a Jesus who is a potential savior of people, but who, after folks die, will send them to eternal torment if they had not accepted his salvation (along with other various requirements) before they died. They preach a Jesus who is not the same in the ages to come, as he is in this age and lifetime.

The next issue he mentions is the potential of their "**continuously receiving a different breath-effect** (or: are repeatedly laying hold of a spirit or attitude that is different in kind and nature) **which you did not receive**." What did he mean by this? In Rom. 8:15 he said,

> "**You see, you folks did** (or: do) **not receive again a spirit of slavery to fear** (or: get slavery's spirit or breath-effect again, unto fear; or: take an attitude which personifies being a slave [as in Egypt or under the Law, leading] into fear again), **but rather you received a spirit of being placed as a son** (or: a Breath-effect which set you in the position of a son; or: you receive an attitude of one having been adopted [in accord with Greek or Roman law]), **within which** (or: in union with Whom) **we are habitually crying out, 'Abba** (Dad), **O Father!'**"

The spirit of slavery comes with keeping the Law, but Paul said in Gal. 5:18, "**Yet since** (or: if) **you folks are continuously being led in spirit** (by [the] Spirit; to [the] Spirit; with a Breath-effect), **you do not exist** (you are not) **under Law** [= Torah; = the flesh system of works; = the Mosaic covenant]." A different spirit would not produce the Fruit of the Spirit:

> "**love** (unrestricted, self-giving acceptance; the drive to overcome existential separation), **joy, peace** (or: harmonious joining), **length before a stirring of emotion** (slowness of rushing toward something; long-enduring; longsuffering; patience; putting anger far away), **useful kindness, goodness** (virtuousness), **faith** (or: faithfulness; trust; trustworthiness; loyalty; reliance; reliability; allegiance; fidelity), **gentle friendliness** (meekness; mildness), **inner strength** (self-control)" (Gal. 5:22-23a).

Remember that Jesus said, "**You will come to be recognizing and fully knowing them from their fruits**" (Mat. 7:16).

And then Paul addresses a third point: "**or a different "good-news"** (a message of ease and well-being which is different in kind and character)." He wrote to Galatia, and in Gal. 1:6,

> "**I am constantly amazed** (or: I continue filled with wonder) **that you folks are so quickly being progressively transplanted** (or, as a middle voice: are thus now quickly transferring yourselves

or changing your stand) **from the One** (or: that [message]) **calling** (summoning) **you people, within Christ's grace** (or: in [the] favor of the Anointed One), **on into a different sort of "message of goodness"** (unto a different evangel, "good news," or gospel; = into an imitation and alternative message of goodness, ease or well-being) – **which is NOT "another" one of the same kind** (= not just another version)!"

Then he addressed these same issues in Gal. 1:

> 7. **But instead that there are certain folks – the ones constantly agitating** (stirring up; disturbing) **you folks – even repeatedly wanting** (or: intending) **to alter and distort** (turn so as to change; pervert; reverse) **Christ's message of goodness, ease and well-being** (or: the good news which is the Anointed One; or: the evangel about and from the [Messiah]).
>
> 8. **However, even if we – or an agent from the atmosphere or sky** (or: a messenger from out of the midst of heaven)! **– should ever bring or announce something as "good news"** (as the message of goodness; as being the evangel or gospel) **to you folks which is to the side of that which we announce** (or: is parallel to what we announced) **to you folks in the message of goodness, ease and well-being, let it be placed on the altar before the Lord** (set up as a result of a divine offering [i.e., to see if it is "accepted" by God, or "rejected," as Cain's was]; or, possibly: cursed).

These same problems have plagued the called-out folks from Paul's day on through to our own.

Now after mentioning "a different 'good news,'" he continues: "**which you did not welcome and accept [i.e., from Paul], are you repeatedly holding back from [him] in an ideal way?**" The Greek is a bit awkward here: the "**[him]**" that I inserted for clarity refers to "**the person**" of the opening clause of this verse. The first parenthetical reading make this a statement, which is either a compliment, or sarcasm (which O'Rourke insists is the case): "you folks are beautifully putting up with and tolerant of [it]!" The "[it]" refers to the "different gospel." The final offering, from other MSS, returns to rendering it as a question: "were you finely holding back from {him; it}?"

Next Paul begins a defense of himself in a way that critiques his opponents at the same time. Witherington suggests that "he is at odds with his opponents… because they do not accept his vision of ministry, that is, a cruciform, Christlike and servant shape" (ibid p 442).

5. **Now you see, I am habitually considering and counting myself to have been in nothing inferior to or deficient from those "very-overly [pretentious and condescending] emissaries** (or: super-folks sent forth with a mission).**"

Paul is probably referring to the Judaizers – those sent out from the Jews in covenant communities that were predominantly composed of Jews. A Judaized gospel was "a different gospel." However, Paul insists that he is "**in nothing inferior to or deficient from**" his opponents, whom he sarcastically categorizes as "**very-overly [pretentious and condescending] emissaries** (or: super-folks sent forth with a mission)." If such folks were steeped in Second Temple Judaism, then they may have overwhelmed the Corinthian community with their vast knowledge of the Law, and perhaps their rhetorical skills. But such things were not the important qualifications for being a representative of Christ, so Paul explains…

6. **Yet even if [I am] non-professional** (ordinary and unskilled) **in word and expression – though certainly not in the intimate and experiential knowledge and insight** (gnosis) **– still, we are men manifesting Light into you folks: in every situation [and] in all things** (or: in every person – in union with and in the midst of all people; in every respect, among all folks).

Paul humbly concedes that he might not be a fine orator: that he may be "ordinary and unskilled" – a "non-professional in word and expression." This describes the folks whom Jesus chose as His first twelve disciples. In 1 Cor. 1:26-27a, Paul sets out the qualifications of those who are called to be Christ's emissaries:

> "**not many wise folks – according to flesh [= the world's wisdom]**
> (or: corresponding to a flesh [system of philosophy or religion]; on the level of [the estranged human situation]; with a consciousness oriented toward a domination System), **not many powerful ones** (those with [political or financial] ability), **not many well-born ones** (ones born to social ease and profit; those of noble birth; folks with distinguished genealogy), **but to the contrary, God collects His thoughts and speaks forth** (or: selects and picks out; chose) **the stupid things** (or: the foolish ones) **of the organized System** (the world of religion, culture and its secular society; or: the cosmos; the universe), **to the end that He could** (or: would; may) **habitually disgrace and bring shame down on the wise ones**."

Next, he affirms that he is not "**non-professional** (ordinary and unskilled)... **in the intimate and experiential knowledge and insight** (*gnosis*)." We read in Eph. 3:

> 3. **that, in accord with an unveiling** (or: down from and in line with a revelation; in keeping with a disclosure), **the secret** (or: mystery) **was made known to me – even as I before wrote** (or: wrote aforetime), **in brief –**
> 4. **toward which [end] you, the folks continually reading** (or: habitually reviewing and recognizing; progressively gathering up knowledge), **are constantly able and continue with power to comprehend** (conceive; understand; apprehend) **my understanding** (insight; confluence; my sending insights together) **in the secret** (or: mystery) **of the Christ**.

Then he nails the main point: "**still, we are men manifesting Light into you folks**." That is the central part of the dispensing: Light to dispel the darkness of a day whose sun has already set. And if this Light was "the Light of humanity," then it was also "the Life" (Jn. 1:4).

Not only that, they were manifesting the Light of Christ: "**in every situation [and] in all things** (or: in every person – in union with and in the midst of all people; in every respect, among all folks)."

7. **Or, do I make a mistake** (or: did I commit a sin) **[by] repeatedly humbling** (or: abasing; lowering) **myself so that you folks can** (or: may; would) **be lifted up** (exalted) **because I announce as good news a free gift – God's good news – to you folks** (or: because without cost I declare the message of ease and well-being to, within and among you: the message of Goodness about, and which, is God)**?**

Hillyer notes that, "Professional Greek rhetoricians (alluded to in vs. 6) would be suspect if they failed to demand fees" (ibid p 1085). Paul is simply wanting them to think about this whole situation that has arisen from the coming of the "super-emissaries." He is asking them to recall how he had come in a cruciform manner, following the example of their Master, who humbled Himself and became a servant. The only way that Jesus was exalted before humans was on a cross. But, in being resurrected,

> "**Going up** (or: Stepping up; Ascending) **into a height** (unto [the] summit) **He led** (or: leads) **captive a captive multitude** (or: He led 'captivity' captive). **He gave** (or: gives) **gifts to mankind** (or: for, in and among the humans; to humanity)" (Ps. 68:18; Eph. 4:8).

Paul uses the same word "**free gift** (without cost)" here, as was used in Eph. 4:8. Paul abased himself to give these Corinthians attentive care, and to dispense "**God's good news**" to them. It was the implanting of the "message of ease and well-being to, within and among" them that "**lifted [them] up**" and "**caused [them] to sit** (or: seated [them]; = enthroned [them]) **together in union with, and among, the heavenly people, and within the things situated upon** [thus, above] **the heavens**" (Eph. 2:6). How, then, could this lowering of himself have been a mistake? The Spirit of Christ that was within them would have made them realize that he had been right to have behaved in this manner.

8. **I encroached upon and took the goods of** (or: rob; despoil) **other called-out folks** (or: groups), **taking** (or: receiving; getting) **rations** (provisions; subsistence pay) **with a view toward the attending service and dispensing pertaining to you people.**

He is reminding them that it was other folks and groups that had been supporting his dispensing, so that he would be able to serve and dispense God's gift to those in Corinth.

9. **Further, being present and facing you, and being put in need** (being made to lack and fall short of means), **I was not a "dead weight" on** (= an idle encumbrance, hence, a financial burden to) **even one person, for the brothers** (= fellow believers) **coming from Macedonia replenished the lacks resulting from my being in need, and in everything I kept and shall continue keeping myself "weight-free" to** (= free from being a burden for) **you folks.**

Here he recalls for them how things actually were, when he was among them. He was not a "free-loader," or "**a dead weight**" on anyone. Folks from the called-out groups in Macedonia "**replenished the lacks resulting from [his] being in need.**" In fact, "**in everything [he] kept and continued keeping [himself] "weight-free" to** (= free from being a burden for) **[them].**" Paul was certainly not building his own "kingdom," or endeavoring to "build his ministry" among them. He came to be their servant, and to be a source of God's gift for them. *Cf* Phil. 4:10-15

10. **Christ's reality** (or: Truth pertaining to, originating in, and which is [the] Anointed One) **continuously exists within me, so that this boast** (or: boasting) **will not be constantly fenced in or hedged about** (thus: stopped or blocked) **unto** (or: for) **me within the slopes** (= regions) **of Achaia!**

Paul was a bearer of God's image: **Reality, which is Christ**, continually existed within him. This Truth was the thing of which he boasted – and was that which He dispensed throughout the region of Achaia, and elsewhere, of course. His boast was like that of Jesus, Who boldly proclaimed,
> "**If ever anyone may continue being thirsty, let him be habitually coming toward** (or: face-to-face with) **Me, and then let the person continuously trusting and progressively believing into Me be constantly** (habitually; repeatedly) **drinking!**" (Jn. 7:37).

That, of course, was a fulfillment of Isa. 55:1, and now Paul was expanding that fulfillment to those in Achaia. He refused to allow this boast in Christ to be "**constantly fenced in or hedged about** (thus: stopped or blocked)." Christ's reality, the Love of God cannot fail (1 Cor. 13:8); the expression of It/Him cannot be blocked or stopped.

11. **Why** (Through what reason or situation)**? Because I am not continuously loving** (giving myself to; urging toward union with) **you folks? God has seen and thus knows!**

Paul will continue his boasting about Christ's reality throughout all the regions of Achaia, because the Truth, which is the Anointed One, constantly exists within him – wherever he goes. But this does not mean that he has forsaken these folks in Corinth; it does not mean that he is "**not continuously loving** (giving myself to; urging toward union with) **[them].**" God is aware of Paul's reasons and purposes, and is also Paul's Witness to the truth of this.

12. **So what I am habitually doing I will still continue doing, to the end that I can cut out the starting point, base of operations, and occasion of those repeatedly wanting and intending a starting point** (base of operations, or, an occasion), **so that they can be found also just as we** (= equal to us), **within that which they are constantly boasting** (= proud)**!**

Paul is one who is led by the Spirit (Rom. 8:14). He will not change his behavior because of criticism or because of the requests and desires of other people. He will "**still continue doing**" what he is "**habitually doing.**" In this particular situation, he is boasting and continuing to proclaim the reality of Christ, "**to the end that [he] can cut out the starting point, base of operations, and occasion of those repeatedly wanting and intending a starting point** (base of operations, or, an occasion)." He did not want these "super emissaries" to have a "base of operation" in Corinth. He wanted to "cut out" their very "starting point" or even "occasion" for getting a foothold in the community.

He wanted these folks to be "**found also just as we** (= equal to us), **within that which they are constantly boasting** (= proud)." He put it this way, in 1 Cor. 11:1,
> "**Progressively come to be imitators of me, correspondingly as I, myself, also [am] of Christ and from [the/an] Anointing**."

He wanted them to give attentive care in a cruciform manner. He wanted them to be imitators of Christ, from following the Anointing. He wanted them to boast in Christ, not in their own abilities or gifts.

13. **For such folks [are] false emissaries** (pseudo-representatives) – **fraudulent and deceitful workers – constantly changing their outward fashion and transforming themselves into emissaries of Christ** (representatives of [the] Anointed One).

Here, he plainly categorizes such folks. They do not truly represent Christ, and they are "**fraudulent and deceitful workers**." Rather than BEING transformed by beholding Christ's glory (3:18, above) or by having their minds renewed (Rom. 12:2), these folks are "**transforming themselves**" by "**constantly changing their outward fashion**." Instead of imitating Christ, they became imitation emissaries. Jesus told his disciples,
> "**You yourselves did not choose Me, but to the contrary I, Myself, selected and picked out** (or: chose) **you folks and placed** (or: set) **you, to the end that you would** (or: can; may) **progressively lead and bring [situations] under control** (or: humbly go your way) **and would** (or: can; should) **be constantly bearing** (bringing forth) **fruit**..." (Jn. 15:16a).

Such folks, as Paul here describes, have chosen themselves and transformed themselves into a role that they have assumed. This is a word of caution, for everyone. Someone once said, "God has no volunteers." No, like with Paul, God apprehends us.

Paul addressed a similar situation in Gal. 2:4,
> "**Yet, through the led-in-at-the-side** (or: smuggled-in) **false brothers** (or: = deceitful or lying fellow believers; or: = imitation members) **– folks who entered alongside to spy out** (to attentively look down and around, observe and take note of) **our freedom which we continuously possess** (constantly have and hold) **within Christ Jesus, to the end that they will utterly enslave us** (or: with a purpose that they shall proceed to bring us down into slavery)."

14. **And no wonder** ([it is] no marvel or cause for astonishment), **for the adversary** (opponent; *satan*) **itself is repeatedly changing its form and outward fashion** (transforming itself) **into a messenger** (person with a message) **of light** (or, as a passive: is from time to time being transformed and changed in its outward expression into an agent from, or that is, [the] Light).

Witherington (ibid p 449) suggests that Paul may be drawing on current Jewish literature in this rhetorical polemic against his opponents (who were obviously Jewish, as vs. 22, below, affirms) in the Corinthian community. In footnote 36 he cites *Life of Adam and Eve*, which is considered to date to the 1st Century AD. Its form is Midrashic and seems to represent Rabbinic traditions, but it exists now only in Greek and Latin MSS. Keep in mind that Paul also drew on Greek poets (e.g. Acts 17:28) to make his points. In 9:1 of this Jewish volume, we read:
> "Then Satan was angry and transformed himself into the brightness of angels and went away to the Tigris River to Eve and found her weeping" (trans. by M.D. Johnson, *The Old Testament Pseudepigrapha, Vol.2*, Hendrickson Pub. 2013 p 260).

If, in fact, Paul was alluding to this text, it does not mean that he was endorsing it as an ontological reality. Johnson instructs us that "it was familiar to early Christians" (ibid p 251), but we do not know what they thought of it. If it was considered to be a Jewish myth, then Paul may have used this imagery to further picture these "super-representatives" as false, fraudulent and deceptive – as were these fanciful tales. He gives this picture, to illustrate his point, without any explanation. In Titus 1:14 he gave this advice:

> "**not habitually holding to** (having [a propensity] toward; heeding and clinging in the direction toward) **Jewish myths** (or: fictions; or, possibly: oral traditions) **and to implanted goals** (impartations of a finished product within; inward directives; commands) **whose source and origin is people** (or: human commandments) **[thus] continually being twisted and turned away from the Truth** (or: reality)." *Cf* 1 Tim. 1:4, 4:7; 2 Tim/ 4:4; 2 Pet. 1:16

So here arises a question: to whom or to what is Paul referring by this term "**the adversary** (opponent; *satan*)"? Paul designates the "false representatives" as being "**its attending servants and dispensers**," in the next verse. In vs. 19, below, he labels them as "**senseless** (foolish; idiotic; imprudent) **people**."

So is the "**adversary**" the fleshly wisdom of the first Adam? Or, is it the worm-infested "manna" (teaching; doctrines; the leaven of the Pharisees) from the past day of the old covenant (e.g., "You have heard that is has been said... But I say unto you..." -- Mat. 5:38-39)? Have not Paul's "opponents" been those who would bring the worn-out Law (Heb. 8:13) into the new creation with its new arrangement? Is it "the Sin," as Paul personified it in Rom. 7:8-20, or "the law of the Sin," and "the body of this Death," in Rom. 7:23-24? Is it

> "**the result of the thinking** (mind-set; effect of the way of thinking; disposition; result of understanding and inclination; the minding; the opinion; the thought; the outlook) **of the FLESH** (= from the human condition or the System of culture and cultus; or: = Torah keeping) **[is; brings] death**.... [or] **the result of the THINKING** (disposition; thought processes; mind-set, outlook) **of the FLESH** (= attention to Torah boundary-markers, custom and cultus; or: = from the human condition) **[is; brings] ENMITY, alienation and discord [streaming] into God** (or: HOSTILITY unto, or active hatred with a view to, God)"? (Rom. 8:6a, 7a)

Duncan Heaster suggests:

> "The individual 'Satan' in the singular referred to in vs. 14, can either be the Jewish system as a whole trying to give a Christian facade (an angel of light, i.e. a minister of Christ, the true light), or an individual leader of the Jewish system.... It needs to be recognized that Paul's writings very often allude to extant Jewish and Gentile literature, sometimes quoting verbatim from them, in order to correct popular ideas. Thus Paul quotes Aratus (Acts 17:28), Menander (1 Corinthians 15:33) and Epimenides (Titus 1:12) – he uses odd phrases out of these uninspired writings by way of illustration... much of the Biblical literature does this kind of thing" (The Real Devil, A Biblical Exploration, www.realdevil.info/5-21.htm).

Next, we must ask: how does this adversary "**repeatedly change its form and outward fashion** (transform itself) **into a messenger** (person with a message) **of light**"? To what is Paul referring, here? Is Paul reaching back to the Garden story (he cited Eve, in vs. 3) and does he thus have the "serpent" in mind, here?

The sphere of "transformation" is seen elsewhere in the Scriptures. If we recall correctly, it is always people that are being transformed, or who, in their deluded thinking, transform themselves. Observe that in vss. 13 and 15 Paul is referring to people "transforming themselves." In both cases, this is not a reality, but a deception. O'Rourke informs us: "No OT text describes the devil under this guise, nor has any other explicit parallel of the description yet been found" (ibid p 288). Paul may have in mind the Judean leadership, who would have been regarded by the masses as a repository of knowledge (light). They were indeed, corporately, "the adversary" of Christ. *Cf* 1 Cor. 3:17-21

Observe that this verse is set between vs. 13, where he describes the false representatives as "**false emissaries** (pseudo-representatives) **– fraudulent and deceitful workers**," and vs. 15 where they "**change their form and outward fashion as though [being]** (or: are habitually transforming or transfiguring themselves [to be] like) **attending servants of eschatological deliverance, justice and equity**." Paul is speaking about people who came in proclaiming a different Jesus, a different spirit and a different message of goodness (vs. 4, above).

Notice, in the parenthetical expansion, that the present participle can also function as a "passive" voice, which means that the action is happening to the adversary, not by the adversary. We find another example of this in the apocalyptic (symbolic) vision in Rev. 20:1-7, where one of God's agents first chains and shuts up the adversary in the abyss, and then later (vs. 7) releases it so that it can deceive the nations in the four quarters of the Land (vs. 8). Both there, in the vision, and here, in Paul, we suggest that where we find the passive voice, it means that God is behind the action (as with Job 1 and 2). Next, observe that the word Light is capitalized. My reason for doing this is that God can transform an adversary into an agent/messenger from the Light. Paul is a classic example of this. On the road to Damascus, before the Light of Jesus shined on him, he was an adversary of Christ (kicking at the goads). The Light, and the Voice, transformed him to be a sent-forth agent of the Light (Christ).

15. **Therefore, [it is] no great thing if its attending servants and dispensers also repeatedly change their form and outward fashion, as though [being]** (or: are habitually transforming or transfiguring themselves [to be] like) **attending servants of eschatological deliverance, justice and equity** (dispensers of the rightwised way pointed out; = ministers of the new covenant) – **whose finish** (or: end in view; finished product; attained goal; consummation; accomplished end) **will proceed in being in accord with, along the line of, to the level of and corresponding to their works and actions** (or: = their outcome will constantly be what they reap from their deeds).

An important thing to notice in the first clause is that these folks are not coming in the guise of satanism, or humanism, or of some other religion: they fashion themselves to be "**like attending servants of eschatological deliverance, justice and equity** (dispensers of the rightwised way pointed out; = ministers of the new covenant)." But they are representatives of "another Jesus" and "a different gospel." A counterfeit is crafted to look just like the real which it is trying to pass itself off as being. The Judaizers were doing exactly that, but they were children that were still in bondage (Gal. 4:25) which Paul compared to the then-present Jerusalem – the representative of the old covenant, in the form of Second Temple Judaism. Such folks were describe by Paul in Gal. 5:

> 3. **Now I continue solemnly asserting** (attesting; affirming; witnessing), **again, to every person** (or: human) **proceeding to be circumcised, that he is, and continues being, a debtor** (one under obligation) **to do** (to perform; to produce) **the whole Law** [= the entire Torah]!
> 4. **You people who in union with** (or: centered in; [remaining] within) **Law continue being "liberated, rightwised and placed in covenant," were at once discharged** (made inactive, idle, useless, unproductive and without effect; or: voided, nullified, exempted) **away from Christ** (or: [the] Anointing) **– you folks fell out from the grace** (or: fall from the midst of the favor)!

Sadly, the history of the majority of institutionalized Christianity shows that they did not heed Paul's words, here in Gal. 5.

Yet, let us consider Paul's rhetoric, here. In vs. 13, above, he termed them as being "**false emissaries** (pseudo-representatives) **– fraudulent and deceitful workers**." They were frauds. They only "**changed their outward fashion**" in order to "**transform themselves into emissaries of Christ**" (vs. 13). Only God can transform a person; He alone is "**the One transforming [a person] to be completely other [than he or she was]**" (5:18, above). He alone is:

> "the One bringing us into another place or state of being, changing us to correspond with other [perceptions and conceptions], altering us to be conformed to another [person], and changing us from enmity to friendship) **in Himself** (or: with Himself; by Himself; to Himself; for Himself), **through Christ**."

So their "**change their form and outward fashion** (habitually transforming or transfiguring themselves) **as though [being] attending servants of justice and rightwised living**" is a sham.

Kaplan astutely points us to verses that elsewhere describe such folks as Paul has encountered:
In Mat. 7:

> 15. **"Constantly apply yourselves to holding off the false prophets – whatsoever ones that are habitually coming to you folks in clothing belonging to sheep** (= disguised as sheep; pretending to have the covering or appearance of sheep), **yet inside they are ravenous, savage wolves.**
>
> 16. **"You will come to be recognizing and fully knowing them from their fruits. People are not normally picking or gathering clusters of grapes from thorn bushes** (prickly plants), **nor ripe figs from thistles or briers.**

In Acts 20:

> 29. **"Now I myself have seen and am aware that, after** (or: with) **my spreading forth as dust and ashes** (= going away, so as to be out of reach), **heavy** (burdensome and oppressive; fierce; vicious) **wolves will enter into the midst of you folks – folks by habit not sparing** (or: treating with tenderness or forbearance) **the little flock,**
>
> 30. **"and men from among you yourselves** (= from your own community) **will of themselves proceed standing up, repeatedly speaking things having been thoroughly turned and twisted** (things that are distorted and not straight), **to progressively drag** (or: draw; [D & p41 read: turn]) **away the disciples behind** (thus: after) **themselves.**

In 2 Pet. 2:1,

> "**Yet false prophets also birthed themselves among the People – as also false teachers will continue existing** (or: being) **among you folks, ones who will proceed to stealthily introduce destructive choices** (or: destructive sects, schools or ways of thinking; sets of principles or courses of action marked by, and which pertain to, loss or destruction) **even repeatedly contradicting or denying** (disowning; disclaiming; saying, "No," of) **the Sovereign Owner having purchased them, continuously bringing swift loss, ruin or destruction upon themselves."**

Eccl. 3:18

> "It is on account of the sons of humanity that God minded to prove and manifest them – and that they might see that they were beasts, of themselves."

Cf Ezk. 22:27-28; Zeph. 3:3-5

We suggest that the pronouncement "**whose finish** (or: end in view; finished product; attained goal; consummation; accomplished end) **will proceed in being in accord with, along the line of, to the level of and corresponding to their works and actions**" is basically a restatement of 1 Cor. 3:15-17, where the work of these folks will not survive God's Fire (i.e., His manifest presence as a Purifier of priests – Mal. 3:2-3), but Whose Fire will, in fact, cleanse and deliver them. Cf 5:10, above, where we all must be manifested so as to receive His decisions regarding our performances. Paul made reference to such folks (as describe here, in vs. 15) in Phil. 3:18-19,

> "**For you see – I was often telling you about them, yet now I am also presently weeping** (lamenting) **in saying it – many continue walking about** (i.e., are living their lives) **as enemies of the cross of the Christ,** [Rev. 3:9] **whose goal** (eventual end; closing act; final stage; result; finished discharge) **[is] ruin and loss** (or: waste and destruction), **whose god [is their] cavity** (or: belly) **and [whose] reputation** (or: glory; opinion) **resides within their shame** (disgrace; embarrassment) **– people continually thinking about** (habitually being intent on; constantly minding) **the things existing upon the earth** (or: upon the Land; or: = folks whose minds are earthbound)." [Rom. 8:6-8; Hos. 4:7; 7:13]

We also have Paul referring to a specific person in 2 Tim. 4:14,

> "**Alexander the coppersmith** (or: metalworker) **displayed many bad** (worthless; evil) **things [in his behavior] to me – the Lord** [= Yahweh or Christ] **will continue awarding to him** (or: giving back in him; paying back for him) **corresponding to his works** (down from his deeds and on the level of his actions)."

All corrective decisions will correspond to the worthless behavior that was done. In Rev. 20:13, we have the apocalyptic vision of a "judgment," and we see that:

> "**And they are judged** (evaluated) **according to their works** (in correspondence with their actions; in line with their deeds)."

Judgment is not based upon who a person is or upon what they believe, but rather "**along the line of, to the level of and corresponding to their works and actions.**" This is how we discipline our own children. But all judgment and discipline from God is done in accordance to His Being and character: with grace and mercy, and to redirect a person's behavior toward the Way pointed out.

16. **I say again** (or: I repeat), **no one should presume to imagine or suppose me to be a senseless fellow** (a fool; one devoid of intellect; an imprudent man). **Still – if not in fact – even if as senseless** (foolish; idiotic; imprudent), **accept and receive me, so that I myself also can boast of something!**

The "say again/repeat" seems to indicate that Paul is returning to his theme which he began in vs. 1, above. This is his rhetorical maneuver to do some boasting – since others are indulging in this (vs. 18, below). But his bottom line is clear: "**no one should presume to imagine or suppose me to be a senseless fellow** (a fool; one devoid of intellect; an imprudent man)." Yet the "**Still**… **even if**…" would bring a smile to his listeners, encouraging them to "**accept and receive [him]**."

17. **What I am presently speaking I am speaking not down from or in accord with [the] Lord** (Master; Owner; [= Christ or Yahweh]), **but to the contrary, as within senselessness** (foolishness; imprudence) **– within this assumed position as a basis for boasting:**

He seems to be playing a role for them, here. They would know that this is not the real Paul, and so would be amused. He is imitating those to whom he refers in the next verse, and we should not miss this rhetorical devise…

18. **since many folks are habitually boasting – according to the flesh** (or: = on the level of the natural being; or: = in the sphere of estranged humanity) **– I myself should also boast,**
19. **for with pleasure you folks – continuously being intelligent, sensible and prudent folks! – habitually put up with the senseless** (foolish; idiotic; imprudent) **people!**

Now comes the sting! His audience would "feel" his point! But just before he "thrusts home," he gives what would appear to be a compliment, in vs. 19 ("**you folks – continuously being intelligent, sensible and prudent folks**"), but which they would embarrassingly realize was sarcasm when he finished the sentence. They lacked wisdom and discernment and would accept the shallow display of "senseless flesh." They would be entertained by it, and welcome it, as we still see today… sadly. Paul could be describing so many situations of religious or secular entertainment in our present cultures. And in both of these spheres, the loss incurred is that folks are led away from the Truth, and into something that is not real. In an honor and shame society, as that in which they lived, this would not have brought them honor!

When he said, "**with pleasure** [note: this is irony] **you folks habitually put up with the senseless** (foolish; idiotic; imprudent) **people**," he was not referring to mentally challenged people within the community, but to the supposed "super representatives of Christ." So those who wanted to be the community leaders would also feel Paul's assessment of them, and his sarcasm.

20. **In fact, you constantly put up with anyone if he is progressively bringing you down to slavery** (or: is completely enslaving you as his habit) **– if someone is repeatedly devouring; if someone is constantly taking [you] in hand; if someone is progressively elevating himself or lifting himself up upon [you]; if someone is continuously bringing the lash into your face** (flaying you with a whip so as to remove the skin and eat into the face)**!**

(= you folks constantly tolerate tyranny, abusive insults, pride and arrogance, as well as being drained of resources, being manipulated and being restrained.)

If we had not seen or experienced such things, we might be tempted to think that Paul is describing what is impossible – no one could be so foolish, could they?! Was he describing what we would call a cult, in our day? We suspect that he was using hyperbole to show his audience what the Judaizers were actually doing to them – and they had been blind to it. In Gal. 2:4 he said that "**through the led-in-at-the-side** (or: smuggled-in) **false brothers who entered alongside...** [it was] **to utterly enslave**" (same verb as used here in vs. 20). We think that he was trying to shock them in order to awaken them from out of the spell these super emissaries had cast on them. Remember Paul's words to the folks of Galatia?

> "**O senseless, unreflecting and foolish Galatians! Who suddenly harmed you with malicious words, or bewitched you folks with the evil eye – before whose eyes Jesus Christ was graphically placarded** (= as though portrayed in writing before your own eyes) **one having been crucified on a stake** (suspended on an execution pole)**?** [*cf* Lu. 24:25] **This only am I intending** (wanting; purposing; willing) **to learn from you people: Did you receive the Spirit** (or: get the Breath-effect; take in hand the Attitude) **from out of works of Law, or from out of a hearing of a report about faithfulness** (= [the] faithful One)?" (Gal. 3:1-2)

For Paul, "**bringing you down to slavery**" meant bringing folks under the Law of the old covenant and the past age (5:17, above).

The phrase "**repeatedly devouring**" refers to an ongoing plunder of their lives – both economically and spiritually! Once again, wolves in sheep clothing. In Lu. 20:46-47, Jesus warned:

> "**Be habitually holding your focus and attention away from the scholars and theologians** (the scribes; the Torah, or, Bible experts).... **folks who [in reality] are habitually devouring the houses** (or: eating down the households) **of the widows... These people will continue and progressively be receiving more excessive result of judgment** (or: will get a more abundant effect of the separating and the decision)."

The thought of "**constantly taking [you] in hand**" speaks of control – a domination system. Paul had certainly also said to them, "**For FREEDOM, Christ immediately set us free! Keep on standing firm, therefore, and do not again be habitually held within a yoke of slavery**" (Gal. 5:1)

As for "**someone is progressively elevating himself**," Jacob had the necessary instruction:

> "**you must consequently be made low** (humbled; demoted; brought to a low station), **in the Lord's sight** (= in [Yahweh's, or Christ's] presence), **and then He will progressively lift you up** (or: continue elevating you)" (Jas. 4:10).

Pride still goes before destruction and a fall (Prov. 16:18). It happened to Eve, in the Garden, and it happens to everyone else.

His description of demeaning and insulting behavior "**bringing the lash into your face**" was surely metaphorical, but it insinuated treating them like children or slaves (for that was common treatment for those two stratum of that society). Hillyer (ibid p 1085) suggests that this might refer to "bullying treatment," i.e., verbal slaps in the face. These who infiltrated the covenant community were certainly seeking to take dominion of the group. The parenthetical paraphrase seems to capture Paul's assessment of the situation.

21. **I am saying [this] down from dishonor** (or: in accord with being devalued), **seeing that** (or: as though) **we, ourselves, had been weak [among you]! Yet in whatever anyone is habitually daring – I say this in senselessness** (I'm talking foolishly and unreasonably) **– I, too, am habitually daring!**

He is speaking from the dishonored and devalued position that the Corinthians seem to have assumed about him and his associates, having been assessed by his opponents as being "weak" (10:10, above) when among them in person. So now he continues the senseless stance taken by the super emissaries, and is daring in the same way that they habitually dare. He is meeting their claims head on, face-to-face, one-on–one. And so he says...

22. **Are they Hebrews? So [am] I! Are they Israelites? So [am] I! Are they a seed of Abraham? So [am] I!**

"'Hebrews.' Referring to the *language* and *nationality*; 'Israelites,' to the *theocracy* and *descent from Israel*, the 'prince who prevailed with God' (Rom. 9:4); 'the seed of Abraham,' to the *claim to a share in the Messiah* (Rom. 11:1; 9:7)" (*Commentary, Practical and Explanatory on the Whole Bible*, Robert Jamieson, A.R. Fausset, David Brown, Zondervan Pub House, 1961 p 1252; emphasis original).

This is the "boasting on the level of flesh" in vs. 18, above. Paul has apparently had similar issues with some of the folks in Macedonia, for he writes in Phil. 3:

> 4. **Even though I myself continue holding** (or: having) **[grounds for] trust and confidence also within flesh, if any other man is in the habit of thinking** (or: is constantly seeming) **or presuming to have come to a settled persuasion, thus having confidence within [his] flesh, I to a greater degree** (more so; for a better reason; rather more)**:**
> 5. **in circumcision, on [the] eighth day;**
> **out of race** (from posterity; by birth; as to class or species), **of Israel;**
> **of Benjamin's tribe; a Hebrew out of the midst of [the] Hebrews**
> (or: = a supreme Hebrew);
> **in accordance to Law, a Pharisee** (or: down from custom, a Pharisee);
> 6. **in accordance to zeal, one constantly pressing, pursuing and persecuting the called-out community;**
> **in accordance to fairness and equity in the way pointed out in the Law, one coming to be, of myself, without defect** (one becoming blameless).

"'An Hebrew of the Hebrews,' not an Hellenist or Greekspeaking Jew, but a Hebrew in tongue, and sprung from Hebrews" (Jamieson, Fausset, Brown ibid).

Obviously the Corinthian community had been awed by the fleshly claims of the intruders, so Paul is setting their so-called superiority at naught by leveling the playing field – in the realm of the flesh. This is his rhetorical method of debunking the claims of these folks. His "boasting" is not bragging, but is his method of waking up his audience from the spell cast by their soulish show. He is saying that their special claims mean nothing. All that is a part of that which has passed by. We are no longer to know or give recognition to anyone based upon the flesh realm (5:16, above).

23. **Are they Christ's attending servants** (dispensers of Christ)**? – I am speaking as one being beside himself** (or: insane) **– I over and above [them]** (or: I more so; = I surpass [them])**! In toilsome labors and weariness more exceedingly; in prisons** (jails) **more often; in blows** (stripes; beatings) **surpassingly; in deaths** (or: near-death situations) **many times** (or: often).

Now he addresses the realm of kingdom activity, but he characterizes even this kind of comparison as insanity. He has to be "**beside himself**" to do such a thing – and he TELLS them so. But then, he gives the actual characteristics of the life of an "**Christ's attending servants**." He begins his list with "**In toilsome labors and weariness more exceedingly**" (and note the superlative comparisons, which are actual facts!), and then continues through vs. 29 in describing his experiences of the cruciform life.

Jamieson, Fausset and Brown (ibid) instruct us that "Clement (*1 Epistle to Corinthians*) describes him as having suffered bonds seven times."

He referred to "**in deaths** (or: near-death situations) **many times** (or: often)" in 1 Cor. 15:31-32,

> "**Daily I am repeatedly facing death** (or: progressively dying)! **Brothers, I swear** (strongly affirm) **by my reason for boasting.... I fight** (or: fought) **in accord with human [means, methods or purposes] with wild beasts in Ephesus**..."

Cf 4:10, above; Acts 9:23; 13:50; 14:5, 6, 19; 17:5, 13.

But before moving on, let us consider the parenthetical alternate rendering of the genitive in his opening rhetorical question: "Are they dispensers of Christ?" Is it Christ that they are dispensing, or Law? Is it the Anointing, or is it ritual religion? We should ask the same concerning those who would lead us. You know a tree by its fruit.

24. **Five times by Jews** (or: under Judeans) **I received forty [stripes; lashes], less one.**
Cf Deut. 25:1-3

25. **Three times I was beaten with rods; once I was stoned; three times I was shipwrecked – I have done night and day within the midst of the depth [of the sea], even hitting bottom;**
Cf Acts 13:4, 13; 14:19, 26; 16:11; 18:18-22; 20:2

26. **on journeys often** (many times); **in dangers** (perils) **of rivers** (or: floods); **in dangers of robbers** (perils of plunderers or insurrectionists; = Zealots); **in dangers from out of [my] race** (kindred); **in dangers from out of the multitudes of ethnic groups** ([the] nations); **in dangers within city; in dangers within a desolate place** (wilderness); **in dangers at sea; in dangers among false-brothers** (= pseudo-believers; or: = Family members who lie and deal falsely);
Cf Acts 11:23; 13:50; 14:2-5, 18-20; 15:1-3; 16:14-23; 17:5; 18:11; 19:23-20:1; Gal. 2:4; 1 Thes. 2:14-15

27. **in exhaustive labor and wearisome toil; in lack of sleep** (or: sleeplessness; or: vigils) **often; in hunger** (or: scarcity of food; or: famine) **and in thirst – in situations of deprivation or need of food** (or: in fastings), **many times; in cold and in lack of sufficient clothing** (or: nakedness);

28. **apart from these external matters** (or: apart from those things [just mentioned] – besides the outside –) **[there is] the thing rushing in on me and giving cares** (the pressure) **from day to day: the anxiety, concern and divided distraction pertaining to all the called-out folks** (or: summoned-forth communities):

29. **Who is continuing weak and I am not proceeding to be weak** (= sharing their weakness)? **Who is habitually snared and caused to stumble or be entrapped, and I, myself, am not being repeatedly made fiery hot** (or: caused to be incensed)?

Verses 28 and 29 proclaim his solidarity with the covenant communities. Recall what he said about members of the body, in 1 Cor. 12:26,

> "**And further, whether one member is continuing to experience the effect of something, or constantly undergoes suffering, all the members continually experience the effect or the suffering together with [it; her; him]; or if a member is being constantly glorified, normally given an assumed appearance, or is progressively receiving a good reputation, all the members are continuously rejoicing together with [him; her; it].**"

Paul lived out his own words.

30. **If** (or: Since) **it is necessary to boast, I will boast concerning the things pertaining to, from, and which are, my weakness.**

Why? Well, he answers this in 12:9b-10, below:

> "**to the end that the ability of the Christ** (or: the Anointed One's power) **can pitch its tent** (or: should tabernacle) **upon me.... for whenever I continue being** (or: may periodically be) **weak, then I am powerful** (or: I then exist being capable)!"

But for the present context, it shows the community his cruciform qualifications. Remember:

> "**If anyone continues intending** (purposing; willing; wanting) **to come on behind Me, let him at once completely say, 'No,' to, deny and disown himself, and then in one move lift up his**

execution stake (pole for suspending a corpse; cross), **and after that proceed to be by habit
continuously following after Me!**" (Jesus: Mat. 16:24).

Do we hear anything like this about the "super emissaries? The "**'very-overly' [pretentious and
condescending] emissaries** (or: representatives)" (12:11b, below) were wanting to "reign" over the
group in Corinth. But Paul later instructs Timothy,

> "**since we are continuously remaining under for support** (or: if we continue patiently
> enduring), **we will also continue reigning** (performing royal activities and influence) **together
> with [Him]**" (2 Tim. 2:12).

Remaining under hard situations, and giving support to those involved, is a cruciform life that calls for
"denying one's self."

31. **The God and Father of the Lord Jesus** (or, in apposition: which is the Master, Jesus) – **the One
continuously being a blessed One** (or: the One constantly existing [as] a Word of ease, a Message of
well-being and [the] *Logos* of goodness) **on into the ages – has seen and thus knows that I am not
lying.**

Paul made a similar acclimation in Rom. 1:9,

> "**God is my Witness** (or: continuously exists being my Evidence) – **to, in and with Whom I
> continuously render service** (or: for Whom I am hired to constantly work), **within my spirit** (or:
> in union with my Breath-effect; in my attitude), **within His Son's good news** (or: in union with the
> message of goodness, ease and well-being pertaining to, coming from, having the character of,
> and which is, His Son)..."

What a clear proclamation of both God's awareness and involvement in our lives: "**God... has seen and
thus knows.**" He also knows that the false teachers ARE lying. This should give the Corinthians pause
to consider to whom they are listening.

32. **In Damascus the ethnarch** (tribal governor; ruler of that culture) **under Aretas, the king, had been
watching with guards to garrison the city of Damascus, intending to seize and arrest me,**
33. **and through a window** (or: small opening) **I was lowered through the wall in a braided hamper**
(like a fish-basket [of ropes or wicker]), **and escaped** (fled out of) **his hands.**

Now Paul ends the generalized list of vss. 23b-29, above, with a specific anecdote of his experience in
the city of Damascus. This episode was narrated in Acts 9:23-26. In that passage, note that it was the
Jews of Damascus who were responsible for those actions against Paul. They were the "*satan*" that was
disguised as messengers of the light.

Chapter 12

1. **It is necessary** (or: binding) **for one to boast from time to time – though indeed not beneficial or
expedient – so I will proceed in coming unto [the subject of] visions and unveilings of [the] Lord**
(or: disclosures from, pertaining to, or given by, [Christ or Yahweh]).

> (or: [other MSS: If (or: Since) it is necessary to continue boasting, {it}; still other MSS: Now to
> repeatedly boast] indeed does not normally bring [people] together, so I will continue moving on
> to sights, apparitions and appearances, as well as revelations and disclosures, whose source and
> origin are [the] Lord, or, which are [the] Lord).

Paul begins this next section by acknowledging a common custom inherent in the human condition: the
need "**for one to boast from time to time,**" and he feels obliged to do so due to the present situation
concerning the "super-emissaries" in Corinth. The verb that I rendered "**necessary**" can also be rendered
"It is binding." Paul either felt compelled by the Lord to say what he was about to disclose, or else this
kind of teacher-disciple relationship required some kind of defense when the teacher came under attack

as to his credentials for being a teacher – especially when it was a community that was involved. Nonetheless, he makes it plain that this was not really "**beneficial or expedient**." Hillyer suggests that "Paul counters his opponents' boasts about their spiritual experiences with one example of his own" (ibid p 1086).

Take note of the variant MS readings of the first clause on offer in the parenthetical expansion. The second alternate text tradition indicates that he is not going to "repeatedly boast." – so he is moving on to discuss "sights and revelations." By the way, a "revelation; unveiling; disclosure" does not necessarily refer to something that is seen. It can refer to an insight or a perception – a *Logos*.

Because it has been assumed that the experience that he describes in vss. 2-3, below, was his own experience, and because in vs. 2 he says that it happened in the past, we do not read Paul as speaking about future experiences, but rather that in this letter he "**will proceed in coming unto [the subject of] visions and unveilings of [the] Lord**." It is for this reason that I inserted "**[the subject of]**," i.e., having just related a physical experience (11:32-33), he now moves to the topic of supernatural experiences.

A "**vision**" can be something seen in the realm of spirit, or simply a "sight; something seen." A good example of the ambiguity of this word can be seen in how we interpret what Peter, Jacob and John saw on the Mount of Transfiguration, in Mat. 17:2-3; in Mat. 17:9, Jesus told them, "**You men should speak of the results of what was seen** (or: tell the vision; speak of the sight) **to no one**..." As seen in the parenthetical expansion, the term can refer to "sights, apparitions or appearances."

The final phrase, "**of [the] Lord**," can be a subjective genitive: "given by the Lord;" it can be an ablative: "from [the] Lord;" a genitive of association: "pertaining to [the] Lord;" or, even apposition: "which is [the] Lord." It can also be an "**unveiling of [the] Lord**," such as John saw in Rev. 1. These options broaden the potential of what Paul will now share...

2. **I have known, and am acquainted with, a person** (or: a man; a human being) **in Christ** (or: within the midst of Christ; in union with [the] Anointed) **more than fourteen years ago – whether in body** (or: in a body), **I am not aware; whether outside of the body, I am not aware; God has seen and knows** (is aware) **– being snatched away** (dragged off; seized and taken) **as such, as far as [the; or: a] third heaven** (or: atmosphere).

This first clause affirmed the then-present fact that the new creation was an existential reality in Paul's day (5:17, above), as well as the accomplished reality that the "old things" (the Law of Moses; the covenant with Israel as a unique nation; the temple cultus arrangement) had passed away, in God's economy. Even though the temple and Jerusalem were still standing, the "new things" had already come into existence. *Cf* Rom. 16:7b; Gal. 1:22

Most scholars conclude that Paul is speaking about himself in the incident that he proceeds to vaguely describe. In our discussion, we will likewise conclude that Paul is speaking of his own experience. Assuming that he wrote this letter circa AD 56, "**more than fourteen years ago**" would place the incident at about AD 41-42. Since Aretas (11:32, above) was the ethnarch until AD 40, Paul's experience probably happened some time after his escape from Damascus (11:33, above).

Next, Paul begins to share the setting, or the situation, and suddenly interjects the uncertainty as to "**whether in body** (or: in a body), **I am not aware; whether outside of the body, I am not aware**." We can almost see him thinking back to the incident as he considers which it was: "**in**" or "**outside**" – "**of the body**." He apparently wants to make the uncertainly clear to his audience, for in beginning the story, in vs. 3, he says this same thing again. It might help us to understand Paul, here, by considering John's situation in Rev. 1:10, where he informs us:

"**I came to be** (or: birthed myself; happened to be) **within spirit** (or: in union with [the] Spirit; in the midst of a Breath-effect)."

There, John says nothing about "**whether in body**," or not. We suspect that Paul was saying the same thing as John said, but he uses different words to explain the circumstances. He also wants his listeners to realize that we don't need to know the details; it is enough for us to realize that "**God has seen and knows** (is aware)" – which he also repeats at the end of vs. 3.

Paul repeats the opening line, "**I have known, and am acquainted with, a person.**" In the next verse, but there, he adds the word "**such**" to set this "person" (we assume: himself) apart from what is average about people. Following the insertion (disclaimer?) that I set off with dashes, he briefly describes the incident: "**[a person] being snatched away** (dragged off; seized and taken) **as such, as far as [the; or: a] third heaven** (or: atmosphere)."

Before we unpack this statement, let us bring in the restatement of the location, to where he was "**snatched away**," from vs. 4a: "**into the Paradise.**" So in Paul's telling of this, he seems to equate "**third heaven** (or: atmosphere)" with "**the Paradise.**" Before we jump to conclusions, let us consider the potential allusions that Paul may be making, and consider the verb that he used. In both vss. 2 and 4, he says "**snatched away** (dragged off; seized and taken)," and we note the passive voice in both verses. This was something that God did; Paul did not work himself up into a frenzy, or empty his mind in deep meditation. This is a very active and even violent verb. Other than in this passage, the verb is used eleven other times in the NT. Let us walk through them:

a) Mat. 11:12,

> "**Now from the days of John the Immerser until right now, the reign and dominion of the heavens** (or: sovereign rule of the kingdom of the atmospheres) **is itself continuously pressing** (or: is progressively pressing and forcing itself) **forward with urgency, and those urging and pressing forward [toward the goal] are one after another GRASPING it and then DRAWING IT UP [to themselves].**"

b) Mat. 13:19b,

> "**the worthless person or the disadvantageous circumstance** (or: the one who brings pain and misery through hard labor; the malevolent and wicked man; the evil one; or: the difficult and wearisome situation) **is repeatedly coming and is habitually snatching up what has been sown** (scattered as seed) **within his heart.**"

c) Jn. 6:15,

> "**Jesus, therefore – experientially and intimately knowing** (or: coming to perceive) **that they are presently about to be coming and to proceed snatching Him away** (seizing and forcefully taking Him away) **to the end that they may make [Him] king...**"

d) Jn. 10:12b,

> "**the wolf continues ravenously snatching them away and progressively scattering and dispersing them.**"

e) Jn. 10: 28b, 29b,

> "**no one will be snatching them** (or: taking them by force) **from out of My hand.... no one has power or is able to proceed to snatch [them; anything] from out of the Father's hand.**"

f) Acts 8:39-40a,

> "**Now when they walked up out of the water, [the] Lord's** [or: = Yahweh's] **wind** (or: a Breath-effect or Spirit [of Christ]; or: a spirit from [Yahweh]) **suddenly snatched Philip away** (i.e.: carried him off), **and the eunuch did not see him any longer.... But Philip was found** (or: discovered) **[entering] into Ashdod...**"

g) Acts 23:10b,

> "**fearing [that] Paul would at some point be torn in two** (or: pulled apart) **by them – commanded the troop** (band of soldiers) **to bring [him] into the barracks after descending to snatch him out of the midst of them.**"

h) 1 Thes. 4:17,

"**Thereupon** (or: After that; As a next step) **we, the presently living folks, the ones presently continuing to be left around, will – at the same time, together with them – proceed being seized and snatched away* within clouds** (or: carried off by force, in union with clouds,) **into the midst of [the] air** (the air that we breathe in; the mist; the haze; the atmosphere around us; [note: this would be in the earth's lower atmosphere, the place where there is air]) **– into the Lord's meeting** ([Christ's or Yahweh's] encounter; an ENCOUNTERING which is the Lord). **And thus** (in this way and such a manner) **shall we always continue being** (or: continue existing at all times) **together with [the] Lord.**"

i) Jude 23,

"**yet on the other hand, be continuously delivering** (or: repeatedly rescuing and saving, restoring to health and wholeness) **others, snatching them from out of the midst of the Fire; be repeatedly extending compassionate mercy**…"

j) Rev. 12:5,

"**And so she brought forth a Son – an adult man** (or: male; masculine one) **Who is about to continuously shepherd** (tend and protect) **all the multitudes** (ethnic groups; nations) **in the sphere of and with relying on the use of an iron staff** (or: rod). **Later, her child was snatched away** (seized and carried off by force) **toward God and to His throne.**"

An interesting association is Paul's experience here in ch. 12, and the apocalyptic description that he gave in 1 Thes. 4:17. Interpreting the Fire of Jude 23 as being the same Fire (God, Himself, manifested thusly in this metaphor) as we find in Rev. 14:10, with US being the agents of the Lamb in both contexts. Jn. 6:15 and Acts 8:39 seem to be physical uses of the verb. Mat. 11:12 and 13:19 appear to be metaphorical uses, as do the uses of it in Jn. 10. Rev. 12:5 we would connect with 1 Thes. 4:17, and also Eph. 2:6 (where this verb is not used, but the action – being spiritual in nature – is the same). We would also associate Paul's experience, here in ch. 12, with that of John in Rev. 4:1-2, where he said, in vs. 2, "**And then, immediately, I in myself came to exist within spirit.**" Paul related a specific incident of a comparable experience, in Acts 22:17,

"**Now it happened to me, after returning into Jerusalem and then during my continuing in projecting thoughts and words toward having events and situations being well** (or: praying), **within the midst of the Temple complex, I came to be** (or: was birthed) **within an ecstasy and then to see Him presently saying to me**…"

So, what about "**[the; or: a] third heaven** (or: atmosphere)"? The concept of "heaven" as a spiritual metaphor (the atmosphere around the earth, and the sky beyond, being those things from which the spiritual metaphor is drawn) was a term for the realm of God, and on earth, the place where His Sprit (Breath-effect; Wind) moved upon the earth (e.g., Gen 1:2). Heaven was "where God lived." But Moses was directed to construct a set-apart tent (tabernacle) so that God could dwell among Israel. The Pattern that Moses was given (when on Mount Sinai) was laid out horizontally in three tiers: a) the outer court; b) the holy place; c) the holy of holies (where Moses met with God, between the cherubim of the mercy seat). We suggest that this lay-out was a figure of the three heavens, and that Paul was snatched-away into the realm of the holy of holies. The entrance to the holy of holies had cherubim woven into the curtain – an echo of Gen. 3:24. The decorations of the holy place was that of a garden. Many scholars consider the Garden of Eden as a prototype of the Tabernacle/Temple. If our reasoning is sound, then we can see why in vs. 4, below, Paul refers to the "third heaven" (vs. 2) as "**the Paradise**," which is the same word that the LXX used for the Heb. word "Garden," in Gen. 2:8,

"Next (or: Later) God planted an enclosed garden (or: **paradise**) within the midst of Eden (Hebrew: delight)…"

The word "paradise" is used two other places in the NT:

a) "**And so Jesus said to him, "Truly it is so** (or: Count on it!)**... I am now saying to you** (or: laying it out for you; [D adds: Take courage])**... Today** (This very day) **you will continue being** (or: keep on existing) **with Me... within the midst of** (or: centered in; in the sphere of; in union with) **Paradise**" (Lu. 23:43);

b) "**In and by the one** (or: To or for the person) **continuously overcoming** (habitually conquering; normally victorious) **I will continue giving by and in him** (or: to him; for him) **to eat from out of the substance of the tree** (wood; log; post) **of the Life which continuously is** (exists being) **within the midst of God's paradise** [a garden of fruit trees]" (Rev. 2:7).

We find a description of the New Jerusalem that echoes the Gen. Garden, in Rev. 22:

1. **And he showed** (points out to) **me a clean, pure river of "water of, and from, life"** (or: Life's water; or: water which is Life), **bright** (resplendent, glistening, clear, sparkling) **as crystal** (clear ice), **continuously flowing** (issuing) **forth from out of God's – even** (or: and) **the little Lamb's – throne!**

2. **Within the midst of her broad place** (plaza; square; street), **and on each side of the river, [is] a tree** (a wood; timber; a log; same word used in Gen. 2:9, LXX; figure for "the cross" in the NT) **of, and which is, life periodically producing twelve fruits, continually yielding** (or: giving away) **according to each month, and the leaves of the tree** (wood; timber) **[are given] for** (or: into) **service** (nurture, care; healing, cure or medical service; a body of household attendants) **of the multitudes** (nations; Gentiles; non-Jews; ethnic groups), [*cf* Ezk. 47:1-12]

Here we will insert an excursus on the metaphorical use of agricultural terms found in both OT and NT:

GOD'S GARDEN

There are many metaphors in Scripture that are taken from the plant kingdom: seeds, vines, agricultural field crops, trees, fruit, branches, leaves, roots. They all are usually a figure to share some truth regarding humanity and God's relationship to humanity.

In John 15, Jesus said that He was the Vine and His disciples were the branches, and He wanted them to bear a lot of fruit. He said that the Father was the vine-dresser who regularly pruned and tended this Vine.

In explaining the parable of the tares of the field, in Matt. 13, Jesus said that the good seed are the sons of the kingdom (a Hebraism which signifies those who have the character and qualities of the kingdom of God), while the field represented the world (i.e., the organized system of culture, religion, economy and government).

Ps. 1 describes an upright person who is in right relationship with God. Vs. 3 tells us, "He is like a tree planted by streams of water, which yields its fruit in season and whose leaf does not wither." Song of Songs 4:12 says, "You are a garden locked up, my sister, my bride..." Ps. 80:8, speaking of Israel says, "You have brought a vine out of Egypt; You have cast out the heathen, and it filled the Land." Isa. Ch. 5 is a song of God's vineyard, and vs. 7 tells us, "The vineyard of the Lord Almighty is the house of Israel, and the men of Judah are the garden of His delight." Jude 12 speaks of people who are "autumn trees, without fruit and uprooted." John the Baptist said, "The ax is already at the root of the trees, and every tree that does not produce good fruit will be cut down and thrown into the fire" (Matt. 3:10). He was speaking of the Jews.

In Gal. 5:12 Paul speaks of the "fruit of the Spirit." In Phil. 1:11 he uses the term "the fruits of righteousness." John the Baptist told the folks to "produce fruit worthy of a change in thinking (or: repentance – Matt. 3:8)."

It seems clear, to us, that God's people are His vine, His fruit trees, His fields of grain. One of the final pictures in our Scriptures includes a wood (a forest – often translated "a tree") of life, producing twelve [crops] of fruit, yielding their fruits each month, and the leaves of the forest (or: trees) have a view unto a curing of the ethnic multitudes (Rev. 22:2). The river of "water of life" flows out of the plaza in the New Jerusalem, and then flows through the midst of this orchard of trees of life.

Now doesn't this sound like a paradise, a garden? In Gen. 2:9, "God made to spring up also out of the earth every tree beautiful to the eye and good for food, and the tree of life in the midst of the garden (or: paradise)…" And in vs. 10, "a river went out of Eden to water the garden (paradise)" (LXX). In vs. 16 God tells the human that he can eat from the trees in this garden. So considering what I have laid forth here, I suggest that the Garden of Eden was a figure for God's people – just as the New Jerusalem, with its garden is called "the bride, the Lamb's wife" (Rev. 21:9-10). Just as Adam and Eve were able to eat of the fruit of the trees in Eden, thus are we able to partake of the fruit of the Spirit being produced by those who abide in the Vine. So why should we think that Eden was a literal garden? God's garden is His people.

A final thought: on the cross, Jesus said to the one worker of ugliness, on the cross beside Him, "Today you will be (or: be existing) with Me in the midst of Paradise" (Lu. 23:43). Jesus was going to Paradise, and Paradise (LXX for garden) is His people. We are encompassed by a great cloud – of witnesses (Heb. 12:1). In our midst are rivers of living water (John 7:38).

The LXX uses the word *paradeisos* thirteen times in Gen. 2-3. God walked and talked with Adam and Eve, in the Garden (Paradise) of Eden. In Gen. 13:10 we read:
> "And Lot, lifting up his eyes, saw all the region round about the Jordan, that all was watered – before God had overthrown Sodom and Gomora – like the orchard of God (or: God's Garden; a paradise from God), and like the land of Egypt until one came to Zogora" (N.E.T.S.; additions mine).

In Num. 24:5-6 we find Balaam's parable:
> "How beautiful are our dwellings, O Jacob, your tents, O Israel! Like wooded valleys giving shade and like orchards (enclosed gardens; paradises) by rivers, and like tents that the LORD pitched…" (N.E.T.S.; additions mine). *Cf Song of Songs* 4:12-13.

We find the LXX version of Ezk. 28:13 of interest:
> "In the delight of the orchard of God (God's garden; the Paradise from God) you were born (you came into existence); you have bound-on every fine stone…" (N.E.T.S.; additions mine).

We trust that these other uses of this term, along with its connection to the "third heaven," will be a catalyst for insight into Paul's experience, as he describes it here in ch. 12. Kaplan points out that our heart is now God's enclosed Garden (as we saw with the Tabernacle/Temple), deep within us.

3. **Further, I have seen and know such a person** (man; human) **– whether in body or apart from the body, I know not; God knows –**
4. **that was snatched away** (seized and taken) **into the Paradise and heard inexpressible gush-effects and utterances** (unutterable sayings and results of a flow; unspeakable results of movement and flux; inexpressible matters and declarations) **which are not being from out of existence** (or: which are not continuing from within the midst of being; or: which it continues being not right; or: for which there is no privilege or authority; which are not being possible; which are not being allowed) **in a person** (to mankind; for a human) **to at any point speak.**

Paul had an unveiling that was similar to that of John, if not being as involved and extensive as what was given to John. Here he "**heard inexpressible gush-effects and utterances**." Other renderings are:
> a) "unutterable sayings and results of a flow";
> b) "unspeakable results of movement and flux";
> c) "inexpressible matters and declarations."

The aspects of "**gush**," "flow" and "flux" are inherent in the root idea of *rhēma*. They picture the movement of God's Spirit when communicating with us.

The next clause gives the literal rendering in, "**which are not being from out of existence,**" and then again in, "which are not continuing from within the midst of being." Next follows four renderings that give more extended meanings of *exon* (out of-being):

      a) "which it continues being not right";

      b) "for which there is no privilege or authority";

      c) "which are not being possible";

      d) "which are not being allowed,"

and then the clause ends with: "**in a person** (to mankind; for a human) **to at any point speak.**"

To help us understand what Paul may have meant by this, let us consider what was instructed to John, when he was about to write down what "the thunders" had said:

> "**And when the Seven Thunders spoke** (gave utterance), **I was about to be writing and I heard a Voice from out of the atmosphere** (or: heaven) **repeatedly saying, 'You must seal** (or: = seal 'up and keep from being disclosed; place a seal on) **what the Seven Thunders uttered** (spoke)," and 'You may not write these things'" (Rev. 10:4).

Neither there, nor here with Paul, are we given the reason why these things were not to be shared with other folks. Perhaps these are just examples for us to learn that we do not always need to tell what we know. Perhaps there was simply no human way to communicate what he had heard. Only his spirit knew it (1 Cor. 2:11).

So where was the sphere to which Paul was "**snatched away** (seized and taken)"? It was not to a physical place, as with Philip (Acts. 8:39), or he would have known that it happened in his body. No, this was not an "outer court" experience. It would not have been to the second heaven (the realm of his soul), but most likely into the higher realm: the holy of holies of his spirit where he continued "joined to the Lord" (1 Cor. 6:17) and was seated with Christ (Eph. 2:6). Secrets were revealed to him that others were not yet in the realm of existence to understand, so he was not allowed to share what he heard. Does this remind you of what Jesus said to His disciples, in Mat. 13:11,

> "**To** (or: For; With) **you folks it has been given to intimately experience and insightfully know the secrets** (mysteries) **of the reign and dominion of the heavens** (or: the kingdom which is the heavens; the royal rule which pertains to and has its origin in the heavens, and which emanates from the atmospheres), **yet it has not been given to those people**"?

5. I will boast over such a person, yet over myself I will not continue boasting – except in my weaknesses, *Cf* 11:30, above.

6. for if I should ever want or intend to boast, I shall not be senseless (unintelligent; unreasonable; imprudent), **for I will continue declaring reality** (truth). **Yet I continue being reticent** (continue refraining, with thrift,) **and so no one should account** (overestimate) **into me above** (or: over) **what he continues seeing [in] and observing [of] me, or hearing from me.**

To "**boast over such a person**" is to boast of existence in Christ, not in one's self or one's ego. *Cf* 10:8, above. So, if he is to boast "**over [himself],**" it will be "**in [his] weaknesses,**" not in his spiritual experiences. By rhetorically putting this experience on a person that he "knew in Christ," he was avoiding personal exaltation.

What "**reality** (truth)" would we expect him to "**continue declaring**"? We suggest that it would be "**the Way, the Truth and the Life**" (Jn. 14:6). Christ is the Way/Path to the Father, who is in the "**third heaven**" (the holy of holies that is deep within us).

7. And now, in the excess of the unveilings (or: with the transcendence of the revelations; by the extraordinary amount and surpassing nature of the disclosures), **through this [situation] and for this reason – so that I could not be progressively exalted** (or: would not continue being overly lifted up [in myself or by others]) **– something with [its] point in [my] flesh is given in me** (or: an impaling-stake for the human nature was given for me; or: a thorn to the natural realm, and a splinter by alienated humanity, was assigned to me): **an agent of, and from, the adversary** (or: an adversarial person with a message), **to the end that he could** (or: should; would) **repeatedly beat me in the face** (or: slap me on the ear) **with his** (or: its) **fist.**

> [comment: this personification of the irritation may well be metaphorical and may refer to his social or cultural-religious situation]

His spirit had been taken extremely high, and "**so that I could not be progressively exalted**" (or, as we say today, "get a big head"), he was given a counter-balance that would keep his feet on the ground. Let us just ponder his blessed situation:

> a) **in the excess of the unveilings**;
> b) with the transcendence of the revelations;
> c) by the extraordinary amount and surpassing nature of the disclosures.

However we render the words, what Paul was told and shown was enough to offset what was revealed to Moses in Mount Sinai. In fact, it replaced it, because the first was the natural, and Paul received: "the spiritual" fulfillment of which the natural was a type and a shadow:

> "**the spiritual [is] not first, but rather the one having the qualities and characteristics of a soul** (the soulish; psychical), **then afterwards, the spiritual** (that pertaining to and having the qualities of Breath-effect and Attitude)" (1 Cor. 15:46).
>
> "**You see, the Law** (= Torah), **holding a shadow of** (having shade from) **the impending good things** (virtues; excellent, agreeable or useful qualities or results) – **not the very image of or the same reproduced likeness from those transactions** (results of executing or performing; effects of practices) – **continues not even once able** (or: still never has power) **at any point to perfect** (bring to the goal and destiny, finish, complete or mature) **those folks repeatedly coming near** (approaching) **by offering the** [other MSS: their] **same sacrifices every year...**" (Heb. 10:1).

Through the excess of the unveilings that were given to, and through, Paul, we can understand that, "**[matters of] eating and drinking, [taking] part of a festival, or of a new moon, or of sabbaths** (= concerning [identity markers] or things that are of a religious nature or cultus), **which things** (= cultic markers) **are a shadow of the things [then] being about to be [which is] now, the body of the Christ** (or: and now the physical form is from, and belongs to, the [Messiah])" (Col. 2::16-17). Christ is "the body" that actually cast the shadow. Paul used the contrast of "body-physical form," to illustrate the reality, as compared to the actual "nothingness" of the "shadow." "With the transcendence of the revelations" came the knowledge and "the extraordinary amount and surpassing nature of the disclosures" in order:

> "**to make known by intimate experience, what [are] the riches of the glory of this Secret** (or: the wealth which has its source in this sacred mystery's manifestation which calls forth praise) **within the multitudes** (among the nations; in the Gentiles; IN UNION WITH the swarms of ethnic groups), **which is** (or: exists being) **Christ within you folks, the expectation of and from the glory**" (Col. 1:27).

So Paul received a special Gift of the Spirit (note the passive voice, which indicates that God was the Giver):

> "**something with [its] point in [my] flesh is given in me;**
>
> or: an impaling-stake for the human nature was given for me;
>
> or: a thorn to the natural realm, and a splinter by alienated humanity, was assigned to me."

What applied to everyone, certainly applied to Paul as well (so we'll quote it again):

> "**you folks must consequently be made low** (humbled; demoted; brought to a low station), **in the Lord's sight** (= in [Yahweh's, or Christ's] presence), **and then He will progressively lift you up** (or: continue elevating you)" – Jas. 4:10, and note here, as well, the "Divine Passive."

Paul was being humbled by the "super emissaries" at the very time that he was writing this letter to Corinth. And why did Paul need this "thorn"? So that he "would not continue being overly lifted up [in himself or by others]." OK, so now we know why, but there remains the question: What was this "**agent**

of, and from, the adversary (or: an adversarial person with a message), **to the end that he could** (or: should; would) **repeatedly beat me in the face** (or: slap me on the ear) **with his** (or: its) **fist**"?

Now let us put this last clause in the context of this letter to Corinth. Who were Paul's opponents, or who were the adversarial people that he was confronting and who had been attacking his credibility? We suggest that Paul is speaking metaphorically about being hit in the face. One's face can speak of one's person or one's reputation. They were attacking both, in Paul. All through Paul's ministry, his main adversaries were either those who still held to the Jewish religion, or the Judaizers who tried to make Paul's converts keep, and adhere to, the Law. They were trying to make the Christian movement into a Messianic branch (or sect) of Second Temple Judaism.

In 11:24, above, we read: "**Five times by Jews** (or: under Judeans) **I received forty [stripes; lashes], less one**." Then in 11:25 we read, "**once I was stoned**" – something from their Law. In. 11:26 we read of him being "**in dangers from out of [my] race** (kindred)," as well as "**in dangers among false-brothers** (= pseudo-believers)." These folks were casting Paul's teachings back into his "**face**." They were people who had a message that was adversarial to Paul and his ministry.

We may receive insight into Paul's metaphor of "a thorn to the natural realm, and a splinter by alienated humanity" by turning to Ezk. 28:24, where this same metaphor was used to exemplify Israel's adversaries, who were:
> "a prickling brier or a painful thorn from any round about them who scorned and despised them."

8. **I called the Lord** [Christ or Yahweh] **alongside for relief, ease and comfort, and entreated [Him] three times over** (or: about) **this, so that he would** (or: should) **at once stand away and withdraw from me,**

He asked the Lord to "paraclete" him – three times (probably from the spheres of all three heavens in which Paul was living: body, soul and spirit). Do you imagine that when these "super emissaries" heard this section read aloud in the congregation that they would be like those hearing Jesus, in Mat. 21:45?
> "**And so, upon hearing His illustrations** (parables), **the chief and ranking priests – as well as the Pharisees – knew by this experience that He had been speaking about them.**"

Paul "**entreated [the Lord] three times over** (or: about) **this.**" This calls to mind Jesus' experience in Gethsemane:
> "**And so, leaving them [and] again going away, He prayed a third time saying the same word** (or: thought; idea)" (Mat. 26:44).

As Jesus concluded, in the first time, "**Nevertheless, more than this, [let it be; it is] not as I continue willing** (wanting; intending), **but to the contrary, as You [will and intend]**" (vs. 39), so here we see in the next verse that Paul apparently accepts the Lord's response, with the explanation that he is given. *Cf* Deut. 3:23-27 for Moses' request to Yahweh, and Yahweh's response.

In this situation, Paul wants "this person" to "**at once stand away and withdraw**." In Gal. 5:12 his desire was:
> "**Would that** (or: I wish that) **those continually unsettling you** (causing you to rise up as in an insurrection; thus: disturbing or exciting you folks) **will also, one after another, cut themselves away** (i.e., amputate themselves from your body [of believers])."

9. **and yet He has said to me – and His declaration stands, "My grace is continuously sufficient in you** (or: My joyous favor is constantly adequate to ward [it] off for you), **for you see, the ability** (or: the [other MSS read: My] power) **is habitually brought to its goal** (or: finished; perfected; matured) **within the midst of weakness** (or: in union with lack of strength and infirmity).**" Most gladly, therefore, I will rather continue boasting in** (or: centered within the midst of; and in union with) **the** [other MSS: my]

weaknesses, to the end that the ability of, and from, the Christ (or: the Anointed One's power; the ability which is the Anointing) **can pitch its tent** (or: would tabernacle) **upon me** (or: = set up residence upon me; = fulfill the Feast of Tabernacles with me; or: = be my house from heaven; [*cf.* 5:1, above; Rev. 21:3])**!**

Ah! That is not what we usually want to hear from the Lord! But, as with Paul, so with us; God has given us these "Gifts of the Spirit" to work on, and in, us. They are used in the final polishing of the golden vessel (i.e., the things that "rub us the wrong way" remove whatever dross would distort His image in us). Our son is a jeweler, and when the piece comes out of the casting mold, then the work begins to remove the sprues and to make it shine. We are made to reflect His GLORY. We recall in 1 Cor. 10:13b Paul instructed us that,

> "**together with the trial** (or: ordeal), **He will also continually make the way out** (the egress; or: He also will habitually do the stepping forth from out of the midst; or: He will even progressively construct the out-come) **to continually enable and repeatedly empower you folks to undergo [it]** (to bear up under [it]; to carry on under [it], sustain [it], and lead on)."

Also, we are informed that, "**He is able to run to the aid of those who cry for help – those being tried** (put through ordeals)" (Heb. 2:18b). *Cf* 2 Pet. 2:9; Eccl. 7:18-19; Isa. 40:29; and then Isa. 41:10,

> "Do not continue fearing (or: Be not constantly fearful): for you see, I am (I exist being) with you! Do not continue wandering (or: Stop being repeatedly going astray into deception)! You see, I Myself AM (continue being) your God – the One being strong within you (or: suddenly giving you inner strength) and I give aid and assistance to you (or: I helped and rescued you) and I, Myself, kept you safe, fastened and secure you with (or: by; in) My just right hand" (LXX, JM).

Other than such as the refining process (taken from Mal. 3:2-3), or the metaphor of "building God's temple" (! Cor. 3), or the pruning of the branches to produce more fruit (Jn. 15), we are left without a direct answer to what Paul was told by the Lord:

> "**you see, the ability** (or: the [other MSS read: My] power) **is habitually brought to its goal** (or: finished; perfected; matured) **within the midst of weakness** (or: in union with lack of strength and infirmity)."

But we have Paul's explanation in 13:4, below:

> "**For even though He was crucified from out of weakness** (or: hung and put to death on a torture stake forth from the midst of weakness), **yet in contrast He is continuously living from out of the midst of God's power and ability. For you see, we ourselves also continue being weak, within** (or: in union with) **Him, but still we will continue on living unto you, together with** [other MSS: within] **Him, from out of the midst of God's power and ability.**"

The weakness is the realm of the cruciform Life. But from that comes the resurrection Life which is displayed after "**the ability and power [has been] brought to its goal.**" The Life is within the Seed, but the Seed must be planted, become weak and die, in order for its "ability" to spring forth and bear fruit. The cruciform Life is US "**being weak, within** (or: in union with) **Him,**" and yet, because He lives, "**we will continue on living,**" and so, "**the ability of, and from, the Christ** (or: the Anointed One's power; the ability which is the Anointing) **can pitch its tent** (or: would tabernacle) **upon [us].**" As Paul put it in Gal. 2:20,

> "**I was crucified together with Christ, and thus it remains... yet I continue living! [It is] no longer I, but it is Christ continuously living and alive within me! Now that which I, at the present moment, continue living within flesh** (= a physical body), **I am constantly living within [His] faithfulness – in and by that [faithfulness] which is the Son of God.**"

"The ability which is the Anointing pitching its tent upon me" is a beautiful picture that calls to mind Rev. 21:3, "**God's tent** (the Tabernacle of God) **[is] with mankind** (the humans), **and He will continue living in a tent** (dwell in a Tabernacle) **with them...**" It is His Presence that is "the power and ability of God." We read in 1 Pet. 4:14,

"**Since** (or: If) **you folks are constantly being insulted and censured in** (or: [because of] union with) **the Name of Christ, [you are] happy ones** (blessed folks), **because God's spirit of glory and power** (or: the Breath-effect of the reputation and from the appearance, along with the ability of God) **is continuously 'resting back upon' you folks.**" *Cf.* Isa. 11:2

10. **Wherefore I habitually delight and take pleasure in weaknesses** (or: in union with lacks of strength and infirmities); **in the midst of outrageous insults and ignominious situations of mistreatment; in union with pressured necessities; in the midst of pursuits for persecution and cramped situations over and on behalf of Christ, for whenever I continue being** (or: may periodically be) **weak, then I am powerful** (or: I then exist being capable)!

The attitude that Paul displays here (**delighting and taking pleasure in** all these things that he lists) actually disempowers all these adverse situations from having a negative effect upon him. He can do this because He knows God, and has experienced God's Spirit empowering him "**whenever [he] continues being** (or: may periodically be) **weak.**" What an example his life was, and what a witness for Christ's faithfulness. *Cf* 13:4, below.

Therefore, when his opponents are saying that Paul is weak (10:10, above), Paul now informs them that if they think that this is the case with him, then at this very moment he is "**powerful** (capable)." Let both the average members of the community, and Paul's opponents, take care! "**For you see, the ability** (or: the [other MSS read: **My**] **power**) **is habitually brought to its goal** (or: finished; perfected; matured) **within the midst of weakness** (or: in union with lack of strength and infirmity)" (vs. 9, above).

We read a similar affirmation in Rom. 5:3-6,

> "**we also keep on celebrating, speaking loudly and boasting within the pressures, while exulting in ordeals, afflictions and tribulations, having seen and thus knowing that the pressure** (or: the ordeal, affliction or tribulation) **is habitually producing a relentless remaining under [situations and circumstances]** (or: the patient ability to give support). **Yet the remaining and abiding under [produces] a quality of being approved by testing; in turn, the quality of being approved by testing [produces] expectation and hope. Now the expectation does not habitually bring down shame** (disgrace; dishonor), **because God's love** (the urge toward reunion and the unambiguous, uniting acceptance from God; God's giving of Himself to [us]) **has been poured out in a gush and shed forth so that it now floods within our hearts, permeating the core of our being, through the Set-apart Breath-effect** (or: Holy Spirit) **being given to us** (in us; for us). **For during our yet existing [as] weak folks and continuing in being without strength, Christ, still corresponding to and in accord with [the] appointed season, died for the sake of the ungodly and irreverent.**"

11. **I have become unreasonable** (senseless; imprudent; foolish) – **you, yourselves, compel me** (press and force me; = drive me to it!) – **for I myself ought to have been being constantly recommended** (placed together with and commended) **by you folks, because not even in one thing did I come behind** (or: am I deficient from or inferior to) **the "very-overly" [pretentious and condescending] emissaries** (or: representatives), **even though I am nothing** (or: since I also exist being nothing!).

Is Paul speaking about this letter, when he says that he has "**become unreasonable**"? Or, was he referring to all his previous dealings with them? In either case, by this rendering of the adjective, do we detect sarcasm or irony in his words? The other renderings, "senseless, imprudent or foolish," may also be read that way, or, he might be offering an apology for seeming to be as those renderings may suggest. It is hard to tell, when we cannot hear the tone of voice or any affectation as the rhetor reads this to the group. Nonetheless, he lays the blame for this at their door: "**you, yourselves, compel me** (press and force me; = drive me to it!)."

They have known him: he was among them for 18 months! The covenant community should have taken Paul's side and defended him against the false teachers – instead of being misled by them so as to doubt Paul. Where was the grace-effect of discernment among them (1 Cor. 12:8-10)? He "**ought to have been being constantly recommended** (placed together with and commended) **by [them]**." Even though he was "**nothing**" (sarcasm, or a declaration that he no longer lived, but Christ lived in him!), still, "**not even in one thing did [he] come behind** (or: [was he] deficient from or inferior to) **the "very-overly" [pretentious and condescending] emissaries** (or: representatives)!" Both truth and sarcasm. He wants them to think over this situation. He is laying it out for them – how could they deny it? In Gal. 2:6 Paul, in speaking of "**the led-in-at-the-side** (or: smuggled-in) **false brothers**" (vs. 4), instructed them:

> "**God is not in the habit of receiving a person's face** (= taking people at face value; or: responding to man's outward appearance or presentation). **So you see, those continuing to be disposed to thinking and imagination** (or: those being supposed to continue with a reputation; those yet forming opinions) **of themselves put nothing new forward for me**."

Well, he goes on…

12. **Indeed, the signs of the emissary** (the sent-forth representative) **were produced and accomplished among you folks in every [situation] of humbly remaining under to give support** (or: in all patient endurance) **– as well as by signs and wonders** (portents; marvels) **and powers** (or: in abilities and capabilities).

In regard to the "**signs of the emissary**," let us review what he said in a previous letter – where he seems to be addressing some of the same issues as here – in 1 Cor. 2:

> 3. **So I, myself, came to be with and toward you, and faced you folks, in lack of strength** (or: in union with weakness), **and in fear – even in much trembling and agitation of mind** (or: very nervous; shaking with reverence and respect; or: = with earnestness and much concern),
> 4. **so my message** (the *Logos*, or word, thought and Information, from me) **and my public proclamation [were; consisted] not in persuasive words of wisdom** (or: ideas from cleverness [MSS add: of, or from, a human]), **but to the contrary [were; consisted] in demonstration of spirit and attitude, as well as of power and from ability**
>> (or: in the midst of a display of clear and logical proof from [the] Spirit, consisting of power and ability; in union with a documented manifestation which was Breath-effect and which was a means of influence and capability),
> 5. **to the end that your trust would not be in human wisdom** (your faith and reliance would not exist in cleverness of people), **but rather in God's power, means, influence and ability.**

In this second letter, he refers to "**signs and wonders** (portents; marvels) **and powers** (or: in abilities and capabilities)." But he adds one more "sign," and this may be the most important of all, because it is a demonstration of Love: "**every [situation] of humbly remaining under to give support** (or: in all patient endurance)." Notice the divine passive in the verb "**were produced and accomplished**." Paul is saying that it was God that did these things. The central sign of the legitimacy of an emissary of Christ is God being in him or her, and acting through him or her. We know them by the Fruit of the Spirit that is produced in them.

But even more striking evidence of his being a sent-forth representative to them was given in 1 Cor. 9:

> 2. **If I am not one sent off with a mission to or for other folks, nevertheless I surely am to and for you people – for you, yourselves, are my seal of the expedition** (or: = the validated document of my sent-off mission), **within, and in union with, the Lord** (or: centered in the Master).
> 3. **[and] this is my defense** (my verbal reply) **to or for those continuously examining me and sifting the evidence about me.**

Furthermore, cf 3:2-3, above, and now consider his words in Rom. 15:18-19,

"**You see, I will not venture to speak anything of which Christ does not work down, produce and bring into effect through me [leading] into a submissive giving of the ear** (or: humble, obedient hearing and paying attention) **from [the] ethnic multitudes** (or: of non-Jews; [the] nations) **by an arranged speech and message as well as by a work – in a power of signs and of miracles, [that is], in [the] power of God's Spirit** (or: in union with an ability from God's Breath; in an ability from an Attitude which is God) **– with a view for me to have filled [the region] from Jerusalem even, around in a circuit, as far as Illyricum [with] the good news of, from, and concerning the Anointed One.**"

13. **So what is there in which you folks were treated as inferior, or made worse off, above** (= more than) **the rest of the called-out folks** (or: communities), **except that for myself, I myself was not a "dead weight" for** (= and idle encumbrance, hence, a financial burden to) **you folks? Give grace to me for this unfairness** (wrong; injustice)**!**

Biting sarcasm. He is holding up the facts for them to look at. Oh, how he had mistreated them! Yes, both sarcasm and irony, again. He is demonstrating his ability in rhetoric – for those false teachers to observe, as well. In 1 Cor. 1:7 he had affirmed to them,

"**you people are not continuing trailing behind or constantly late, so as to be deficient or fall short – not even in one effect of grace** (or: result of favor) **– being ones habitually receiving and taking away into your hands from out of our Lord's unveiling: Jesus Christ.**"
And then in 1 Cor. 9:12 he reminded them:

"**Since others are continually sharing and participating in your right from existing** (privilege), **[why] not rather** (or: all the more) **we? But to the contrary, we did not make use of this right, but rather we are habitually putting a roof over, and thus covering** (perhaps: = putting up with) **all people, and all things** [or: situations], **so that we should not give any hindrance to the progress of Christ's good news.**"

14. **Look** (or: Consider)**! This third time I continue holding [myself] ready and prepared to come to** (or: go toward) **you folks – and I will not proceed in being "dead weight"** (an encumbrance or burden), **for I am not habitually seeking your "things"** (your possessions), **but to the contrary, you. For the children ought not to be habitually storing up and accumulating [material resources] for the parents, but rather, the parents [should do this] for the children.**

Note the opening interjection: "**Look** (or: Consider)!" He wants them to think about what he is about to say. He lays out both his integrity, and his relational philosophy. He has reminded them that he is a parent to them. Recall his words in 1 Cor. 4:15b, "**because in one moment I, myself, fathered** (gave birth to; generated) **you people within and in union with Christ Jesus.**" And, "**the children ought not to be habitually storing up and accumulating [material resources] for the parents, but rather, the parents [should do this] for the children.**" So of course he is "**not habitually seeking [their] 'things'** ([their] possessions)," and furthermore he "**will not proceed in being 'dead weight'**" on them, should he proceed in coming for a visit. Can you imagine this: he is not demanding an honorarium!! OK, a little of my own sarcasm (I blame Paul).

We read in Acts 20:33 Luke recording Paul saying,

"**I did not covet, have an over-desire for, or set my heart upon silver or gold or clothing which belongs to even one person.**"

He calls the Corinthians his "**beloved children,**" in 1 Cor. 4:14, so he is taking the position and attitude of a parent toward them in the last sentence of this verse.

15. **So I myself most gladly shall spend** (pay the expenses) **– even be completely spent** (exhausted; bankrupted) **– over** (on behalf of) **your souls. Even if I am constantly loving you excessively, I am**

habitually being loved or accepted less. (or: And since I am continuously loving you and seeking union with you more abundantly {or: too much}, am I being loved less?)

To the folks at Philippi he said,
> "**But even more, since** (or: if) **I am also repeatedly poured out as a drink offering upon the sacrificial offering and public service pertaining to your faith**..." (Phil. 2:17).

This same attitude was also shown to those in Thessalonica:
> "**Thus, continuously being your affectionately "attached-ones"** (ones having a like-flow [of nourishment from our Nursing Mother]), **we were habitually delighted** (thinking it good; well-pleased) **to share or impart to you not only God's message of goodness and well-being** [other MSS: the good news which is Christ], **but rather even our own souls** (= inner beings and lives; or: = selves), **because you have been birthed** (or: come to be) **beloved ones to us**."

So now he lays out the truth and reality of his heart: He would do anything for them – even if they don't really appreciate it. Even if, in fact, he is "**habitually being loved or accepted less!**" Where did Paul get this "unconditional love"? Can you even imagine that some people doubt that God, Himself/Herself, Loves unconditionally? This is GOD, in Paul, saying, "And since I am continuously loving you and seeking union with you more abundantly {or: too much}, am I being loved less?" Observe his (and God's) next statement, in vs. 16: "**Yet, let it continue to be.**" Paul was an image-bearer of God (Gen. 1:26). This was because he was in Christ (5:17, above). *Cf* his comment about them in 6:12, above.

16. **Yet, let it continue to be** (or: so be it; be that as it may; let it be). **I myself do not** (or: did not) **overburden or weigh you down. Nonetheless, being inherently ready to do anything and capable for every work, [you say that] I caught you, taking you by bait** (as used for fish)!

Yes, "So be," or, "Be that as it may," he will still not overburden them or weigh them down. Paul is whispering words of wisdom, "let it be." His next statement about not overburdening them is an echo of 11:9, above – the rhetoric of repetition, so that his audience gets the point.

The next statement can be taken in more than one way (Surprise!). David Bentley Hart renders it, "But, being wily, I took you with guile." That is a good rendering, but considering Paul's employment of rhetoric in this passage, I put this in the mouth of his accusers, by inserting, "**[you say that]**." The *ESV* does this, as well, as does Nyland, and the *New World Translation*. But the NASB reads it like Hart: "Nevertheless, crafty fellow that I am, I took you in by deceit." Rotherham gives a similar straightforward rendering, but offers this footnote: "As if: 'is *that* what you say?' – which he then indignantly denies." Here, Hillyer comments: "some insinuate that being *crafty* he will obtain money by filching funds collected in Corinth by his agents" (ibid p 1087). Witherington interprets this verse in a similar way that Hillyer does, and posits that this verse must be read as irony (ibid p 467).

What others have rendered as "guile" (can we really imagine Paul using guile, or as him being "crafty"?) I have offered the more literal renderings: "**being inherently ready to do anything and capable for every work.**" You see, this term can also have a positive nuance. Also, instead of rendering the dative noun "with guile," or, "by deceit," as noted above, I rendered it literally. The word *dolos* strictly refers to "*bait* for fish" (*Analytical Lexicon of the Greek NT*, Friberg, Friberg, Miller, Baker Books, 2000). May God's Spirit enable you to decide how Paul was speaking here, and therefore, what he meant by this somewhat ambiguous statement. But as Rotherham points out, consider his next, forceful affirmation...

17. **Not anyone whom I have sent off to you folks [did this]! Did I take advantage of you through him?**

So we see that Paul denies that any people whom he sent to them "**caught [them or took them] by bait**." They were not deceitful, wily or full of guile. Next, he asks the covenant community if he, himself, had taken advantage of anyone through the person that he had sent to them. This rhetorical question expects a "NO!" response. Paul is calling these folks to their senses. *Cf* 7:2, above.

18. **I called Titus alongside, urged [him] and sent [him] off, together with the** (or: [his]) **brother** (or: = fellow believer and member of the Family), **as an emissary** (sent-off representative). **Surely Titus did not take advantage of you! Do we not walk about in the same Spirit** (or: = Do we not live and order our lives with the same attitude)**? Not in the same footprints?**

Recall Paul's supportive statements of Titus in 8:6, 16 and 18, above. He is confident that Titus took no advantage of them. So he reasons with them with another rhetorical question: "**Do we not walk about in the same Spirit?**" This could also be read as on offer in the parenthetical expansion: "Do we not live and order our lives with the same attitude?" Then he expands this thought with an even more detailed metaphor: "**Not in the same footprints?**" That means that a person is walking the same Path/Way, and in the very same way, as another person. He and Titus live congruent lives – and both of these live the Way that Christ lived.

19. **All this time** [other MSS: Again] **do you folks continue thinking** (supposing; presuming) **that we are repeatedly making a verbal defense to YOU? Down [here] in God's stead and place, we are constantly speaking within Christ and in union with [the] Anointing! And the whole** (all [these] things), **beloved ones, [is** (are)**] over** (on behalf of) **your edification** (your upbuilding; the construction of your house).

The term "**a verbal defense**" was "a technical legal term" (Nyland, ibid p 349 n 10). Hillyer (ibid p 1087) suggests that Paul is using it "as in a court," and thus, "to YOU" would position the Corinthians as being their "judges." But let us recall Paul's attitude on such a case, in 1 Cor. 4:3a,

> "**Now to** (or: for) **me, it is of little importance** (a very trivial matter) **that I am being constantly critiqued** (sifted, critically reviewed and evaluated; put up for judgment) **by you folks…**"

Cf 5:12, above.

The *CLNT* does not render the first sentence as a question, but rather (and following the other MSS) as an affirmation: "Again, you are presuming that we are defending ourselves to you." The *NASB* is similar to *CLNT*, but following this statement it inserts the word "*Actually*" as the beginning of the next sentence. Although following the later textual tradition that places a question mark at the end of the first statement, by emphasizing the plural, dative pronoun "**to YOU**" (by using all upper case), my rendering suggests a reading that agrees with these three previous translations. Rotherham presents this same reading by using diacritical marks to indicate the "YOU" is emphatic.

Whether Paul meant it as a question or as a statement, the next sentence is his answer and main point: "**Down [here] in God's stead and place, we are constantly speaking within Christ and in union with [the] Anointing!**" By speaking "within Christ" and "in union with the Anointing" (a conflation of two potential renderings of the same Greek phrase), he is speaking the Truth – and this is what ultimately matters (*cf* 11:31, above; Rom. 9:1). What a statement! They are God's mouthpiece; they are His prophets – His witnesses. They are "as God" to the Corinthians (Ex. 7:1)! Paul used this same adverb in 2:17b, above, where he virtually says the same thing.

And now he speaks of everything that he has been saying to them: "**And the whole** (all [these] things), **beloved ones, [is** (are)**] over** (on behalf of) **your edification.**" This says again what he said in 4:15a, above,

> "**for you see, all things [are]** (the whole – everything – [is]) **because of you folks.**" *Cf* 1 Cor. 10:33

But here he adds the explanation of what he means: it is for their "**edification.**" The alternate renderings, "your upbuilding; the construction of your house," give us an allusion to 1 Cor. 3:9-17. The Greek word for edification is a cognate of the word for "house; building," and thus it literally means the construction and upbuilding of a house. Paul subtly brings them back to the fact that they are God's House, His Temple.

20. **So you see, I continue being afraid, lest somehow – on coming – I may not find you folks such as I habitually intend** (purpose; desire) **– and I myself may be found by you [to be one] such as you folks continue not desiring – lest somehow [I may find] strife** (contention; quarreling), **jealousy, outbursts of emotions or swellings of anger, selfish ambition and factious rivalry, backbitings** (down-babblings; slanderous conversations), **whisperings** (occasions of malicious gossiping), **situations of puffing up** (inflations of pride), **disorders** (situations of unrest; turbulences; losses of tranquility; instabilities).

Up to this point, Paul has been through a lot with these folks, over the last (perhaps) couple years. They have demonstrated a lack of stability. Recall his words to them in 1 Cor. 4:21,
> "**What do you folks want** (presently desire; normally intend; by habit purpose)**? Should I come to you people within [the realm of] a rod** (staff; = with corrective measures), **or within love** (solidarity), **and in a spirit of gentle friendliness and tender kindness** (or: meekness)**?**"

It seems like nothing had changed over the last year and a half.

21. **My God will** [other MSS: may] **not again be repeatedly humbling me toward you folks, at my coming, and yet I may mourn and grieve over many of those having previously been failing** (missing the goal; sinning), **continuing thus and not at any point changing thinking to a new state of consciousness and attitude regarding the uncleanness and fornication** (sexual immorality; prostitution) **and loose conduct** (licentiousness) **which they practice.**

Recall, again, 2:1 and 4, above. He is once more calling this to their attention. But this seems to have been a common situation among these fledgling congregations:
> "**For you see – I was often telling you about them, yet now I am also presently weeping** (lamenting) **in saying it – many continue walking about** (i.e., are living their lives) **as enemies of the cross of the Christ** (the Anointed One's execution-stake and suspension-pole)" (Phil. 3:18). *Cf* Rev. 3:9

Chapter 13

1. **I am habitually coming to you folks – this third time, now!**
> "**Upon [the] mouth of two witnesses – and of three – every effect of a flow** (gush-effect; matter; declaration; saying) **will continue being made to stand.**" [Deut. 19:15]

Is he referencing this OT text to signify that each of his visits is a "witness" on his behalf? Or is this quote meant to rhetorically set-up his repeated "sayings," that he refers to in vs. 2, and then the "**proof**" that his audience continues seeking, in vs. 3, below?

2. **I have said before, and I continue foretelling** (laying it out beforehand) **– as if continuing present, the second time, and yet now continuing absent – to those having before failed** (deviated; sinned), **and still continuing thus – and to all the rest – that if I should ever come again into the [area], I will not continue to being thrifty, so as to spare or refrain,**

Here he gives his opponents a warning, in the last clause. Notice his use of two verbs in the first clause: the first the more ordinary verb (*proeipon*) for saying or speaking, here in the perfect tense; the second (*prolegō*) which has the root idea of "laying it out beforehand," but in the present tense (ongoing action). He had already told them this in the past, and he continues foretelling them while laying out more details. He does this while being absent from the presence, but he speaks "**as if continuing present**." The

Logos in his words are spirit, and there is no distance between his words and his audience: "**every effect of a flow** (gush-effect; matter; declaration; saying) **will continue being made to stand**."

His warning implies that he expected "**those having before failed** (deviated; sinned)" NOT to "**still continue thus**." We observe his use of the subjunctive mood (**should**) along with the particle, "**if ever,**" when he speaks of a potential visit in the future. We can never be sure of any future plans or actions.

3. since you continue seeking a proof of the Christ continuously speaking within and in union with me – Who [having come] into you folks is not being weak, but rather continues powerful (or: capable) **within and in union with you folks.**

The first clause reminds us of Mat. 10:20, where Jesus told His disciples:
> "**You see, you, yourselves, are not the ones then speaking, but rather, [it is] the Spirit** (Breath-effect; Attitude) **of your Father repeatedly speaking within you**."

The forewarning of potential corrective action, on Paul's part, is elicited by the fact of their "**continued seeking a proof of the Christ continuously speaking within and in union with [him]**." But then he reminds them that Christ Himself has already come "**into [them],**" and He "**is not being weak, but rather continues powerful** (or: capable) **within and in union with you folks**." You see, God is within His Temple (His home), i.e., within the Corinthians themselves – who are His Temple (6:16, above; 1 Pet. 2:5). Paul had already told them this same thing, in 1 Cor. 6:19. This fact seems to be hard for people to grasp – even in our day.

Let us really think about Paul's words here: God "**continues powerful** (or: capable) **within and in union with [US]**." Selah!

We read another affirmation of Christ speaking through Paul, in 1 Cor. 9:2,
> "**If I am not one sent off with a mission to or for other folks, nevertheless I surely am to and for you people – for you, yourselves, are my seal of the expedition** (or: = the validated document of my sent-off mission), **within, and in union with, the Lord**."

How quickly people forget.

4. For even though He was crucified (or: hung and put to death on a torture stake) **from out of the midst of weakness, yet in contrast, He is continuously living from out of the midst of God's power and ability. For you see, we ourselves also continue being weak, within** (or: in union with) **Him, but still we will continue on living together with** [other MSS: within] **Him, unto** (or: with a view to) **you folks, from out of the midst of God's power and ability.**

Ponder the implications of the second clause of Paul's first statement. He had just posited that **Christ** continues **powerful and able within [them]** (and, therefore, within US; 3b, above); now he states that "**He (Christ) is continuously living from out of the midst of God's power and ability!**" Paul gave us a picture of this in Eph. 1:19-20,
> "**His ability and power [being given] unto, and into, us... in accord with the operation** (or: energizing; internal working) **of force** (or: might) **of His strength, which is operative** (or: which He exerted and inwardly worked) **within the Christ** (the Anointed One), **awakening and raising Him forth from out of the midst of dead folks and then seating Him within** (or: = at) **His right [hand] within the things** (or: places or realms) **situated upon the heavens and in union with the imposed atmospheres.**"

But this also implies that Christ lives within us, and shows us one aspect of HOW He lives, within US! This is just one of Paul's "**two witnesses**" (vs. 1). Let us visit another witness:
> "**but to the contrary, He empties Himself** (or: removed the contents of Himself; made Himself empty), **receiving** (or: taking; accepting) **a slave's form** (external shape; outward mold), **coming to be** (or: birthing Himself) **within an effect of humanity's** (mankind's; people's) **likeness. And**

so, being found in an outward fashion, mode of circumstance, condition, form-appearance (or: character, role, phase, configuration, manner) **as a human, He lowers Himself** (or: humbled Himself; made Himself low; degrades Himself; levels Himself off), **coming to be a submissive, obedient One as far as** (or: to the point of; until) **death – but death of a cross!**" (Phil. 2:7-8).

Another affirmation of what Paul states in the first sentence is seen in 1 Pet. 3:18b,

"[He], on the one hand, being put to death in flesh (= a physical body), **yet on the other hand, being made alive in spirit** (or: indeed, being put to death by flesh {or: = the estranged human condition}, yet, being engendered a living one by Breath-effect {or: [the] Spirit})."

So Paul connects Christ's being "**crucified from out of weakness**" to the continued "**being weak, within** (or: in union with) **Him**" (the cruciform life) of Paul and his associates. "**But still**," he affirms, "**we will continue on living together with** [other MSS: within] **Him**." [Cf 10:3-4, above.] Notice the parenthetical expansion of "**unto you**," which literally can read "with a view to you." Paul sees his life in Christ as being "with a view to" them, and to the point of existential solidarity where his spirit reaches "into the midst of [them]" (an expanded meaning of the preposition eis). This is union; this is common being and common participation of mutual indwelling – just as we have by being "in God."

But Paul does not end with this. No, he repeats the same phrase that he had just said about Christ's "**continuously living**," but now applies it to himself and his associates (and by implication, to US): they, and we, were/are living is "**from out of the midst of God's power and ability**." What a "powerful" statement! This is possible because of our being joined to Him (1 Cor. 6:17) and because of our "**continuously living together with** [other MSS: within] **Him**." Paul expressed something similar in Rom. 6:4,

"**Christ was roused and raised forth from out of the midst of dead folks THROUGH** (through means of) **THE GLORY** (the glorious manifestation of splendor which calls forth praise; the assumed appearance) **of, from, and which is, The Father; thus also we can walk around within newness of life**."

That was true for them, then, and it is true for us, now.

5. Keep on examining and making trial of yourselves, since you exist being in union with the Faithfulness (or: whether you continue being centered within the midst of this Trust); **repeatedly test and assay yourselves so as to approve of yourselves and come to meet the desired specifications. Or are you not now fully aware nor presently recognizing yourselves, with accurate insight: that Jesus Christ constantly exists being within the midst of, and in union with, you people? – since you are surely not unable to stand the test, nor are you unproven or disapproved!** (or: – except you are somewhat disqualified.)

Following the imperative to "**Keep on examining and making trial of [themselves]**," the dependent clause can be read two different ways – depending upon how we read the particle "ei," ("since," or "if; whether"). The bold rendering makes a declarative statement: "**since you exist being…**" Because of the sphere of their existence "**in union with the Faithfulness**" (of Christ), they are qualified and empowered to examine themselves. Chrysostom said, "Look into yourselves and you will find that you have Christ in you," and Ambrosiaster stated: "A person who has a sense of faith in his heart knows that Jesus Christ is within him" (Homilies on the Epistles of Paul to the Corinthians, Ancient Christian Commentary on Scripture, NT Vol. 6, 1-2 Corinthians, InterVarsity Press, 1999 p 314).

The parenthetical rendering, "whether you continue being," assumes their ability to discern their true state of being, and thus Paul would be telling them to "make trial of themselves" to see "whether [they] continue being centered within the midst of this Trust." He leaves it ambiguous (thus not making a new "law") about how they should do this. We suggest that they would do it in union with God's Spirit that indwells them… listening to His inner voice. Cf 1 Cor. 11:28

Next he goes on to expand his thought with the added imperative: "**repeatedly test and assay yourselves so as to approve of yourselves and come to meet the desired specifications**." This redundant imperative ends with the idea of meeting "the desired specifications." Since this second imperative is parallel to the first one, we can assume that "**the desired specifications**" are "**being in union with the Faithfulness** (or: this Trust)." The phrase is equivalent to being "in Christ," for "the Faithfulness" was His Faithfulness. Or, reading the phrase as "being centered with the midst of this Trust," it still points to Christ Who personified, and embodied, Trust in God. He was the Just One who walked in the Way pointed out. Faith, trust, and faithfulness are synonymous terms with different nuances, but they all are aspects of "the Anointing," or, "the fruit of the Spirit' (Gal. 5:22). In fact, Gal. 5:22-24) gives an excellent description of "**the desired specifications**" of the cruciform life.

Next Paul gives his audience a rhetorical question, "**Or are you not now fully aware... that Jesus Christ constantly exists being within the midst of, and in union with, you people?**" This reminds them of what he had just told them in 4b, above. Repetition drives the point home. Let us recall Jesus' words to the Father, in Jn. 17:9b-10,

> "**those whom You have given to Me, and I possess**... **continuously exist** (or: are) **in You** (or: by You; for You; with You). **Thus, all My possessions are Yours, and Your possessions are Mine, and I have been – and remain – glorified** (made to be a recognized appearance and a manifestation which calls forth praise) **in and among them**."

In Rom. 8:10 we have another of Paul's beautiful declarations:

> "**But since Christ [is] within you folks, on the one hand the body is dead, BECAUSE OF sin** (through failure, deviation and missing the target), **yet on the other hand, the Spirit, Attitude and Breath-effect [is] Life BECAUSE OF an eschatological act of justice that brought a rightwising deliverance into equitable, covenantal relationships within the Way pointed-out** (or: on account of the covenantal Faithfulness of a liberating Turn into the Right Direction of the Living Way/Path)."

Next, he rounds off the point that he has just made by another dependent clause that opens with the same particle, "**since**," but here he makes another declarative affirmation – using double negatives: "**you are surely not unable to stand the test**," and this same clause can read, "**nor are you unproven or disapproved!**" (Yes, I conflated two rendering into one clause!). Now these is still another reading that conveys a nuance of doubt about their situation: "except you are somewhat disqualified." On this reading, *cf* 1 Cor. 9:27. Each person in his audience is presented with a chance to "examine himself" by this rhetorical ambiguity: if the shoe fits, wear it (as the saying goes).

6. Yet I continue expecting that you folks will progressively come to know by intimate experience that we ourselves are not unable to stand the test, nor are we unproven, disapproved or disqualified!

This is brilliant rhetoric: he knows that most likely, upon their self-examination, they will come to the conclusion that they DO pass the test and ARE, in fact, proven, approved and qualified. Thus, he reasons, they "**will progressively come to know by intimate experience**" that so do Paul and his associates. Paul repeats his double-negative affirmation (**not un-**) to counter the accusations of the false intruders. By what he says here, he is displaying confidence in them. He is turning them to his side of the conflict. His *logos*, which is Sprit and Life (Jn. 6:63), builds them up and points them to the Way.

7. Now we habitually hold good thoughts, having wishes of ease and well-being face-to-face with (or: toward) **God, asking [that] you folks do nothing worthless or of bad quality – not so that we, ourselves, can appear** (or: should be made to be seen) **as proven, approved or qualified, but rather so that you yourselves can** (or: should; would) **be habitually doing** (performing; creating) **that which is beautiful** (or: constantly constructing the ideal; repeatedly making what is fine), **even though we**

ourselves may be as ones unproven, disapproved and disqualified (= should look as if we had failed the test and are discredited),

Here Paul describes the mental attitude concerning the Corinthians, and the setting in which they are "**habitually hold good thoughts, having wishes of ease and well-being**." They live "**face-to-face with** (or: [oriented] toward) **God**." We find this same phrase in Jn. 1:1 where the *Logos* (Word; Thought; Verbal Expression, etc.) is "face-to-face with God." Paul's "**asking**" God, on behalf of the Corinthians, comes in a form of good thoughts and wishes of ease and well-being. This present tense verb is normally rendered "praying," but Concordant Keyword Concordance gives the Greek elements as "well-wish." The CLNT therefore renders the verb, "we are wishing." The verb, *euchomai*, has the root idea of having or holding (a cognate of *echō*: to have or hold) prefixed by *eu-* (goodness; ease; well-being). So in the presence of God, Paul and his friends hold good thoughts toward God as they ask that the Corinthians "**do nothing worthless or of bad quality**." The idea of "having wishes" expressed as we gaze into the face of God (3:18, above) is like having a conversation with Him. Bottom line: Paul and his group want only goodness, ease and well-being for the covenant community.

He is not concerned about how they themselves appear to other folks, "**but rather so that you yourselves can** (or: should; would) **be habitually doing that which is beautiful** (or: constantly constructing the ideal; repeatedly making what is fine)." He wants them to repeatedly "perform and create" goodness, ease and well-being within their community – regardless of how folks in Corinth think of Paul and his associates. Recall 6:9, above.

8. **for it follows that we continue with no power** (are unable and incapable) **[to do] anything against** (or: [to be] putting down) **this Reality or the Truth, but to the contrary, [we have power and ability] for the sake of the Truth, and over [the situation] of this Reality.**

The conjunction that begins this verse, which I have rendered "**for it follows that**," indicates that he is continuing his thoughts presented in vs. 7, and what follows is an expansion of his explanation concerning his and his fellow-workers' existential situation in the Lord, as being attending servants and dispensers of Christ.

So what does he mean by this somewhat enigmatic explanation? What follows, "**but to the contrary**," gives us the answer. Their entire mission and attending service is to Christ (Mat. 25:40b) – Who Is "**the Reality and the Truth** (a conflation of the two central ideas of *alētheia*; *cf* Jn. 14:6). Their power and ability is THROUGH the new arrangement (covenant) of this new Reality of the new creation (5:17, above): it is the Truth (Christ) that empowers them "**for the sake of the Truth, and over [the situation] of the Reality**." On offer are both the literal and the common extended meaning of the preposition that is used in the final phrase of the verse: "**over**" (the literal concept); "**for the sake of**" (the extended meaning). Both meanings apply: their power is for the sake of Christ (which includes His corporate body), and is over the realm of this new Reality (*cf* Eph. 2:6).

As Jesus said, "**every city or household being parted down against itself will not continue standing** (= be surviving)" (Mat. 12:25b). Therefore, it follows that Christ's servants "**continue with no power** (are unable and incapable) **[to do] anything against** (or: [to be] putting down) **this Reality or the Truth**." And so, he continues...

9. **So we are constantly rejoicing whenever we ourselves may continue being weak, yet you, yourselves, may continue being able and powerful. We are also constantly holding this good thought, asking with wishes of ease and well-being: your complete adjustment** (your thoroughly being knitted together, made completely equipped in full readiness, and adapted in perfect unity).

The first statement encapsulates the point of the argument that he has been making to them. The parents provide for the enhancement of their children… they "paraclete" them. And often to the point of "weakness" in doing so! Here let us remember 1 Cor. 4:10,

> "**We [are] stupid folks** (fools; ones led by nonsense) **because of Christ, yet you folks [are] sensible and intelligent ones** (ones with understanding) **within, and in union with, Christ; we [are] weak ones, yet you people [are] strong ones; you [are] folks in glory and illustrious reputation, yet we [are] dishonored and unvalued ones**."

There, the rhetoric was different from here, but once again Paul contrasts the situation of the "dispensers" to that of those in Corinth, in order to cause them to reconsider their attitudes, and reassess their own situation.

The next declaration repeats the first clause of 7a, above, but now puts what follows, "**but rather…**," in the center of that verse and in different words: "**your complete adjustment**." Adjustment to what? To the image of God; to the glory that truly manifests Christ to their world. Now (as by this time it should be expected!) the noun in this final phrase has a semantic range, so we will examine these options:

> a) "thoroughly being knitted together": the idea of "knitted together" offers a mental picture of being a part of a whole cloth where each stitch is joined to all the other stitches in a union of functions and existential reality;
>
> b) "made completely equipped in full readiness": this picture is of folks being trained to do a job, or of being alert and capable to handle any situation that arises;
>
> c) "adapted in perfect unity": this description speaks of positive corporate relationships that can productively function in this new Reality.

Another thought on "complete adjustment" can be seen in the metaphor of God's complete soldier's equipment in Eph. 6:14-17. The things that are strapped to the body have to be adjusted to each individual (remember how Saul's armor did not fit the young David?). Corporately speaking, the covenant community needed to be adjusted, adapted, equipped and knitted together in order to address the kinds of intrusions that they were at that time experiencing with those "super emissaries," or just to deal with the carnality and immaturity such as he had addressed in his first letter to them. We find an echo of this verse in 1 Thes. 3:9b-10,

> "**we are continually rejoicing because of you – before** (or: in front of; in the place facing toward and in the presence of) **our God, while night and day, over-excessively repeatedly begging regarding our need to see your face** (= to see you face to face), **and then to freshly adjust to correspondence** (or: thoroughly equip, fit, knit together, mend and bring into agreement) **the things lacking** (the shortcomings or deficiencies) **of your faith and with regard to your loyal trust!**"

Everyone needs this kind of "adjustment (etc.)." Christ gave those such as Paul and his associates to the called-out folks,

> "**facing and with a view toward the bringing down of the fresh and timely, for the preparation** (mending; knitting together; adjusting; fitting; repairing; perfectly adjusting adaptation; equipping; completely furnishing) **of the set-apart folks unto a work** (or: into an action; into the midst of a deed or task) **of attending service and dispensing, [leading] unto** (or: into) **construction** (house-building) **of the body which is the Christ** (or: whose source, character and quality is from the Anointed One; or: the body formed by the Anointing)" (Eph. 4:12). *Cf* vs. 11, below.

10. Therefore, being absent, I am now writing these things, to the end that [when] being present I may not severely employ the rights that accord with the authority (or: harshly behave in the sphere from out of [my] existence; act in a cutting-off way along the line of what is out of Being) **which the Lord** [= Christ or Yahweh] **gave, and gives, to and in me, with a view into building the house up** (construction of a household), **and not into tearing [it] down.**

This statement is straightforward and hardly needs any explanation. But we will separate out the renderings that follow, "**being present I may not**…" to facilitate consideration of the options:

a) **severely employ the rights that accord with the authority**;

b) **harshly behave in the sphere from out of [my] existence**;

c) **act in a cutting-off way along the line of what is out of Being**.

Just as a reminder, "authority" is *ex-ousia*: "out of, or from out of," and "being; existence; Being (God)." Now, of course, this is his goal and desire, but if the community does not respond to this letter, then he was prepared to "employ; behave or act" in these ways. Why? Well, because all of his attentive care of them was "**with a view into building the house up** (construction of a household)."

It seems appropriate to quote Paul's instructions to Titus:

"**be repeatedly cross-examining them abruptly while cutting away [at the case] and bringing the question to the proof, so as to test and decide the dispute and expose the matter – to the end that they can be sound and healthy within the midst of the Faithfulness, in union with the Trust and centered in that Loyalty**" (Tit. 1:13).

Also, again notice the ambiguous dative of the pronoun "**me**." The Lord "**gave**" and "**gives**" (two potential renderings of the aorist tense – the "fact" or, in an English rendering, "tense-less" tense) these "**rights**" (that come with the granted "authority") to Paul and in Paul. But – and this is critical – his new existence, and the right that came from the Being were "**not into tearing [the community] down**."

11. **As to the rest, brothers** (= fellow believers and members – Family), **be habitually rejoicing** (or: be progressively happy); **be continuously adjusted so as to be completely equipped and fully made ready while being thoroughly knitted together into perfect unity; be repeatedly called alongside to give, or be given, aid, relief, comfort and encouragement; constantly mind the same thing and agree, being of the same opinion** (have the same frame of mind and be mutually disposed); **continuously dwell in and with peace** (habitually maintain the joining; be and live in joined-harmony) – **and the God of the Love and Peace** (or: the God Who is the Self-giving urge toward reunion and joining-harmony) **will continue being with you folks.**

The opening term here, "**As to the rest**," can literally be rendered "a leftover [thing; topic; issue; etc.]." This is not just a "final word to them," but rather the admonitions that follow apply to any other issues that the community might experience. So no matter what arises (throughout the "rest" of their lives), these imperatives apply:

a) **be habitually rejoicing** (or: be progressively happy) – does he really mean this? Yes!

b) **be continuously adjusted so as to be completely equipped and fully made ready while being thoroughly knitted together into perfect unity** – here he repeats the thoughts of 9b, above, so we should assume that it is a very important point, in Paul's mind; Note the passive voice;

c) **be repeatedly called alongside to give, or be given, aid, relief, comfort and encouragement** – habitually be paracletes to others; again: passive voice: be led by the Spirit (Rom. 8:14);

d) **constantly mind the same thing and agree, being of the same opinion** – or, "have the same frame of mind and be mutually disposed [to one another];" *Cf* Rom. 12:16; 1 Cor. 1:10; 1 Pet. 3:8

e) **continuously dwell in and with peace** – or, "habitually maintain the joining; be and live in joined-harmony." *Cf* Rom. 15:33

These imperatives are all based upon the "indicatives" (the declarative statements of affirmation) that Paul proclaims: e.g., they are in Christ; they are God's Temple (God lives within them); they have been made alive from the dead and raised up and are seated in the heavenly realms, with Christ (Eph. 2:1-6). These imperatives are like Jesus telling His disciples to abide/dwell in Him as a branch does in a Vine (Jn. 15:1ff). When, by the ability, power, Life and strength of the Spirit that is incarnated in us, we live and walk the Path in this manner that Paul just laid out, then "**the God of the Love and Peace** (or: the God Who is the Self-giving urge toward reunion and joining-harmony) **will continue being with [them]**." This affirmation demonstrates the "durative," or "ongoing," function of the future tense. God was at that moment "with them" – Paul was not talking about some "future" situation, or listing these imperatives that must be met in order for this situation to happen for them. The declaration in Rev. 21:3 was a present reality:

> "**God's tent** (the Tabernacle of God) **[is] with mankind** (the humans), **'and He will continue living in a tent** (dwell in a Tabernacle) **with them, and they will continue being** (will constantly exist being) **His peoples, and God Himself will continue being with them**."

Before moving on, let us emphasize the alternate rendering in this last statement, which declares the attributes of "**the God of the Love and Peace**":

> "the God Who is the Self-giving urge toward reunion and joining-harmony."

Hillyer comments that "The closing fourfold appeal aptly summarizes his letter" (ibid p 1088).

12. **Greet and embrace one another within a set-apart expression of affection** (or: centered in, and in union with, a holy and sacred kiss; in the sphere of [the] Sacred Kiss).
13. **All the set-apart folks** (holy ones; sacred people) **constantly embrace you folks and send you their best.**

The rendering "**a set-apart expression of affection**" offers the broad semantic range of the Greek expression. The qualifying "**set-apart**" indicates that it is not a "common or profane" expression. Cultures, and individual personalities, differ. Personal experiences that have scarred people need to be considered. This rendering allows for "ease" to prevail within the communities. Those who are not "**habitually walking about** (= living your life) **in spirit** (or: by [the] Spirit; with a Breath-effect)" (Gal. 5:16) can, and have, abused this admonition – and have caused offense. I have known many who do not enjoy or appreciate a physical kiss from someone to whom they are not physically related. Love is sensitive to the sensitivities of other people.

The greeting is to be "centered in, and in union with" a "kiss" that is "holy and sacred." The fact that Paul felt the need to qualify this kind of "kiss" or "expression of affection" should inform us that he was speaking of something other than an expression that was in the "flesh" realm – for we do not know one another in this realm (5:16, above).

Now how about the final offering: "in the sphere of [the] Sacred Kiss"? Does this take us into another layer of understanding – that our greeting is in the sphere of God kissing us? Remember the relationship of Christ to His body is also the relationship of the divine Husband to His wife.

Verse 13 expresses the love of the greater body of Christ that in this case is directed to the community in Corinth. Paul uses the same verb "**Greet and embrace**" in both sentences. In vs. 13 I rendered the idea of "greet" in the common form, "**send their best**." Of course in this verse the sense of "**embrace**" (being via a letter) indicates a mental, heart and spiritual embrace – which includes both emotions and attitude.

14. **The grace and joyous favor of, from and which is the Lord, Jesus Christ – even the Love which is God** (or: and the unambiguous, uniting acceptance and participation of, from and which characterizes God), **and the common-existence, partnership, sharing, communion and participation which is the set-apart Breath-effect** (or: of and from the Holy Spirit and that sacred spirit-attitude) – **[continue being; are] with all of you folks. It is so** (Count on it; Amen)!

As in all my translation of Paul's closing statements, I offer a different form of the copula to supply the ellipse (the missing of the verb). Instead of inserting that common form "be," as though this is a wish for them (which would be contrary to the entire Pauline corpus), I offer different forms of this same verb, reading Paul as making one last affirmation to them: grace/joyous favor, Love and the common-existence (etc.) of and from the Holy Spirit, "**[continue being; are] with all of you folks**." Likewise, along with the common transliteration "Amen," I offer the more emphatic affirmations that these things "ARE" with them: "**It is so** (Count on it)!" Hillyer comments:

> "It would accord with Paul's virile faith to take his closing verse not as a prayer but as a statement: 'Grace, *etc.*, are with you all! So – go forward on this foundation!" (ibid p 1088).

Since the letter that Paul wrote to the Romans is dated circa AD 57, approximately one year after the date assigned to 2 Corinthians, and since scholars generally agree that it was written to Rome FROM Corinth, we may conclude that 2 Cor. was a success for Corinth, and that the relationship between them and Paul was fully restored. Amen.

CPSIA information can be obtained
at www.ICGtesting.com
Printed in the USA
LVHW052358121020
668649LV00017B/542